ASCENT®

CENTER FOR TECHNICAL KNOWLEDGE

Autodesk® InfraWorks® 2025 Fundamentals

Learning Guide

Imperial Units - Edition 1.0

ASCENT - Center for Technical Knowledge®
Autodesk® InfraWorks® 2025
Fundamentals
Imperial Units - Edition 1.0

Prepared and produced by:

ASCENT Center for Technical Knowledge
630 Peter Jefferson Parkway, Suite 175
Charlottesville, VA 22911

866-527-2368
www.ASCENTed.com

Lead Contributors: Jeff Morris and Heather Adams

ASCENT - Center for Technical Knowledge (a division of Rand Worldwide Inc.) is a leading developer of professional learning materials and knowledge products for engineering software applications. ASCENT specializes in designing targeted content that facilitates application-based learning with hands-on software experience. For over 25 years, ASCENT has helped users become more productive through tailored custom learning solutions.

We welcome any comments you may have regarding this guide, or any of our products. To contact us please email: feedback@ASCENTed.com.

AS-IFW2501-FND1IM-SG // IS-IFW2501-FND1IM-SG

Contents

Appendix A: Road Tools A-1

Appendix B: Point Cloud Modeling B-1

Preface

The *Autodesk® InfraWorks® 2025: Fundamentals* guide provides you with a fundamental knowledge of the accelerated design process that uses data-rich 3D models with high-end visualizations. This enables you to create, evaluate, and better communicate 3D site plan proposals for faster approvals.

Topics Covered

Roadway Design:

- Create property boundaries for parcels, easements, and right of ways.
- Create and modify design roads with precise parameters.
- Add components and decorations to roads.
- Adjust roadside grading.
- Apply and review superelevations in component roads.
- Modify how design roads intersect using a standard intersection or roundabout.
- Optimize the vertical design of a roadway.
- Create gradient maps based on selected feature sets to identify areas with low impact for site or corridor optimization.
- Find an optimal horizontal design of the roadway which yields a cost-effective and environmentally friendly solution.
- Run traffic simulations to analyze and animate design traffic.

Bridge and Tunnel Design:

- Add bridges and tunnels to a design roadway.
- Work with bridge deck and girder cross sections.
- Perform analysis and design checks on all the pre-stressed girders of your bridge.

Drainage Design:

- Run a watershed analysis.
- Create or modify culverts.
- Create a pavement drainage network.
- Analyze the pavement drainage network.

Point Cloud Modeling:

- Preparing the point cloud.
- Create a terrain from a point cloud.
- Create features from a point cloud.

Prerequisites

Access to the 2025 version of the software, to ensure compatibility with this guide. Future software updates that are released by Autodesk may include changes that are not reflected in this guide. The practices and files included with this guide are not compatible with prior versions (e.g., 2024).

Note on Software Setup

This guide assumes a standard installation of the software using the default preferences during installation. Lectures and practices use the standard software templates and default options for the Content Libraries.

The Traffic Simulation Analysis tool in InfraWorks requires that a suppoted Java Runtime Environment be installed on your system. If you receive a message that the Java Runtime is not found, you will need to install a supported Java Runtime Environment. For more information, search for **Java Requirements for Autodesk InfraWorks** in the InfraWorks Help documentation.

Note on Learning Guide Content

ASCENT's learning guides are intended to teach the technical aspects of using the software and do not focus on professional design principles and standards. The practices aim to demonstrate the capabilities and flexibility of the software rather than following specific design codes or standards.

Lead Contributor: Jeff Morris

Specializing in the civil engineering industry, Jeff authors training guides and provides instruction, support, and implementation on all Autodesk infrastructure solutions.

Jeff brings to bear over 25 years of diverse work experience in the civil engineering industry. He has played multiple roles, including Sales, Trainer, Application Specialist, Implementation and Customization Consultant, CAD Coordinator, and CAD/BIM Manager, in civil engineering and architecture firms, and Autodesk reseller organizations. He has worked for government organizations and private firms, small companies and large multinational corporations and in multiple geographies across the globe. Through his extensive experience in Building and Infrastructure design, Jeff has acquired a thorough understanding of CAD Standards and Procedures and an in-depth knowledge of CAD and BIM.

Jeff studied Architecture and a diploma in Systems Analysis and Programming. He is an Autodesk Certified Instructor (ACI) and holds the Autodesk Certified Professional certification for Civil 3D and Revit.

Jeff Morris has been a Lead Contributor for *Autodesk InfraWorks: Fundamentals* since 2021.

Lead Contributor: Heather Adams

Heather is an Education Specialist Manager with more than 15 years of technical experience in software installation, customization, training, and template development. As part of her role, she helps to enhance training content and class delivery, in addition to training students in the Infrastructure division.

Heather is an Authorized Certified Instructor (ACI) and has achieved the Autodesk Certified Professional certification for both Civil 3D and AutoCAD. Before entering the Autodesk business, she worked for consulting firms.

Heather received her Bachelor of Science in Civil Engineering from the University of Tennessee. She later earned her PE in Water Resources.

Heather Adams has been a Lead Contributor for *Autodesk InfraWorks: Fundamentals* since 2021.

In This Guide

The following highlights the key features of this guide.

Feature	Description
Practice Files	The Practice Files page includes a link to the practice files and instructions on how to download and install them. The practice files are required to complete the practices in this guide.
Chapters	A chapter consists of the following: Learning Objectives, Instructional Content, Practices, Chapter Review Questions, and Command Summary. • **Learning Objectives** define the skills you can acquire by learning the content provided in the chapter. • **Instructional Content**, which begins right after Learning Objectives, refers to the descriptive and procedural information related to various topics. Each main topic introduces a product feature, discusses various aspects of that feature, and provides step-by-step procedures on how to use that feature. Where relevant, examples, figures, helpful hints, and notes are provided. • **Practice** for a topic follows the instructional content. Practices enable you to use the software to perform a hands-on review of a topic. It is required that you download the practice files (using the link found on the Practice Files page) prior to starting the first practice. • **Chapter Review Questions**, located close to the end of a chapter, enable you to test your knowledge of the key concepts discussed in the chapter. • **Command Summary** concludes a chapter. It contains a list of the software commands that are used throughout the chapter and provides information on where the command can be found in the software.
Appendices	Appendices provide additional information to the main course content. It could be in the form of instructional content, practices, tables, projects, or skills assessment.

Practice Files

To download the practice files for this guide, use the following steps:

1. Type the URL *exactly as shown below* into the address bar of your Internet browser to access the Course File Download page.

   Note: If you are using the ebook, you do not have to type the URL. Instead, you can access the page by clicking the URL below.

   https://www.ascented.com/getfile/id/piauhyensisPF1

   https://www.ascented.com/getfile/id/piauhyensisPF2

   https://www.ascented.com/getfile/id/piauhyensisPF3

   https://www.ascented.com/getfile/id/piauhyensisPF4

2. On the Course File Download page, click the **DOWNLOAD NOW** button, as shown below, to download the .ZIP file that contains the practice files.

3. Once the download is complete, unzip the file and extract its contents.

   The recommended practice files folder location is:
   C:\InfraWorks Practice Files

   Note: It is recommended that you do not change the location of the practice files folder. Doing so may cause errors when completing the practices.

Chapter 1

Navigating the User Interface

In this chapter, you will learn about Building Information Modeling (BIM) and how it is used in the Autodesk® InfraWorks® software. This includes examining the software terminology and interface, learning how to navigate and work with an InfraWorks model, creating different versions of the model (known as proposals), and becoming familiar with the basic navigation controls and predefined views (known as bookmarks).

Learning Objectives

- Locate basic features and commands in the Autodesk InfraWorks software interface.
- Navigate a model using the mouse, ViewCube, and bookmarks.
- Create new proposals in a model to provide additional design options.
- Review the basic commands that are available to make changes to model elements.

1.1 Building Information Modeling

Autodesk InfraWorks is a powerful Building Information Modeling (BIM) program that streamlines site design and the design process for different types of infrastructure projects by using a 3D model. The BIM process supports the ability to coordinate, update, and share design data with team members throughout the design, construction, and management phases of a project's life cycle.

The Autodesk InfraWorks software creates data-rich models using information about the existing environment. Using these models supports more informed decision-making and an accelerated site design process. You can create multiple design alternatives in one model (known as proposals), enabling you to quickly estimate the budget, scope, and schedule with an appropriate level of detail from the beginning of a project. The high-impact visuals that are automatically created during the design process better communicate the design intent to stakeholders.

Autodesk InfraWorks coordinates with other software, such as Autodesk® Civil 3D® and Autodesk® Revit®, to reduce rework and seamlessly enable coordination between project team members.

Launching the Software

The Autodesk InfraWorks software can be launched by double-clicking the (Autodesk InfraWorks) icon on the desktop or selecting it from the Start menu.

When you open the software for the first time (and periodically thereafter), you must sign in to your Autodesk Account. The Autodesk Account Sign in screen displays automatically, as shown in Figure 1–1. Enter your account email and click **NEXT**, then enter your password and click **SIGN IN**.

Figure 1–1

1.2 Overview of the Interface

The Autodesk InfraWorks user interface is designed for intuitive and efficient access to commands and views. It includes the *Home* screen and the model view.

Home Screen

When Autodesk InfraWorks is initially launched, the *Home* screen displays, as shown in Figure 1–2. This screen enables you to:

- Preview recent models
- Access Model Builder
- Open existing models or create new models
- Review notices
- Collaborate with others

Figure 1–2

Note: *A* ***Save*** *option is not available because the model is a database file (SQLite), which saves after every action. The* ***Duplicate*** *command, found under Settings and Utilities, enables you to save an existing model to a new file.*

Three dots display in the lower-right corner of the thumbnail, as shown in Figure 1–3, or to the far right side in list view. When you click the dots, the following options are available:

- **Open Model**
- **Duplicate Model**
- **Delete Model**
- **Remove from Recent**

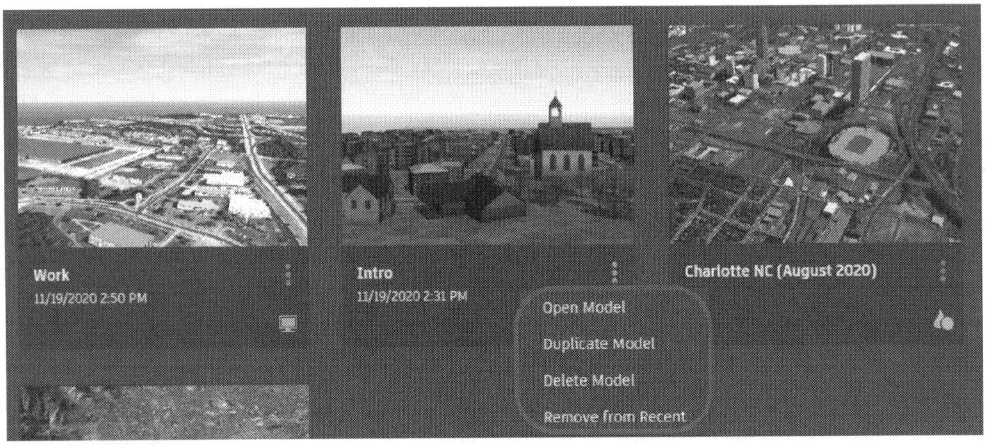

Figure 1–3

How To: Open a Model

On the *Home* screen, click on the preview thumbnail for the model you wish to work in.

- If the model you need to open is not visible on the *Home* screen, click the **Open** button in the sidebar, then browse for the file location, select the file, and click **Open**.
- If the model has a yellow alert symbol next to it, it was saved in an older version of the software, as explained in the tooltip that displays if you hover the cursor over the symbol, as shown on the left in Figure 1–4. You can choose to either **Upgrade Model** or **Upgrade a Copy**, as shown on the right in Figure 1–4.

***Note:** All team members should sync their changes before any cloud model is upgraded.*

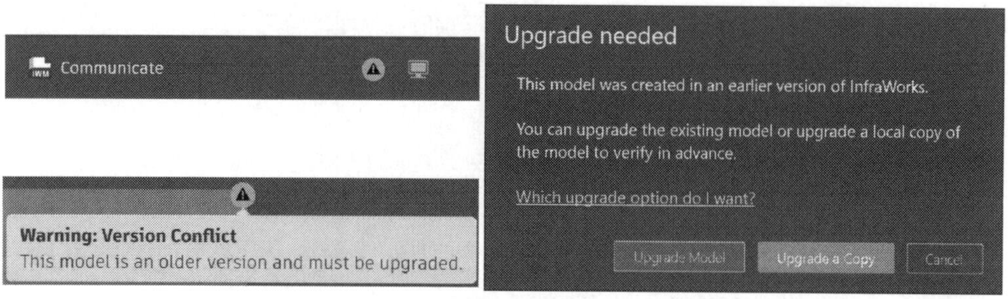

Figure 1–4

- If the model has a  (Sample model) icon in the tile, as shown in Figure 1–5, it is a sample model that will need to be downloaded from the cloud, which can take some time.

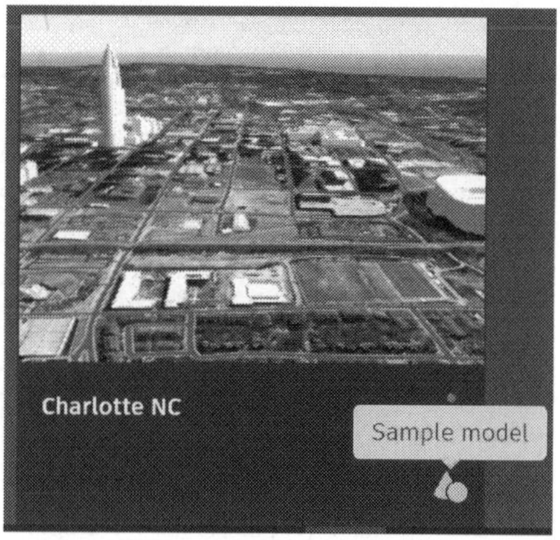

Figure 1–5

Hint: Creating Thumbnails for the Home Screen

You can set a specific view of the model to be displayed on the *Home* screen (when in Tile mode).

1. Navigate to the view you want to save as the thumbnail.
2. If needed, adjust the **Sun and Sky** settings (covered later in this guide).
3. In the *Utilities* drop-down list, select **Set Home Thumbnail**, as shown in Figure 1–6.

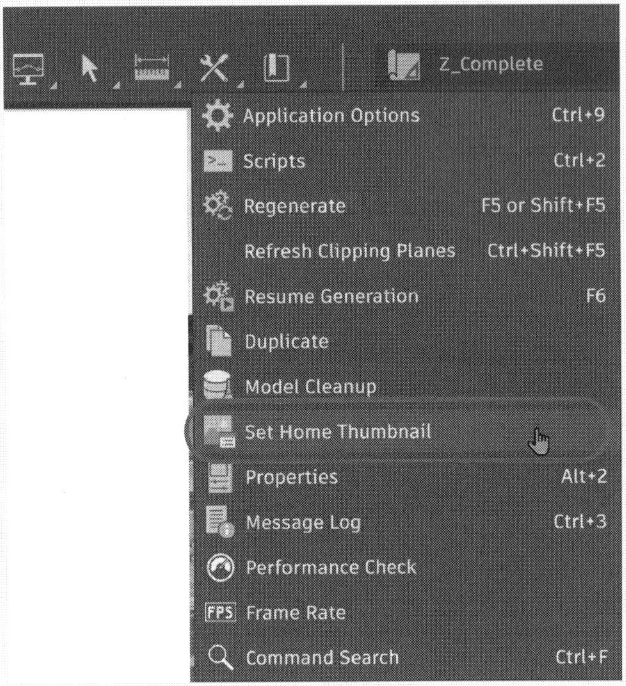

Figure 1–6

Model View

The model view displays when a model is created or opened from the *Home* screen. Figure 1–7 shows the components in the model view user interface.

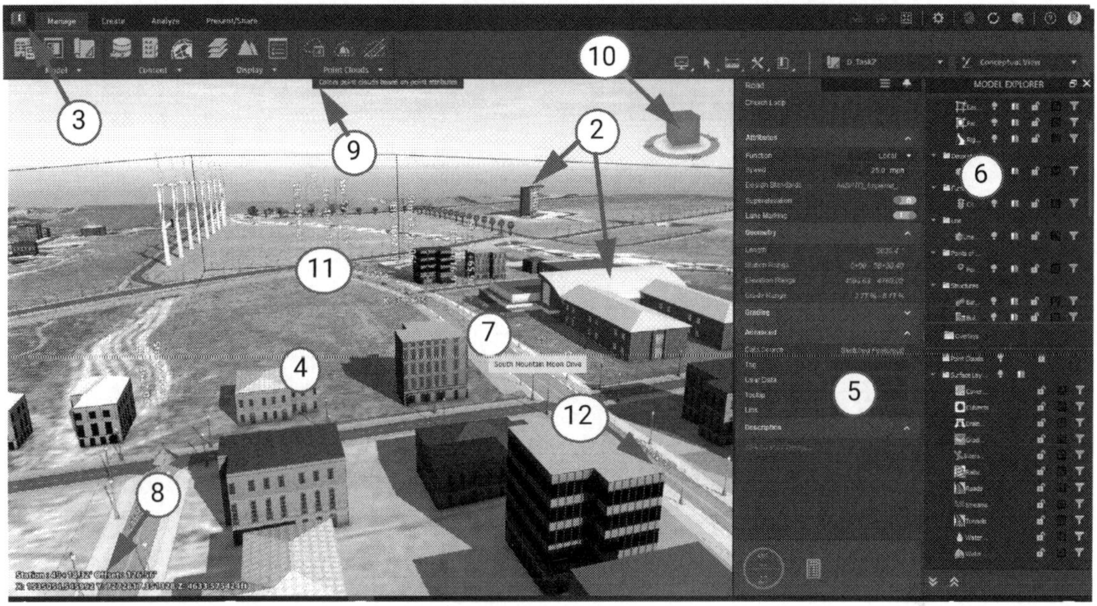

Figure 1–7

1. Toolbar	5. Asset Card	9. Tooltips
2. Buildings from Revit	6. Model Explorer	10. ViewCube
3. Switch to *Home*	7. Automatic Labels	11. Station labels
4. Buildings from Model Builder	8. Model Coordinates	12. Selected Feature

Toolbar

The toolbar (shown in Figure 1–8) provides a variety of frequently used tools.

- Project Tools are the tabs found on the left side of the toolbar. They include planning, design, analysis, and presentation tools.
- Utilities are found on the right side of the toolbar. These include tools for measurement, performance, view settings, bookmarks, collaboration options, application options, and account administration.
- Clicking (Switch to *Home*) in the upper-left corner of the toolbar takes you back to the *Home* screen.

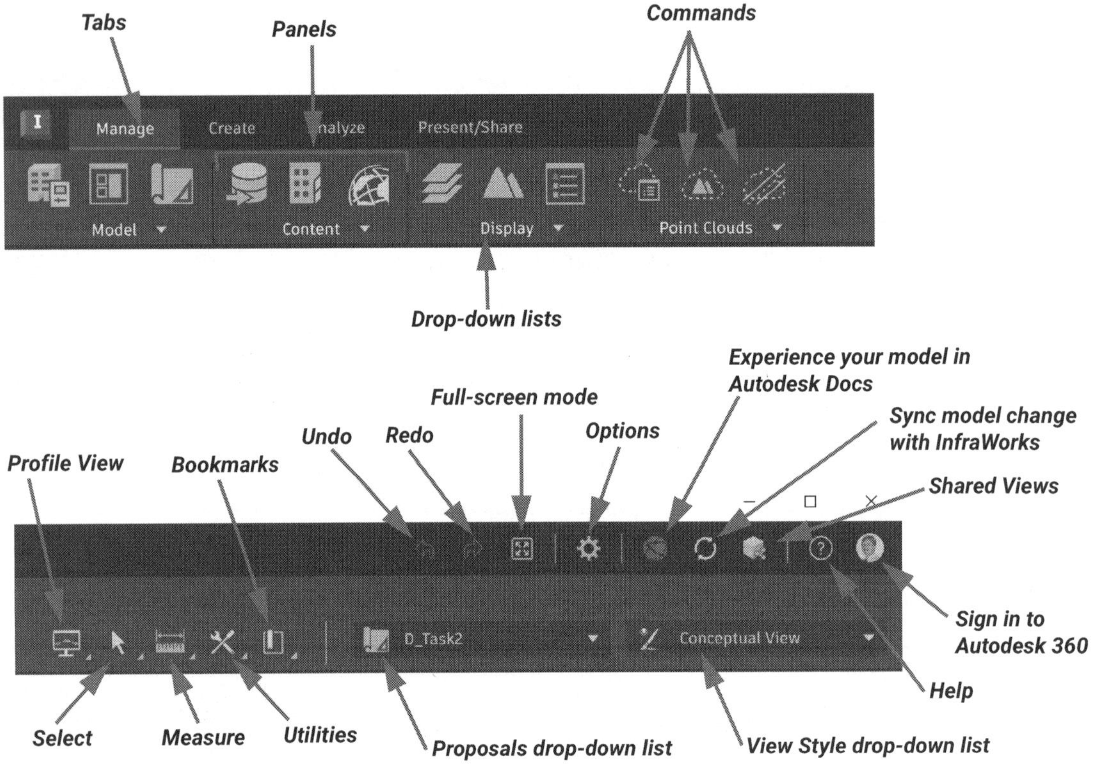

Figure 1–8

Project Tools

The Project Tools are grouped together in tabs representing the phases of a work project (*Manage, Create, Analyze, Present/Share*). Each tab includes panels that contain the main commands for that topic, as shown in Figure 1–9. You can access further commands using the drop-down lists for each section.

Manage tab

Create tab

Analyze tab

Present/Share tab

Manage tab> Display drop-down list

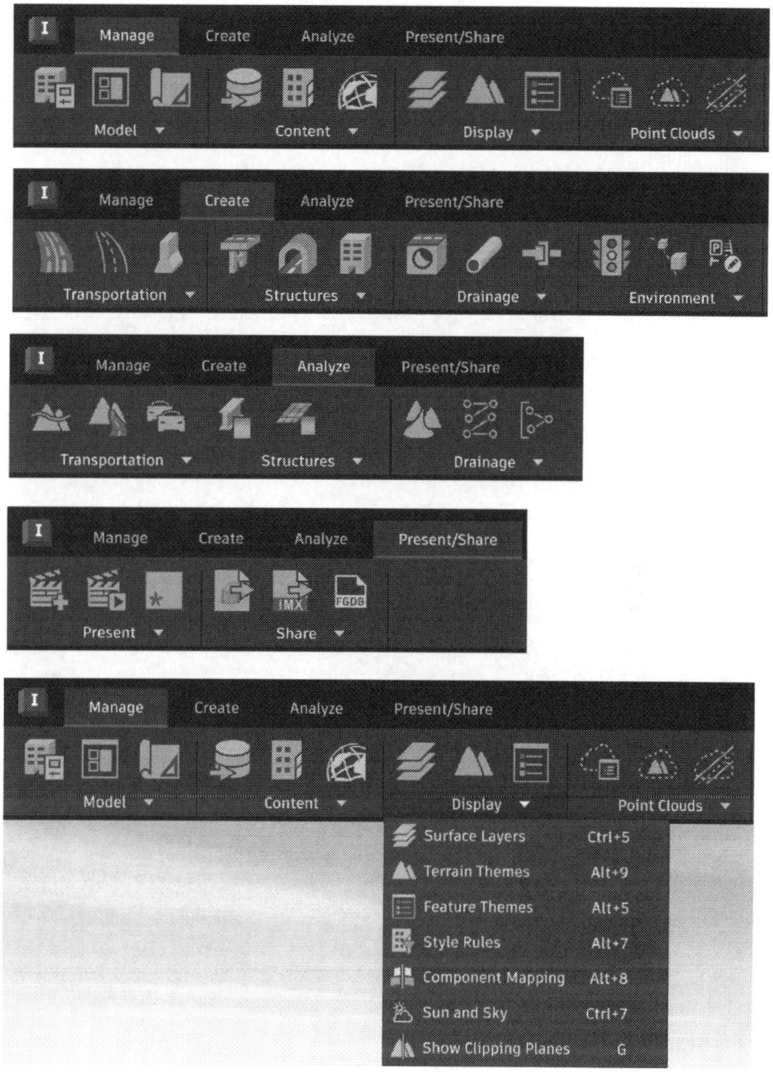

Figure 1–9

Asset Cards

Asset cards and stacks are used to modify the model. They display when certain commands are active or certain design features are selected in the model, as shown in Figure 1–10. Asset cards offer relevant information for the currently selected feature. They enable you to do the following:

- View preview thumbnails for selected styles and colors.
- View and modify the properties of multiple features of the same type at the same time.
- Use the mini picker to change styles and colors of features.
- View warnings for attributes that violate specific parameters.

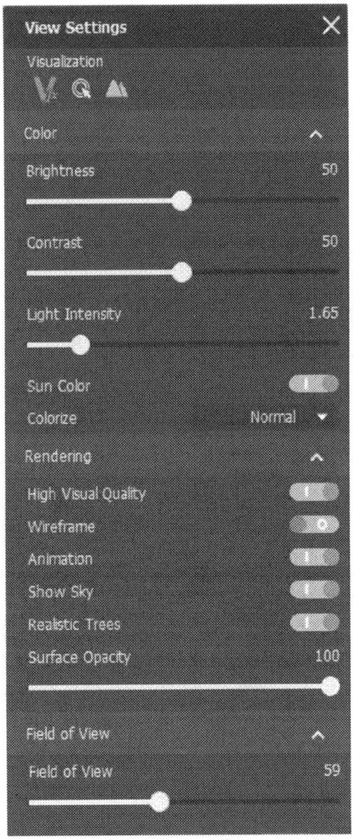

Command asset card (View Settings asset card/Visualization stack)

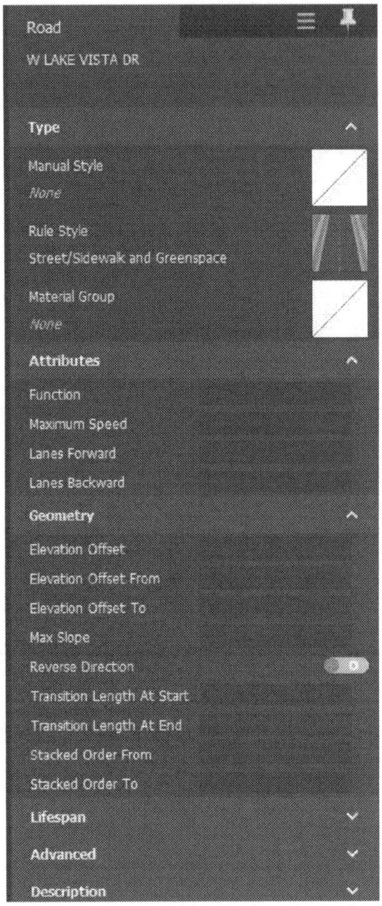

Feature asset card (Road asset card)

Figure 1–10

The contextual stacking of panels enables you to arrange and manage panels by doing the following:

- Maximize your model view by dragging panels to a second monitor.
- Show or hide specific attributes in a stack (customizable per asset type).
- Attach and detach individual panels to create stacks of information.
- Arrange panel sequences based on the information you need.
- Manage the display of information by collapsing and expanding individual panels.
- Hide or show panels using a menu on the top right of the stack.
- Reset the stack layout back to the default layout.
- Autohide the panels so that they only display when you are actively working with (hovering over) a stack area.

Model Explorer

The *Model Explorer* (shown in Figure 1–11) lists the layers that have been added to the model and enables you to hide or display individual model layers. To access the *Model Explorer*, in the *Manage* tab>*Model* panel, click  (Model Explorer).

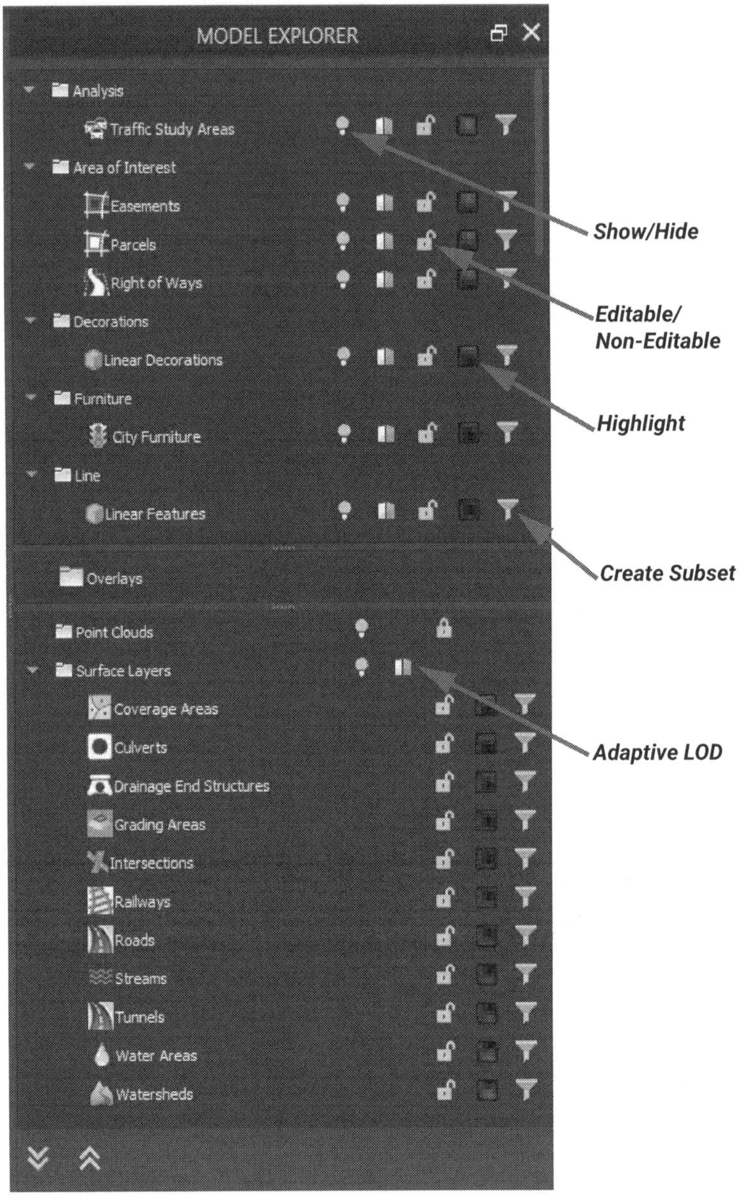

Figure 1–11

Model Window

The model window (shown in Figure 1–12) is the working area in which you create model elements.

Figure 1–12

How elements display in the model window depends on the view style selected in the toolbar. Different view settings can be set up to support different workflows, as shown in Figure 1–13. When working on proposed roads, you might want to display the surface and buildings in wireframe in order to view their triangular irregular network (TIN). In contrast, when you are communicating the design to stakeholders, you might want a more realistic appearance to communicate what the design should look like when the construction is complete.

Engineering view style used for creating design elements

Conceptual view style used for communicating the design

Figure 1–13

Model Coordinates

Each model is assigned a coordinate system that defines the project's location in the world. Once assigned, model coordinates display in the bottom-left corner of the model window, as shown in Figure 1–14. The coordinates display the cursor's location in the model in the X, Y, and Z planes. They automatically update as the cursor moves around in the model.

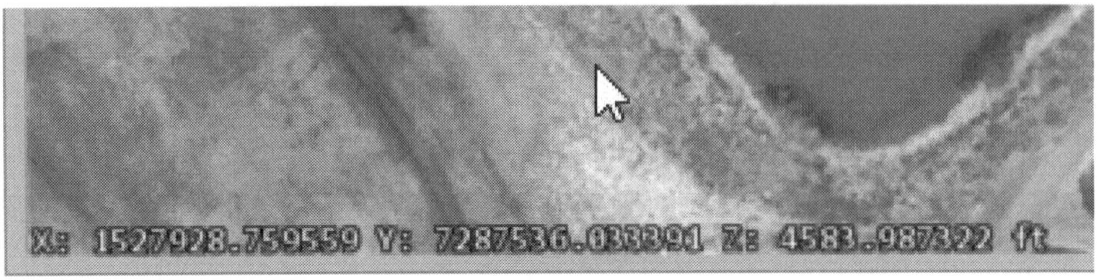

Figure 1–14

Tooltips

Tooltips display when you hover the cursor over a command or feature in the model. These tooltips are labels and short descriptions that display to help ensure that you are selecting the correct items. Figure 1–15 shows an example of a feature tooltip on the left and a command tooltip on the right. If tooltips do not display as you hover over an item, you need to enable them.

> **Note:** *When a model is created using the Model Builder, OpenStreetMap feature names display as tooltips (if available).*

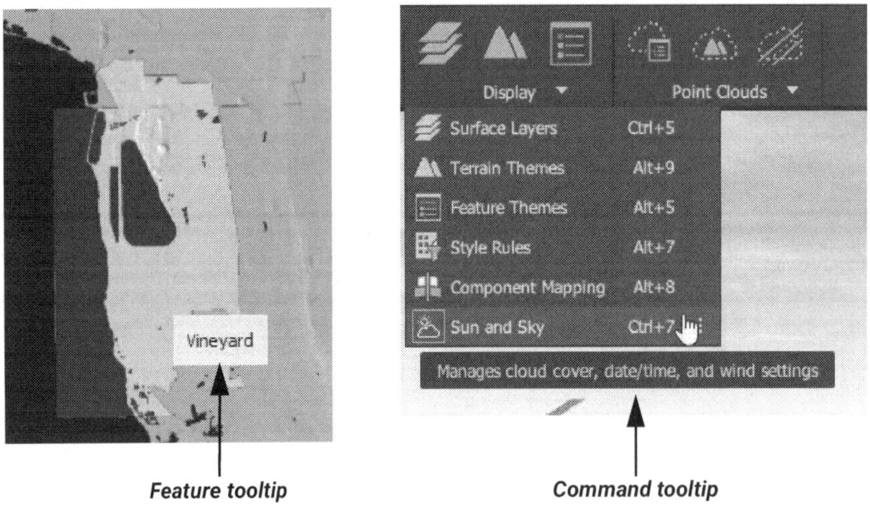

Figure 1–15

To toggle tooltips on or off, in the toolbar, expand the *View Style* drop-down list and click (Configure current view), as shown in Figure 1–16. In the *View Settings* asset card, click (Change navigation and application feedback settings) to open the *Interaction* stack. Under *Information Labels*, click the **Tooltips** slider to toggle them on or off, as shown in Figure 1–17.

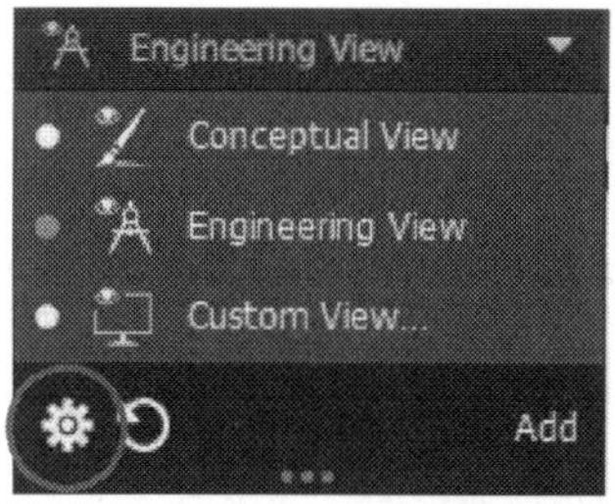

Figure 1–16

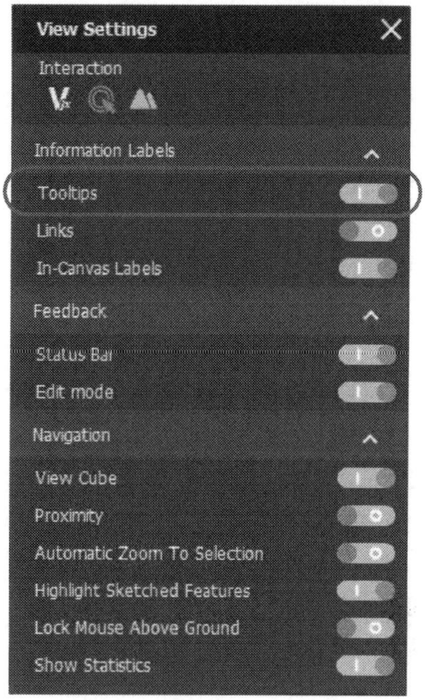

Figure 1–17

ViewCube

The ViewCube (shown in Figure 1–18) provides visual clues indicating the camera position in the model and the direction in which the camera is pointed. The ViewCube helps you to quickly move around the model by providing access to predefined views. This is discussed further in the next section.

Figure 1–18

1.3 Navigating the Model

Navigation commands are critical for working efficiently in any drawing program. Sometimes you need to display the entire model, while other times you need to display more detail. When navigating the Autodesk InfraWorks model, you can change the camera position to obtain a better view of the design.

Mouse

The mouse is the main model navigation tool. A three-button mouse can be used to pan around the model, zoom in/out, and orbit the model in 3D, as shown in Figure 1–19.

Note: *Unlike AutoCAD-based software, holding the mouse wheel to pan does not work in the Autodesk InfraWorks software.*

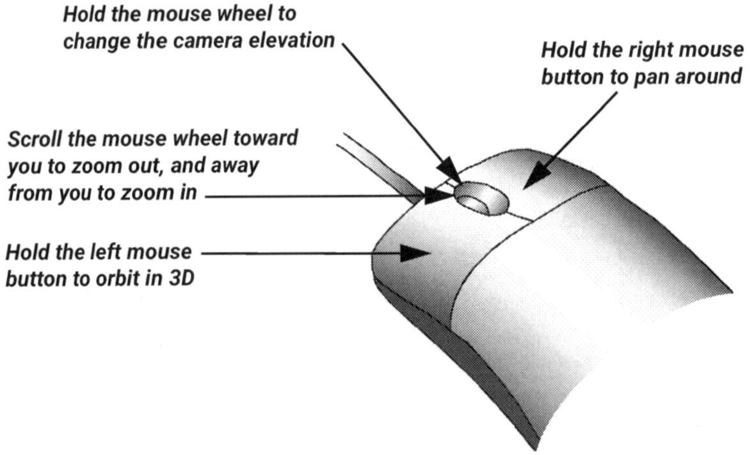

Figure 1–19

ViewCube

The ViewCube provides quick access to many different predefined views. As you move the cursor over it, each face or corner highlights. Once highlighted, you can click the face or corner to reorient the model to the highlighted predefined view, as shown in Figure 1–20. If you hover the cursor over the ViewCube, (*Home*) and (Context Menu) both display, as shown in Figure 1–20.

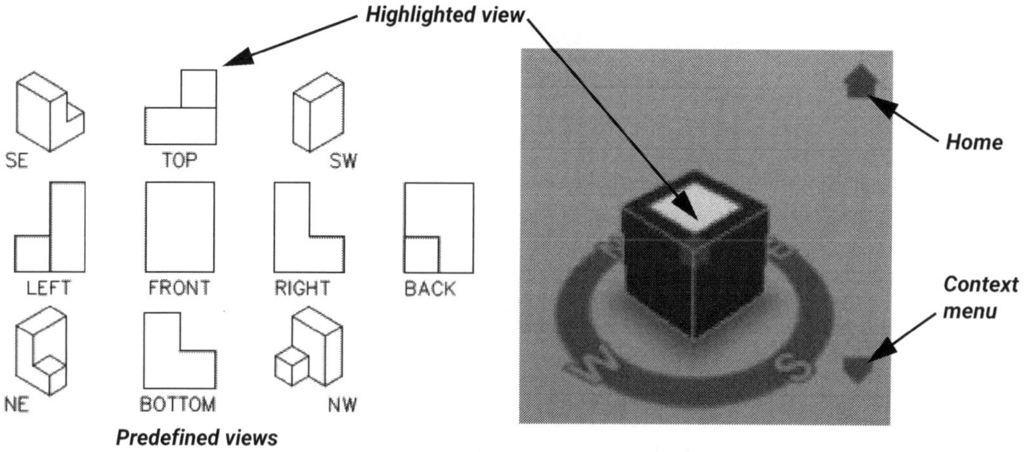

Figure 1–20

Home View

The default *Home* view is a top view that displays the entire model, or it can be a specified view that you define. To quickly go back to the *Home* view, hover the cursor over the ViewCube and click (*Home*). Alternatively, you can press <*Home*> or <F4>.

How To: Change the *Home* View

1. Move the camera to the view that you want to use as the new *Home* view.
2. Click (Context Menu) or right-click on the ViewCube and select **Set current view as home**.

ViewCube Properties

The *ViewCube Properties* dialog box (shown in Figure 1–21) controls whether the ViewCube displays in the model, as well as its location, size, and opacity.

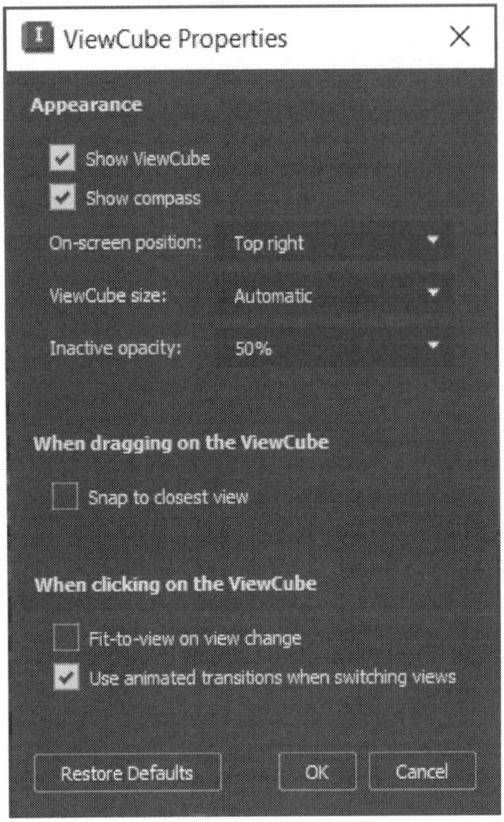

Figure 1–21

The ViewCube can display in any of the four corners of the model: top left, top right, bottom left, or bottom right. To open the *ViewCube Properties* dialog box, click (Context Menu) or right-click on the ViewCube and select **Properties**.

To toggle the ViewCube on or off, in the toolbar, expand the *View Style* drop-down list and click (Configure current view). In the *View Settings* asset card, click (Change navigation and application feedback settings) to open the Interaction stack. Under *Navigation*, click the **ViewCube** slider to toggle it on or off, as shown in Figure 1–22.

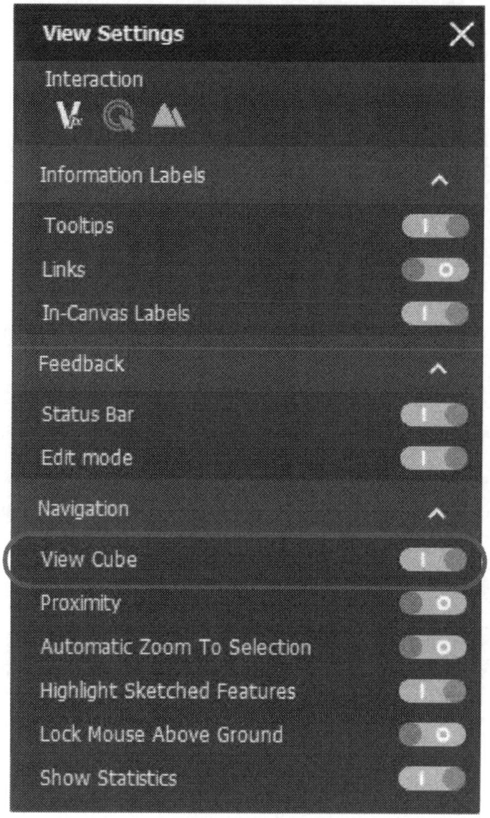

Figure 1–22

Bookmarks

Bookmarks are saved views that quickly reorient the view from one location of the model to another. You can create, preview, and search bookmarks. In addition, you can share bookmarks via Shared Views.

In the toolbar, when you click  (Bookmarks), a list of bookmarks with preview thumbnails displays, as shown in Figure 1–23.

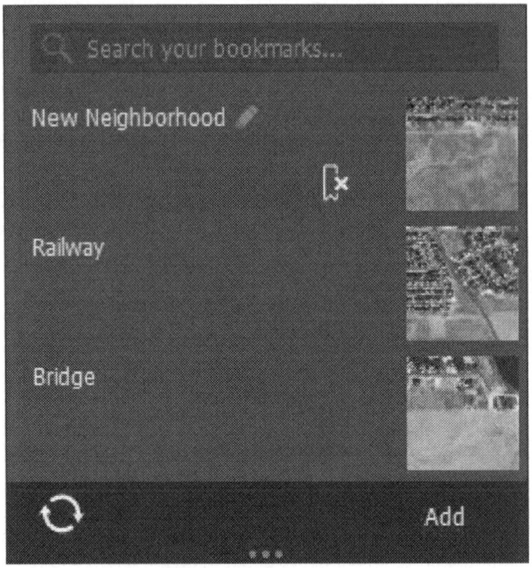

Figure 1–23

Hovering the cursor over a bookmark causes additional tools to display. The table below describes each tool available in the *Bookmarks* drop-down list.

Icon	Description
	Enables you to rename a specific bookmark.
	Deletes the specific bookmark.
	Refreshes the preview thumbnails for all bookmarks according to what displays in the current proposal.
Add	Adds a new bookmark for the current model view.

Other Navigation Tools

Lock Mouse Above Ground

Designers are usually more concerned with what is happening above ground than below ground. You are able to lock the camera position so that is remains above the terrain.

How To: Lock the Camera Position Above the Terrain

1. In the toolbar, expand the *View Style* drop-down list and click (Configure current view).
2. In the *View Settings* asset card, click (Change navigation and application feedback settings) to open the *Interaction* stack.
3. Under *Navigation*, click the **Lock Mouse Above Ground** slider to toggle it on or off, as shown in Figure 1–24.

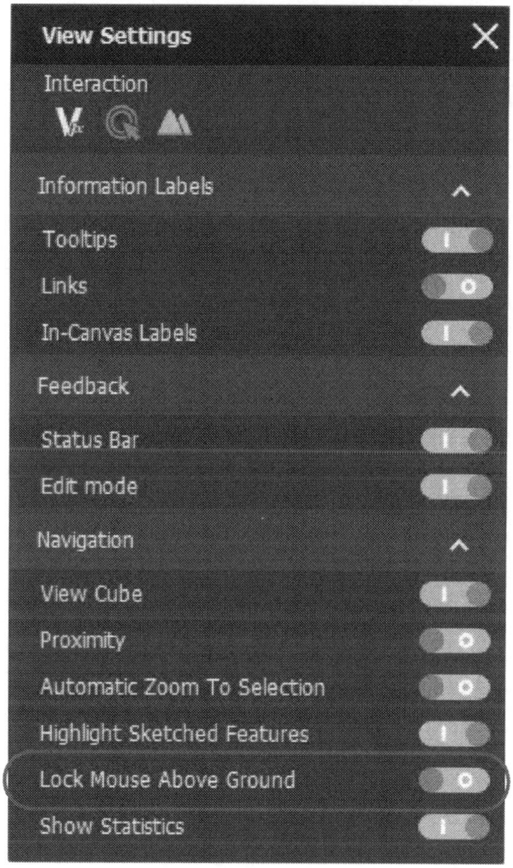

Figure 1–24

Elevate/Lower Camera

To move the camera position in the Z-direction, press <Q> or <1> to elevate the camera, or <E> or <0> (zero) to lower the camera elevation.

> ***Note:*** *Using <1> or <0> to change the camera elevation only works on the numeric keypad of the keyboard.*

Look Up/Down

The camera angle can be tilted up or down by pressing <S> to look up or <W> to look down.

Zoom to Selected

(Zoom to Selected) is used to zoom to a point of interest in the model.

How To: Zoom In on a Selected Feature

1. In the model, click on the feature to select it.
2. In the toolbar, expand the (Select) drop-down list and click (Zoom to Selected), as shown in Figure 1–25.

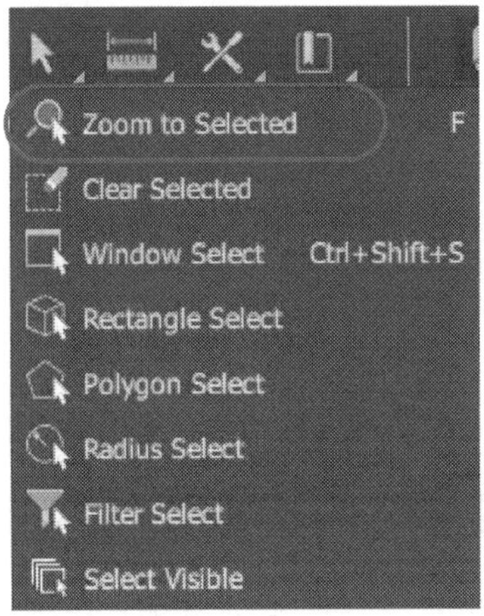

Figure 1–25

Alternatively, you can double-click in the model at the point of interest. Double-clicking inside the model to zoom in also rotates the view as it zooms.

1.4 Basic Commands

To work with features in the model, you must be able to select them. The same selection tools are used to select features from imported source data and features that you have created. Knowing which selection tools are available and how to use them helps you to be more efficient.

Selecting Features

Before you can edit an item, you must be able to select it. By default, you can click on any entity in the model to select it. The following selection options are available from the (Select) drop-down list in the toolbar:

Icon	Description
(Zoom to Selected)	Zooms in and centers on the selected feature(s).
(Clear Selected)	Clears the current selection. You can also use the keyboard shortcut by pressing <Esc>.
(Window Select)	Enables you to select an area based on two opposite corners of a rectangle by dragging the cursor over a region of the model. Any features that are within or touching the edge of the window are selected.
(Rectangular Select)	Enables you to define a box with three points (*Min/Max* for *X*, *Y*, and *Z*). Any features that are completely inside the box are selected. Note: You must double-click on the last point to complete the command.
(Polygon Select)	Enables you to define any shape based on three or more points. Any feature(s) that are inside or touching the edge of the polygon are selected. Note: You must double-click on the last point to complete the command.
(Radius Select)	Enables you to define a circular region by selecting the center point. Any features that are completely inside the defined circle are selected. Note: You must double-click to set the distance from the center and complete the command.
(Filter Select)	Enables you to define an expression to select features according to specific attributes. When clicked, the *Create an attribute filter* dialog box opens, which enables you to create filter expressions to use with this selection option.
(Select Visible)	Enables you to select all objects that are visible from your current vantage point. The objects remain selected (highlighted) even when you change your vantage point.

- Multiple selections can be made by holding down <Ctrl> when selecting features in the model.
- To select a feature, the feature class or layer must be unlocked in the *Model Explorer*, and *Edit mode* must be toggled on in the *View Settings* asset card.

How To: Toggle Edit Mode On/Off

1. In the toolbar, expand the *View Style* drop-down list and click (Configure current view).
2. In the *View Settings* asset card, click (Change navigation and application feedback settings) to open the Interaction stack.
3. Under *Feedback*, click the **Edit mode** slider to toggle it on or off, as shown in Figure 1–26.

   Note: *This only toggles Edit mode for the current view style.*

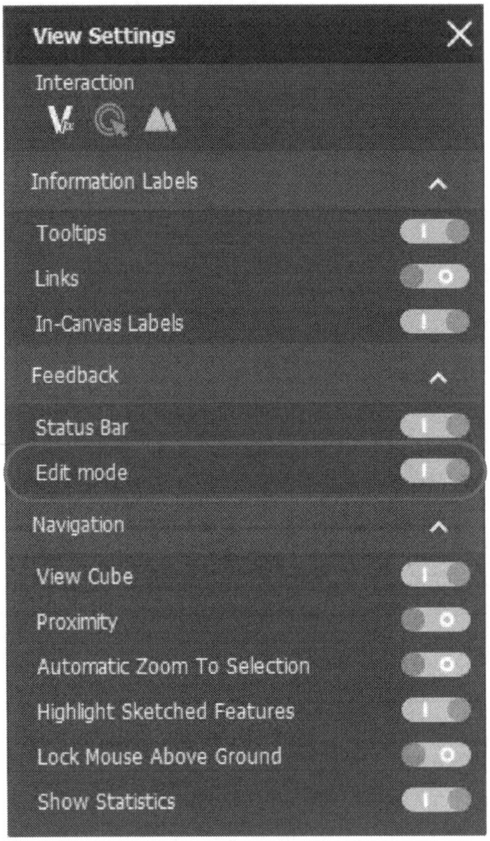

Figure 1–26

Shortcut Commands

Many Windows programs use common shortcut keys. Many of these keys can also be used in the Autodesk InfraWorks software. Shortcut keys can be used in conjunction with the clipboard to share features between different proposals or models.

The following table describes some of the available shortcut keys:

Command/ Icon	Keyboard Shortcut	Description
Select All	<Ctrl>+<A>	Selects all of the contents (i.e., created features and data sources) in the current model.
Invert Selection	<Alt>+<I>	Inverts the currently selected contents. These are cleared, while previously unselected objects become selected.
Deselect	<Esc>	Clears the selection of any objects that were selected in the model.
Zoom Selected	<F> (or double-click on the object)	Zooms in on the currently selected objects in the model.
Copy	<Ctrl>+<C>	Copies features to a clipboard for use later. You can copy an individual feature, an entire feature class, or multiple feature classes using the **Copy** command.
Duplicate	<Ctrl>+<D>	Copies features without copying to the clipboard. You can duplicate an individual feature, an entire feature class, or multiple feature classes using the **Duplicate** command. Note: You can press <Shift>+<Ctrl> while dragging selected features to duplicate them without using the clipboard.
Paste	<Ctrl>+<V>	Pastes items from the clipboard into the model. Hold <Ctrl>+<V> and double-click in the model where you want the copied feature to be placed.
Paste in Place	<Shift>+<Ctrl>+<V>	Pastes items at their original locations.
Delete	<Delete>	Removes selected features from the model.
Cut	<Ctrl>+<X>	Removes selected features from the model and places them on the clipboard for use later. You can cut an individual feature, an entire feature class, or multiple feature classes using the **Cut** command.
 (Undo)	<Ctrl>+<Z>	Undoes the last command used in the model. Repeating the **Undo** command undoes commands in the order in which they were executed. The icon is found in the toolbar.

Command/ Icon	Keyboard Shortcut	Description
(Redo)	<Ctrl>+<Y>	Reverses an **Undo** command, reissuing the last command that was undone in the model. Repeating the **Redo** command reissues commands in the order in which they were undone. The icon is found in the toolbar. Note: **Redo** only reissues commands that were successive. For example, if you undo five commands, redo three of those commands, and then issue a new command, the **Redo** command is disabled when you execute the new command.

Command Search

A Command Search is available by pressing <Ctrl>+<F>. A small search box opens near the location of the mouse cursor to search for commands in InfraWorks. As you begin to type, the box populates with matches, as shown in Figure 1–27

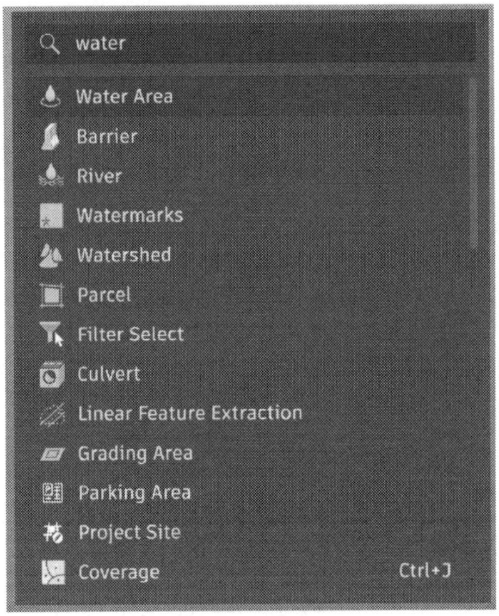

Figure 1–27

When a command is invoked from the search, a Tip box in the lower center of the screen is displayed, as shown in Figure 1–28.

Figure 1–28

Gizmos

Gizmos enable you to quickly modify model features, similar to the way grips are used in AutoCAD-based programs. In the model, click the entity you wish to edit to cause gizmos to display when objects are selected. Different gizmos display depending on the type of feature that is selected when you access the Edit Features mode.

The following table describes a few of the available gizmos:

Gizmo	Transformation	Description
	**Elevation**	Used with linear features (e.g., roads, railways, and coverages). In a 3D view, it stretches features vertically by changing the elevation of a linear feature vertex.
	**Height**	Only used with buildings, city furniture, and trees. Changes the height of a building while leaving the footprint unchanged. Changes the scale of trees and city furniture proportionally.
	**Rotate**	Rotates a feature around the Z-axis.
	**Control Point**	Displays at each corner, point of intersection, or base of features. Stretches linear features (e.g., roads, rails, coverages, and building outlines) by moving the selected vertex of the feature. Moves the location of point features (e.g., trees or city furniture). Note: Additional control points can be added by holding down <Alt> and selecting the new control point location(s).
	**Move**	Moves the selected feature or vertex.

The *Move* gizmo has four handle options for moving model elements. These handles can be selected to move features in specific planes. The available handles are as follows:

Handle	Transformation	Description
	**Move in XY Plane**	Select the square between the X- and Y-axes to move a feature to a new location in the XY plane.
	**Move in X Axis**	Select the red arrow to constrain the movement of a feature to a new location along the X-axis.
	**Move in Y Axis**	Select the green arrow to constrain the movement of a feature to a new location along the Y-axis.
	**Move in Z Axis**	Select the blue arrow to constrain the movement of a feature to a new location along the Z-axis.

1.5 Working with Proposals

A proposal is a design alternative in the model and should be created for each design alternative that you plan to explore or propose to the client. By default, every model has at least one proposal called the **master**.

It is recommended that you only include base model information (existing conditions) in the master proposal. Then, create a new proposal for each new design alternative based on the master proposal. Everything in the current proposal is included in the new proposal.

For example, if you sketch new model elements in a proposal, any new proposals based on that proposal contain those model elements. By ensuring that the master proposal only contains the existing conditions, you can always create a clean proposal.

If you use pieces from multiple proposed designs, you can merge them to create one proposal that includes everything contained in the other proposals. You can then remove all but the required elements.

You can switch between proposals by expanding the  (Proposals) drop-down list in the toolbar and selecting the proposal that you want to be active, as shown in Figure 1–29.

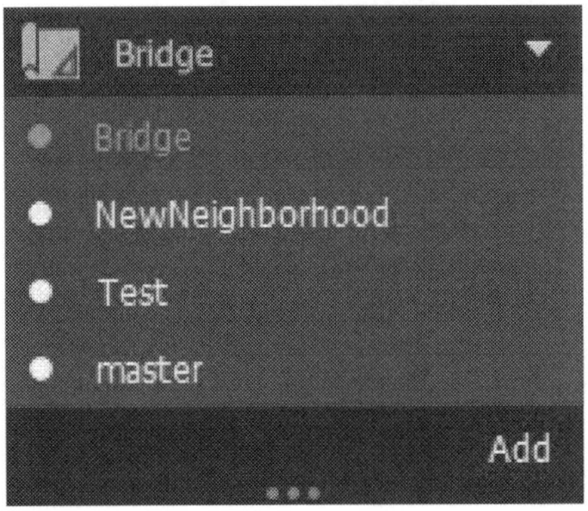

Figure 1–29

Proposals Panel

The *Proposals* panel contains statistics about the proposals you have created, as shown in Figure 1–30. The statistics include the number of items added or removed per feature type. You can also quickly display measurements for added features, such as length, area, and volume. To display statistics for specific features, expand the details under the feature type, and then expand the specific feature ID to display its measurements.

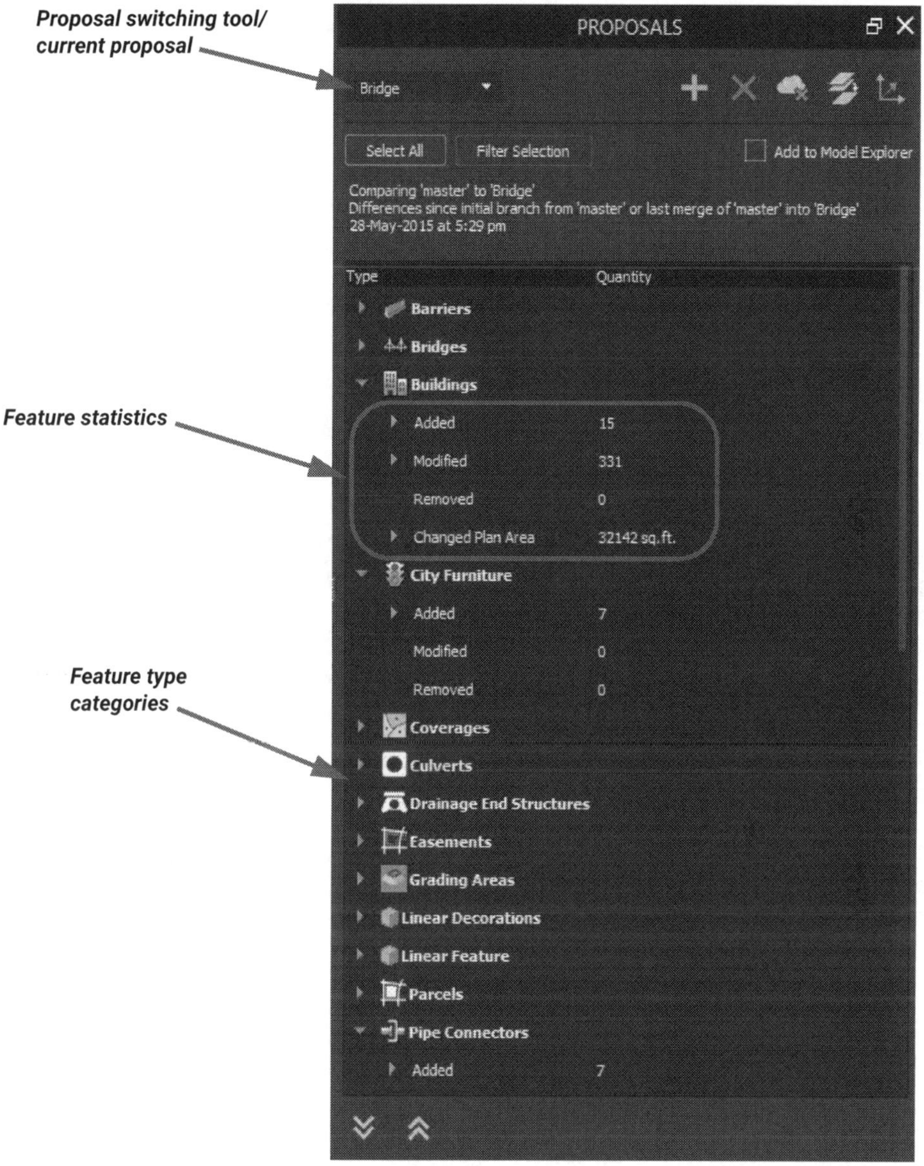

Figure 1–30

Proposal Tools

The following tools can help you manage the proposals in the current model. They are located at the top of the *Proposals* panel.

Icon	Description
(Add new proposal)	Creates a new proposal based on the current proposal. It includes everything in the current proposal.
(Delete current proposal)	Removes the current proposal from the model.
(Delete proposal from the cloud model)	Removes the current proposal from the model that is stored in the cloud (BIM 360).
(Merge proposals)	Combines a selected proposal's edit history with the edit history in the current proposal.
(Toggle 2D/3D sketch display)	Displays sketched features as 2D linework when in 2D mode or as a 3D model when in 3D mode, as shown in Figure 1–31.

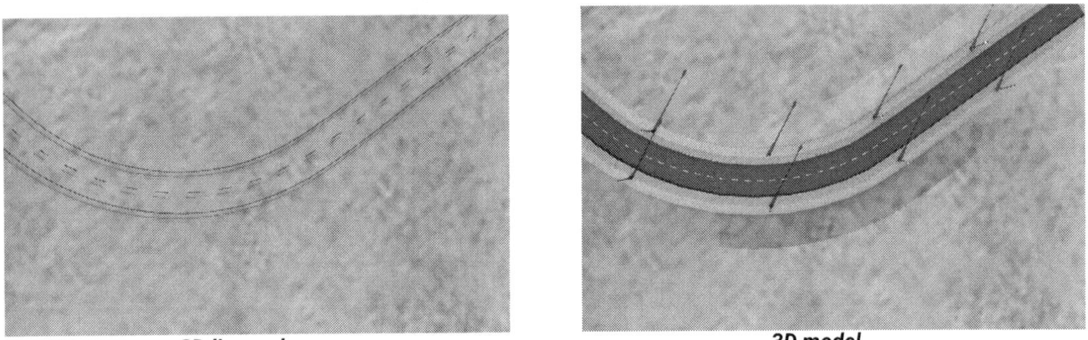

2D linework ***3D model***

Figure 1–31

How To: Create a New Proposal

1. Create a base model in the master proposal by importing data from various sources.
2. In the *Manage* tab>*Model* panel, click (Proposals) to display the **Proposals** panel.
3. In the *Proposals* panel, select the proposal that you want to use as the base, as shown in Figure 1–32.

Figure 1–32

4. In the *Proposals* panel, click (Add new proposal).
5. In the *Add New Proposal* dialog box, type a name for the proposal and click **OK**.

Alternatively, you can:

1. Select the proposal that you want to use as the base from the (Proposals) drop-down list to make it active.
2. Click **Add** from the (Proposals) drop-down list (in the lower-right corner).
3. In the *Add New Proposal* dialog box, type a name for the proposal and click **OK.**

How To: Merge Proposals

1. In the *Manage* tab>*Model* panel, click (Proposals) to display the *Proposals* panel.
2. Select the proposal into which you want to merge the features, as shown in Figure 1–33.

Figure 1–33

3. At the top of the *Proposals* panel, click (Merge proposals).

4. In the *Merge Into Current Proposal* dialog box, select the proposal that you want to merge into the current proposal, as shown in Figure 1–34.

   Note: *To easily browse added or modified features, the Merge panel provides a* ***Zoom to Selected*** *option.*

Figure 1–34

5. Click **OK**.

Practice 1a
Navigate the User Interface

Practice Objectives

- Navigate around a 3D model using preset views, manual orbiting tools, and the ViewCube.
- Check the units of measurement.
- Manage proposals by creating new proposals and merging existing proposals.

In this practice, you will access preset views, orbit the drawing, and return to a previous view. Additionally, you will create a new proposal and merge it with another proposal.

Task 1: Navigate the model.

1. On the *Home* screen, click **Open**.
2. Navigate to the *InfraWorks Practice Files\1-Navigation* folder and select **INTRO.sqlite**. Click **Open**.
3. Click (Bookmarks) and select **Pier 3D**. You find this at the bottom of the list - Bookmarks are not sorted alphabetically.
4. In the toolbar, select **Z-Complete** from the (Proposals) drop-down list, as shown in Figure 1–35.

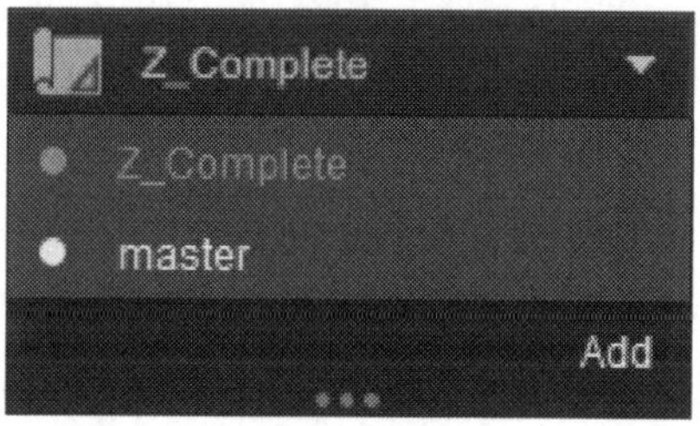

Figure 1–35

5. Scroll the middle mouse button toward you to zoom out.

6. Hold the left mouse button (Orbit) and drag the mouse to orbit the model so it displays as an elevation view with the camera south of the bridge, as shown in Figure 1–36.

Figure 1–36

7. Hold the right mouse button (Pan) and drag the mouse to the left to pan the model to the intersection of the pier road with S Redwood Rd (the road that is running north and south), as shown in Figure 1–37. You may have to zoom out and orbit as well.

Figure 1–37

8. Click on the **S Redwood Rd** road and note that the station information is displayed.
9. Double-click on the Railway next to the road and you are zoomed in to the particular component of the rail you selected.
10. Zoom out and select a building in the model by single-clicking on it. This time, press <F> (on your keyboard) to zoom in to the feature.
11. Note the gizmos on the selected object. Press <Esc> to deselect the object.
12. Click (Bookmarks) and select **Project Area**, near the top of the list.

13. In the toolbar, select **master** from the (Proposals) drop-down list.

14. Click (Bookmarks) and select **Hotel 3D**. With the bookmark list still expanded, select the **Hotel-Interior** bookmark, as shown in Figure 1–38. Note how the view smoothly transitions to the new vantage point. Select **Church 3D** to traverse to a new area in the model.

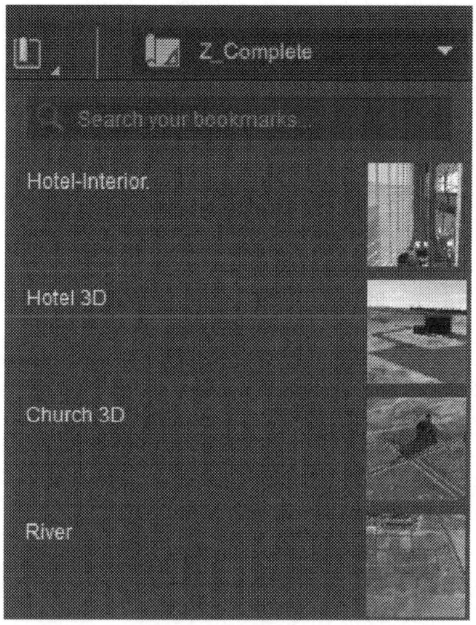

Figure 1–38

15. Change the proposal back to **Z-Complete**, then select **Hotel 3D**, and then **Hotel-Interior** bookmark.

Task 2: Check units of the model.

1. Select **Church 3D bookmark.**

2. In the toolbar, expand the 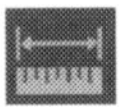 (Measure) drop-down list and select **Point to Point Distance**, as shown in Figure 1–39.

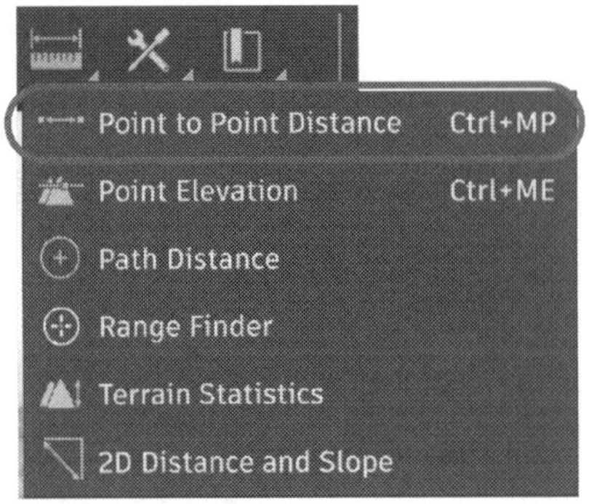

Figure 1–39

3. In the model, click on one point. When you move the mouse for the second point, a tooltip appears displaying the running distance. Once you select the second point, the distance is measured. You can select other points to measure.
4. The units of measurement will either be imperial or metric, as shown in Figure 1–40.

Figure 1–40

5. Once you press <Esc>, all measurements vanish.
6. In the toolbar, expand the 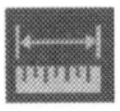 (Measure) drop-down list and select **Point Elevation**.
7. In the model, click a point on the church steeple. When you move the mouse a leader appears. Click a point and the elevation is displayed as a tooltip appears. Select a second point to position the elevation readout.
8. You can select other points to measure the elevation.

9. The units of measurement will either be imperial or metric, as shown in Figure 1–41.

Figure 1–41

10. Press <Esc> to clear all measurements.
11. If you need to change the units of measurement, this will be covered later in this guide.

Task 3: Search for a command.

1. Press <Ctrl>+<F>. A small search box opens near the location of the mouse cursor.
2. Type in **park** and note how the suggestions are populated with each keystroke, as shown in Figure 1–42

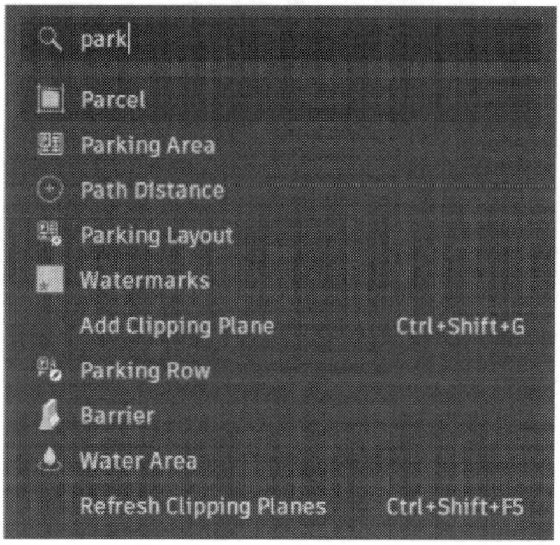

Figure 1–42

3. Select **Parking Area** in the list.

4. The **Parking Area** command is invoked along with a Tip box in the lower center of the screen, as shown in Figure 1–43.

Figure 1–43

5. You will not be placing parking area yet, so press <Esc> to cancel the command.

Task 4: Create a new proposal and merge proposals.

1. In the toolbar, expand the (Proposals) drop-down list and set the current proposal to the **master** proposal.
2. At the bottom of the *Proposals* drop-down list, click **Add** to add a new proposal.
3. In the *Add New Proposal* dialog box, type **Combination** for the proposal name and click **OK**. **Combination** is now the active proposal and includes everything that was in the master proposal.
4. In the *Manage* tab>*Model* panel, click (Proposals) to open the *Proposals* panel.
5. Click (Bookmarks) and select **Railway**.
6. At the top of the *Proposals* panel, click (Merge proposals).
7. In the *Merge Into Current Proposal* dialog box, select the **Bridge** proposal to merge it into the *Combination* proposal, as shown in Figure 1–44.

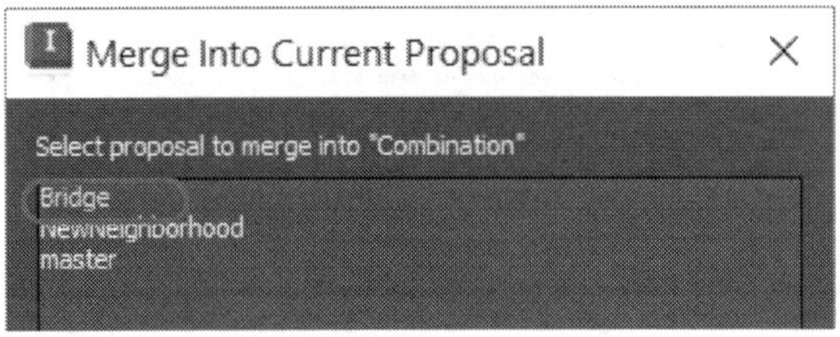

Figure 1–44

8. Click **OK**. After some processing time, the bridge displays in the right side of the view, along with other features of the *Bridge* proposal.
9. At the top of the *Proposals* panel, click (Merge proposals).

10. In the *Merge Into Current Proposal* dialog box, select the **NewNeighborhood** proposal to merge it into the *Combination* proposal, as shown in Figure 1–45.

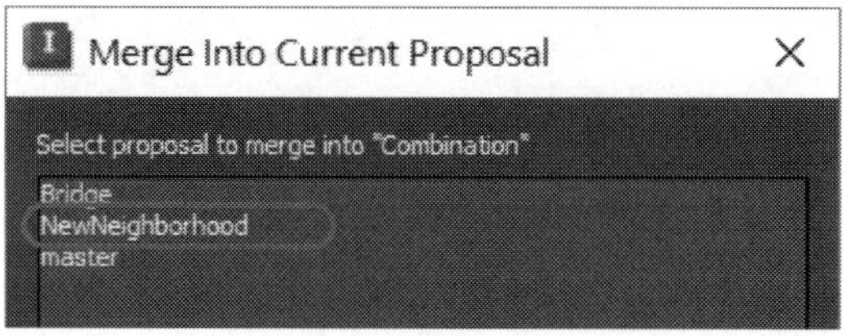

Figure 1–45

11. Click **OK**. After some more processing time, a new neighborhood with roads and buildings displays in the view.
12. Close the *Proposals* panel.

Task 5: Configure the view interaction settings.

1. Orbit or pan down below ground level and note you can look above from below ground level.
2. In the toolbar, expand the *View Style* drop-down list and click (Configure current view), as shown in Figure 1–46.

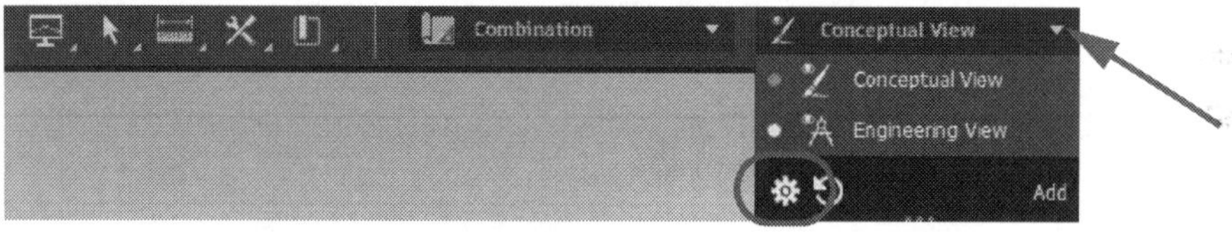

Figure 1–46

3. In the *View Settings* asset card, click (Change navigation and application feedback settings) to open the *Interaction* stack.

4. Under *Navigation*, click the **Lock Mouse Above Ground** slider to toggle it on, as shown in Figure 1–47. Ensure that **Tooltips** and **ViewCube** are also on.

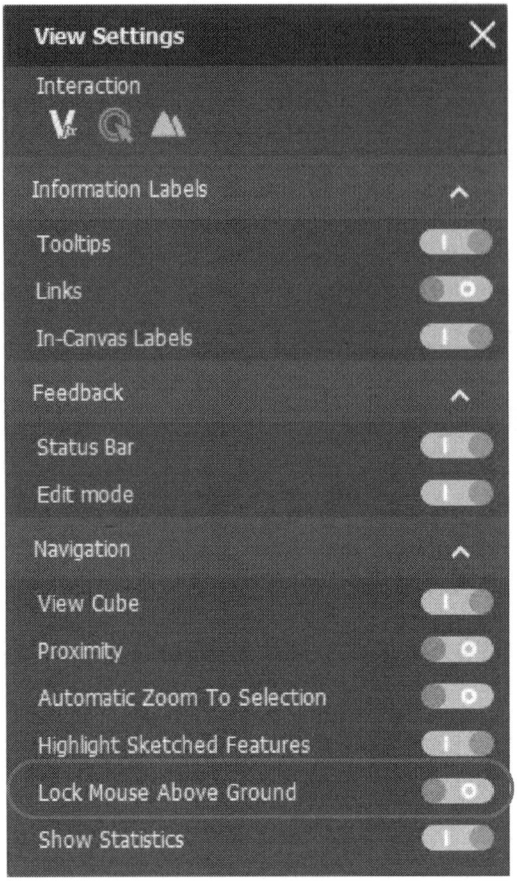

Figure 1–47

5. Close the *View Settings* panel.
6. Orbit or pan down near ground level. Note that you can no longer go below the ground level.
7. There is no "Save" option in InfraWorks. All changes are immediately saved.
8. Click on  (Switch to *Home*) in the upper-left corner of the toolbar to go to the *Home* screen.

End of practice

Chapter Review Questions

Use Figure 1–48 to answer Questions 1 and 2.

Figure 1–48

1. In Figure 1–48, which part of the user interface is indicated by number 1?
   a. Toolbar
   b. ViewCube
   c. Model Explorer
   d. Model Window

2. In Figure 1–48, which part of the user interface is indicated by number 2?
   a. ViewCube
   b. Asset Card
   c. Toolbar
   d. Tooltips

3. Bookmarks are used to quickly change the view to a specific area of the model.
    a. True
    b. False

4. Which of the following should be used to display different design variations for the project?
    a. Bookmarks
    b. Proposals
    c. Coverages
    d. Model Explorer

5. How do you pan in a model?
    a. Click and drag the right mouse button.
    b. Click and drag the mouse scroll wheel.
    c. Scroll with the mouse scroll wheel.
    d. Click and drag the left mouse button.

6. How do you quickly zoom in to a selected object in a model? (Select all that apply.)
    a. Select the object and use the  (Select) drop-down list in the toolbar.
    b. Select the object and press <Pg Up>.
    c. Double-click on the object.
    d. Select the object and press <F>.

Command Summary

Button	Command	Location
	**Application Options**	• **Toolbar**
	**Bookmarks**	• **Toolbar**
	**Change navigation and application feedback settings**	• ***View Settings* asset card**
	**Configure current view**	• **Toolbar:** *View Style* drop-down list
N/A	**Elevate Camera Down**	• **Mouse:** Hold scroll wheel • **Shortcut key**: <E> or <0> (zero)
N/A	**Elevate Camera Up**	• **Mouse:** Hold scroll wheel • **Shortcut key**: <Q> or <1>
 / 	***Home* view**	• **ViewCube** • **Shortcut key:** <*Home*> or <F4>
N/A	**Lock Above Terrain**	• ***View Settings* asset card:** *Interaction* stack
	**Merge proposals**	• ***Proposals* panel**
	**Model Explorer**	• **Toolbar:** *Manage* tab>*Model* panel
N/A	**Open**	• ***Home* screen**
N/A	**Pitch Down**	• **Shortcut key**: <W>
N/A	**Pitch Up**	• **Shortcut key**: <S>
	**Proposals**	• **Toolbar** • **Toolbar:** *Manage* tab>*Model* panel
	**Select**	• **Toolbar**
N/A	**Tooltips**	• ***View Settings* asset card:** *Interaction* stack
N/A	**ViewCube**	• ***View Settings* asset card:** *Interaction* stack
N/A	**Zoom In**	• **Mouse:** Scroll wheel • **Shortcut key**: <+>
N/A	**Zoom Out**	• **Mouse:** Scroll wheel • **Shortcut key**: <->

Button	Command	Location
	**Zoom Selected**	• **Shortcut key:** <F> • **Toolbar:** Select drop-down list • **In model**: Double-click on point of interest

Chapter

2

Connecting to Data Sources

Firms that use existing GIS data during the project planning or bid phases of a project can offer a more complete analysis of the project and better proposals to stakeholders. In this chapter, you will learn how to create a new model and then how to connect additional existing data sources. Finally, you configure the data sources to display correctly in the model.

Learning Objectives

- Create a new model using the Model Builder.
- Create a new model from scratch.
- Set the model coordinate system, units, and extents.
- Connect to select data source types to display the existing conditions in a model.
- Configure the connected GIS data for correct display.

2.1 Geographic Information Systems Overview

All Autodesk® InfraWorks® models begin by importing existing data from various sources. These sources include building outlines, roads, utilities, terrain, images, etc. Typically, the data you start with comes from a Geographic Information System (GIS). A GIS enables organizations to better store, manage, and analyze geographical data.

In its most simple definition, a GIS is the creation of a smart map in which data is attached to geographical elements. It attempts to explain or predict spatial distribution or variation in human activity and its connection to physical features on the earth's surface.

Most GIS sources include multiple files. The most basic GIS data source often includes a raster or vector file and a database file containing information referenced by the raster/vector features. For example, an ESRI Shape File includes the vector file (.SHP), a database file (.DBF), a projection file (.PRJ), etc., as shown in Figure 2–1.

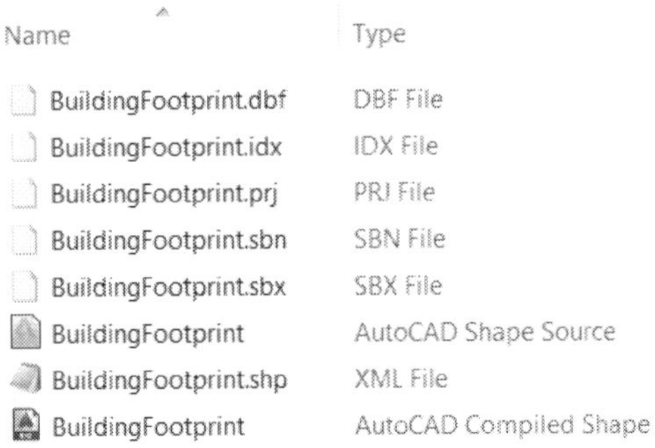

Figure 2–1

Sample GIS Data

Many different agencies take advantage of the benefits of using GIS to analyze and manage their infrastructure and data. Uses of GIS data include the following:

- Cities store street centerline maps connected to pavement management system databases, ensuring the correct maintenance and repair of city roads.
- Utility companies store electronic maps indicating where pipes, manholes, and other utilities are buried to provide blue stake services to anyone needing a digging permit. If a utility is damaged due to a natural or man-made disaster, data connected to the utility maps can be used to quickly notify the affected residents about how long they are going to be without service.
- Retailers use GIS data to better analyze which customers buy certain goods. This enables them to send coupons and other marketing material directly to the customers that are most likely to buy their products. The data is also used to help them strategically locate merchandise in the store.

- GIS data is often created, managed, and stored by government agencies to help them track public infrastructure. During a project's planning phase, planners, developers, and civil engineers use GIS data to help select the best location for the proposed project. During this phase of the project, existing GIS data is collected from various agencies.

Model Builder

The easiest way to find GIS data is to use the Model Builder. To use this feature, access to the Internet is required. The Model Builder creates a new model and includes existing datasets from the following sources:

Data Type	Source
Elevation	Terrain data for the United States and its territories uses 10 and 30 meter DEMs from the National Elevation Dataset (NED). The rest of the globe (between -60 degrees latitude) uses SRTM 90m DEM data processed by CIAT-CSI.
Imagery	Satellite imagery from Microsoft® Bing® Maps is draped over the model terrain.
Roads and Highways	OpenStreetMap's (OSM) Highway and Railway datasets are readily available. They are used to create roads and railway features in the model. If feature names are available from OSM, they appear as tooltips and provide a hyperlink to the source feature that opens in the default web browser.
Buildings	The building data is also from the OpenStreetMap dataset.

How To: Create a New Model Using Model Builder

1. On the *Home* screen, click **Model Builder**.
2. In the *Model Builder* interface, type the project address in the search field or, using the mouse, zoom in and pan on the project area using the map in the right pane.
3. Once you have selected an area (that is below the maximum area limit) the *Model Identification* window opens, as shown in Figure 2–2.

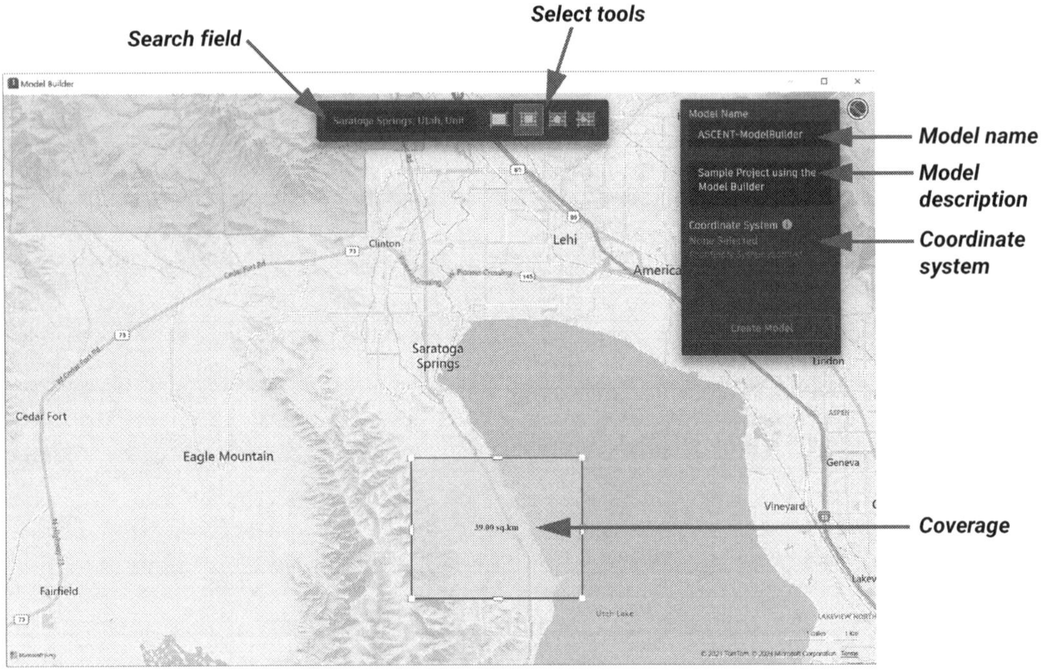

Figure 2–2

4. Use one of the **Select** tools to define the area of interest (AOI) to include in the model. You can choose between the following:
   - Select current map extents.
   - Draw a rectangle to select an AOI.
   - Draw a polygon to select an AOI.
   - Import a polygon to select an AOI.

   ***Note:** There is a **200 sq. km** maximum area limit.*

5. Once you have selected an area (that is below the maximum area limit) the *Model Identification* window opens, as shown previously in Figure 2–2. Enter the following:
    - Name for the model
    - Description for the model
    - Coordinate system for the model
6. Click **Create Model**.
7. The model will be created in the background. Click **Close** in the *Model Builder* dialog box.
8. You are notified by email when the model is ready.
9. Close the *Model Builder*.
10. On the *Home* screen, click on the newly created model to open it, as shown in Figure 2–3.

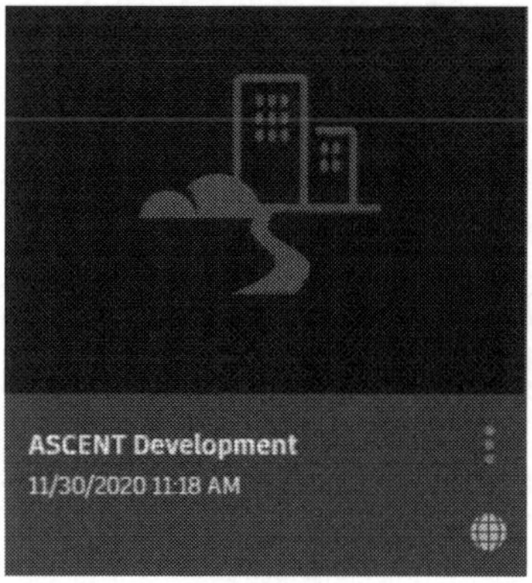

Figure 2–3

11. In the dialog box asking where to store the model, click **Local** to save it to your computer's C: drive or **Autodesk Docs** to save it in a predefined Autodesk Docs project, as shown in Figure 2–4.

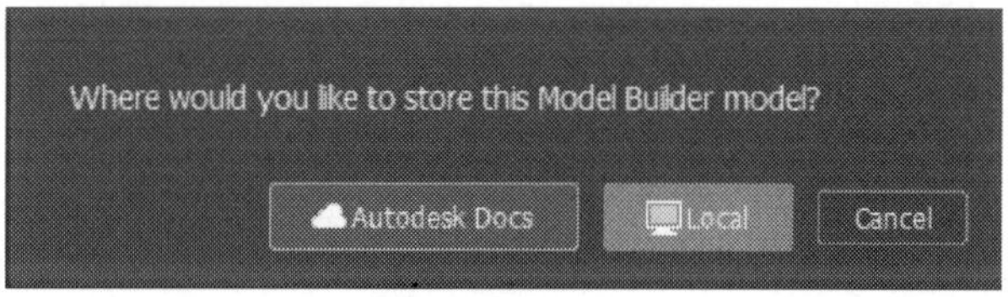

Figure 2–4

If you choose Local, the model will be stored in the default location with a numeric folder name. The default location is *C:\Users\login-name\Documents\Autodesk InfraWorks Models\Autodesk 360*. This default can be changed in the *Application Options*.

How To: Change the Location of the Cloud Models

1. On the *Home* screen, click (Application Options) in the toolbar.

2. In the *Application Options* dialog box, in the left pane, note that **General** is the current page. In the right pane, for the *Cache location for cloud models* field, you can either type in the desired path or click on the ellipsis (...) to browse to the desired location, as shown in Figure 2–5.

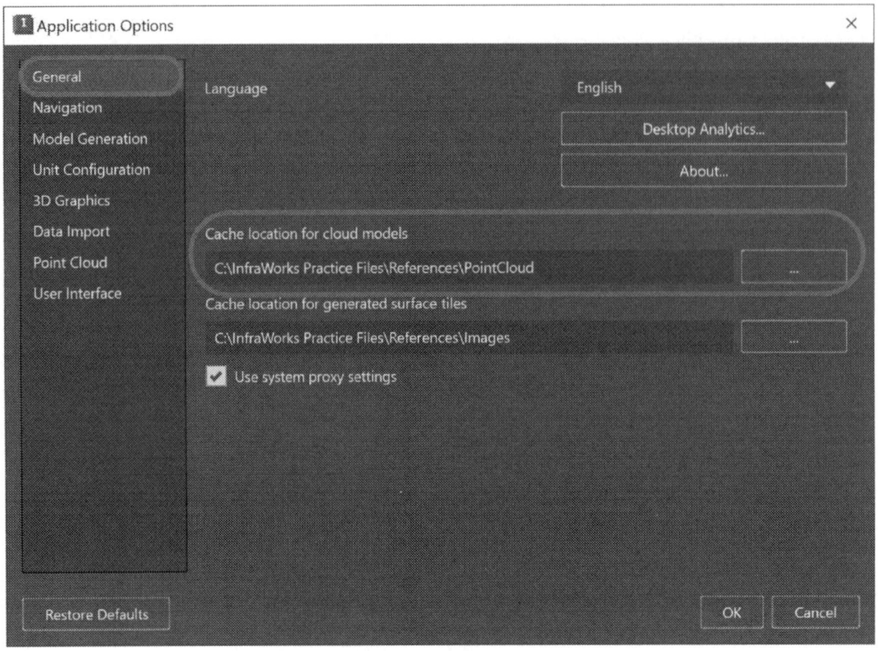

Figure 2–5

3. Click **OK**.

Finding GIS Data

Another way to find GIS data for your project site is to perform an Internet search for the city, state, and/or country where the project is located. Include the keywords **GIS data** in your search. Several agencies recognize the value that GIS data brings to a project and the importance of sharing it due to the exhausting cost of its collection.

> **Note:** *The data for this guide was downloaded from the Automated Geographic Reference Center (AGRC) (found at gis.utah.gov) and the Utah County Government GIS site (utahcounty.gov).*

A large number of Internet sites provide free GIS data to the public, such as *USGS.gov*. There are also private and government organizations around the world that collect GIS data and act as a central resource for GIS data, which you can purchase or download for free. Ensure that when you download the data sources, you include all of the connected file types and download them to the same directory.

You can also connect to ArcGIS data directly through the ArcGIS Connector described later in this chapter.

Geographic Coordinate Systems

When working with GIS data, note that it can be created in many different geographic coordinate systems. A geographical coordinate system is a mathematical equation that takes the earth's features (formed on a sphere) and projects them onto a flat sheet of paper. Cartographers first developed coordinate systems to help them map locations on Earth by assigning numbers or letters for ease in plotting them on a map. One or two numbers represent the horizontal position (*x, y* or *latitude* and *longitude*), and one number represents the vertical position (*z* or *elevation*).

Several coordinate systems have been developed over the centuries to assist in plotting elements on the Earth's surface. They include cylindrical, conical, and azimuthal, as shown in Figure 2–6. In each of the projection types, there are two ways to line up the projection plane:

- One is to make it *tangent* to the earth's surface so that there is only one line or point where the distances are 100% accurate.
- Another is to make it *secant* to the earth's surface. This provides two lines where distances are 100% accurate. The distances between the secant lines are within civil engineering error tolerances.

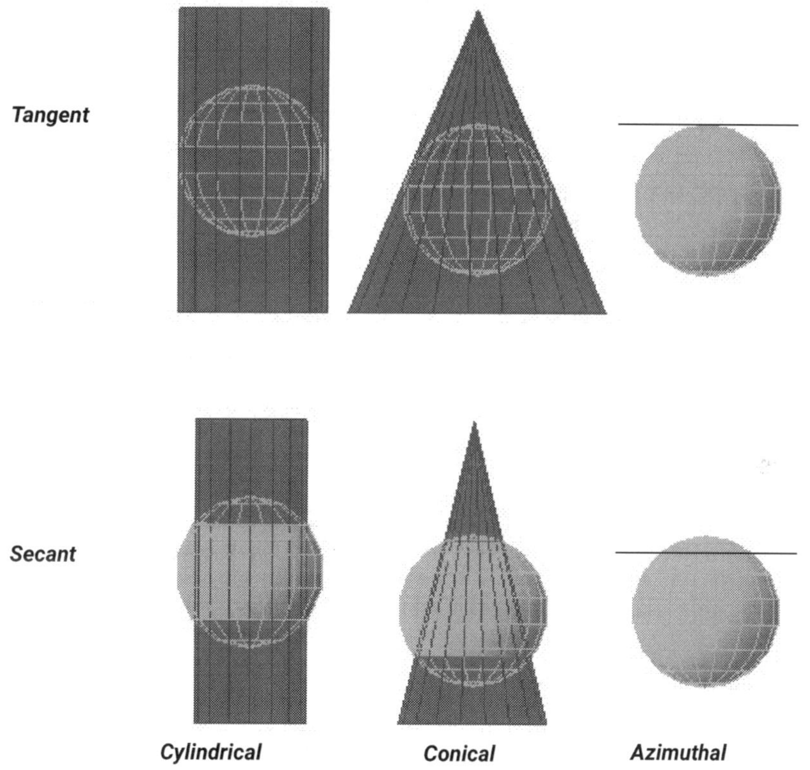

Figure 2–6

Setting Coordinate Systems and Model Extents in the Autodesk InfraWorks Software

> ***Note:*** *When a model is created using the Model Builder, the coordinate system is automatically set to LL84 (WGS84 datum, Latitude- Longitude; Degrees).*

When a new model is created using the Autodesk InfraWorks software, the coordinate system and model extents can be set immediately. Setting the model extents focuses the model on the project area and reduces the size of the model file. The minimum and maximum X- and Y- values can be entered into the software.

Setting the coordinate system indicates which mathematical equation is going to be used for setting the coordinates of your project and which values display in the bottom-left corner of the model area, as shown in Figure 2–7.

Figure 2–7

When you import data from other sources, the Autodesk InfraWorks software automatically transforms the data to your project's coordinate system and can trim the data at the project extents (minimum and maximum X,Y values). Over 6,000 coordinate systems are stored in the software.

When starting a new project, you might not know the coordinates for the model extents. In this situation, or if you used Model Builder to create the model, you can set the model extents and/or coordinate system after you import the data. In the *Manage* tab>*Model* panel, click (Model Properties). You can import the model extents from any of the following file formats:

• .ADF	• .ASC
• .BT	• .DB
• .DEM	• .DOQ
• .PNG	• .SDF
• .SQLITE	• .SHP
• .TIF	• .SID

This is helpful if you often work in the same geographical areas, or if you plan to set the model limits to the extents of an aerial image or .DEM file.

Design Standards

Design standards are used to set the horizontal and vertical design control for creating component roads. It is important to set the design standard if you plan to create component roads. Different design standards should be used depending on the location of the project and the units in which the project is being designed.

The Autodesk InfraWorks Roadway Design tools provide the opportunity to control curve radii, grades, and other parameters associated with road geometry.

How To: Start a New Model with the Correct Coordinate System

1. On the *Home* screen, click **New**.
2. Type a file name in the *Name* field and a description in the *Description* field.
3. Set the location for storing the file:
    - If you select *Collaborate*, you will also need to select the BIM 360 project folder with which to share the file.
    - If you select *Work Local*, you will also need to set the directory path.
4. Click **Model Extents** to expand the *Model Extents* area, as shown in Figure 2–8.

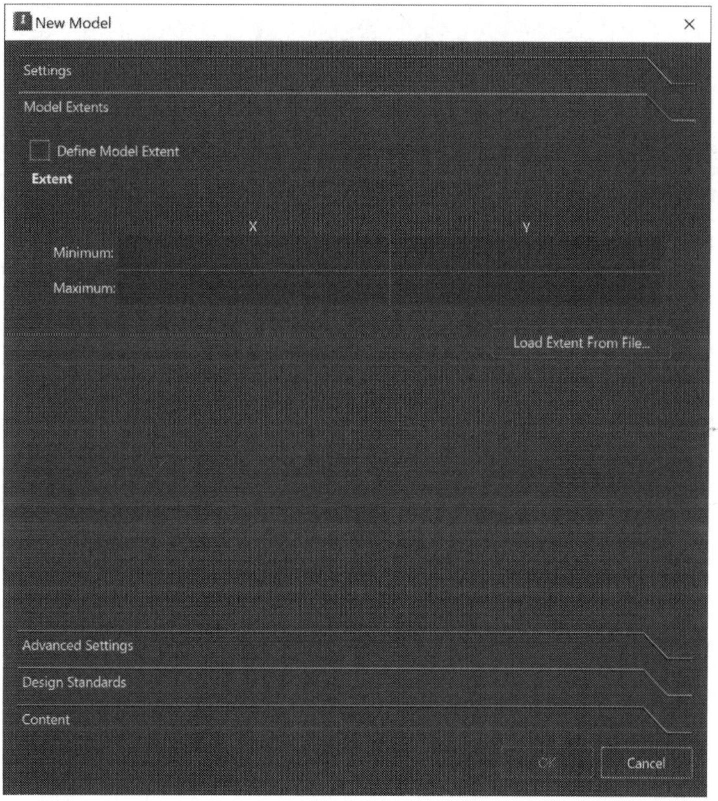

Figure 2–8

5. Select the **Define Model Extent** option to set the minimum and maximum X and Y values to set the model extents.
6. Click **Advanced Settings**.
7. In the *Advanced Settings* area under *Display Coordinates*, click (Choose coordinate system) in the *User Coordinate System (UCS)* field. Select a category in the left pane, and then double-click on the project coordinate system in the right pane, as shown in Figure 2–9.

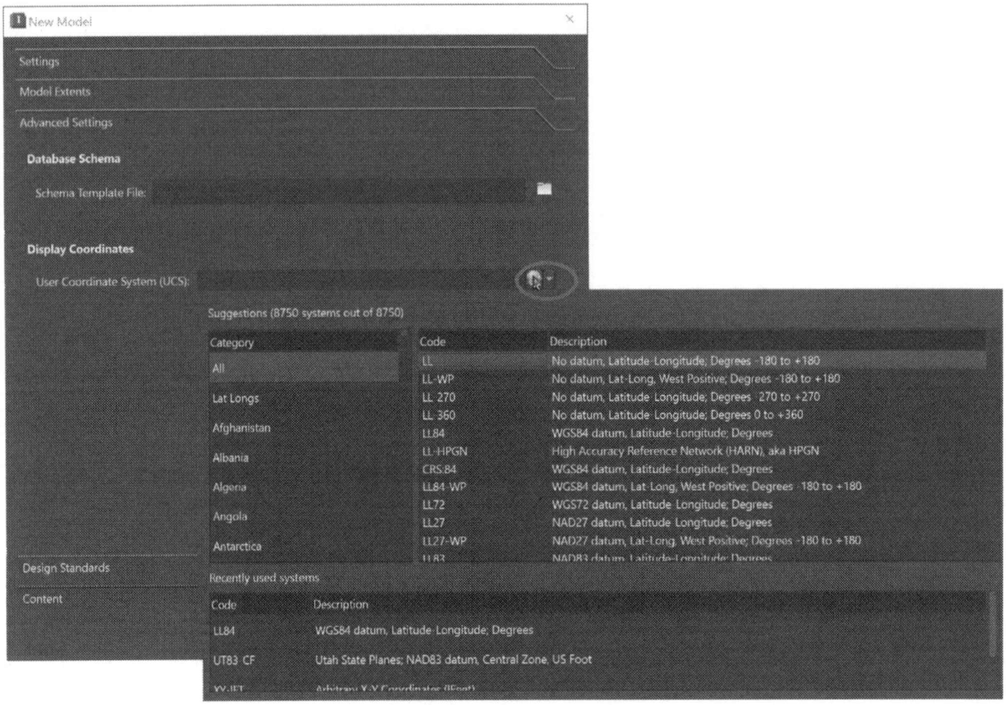

Figure 2–9

8. Click **Design Standards**.

9. In the *Road Standards* drop-down list, select the appropriate standards for your project, then indicate the *Driving Direction* by selecting which side of the road traffic travels on, as shown in Figure 2–10.

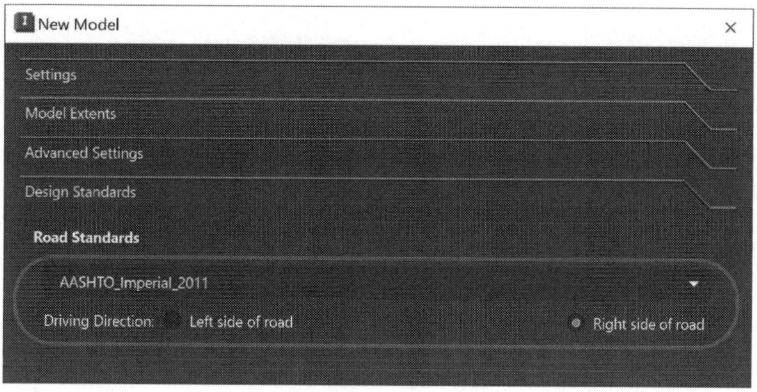

Figure 2–10

10. Click **OK** to create the model.

How To: Set the Coordinate System of an Existing Model

1. In the *Manage* tab>*Model* panel, click (Model Properties).
2. In the *Model Properties* dialog box, in the *Coordinate Systems* area, in the *UCS* field, click (Choose coordinate system).
3. Select a category in the left pane, then double-click on the project coordinate system in the right pane.

   Note: *If Model Builder was used to create the model, the model extents are defined during the creation process.*

4. To change the model extents, clear the **Use Entire Model** option and use one of the following methods to set the model extents, as shown in Figure 2–11.
   - Use the **Define Interactively** tool and select either the **BBox** (bounding box) or **Polygon** option.
   - Enter the minimum and maximum X- and Y-values.
   - Load the values from an external file by clicking **Load Extent From File**.

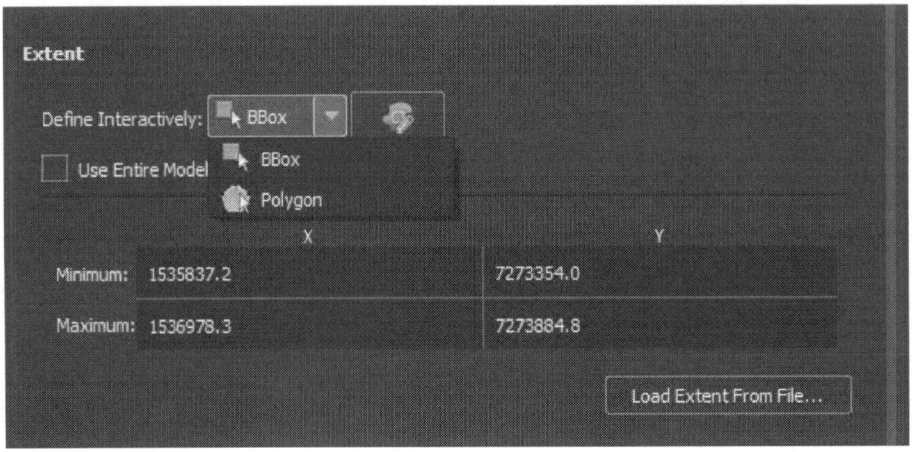

Figure 2–11

5. Click **Save**.

Metadata

Most GIS sources provide metadata in the form of an HTML or PDF file. This metadata file contains information on the contents of the file, coordinate system used in the file, limitations of the file, and the kind of data contained in each of the database fields.

Understanding how the GIS data was created helps you to understand how the data can be used, and how much you can rely on its accuracy. Metadata for all of the GIS source files used in this guide is located in the practice files *Metadata* folder.

Hint: Locating the Information About the Database Fields

If the metadata file does not describe each of the fields in the database connected to the geographic features, you can use the AutoCAD® Map 3D software or the Autodesk® Civil 3D® software to determine the information. Connect to the data using the **Planning** and **Analysis** tools and open the data table.

Units

The assigned coordinate system indicates which units are used for the model (feet or meters). However, those units do not display automatically. The default units that display in the model are meters. Once changed, the new units remain the display units for all the models opened in the Autodesk InfraWorks software until changed.

Hint: Imperial Units - Feet vs. US Survey Feet

If you are using imperial units, you can display them in feet or US Survey feet. The difference between the two measurements is only 2 parts per million. However, that difference is measured from the origin and results in a difference of 2 feet for every 189 miles from the origin point. Therefore, it is important to use the same units as the coordinate system.

How To: Set the Display Units for the Model

1. On the *Home* screen, click (Application Options) in the toolbar.
   - Alternatively, if you already have a model open, in the toolbar, use the (Utilities) drop-down list to select (Application Options).
2. In the *Application Options* dialog box, in the left pane, select **Unit Configuration**. In the right pane, select the required *Default Units* for the model, as shown in Figure 2–12.

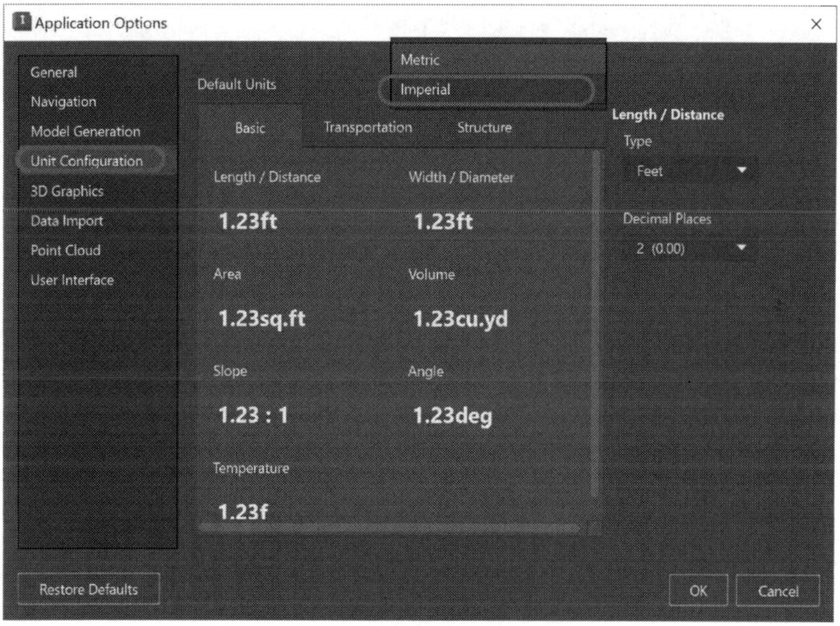

Figure 2–12

3. Click **OK**.

Practice 2a
Create a New Model from Scratch

Practice Objectives

- Create a new model from scratch.
- Set the coordinate system and units for the model.

In this practice, you will create a new model from scratch while simultaneously setting the coordinate system for the model.

1. On the *Home* screen, click **New**..., as shown in Figure 2–13.

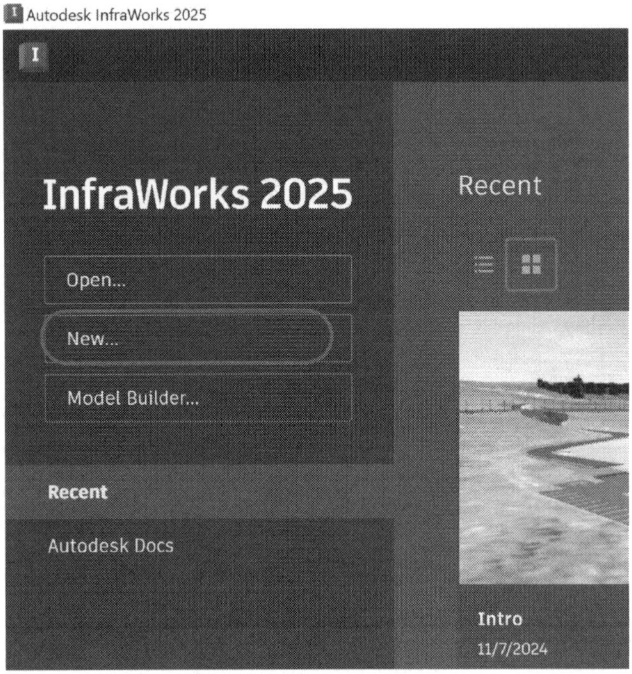

Figure 2–13

2. In the *New Model* dialog box, set the following, as shown in Figure 2–14:
   - *Name*: **ASCENT-Scratch**
   - *Description:* **Sample Project starting from scratch**
   - Select the **Work Local** option.
   - *Work Local:* **InfraWorks Practice Files/2-Connect-Data**

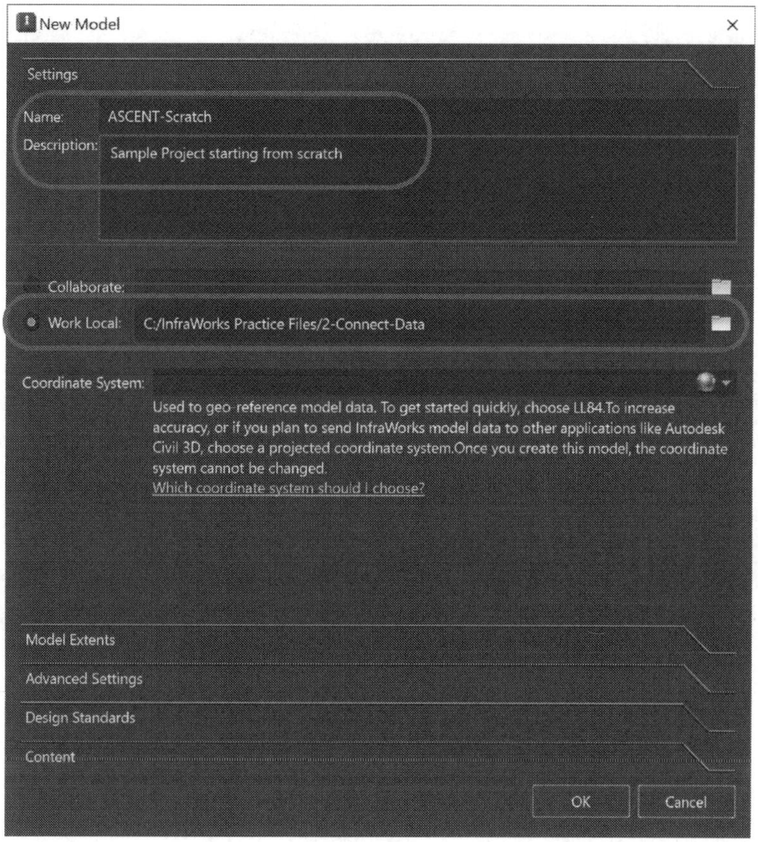

Figure 2–14

3. For the *Coordinate System* field, click (Choose coordinate system). Under *Category*, select **USA, Utah**. Under *Code*, double-click on the **UT83-CF** coordinate system, as shown in Figure 2–15.

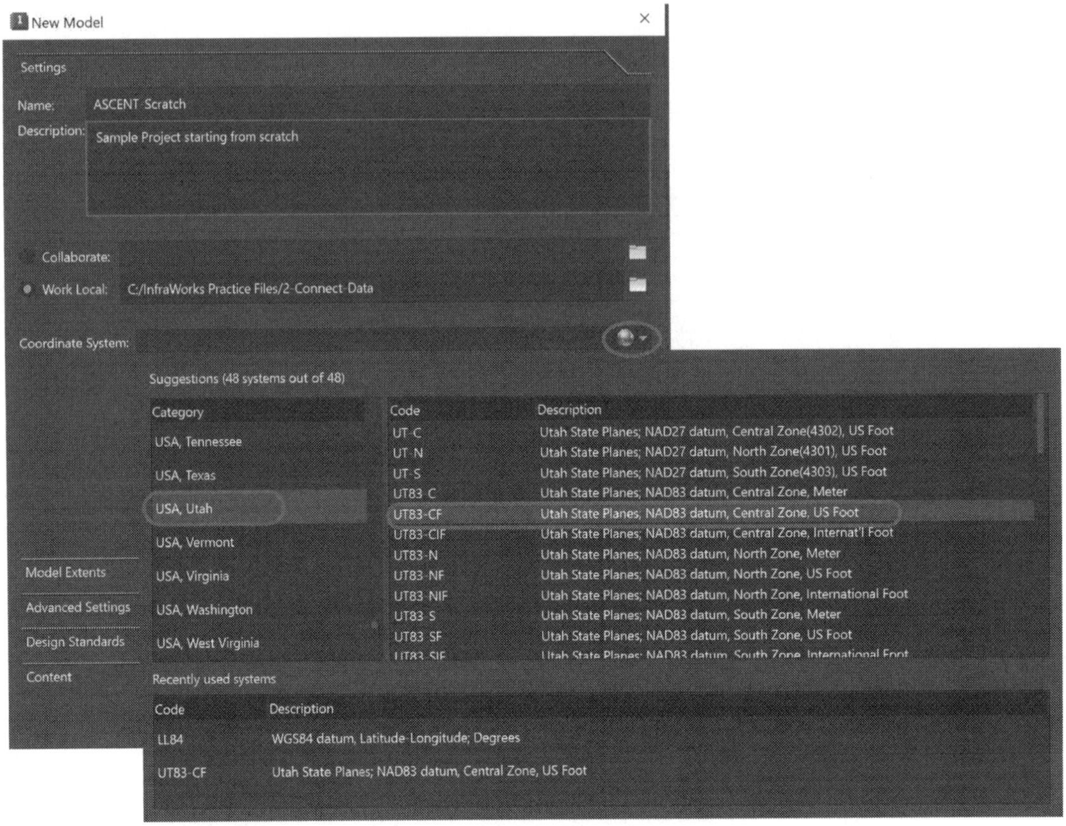

Figure 2–15

4. Click **OK** to create the model. When done processing, you will see a blank canvas consisting of a blue sky and a dark blue surface in the model window. There is no data yet to display.

5. In the toolbar, click (Application Options).

6. In the *Application Options* dialog box, select **Unit Configuration**. Expand the *Default Units* drop-down list and select **Imperial**, as shown in Figure 2–16.

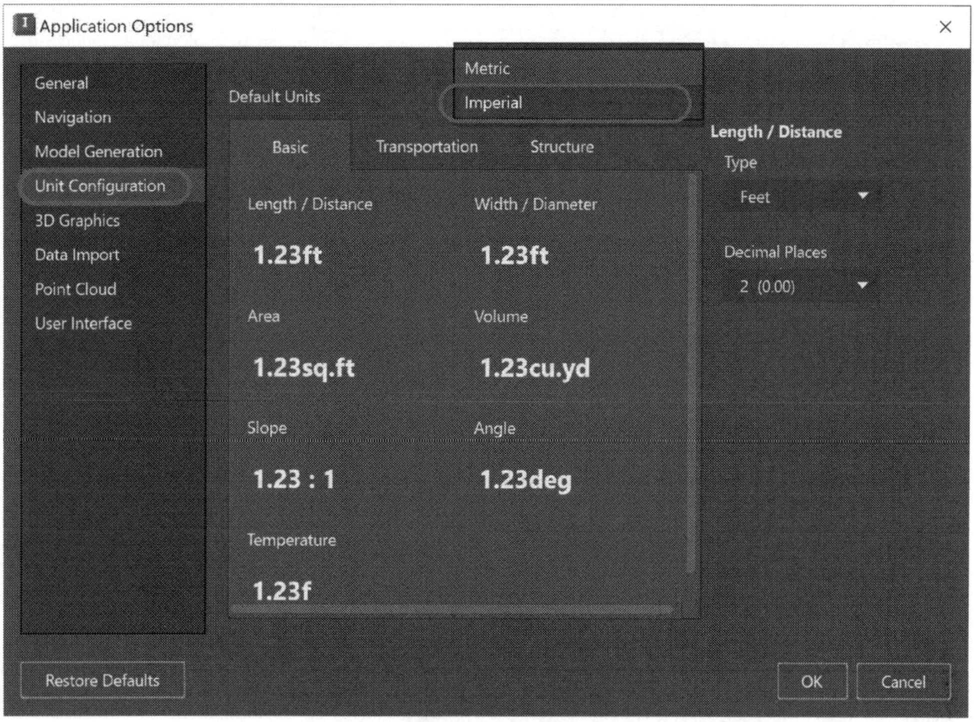

Figure 2–16

7. Click on the *Transportation* tab and the *Structure* tab to review the units, but do not change anything.
8. Click **OK**.

End of practice

Practice 2b
Create a New Model Using Model Builder

Practice Objectives

- Create a new model with existing GIS data.
- Set the coordinate system and units for the model.

In this practice, you will create a new model using the Model Builder and add existing GIS data to it automatically during the creation process. Then, you will change the coordinate system and units for display.

Note: *To complete this practice, access to the Internet is required.*

1. On the *Home* screen, click **Model Builder...**, as shown in Figure 2–17.

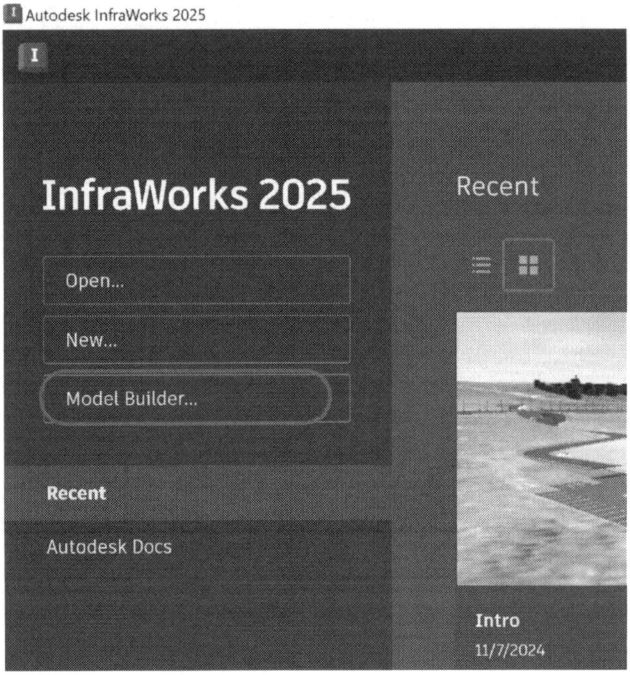

Figure 2–17

2. In the *Model Builder* dialog box, in the search field, type **Saratoga Springs, Utah**.

3. To set the area of interest, click (Draw a rectangle to select an AOI). Zoom in and select the area indicated in Figure 2–18.

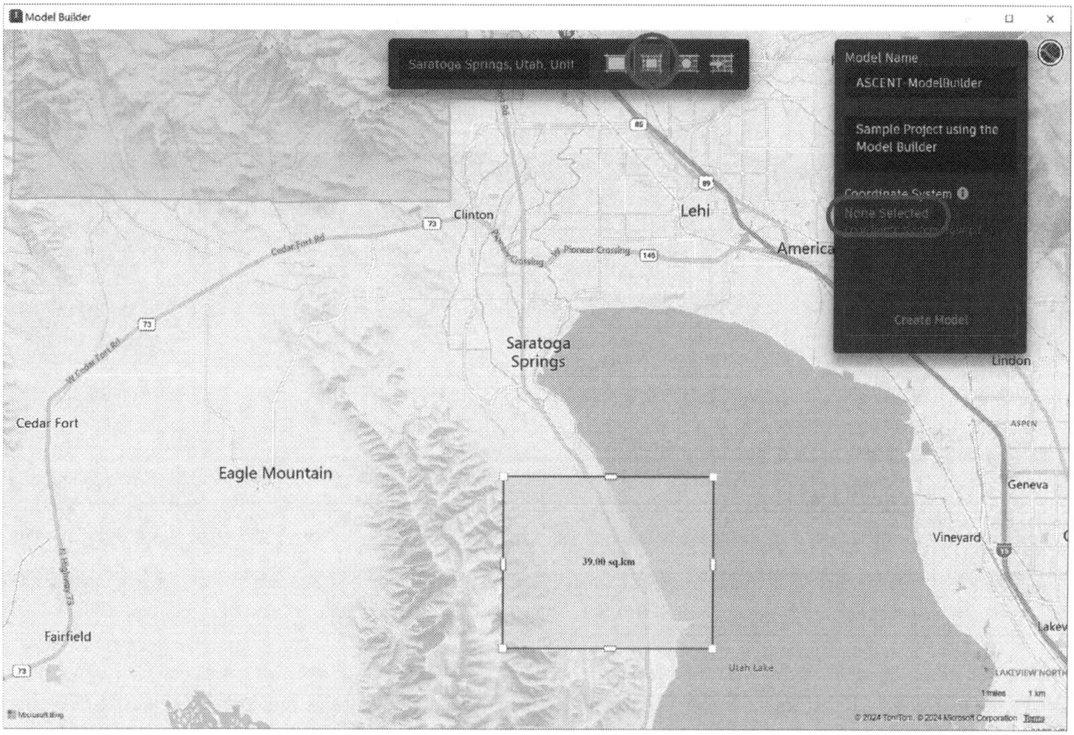

Figure 2–18

4. Set the *Model Name* to **ASCENT-ModelBuilder**.
5. Click the **Add description** blue text to add a model description. Enter **Sample Project using the Model Builder**.
6. Click the **None Selected** blue text under *Coordinate System*.

7. For the *Category*, select **USA, Utah**. In the right pane, double-click on the **UT83-CF** coordinate system, as shown in Figure 2–19, and click **OK**. As an option, you can type **ut83** in the *Search* field in the top-right corner to filter the results.

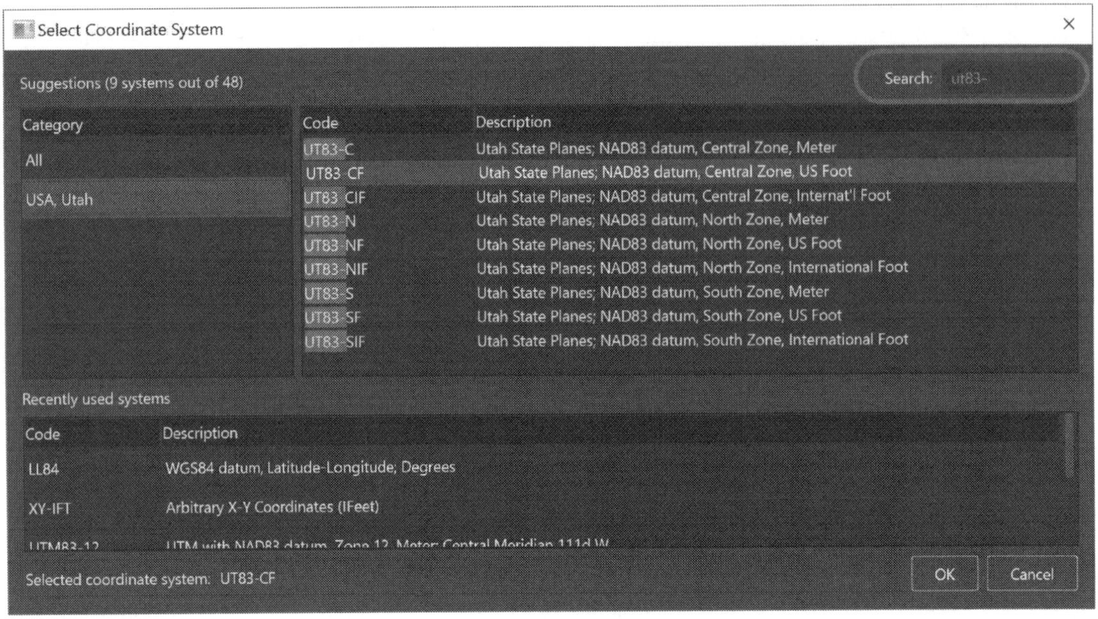

Figure 2–19

8. Note the new message in orange explaining that the coordinate system cannot be changed once the model has been created.
9. Click **Create Model**.
10. A dialog box displays, informing you the model is being prepared. By clicking the **Show details** blue text, you can review the model information, as shown in Figure 2–20.

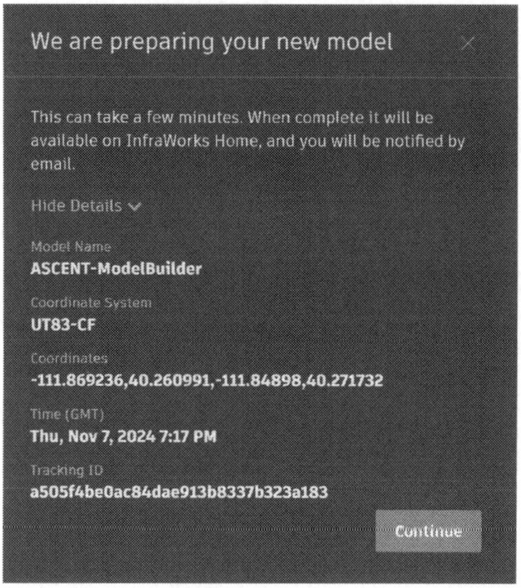

Figure 2–20

11. Click **Continue**.
12. It will take a few minutes before the model displays on the *Home* screen. Click the **X** in the top-right corner to close the *Model Builder* interface.
13. You will receive an email when the model is ready, as shown in Figure 2–21.

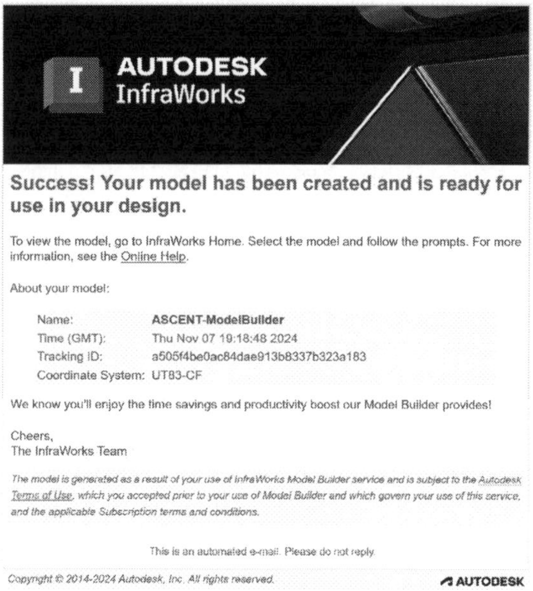

Figure 2–21

14. On the *Home* screen, a new entry for the **ASCENT-ModelBuilder** model will display, as shown in Figure 2–22. Note the globe symbol, indicating it is a Model Builder model.

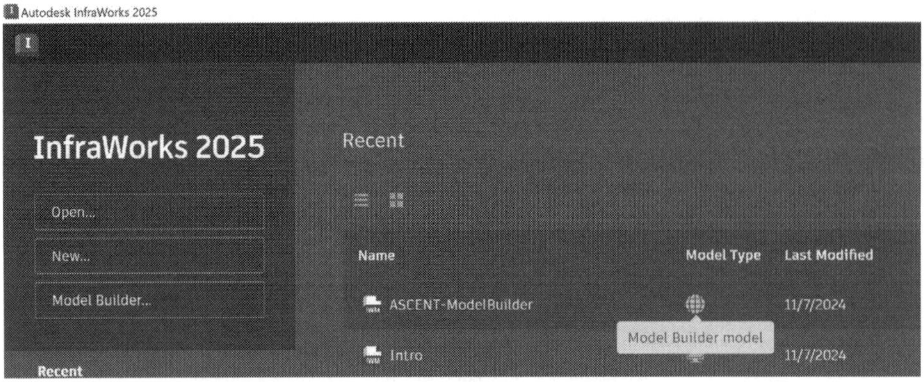

Figure 2–22

15. In the dialog box asking where to store the model, click **Local**. This will save the model in its default location, which is displayed when you hover over the computer icon on the *Home* screen, as shown in Figure 2–23.

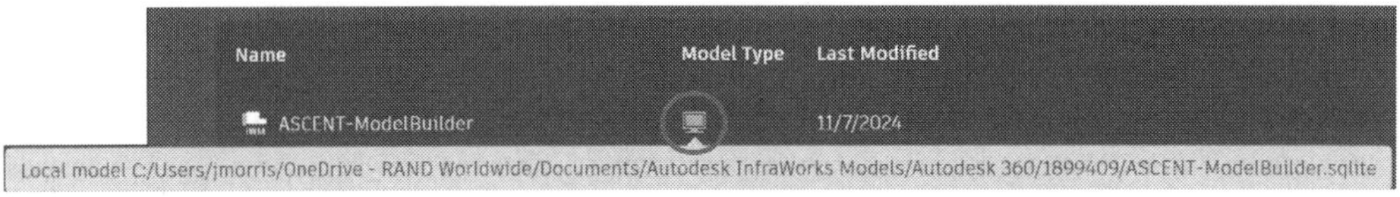

Figure 2–23

16. The model will download from the cloud, which may take some time. When finished, the model opens.

17. In the toolbar, click (Application Options).

18. In the *Application Options* dialog box, select **Unit Configuration**. Expand the *Default Units* drop-down list and select **Imperial**, as shown in Figure 2–24.

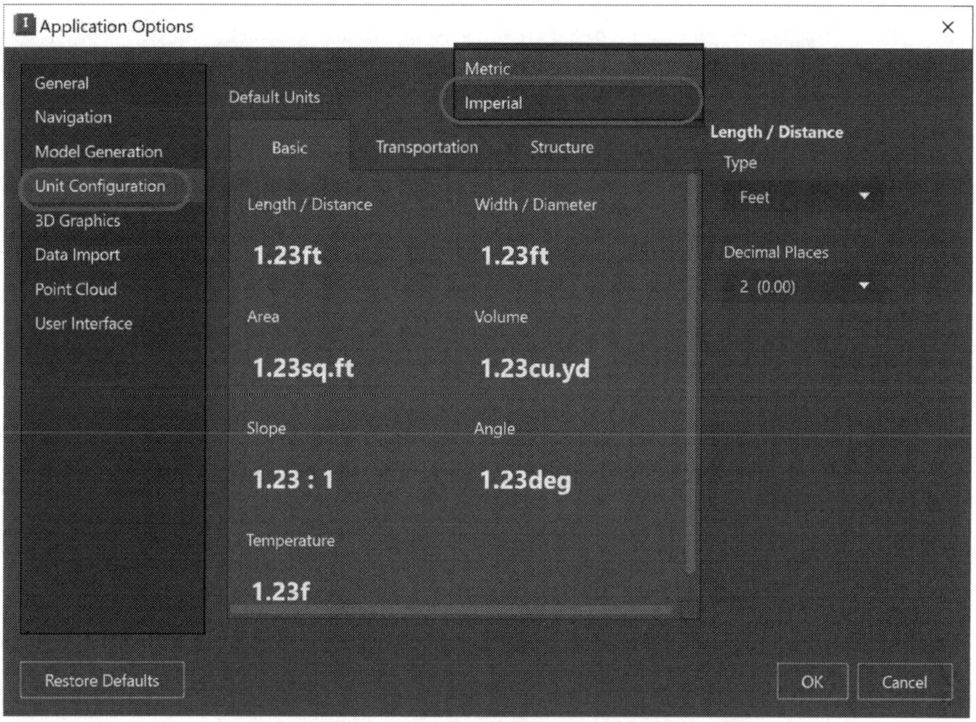

Figure 2–24

19. Click on the *Transportation* tab and the *Structure* tab to review the units, but do not change anything.
20. Click **OK**.

End of practice

2.2 Connect to Data Sources

External GIS data is imported into the model as layers using the Model Builder or the *Data Sources panel*, as shown in Figure 2–25. The *Data Sources* panel opens when a new, empty model is created. If you close it before you have finished adding data, you can reopen it with the Project Tools.

In the *Data Sources* panel, connected data is listed in the top area, while information about the data is listed in the bottom area. Three categories of data sources can be used in the model:

- File data sources, which can be added by clicking  (Add file data source).
- Database data sources, which can be added by clicking  (Add database data source).
- ArcGIS data sources, which can be added by clicking  (Add ArcGIS data source).

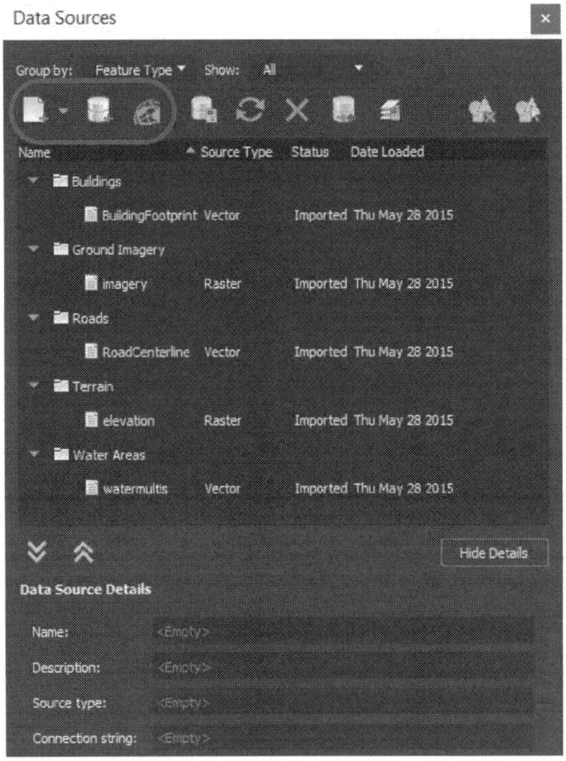

Figure 2–25

File Data Sources

A file data source can be a raster or vector file. Several different file data sources can be imported into the Autodesk InfraWorks model, as shown in Figure 2–26. For each file data source type, multiple file formats can be used. To add a file data source, click  (Add file data source) in the *Data Sources* panel.

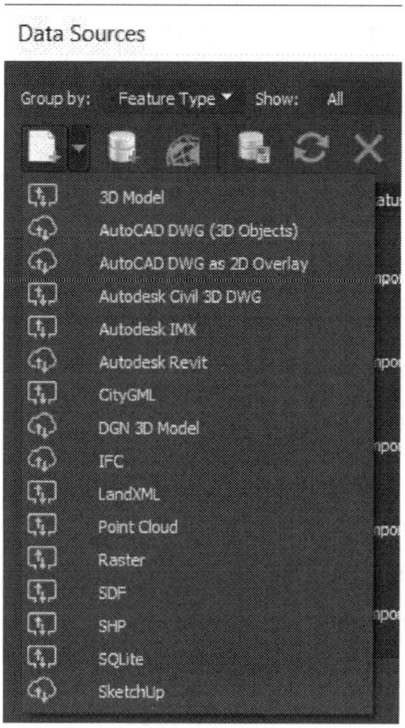

Figure 2–26

The uses of each data file format are as follows:

Data File Format	Use and Accepted File Extensions
3D Model	Used to import local 3D models (.3DS, .DAE, .DXF, .FBX, .OBJ).
Autodesk Civil 3D DWG	Used to import Autodesk Civil 3D objects, which include corridors, surfaces, pipes, and pipe networks (.DWG). To use this file format, you must have the Autodesk Civil 3D software installed.
AutoCAD DWG (3D Objects)	Used to import local or cloud-based 3D objects, including 3D solids, surfaces, and meshes (.DWG). To use this file format, you must have a connection to the Internet and an Autodesk 360 (A360) account.

Data File Format	Use and Accepted File Extensions
AutoCAD DWG as 2D Overlay	Used to import local or cloud-based 2D line data from AutoCAD files (.DWG, .DXF). To use this file format, a connection to the Internet and an A360 account are required.
Autodesk IMX	Used to import local Autodesk Civil 3D design elements, such as surfaces, pipes, alignments, profiles, and corridor shapes (.IMX).
Autodesk Revit	Used to import Autodesk Revit files (.RVT, .RFA). To use this file format, a connection to the Internet and an A360 account are required.
CityGML	Used to import virtual 3D city models (.CITYGML, .GML, or .XML). To use this file format, you must install and use the free CityGML Importer for InfraWorks.
DGN 3D Model	Used to import cloud-based or local 2D and 3D line work from Bentley v7 or v8 software (.DGN). To use this file format, a connection to the Internet and an A360 account are required.
IFC	Used to import cloud-based or local Industry Foundation Classes (IFC) models (.IFC). To use this file format, a connection to the Internet and an A360 account are required.
LandXML	Used to import local terrain or surface models (.XML, .LANDXML).
Point Cloud	Used to import local 3D laser scans (.RCS, .RCP). Note: Point clouds must be imported into Recap first to be configured. If you do not do this step, the point cloud does not render.
Raster	Used to import local terrain or surface data from raster or vector-based data as well as imagery (.ADF, .ASC, .BT, .DDF, .DEM, .DT0, .DT1, .DT2, .GRD, .HGT, .DOG, .ECW, .IMG, .JP2, .JPG, .JPEG, .PNG, .SID, .TIF, .TIFF, .WMS, .XML, .VRT, .ZIP, .GZ).
SDF	Used to import local Autodesk Spatial Data Files 3.0 (.SDF).
SHP	Used to import local ESRI Shape Files (.SHP). Note: It is important to ensure that you have all of the files that are associated with a shape file that is stored in the same location as the shape file (.PRJ, .SHX, .SBN, .DBF, .IDX, .SBX, etc.).
SketchUp Files	Used to import cloud-based or local SketchUp (up to 2016) files (.SKP). To use this file format, a connection to the Internet and an A360 account are required.
SQLite	Used to import SQLite 3.6 files (.SDX, .SQLITE, .DB).

How To: Connect to File Data Sources

1. In the *Manage* tab>*Content* panel, click  (Data Sources) to open the *Data Sources* panel.
2. In the *Data Sources* panel, expand  (Add file data source) and select a file format, as shown in Figure 2–27.

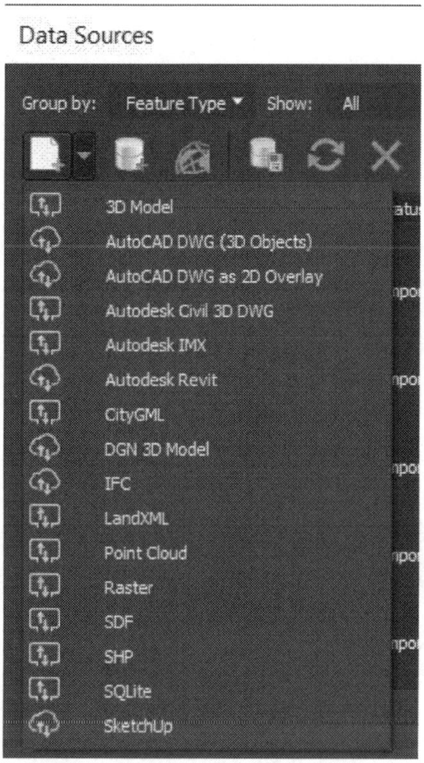

Figure 2–27

Note: *Hold <Shift> or <Ctrl> to select multiple files from the directory.*

3. Browse to the directory in which the file is located. Select the required file(s) and click **Open**.

Hint: Cloud vs. Local Import

When importing files, the Autodesk InfraWorks software converts the files into a usable format. This conversion is usually completed in the cloud. You can modify the application options to enable local processing of supported formats.

If you want to use the Autodesk Navisworks software (rather than the cloud) to process files, in the toolbar, use the (Utilities) drop-down list to select (Application Options). In the *Application Options* dialog box, on the *Data Import* page, select **Navisworks based Local Import**, as shown in Figure 2–28.

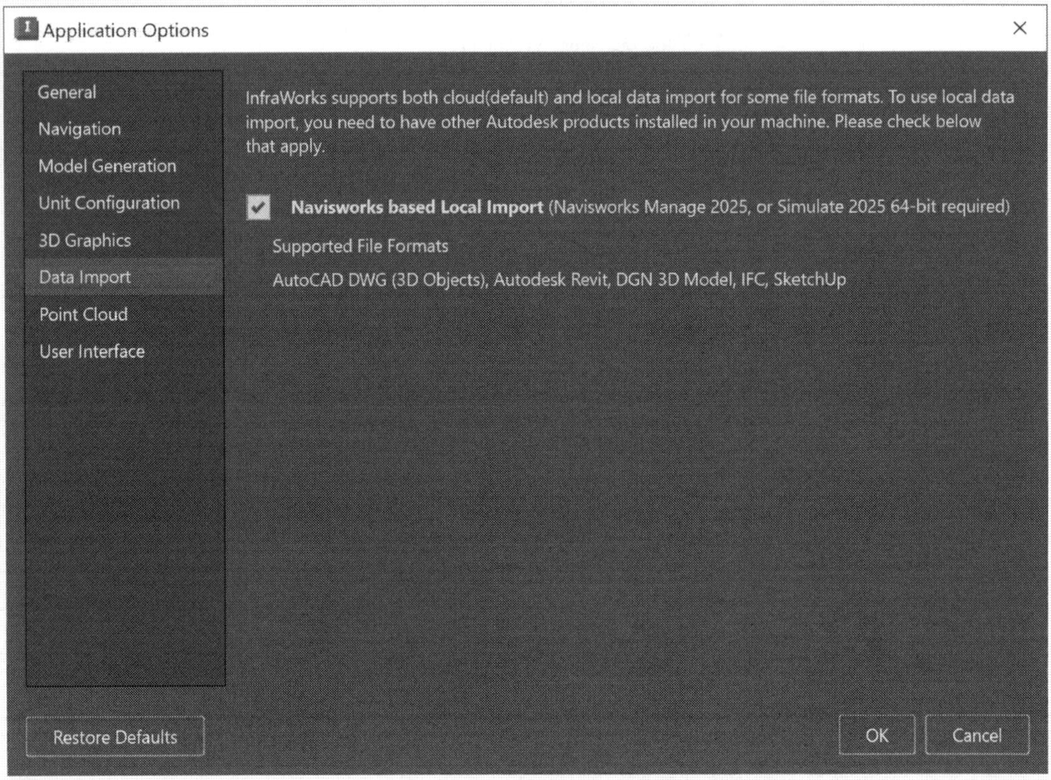

Figure 2–28

Database Data Sources

A database data source can be a vector, ODBC, or OpenGIS raster file. Seven different database types can be added to the Autodesk InfraWorks model. To connect to a database, click  (Add database data source) in the *Data Sources* panel. In the *Connect to Data Source* dialog box, select the database type in the *Connection type* drop-down list (as shown in Figure 2–29) and fill in the required fields.

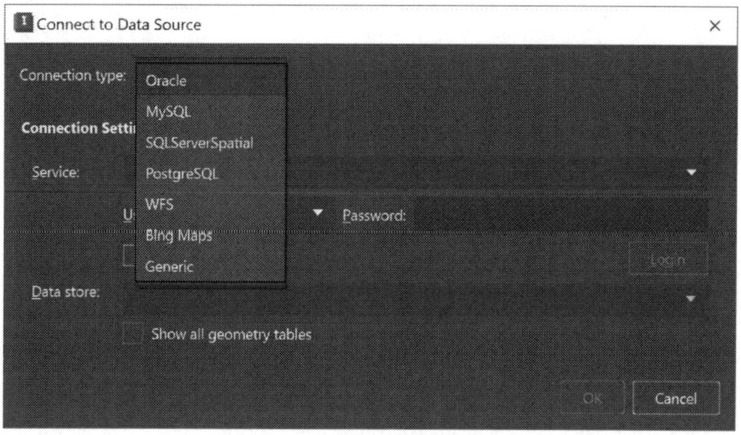

Figure 2–29

The types of database data sources are as follows:

Database	Description
Oracle	Imports Oracle Express, Standard, and Enterprise Editions (Oracle 11g, Release 2 or Oracle 12c, Release 1). Note: The Oracle Client or Instant Client must be installed and configured before the file can be connected.
MySQL	Imports MySQL 5.7. Note that to connect to your MySQL data source, you need to copy **libmySQL.dll** into the *Autodesk\InfraWorks* folder.
SQL Server Spatial	Imports Microsoft SQL Server 2008 R2, 2012, 2014, or 2016, which supports Standard and Enterprise Editions.
PostgreSQL	Imports PostGIS 2.2 and PostgreSQL 9.5.
WFS	Imports WFS 2.0.0.
Bing Maps	Imports imagery, which can be one tile at ground resolution of 78,271.5170 m/pxl, up to 19 tiles at ground resolution of 0.2986 m/pxl.
Generic	Imports a number of generic database types, such as ArcSDE 9.3 SP1, 10.2, 10.3, 10.3.1, 10.4, TIGER, DGN, UK.NTF, etc. Note: ArcSDE connections require a script that is unique to each instance.

How To: Connect to Database Data Sources

1. In the *Manage* tab>*Content* panel, click (Data Sources) to open the *Data Sources* panel.
2. In the *Data Sources* panel, click (Add database data source). In the *Connect to Data Source* dialog box, select the database type in the *Connection type* drop-down list, as shown in Figure 2–30.

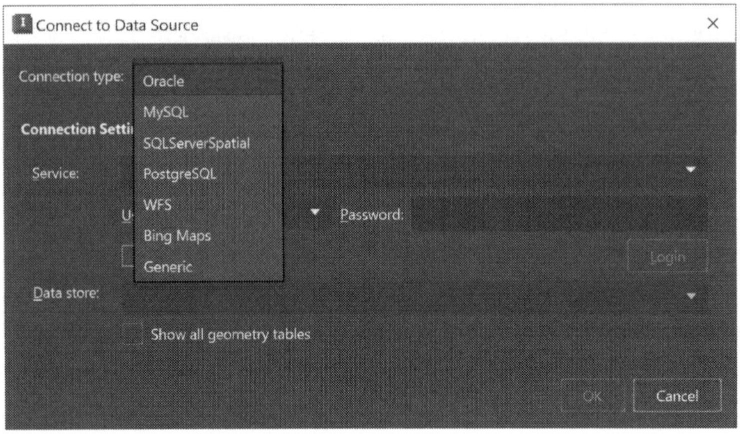

Figure 2–30

3. Fill in all of the required login information for the selected database and click **OK**.

Hint: Missing Data Source Files

When InfraWorks projects use data from *Model Builder*, the data sources cannot be modified. A warning message displays, as shown in Figure 2–31.

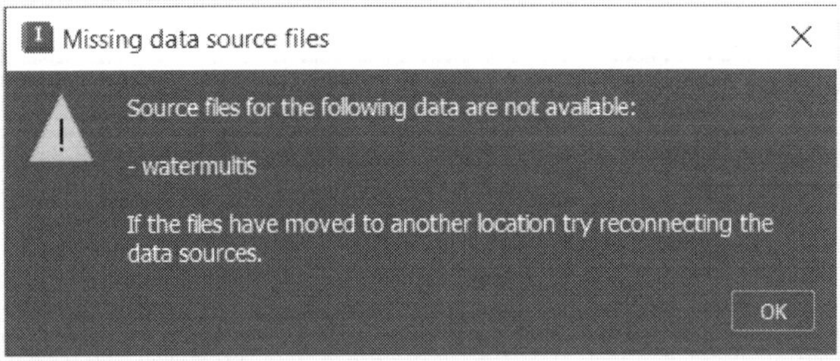

Figure 2–31

Autodesk Connector for ArcGIS

For ESRI ® ArcGIS Online and Enterprise portals, you can connect directly to these sources using your ESRI ArcGIS login information to connect within the *Data Sources* panel, as shown in Figure 2–32.

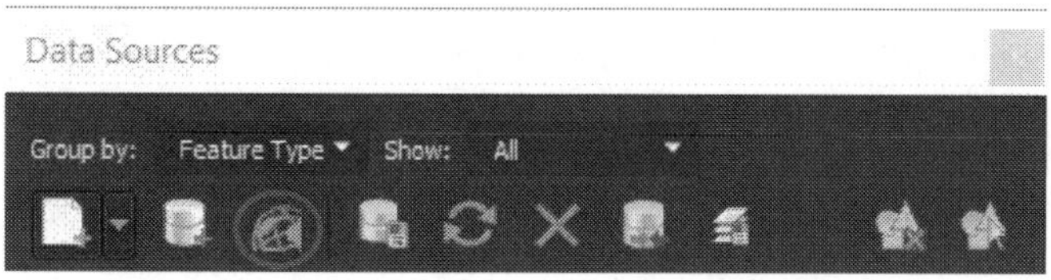

Figure 2–32

You may require ESRI login credentials to enter the portal, as show in Figure 2–33.

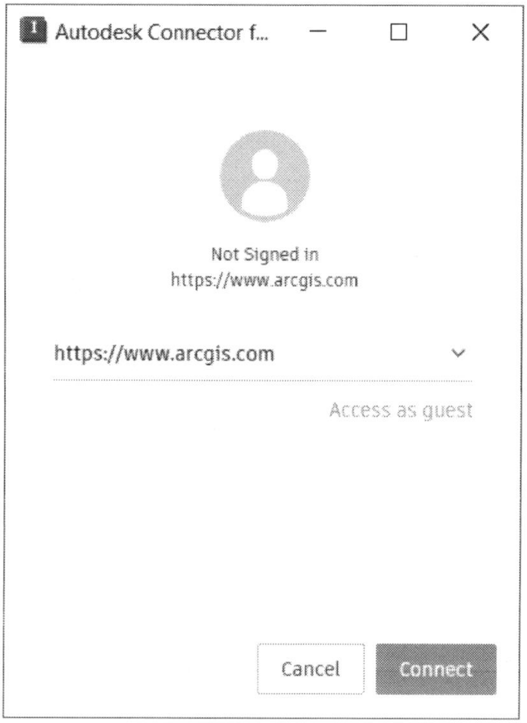

Figure 2–33

Inside the portal, you can navigate to your project site by entering an address, location name, or longitudinal and latitudinal coordinates (as shown in Figure 2–34).

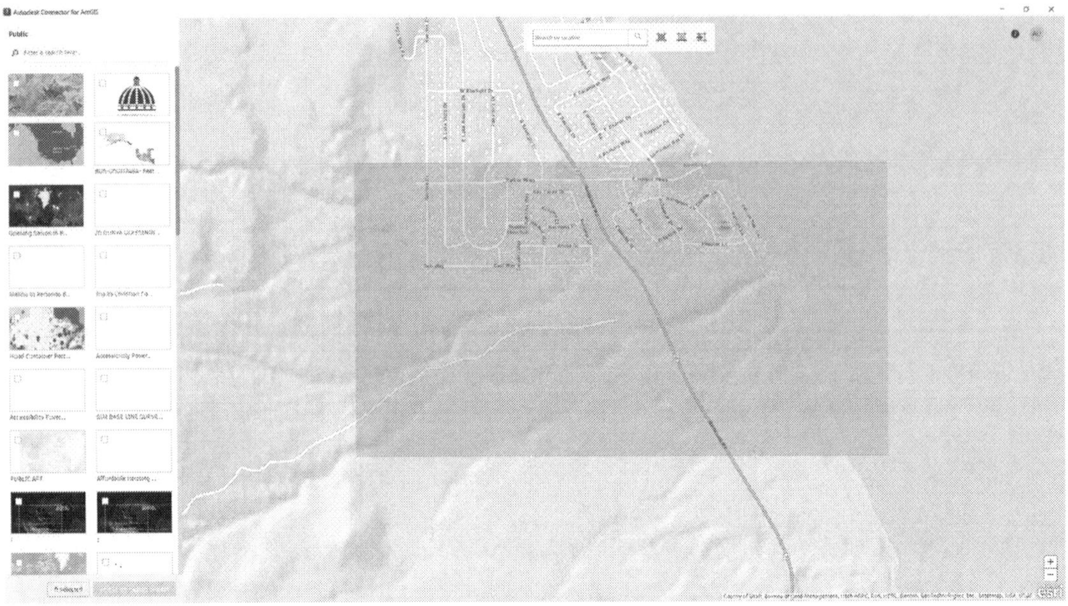

Figure 2–34

From there, you can browse through available datasets contained within your organization's ArcGIS Online content to be included with your project.

Practice 2c
Import GIS Data

Practice Objective

- Connect to existing GIS data.

In this practice, you will connect additional data to the model that you obtained from the local government agencies. This data includes a more accurate DEM file, a higher resolution aerial image, and various shape files that contain roads, water bodies, buildings, etc. You can choose to add data to the blank canvas of the model created in ***Practice 2a: Create a New Model from Scratch*** or you can add more accurate data to the model created using the Model Builder in ***Practice 2b: Create a New Model Using Model Builder***.

However, the model created for this exercise includes predefined bookmarks to help you navigate the model more efficiently.

1. Open **CreateModel.sqlite** from the *InfraWorks Practice Files\2-Connect Data* folder.
2. In the toolbar, ensure the **master** proposal is active to base a new proposal on, as shown in Figure 2–35.

Figure 2–35

3. Expand the  (Proposals) drop-down list and click **Add** to create a new proposal, as shown above in Figure 2–35. Name it **XXX_Proposal** (substituting **XXX** with your initials).
4. In the *Manage* tab>*Content* panel, click  (Data Sources).

   Note: *The data that is already in the model came from Model Builder.*

5. In the *Data Sources* panel, take note of the data that is already connected to the model. Zoom in and view the data in the model a little closer.

In the *Data Sources* panel, double-click on any of the data sources. You should receive an error because you cannot modify data source connections that came from *Model Builder*, as shown in Figure 2–36.

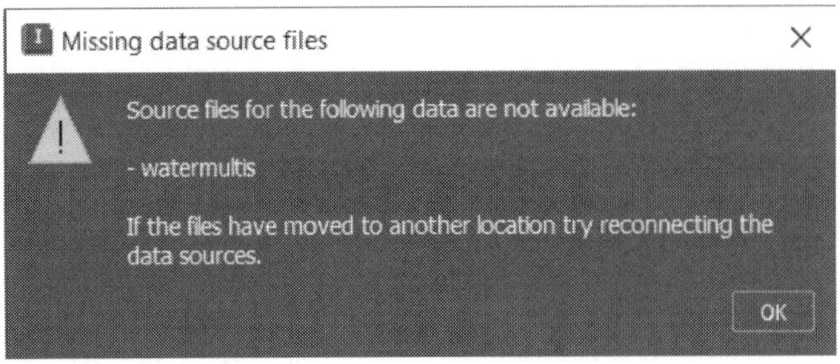

Figure 2–36

6. Click **OK** to dismiss the warning.

7. In the *Data Sources* panel, expand  (Add file data source) and select **Raster**, as shown in Figure 2–37.

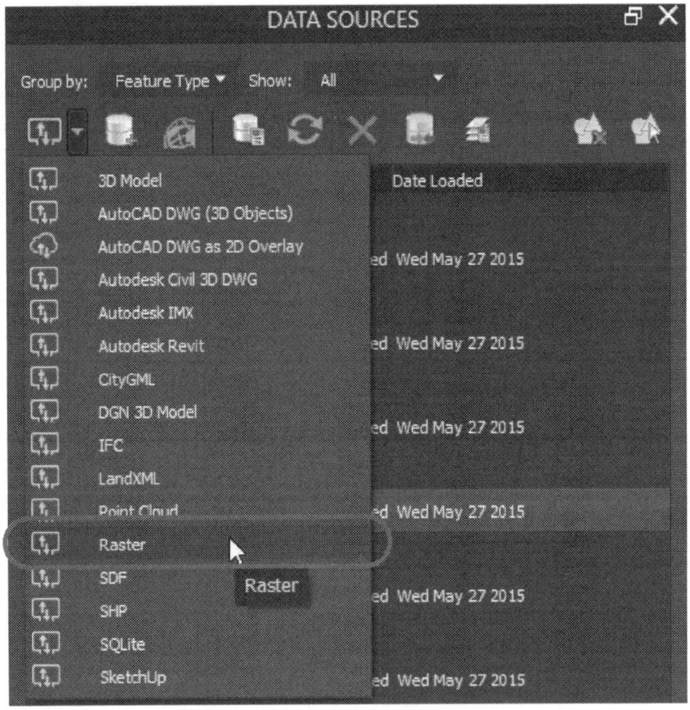

Figure 2–37

***Note:** Use <Ctrl> when choosing the files to select multiple files.*

8. Browse to the *InfraWorks Practice Files\References\Images* folder. Select the three DEM files[1] in the folder and click **Open**.
9. Note that these are now entered under the **Terrain** branch of the *Data Sources* panel, as shown in Figure 2–38.

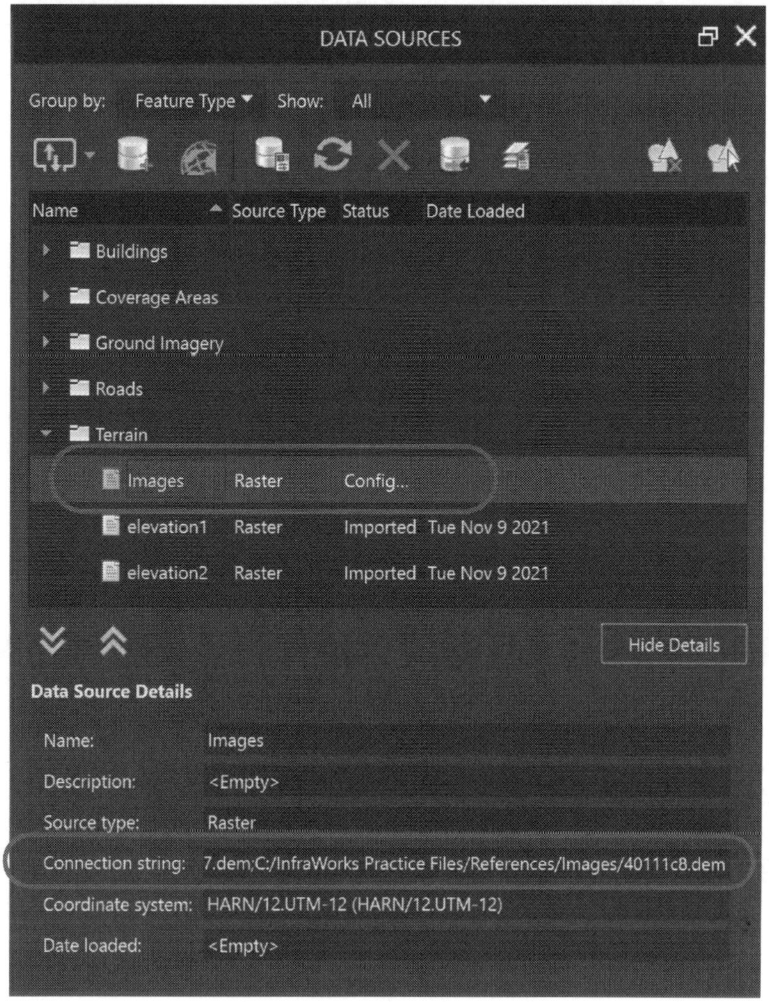

Figure 2–38

1. (AGRC), Utah Automated Geographic Reference Center, 2007; (AGRC), Automated Geographic Reference Center, 2012; Department, GIS Division of the Utah County Information Systems, 2013

10. Repeat the process for adding the **12TVK240580.tiff** and the **12TVK260580.tiff**.

11. Note that these are now entered under the **Ground Imagery** branch of the *Data Sources* panel, as shown in Figure 2–39.

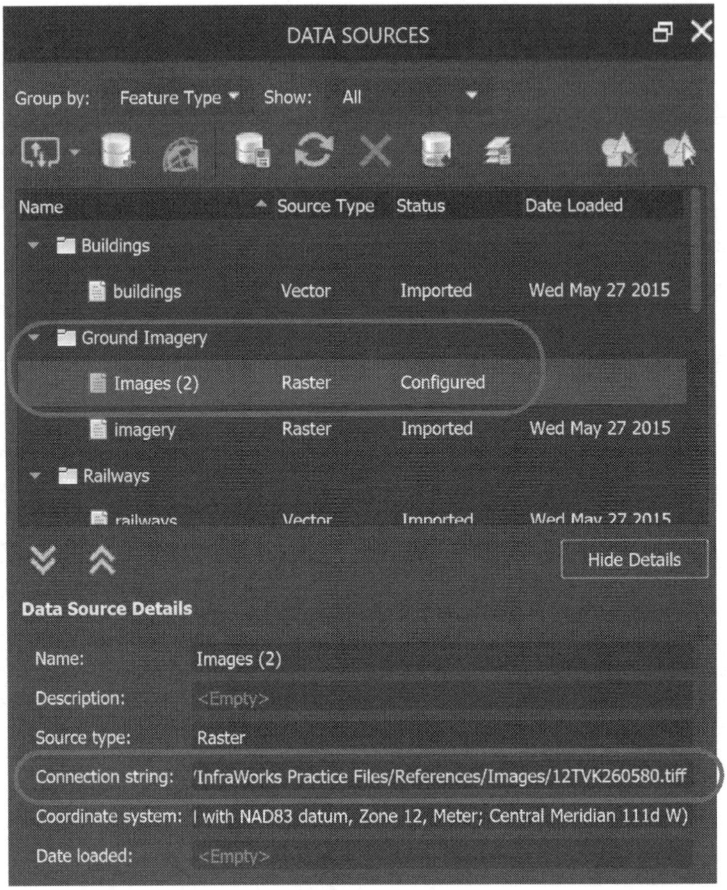

Figure 2–39

12. In the *Data Sources* panel, expand (Add file data source) and select **SHP**, as shown in Figure 2–40.

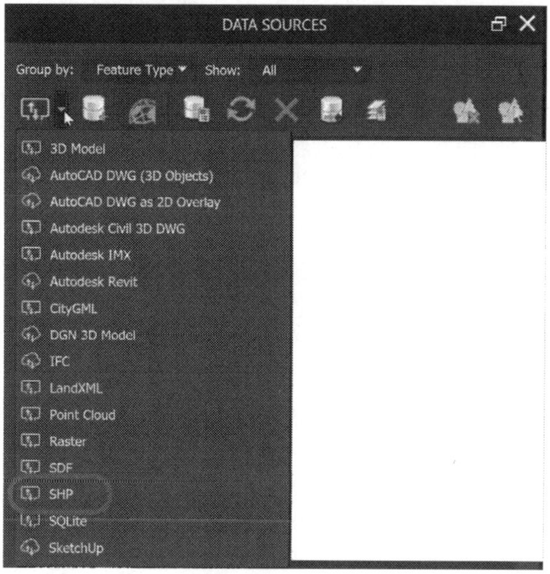

Figure 2–40

13. Browse to the *InfraWorks Practice Files\References\GIS* folder. Select all the *.SHP files in the folder and click **Open**. After you select the first file, then use <Shift> and select the last file. All files in between are selected.
14. The *Data Sources* panel now displays these GIS sources as being **Not Configured**, as shown in Figure 2–41.

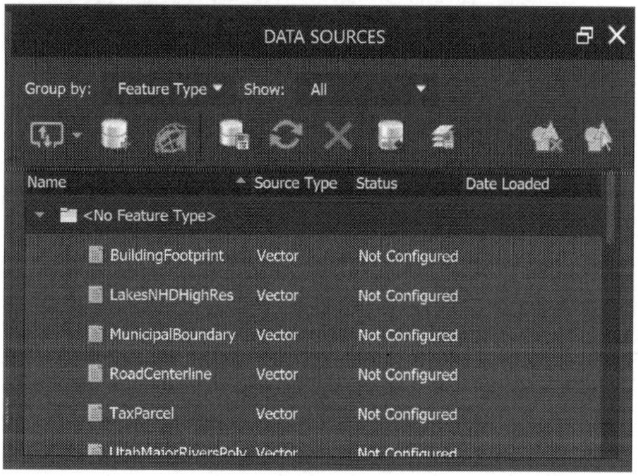

Figure 2–41

15. In the next practice, you will configure these data sources.

End of practice

2.3 Configure and Display Data Sources

Although the source data has been connected, it does not display in the model because the data must be configured first. Configuring the data is important because it enables you to:

- Set the coordinate system in which the source data is located.
- Map database fields located in the source data database file to the properties specified in the model template.

The more database fields you can map to your model, the more analysis can be done with the model. You can also add more accuracy to the model if database fields specify elevations, heights, and other numerical information about the raster or vector to which they pertain.

Data Source Configuration

Once a data source has been imported, it is configured in the *Data Sources* panel by either double-clicking on the data source or selecting the data source and clicking  (Configure Data), as shown in Figure 2–42.

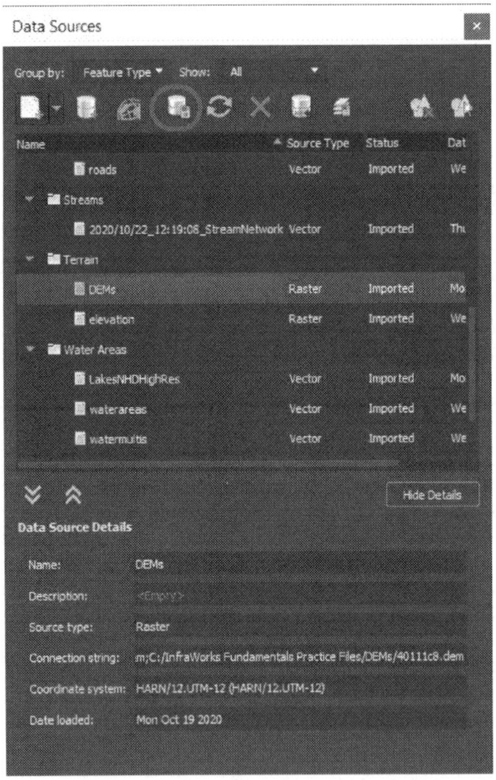

Figure 2–42

Hint: Terrain Data

It is essential that terrain data be added to the model first, since all other data sits on top of the terrain. Without a terrain surface, other data cannot be displayed. Additionally, only one terrain surface can display at any one time. If multiple terrain surfaces exist in a model, the visibility of the surfaces can be determined by setting the display order in the *Surface Layers* dialog box. Click and drag the new surface from the *Uncategorized* branch of the *Terrain Surfaces* list to the *Ground Surface* branch, then drag it up or down to set the display priority (as shown in Figure 2–43).

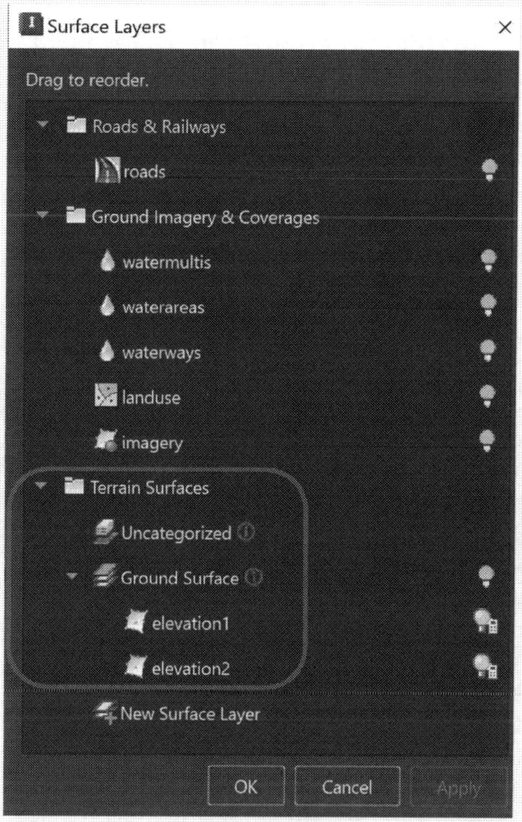

Figure 2–43

The *Surface Layers* dialog box can be accessed from multiple places:

- Click (Manage the order and visibility of surface data) in the *Data Sources* panel.
- In the *Model Explorer* panel, right-click on *Surface Layers* and select **Surface Layers**.
- In the *Manage* tab>*Display* panel, click (Surface Layers).

Data Source Details

When a data source is selected in the *Data Sources* panel, details about the source display in the *Data Source Details* area. The details include the name, description, source type, connection string (indicating where the source file is located), coordinate system, and date that the source was loaded into the model.

If a data source file is moved to a new location, the connection to the file is lost and errors might occur when working with features from that data source. Therefore, avoid moving files once you have connected them to an Autodesk InfraWorks model unless doing so is absolutely necessary.

If the data source files must be moved, you must reassociate them from the new location.

How To: Reassociate Moved Data Sources

1. Select the data source in the *Data Sources* panel and click  (Manage paths of file data sources).
2. In the *File Data Source Reconnection* dialog box, click the ellipsis (...) for browsing under the *New* column, as shown in Figure 2–44. Locate and select the file.

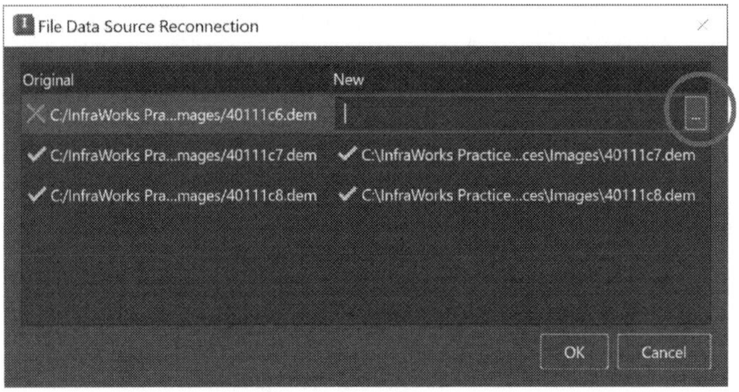

Figure 2–44

- This must be done for every proposal in which the data source is located.
- If more than one file is listed under the source data and both are located in the same directory, the paths for the additional files in the *File Data Source Reconnection* dialog box should automatically be populated.

General Information

In the area at the top of the *Data Source Configuration* dialog box, every layer includes a *Name*, *Description*, *Source*, and *Type* field, as shown in Figure 2–45. The *Description* and the *Type* are usually the only two fields that require you to input information.

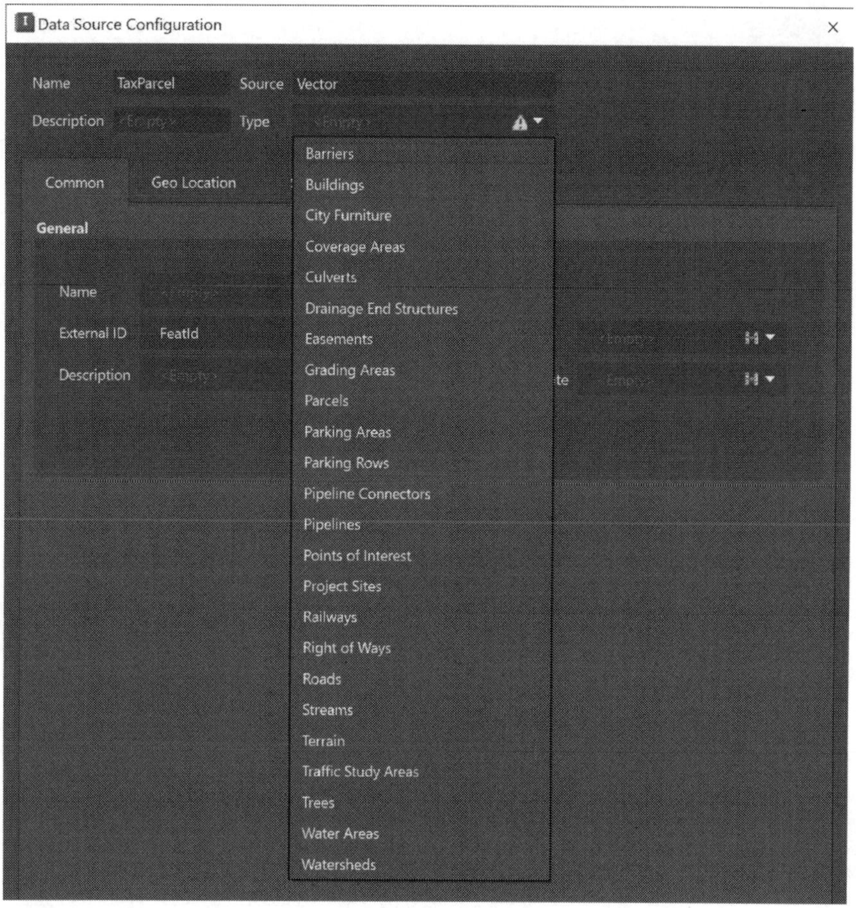

Figure 2–45

The *Type* field is the most important field in this area. It determines the table and other settings that become available for the data source. Once the type has been configured in a model, it cannot be changed. The available configuration types are as follows:

- Barriers
- Building
- City Furniture
- Coverage Areas
- Culverts
- Drainage End Structures
- Easements
- Land Areas
- Parcels
- Parking Areas
- Parking Rows
- Pipeline Connectors
- Pipelines
- Points of Interest
- Project Sites
- Railways
- Right of Ways
- Roads
- Streams
- Terrain
- Traffic Study Areas
- Trees
- Water Areas
- Watersheds

Common Tab

Note: *There are multiple ways to set styles in the Autodesk InfraWorks software. Note that each data type has different fields available on the various tabs.*

The *Common* tab (shown in Figure 2–46) maps database fields to specific model properties and sets the styles to display the data source features.

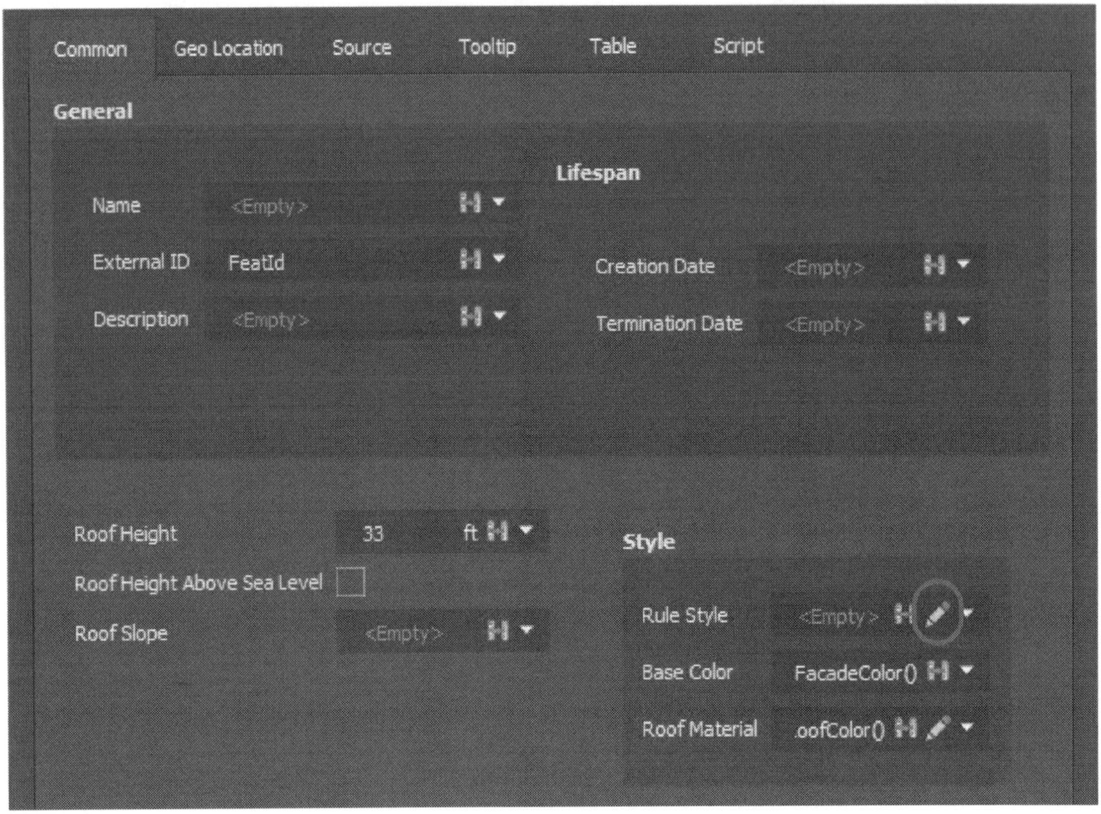

Figure 2–46

How To: Select a Style for Data Source Features

1. In the *Style* field, click (Style Chooser), as shown previously in Figure 2–46. Select the required style in the *Select Style / Color* dialog box, as shown in Figure 2–47.

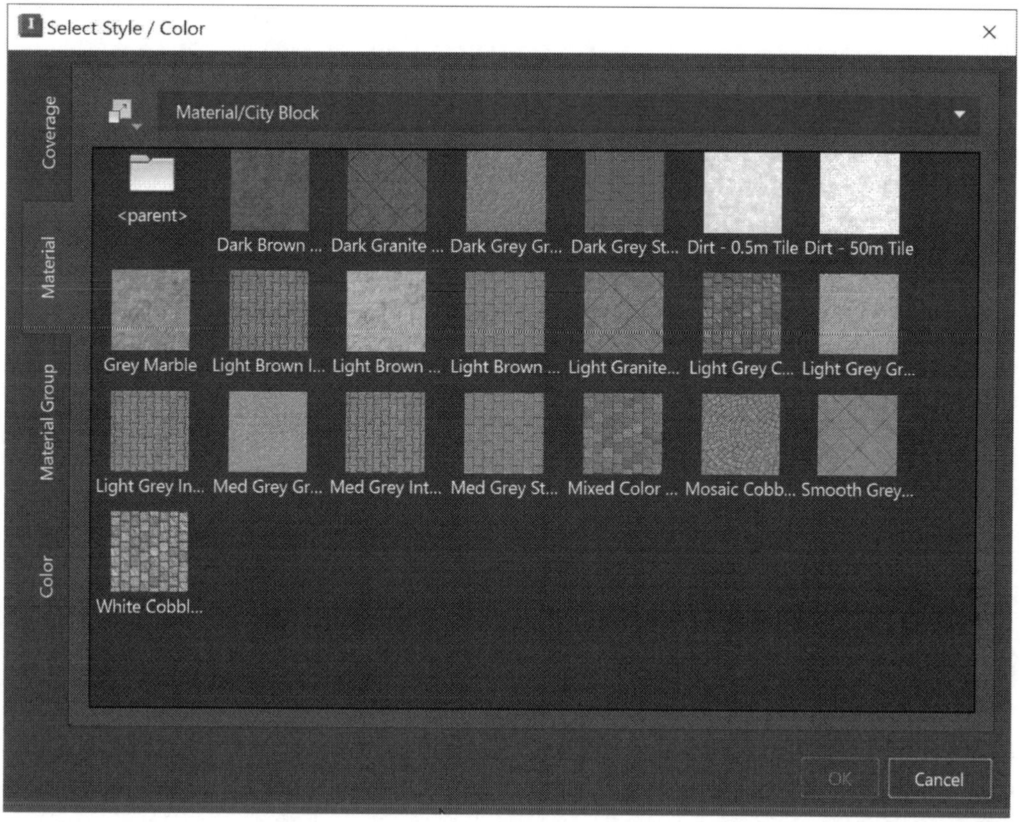

Figure 2–47

2. Click **OK**.

Geo Location Tab

The *Geo Location* tab (shown in Figure 2–48) sets the source data's original geographic coordinate system. It is important to ensure that the *Coordinate System* field is correct because it is used to project the source data to the model coordinate system. If the wrong coordinate system is selected, the features display in the wrong location in the model.

If required, you can change the coordinate system using the *Coordinate System* drop-down list. Additional commands in the *Geo Location* tab enable you to manually set the insertion point, scale, and rotation factors, or interactively place the data source.

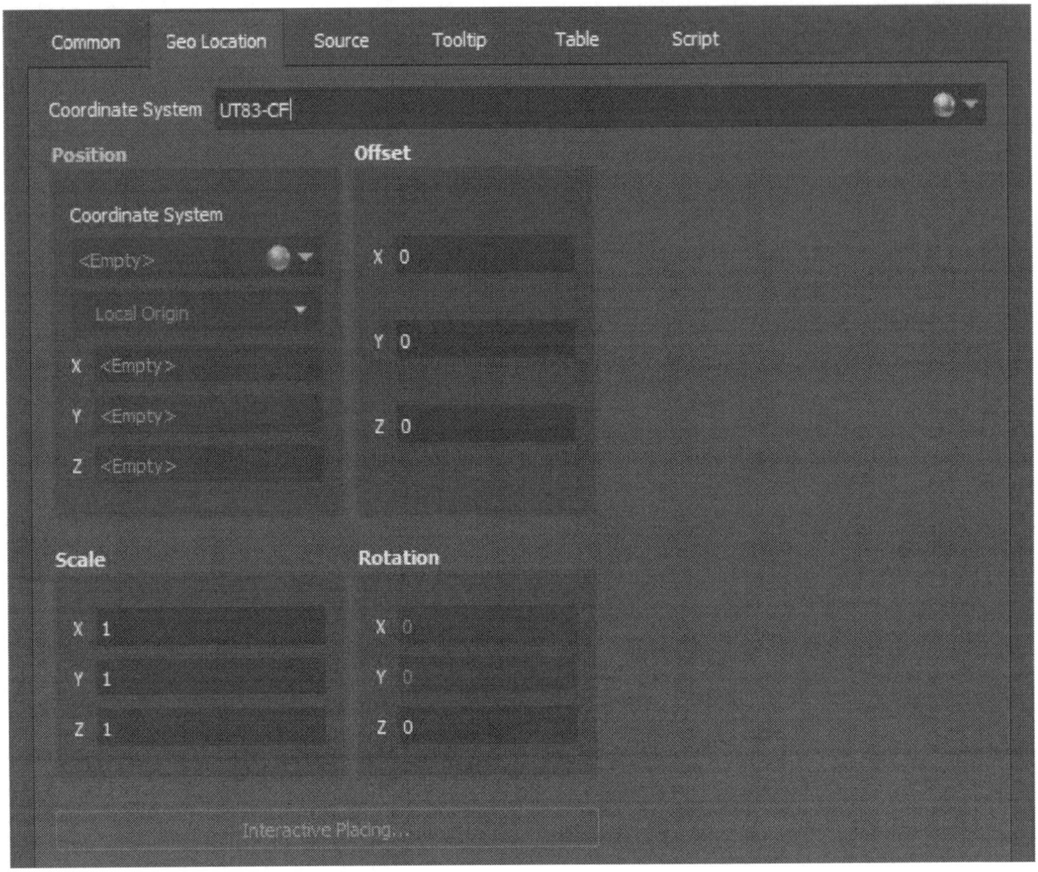

Figure 2–48

Source Tab

The *Source* tab imports a subset of the original data by creating a source filter. The source filter can be a property filter or location filter. If the option to **Clip to model extent** is selected, the source data is automatically trimmed to the model extents.

Note: *Clipping to the model extents helps keep the file size down.*

The *Source* tab also enables you to control whether features are placed at a set elevation according to a property or draped on the terrain surface. The following three options are available for the elevation:

Option	Description
Don't drape	Features are not assigned an elevation. Instead, they are imported at the elevation at which they were originally created.
Drape	Feature elevations are automatically taken from the terrain surface elevations.
Set Elevation	Enables you to select a field in the data table to be used to set the elevation.

If you are importing a source file that consists of polylines, you can select the option to **Convert closed polylines to polygons**, as shown in Figure 2–49.

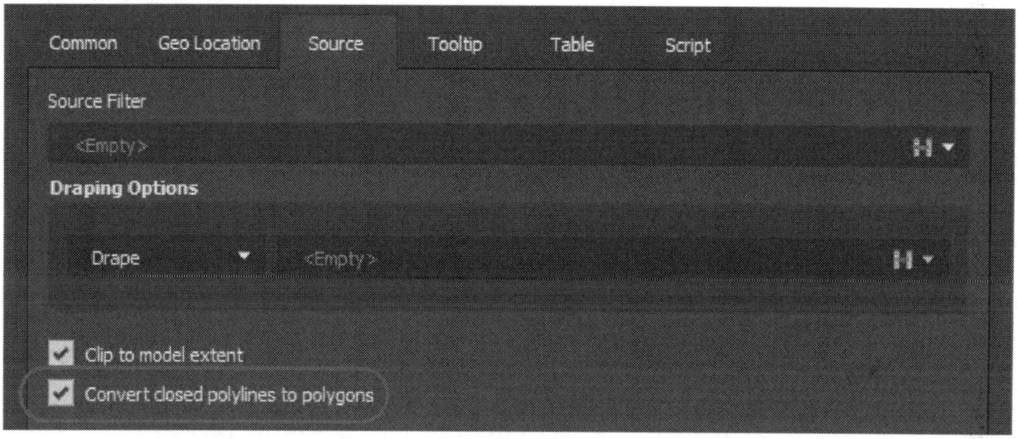

Figure 2–49

Tooltip Tab

The *Tooltip* tab temporarily labels a model element by displaying a selected property when the cursor hovers over a feature. The tooltip in Figure 2–50 shows the name of the city when the cursor hovers over any part of the city. Additionally, hyperlinks can be added to link features to a specific web page or other file.

> ***Note:*** *Tooltips are automatically added to data obtained from Model Builder.*

Figure 2–50

How To: Add a Tooltip to a Data Source

1. In the *Tooltip* tab, select the *Html* tab and click (Insert Property).
2. In the *Select Property* dialog box, select the property that you want to display, as shown in Figure 2–51.

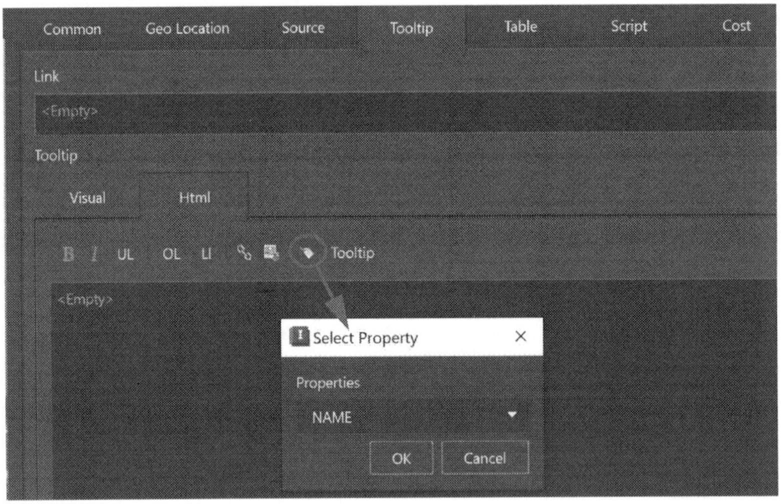

Figure 2–51

3. Click **OK**.

Table Tab

The *Table* tab maps (connects) fields from the original GIS data source database to the list of properties for the current data type. You must map any key fields that you plan to use later for stylizing and analyzing the model. In the example shown in Figure 2–52, the current market value (**MKT_CNTVAL**) is mapped to the *User Data* property for a parcel coverage. This data can be used to display the coverage, with various fill patterns or colors, according to the property value.

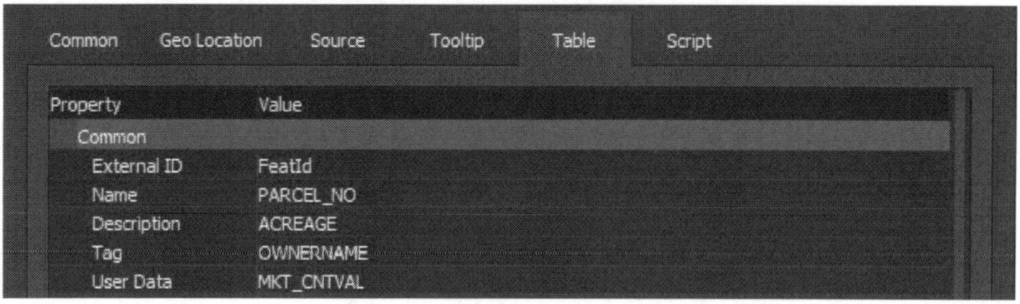

Figure 2–52

Script Tab

The *Script* tab specifies advanced import settings using JavaScript. The example script shown in Figure 2–53 varies the style for streets based on their values for the *Elevation* property.

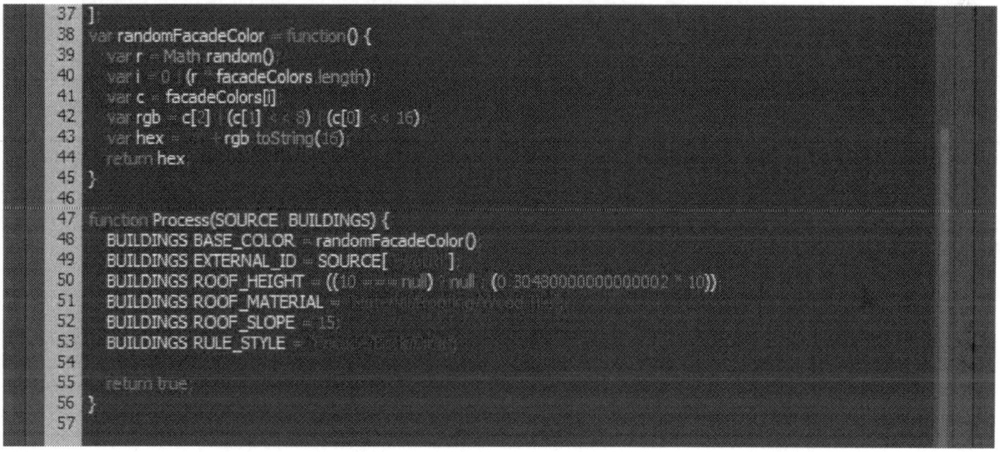

Figure 2–53

Hint: Refreshing Data Sources with scripts

Scripts are a method are importing malicious code for phishing and hacking. When reconnecting or refreshing to a data source that has scripts, a warning appears about the dangers involved, as shown in Figure 2–54.

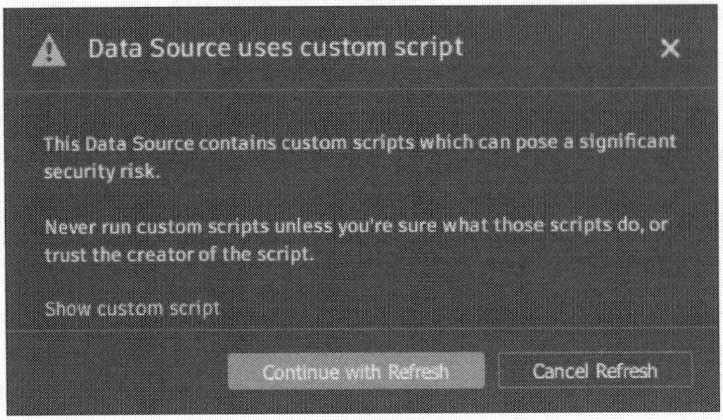

Figure 2–54

Only agree to refreshing such data sources if you are certain of the source (and author) of the scripts.

Expressions

Expressions are required when mapping a database field that does not directly match a property in the model. For example, the source data might list the number of floors or stories in a building, but not the actual roof height. To display the building with an accurate roof height, you need to create an expression in the *Roof Height* field that multiplies the number of floors by an average floor height.

How To: Create an Expression

1. In the *Data Source Configuration* dialog box, select the tab containing the field that you want to calculate (e.g., *Common*, *Table*, etc.).
2. In the field next to the property that you want to calculate, click (Expression Editor), as shown in Figure 2–55.

    Note: *If (Expression Editor) is not displayed, select the field to make it display.*

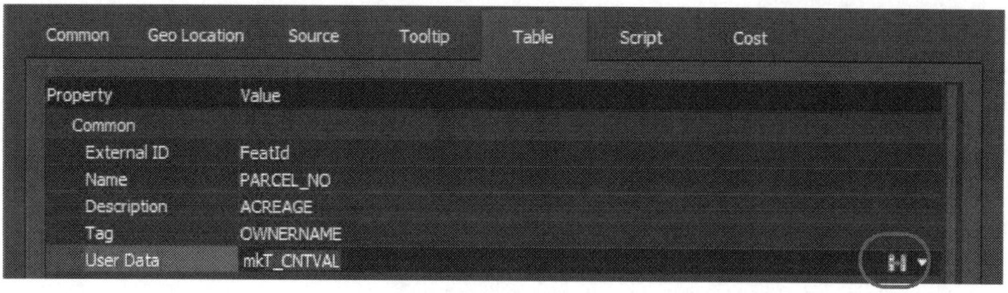

Figure 2–55

3. In the *Expression Editor*, create a simple numeric expression, as shown in Figure 2–56:
   - Select a property in the expanded **Properties** list.
   - Select an operation in the expanded **Operators** list.
   - Enter the value by which to modify the property.

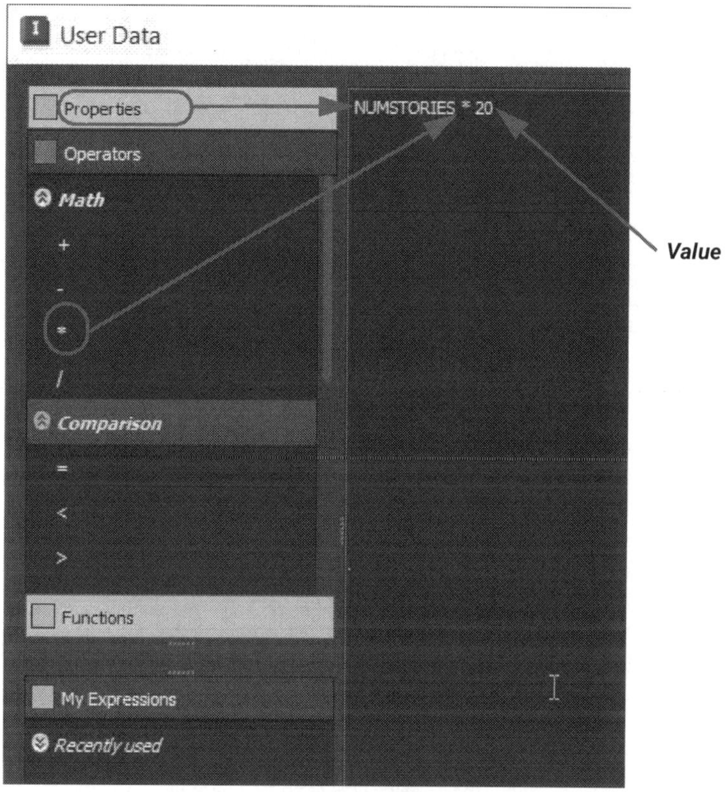

Figure 2–56

4. Click **OK**.

Model Explorer

Using the *Model Explorer*, you can hide/display, lock/unlock, and highlight layers that have been added to the model, such as shape files, raster images, and DEM files. You can also filter the data that displays to focus on a specific attribute or to only display data in a specific area. To display the *Model Explorer*, in the *Manage* tab>*Model* panel, click  (Model Explorer).

In the *Model Explorer*, layers are listed on the left with icons on the right identifying their display and selectability status, as shown in Figure 2–57.

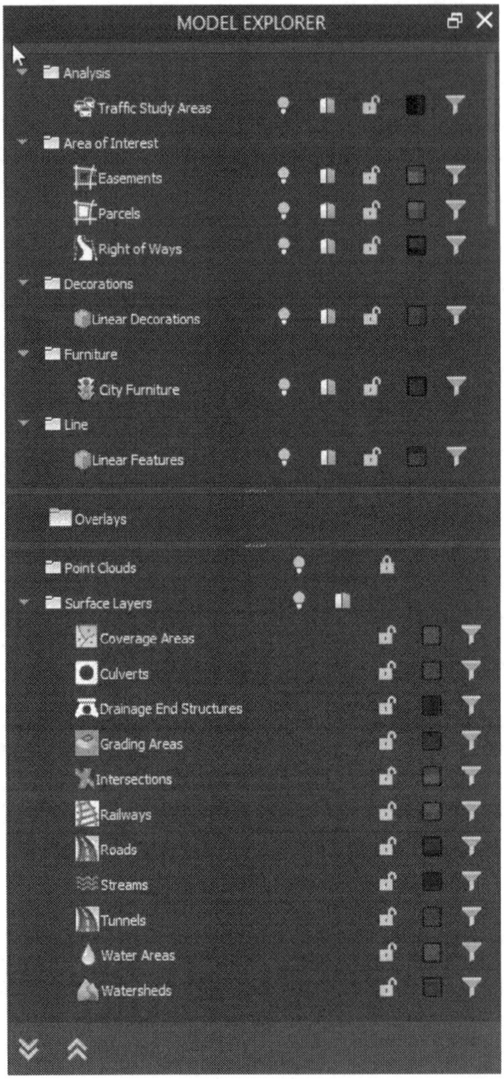

Figure 2–57

The icons in the *Model Explorer* are described in the following table.

Icon	Purpose
(Display/Hide Layers)	Indicates whether the layer is displayed in the model. Yellow indicates that the layer is displayed, while gray indicates that the layer is hidden.
(Level of Detail)	Specifies the level of detail displayed for various layers according to the zoom distance. Higher levels display more detail, while lower levels display less detail. By default, *Level of Detail* is set to **Adaptive**, which displays objects that are closer with more detail and objects that are further away with less detail.
(Selectable/ Unselectable)	Makes items in the layer selectable when the lock is in the open position. When the lock is in the closed position, the layer cannot be selected.
(Highlight)	Highlights the layer features in the model. Note: The highlight is only used for identification. Highlighting a layer does not mean it has been selected for editing.
(Create Subset)	Filters the layer to only display the number of features that you specify.

Practice 2d
Configure Source Data for Display

Practice Objectives

- Display connected GIS data in the model.
- Set the model extents for the new model.

In the previous practice, you imported multiple data sources. In the *Data Sources* panel, the data is separated into three categories: *No Feature Type*, *Ground Imagery*, and *Terrain*. All of the DEM files are under the **Terrain** layer and can be configured at the same time. All of the aerial images are under **Ground Imagery** and can also be configured at the same time. However, all of the shape files are listed in the *No Feature Type* category and must be configured individually.

Task 1: Configure terrain source data.

In this task, you will configure the new DEM files for display.

1. Continue working in the same model as the last practice or open **CreateModel.sqlite** from the *InfraWorks Practice Files\2-Connect Data* folder.
2. If you did not complete the previous task or are not confident it was successful, you can switch to the **A_Task1** proposal.
3. In the *Manage* tab>*Content* panel, click  (Data Sources).
4. In the *Data Sources* panel under *Terrain*, double-click on the **Images** layer, which represents the three DEMs[2] together.

2. (AGRC), Utah Automated Geographic Reference Center, 2007

5. Note that *Type* is set to **Terrain** automatically. On the *Geo Location* tab, ensure that the *Coordinate System* is set to **HARN/12.UTM-12**, as shown in Figure 2–58.

   Note: *The coordinate system was set automatically because a projection file was included with the DEM file.*

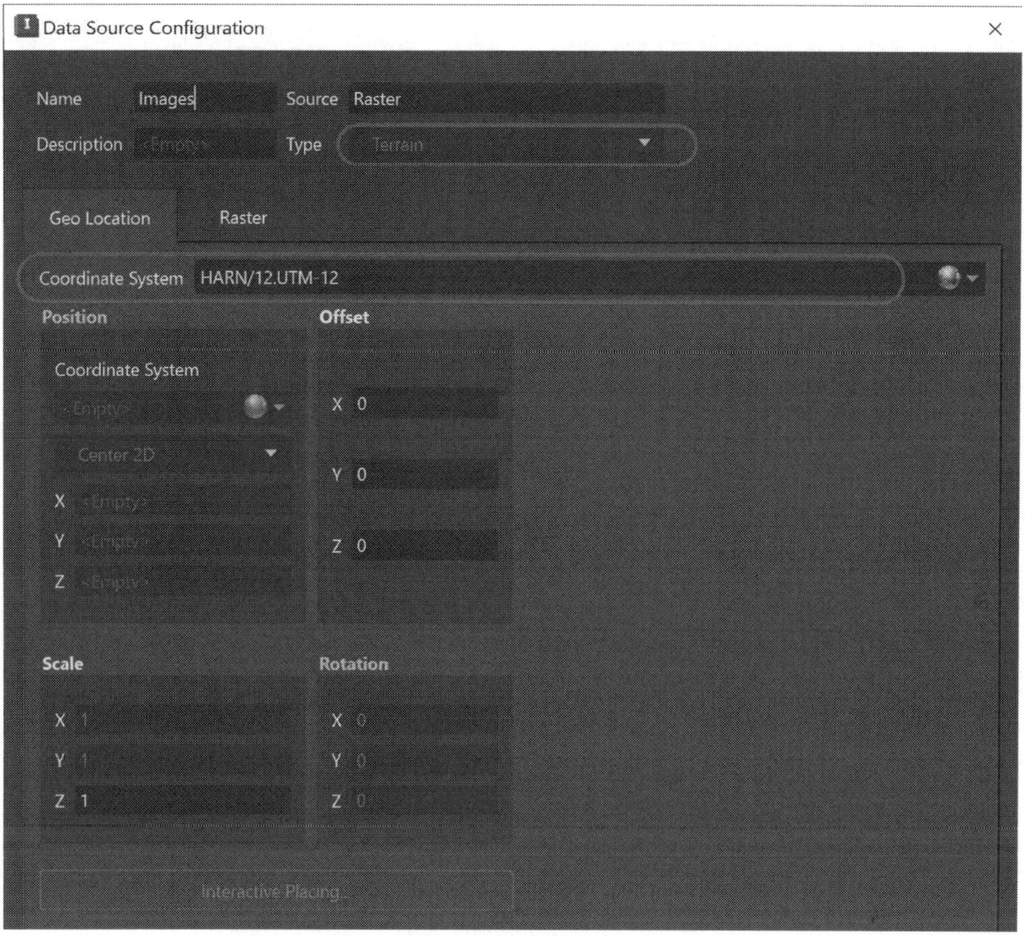

Figure 2–58

6. On the *Raster* tab, select the **Clip to Model Extent** option, as shown in Figure 2–59.

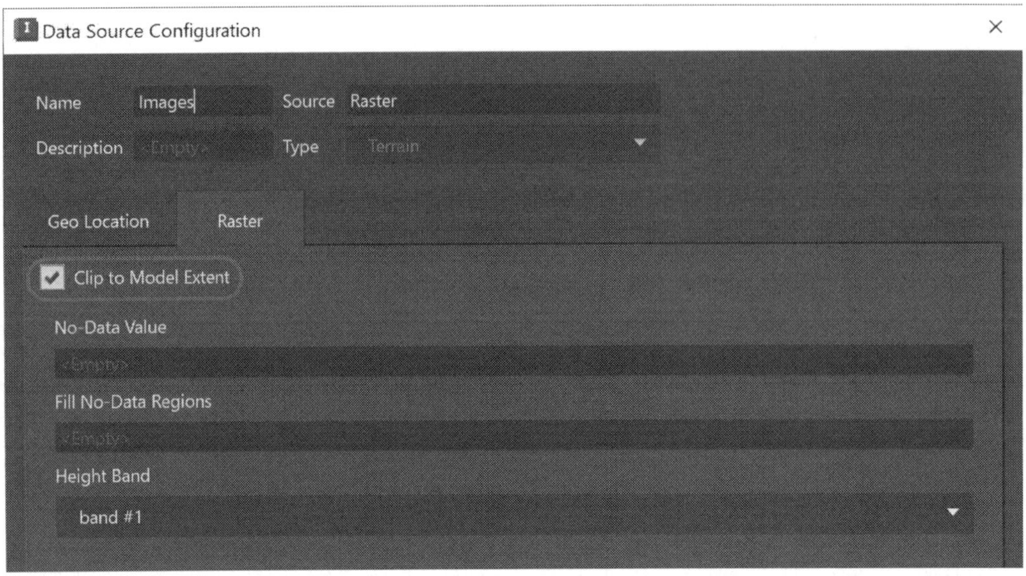

Figure 2–59

Note: *You might not notice a difference unless you started from the blank model created in Figure 2–59.*

7. Click **Close & Refresh** to display the terrain in the model.
8. Since you are adding another terrain source in the form of DEMs, InfraWorks displays the message shown in Figure 2–60 about the surface not being categorized.

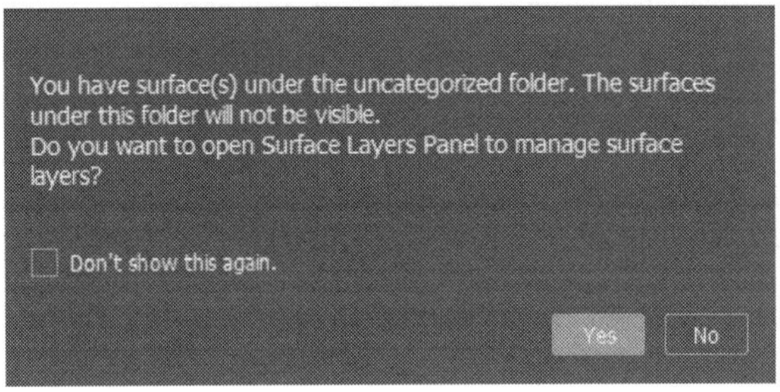

Figure 2–60

9. Click **Yes** to categorize the surface.

Note: *You can also open the Surface Layers dialog box by clicking*  *(Surface Layers) in the Manage tab>Display panel.*

10. In the *Surface Layers* dialog box, double-click on *New Surface Layer* to rename it to **DEMs**.

11. Click the **Images** layer under *Uncategorized* and drag it to the newly named *DEMs* layer, as shown in Figure 2–61. Turn on the light bulb icon so the images are displayed in the model.

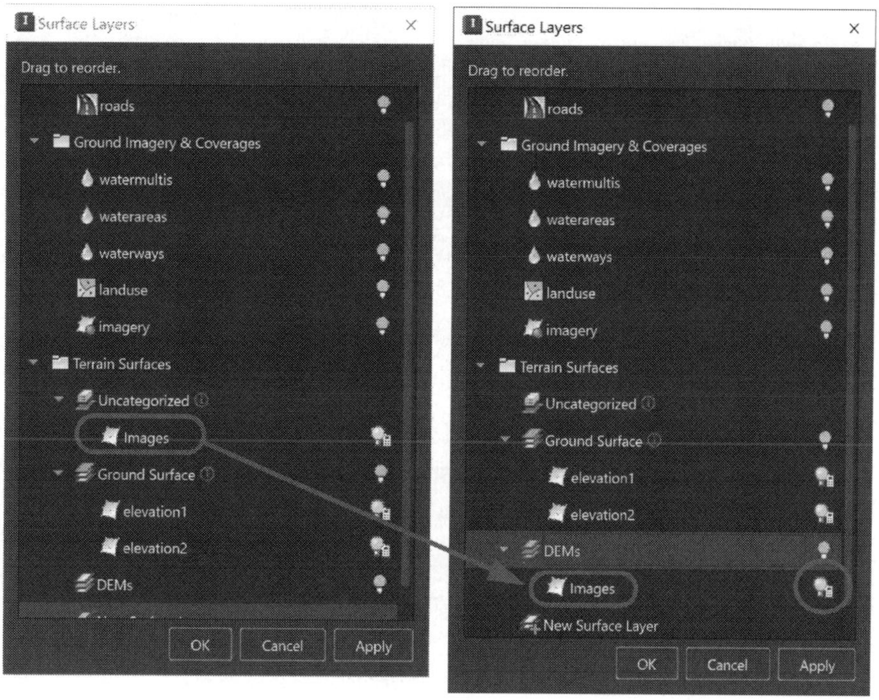

Figure 2–61

12. Click **OK** to close the *Surface Layers* dialog box.

Task 2: Configure image source data.

In this task, you will configure a higher quality image for display in the project area.

1. If you did not complete the previous task or are not confident it was successful, you can switch to the **A_Task2** proposal.
2. In the toolbar, click  (Bookmarks) and select **Image Quality**.
3. In the *Data Sources* panel under *Ground Imagery*, double-click on the **Images(2)**[3] layer to open the *Data Source Configuration* dialog box.

   Note: *The coordinate systems often vary for different data sources, depending on who created them and when.*

4. Note that the *Type* is set to **Ground Imagery**. On the *Geo Location* tab, ensure that the *Coordinate System* is set to **UTM83-12**. You can type this coordinate system in, then pick it from the supplied list.

3. (AGRC), Automated Geographic Reference Center, 2012

5. On the *Raster* tab, ensure that the **Clip to Model Extent** option is selected. In the *Classification* drop-down list, select **Aerial**, as shown in Figure 2–62.

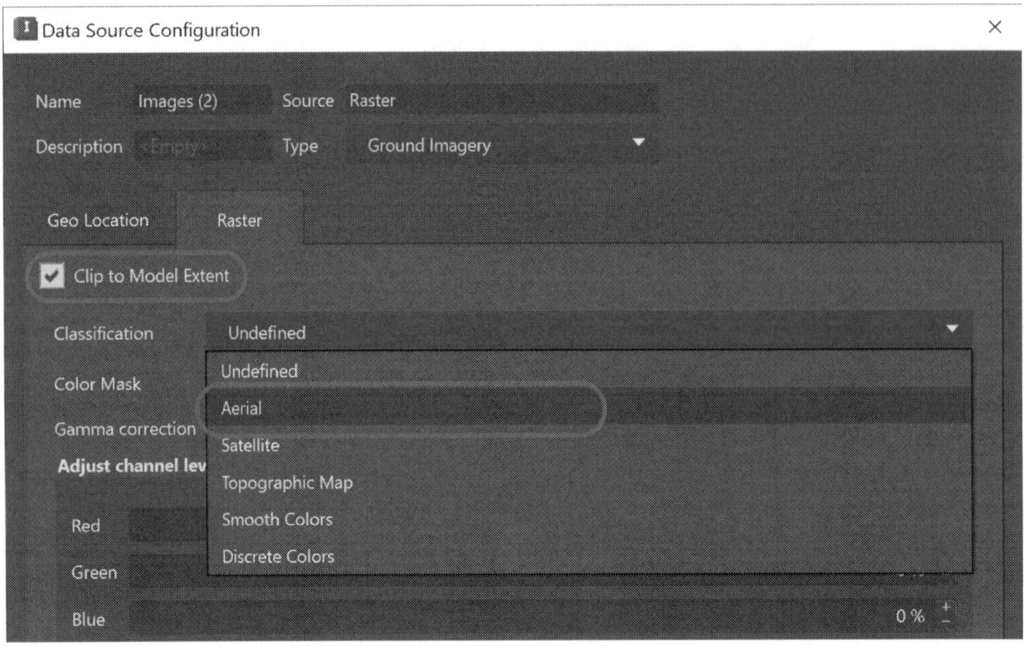

Figure 2–62

6. Click **Close & Refresh** to display the images in the model. The quality of the new image is much better than the one inserted by the *Model Builder,* as shown in Figure 2–63.

   *Note: Since nothing changed in the Data Source Configuration dialog box, you could have also selected **Images** and clicked (Refresh data source).*

Original image

New image

Figure 2–63

Task 3: Add tags to data sources.

In this task, you will take advantage of tags as you configure data sources for display.

1. On the ViewCube, click (*Home*) to view the entire model.
2. In the *Data Sources* panel, double-click on the **MunicipalBoundary**[4] layer to open the *Data Source Configuration* dialog box.
3. Set the *Type* to **Coverage Areas**.
4. In the *Geo Location* tab, ensure that *Coordinate System* is set to **UT83-CF**.
5. In the *Source* tab, set the *Draping Options* to **Drape** and select the **Clip to model extent** option, as shown in Figure 2–64.

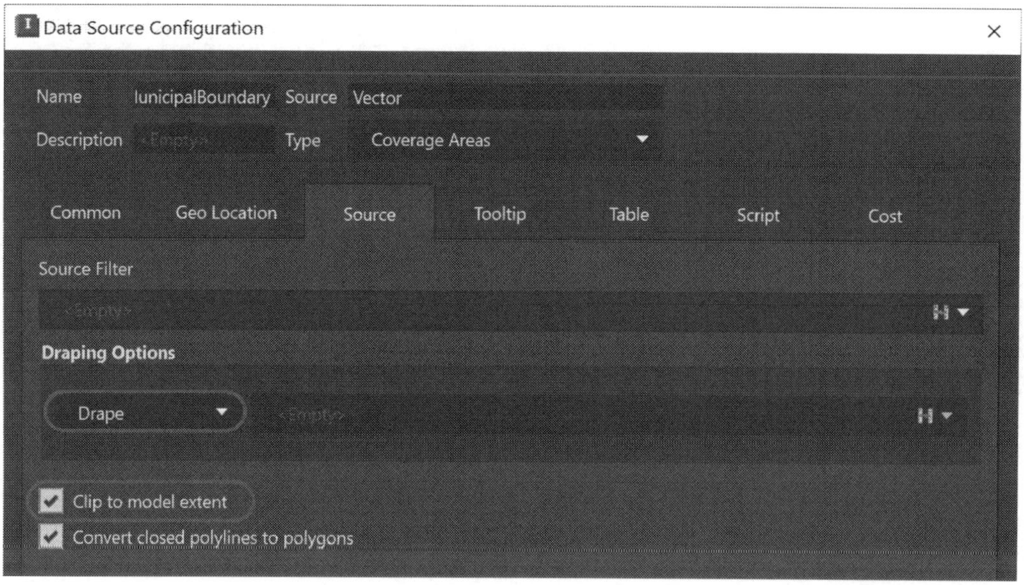

Figure 2–64

4. Department, GIS Division of the Utah County Information Systems, 2013

6. Go back to the *Common* tab, and in the *Rule Style* field, click (Style Chooser), as shown in Figure 2–65.
7. In the *Select Style / Color* dialog box, on the *Coverage* tab, select **Boundary** for the style, as shown in Figure 2–65. Click **OK** to close the *Select Style / Color* dialog box.

Note: *The Boundary style was created for these practices and only exists in the* ***CreateModel.sqlite*** *model.*

Figure 2–65

8. On the *Table* tab, set the following parameters by selecting them from the drop-down lists using the down-arrow icon, as shown in Figure 2–66:
   - *Name:* **NAME**
   - *Description:* **TYPE**

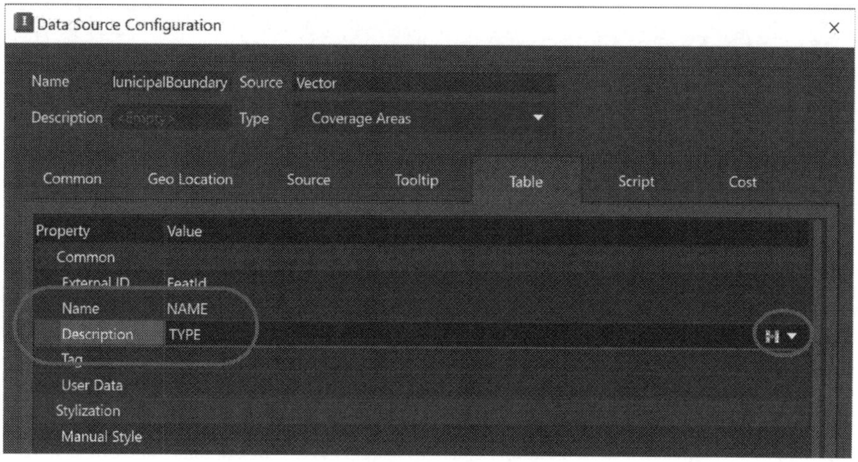

Figure 2–66

9. On the *Tooltip* tab, select the *Html* tab and click in the content area. Click (Insert Property).
10. In the *Select Property* dialog box, expand the drop-down list using the down-arrow icon and select **NAME**, as shown in Figure 2–67. Click **OK**.

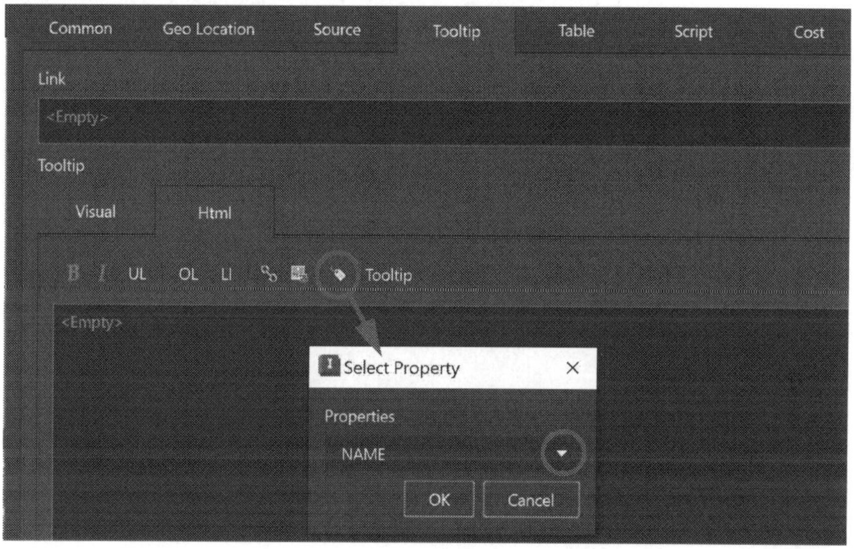

Figure 2–67

11. If there is a text entry of **<Empty>** after the green *%NAME%* in the *Tooltip* script area (as shown in Figure 2–68), highlight and delete it.

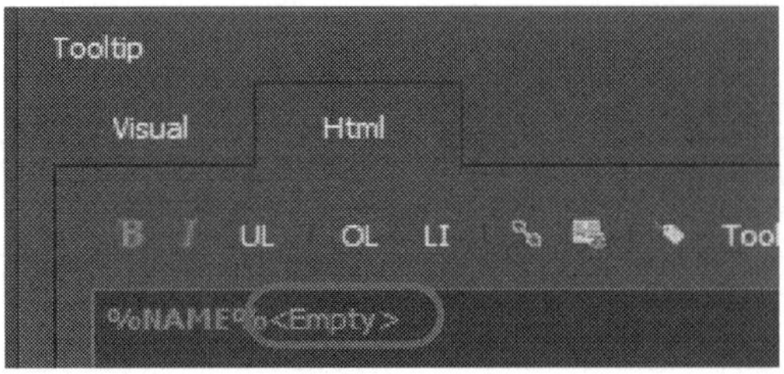

Figure 2–68

12. Click **Close & Refresh** to display the city boundaries in the model.

13. In the toolbar, click (Bookmarks) and select **Project Area**.

14. In the model, hover the cursor over some areas and note that a tooltip displays indicating the parcel belongs to the Pelican Bay municipality, as shown in Figure 2–69.

Figure 2–69

15. In the *Data Sources* panel, double-click on the **TaxParcel**[5] layer to open the *Data Source Configuration* dialog box, as shown in Figure 2–70. Set the following parameters:

- *Type:* **Coverage Areas**
- *Geo Location* tab, *Coordinate System*: **UT83-CF**
- *Source* tab, *Draping Options*: **Drape**
- *Source* tab: **Clip to model extent**
- *Table* tab, *Name*: **PARCEL_NO**
- *Table* tab, *Description*: **ACREAGE**
- *Table* tab, *Tag*: **OWNERNAME**
- *Table* tab, *User Data*: **MKT_CNTVAL**

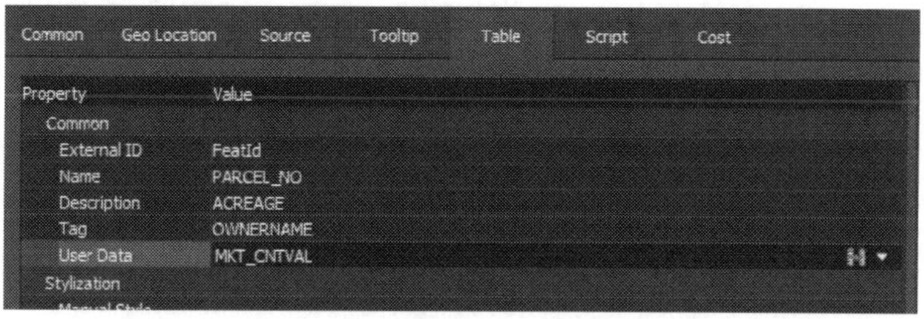

Figure 2–70

16. On the *Tooltip* tab, select the *Html* tab. Click (Insert Property), as shown in Figure 2–71.

17. In the *Select Property* dialog box, expand the drop-down list and select **TAG**, as shown in Figure 2–71. Click **OK**.

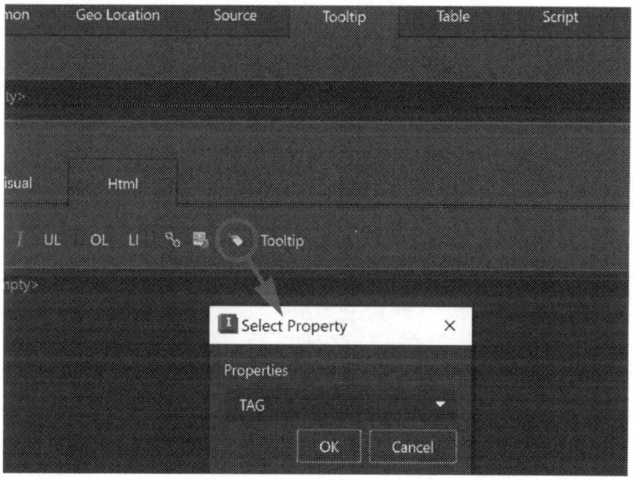

Figure 2–71

5. Department, GIS Division of the Utah County Information Systems, 2013

18. As before, delete the **<Empty>** text entry after the green%*TAG*% entry in the *Tooltip* script area, if required.
19. Click **Close & Refresh** to display the parcel boundaries in the model. **Note:** Because a style was not set, the model will display as though nothing has changed. However, when you move the cursor over the terrain, the parcels of land highlight as shown in Figure 2–72. If required, click (Bookmarks) and select **Project Area**.

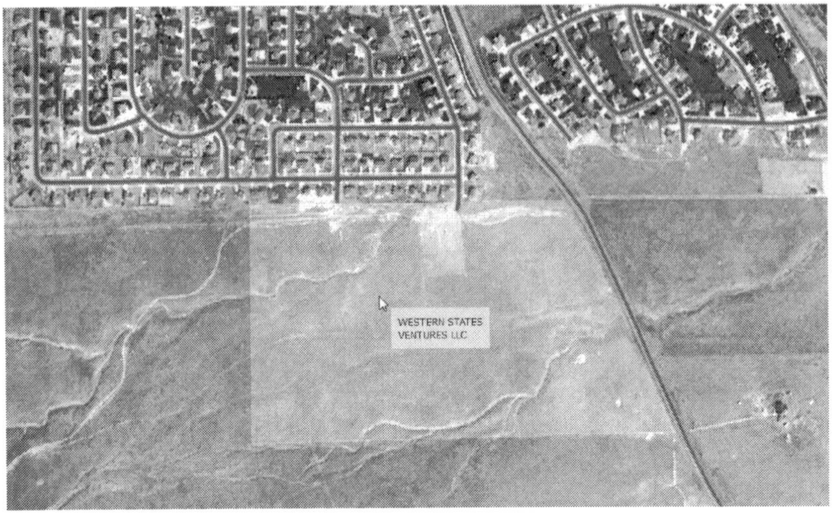

Figure 2–72

Task 4: Display data sources using expressions.

In this task, you will take advantage of expressions as you configure data sources for display.

1. If you did not complete the previous task or are not confident it was successful, you can switch to the **A_Task3** proposal.
2. On the ViewCube, click (*Home*) to view the entire model.
3. In the *Data Sources* panel, double-click on the **RoadCenterline**[6] layer to open the *Data Source Configuration* dialog box. Set the following parameters:
   - *Type:* **Roads**
   - *Geo Location* tab, *Coordinate System*: **UT83-CF**
   - *Source* tab, *Draping Options*: **Drape**
   - *Source* tab: **Clip to model extent**

6. Department, GIS Division of the Utah County Information Systems, 2013

4. On the *Common* tab, in the *Elevation Offset* field, click (Expression Editor).
5. In the *Expression Editor*, expand *Properties>Numeric* and double-click **ROADLEVEL**, as shown in Figure 2–73.

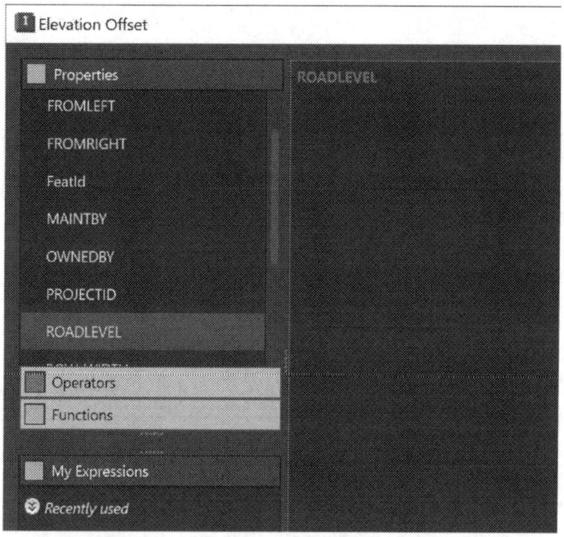

Figure 2–73

6. In the *Expression* area, after **ROADLEVEL**, type ***12**, as shown in Figure 2–74.

   Note: *The ROADLEVEL field has three values: -1, 0, and 1. Multiplying it by 12 sets the elevation to 12 feet above or below ground level (used for overpasses or underpasses), or drapes on the terrain for zero values.*

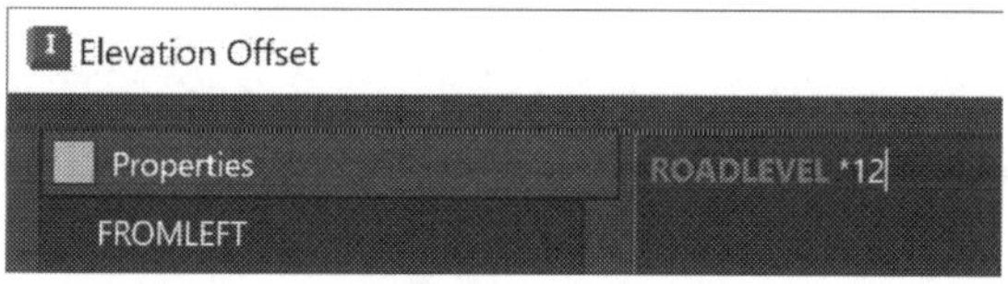

Figure 2–74

7. Click **OK**.
8. On the *Common* tab, in the *Rule Style* field, click (Style Chooser).

9. In the *Select Style* dialog box, on the *Road* tab, select **Sidewalk and Greenspace**, as shown in Figure 2–75. Click **OK** to close the *Select Style* dialog box, but remain in the *Data Source Configuration* window.

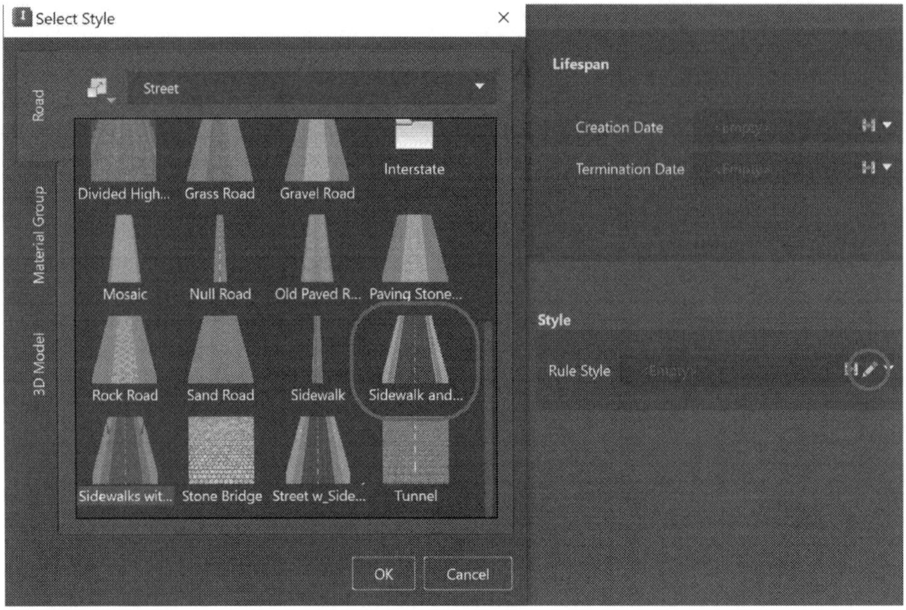

Figure 2–75

You will now map the data fields in the connected database file to the fields created by the Autodesk InfraWorks data scheme. This step is important if you plan to use the database information to label or analyze the model. In this case, you will map the *Roadclass* database field to the *Description* field so that you can use that information to set style rules later.

10. On the *Table* tab, set the following parameters using the values found in the drop-down lists, as shown in Figure 2–76:

- *Name:* **FULLNAME**
- *Description:* **ROADCLASS**
- *Tag:* **ALTROADNAM**
- *User Data*: **ROW_WIDTH**

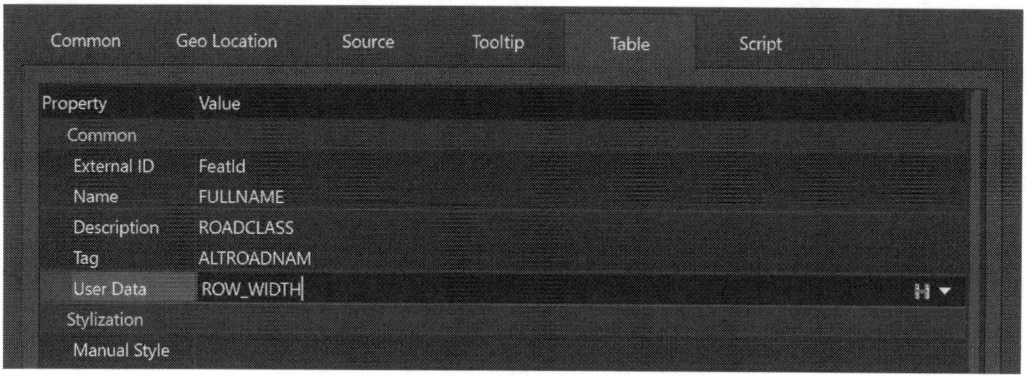

Figure 2–76

11. On the *Tooltip* tab, select the *Html* tab and click (Insert Property). In the *Select Property* dialog box, select **NAME** and click **OK**.
12. As before, if a text entry of **<Empty>** is after the green *%NAME%* entry in the *Tooltip* script area, delete it.
13. Click **Close & Refresh** to display the road centerlines in the model. If you started the model using *Model Builder*, it is likely that roads already existed in the model, which causes confusion regarding which roads to display (as shown in Figure 2–77). In cases like this, it is best to remove one or the other set of roads. Since you will use the information in the database to set road styles later, you need to remove the roads created in *Model Builder*.

Figure 2–77

14. In the *Data Sources* panel under *Roads*, select **roads** and click (Remove data source). When the warning box displays, click **Yes**.
15. In the toolbar, click (Bookmarks) and select **Buildings**.

16. In the *Data Sources* panel, double-click on the **BuildingFootprint**[7] layer to open the *Data Source Configuration* dialog box. Set the following parameters:
    - *Type*: **Buildings**
    - *Geo Location* tab, *Coordinate System*: **UT83-CF**
    - *Common* tab, *Roof Height*: **20**
    - *Source* tab, *Draping Options*: **Drape**
    - *Source* tab: **Clip to model extent**
17. Click **Close & Refresh** to display the buildings in the model. It can take some time for the model to refresh itself.
18. Use the mouse and/or ViewCube to view the model from different angles, as shown in Figure 2–78.

Figure 2–78

Task 5: Set the model extents.

The model that you have configured includes several cities. The project you will create is a multi-use development on the west side of the lake. The development will connect to the east side of the lake using a bridge. To focus on the area of interest and trim the data to this area, you will set the model extents.

7. Department, GIS Division of the Utah County Information Systems, 2013

1. In the model, move the cursor around and note how the coordinates change in the bottom-left corner of the model area, as shown in Figure 2–79. The minimum and maximum X and Y values required for the model determine the values you will set for the model extents.

Figure 2–79

2. In the *Manage* tab>*Model* panel, click  (Model Properties).
3. In the *Model Properties* dialog box, clear the **Use Entire Model** option. Set the following parameters listed in the table below and as shown in Figure 2–80.

Field	X	Y
Minimum	1532500	7267000
Maximum	1543000	7274500

Note: *Alternatively, you could have chosen to define the extents using a bounding box or polyline.*

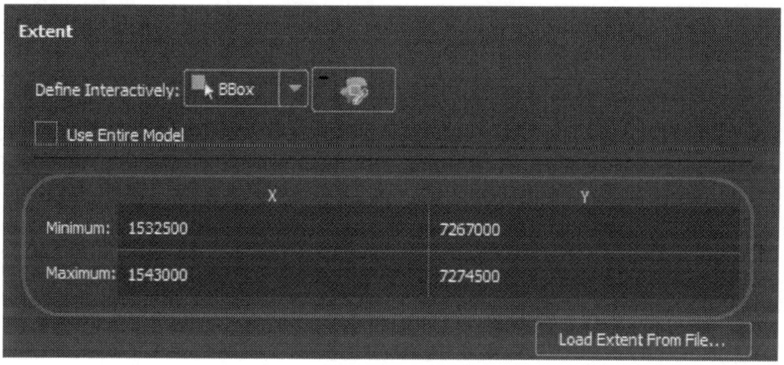

Figure 2–80

4. Click **Apply**, then click **OK**. The model will adjust to its new extents, as shown in Figure 2–81.

Figure 2–81

Note: *The model does not need to be saved as it has been automatically saved while you were working.*

Task 6: Hide model elements.

In this task, you will hide and lock a specific layer to help focus on the project area.

1. Click (Bookmarks) and select **Project Area** to return to the previously saved view where the project will be focused. Note: When you hover the cursor over an area, a parcel is highlighted instead of the city outline.

2. In the *Manage* tab>*Model* panel, click (Model Explorer).

   Note: *The surface layers are combined to make it easier to control all of them at the same time. This includes the DEM files, images, and other GIS data that was imported into the model.*

3. In the *Model Explorer* panel, right-click on **Surface Layers** and select **Surface Layers** (as shown in Figure 2–82) to manage the surface layers separately.

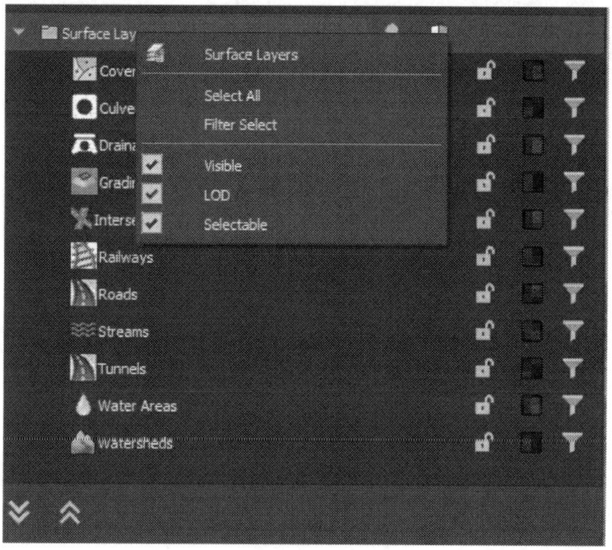

Figure 2–82

4. In the *Surface Layers* dialog box, click  to the right of the **TaxParcel** layer to toggle it off, as shown in Figure 2–83.

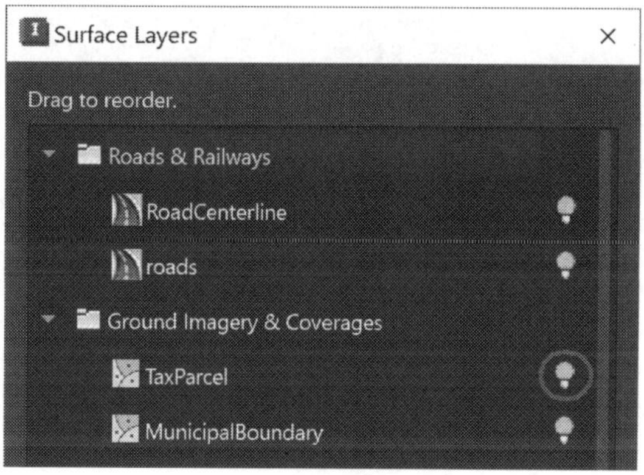

Figure 2–83

5. Click **Apply,** then click **OK**.
6. Click **OK** to close the *Surface Layers* dialog box.
7. Move the cursor over the model and note that the city is highlighted rather than the parcel.

Task 7: Lock the existing GIS layers.

1. Click (Bookmarks) and select **Buildings**.
2. In the model, select one of the buildings. Note that the bottom of the building has gizmos that enable you to edit it, as shown in Figure 2–84. Press <Esc> to clear the selection of the building.

Figure 2–84

3. In the *Model Explorer* panel, expand the *Structures* branch, then click to the right of the **Buildings** layer, as shown in Figure 2–85. The icon will change to a locked state ( ).

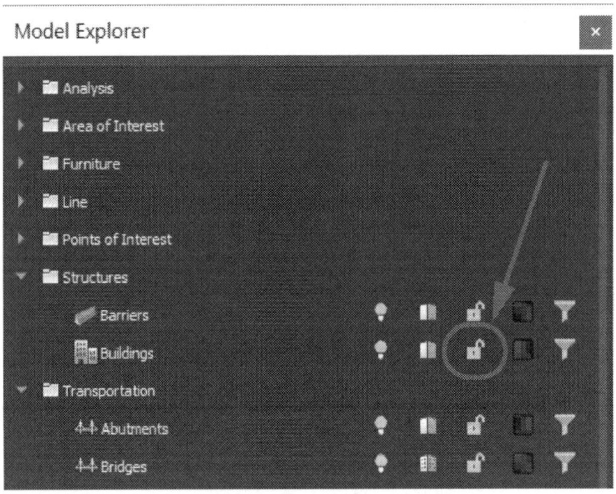

Figure 2–85

4. Try to select a building in the model. Note that the buildings can no longer be selected.
5. Close the *Model Explorer* panel.
6. Close the model.

End of practice

Chapter Review Questions

1. Why is the source data not displayed once it has been imported into the model?
   a. By default, it is toggled off in the Model Explorer.
   b. It needs to be configured before it can be displayed.
   c. The graphics card is not powerful enough to display the data.
   d. It might be hidden under another data source.

2. How can you determine whether the GIS data is usable for your project's needs? (Select all that apply.)
   a. Communicate with the owner of the GIS data source.
   b. Download and read the metadata included with the GIS data source.
   c. Connect to the data in the AutoCAD Map 3D or Autodesk Civil 3D software to preview the data and its data table before importing it into the Autodesk InfraWorks model.
   d. There is no way of determining its usability.

3. Which of the following types is not available as an option when configuring data sources?
   a. Barriers
   b. Bridges
   c. Buildings
   d. Railways

4. Which configuration tab would you use to drape data on a terrain surface?
   a. Common
   b. Geo Location
   c. Source
   d. Script

5. Which configuration tab would you use to display feature attributes in the model as you hover the cursor over them?
    a. Common
    b. Source
    c. Table
    d. Tooltip

6. Why is it important to set both the model coordinate system and the data source coordinate system?
    a. So that the software can automatically re-project the data sources for you and make everything line up with the correct insertion point, scale factor, and rotation value.
    b. So that the correct units (feet or meters) display in the model.
    c. So that the visual styles for the data sources all coordinate with the project.
    d. You only have to set one or the other, not both.

Command Summary

Button	Command	Location
	**Add ArcGIS data source**	• ***Data Sources* panel**
	**Add database data source**	• ***Data Sources* panel**
	**Add file data source**	• ***Data Sources* panel**
	**Application Options**	• ***Home* screen** • **Toolbar** • **Toolbar:** *Utilities* drop-down list
	**Data Sources**	• **Toolbar:** *Manage* tab>*Content* panel
N/A	**Deselect**	• **Shortcut key:** <Esc>
 / 	**Layer Lock/Unlock**	• **Model Explorer**
	**Layer On/Off**	• **Model Explorer**
	**Model Explorer**	• **Toolbar:** *Manage* tab>*Model* panel
	**Model Properties**	• **Toolbar:** *Manage* tab>*Model* panel
N/A	**New Model**	• ***Home* screen**
N/A	**Select All**	• **Shortcut key:** <Ctrl>+<A>
	**Surface Layers**	• ***Data Sources* panel** • **Model Explorer** (right-click Surface Layers) • **Toolbar:** *Manage* tab>*Display* panel

Chapter 3

Stylize Data Sources

Model features are thought of as a single category. However, it might occasionally be necessary to display features in the same data source differently. For example, a highway typically has more lanes than a local road. Additionally, a local road often has a sidewalk and lamp posts running alongside, while a highway does not have these design elements. In this chapter, you will learn how to use scripts, expressions, and style rules to display data sources according to information connected to the model (e.g., in database fields). You will also learn how to override style rules to manually change the display of specific features. If the required style is not available, it might be necessary to create a custom style to suit the project's needs. You will learn how to create and share styles from one project to another.

Learning Objectives

- Display a data source according to specific data in the database that is connected to the feature.
- Change the style of selected features to override any style rules being used.
- Create/edit styles in catalogs.
- Share style catalogs with other users.

3.1 Using Multiple Styles to Display Features

You have learned how to select one style for an entire data source during the data configuration process using (Style Chooser).

Alternatively, you can set the style for a data source subset by clicking (Expression Editor) in the *Rule Style* field in the *Data Configuration* dialog box (as shown in Figure 3–1).

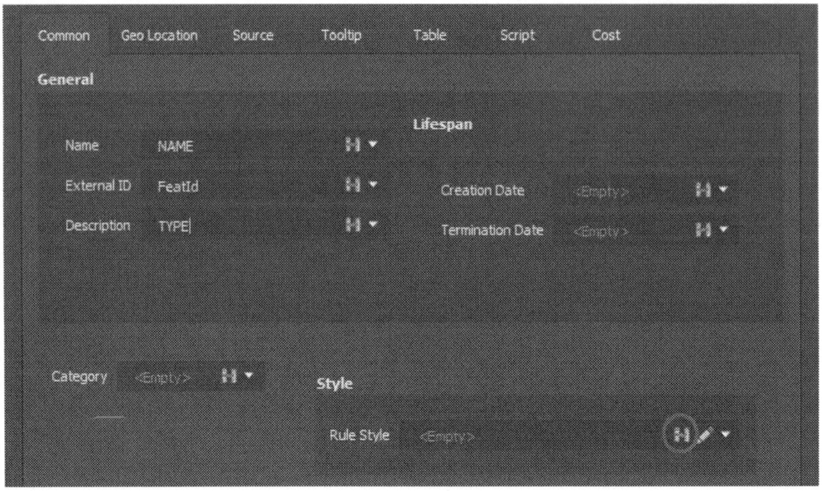

Figure 3–1

Create Filter Expressions

To automatically stylize a feature based on the connected database data, you must create an expression. The *Create Filter Expression* dialog box enables you to create two types of filter expressions:

- Location filters
- Property filters

Location Filters

In the *Create Filter Expression* dialog box, click **Spatial**. The five types of location boundaries available are as follows:

Disjoint	Selects all features that do not overlap the shape you draw.
Inside	Selects all features that lie inside the shape you draw.
Intersects	Selects all features that intersect with the shape you draw.
Overlaps	Selects all features that overlap any part of the shape you draw.
Within	Selects all features that are within the shape you draw but are not touching the edges of the shape.

Property Filters

In the *Create Filter Expression* dialog box, click **Properties** and select a property from the list. The available properties vary according to the database fields that are connected to the data source. After selecting a property, you need to set the values in the data field that you want to use to define the style. An operator is required to help filter the list of values. Some of the available comparison operators are shown in Figure 3–2.

> **Note:** *The title of the dialog box varies depending on the database field you want to create the expression for. Typically the title will contain the name of the field, such as Name, Description. If you are building a Rule Style, that will be the name of the dialog box.*

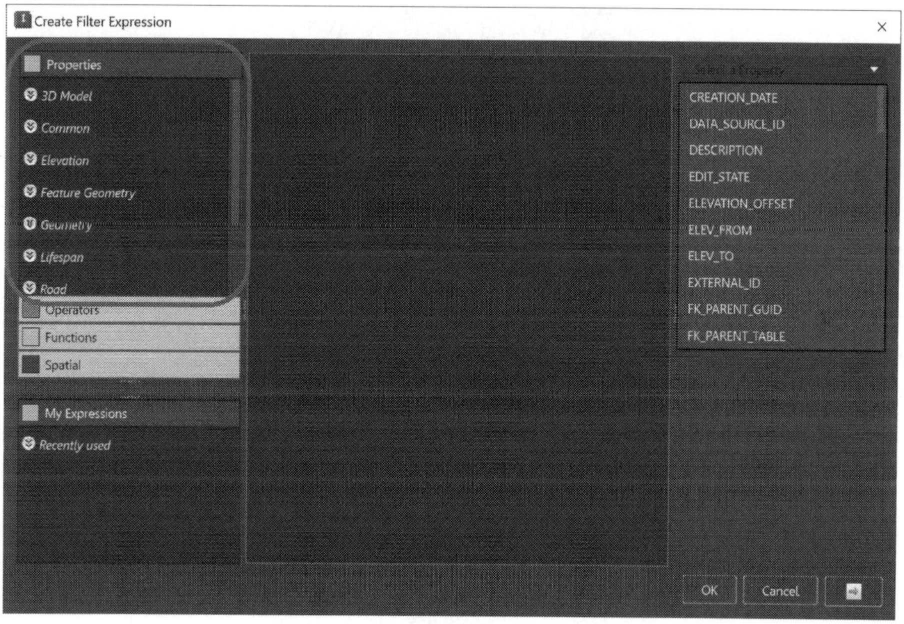

Figure 3–2

Find Available Values

It is important to determine which values are available in each property to determine which operator to use. You can determine the available values in a property by clicking (Show/Hide the Values pane) in the *Create Filter Expression* dialog box. If you have selected a numeric property, you can use operators, such as **Greater Than**, **Less Than**, or **Equal To**, to refine the selection. If a text property is selected, you must use a text operator, such as **Like**, **Not Like**, or **Null**. These and other operators are accessed by clicking **Operators** in the *Create Filter Expression* dialog box.

How To: Find Available Values

1. In the *Create Filter Expression* dialog box, click (Show/Hide the Values pane) to display the ***Values*** pane.
2. In the *Values* pane, select a property to retrieve from the drop-down list, as shown in Figure 3–3. The list of available values displays. If required, you can filter the list of values by entering keywords into the *Filter the list of values* text box.

Figure 3–3

3. Select a value from the list, as shown in Figure 3–4, and double-click on it to populate the value in the *Expression Editor*.

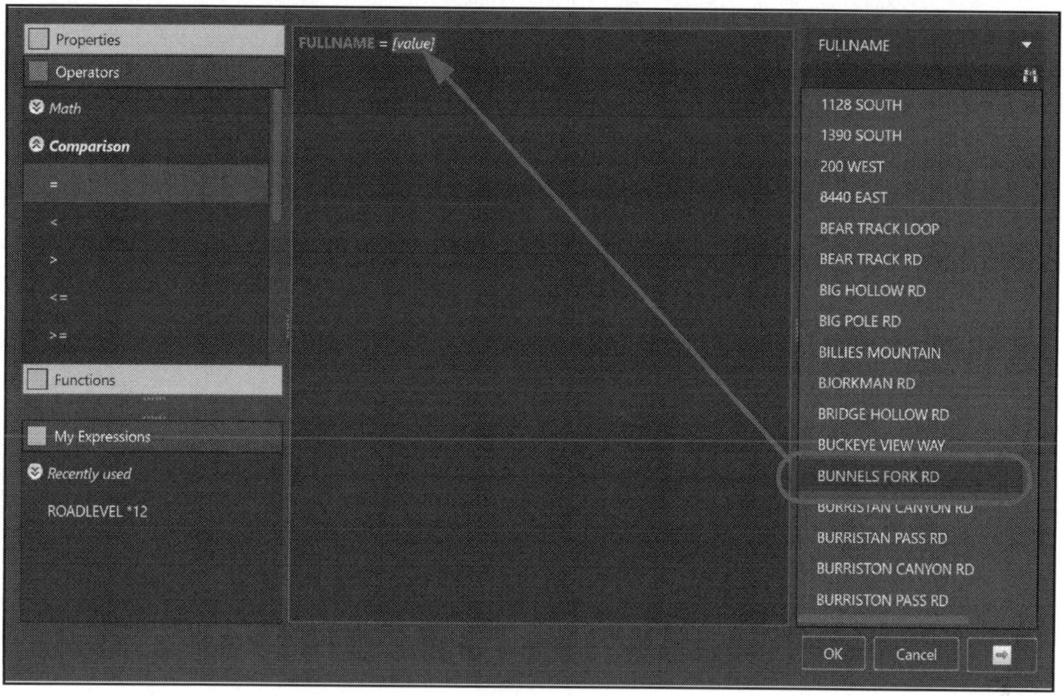

Figure 3–4

Operators

There are four groups of operators: **Math**, **Comparison**, **Logical**, and **Other**. The available operators are as follows:

Math Operators		
+	**Add**	Sums numerical properties.
-	**Subtract**	Subtracts numerical properties.
*	**Multiply**	Multiplies numerical properties.
/	**Divide**	Divides numerical properties.
Comparison Operators		
=	**Equal To**	Text or numerical properties hold an exact value.
<	**Less Than**	Numerical properties are less than an exact value.
>	**Greater Than**	Numerical properties are greater than an exact value.
<=	**Less Than or Equal To**	Numerical properties are less than or equal to an exact value.
>=	**Greater Than or Equal To**	Numerical properties are greater than or equal to an exact value.
<>	**Not Equal To**	Does not equal a specific value.
LIKE	**Matching**	Text matches a pattern.
NOT LIKE	**Not Matching**	Text does not match a pattern.
IN	**Equal To Any**	Matches any value in a list.
NOT IN	**Not Equal To Any**	Does not match any value in a list.
IS NULL	**Empty**	Returns if property is empty.
IS NOT NULL	**Not Empty**	Returns if property has any value.
Logical Operators		
AND	**Exclusive**	Must meet all conditions.
OR	**Inclusive**	Matches any one of the conditions.
NOT	**Selective**	Negates the expression.
Other		
( )	**Group**	Group the selection in the parentheses.

How To: Create a Filter Expression

1. In the *Create Filter Expression* dialog box, expand *Properties* and double-click on the property containing the appropriate values to select, as shown in Figure 3–5.

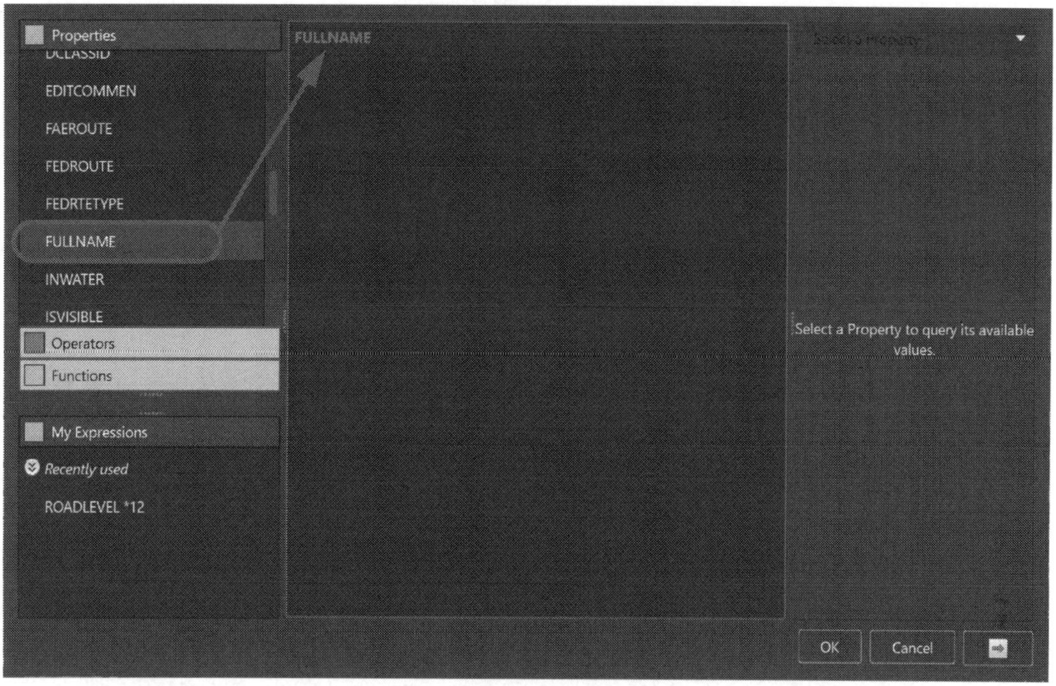

Figure 3–5

2. Select an appropriate operator.

3. Click  (Show/Hide the Values pane) to display the *Values* pane.

4. In the *Values* pane, select the required property from the drop-down list, as shown in Figure 3–6.

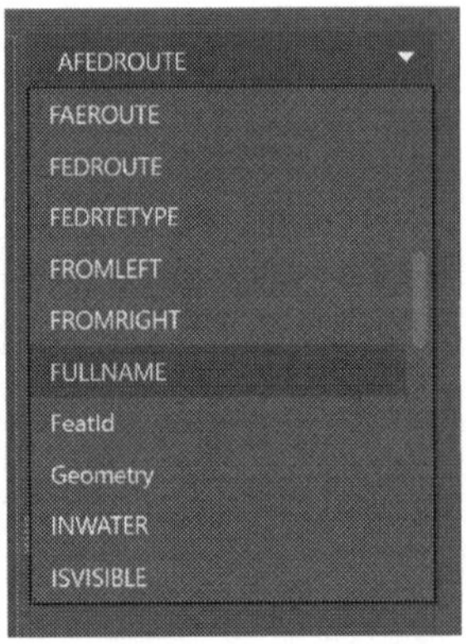

Figure 3–6

5. Double-click the **[value]** in the center pane to highlight it, then select a value from the list in the *Values* pane, as shown in Figure 3–7, and double-click on it to populate the value in the *Expression Editor*.

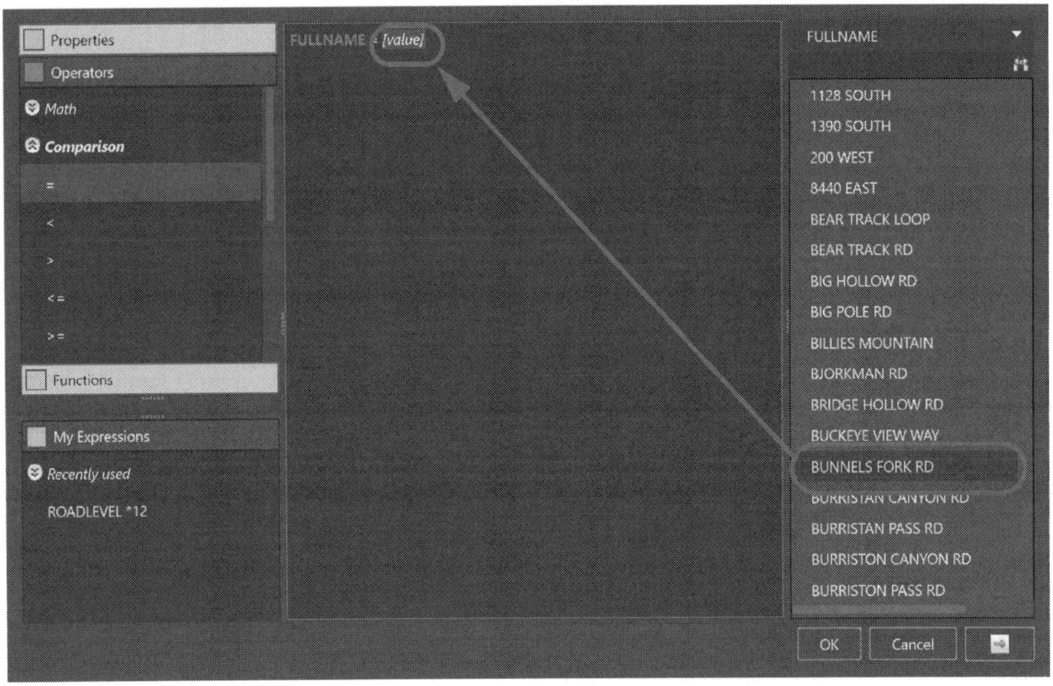

Figure 3–7

Using Scripts to Set Multiple Feature Styles

Scripts can be used to assign multiple styles simultaneously for one data source. For example, this can happen when you import a building's data source into the model. The buildings use random facade and roof colors from a default script, as shown in Figure 3–8. JavaScript® is used to create scripts that are used in the *Script* tab in the *Data Configuration* dialog box.

> ***Note:*** *Custom scripts for an Autodesk InfraWorks model can be created by anyone with a knowledge of JavaScript.*

Figure 3–8

How To: Use a Script to Modify Feature Styles

1. In the *Manage* tab>*Content* panel, click (Data Sources).
2. In the *Data Sources* panel, double-click on the layer that you want to change.
3. In the *Data Configuration* dialog box, in the *Script* tab, click **Edit**.

4. Using JavaScript, make the required changes. Figure 3–9 shows a script that varies the road styles based on the property value for *Elevation*.

```
function Process() {
   ROADS.ELEV_FROM = SOURCE.ElevStart;
   ROADS.ELEV_TO = SOURCE.ElevEnd;
   ROADS.LANES_BACKWARD = SOURCE.LanesTo;
   ROADS.LANES_FORWARD = SOURCE.LanesFrom;
   ROADS.NAME = SOURCE.Name;
   if ((ROADS.ELEV_FROM > 0) || (ROADS.ELEV_TO > 0)){
      ROADS.RULE_STYLE = "DefaultStreetStyles:Bridge0";
   if ((ROADS.ELEV_FROM > 0) || (ROADS.ELEV_TO > 0)){
      ROADS.RULE_STYLE = "DefaultStreetStyles:Tunnel0";
   } else {
      ROADS.RULE_STYLE = "DefaultStreetStyles:Street0";
   }
}
```

Figure 3–9

5. Click **Close & Refresh** to display the changes in the model.

Create Style Rules

You can also use style rules to modify how features display in the model according to data connected to each feature. Style rules override anything that was set during the data configuration process. Each feature class is stylized separately and has a tab in the *Style Rules* dialog box. In the example shown in Figure 3–10, the *Roads* class tab is active and three rules are listed.

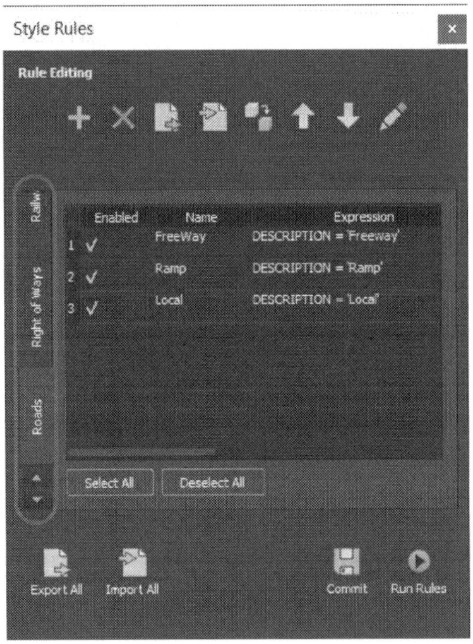

Figure 3–10

Each class of features is stylized separately using expressions. Expressions can use values from source data fields or a location to stylize features. Once an expression has been created, a style is assigned to the rule.

How To: Create a New Style Rule

1. In the *Manage* tab>*Display* drop-down list, click (Style Rules).
2. At the top of the *Style Rules* dialog box, click (Add a new Rule).
3. In the *Add Style Rule* dialog box, enter a name for the new style rule, as shown in Figure 3–11. Click **OK**.

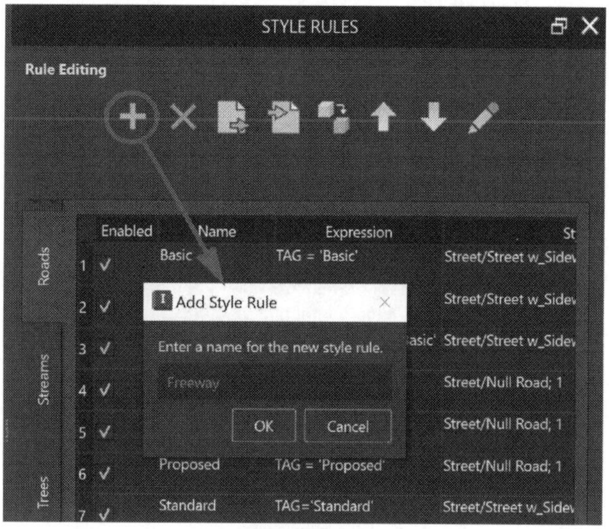

Figure 3–11

4. In the *Style Rules* dialog box, select the new rule and click (Edit properties).

5. In the *Rule Editor* dialog box, in the *Expression* area, click  (Edit), as shown in Figure 3–12.

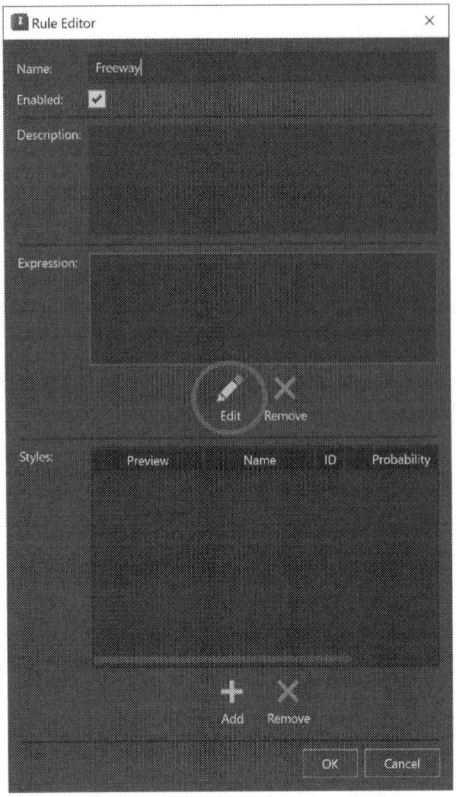

Figure 3–12

6. In the *Create Filter Expression* dialog box, define the required expression (as described in the previous section) and click **OK**.

7. In the *Rule Editor* dialog box, in the *Styles* area, click  (Add an existing style), as shown in Figure 3–13.

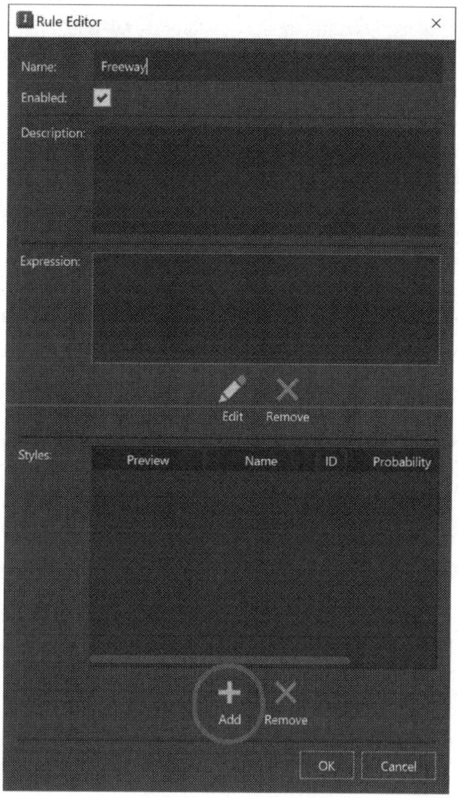

Figure 3–13

8. In the *Select Style* dialog box, on the *Road* tab, select a style, as shown in Figure 3–14. Click **OK**.

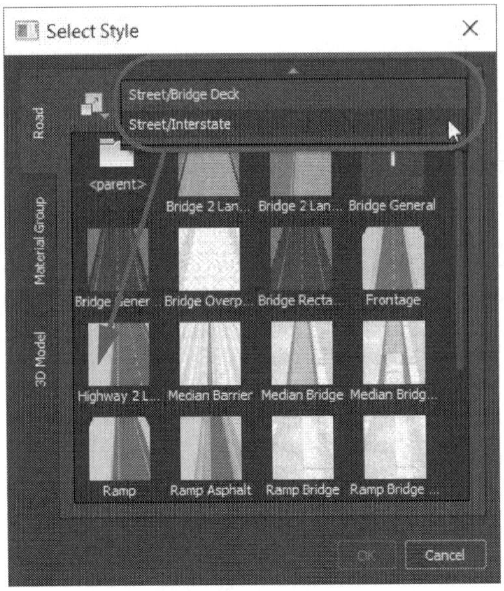

Figure 3–14

9. In the *Rule Editor* dialog box, click **OK** to return to the *Style Rules* dialog box.

10. In the *Style Rules* dialog box, click  (Run Rules) to display the results of the style change.

Reuse/Share Style Rules

If the same rules are used repeatedly to stylize different models, it is possible to save the rules in a ***.rules.json** file. Such **rules.json** files can be reused in other proposals in the same model or imported into other models.

> ***Note:*** *Import and run scripts with caution. Text files such as scripts can contain malicious content which can compromise your computer. Only import and run scripts from trusted sources.*

How To: Export Style Rules

1. Open the Autodesk InfraWorks model and proposal that contains the style rules that you want to reuse.
2. In the *Manage* tab>*Display* drop-down list, click 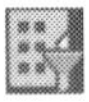 (Style Rules) and review the rules.

3. At the bottom of the *Style Rules* dialog box, click (Export All), as shown in Figure 3–15.

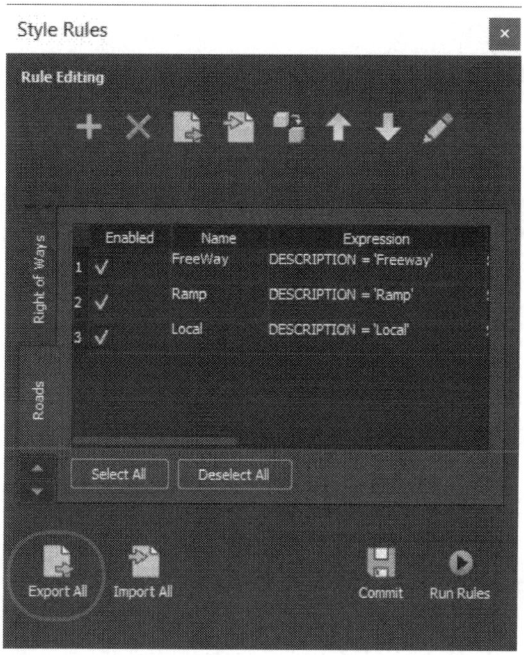

Figure 3–15

4. Select the path and enter a file name for the style rules (*.rules.json) file. Click **Save**.
5. Close the *Style Rules* dialog box.

How To: Import Style Rules

1. Open the Autodesk InfraWorks model into which the style rules are to be imported.

   Note: *Rules in the saved file that have the same name as an existing rule in the model cannot be imported. Therefore, it is important to delete or change the names of any existing rules if you want to use the imported rules.*

2. In the *Manage* tab>*Display* drop-down list, click (Style Rules) and review the rules.

3. At the bottom of the *Style Rules* dialog box, click (Import All), as shown in Figure 3–16.

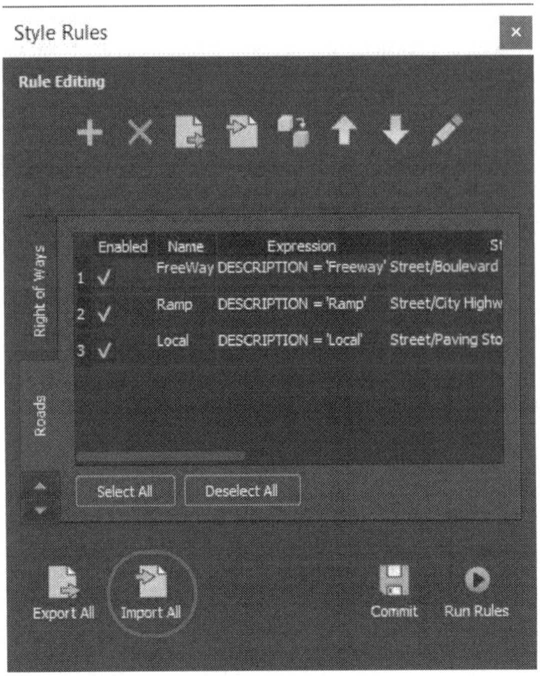

Figure 3–16

4. Select the path and file name for the style rules (*.rules.json) file that contains the required style rules. Click **Open**.
5. A warning is displayed explaining the dangers of running custom scripts, as shown in Figure 3–17. If the script is from a trusted source, continue with the refresh. If there is doubt, click **Cancel Refresh** and check the script's authenticity.

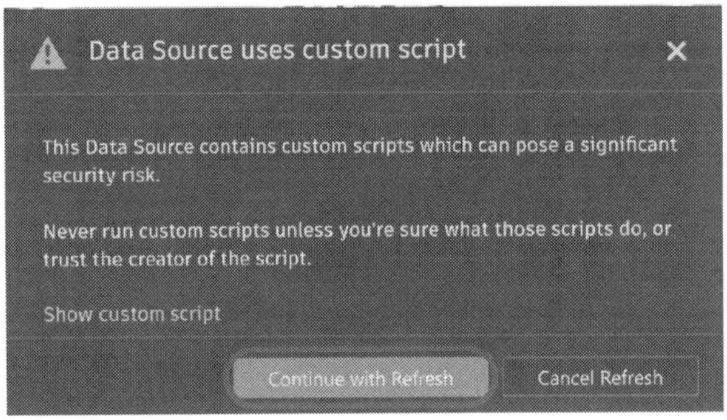

Figure 3–17

6. Close the *Style Rules* dialog box.

3.2 Overriding Style Rules

There always seems to be at least one exception to every rule. For example, it is common to stylize roads according to their road classification. However, if the road has a bridge on one of its sections, it might be necessary to override the road classification style given to that section with a bridge style, as shown in Figure 3–18.

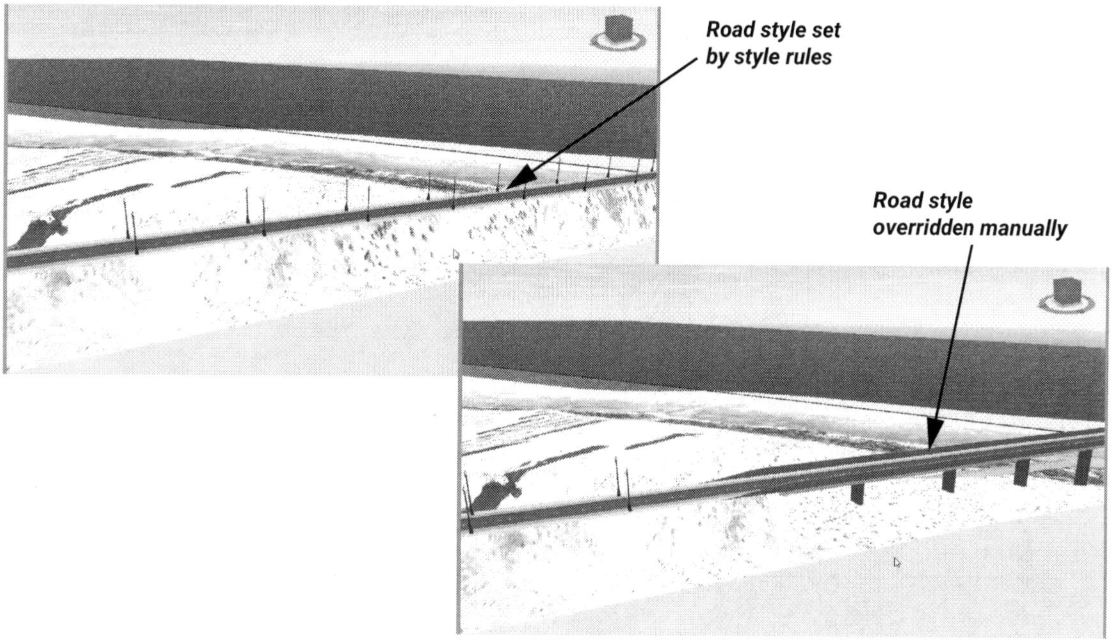

Figure 3–18

How To: Change a Style Using the Style Palette

1. In the *Manage* tab>*Control* panel, click  (Style Palette) and select the appropriate tab for the feature you are changing.

2. Select the style from the preview area and drag and drop it onto the feature to apply the style, as shown in Figure 3–19.

Figure 3–19

3. Close the *Style Palette*.

How To: Change a Style Using Feature Properties

1. In the model, select the model feature, right-click on the feature, and select **Properties**.
2. In the *Properties* panel, change the style in the *Manual Style* field, as shown in Figure 3–20.

   Note: *You can remove a style override by deleting the Manual Style from the Properties panel and updating the model.*

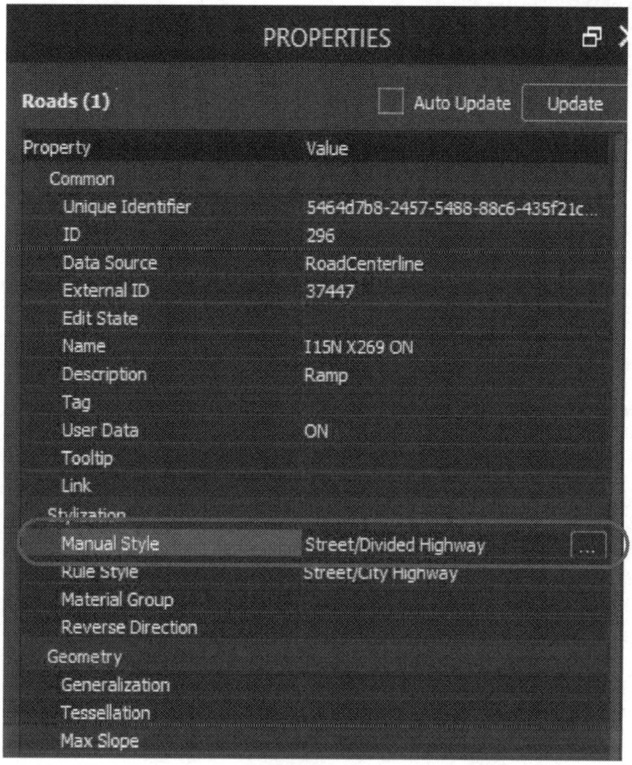

Figure 3–20

3. Click **Update** to display the change in the model.

How To: Change a Style Using a Feature's Asset Card

1. In the model, select the model feature.
2. In the feature asset card, click on the *Manual Style* thumbnail and select a frequently used style. You can also click **More Styles** to select a style from the *Select Style* dialog box, as shown in Figure 3–21.

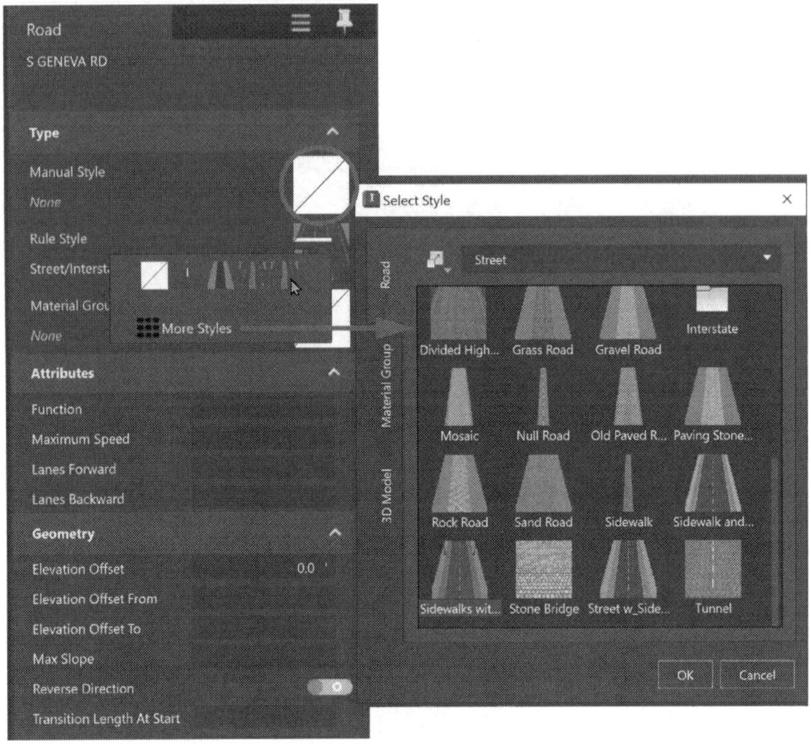

Figure 3–21

3. Click **OK**.

Practice 3a
Stylize Data Sources

Practice Objective

- Change the visual style assigned to a model feature using scripts, style rules, and style overrides.

In this practice, you will use scripts, style rules, and style overrides to change the display of model features.

Task 1: Use scripts to change the display of model features.

A default script is currently being used in the model to randomly set the color of the buildings. Additionally, all of the buildings in the model are currently the same height. A JavaScript expert has created a script for you that will randomize the building styles and heights throughout the model. In this task, you will use this script to automatically modify the building styles.

1. On the *Home* screen, click **Open**.
2. In the *InfraWorks Practice Files\3-Styles* folder, select **Styles.sqlite** and click **Open**.
3. Click (Bookmarks) and select **Buildings**. Ensure that **A_Task1** is the current proposal.
4. If the *Data Sources* panel is not already displayed, in the *Manage* tab>*Content* panel, select (Data Sources).
5. In the *Data Sources* panel, double-click on the **BuildingFootprint** layer.
6. In the **Start** menu on your computer, launch **Notepad**.
7. In the Notepad window, expand the **File** menu and select **Open**.
8. In the *InfraWorks Practice Files\References\Data\Scripts* folder, select **BuildingScript.txt** and click **Open**.
9. Press <Ctrl>+<A> to select all of the contents of the file. Press <Ctrl>+<C> to copy the file contents.
10. Return to the Autodesk InfraWorks software.
11. In the *Data Configuration* dialog box, in the *Script* tab, click **Edit**.
12. Click anywhere inside the script area and press <Ctrl>+<A> to select all of the content of the script. Press <Delete> to remove the content of the script.
13. Press <Ctrl>+<V> to paste the contents from the text file into the script area.
14. Click **Close & Refresh** to display the changes in the model. Note that each building now has a different facade (including color and windows), a different height, and a different roof style.

15. A warning is displayed explaining the dangers of running custom scripts, as shown in Figure 3–22. Sine this is from a trusted source, you can continue with the refresh. If however you feel uncomfortable running the script, cancel the refresh and set the **A_Task2** proposal to current for the next task.

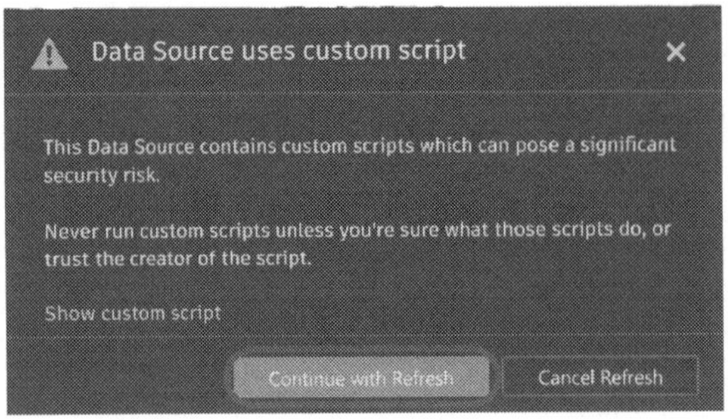

Figure 3–22

Note: *If the buildings do not change styles randomly according to the script, you might need to remove the* **BuildingsFootprint** *layer from the Data Sources panel and re-import the buildings.*

16. Close the *Data Sources* panel.

Task 2: Use style rules to change the display of the model features.

The roads in this model are currently only using one style. However, there are a number of different types of roads and many of them follow a similar pattern according to their road class. The **RoadCenterline.shp** file[1] lists each road's classification in a database field called *ROADCLASS*. When the layer was imported and configured, the *ROADCLASS* field was mapped to the *Description* property in the *Table* tab in the *Data Source Configuration* dialog box. In this task, you will use this property to set the styles for the road centerlines.

Note: *If you did not complete the previous task, set the* ***A_Task2*** *proposal to current.*

1. Click (Bookmarks) and select **Road Styles**.
2. In the *Manage* tab>*Display* drop-down list, select (Style Rules). Note that pressing <Alt>+<7> will also toggle the *Style Rules* on and off.
3. In the *Style Rules* dialog box, use the down arrow in the lower-left area of the panel to find the *Roads* tab and select it. There are several road rules already created.
4. At the top of the *Style Rules* dialog box, click (Add a new Rule).

1. Department, GIS Division of the Utah County Information Systems, 2013

5. In the *Add Style Rule* dialog box, type **Freeway**, as shown in Figure 3–23. Click **OK**.

   Note: *If the rule style already exists, click (Delete Rule) to remove it so you can recreate it.*

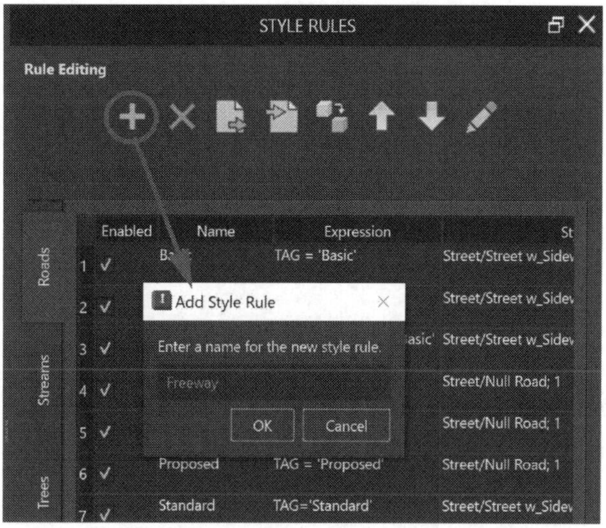

Figure 3–23

6. In the *Style Rules* dialog box, double-click on **Freeway** to edit the rule.
7. In the *Rule Editor* dialog box, in the *Expression* area, click (Edit), as shown in Figure 3–24.

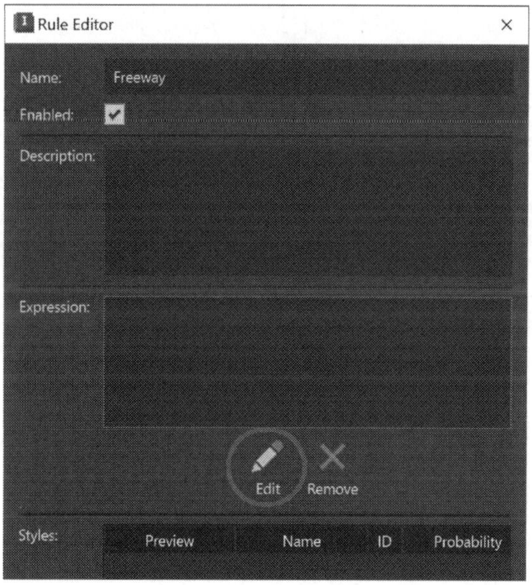

Figure 3–24

8. In the *Create Filter Expression* dialog box, do the following (as shown in Figure 3–25):
   - Expand **Properties**. Under *Common*, double-click on **DESCRIPTION**.
   - Expand **Operators**. Under *Comparison*, double-click on **=**.
   - If the *Values* pane is not open, click  (Show/Hide the Values pane) in the lower-right corner (next to the **Cancel** button) to display a list of possible properties.
   - Expand the *Properties* drop-down list and select **DESCRIPTION**.
   - In the *Expression Editor*, double-click on **[value]**.
   - In the *Values* pane, double-click on **Freeway**.
   - Click **OK**.

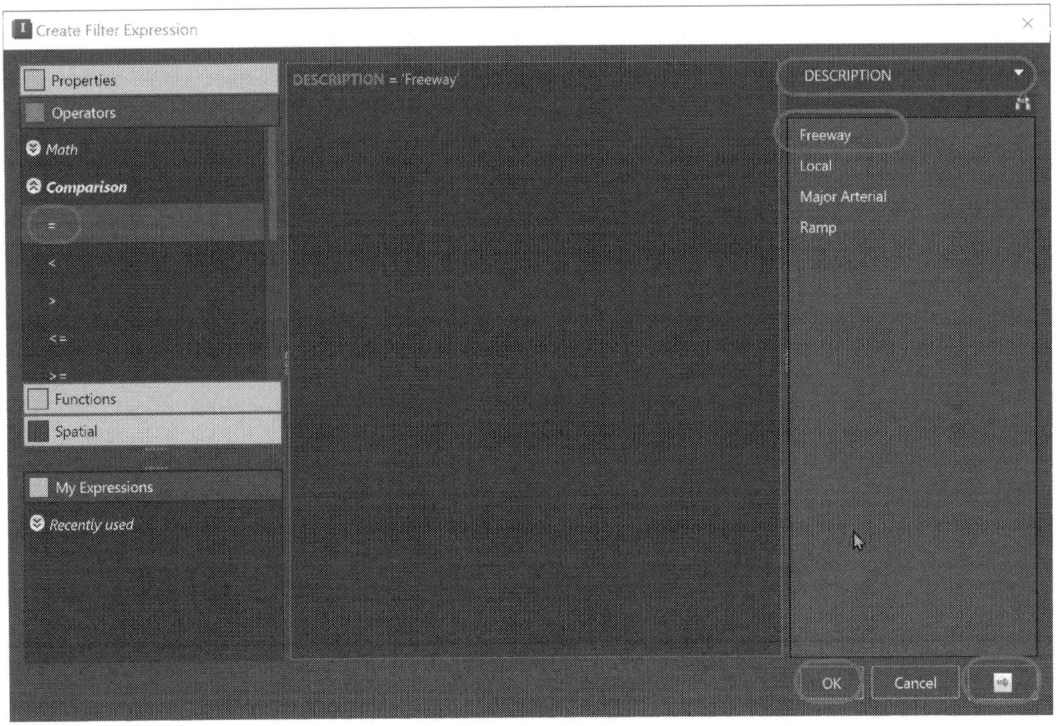

Figure 3–25

9. In the *Rule Editor* dialog box, in the *Styles* area, click  (Add an existing style), as shown in Figure 3–26.

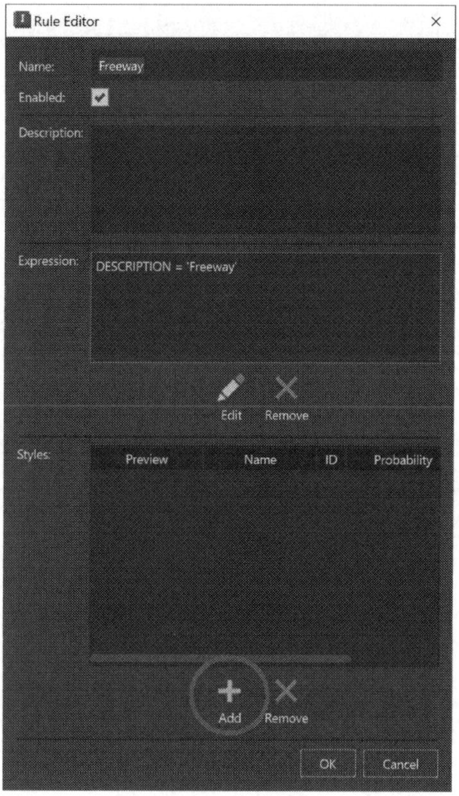

Figure 3–26

10. At the top of the *Select Style* dialog box, in the *Road* tab, expand the drop-down list and select **Street/Interstate** (you may have to use the small drop-down arrow to select it form the drop-down list).

    Note: *Sometimes the Select Style dialog box moves under the Rule Editor dialog box. Therefore, move the Select Style dialog box to the right or left so it is selectable.*

11. In the *Preview* area, select **Highway 2 Lane Forward**, as shown in Figure 3–27, and click **OK**.

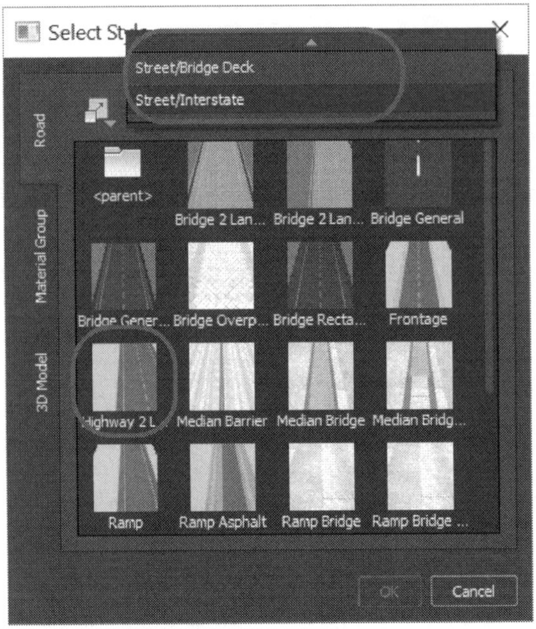

Figure 3–27

12. In the *Rule Editor*, click **OK** to return to the *Style Rules* dialog box.

13. In the *Style Rules* dialog box, click (Run Rules) to display the results of the style change.

Note: If a rule style already exists, click (Delete Rule) to remove it.

14. Repeat Steps 4 to 12 to add the following rules and styles:

Name	Expression	Style
Ramp	DESCRIPTION=Ramp	Street/Interstate/Ramp Asphalt
Major Arterial	DESCRIPTION=Major Arterial	Street/Interstate/Street 2 Lane-1 LT Turn
Local	DESCRIPTION=Local	Street/Old Paved Road, Grass Shoulder

15. In the *Style Rules* dialog box, click (Run Rules) to display the results of the style changes.
16. Close the *Style Rules* dialog box by clicking on the **X** in the upper-right corner.

Task 3: Override the style rules.

Stylizing the road centerlines according to the road class helps create a more realistic model. In this model, part of the frontage road has been given the wrong styles and does not match what is actually there. In this task, you will override a style rule to give the road the correct style.

> ***Note:*** *If you did not complete the previous task, set the* ***A_Task3*** *proposal to current.*

1. Click (Bookmarks) and select **Road Styles**.
2. In the *Manage* tab>*Content* panel, select (*Style Palette*).
    - Note that pressing <Alt>+<6> will toggle the *Style Palette* on and off.
3. In the *Style Palette*, use the down arrow in the lower-left area of the panel to find the *Roads* tab and select it.
4. At the top of the *Style Palette*, expand the drop-down list and select **Street/Interstate**. Click and drag **Street 2 Lane-1 LT Turn** from the *Style Palette* to the model and drop it on the segment of frontage road that was styled incorrectly, as shown in Figure 3–28.

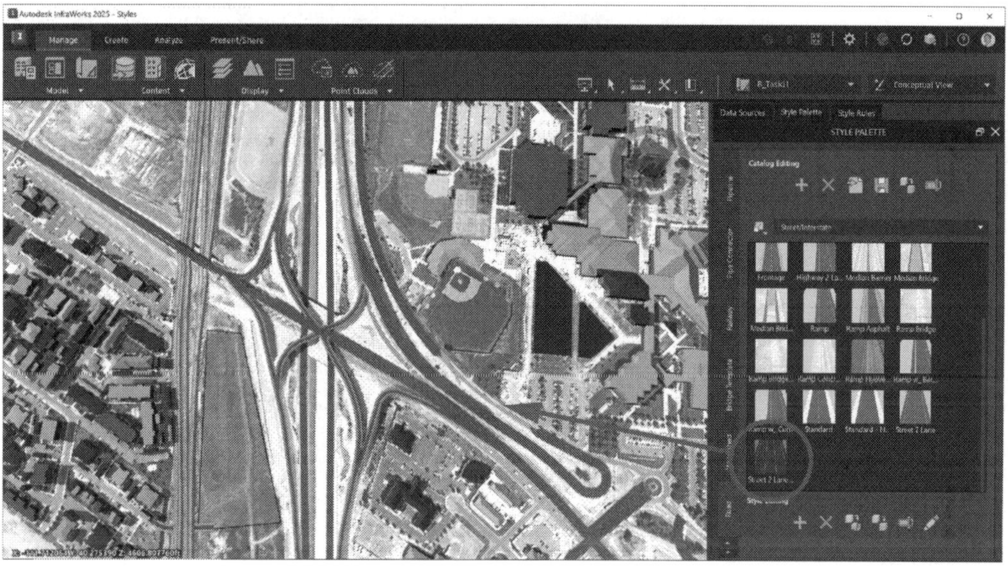

Figure 3–28

5. Close the *Style Palette*.

End of practice

3.3 Create and Share Styles

Although many styles come with the Autodesk InfraWorks software, you might need to create additional styles for your project. You can do so by creating a new catalog of styles or by adding a new style to an existing catalog.

Catalogs

A catalog is a collection of styles that are sorted by feature category. The catalog is listed in a drop-down list at the top of the *Style Palette*. You can manage style catalogs using the tools at the top of the *Style Palette*, as shown in Figure 3–29.

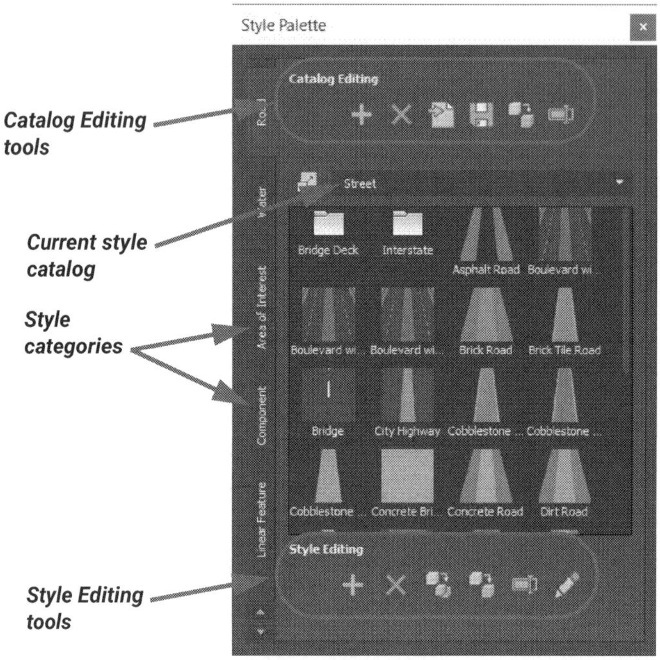

Figure 3–29

Catalog Editing Tools

The Catalog Editing tools at the top of the *Style Palette* only affect the style catalogs. The tools control how the styles are grouped together.

Icon	Description
(Add New Style Catalog)	Creates a new style catalog, which is added to the *Style Palette* and becomes the active catalog.
(Delete Selected Style Catalog)	Removes the current style catalog from the *Style Palette*. Note: Style catalogs can be re-imported, if required. The catalogs are saved externally in an .XML file, which is not deleted when the catalog is removed from a model.
(Import Style Catalog From File)	Imports a style catalog from a specified file. The catalog is added to the *Style Palette* and becomes the active catalog.
(Export Selected Style Catalog)	Creates an external file of the current style catalog. The copy is stored in a specified location.
(Copy Selected Style Catalog)	Makes a copy of the current style catalog, which then becomes the active catalog. The copy is stored in a specified location.
(Rename Selected Style Catalog)	Enables you to enter a new name for the current style catalog.

Styles

Styles are used to make a model look more realistic. Each style category contains unique settings that must be set to create a style.

The quickest way to create new styles is to create a new style based on an existing style. You can also create new styles from scratch or from 3D models. If you plan to make changes to an existing style, it is recommended that you copy the style first, and then make changes to the copy.

Hint: Creating Styles for a Model

The Autodesk InfraWorks Online Help has additional information on creating specific styles. To open the Autodesk InfraWorks Online Help, press <F1>.

Style Editing Tools

The Style Editing tools, located at the bottom of the *Style Palette*, only affect the currently selected style. Using these tools enables you to copy and edit the available styles.

Icon	Description
(Add New Style)	Creates a style in the current catalog. A blank style entry displays in the preview area. Double-click on the style to specify the style components.
(Delete Selected Style Catalog)	Removes the selected style from the current style catalog.
(Copy Selected Style to Another Catalog)	Makes a copy of the selected style and moves the copy to another style catalog in the current feature category.
(Copy Selected Style Locally)	Makes a copy of the selected style in the current style catalog.
(Rename Selected Style)	Enables you to enter a new name for the selected style.
(Edit Selected Style)	Opens the Style Editor, in which you can change the properties of the selected style.

Material Styles

Defining a material style enables you to create a fill pattern for any other style. Selecting a **Color** material style type enables you to use a color from the palette or to create a custom color using HSV or RGB values. You can use a custom image by selecting the **Texture** material style type. If you use a custom image file to create the fill pattern, you can set the size of the image to control the size of the pattern in the model. The *Define New Material* dialog box is shown in Figure 3–30.

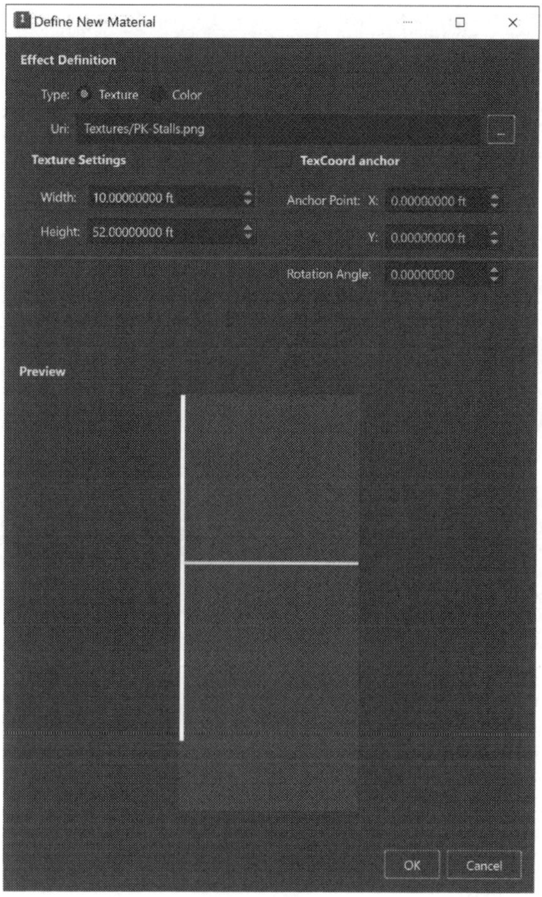

Figure 3–30

Barrier Styles

Barriers are often used to control traffic of various types, such as vehicular, bike, or pedestrian traffic. Defining a barrier style enables you to change the barrier segment length, the barrier height, the material for the barrier faces, and the spacing between each barrier. Changing the thickness changes the buffer along the polyline representing the barrier. The *Configure Barrier* dialog box is shown in Figure 3–31.

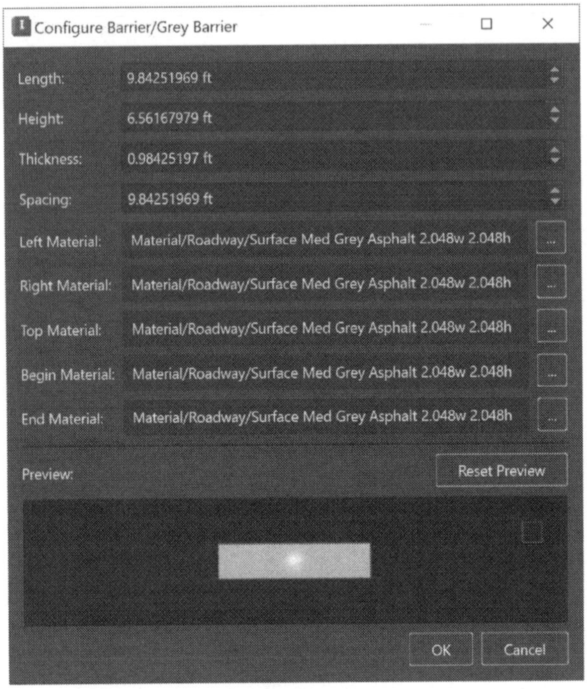

Figure 3–31

Coverage Styles

Coverages can represent parking areas, empty lots, parks, etc. Defining a coverage style enables you to select the material used to fill the interior area and select a material and width for the outline. InfraWorks also has dedicated parking layout tools that will be explored later in this guide.

The *Define New Coverage* dialog box is shown in Figure 3–32.

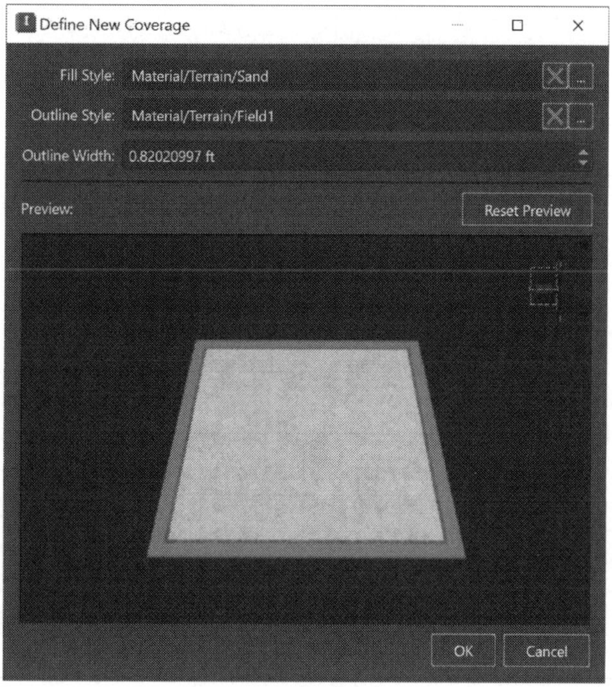

Figure 3–32

Planning Road Styles

> ***Note:*** *Component roads do not have styles, but components. These are covered in a different chapter of this guide.*

Planning road styles are more complex than most other styles. Defining a road style enables you to define the types of materials used by different parts of the road and the number of default travel lanes that are available. It also enables you to add barriers and other safety features to a road, such as lighting, park strips, and sidewalks. The *Configure Street/Interstate* dialog box has four areas, as shown in Figure 3–33.

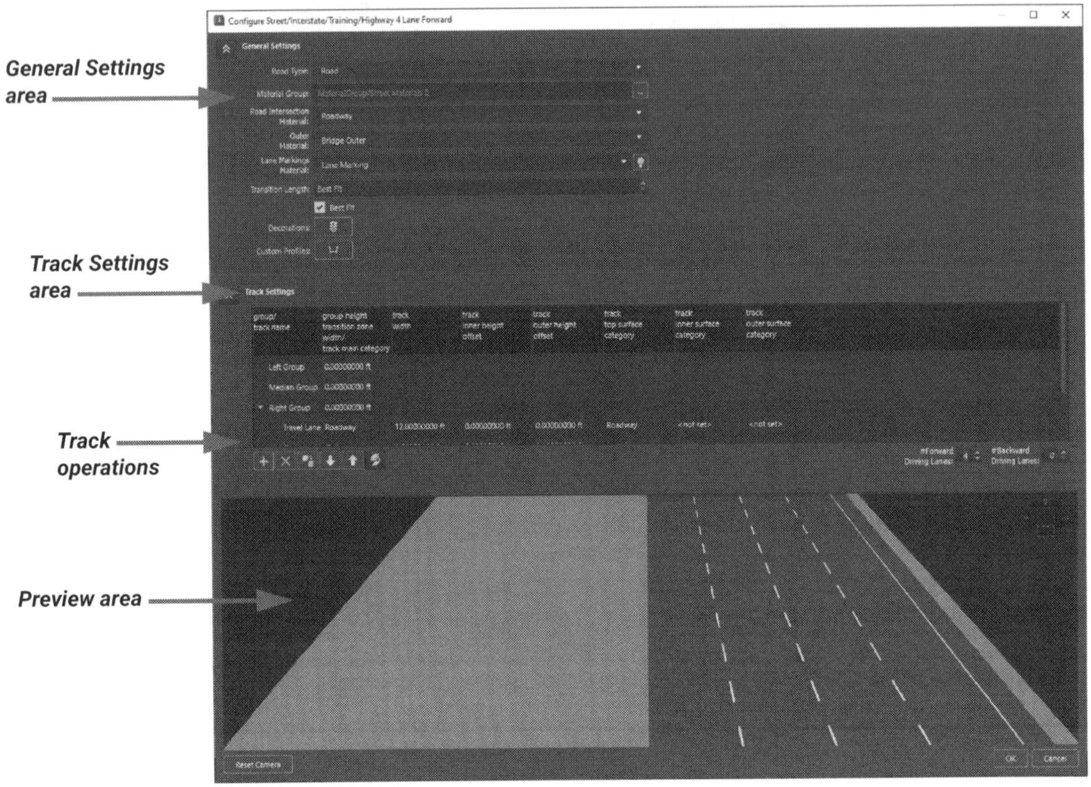

Figure 3–33

General Settings

The *General Settings* area enables you to specify the road type, road intersection material, lane marking material, and decorations.

- **Road Type:** Defines the road as a regular above-ground road, a bridge, or a tunnel.
- **Material Group:** Maps the materials that are assigned to different parts of a road. Each component of the material group can be defined separately in its catalog.

- **Road Intersection Material:** Specifies the category of material that is to be used for areas where road segments cross each other. If two roads with different styles share a crossing region, the road style of the road with the highest value in the *Importance* property displays. The *Importance* property is located in the road's *Properties* panel, as shown in Figure 3–34. You can access it by selecting the road, right-clicking, and selecting **Properties**.

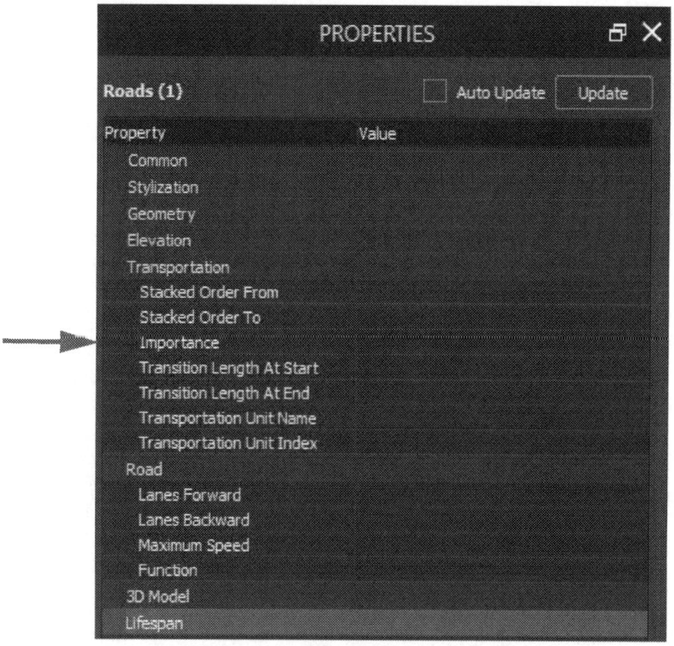

Figure 3–34

- **Outer Material:** Specifies the material applied to the terrain along the outer-most track.
- **Lane Markings Material:** Specifies the category of material to be used for lane markings.

  Lane markings can be toggled on or off using to the right of the *Lane Markings Material* field. By default, lane markings are not generated for intersecting regions.
- **Transition Length:** Specifies the default transition length for the style. Selecting the **Best Fit** option permits the software to set the transition length.

Note: *Decorations is discussed in greater detail in the Roadways chapter.*

- **(Decorations):** Opens the *Decoration Editor* dialog box, as shown in Figure 3–35. It enables you to add 3D models to the roadway at specified intervals. The 3D models can include barriers, signs, light poles, and other city furniture. In the *Decoration Target* field, select the location that you want the 3D model to display in. Click to select a 3D model (this will open the *Select Style* dialog box). Finally, set the spacing and rotation for the 3D model in the *Decoration Settings* area.

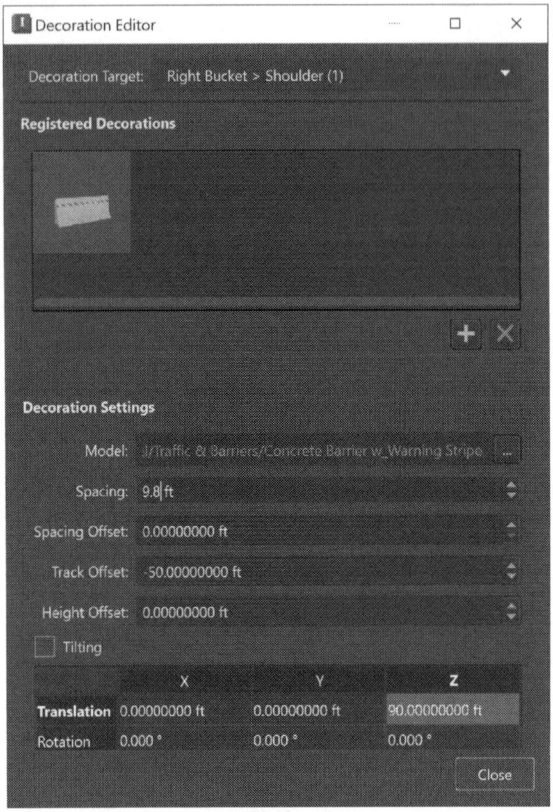

Figure 3–35

- **(Custom Profiles):** Specifies a 2D cross section (.SDF or .SQLite file format) to create or display decorations that follow the path along curved roads. This is most useful for customizing the profile of medians, bike-ways, curbs, green space, sidewalks, etc.

Track Settings

The *Track Settings* area defines the road elements. Each row of the table sets the width, height, and surface categories for one element or track for the road. There is usually only one row dedicated for lane elements because the number of lanes is defined by the *#Forward* and *#Backward Driving Lanes* fields, as shown in Figure 3–36.

***Note:** The order of the tracks in the Track Settings area determines the order in which they display in the model.*

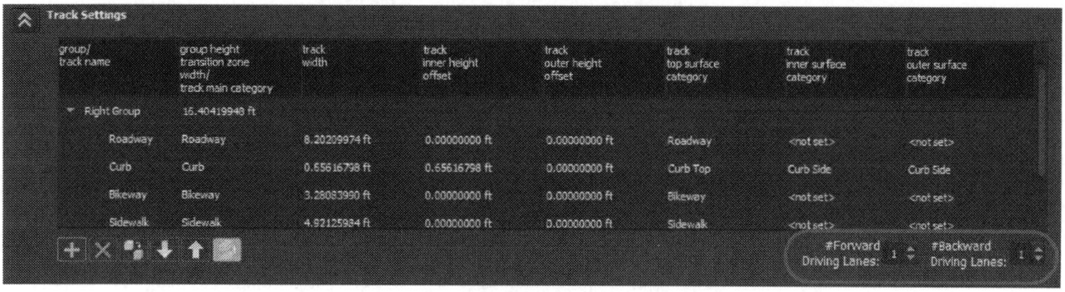

Figure 3–36

By default, only the right side of the road displays in the *Preview* area because the software mirrors the right side of the road to create the left side in the model. To create an asymmetric road and display the left side, click (Create Asymmetric Road) below the table. You can create additional rows/tracks by clicking (Add New Element) below the table. The columns in the *Track Settings* area are as follows:

Column	Description
group/track name	The track name identifies the track use. The group name identifies where the track falls: either in the median or on the left/right side of the road.
group height transition zone width/track main category	The *track main category* is the basic material type for the road element. Options in this column depend on the material group selected in the *General Settings* area. The *group height transition zone width* category applies to the group.
track width	Sets the width for the corresponding road element.
track inner height offset	Sets the starting height of the corresponding road element relative to the previous track. Note: The initial height is based on the centerline of the road.
track outer height offset	Sets the finishing height of the corresponding road element relative to the next track.
track top surface category	Sets the material to be used for the top surface of the road. Options in this column depend on the material group selected in the *General Settings* area.
track inner surface category	Sets the material to be used for the vertical geometry that is created if the inner offset height value is not equal to zero.
track outer surface category	Sets the material to be used for the vertical geometry that is created if the outer offset height value is not equal to zero.

Track Operations

The track operations area (shown in Figure 3–37) is where you set the number of lanes for the road, both forward and backward. It is also used to modify the *Track Settings* table.

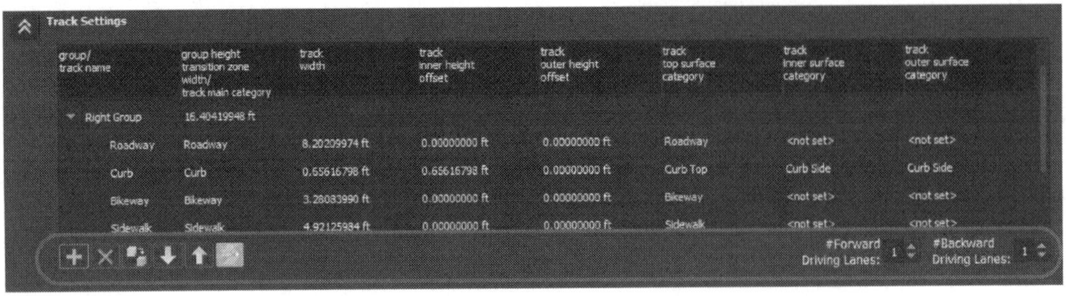

Figure 3–37

The available icons and their uses are as follows:

Icon	Description
(Add New Element)	Creates a new road element in the *Track Settings* area.
(Delete Selected Element)	Removes the selected road element or group from the *Track Settings* area.
(Copy Selected Element)	Makes a copy of the selected road element in the *Track Settings* area.
(Move Element Up)	Moves the selected road element up in the track list and changes its location in the *Preview* area.
(Move Element Down)	Moves the selected road element down in the track list and changes its location in the *Preview* area.
(Create Asymmetric Road)	Adds a median group and a left group to the track list, which enables you to create an asymmetric road.

Preview Area

The preview area displays an image of how the road is going to display when applied to road centerlines in the model. The camera position can be moved using the ViewCube in the preview area or by using the mouse, similar to working in the model.

Practice 3b
Create Styles

Practice Objective

- Create new visual styles for model features.

In this practice, you will create a coverage style for a parking lot and a road style.

Task 1: Create and use a coverage style.

A new commuter parking lot is being built next to the freeway entrance. Coverages are a great way to grade parking lots and other grading sites. Using a custom coverage style provides the opportunity to make the graded site look however you would like. In this task, you will create a material style and a coverage style that looks like a parking lot and apply the style to a coverage in the model.

InfraWorks also has dedicated parking lot tools available, which will be explored later in this guide.

1. Continue working in the same model as the last practice. If you closed the file, on the *Home* screen, click **Open**. In the *InfraWorks Practice Files\3-Styles* folder, select **Styles.sqlite** and click **Open**.

   Note: *If you did not complete the previous practice, set the* ***B_Task1*** *proposal to current.*

2. Click (Bookmarks) and select **ParkingLot**.

3. In the *Manage* tab>*Content* panel, select (Style Palette). In the *Style Palette*, use the down (or up) arrow in the lower-left area of the panel to find the *Material* tab, as shown in Figure 3–38.

   ***Note:** Remember that <Alt>+<6> toggles the Style Palette on and off.*

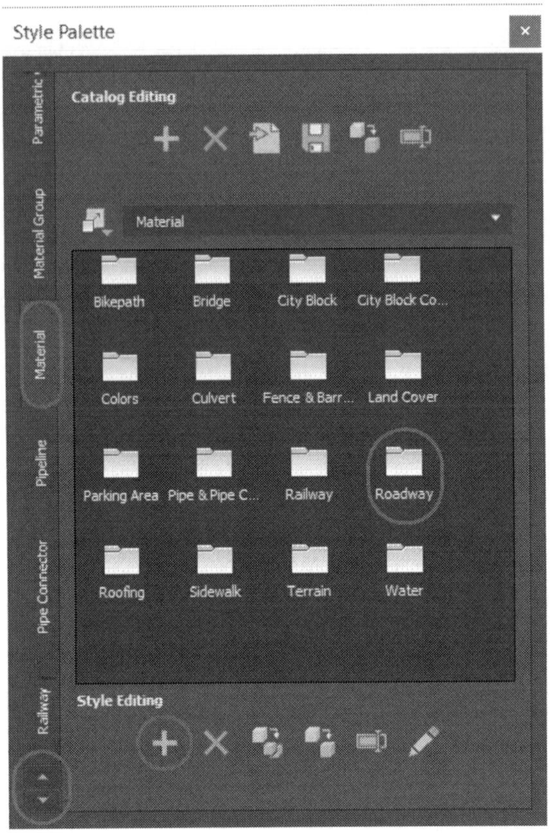

Figure 3–38

4. Double-click on **Roadway** to display all of the available road materials.

5. In the *Style Editing* area at the bottom of the *Style Palette*, click (Add new style).

6. In the *Define New Material* dialog box, do the following:
   - For the *Type*, select **Texture**.
   - To the right of the *Uri* field, click the ellipsis (...) for browsing, navigate to the *InfraWorks Practice Files\References\Images* folder, select **PK-Stalls.png**, and click **Open**.
   - Click **OK** in the *Added Texture File to Model Resources* dialog box.
   - In the *Texture Settings* area, type **10** for the *Width* and type **52** for the *Height* (as shown in Figure 3–39).
   - Click **OK**.

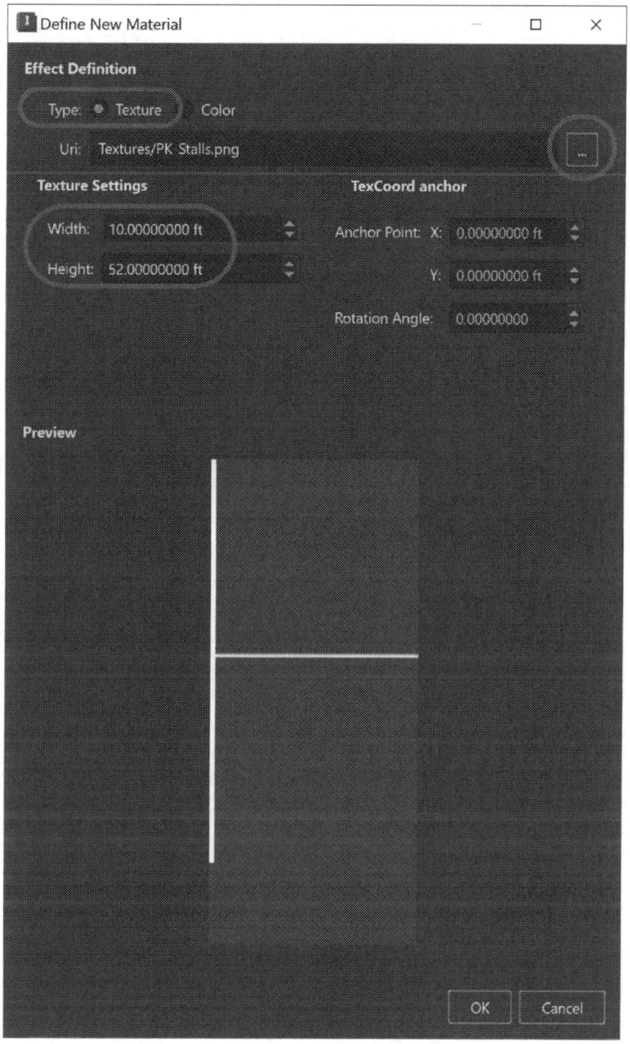

Figure 3–39

7. Click on the name of the newly created material (*New Material*) to rename it. Type **PK-Stalls** and press <Enter>.
8. In the *Style Palette*, select the *Coverage* tab (near the top of the tab list), as shown in Figure 3–40.

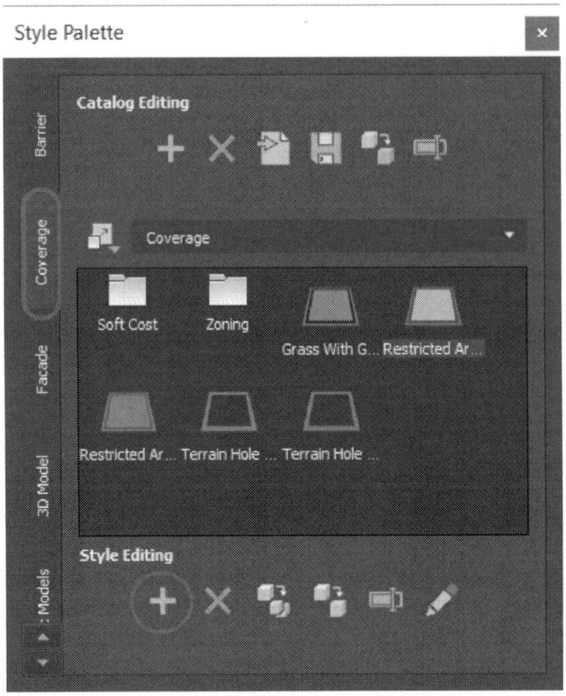

Figure 3–40

9. In the *Style Editing* area at the bottom of the *Style Palette*, click **+** (Add new style).
10. In the *Define New Coverage* dialog box, to the right of the *Fill Style* field, click the ellipsis (...) for browsing.

11. In the *Select Style / Color* dialog box:
    - Select the *Material* tab.
    - Double-click on **Roadway**.
    - Select **PK-Stalls**, as shown in Figure 3–41. Click **OK**.

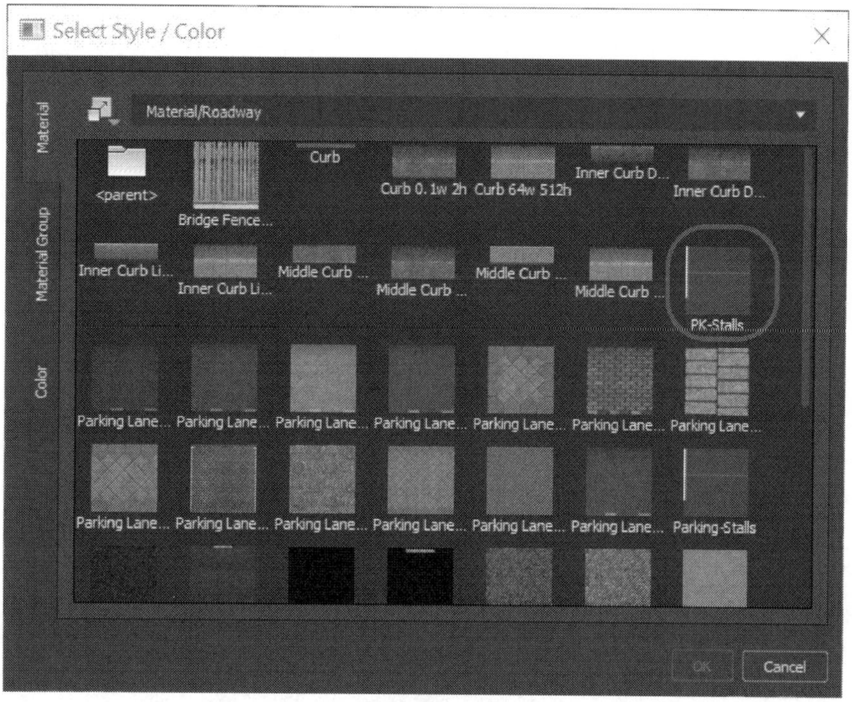

Figure 3–41

12. In the *Define New Coverage* dialog box, to the right of *Outline Style*, click the ellipsis (...) for browsing.

13. In the *Select Style / Color* dialog box, do the following:
    - Select the *Material* tab.
    - Double-click on **Roadway**.
    - Select **Curb 0.1w 2h**, as shown in Figure 3–42.
    - Click **OK**.

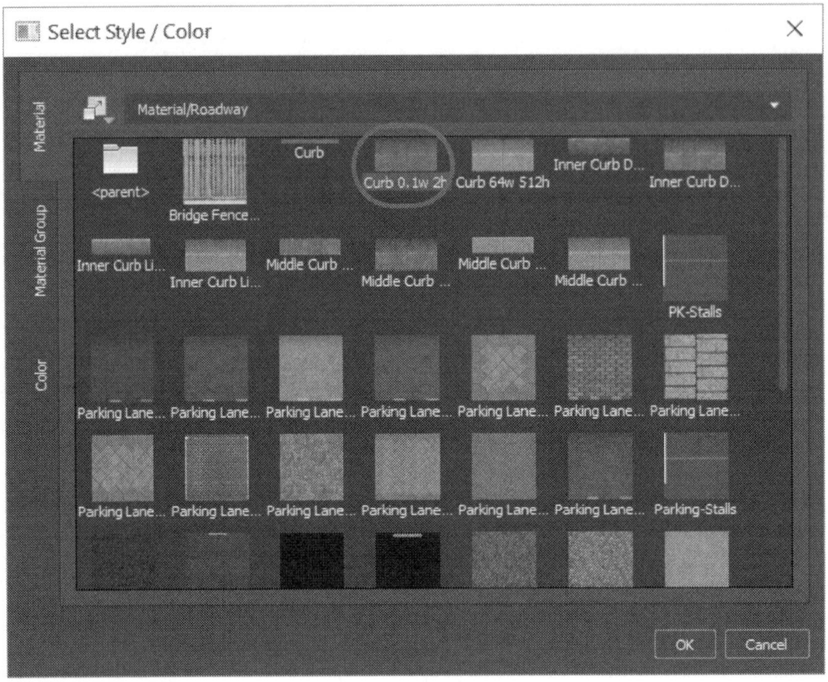

Figure 3–42

14. Leave the *Outline Width* set to **0.82....** and click **OK**.
15. For the coverage style name, type **ParkingLot** and press <Enter>.

16. Drag the new **ParkingLot** coverage style to the new commuter parking lot shown in Figure 3–43.

Figure 3–43

Task 2: (Optional) Create a new road style.

Stylizing the road centerlines according to the road class helps create a more realistic model. However, the road style used to display the I-15 corridor does not have enough lanes and needs to have the correct barriers to protect drivers from running off the road or into oncoming traffic. In this task, you will create a new catalog and create a copy of the style that is currently used for I-15. You will make the required modifications to the style and apply it to the style rules.

> ***Note:*** *If you did not complete the previous task, set the* ***B_Task2*** *proposal to current.*

1. Click (Bookmarks) and select **Road Styles**.
2. In the *Style Palette*, select the *Road* tab.
3. Expand the drop-down list and select **Street/Interstate**.
4. In the *Catalog Editing* area at the top, click (Add New Style Catalog).
5. Click on the name of the newly created catalog (*New Catalog*) to rename it. Type **Training** and press <Enter>.

6. In the style preview area, select the **Highway 2 Lane** style.
7. In the *Style Editing* area at the bottom of the *Style Palette*, click (Duplicate the selected style to another catalog).
8. In the *Copy Item* dialog box, select the **Street/Interstate/Training** option, as shown in Figure 3–44. Click **OK**.

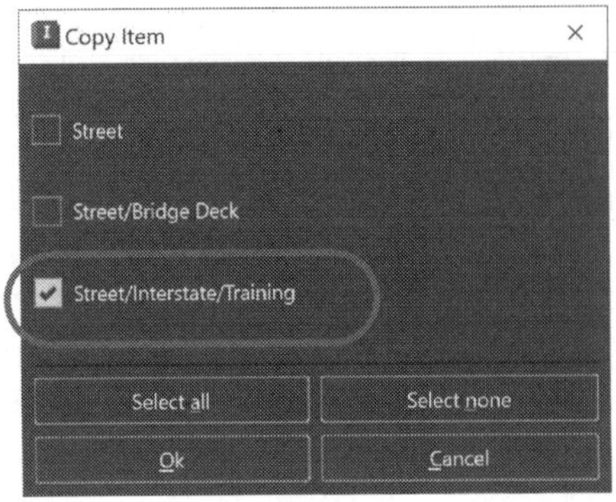

Figure 3–44

9. Expand the drop-down list and select **Street/Interstate/Training**.
10. In the *Style Preview* area, select the **Highway 2 Lane** style.
11. In the *Style Editing* area at the bottom of the *Style Palette*, click (Rename Selected Style). Type **Highway 4 Lane Forward** and press <Enter>.
12. In the *Style Editing* area at the bottom of the *Style Palette*, click (Edit Selected Style).

13. In the *Configure Street/Interstate/Training* dialog box, do the following (as shown in Figure 3–45):

- In the lower-right corner of the *Track Settings* area, set the *#Forward Driving Lanes* to **4**.
- Click  (Create asymmetric road) so that the icon is not greyed to make the road asymmetrical.
- Click  (Decorations).

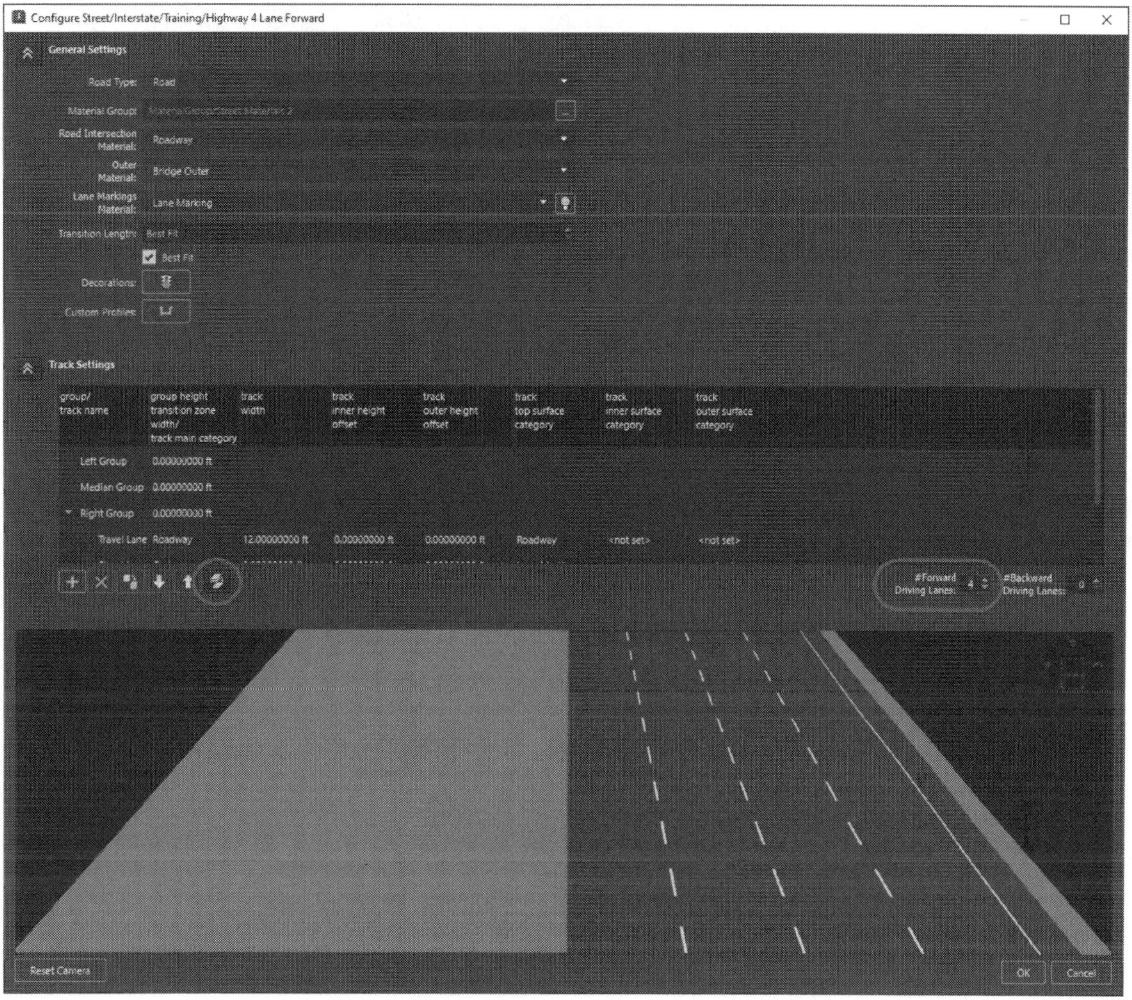

Figure 3–45

14. In the *Decorations Editor* dialog box, the *Decoration Target* drop-down list should be set to **Right Bucket>Travel Lane**.

15. Click (Add 3D Model) to open the *Select 3D Model Style* dialog box. Do the following:

- Double-click on **<parent>**, then select **Vehicles**.
- Select **BMW 7 Series**, as shown in Figure 3–46.

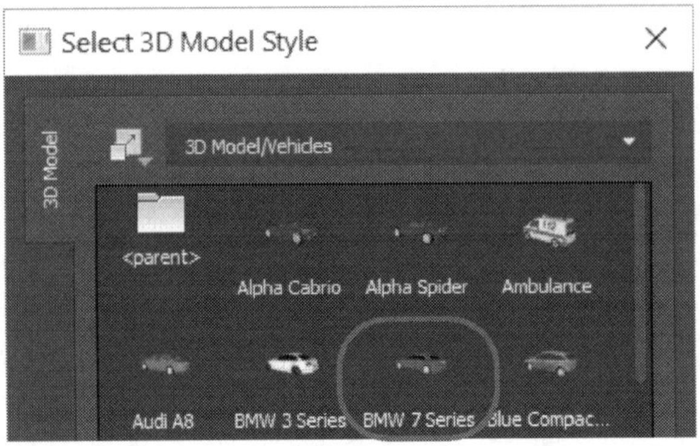

Figure 3–46

16. Click **OK**.

17. Move the *Decoration Editor* dialog box so that the preview area in the *Style Configuration* dialog box can be seen. Set the following in the *Decoration Editor* dialog box, as shown in Figure 3–47:

    * *Spacing*: **50**
    * *Track Offset:* **6**

    Note: *If you live in any country that drives on the right side of the road, then in the Z column, change the Rotation to **180**.*

    Note the change in the preview area.

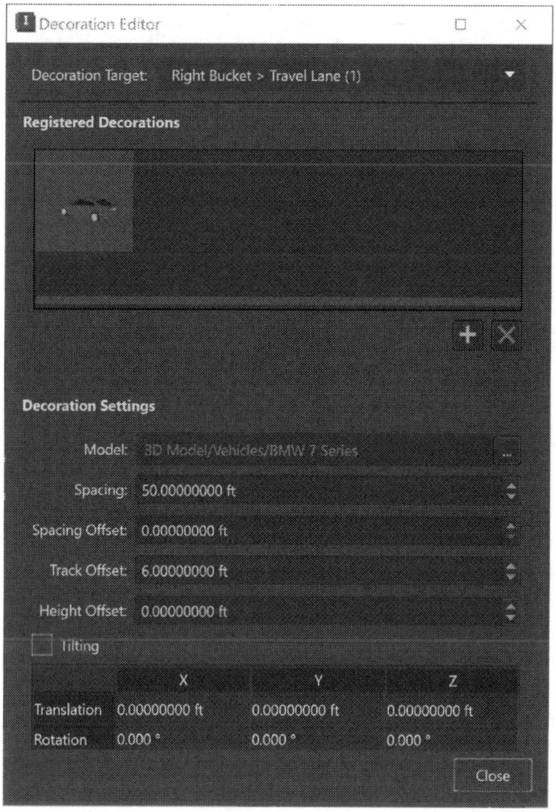

Figure 3–47

18. In the *Select 3D Model Style* dialog box, click (Add 3D Model) and select **Blue Compact Car**. Set the following in the *Decoration Editor* dialog box, as shown in Figure 3–48:
    - *Spacing*: **55**
    - *Track Offset*: **30**

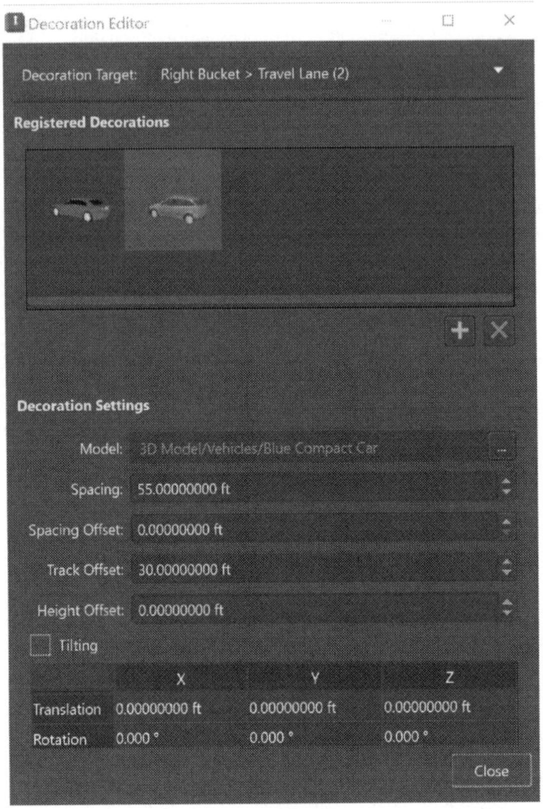

Figure 3–48

19. In *Decoration Target* drop-down list, select **Right Bucket>Shoulder**, as shown in Figure 3–49.

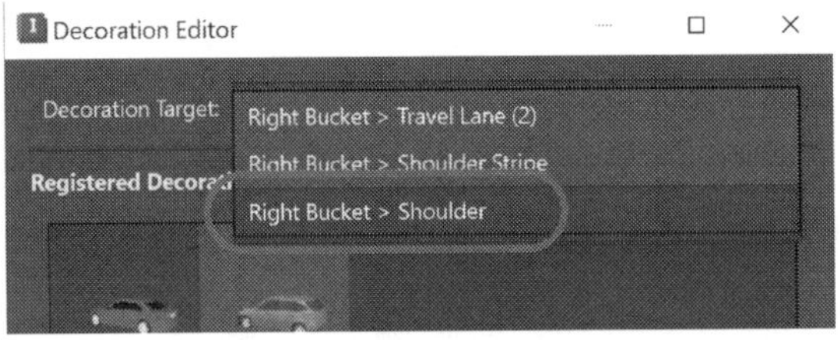

Figure 3–49

20. In the *Select 3D Model Style* dialog box, click  (Add 3D Model) and double-click on **Concrete Barrier Grey**, which is in the *3D Model/Traffic & Barriers* folder.

21. Move the *Decoration Editor* dialog box so that the preview area in the *Style Configuration* dialog box can be seen. Set the following in the *Decoration Editor* dialog box, as shown in Figure 3–50:

    - *Track Offset*: **-50**
    - *Z Rotation*: **90**

    Note the change in the preview area.

22. To the right of the *Spacing* field, click the up and down arrows until the barriers abut each other in the preview area in the *Style Configuration* dialog box (the *Spacing* should be close to **9.8 ft**), as shown in Figure 3–50.

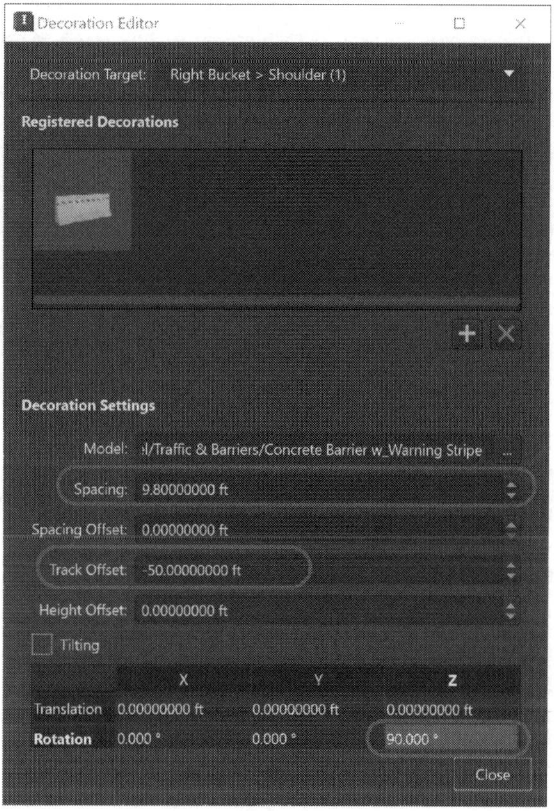

Figure 3–50

23. Click **Close**.

24. In the *Style Configuration* dialog box, click **OK** to accept the changes.

25. Open the *Style Rules* panel and change the **Freeway** style rule to make it use the **Highway 4 Lane Forward** style that you just created, as shown in Figure 3–51.

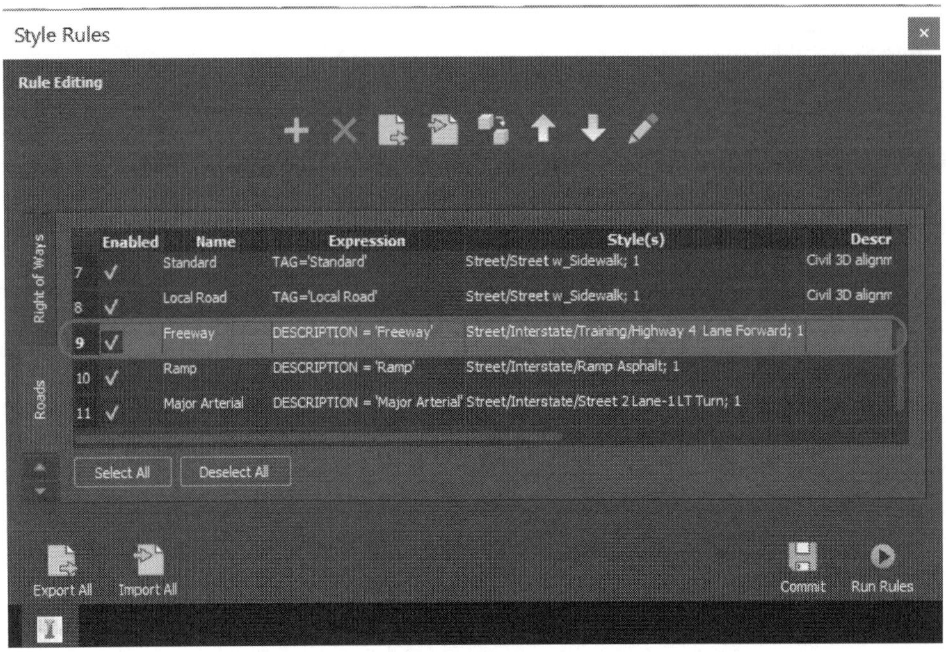

Figure 3–51

26. Click (Run Rules) to display the changes in the model.
27. Close the model.

End of practice

Chapter Review Questions

1. Which programming language is used to change the appearance of data sources on import?
   a. HTML
   b. C++
   c. .Net
   d. JavaScript

2. When working with expressions, which of the following operators can be used for text fields?
   a. Like
   b. Not Like
   c. = (Equal To)
   d. All of the above

3. When changing a model feature's style automatically, two filter types are available: Location and Property.
   a. True
   b. False

4. When creating new styles, which of the following cannot be set for a barrier style?
   a. Length
   b. 3D Model
   c. Height
   d. Spacing

5. When creating new styles, in which of the following areas would you set the number of lanes for a road style?
   a. General Settings area
   b. Track Settings area
   c. Track operations area
   d. Preview area

Command Summary

Button	Command	Location
	**Style Palette**	• **Toolbar:** *Manage* tab>*Content* panel
	**Style Rules**	• **Toolbar:** *Manage* tab>*Display* drop-down list

Chapter 4

Roadways

Using planning design tools, you can add roads, railway lines, bodies of water, and coverage areas to a model. In this chapter, you will learn how to add many of these model elements and how to edit the elements once they have been created.

There are two types of roads that can be created in the Autodesk® InfraWorks® software: planning roads (existing roads) and component roads (proposed design roads). You can use the component roads to add engineering parameters to road designs and the rule-based tool sets to lay out a preliminary roadway design. During the creation process, you can instantly visualize the designed road in context with its surroundings.

In this chapter, you will learn how create both planning and component roads, as well as how to set design speeds, adjust curve radii, and improve traffic flows through detailed interchanges and roundabouts.

Learning Objectives

- Create planning designs of roads, bridges, and tunnels.
- Create right of ways and easements for road corridors.
- Design an engineered road with precise design parameters (such as design speed, tangent length, and specific curve radii).
- Modify the horizontal layout of a component road.
- Modify the vertical layout of a component road.
- Add superelevations to a component road.
- Modify how two component roads intersect using the *Intersection* asset card or stack.

4.1 Create Planning Roads in a Model

Every design project needs to be accessed in some way, and this is easily done by creating a new road or simple driveway into the site. Using the **Planning Roads** command, you can add roads, bridges, and tunnels to a model. Which of these three features you create depends on the style of road that you select in the *Select Draw Style* asset card, shown in Figure 4–1, when starting the **Planning Roads** command. To find a required style faster, you can filter the available styles by typing in the *Search* field.

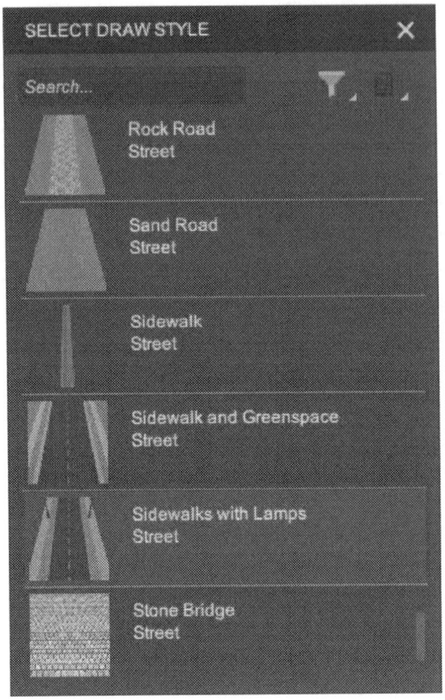

Figure 4–1

How To: Create a Planning Road

1. In the *Create* tab>*Transportation* panel, click (Planning Road).
2. The *Select Draw Style* asset card opens, as shown in Figure 4–2. Select the required style.

   Note: *Once you have selected the first road style in the model, that style becomes the active style. To change the active style, click (Planning Road) and select a different style from the Select Draw Style asset card.*

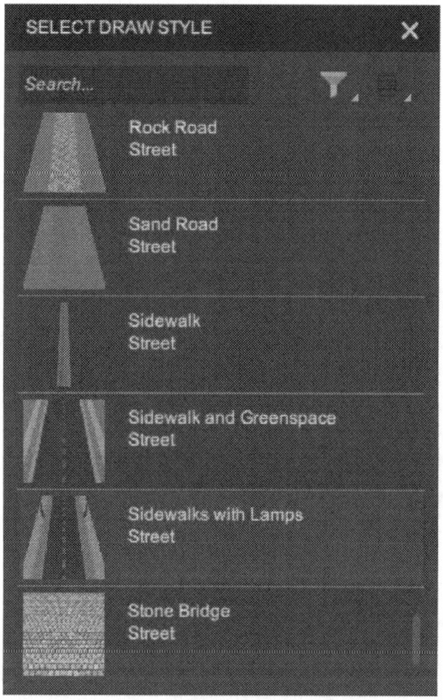

Figure 4–2

3. Click in the model where you want to start the road, bridge, or tunnel.
4. Move the cursor in the direction the road needs to follow. Type a distance to the first point of intersection (PI). Click the model at the locations of each additional required PI.
5. If crossing existing roads, ensure that you place a PI at the intersection to ensure that the intersection is created correctly.
6. For the final PI, double-click on the location at which you want to end the road, bridge, or tunnel. Doing so ends the **Planning Road** command.
7. Press <Esc> to clear the selection of the newly created road, bridge, or tunnel.

Edit Planning Roads

Once a planning road, bridge, or tunnel has been created, you can change the design options. For example, you might need to add more curves to the road or change the elevation at specific locations. To edit a road, select it and use the gizmos to make changes. You can also right-click on the road to access the following options.

Icon	Command	Description
	**Add Vertex**	Adds a point of intersection (PI) at the point at which you right-clicked.
	**Remove Vertex**	Removes the PI on which you right-clicked.
	**Split Feature**	Breaks the planning road, bridge, or tunnel into multiple features at the point at which you right-clicked.
	**Drape Feature**	Drapes the roadway on the surface terrain, reducing the need to add points of vertical intersections (PVIs) along the road.
N/A	**Convert to planning road**	Converts a planning road to a component road, enabling you to add more design parameters (curve radius, daylight slope, etc).
N/A	**Properties**	Opens the *Properties* palette, in which you can change the style, number of lanes, elevation offset, etc.

When working with roads created using the **Planning Road** tool, you must add a vertex where you need to add a horizontal or vertical curve to the road. This helps reduce the amount of cut and fill required to build the road, as shown in Figure 4–3.

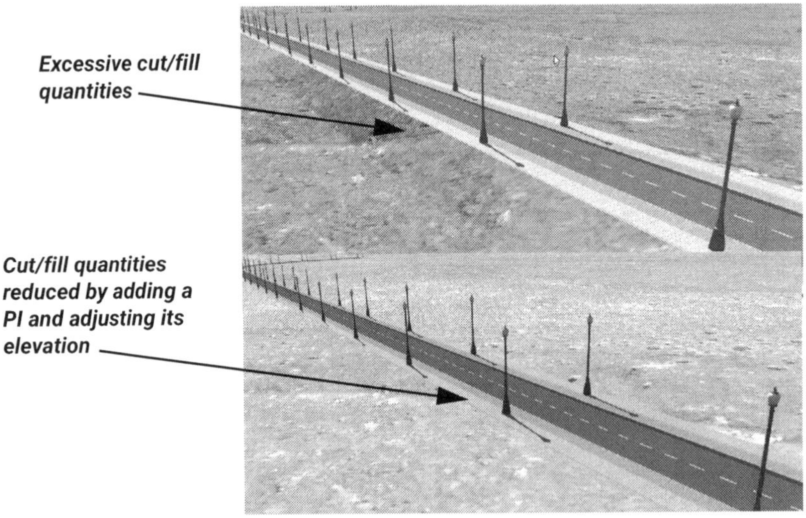

Figure 4–3

If you only need to change the style of planning road for part of the roadway, use the **Split Feature** command, then use the *Road* asset card or *Properties* to change the style for the segment of road that needs to be changed. In the *Properties* palette, select an option in the *Manual Style* field and click **Update**, as shown in Figure 4–4.

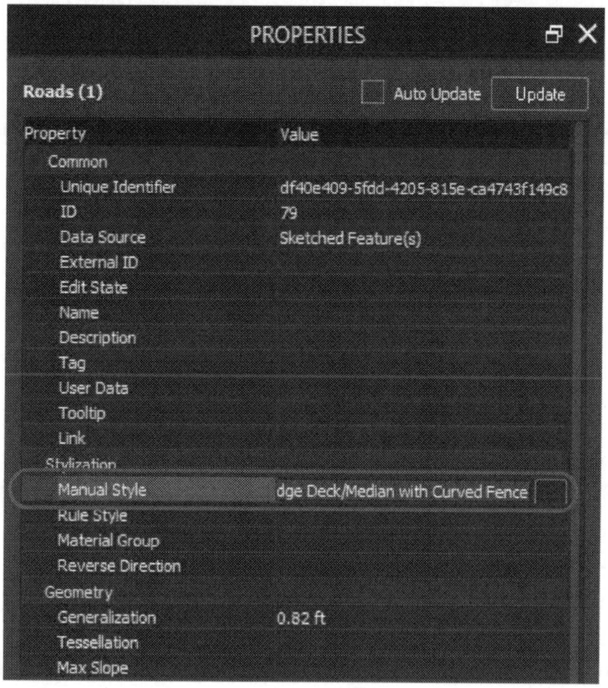

Figure 4–4

Practice 4a
Create Planning Roads in the Model

Practice Objective

- Create multiple planning roads in the model to display the design concept.

In this practice, you will create a planning road that ends at a pier. You will use a bridge style to create the pier. You will then create additional roads for a new subdivision that will connect to an existing subdivision.

> **Note:** *The road designs in these practices are meant as a learning exercise rather than proper road design. Therefore, the engineering and layout may not be optimal or appropriate for real-world use.*

Task 1: Create a planning road.

1. On the *Home* screen, click **Open**.
2. In the *InfraWorks Practice Files\4-Roads* folder, select **CreateRoads.sqlite** and click **Open**.
3. In the (Proposals) drop-down list, select the **A_Task1** proposal to make it your current proposal.
4. Click (Bookmarks) and select **Pier Road**. The view displays as shown in Figure 4–5.

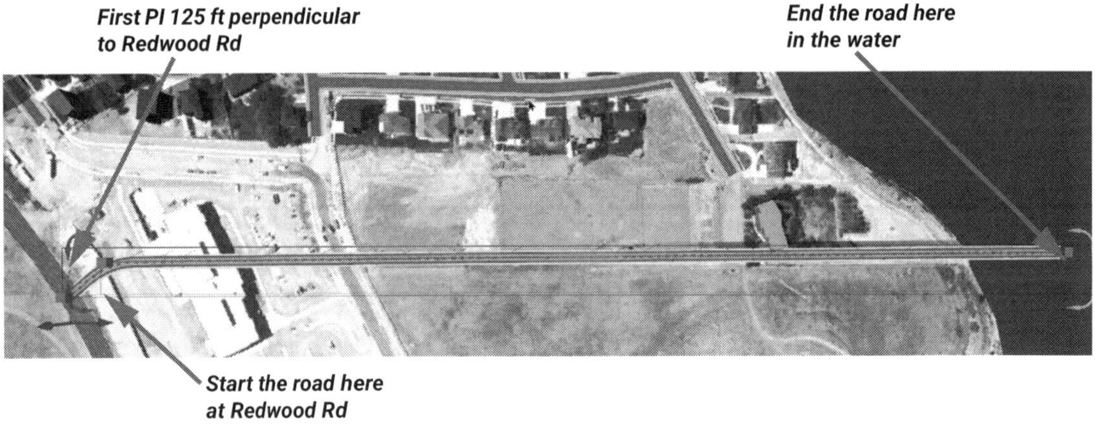

Figure 4–5

5. In the *Create* tab>*Transportation* panel, click (Planning Road).

6. In the *SELECT DRAW STYLE* asset card, type **sidewalk** in the *Search* field. Select **Sidewalk with Lamps Street**, as shown in Figure 4–6.

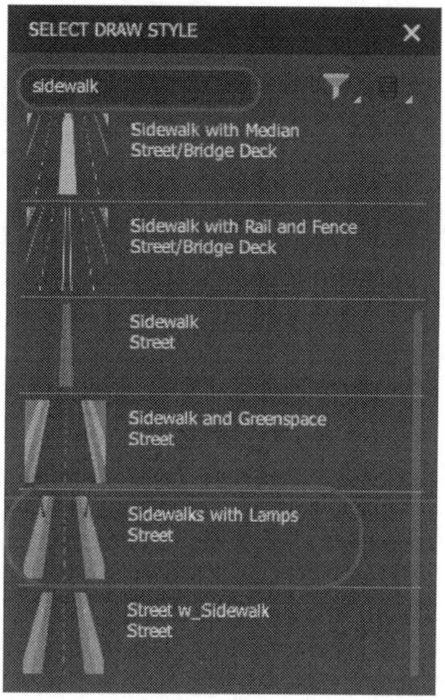

Figure 4–6

7. Close the *SELECT DRAW STYLE* asset card.
8. To start the planning road in the model, click near the centerline of **Redwood Rd** (as shown in Figure 4–5). Type **125**, press <Enter>, and then click northeast of that point to make the road perpendicular to **Redwood Rd**, overlaying the existing dirt road. If the distance field does not display initially, move the cursor further away from the starting point until it displays.
9. If you need to try again, press <Esc> and relaunch the **Planning Road** command. InfraWorks remembers the last style used, so you do not need to select the style again.
10. Move the cursor due east and double-click to end the planning road inside the water, about **2,550 feet** from shore, as shown in Figure 4–5.
11. Press <Esc> twice to end the command and release the roadway selection.

Task 2: Edit the planning road.

1. Continue working in the same model. If you did not complete the last task, select the **A_Task2** proposal to make it current.
2. In the model, select the new road.

3. In the *Road* asset card, near the top, type **Pier Lane** as the road's name, as shown in Figure 4–7, and press <Enter>.

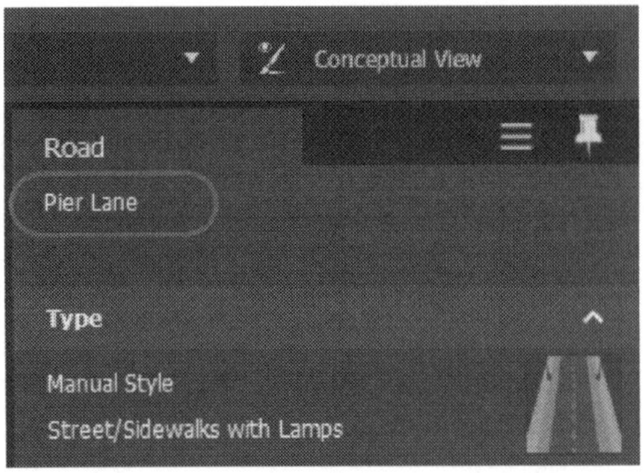

Figure 4–7

4. Right-click near the midpoint of the road and select **Split Feature**, as shown in Figure 4–8. Do not pick the road.

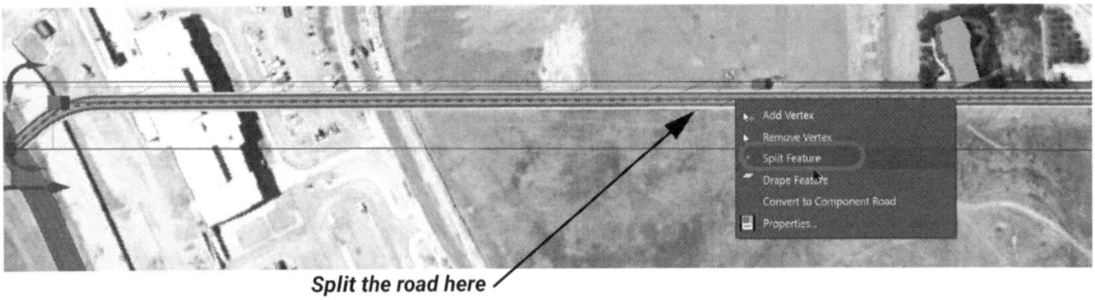

Figure 4–8

5. Select the segment of road to the right of the split. This section will become the new pier. You might need to select close to the split point to select the correct portion of the planning road.
6. In the *Road* asset card, click the *Manual Style* thumbnail and select **More Styles**.
7. In the *Select Style* dialog box, select the **Street** catalog, then the **Bridge** style, as shown in Figure 4–9. Click **OK**.

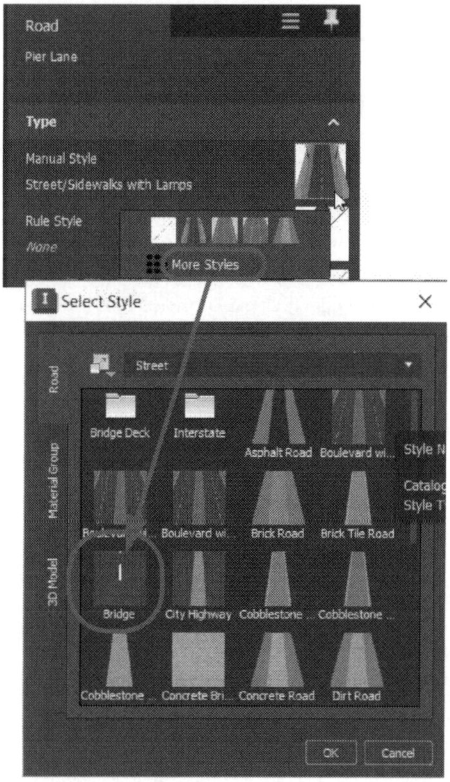

Figure 4–9

8. Click (Bookmarks) and select **Pier 3D**. The view displays as shown in Figure 4–10.

Figure 4–10

9. The bridge goes down into the water. Select the bridge and click on the cyan cone of the (Elevation Gizmo) to raise the right side of the bridge so that it is parallel with the water line, as shown in Figure 4–11.

Figure 4–11

Task 3: Create subdivision roads.

1. Continue working in the same model. If you did not complete the last task, select the **A_Task3** proposal to make it current.

2. Click (Bookmarks) and select **Project Area**.

3. In the *Create* tab>*Transportation* panel, click (Planning Road). The **Sidewalk with Lamps** road style is automatically selected because it was the last style that was used. Continue using this style.

   Note: Placing the west PIs causes the road to form one large curve. This is corrected in the next step.

4. In the model, create the road shown in Figure 4–12 by typing the distances and pressing <Enter> before clicking to place each PI. Double-click the last PI to end the command.

Figure 4–12

5. Press <Esc> to end the command and show the road's gizmos.
6. Orbit the model more than 45° past the plan view orientation to display the vertical gizmos. Orient the view so that you are looking east, similar to the view shown in Figure 4–13.

   Note: This vertex reduces the curve radii of the horizontal curves at the north and south ends of the road.

7. Add a new vertex at the approximate midpoint of the north-south segment of the new road, as shown in Figure 4–13. To add a vertex, right-click where you want to place the vertex and select **Add Vertex**. Adjust the elevation of the new vertex using the cyan cone of the (Elevation Gizmo).

Add vertices here, then adjust elevations

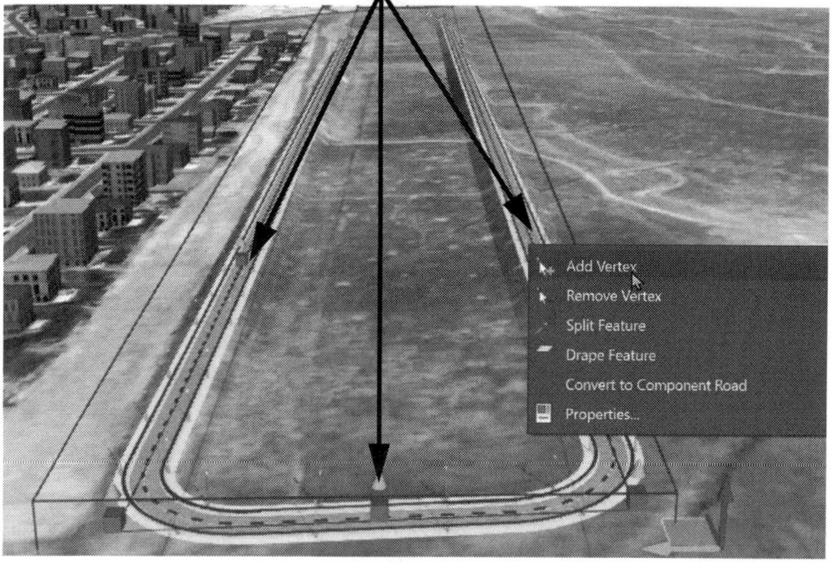

Figure 4–13

8. Add additional vertices, as required, to reduce the cut and fill volumes for the new road.
9. Click (Bookmarks) and select **Project Area**.
10. Add additional neighborhood planning roads, as shown in Figure 4–14. Place vertices at locations where one road intersects another by clicking on the midpoint of the roads where they will intersect. Doing so results in clean intersections, rather than overpasses or underpasses. Also add vertices to the southern road to decrease the curve radii.

Figure 4–14

11. Press <Esc> to clear the selection of all of the roads.

End of practice

4.2 Parcels, Right of Ways, and Easements

Before a road can be built, it is important to ensure that the proper permissions are legally granted to anyone planning on using the road. This is done by will, by deed, or by contract. An easement grants the right to use property that is owned by another. Easements are most often used to deliver utilities (e.g., water, sewer, and electrical) to parcels. Right of ways are easements that permit a person to travel or pass through a parcel of land that is not owned by the traveler. Easements on a deed generally remain with the land in perpetuity, while a right of way is often granted with an explicit expiration date.

Information about existing right of ways, easements, and parcel boundaries can be obtained from the local recorders office or other government entities. Several government agencies provide electronic files representing parcel boundaries (in the form of Geographic Information data) either for free or for a small fee.

Import Property Boundaries

Some right of ways have been put aside by government agencies for road development for years. In cases like this, it is necessary to import existing property boundaries to ensure that your road proposals stay within the designated corridors. Importing parcel, easement, and right of way data is no different than importing any other GIS data. Once imported and configured, parcels, easements, and right of ways are listed in the *Model Explorer* under *Area of Interest*. Once imported, you can view existing and proposed surface contours within the property boundaries and control the contour intervals.

How To: Import Existing Parcel Boundaries

1. In the *Manage* tab>*Content* panel, click  (Data Sources).
2. In the *Data Sources* panel, expand  (Add file data source) and select the type of file required, as shown in Figure 4–15.

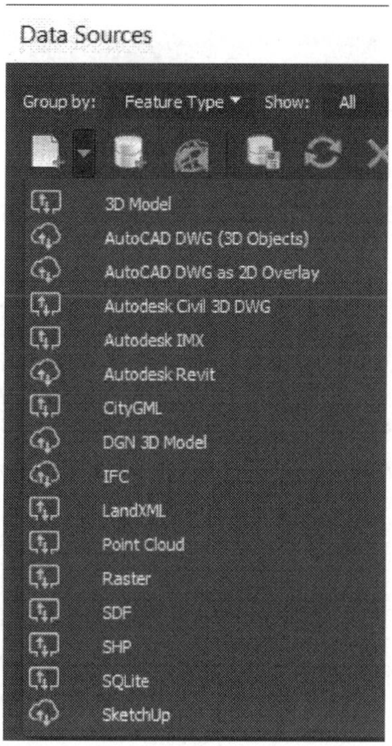

Figure 4–15

3. Select the file containing the property boundary data. Click **Open**.
4. In the *Data Sources* panel, double-click on the property boundary layer to open the *Data Source Configuration* dialog box.

5. Set the *Type* to **Parcels**, **Easements**, or **Right of Ways** (as shown in Figure 4–16), then check the following:
   - On the *Geo Location* tab, confirm that the *Coordinate System* is set correctly.
   - On the *Source* tab, set the *Draping Options* and set **Clip to model extent**, as required.
   - On the *Table* tab, fill in as many table fields as you can.

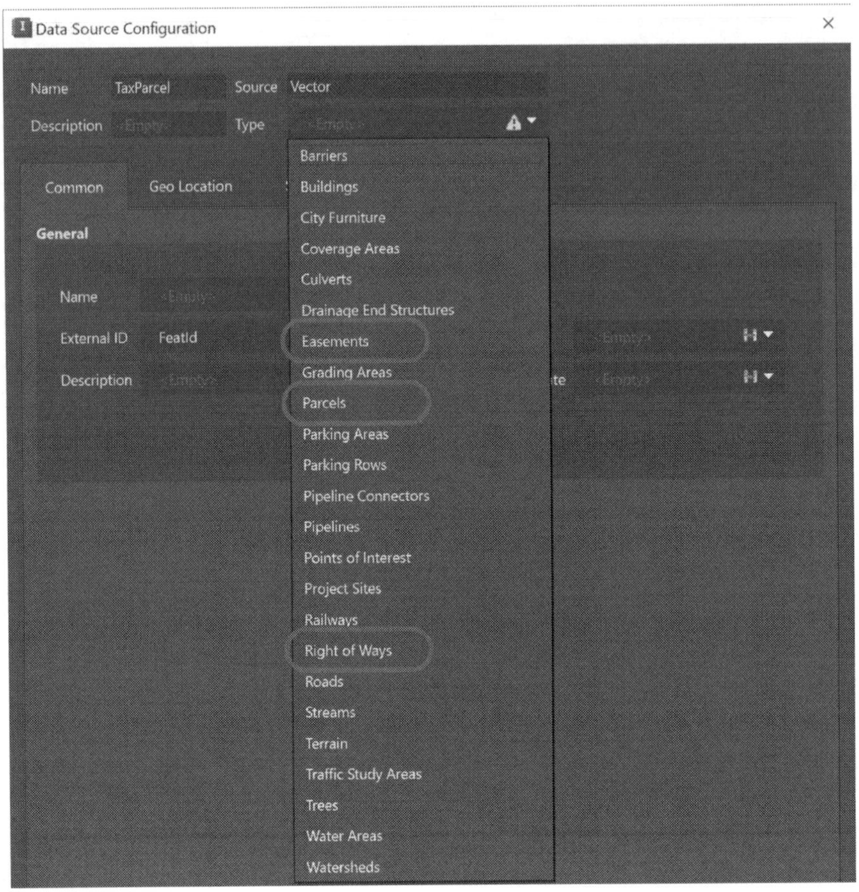

Figure 4–16

6. Click **Close & Refresh**.

Create Parcels and Easements

If electronic versions of the property boundaries are not available, you might need to manually create a parcel or easement. This can be done using the tools that are available in the Project Tools toolbar.

How To: Manually Create Parcels or Easements

1. In the *Create* tab>*Environment* drop-down list, click either (Parcels) or (Easements), as required.
2. In the model, click the first vertex for the starting point of the property boundary.
3. Move the cursor in the direction of the next vertex. If you know the required distance, type it and press <Enter> to lock in the distance. Click to set the vertex when the angle seems correct.
4. Repeat Step 3 for all but the last vertex.
5. Move the cursor in the direction for the last vertex. If you know the required distance, type it and press <Enter> to lock in the distance. Double-click to set the last vertex when the angle looks correct.

Create Right of Ways

You create right of ways (ROW) slightly differently than parcels and easements. When drawing a ROW, there are three options:

- **Free-Form Shape:** Enables you to create free-form polygons.
- **Parallel Drawing:** Enables you to offset an existing feature parallel to its centerline, with equal or varying values on each side.
- **Road Offset:** Enables you to select a road to offset with equal or varying values on each side. The length can also be adjusted for the ROW, as required.

How To: Create a Right of Way from a Road

1. In the model, select the planning road.
2. Right-click and select **Add Right of Way**.

How To: Manually Create a Right of Way

1. In the *Create* tab>*Transportation* panel, click (Right of Ways).
2. In the model, click the starting point centerline for the ROW.
3. Move the cursor in the direction of the next centerline vertex. If you know the required distance, type it and press <Enter> to lock in the distance. Click to set the centerline vertex when the angle looks correct.
4. Repeat Step 3 for all but the last centerline vertex.
5. Move the cursor in the direction of the last centerline vertex. If you know the required distance, type it and press <Enter> to lock in the distance. Double-click to set the last vertex when the angle looks correct.

Display Contours

The advantage of adding parcels, easements, and right of ways to the model is that you can display the existing or proposed ground contours in them. This helps improve terrain visualization and enables you to better understand the drainage and slope on the site. Once a parcel is created or imported, select the boundary. In its asset card, toggle on the contours and set their interval, as shown in Figure 4–17.

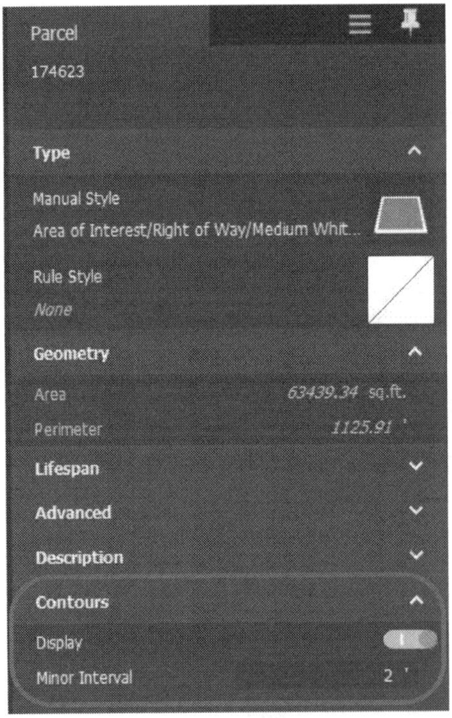

Figure 4–17

Practice 4b
Work with Parcels

Practice Objectives

- Import existing parcel lines from GIS data.
- Create right of ways for the new roads.

In this practice, you will import GIS data provided by the city and configure it as parcels. You will then create new right of ways for proposed roads.

1. On the *Home* screen, click **Open**.
2. In the *InfraWorks Practice Files\4-Roads* folder, select **CreateRoads.sqlite** and click **Open**.
3. In the toolbar, select **B_Task1** from the (Proposals) drop-down list.
4. Click (Bookmarks) and select **ProjectArea**. If the *Data Sources* panel is not already displayed, in the *Manage* tab> *Content* panel, select (Data Sources).
5. In the *Data Sources* panel, expand (Add file data source) and select **SHP** for the type of file, as shown in Figure 4–18.

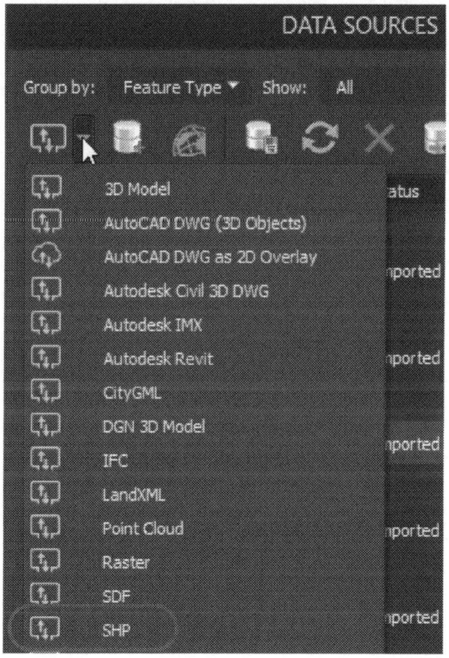

Figure 4–18

6. Browse to the *InfraWorks Practice Files\References\GIS* folder, select **TaxParcel.shp**, and click **Open**.

7. In the *Data Sources* panel, double-click on the **TaxParcel**[1] layer to open the *Data Source Configuration* dialog box, as shown in Figure 4–19. Set the following parameters:

   - *Type*: **Parcels**
   - *Geo Location* tab, *Coordinate System*: **UT83-CF**
   - *Source* tab, *Draping Options*: **Drape**
   - *Source* tab: **Clip to model extent**
   - *Table* tab, *Name*: **PARCEL_NO**
   - *Table* tab, *Description*: **ACREAGE**
   - *Table* tab, *Tag*: **OWNERNAME**
   - *Table* tab, *User Data*: **MKT_CNTVAL**

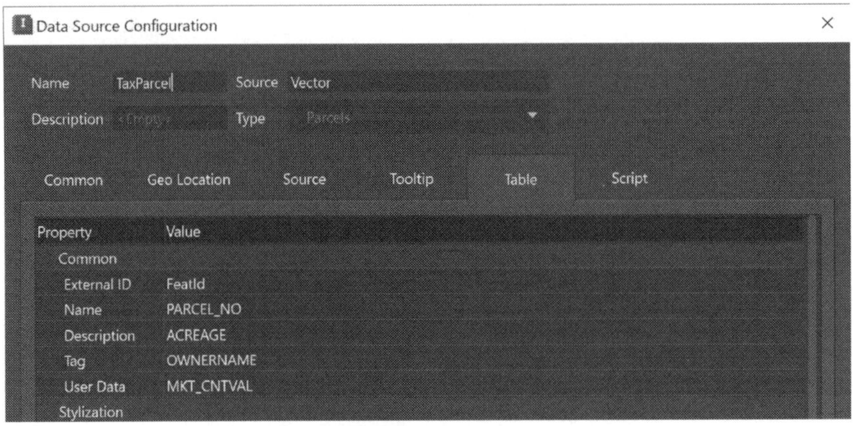

Figure 4–19

8. Click **Close & Refresh**.

9. In the *Manage* tab>*Model* panel, click (Model Explorer) to open the *Model Explorer*.

10. Make sure the **Parcels** and **Right of Ways** layers under *Area of Interest* are turned on, as shown in Figure 4–20. **Right of Ways** will be discussed in the next section.

1. Department, GIS Division of the Utah County Information Systems, 2013

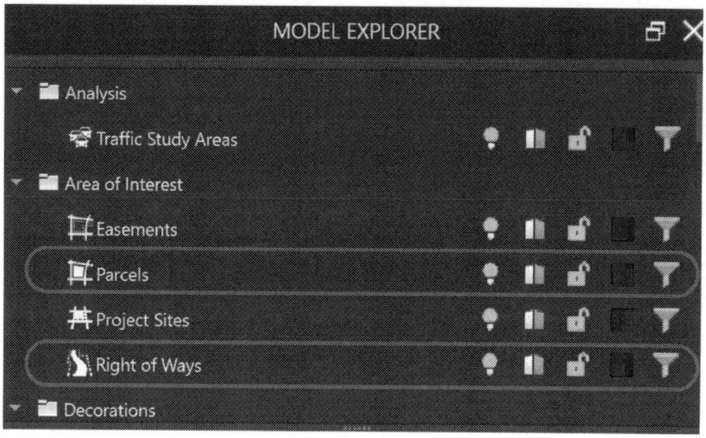

Figure 4–20

11. Close the *Model Explorer*.
12. In the model, select the three parcels within the display, one at a time, by clicking on their border lines. In their asset cards, toggle on the contour display for each one. Note how each parcel then displays contour lines, as shown in Figure 4–21.

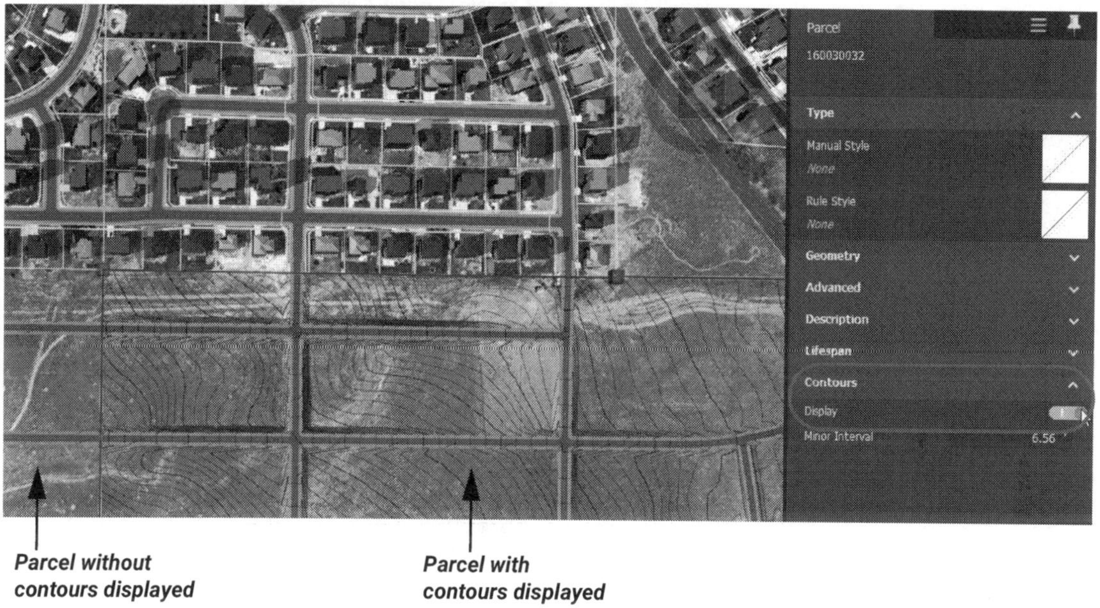

Figure 4–21

13. Turn the contours off for all parcels.
14. Press <Esc> to release the last parcel.

End of practice

4.3 Creating Component Roads

Component roads are used to create design roads in InfraWorks. Component roads follow two sets of standards: **road design standards**, which are preprogrammed into the software, and **project design standards**, which are manually input by you.

The road design standards parameters are set when creating the model in the *New Model* dialog box, under the *Design Standards* section (as shown in Figure 4–22). The American Association of State Highway and Transportation Officials (AASHTO) design criteria is the most commonly used standard within the United States of America. In addition to setting the standards, you can set the driving direction for the road to be the left or right side of the road. Alternatively, if the design standards were not set when creating the model, you can set them during the design process using the *Model Properties* dialog box, as shown in Figure 4–23. You can set the driving direction to be the left or right side of the road here as well.

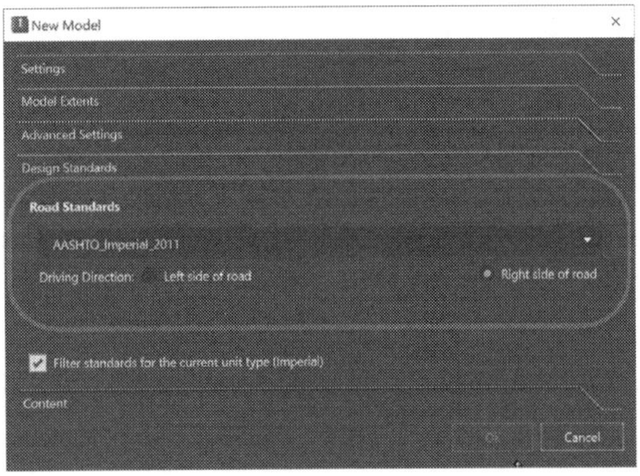

Figure 4–22

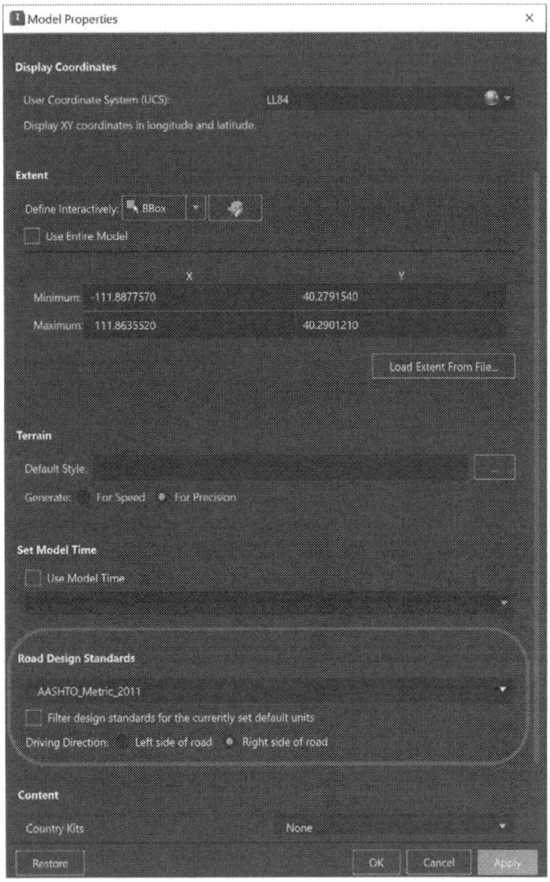

Figure 4–23

Component roads provide much more flexibility and control when designing them than planning roads do. They enable you to add, delete, and modify each component of the road (lanes and curbs) separately, as shown in Figure 4–24.

This means that you do not have to create a new road style for every minor change to the road cross section. If planning roads already exist in the model, you can convert them into component roads. When a planning road is converted to a component road, the following occurs:

- The number of lanes and the track width are preserved.
- All component depths are set to the default 0.2 meters for lanes and sidewalks.
- The track top surface category material is applied to the entire component when converting from a planning road style.

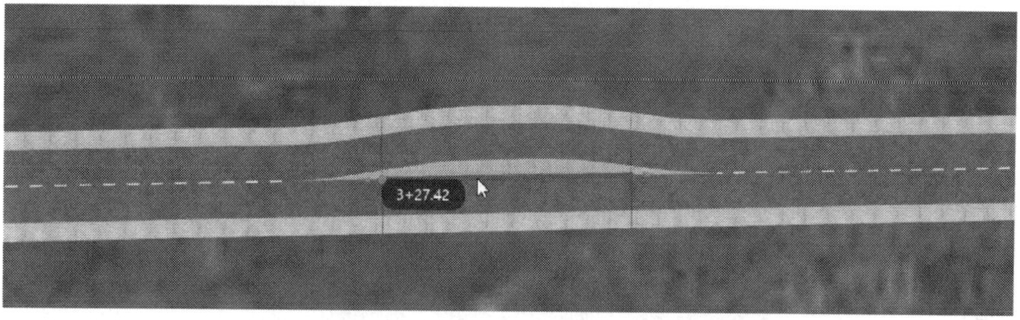

Figure 4–24

Hint: Upgraded Models

Earlier versions of the InfraWorks software contained both design roads and component roads. When you open a model that contains the earlier design roads, they are automatically converted to planning roads. The original design road styles are matched to component road assemblies, which makes the upgrade process seamless.

Road Function

Selecting the correct *Function* is a crucial part of setting the design parameters. Four road functions are available in the *Road* asset card, as shown in Figure 4–25. The road function automatically sets the default design speed to be used for the roadway design. It is recommended that you name the road for easy identification.

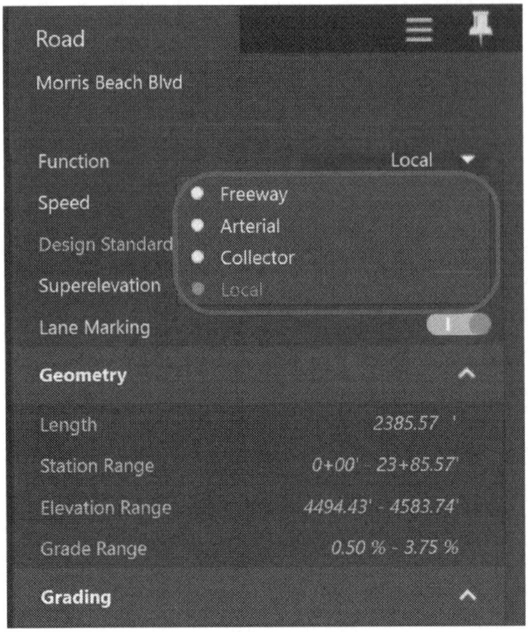

Figure 4–25

The *Design Speed* is the maximum speed that the road is designed for and should not be confused with the legally permitted travel speed. The default design speed for a roadway depends on the function of the road being designed. A full list of the available options is shown in the table below.

Road Function	Maximum Design Speed
Freeway	70 mph
Arterial	50 mph
Collector	40 mph
Local	25 mph

If a road's design speed changes, you can edit it during the creation process by typing the new speed in the *Speed* field that displays next to the cursor, as shown in Figure 4–26. You can also change it in the *Road* asset card any time the road is selected.

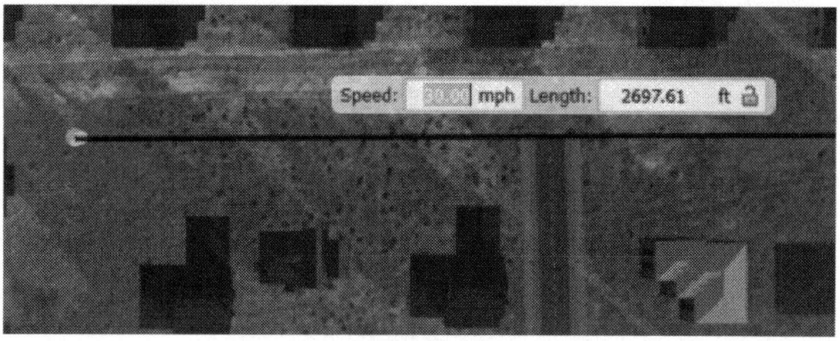

Figure 4–26

Horizontal Curves and Spirals

The design speed property of a roadway sets the minimum and maximum permitted curve radius and spiral lengths for a given point of intersection (PI) along a roadway. The default curve type is set to *Spiral Curve Spiral*. To change the curve type used at a PI, right-click on the curve to display a fly-out menu. On the *Convert Geometry* menu, you can change the curve type (shown in Figure 4–27). As you set the PIs, tangent lines (which project all of the way to the actual point of intersection) display in white, curves display in green, and spirals display in magenta. Geometry dimensions also display, as shown in Figure 4–27.

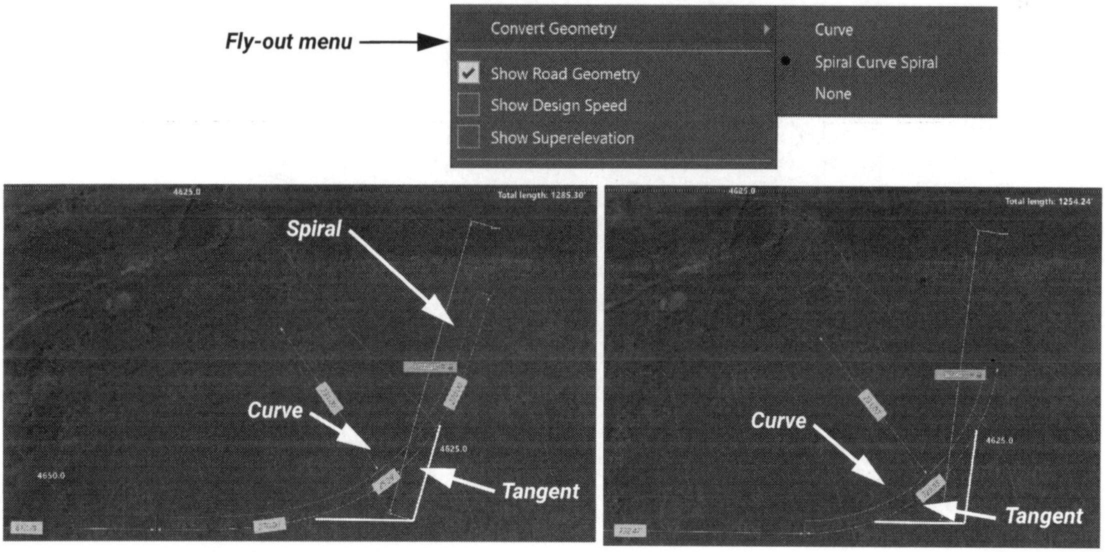

Spiral Curve Spiral ***Curve***

Figure 4–27

How To: Convert a Planning Road to a Component Road

1. In the model, select a planning road.
2. Right-click on the planning road and select **Convert to Component Road**, as shown in Figure 4–28.

Figure 4–28

3. The order by which you convert Planning Roads is important. Occasionally a planning road may not be able to be converted if other planning roads connect to it. In that case, try converting the connecting planning roads first, and then try the obstinate planning road again.
4. When Planning Roads have been created from Model Builder, they are segmented into individual parts between intersections, as shown in Figure 4–29. When converting them into Component Roads, it is recommended to convert only one segment, erasing the other segments and then stretching the resulting Component Road so it becomes one continuous road.

Figure 4–29

Hint: Interoperability with Autodesk Civil 3D Roads

Roads that you import from the Autodesk Civil 3D software or from an .IMX file automatically become component roads. When you open an InfraWorks model in Civil 3D that has component roads, the roads include surfaces and subassemblies. Roads with spiral curves in Civil 3D maintain their spiral types when brought into InfraWorks but cannot be changed.

How To: Create a Component Road from Scratch

1. In the *Create* tab>*Transportation* panel, click (Component Road).
2. In the *Road* asset card, select the following (as shown in Figure 4–30):

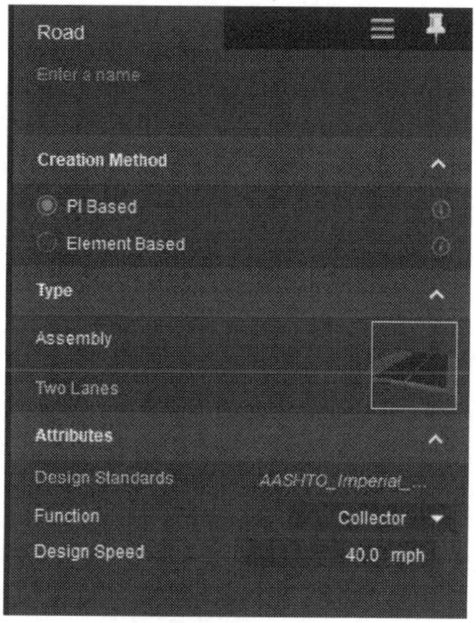

Figure 4–30

- *Creation Method* (two options to choose from):
    - **PI Based:** Pick points for the points of intersection along the centerline of the road, as shown in Figure 4–31. The InfraWorks software automatically places lines, curves, or spirals for you according to the function and design speed.
    - **Element Based:** Click to place the endpoints of objects (tangents and curves) along the centerline of the road, as shown in Figure 4–32.

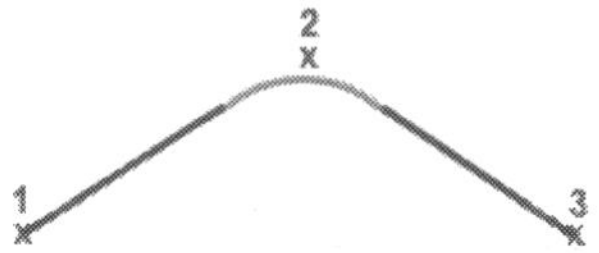

Figure 4–31

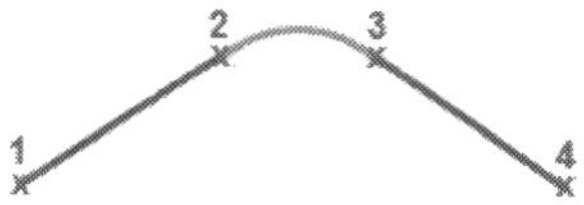

Figure 4–32

- *Type:* Click on the assembly name to change which assembly the road uses.
- *Attributes:*
    - Select the appropriate *Function* for the component road.
    - Modify the *Design Speed*, as needed.

3. In the model, click to set the starting point of the new roadway.
4. Move the cursor toward the next PI or element. Type a *Speed* and *Distance* in the respective fields and press <Enter> to set the values. Click to set the second PI or element endpoint when the angle looks correct.
5. Move the cursor in the direction toward the next PI or element and right-click to display the curve options.
6. According to the project requirements, select **Curve** or **Spiral Curve Spiral** for the transition between tangents, as shown in Figure 4–33.

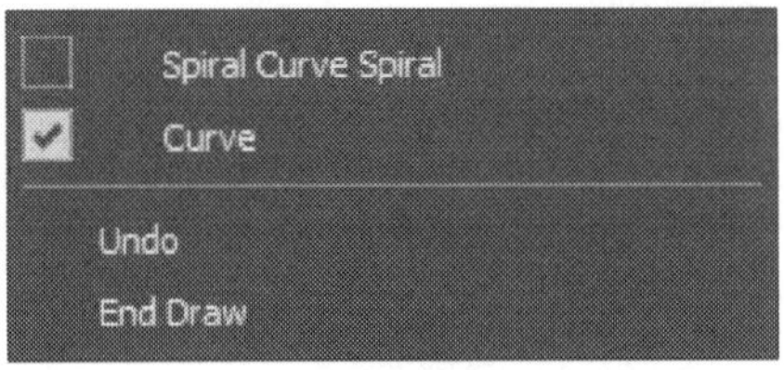

Figure 4–33

7. Repeat Steps 5 and 6 until all but the last horizontal PI is set for the roadway design.
8. Double-click to set the last PI or right-click and select **End Draw**.

Design Standard Warnings

When a curve on the component road is selected, an orange color represents a violation of the minimum radius. Selecting the radius cell will display a warning stating the violation of the selected design standards, as shown in Figure 4–34.

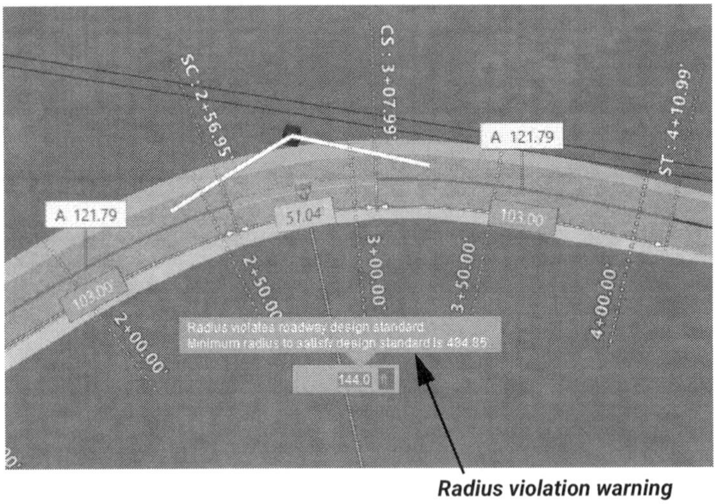

Figure 4–34

Practice 4c
Convert and Create Component Roads

Practice Objectives

- Replace planning roads with component roads in order to apply design parameters to them.
- Create component roads from scratch.

In this practice, you will create a new proposal. You will then turn an existing sketched road into a component road in order to add engineering parameters.

Task 1: Convert a sketched road to a component road.

1. Continue working in the same model as the last practice. If you closed the file, on the *Home* screen, click **Open**. In the *InfraWorks Practice Files\4-Roads* folder, select **CreateRoads.sqlite** and click **Open**.
2. If you did not complete the last task, select **B_Task2** in the (Proposals) drop-down list to make it current.
3. Click (Bookmarks) and select **ProjectArea**. Expand the (Proposals) drop-down list and click **Add**.
4. In the *Add New Proposal* dialog box, type **DesignRoad** for the name and click **OK**.
5. In the model, select the road shown in Figure 4–35.

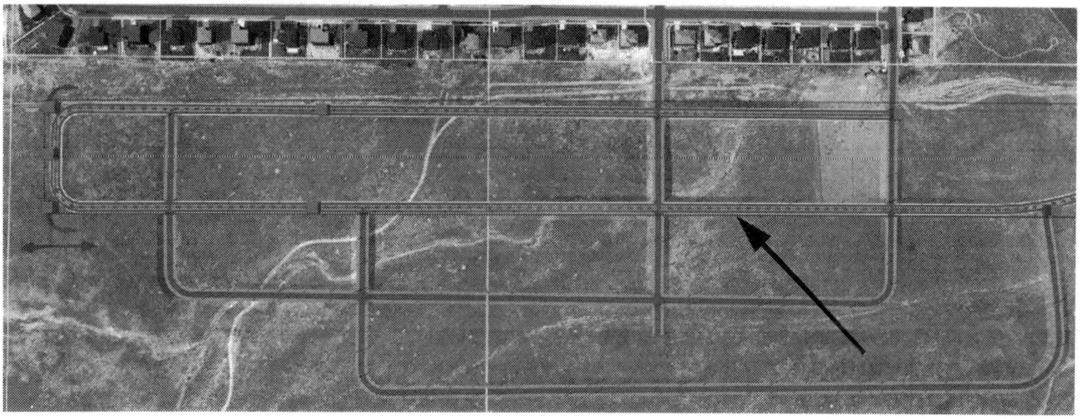

Figure 4–35

6. Right-click on the road and select **Convert to Component Road**, as shown in Figure 4–36.

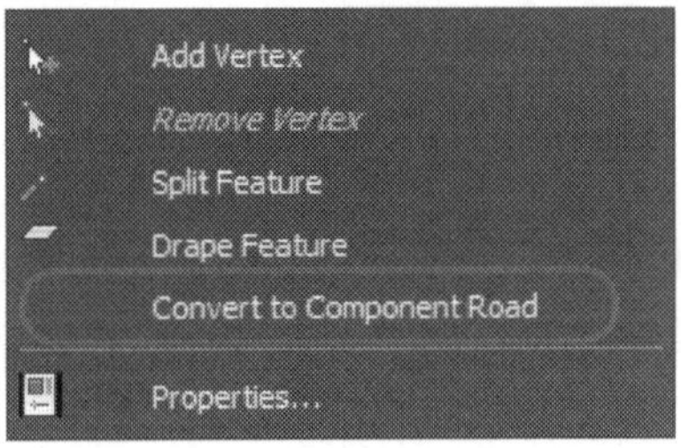

Figure 4–36

7. In the *Road* asset card that displays, name the road **Church Loop**, then expand the *Attributes* area and ensure that the *Function* is set to **Local**, as shown in Figure 4–37.

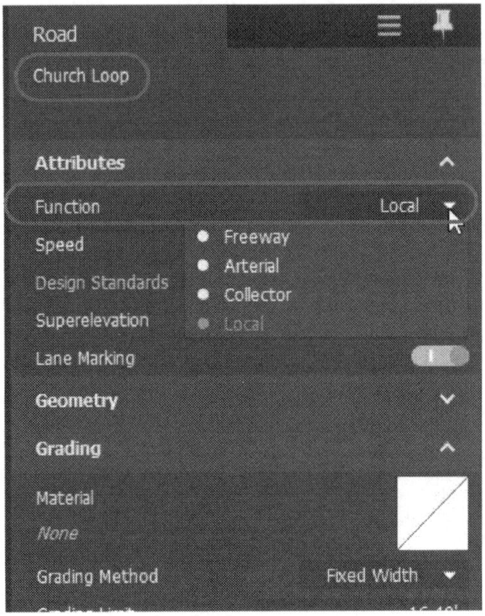

Figure 4–37

8. Press <Esc> to release the road selection.

9. In the model, select the road shown in Figure 4–38.

Figure 4–38

Note: *Naming roads will facilitate importing data into Civil 3D.*

10. Repeat Steps 6 to 8, naming the road **Adams Ave** and ensuring the *Function* is set to **Local**.

11. Click (Bookmarks) and select **Project Area**.
12. In the model, select **S Redwood Rd** (shown in Figure 4–39).

Figure 4–39

13. In the *Road* asset card, change the style from *Street 2 Lane-1LT Turn* to **Street 2 Lane**. You will need click on the icon within the *Manual Style* field, then click on **More Styles**. This will open the *Select Style* dialog box, from which you can pick the **Street 2 Lane** style, as shown in Figure 4–40.

    Note: *When the planning roads were created from Model Builder, these styles were applied. You need to change the styles so the converted component road will have the appropriate components.*

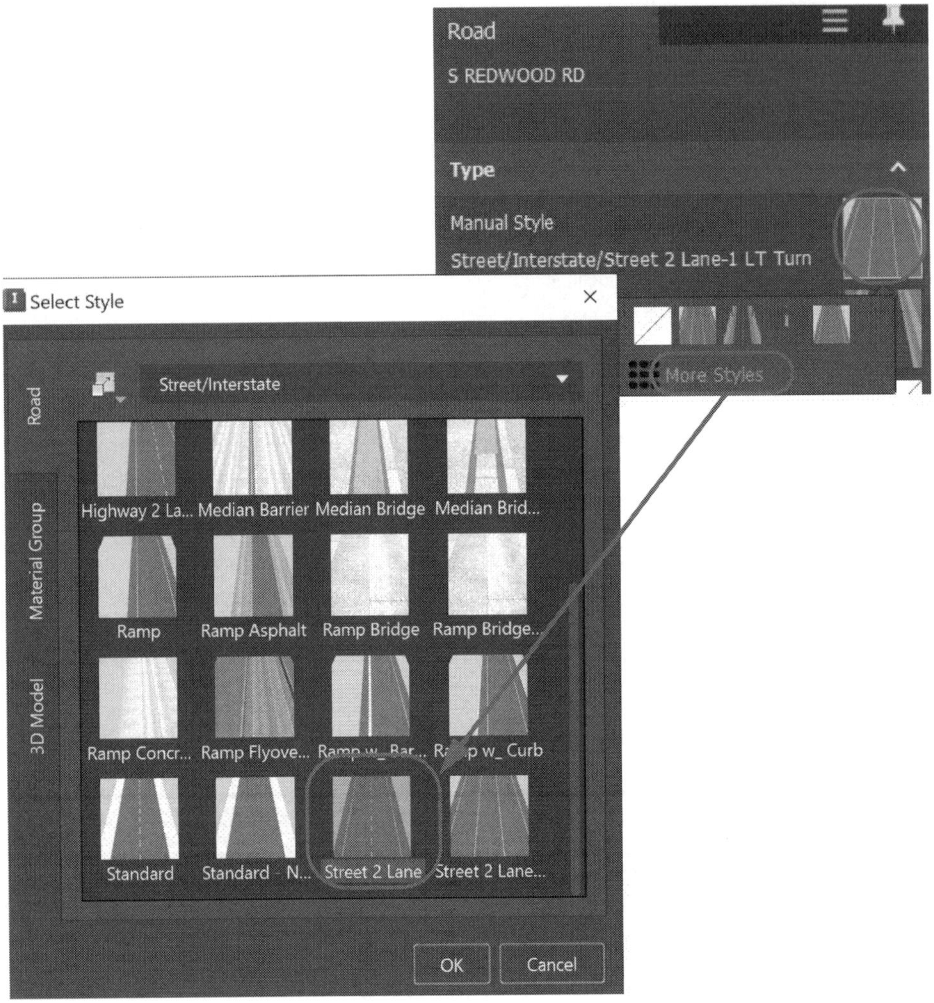

Figure 4–40

14. Right-click on the road and select **Convert to Component Road**.
15. A dialog box about planning roads being converted to component roads may display. Click **OK** to dismiss it.

16. In the *Road* asset card, expand the *Attributes* area and set the *Function* to **Collector**, as shown in Figure 4–41.

    Note: *Verify that the name has been ported over from the planning road.*

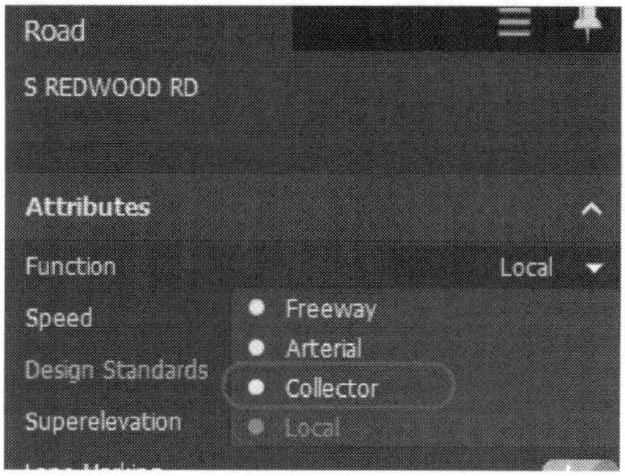

Figure 4–41

17. In the *Speed* field, type **45** and press <Enter>.
18. Press <Esc> to clear the road selection.
19. Select the upper (northern) section of **S Redwood Rd**, as shown in Figure 4–42.

Figure 4–42

20. Repeat Step 13 to change its style.
21. Attempt to convert the road to a component road (using the right-click menu) as you had done previously. You receive the error message shown in Figure 4–43, stating that InfraWorks is unable to convert this planning road. Not all planning roads from Model Builder can be converted. You may need to delete the planning road and create the desired component road manually.

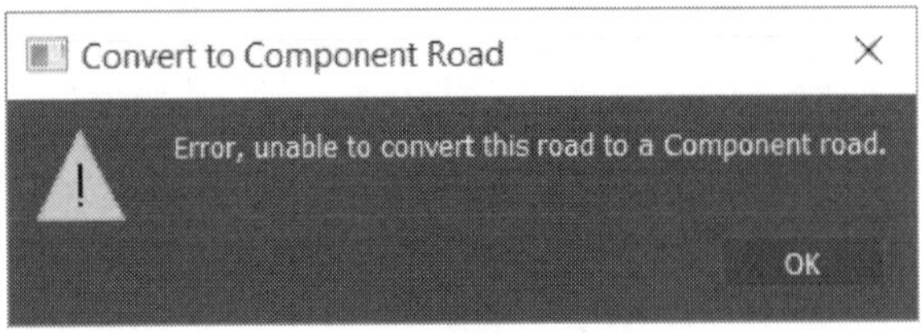

Figure 4–43

22. Click **OK** to close the *Convert to Component Road* dialog box.

Task 2: Create a right of way from a road.

1. In the model, select the **Adams Ave** component road, shown in Figure 4–44. If needed, restore the **Project Area** bookmark.

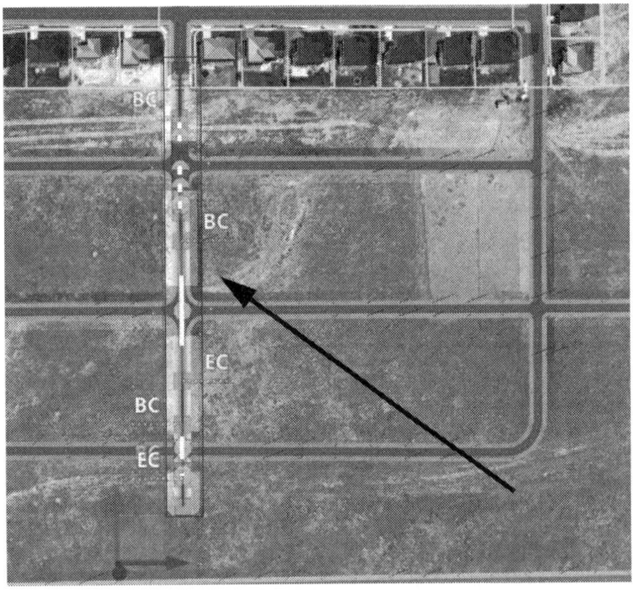

Figure 4–44

2. Right-click and select **Add Right of Way**. You will note that white ROW lines now surround the component road, as shown in Figure 4–45. If you do not see the ROW lines, make sure they are turned on in the *Model Explorer* under *Area of Interest*.

Before ***After***

Figure 4–45

3. Press <Esc> to release the selection.
4. In the *Manage* tab>*Model* panel, click (Model Explorer).
5. In the *Model Explorer*, under *Area of Interest,* click (Layer Visible) to the right of **Parcels** and **Right of Ways** to toggle them off. This causes both the parcel lines and the contours, as well as the right of way lines you just created, to be hidden. The contours may not be displayed if you closed the model after you made them visible in the previous task.
6. Close the *Model Explorer*.

Task 3: Create a new element-based component road.

In this task, you will create a new component road. Point of interest (POI) tacks have been placed to help you pick the points of intersection (PIs).

1. Continue working in the same model as the last task. If you did not complete the last task, select the **B_Task3** proposal to make it current.
2. Click (Bookmarks) and select **Hotel**.
3. In the *Create* tab>*Transportation* panel, select (Component Road).
4. In the *Road* asset card, name the road **Ascent Hotel Dr**.
5. Under *Creation Method*, select **Element Based**. Under *Type*, click the assembly name to select a different assembly, as shown in Figure 4–46.
6. In the *Select Assembly* asset card, select **Component>Assembly>Two Lanes** (at the bottom of the list), as shown in Figure 4–46.

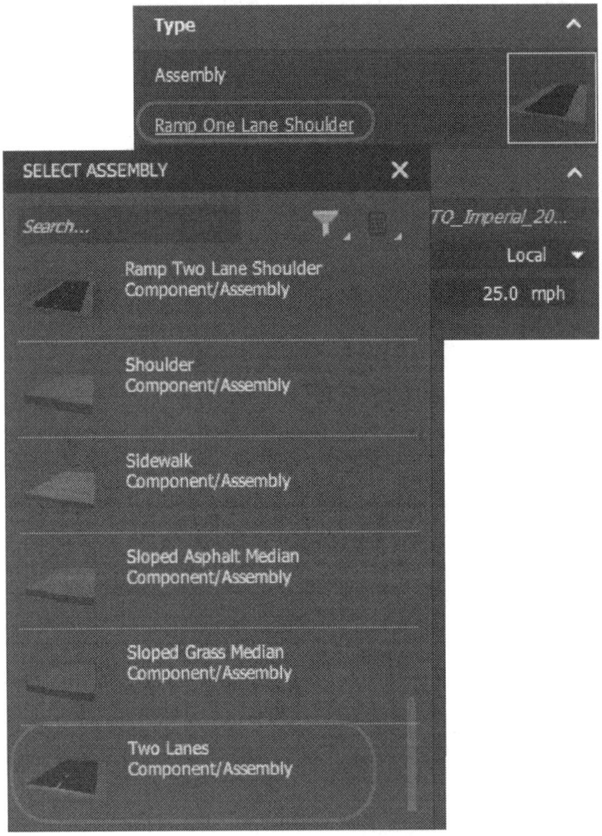

Figure 4–46

7. Close the *Select Assembly* asset card.
8. In the model, click to set the starting point of the new roadway at the **Point 1** blue POI tack at the center of the component road shown in Figure 4–47. This is the first element. If the blue POI tacks are not visible, ensure that one of the **B_Task** proposals is current.

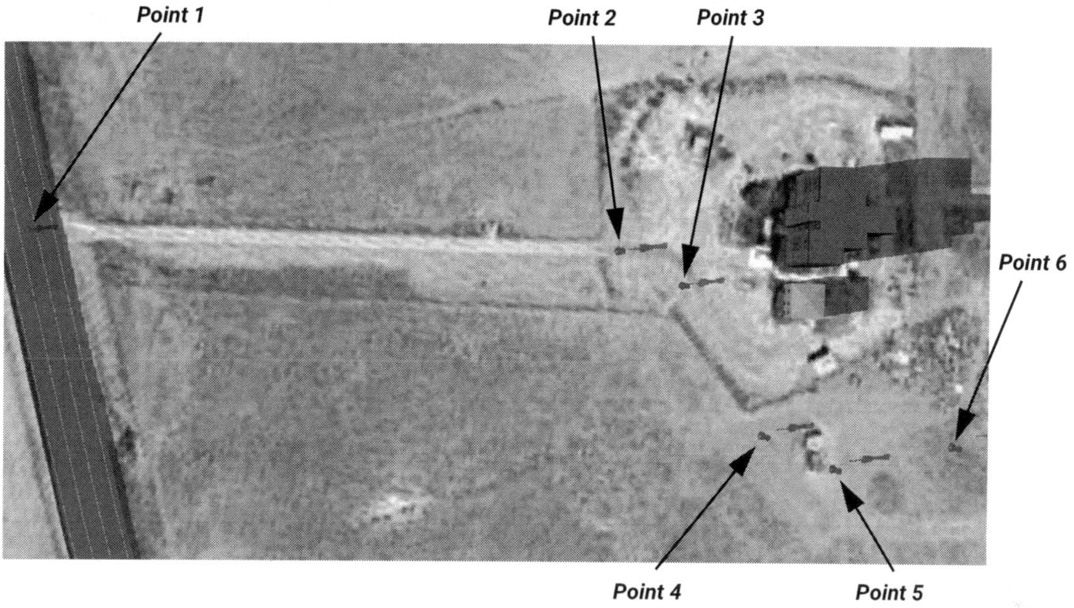

Figure 4–47

9. In the model, move the cursor to the east and click on the **Point 2** POI tack shown in Figure 4–47. This is the tangent line and the beginning of the curve element.
10. Move the cursor to the southeast and click on the **Point 3** POI tack shown in Figure 4–47. This is the curve element and the beginning of the second tangent line.
11. Complete the **Ascent Hotel Dr** by clicking near the remaining blue POI tacks, then double-clicking near the last one, as shown in Figure 4–47.

12. The final road should look similar to Figure 4–48. You will refine the curves and vertical heights later.

Figure 4–48

Task 4: Create a new PI-based component road.

In this task, you will create a new component road. POI tacks have been placed to help you pick the PIs.

1. Continue working in the same model as the last task. If you did not complete the last task, select the **B_Task4** proposal to make it current.
2. Click (Bookmarks) and select **Beach Access**.
3. In the *Create* tab>*Transportation* panel, select (Component Road).
4. In the *Road* asset card, name the road **Morris Beach Blvd**.
5. Under *Creation Method*, select **PI Based**. Under *Type*, ensure that it is still set to **Two Lanes**. Even though it will be a boulevard, you will start with two lanes and add components later.

6. In the model, click to set the starting point of the new roadway at the **Point 1** green POI tack at the center of the component road, shown in Figure 4–49 for the first element. If the green POI tacks are not visible, ensure that one of the **B_Task** proposals is current.

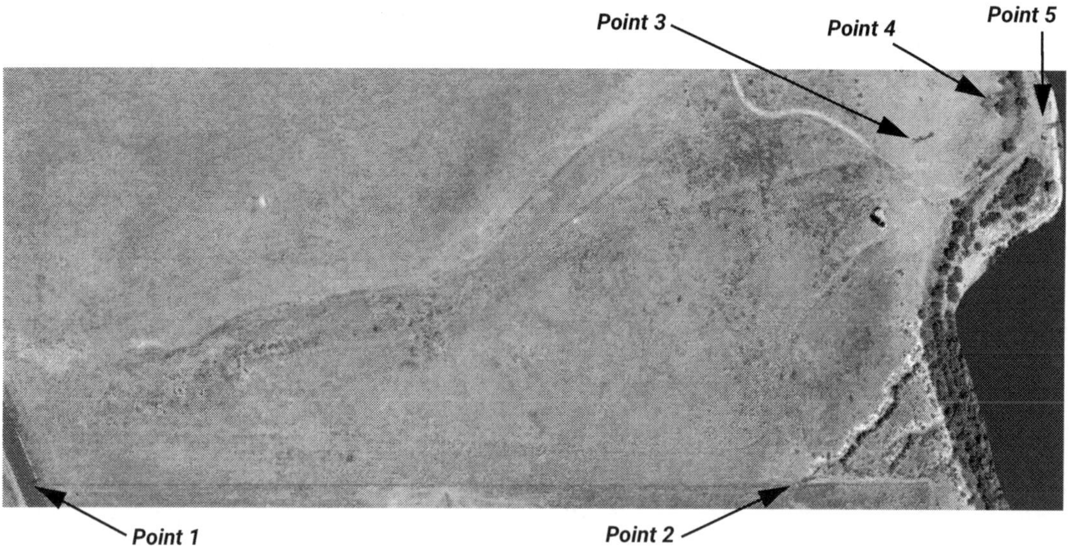

Figure 4–49

7. In the model, move the cursor to the east and click on the **Point 2** green POI tack shown in Figure 4–49. This is the tangent line and the beginning of the curve element.
8. Move the cursor to the northeast and click on the **Point 3** green POI tack shown in Figure 4–49. This is the of the curve element and the beginning of the second tangent line.
9. Complete the **Morris Beach Blvd** by clicking near the remaining green POI tacks, then double-clicking near the last one, as shown in Figure 4–49.

10. The final road should look similar to Figure 4–50. You will refine the curves and vertical heights later. The last PI is too tight to insert a curve, so none is created. This too will be fixed in a later practice.

Figure 4–50

11. (Optional) Delete all the green and blue tacks, since they are no longer needed. You can either select each one or use the window select method, then press <Delete> to erase them. Be careful not to select the roads; if you do, you can press <Ctrl> and click them again to deselect them.

End of practice

4.4 Add Detail to Component Roads

Not every road is created the same. Typical road cross sections vary according to their location and use. A freeway has a much different cross section than a local road. Even local road cross sections can vary as the road crosses into a new governing jurisdiction.

Consider the following examples:

- One city might require a meandering sidewalk for pedestrians and bikes, while another might have bike lanes that are adjacent to vehicular traffic.
- One city might require a curb and gutter, while another might not, as shown in Figure 4–51.
- One area of a city might require a specific type of street light, while another area might require something different, as shown in Figure 4–51.
- One soil type may allow for a 2:1 slope for the daylight lines, while other soil types might require a more gradual slope.

Figure 4–51

When working with component roads, you can add new components (sub-assemblies) and decorations, as required, along specific stations. In addition, you can easily change entire assemblies along component roads and the grading of the daylight lines as the road crosses different soil types.

> ***Note:*** *Decorations can be imported from Revit Families into the style palettes.*

How To: Add Components to a Component Road

1. In the model, select the component road.
2. Right-click on the component road and select **Insert Road Component**.
3. In the *Select Component* asset card, select the assembly you want to insert.
4. In the model, proceed as follows:
   - Place the cursor so that the orange line is located where the new component belongs, as shown in Figure 4–52.
   - Double-click to place the component and end the command.
   - Alternatively, you can click once to place the component, and then adjust the length using the component's gizmo, as shown in Figure 4–53. Once you have adjusted the component's length, press <Esc> to end the command.

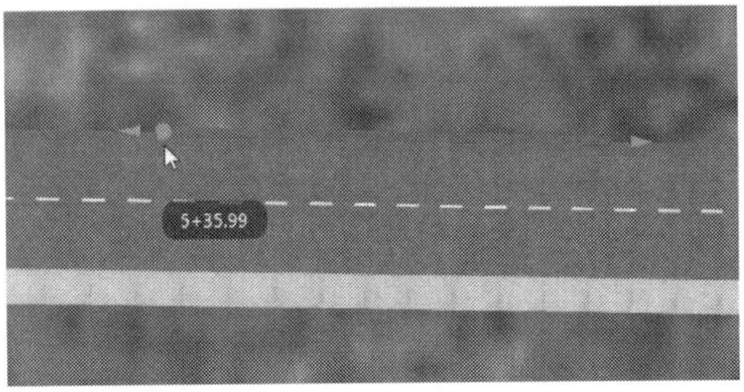

Figure 4–52

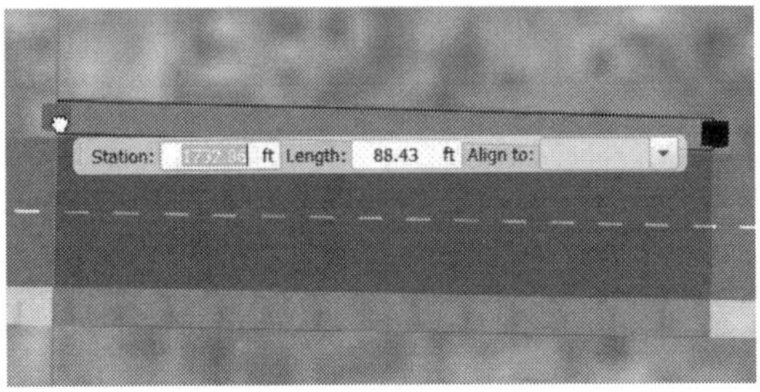

Figure 4–53

   - When adjusting a component's length, you can have it snap to the **Start of road**, as shown in Figure 4–54, or to the **End of road**.

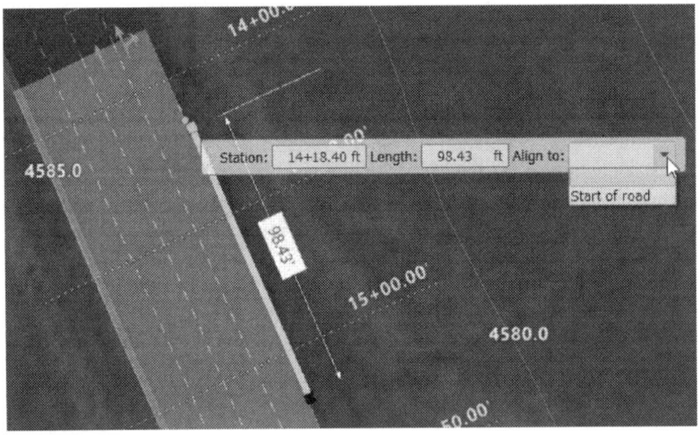

Figure 4–54

5. Select the new component and make any required changes to its length using the component's gizmo. Also, make any required changes to its properties using its stack, as shown in Figure 4–55.

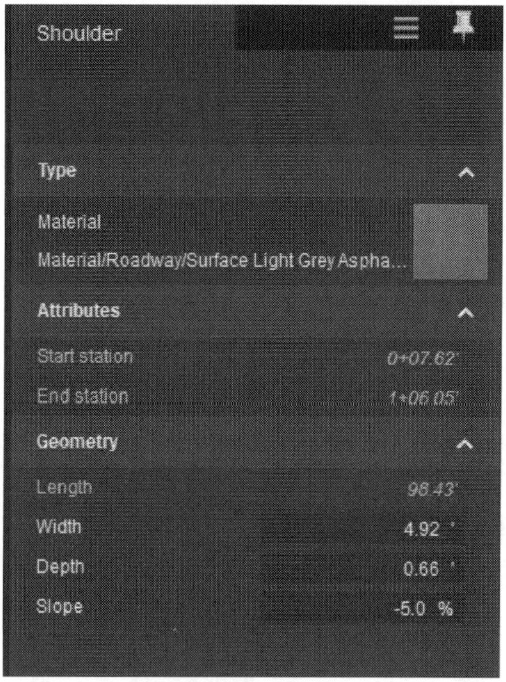

Figure 4–55

6. Press <Esc> to clear the selection of the component.

How To: Add Decorations to Component Roads

1. In the model, select the component road.
2. Right-click on the component road and select **Place Decorations**.
3. In the *Select Decoration* asset card, select the city furniture you wish to insert.You can use the filter at the top to narrow your search for decorations.
4. In the model, place the cursor so the orange line is located where the new decoration belongs and double-click to place the component.

5. Select the new component and make any required changes to its length using the component's gizmo. Also, make any required changes to its properties using its stack, as shown in Figure 4–56.

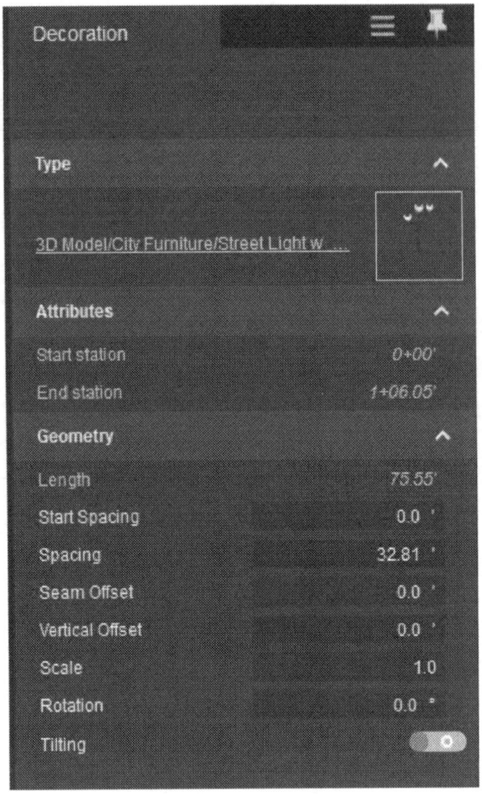

Figure 4–56

6. Press <Esc> to clear the selection of the component.
7. Decoration gaps are maintained when the host road goes through intersections and roundabouts.
8. You can use unattached free form linear decorations, which are independent of a road alignment.

Hint: Legacy Decorations

Road Decorations have been significantly changed. If the decorations are from a legacy version, a message bar is displayed: *This is an old version of decoration that must be converted before editing. Right-click to view conversion options.*

Reuse Assemblies

Once you create a component road assembly, you can save it for reuse on other roads.

How To: Save an Assembly for Reuse

1. In the model, select the component road you wish to reuse.
2. Right-click on the component road and select **Add to Library**.
3. In the model, click to select a cross section of the component road to add to the library.
4. In the *Add To Library* asset card, type a name and press <Enter>.

Practice 4d
Add Detail to Component Roads

Practice Objective

- Modify the component road using the asset card and gizmos.

In this practice, you will remove components, then add components and decorations to S Redwood Rd.

Task 1: Modify the component road.

1. Continue working in the same model as the last practice. If you closed the file, on the *Home* screen, click **Open**. In the *InfraWorks Practice Files\4-Roads* folder, select **CreateRoads.sqlite** and click **Open**.
2. If you did not complete the last task, select **C_Task1** in the  (Proposals) drop-down list to make it current.
3. Click  (Bookmarks) and select **Hotel**. Zoom in to the intersection.
4. In the model, select **S Redwood Rd**. Click on the left (west) shoulder on the outside edge of the road, as shown in Figure 4–57. In the *Shoulder* stack, under *Geometry*, note that the *Width* is **4'**.
5. Right-click and select **Delete Component**. You will add something in its place later.

   Note: Be careful when deleting the shoulders. You can tell what is selected by looking at the asset card that displays.

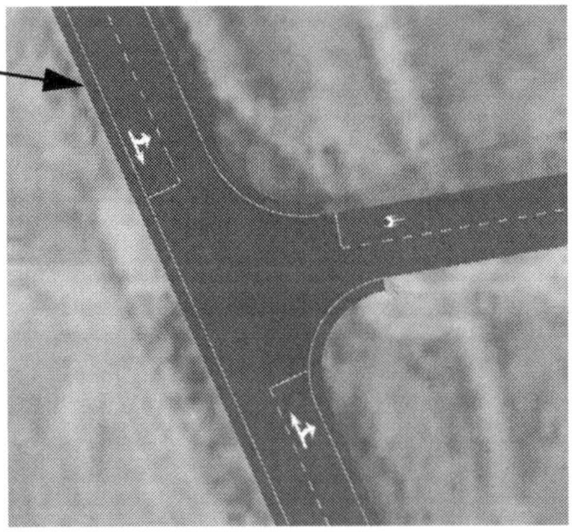

Figure 4–57

6. Select the left (west) lane. In the *Lane* stack, under *Geometry*, change the *Width* to **14**. Repeat for the right lane.

7. Select **Ascent Hotel Dr**, then right-click and select **Insert Road Component**.
8. In the *Select Component* asset card, scroll down and select **Shoulder**, as shown in Figure 4–58. In the *Shoulder* stack, under *Geometry*, ensure that the *Width* is **4'**.

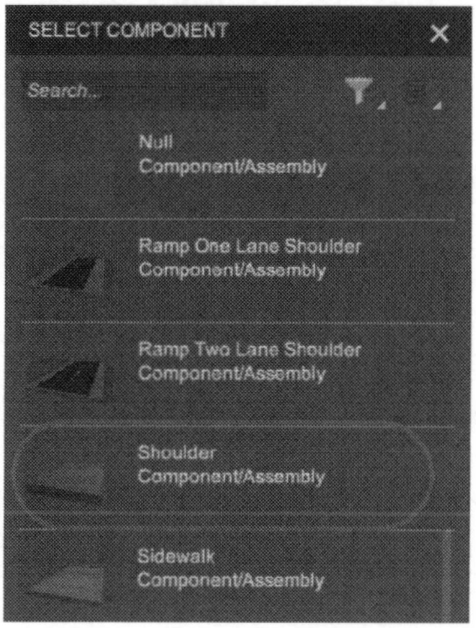

Figure 4–58

9. In the model, do the following:
   - Note that there are three choices for inserting the shoulder component. Place the cursor so the orange line is located on the upper north side of the road, as shown in Figure 4–59. Click once to place the lane.
   - Right-click on the assembly and uncheck **Transition In** and **Transition Out**, as shown in Figure 4–60.
   - Move the *Assembly Length* gizmo to match up with the shoulder of the intersecting road.
   - Adjust the assembly length using the right gizmo so the shoulder goes to the end of the road.

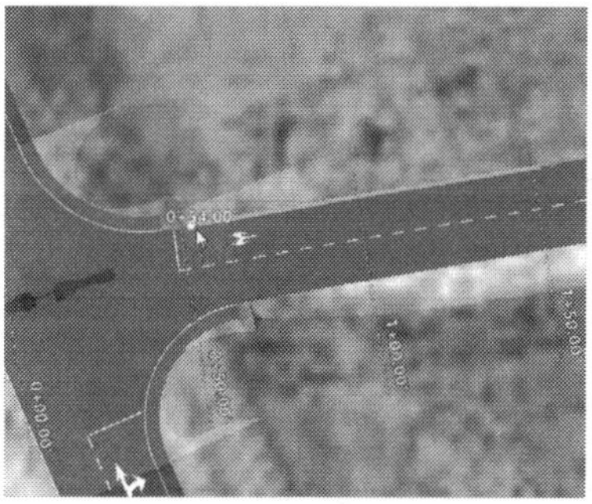

Figure 4–59

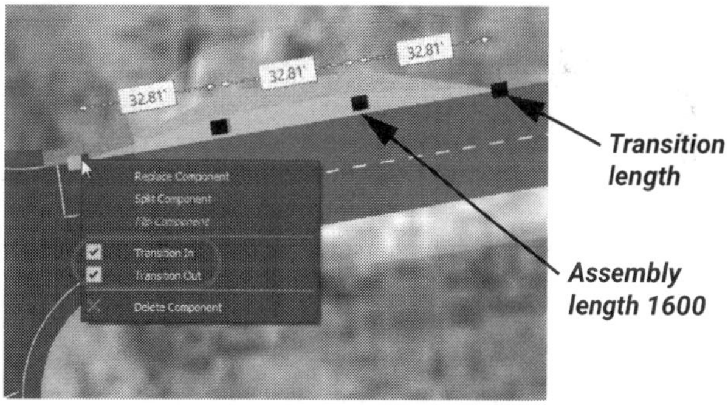

Figure 4–60

10. Repeat Steps 7 to 9 for the southern side of **Ascent Hotel Dr** to add another shoulder.
11. Use what you just learned to add shoulders to **Morris Beach Blvd**. Note that when you reach the edge of the screen area as you drag the gizmos, the screen will pan in that direction.

    Note: *The road extends beyond the model limits you had set earlier, but that is not an issue.*

12. Select **S Redwood Rd**. In the *Road* asset card, under *Geometry*, note the *Length* and *Station Range* of the road, as shown in Figure 4–61. You will use these values to adjust the additional components you will be adding next.

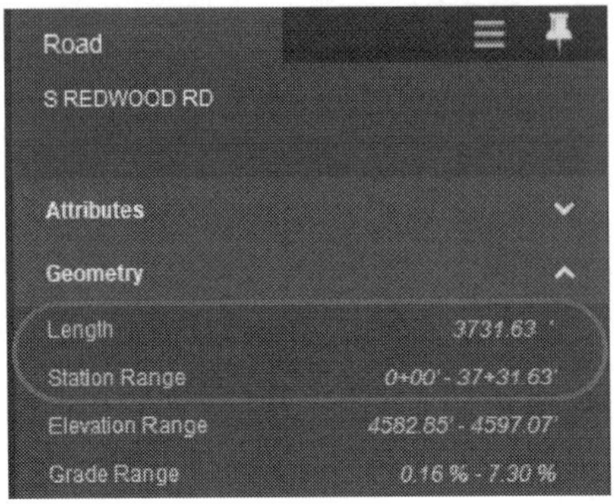

Figure 4–61

13. Click  (Bookmarks) and select **S Redwood Start**.
14. Select **S Redwood Rd**, right-click, and add the **Curb & Gutter** assembly to the left (south) edge of the road.
    - Place the component at the beginning of the road (Station 0.00).
    - As you drag the gizmo, you can enter either the *Length* of the component or the *Station* value you had noted earlier, as shown in Figure 4–62. Type in **3731.63** for the *Length*.

Figure 4–62

15. Add the following components:
    - Add the **Sloped Grass Median** to both sides of the road for the entire length, as you had just done, with no transitions in or out.
    - Add the **Sidewalk** assembly to the left (south) edge of the road for the entire length. In the *Sidewalk* stack, under *Geometry*, ensure that the *Width* is **5'**.
16. Select the shoulder component on the right side. Right-click on it and select **Replace Component** from the menu. In the *Select Component Style* dialog box, select the **Curb & Gutter** assembly, as shown in Figure 4–63.

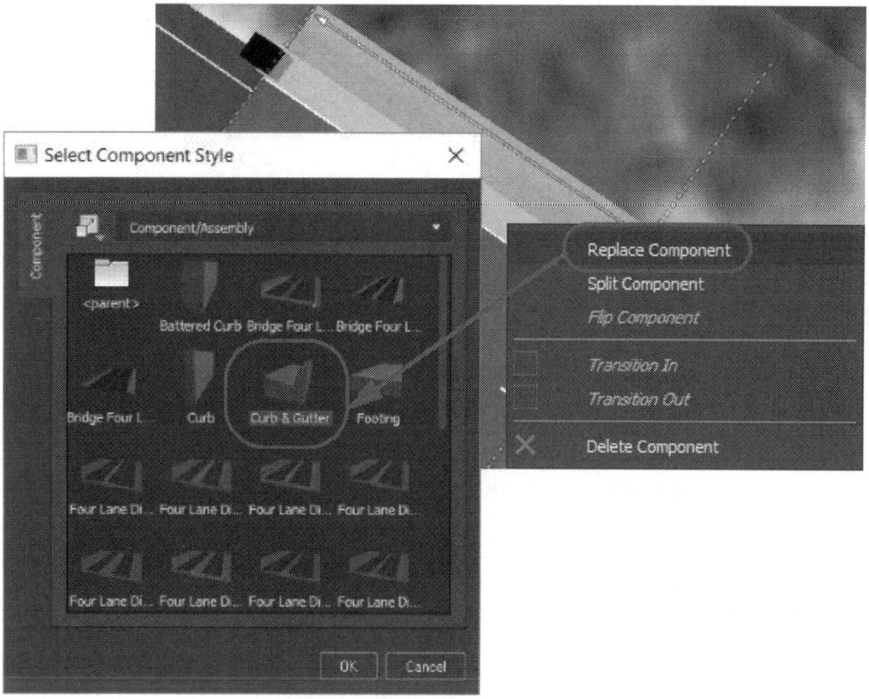

Figure 4–63

17. Right-click on *S Redwood Rd* and select **Place Decorations**.
18. In the *Select Decoration* asset card, type **Light** in the search, then select **Street Light w_3 Bulbs**.

19. In the model, place the cursor so that the insertion line follows the edge of the sidewalk and grass median on the left (west) side of the road, as shown in Figure 4–64. Click to place the decoration.

Figure 4–64

20. In the *Decoration* stack, under *Geometry*, set the *Spacing* to **50'** and the *Seam Offset* to (negative) **-2'** to place the lights into the grass median.

   Note: *The lights only go to station 1650 since both components surrounding it only extend that far. To add lights to the end of the road, you would have to add another decoration.*

The client wants to see what a less expensive light looks like. On the right (east) side of the road, you add a different style of light to show them how it looks in contrast with the first light. Once they decide which light they like best, you can simply change the assembly on one side of the road.

21. Right-click on *S Redwood Rd* and select **Place Decorations**.
22. In the *Select Decoration* asset card, type **Light** in the search, then select **Street Light w_1 Bulb**.

23. In the model, place the cursor so the insertion line follows the edge of the sidewalk and grass median on the right (east) side of the road, as shown in Figure 4–65. Orbit the model so that you can see the results.

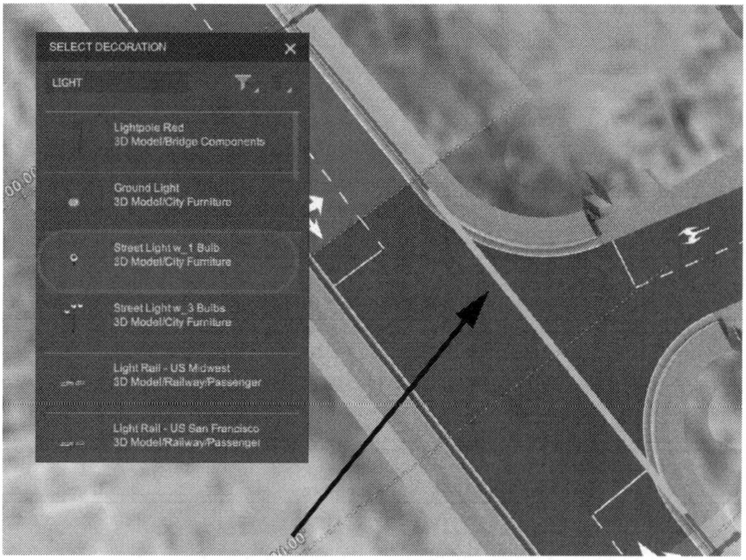

Figure 4–65

24. In the *Decoration* stack, under *Geometry*, set the *Spacing* to **50'** and the *Seam Offset* to (negative) **-2'**, as shown in Figure 4–66.

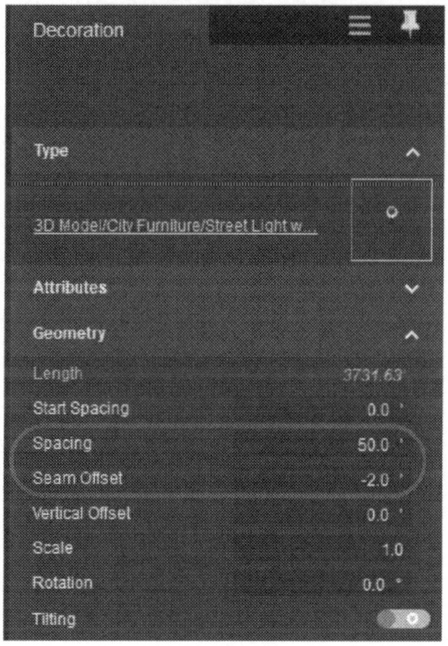

Figure 4–66

25. Press <Esc> to clear the selection of the decoration. Examine the model.

The client has decided that they prefer the more expensive three-bulb street light. Rather than remove the single light pole, you can simply change the decoration.

26. In the model, click on the light decoration on the right (east) side of the road to display the *Decoration* stack.
27. In the *Decoration* stack, click on the style name.
28. In the *Select Component* dialog box, select **3D Model/City Furniture/Street Light w_3 Bulbs**.
29. Press <Esc> twice to clear the selection of the decoration and the component road.

Task 2: Save a new assembly.

1. If you did not complete the last task, select the **C_Task2** proposal to make it current.
2. In the model, select **S Redwood Rd**.
3. Right-click on *S Redwood Rd*, hover over *Road Assembly*, and select **Add to Library**.
4. In the model, click to select a cross section of *S Redwood Rd*, as shown in Figure 4–67.

Figure 4–67

5. In the *Add To Library* asset card, type **ASC-Collector** for the name and press <Enter>.

End of practice

4.5 Modifying Horizontal Layouts

You can change the horizontal layout of a component road using gizmos or the *Road* asset card. When making a lot of changes to the roadway, you may want to delay the model regeneration for component roads. This allows you to reduce how much time you spend waiting on the model to regenerate. By default, each time any road centerline modifications are made, it cause the entire model to regenerate.

How To: Delay Road Regeneration

1. In the toolbar, click  (Application Options).
2. In the left column of the *Application Options* dialog box, select **Model Generation**.
3. Select the **Delayed Road Regeneration** checkbox, as shown in Figure 4–68.

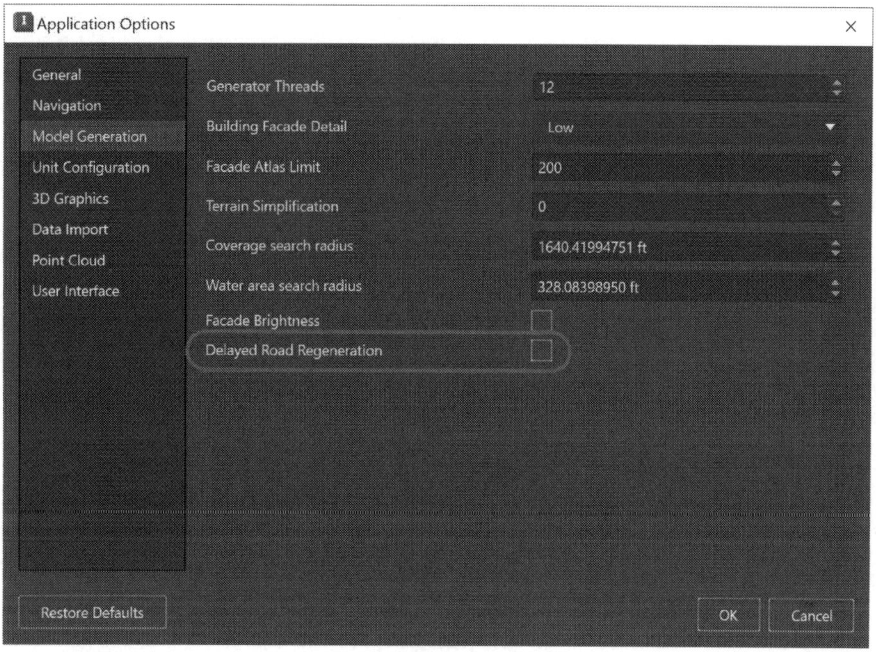

Figure 4–68

4. Click **OK**.

Horizontal Gizmos

When the component road is selected, gizmos display at various points along the road. Each gizmo is used to modify the roadway in specific ways, as described in the table below.

Gizmo	Location	Description
	**Point of Intersection (PI)**	Located at the endpoint of a road or at the horizontal point of an intersection. Changes the endpoint or PI location in the plan view, which changes the bearing and distance of the tangent.
	**Curve Radius**	Located at the midpoint of a curve. Changes the horizontal curve radius, affecting the curve's start/end points and length. Note that Spiral Curve Spiral curves do not contain this gizmo.
	**Beginning of Curve or End of Curve**	Located at the endpoint of a curve where it meets a tangent. Changes the horizontal curve radius, affecting the curve's start/end points and length. Note that Spiral Curve Spiral curves do not contain this gizmo.

When you right-click on different gizmos or segments of the road, different fly-out menus or fields display next to the cursor. Right-clicking on a curve displays the menu shown in Figure 4–69. This menu enables you to change the curve into a spiral.

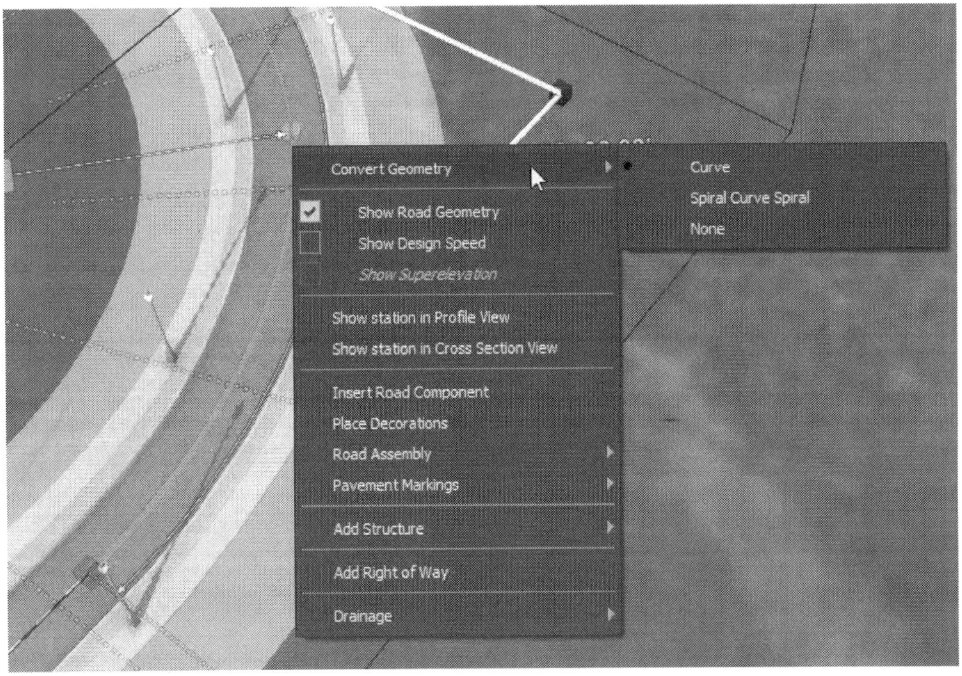

Figure 4–69

Component Road Asset Card

The *Component Road* asset card has multiple edit modes (stacks). The current edit mode, or stack, is determined by what is selected on the road, as shown in Figure 4–70. Each stack provides options for editing different parts of the component road.

Entire road selected

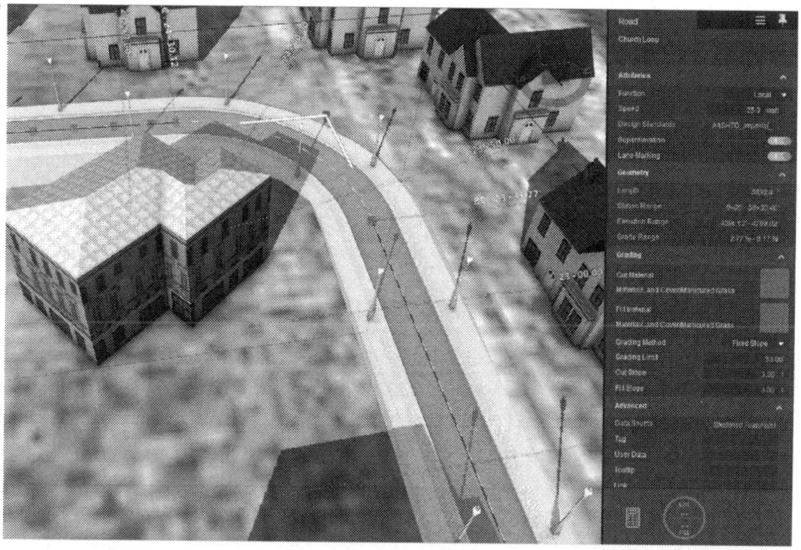

Curve or tangent segment selected

Figure 4–70

- The top of the *Road* asset card lists the road name, which can be modified. Underneath the name, a description of the road can be added.

Entire Road Edit (Road Asset Card)

The edit mode for the entire road (shown on the top in Figure 4–70) displays information about the road. Editable fields display in white text.

- The *Attributes* area contains the *Function*, *Speed*, *Design Standards*, *Superelevation*, and *Lane Marking* fields. Only the design standards cannot be changed in the *Attributes* area. Changing the *Function* should also change the design speed.
- The *Geometry* area displays the total length of the road, the range of elevations, and the range of grades along the road. Nothing in the *Geometry* area can be modified.
- The *Grading* area displays the *Material* and *Grading Method* used and any *Grading Limits* you set.
- The *Advanced* area enables you to add **Tags**, **User Data**, **Tooltips**, and **Links**.

If a segment (tangent or curve) is selected instead of the whole road, only the *Attributes* and *Grading* stacks are available (as shown on the bottom in Figure 4–70).

How To: Replace Assemblies on Component Roads

1. In the model, select the component road.
2. Right-click on the component road, hover over *Road Assembly*, and select **Replace Assembly**.
3. In the *Select Draw Style* asset card, select the required assembly.
4. In the model, either:
   - Hover over the component road and double-click to place the assembly over a selected section

   OR

   - Single-click to begin drawing the assembly at a specific station. Click again to indicate at which station the assembly should end.
5. Press <Esc> to clear the selection of the component.

Road Annotation

When a component road is selected in the model, station annotations display at set intervals and at certain geometry points, as shown in Figure 4–71. Clicking on a geometry label allows you to modify the geometry.

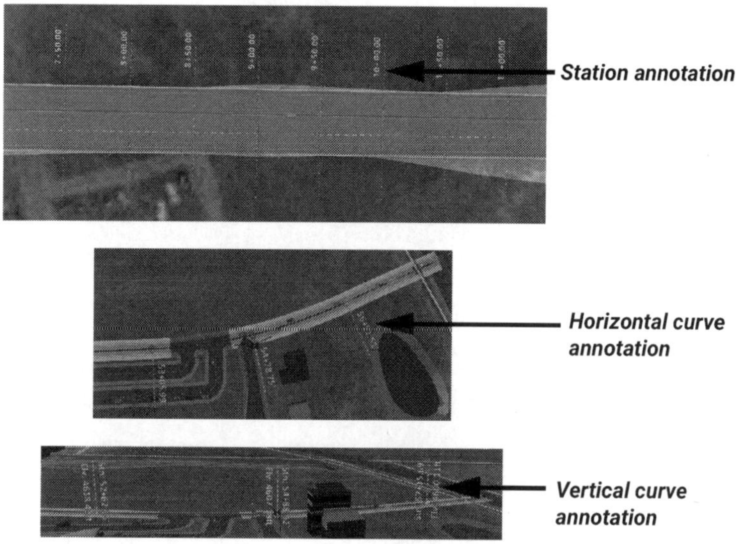

Figure 4–71

If specific geometry, such as a curve or tangent, is selected, the geometry annotation displays and adjusts in real-time as you drag gizmos during the modification process, as shown in Figure 4–72.

Figure 4–72

InfraWorks calculates the minimum radius required based on roadway design standards and design speeds. It warns when such standards aren't met, as shown in Figure 4–73.

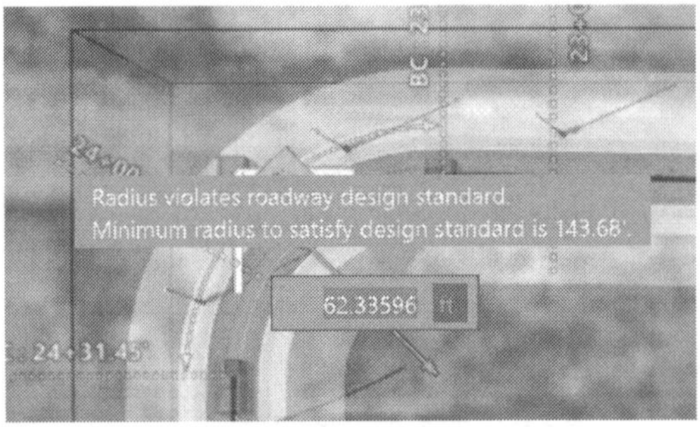

Figure 4–73

Roadside Grading

Grading components enable you to set the daylight slopes from the edge of the assembly to the existing ground surface. Roadside grading for a component road can be controlled in its asset card. You can set the material, slope, and width.

You can choose between a fixed width or fixed slope grading method. When the **Fixed Width** option is selected, you can only set the *Grading Limit* parameter for the road, as shown in Figure 4–74. However, selecting the **Fixed Slope** option enables you to change the *Material*, *Cut Slope*, *Fill Slope*, and *Grading Limit*, as shown in Figure 4–75.

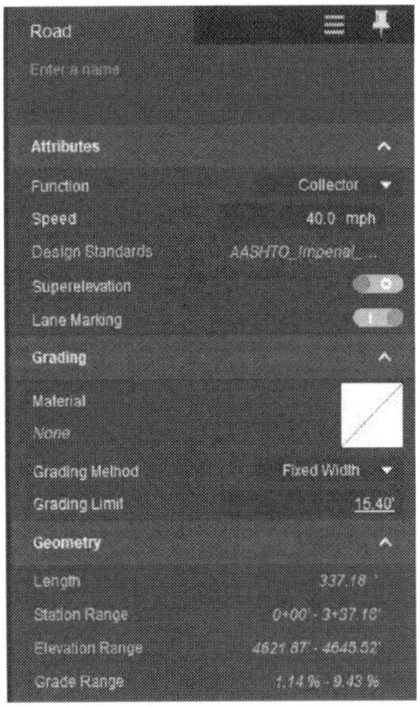

Figure 4–74

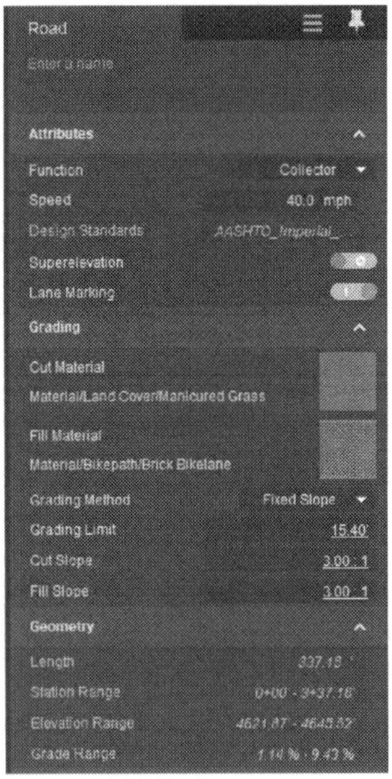

Figure 4–75

Altering the grading using the *Road* asset card applies the grading parameters for the entire road, as well as both sides of the road. Selecting one grading component on one side of the road enables you to modify the grading on each side of the road separately. You can also split grading slopes as required to transition from one slope (2:1) to another (3:1) and change the material on each, as shown in Figure 4–76.

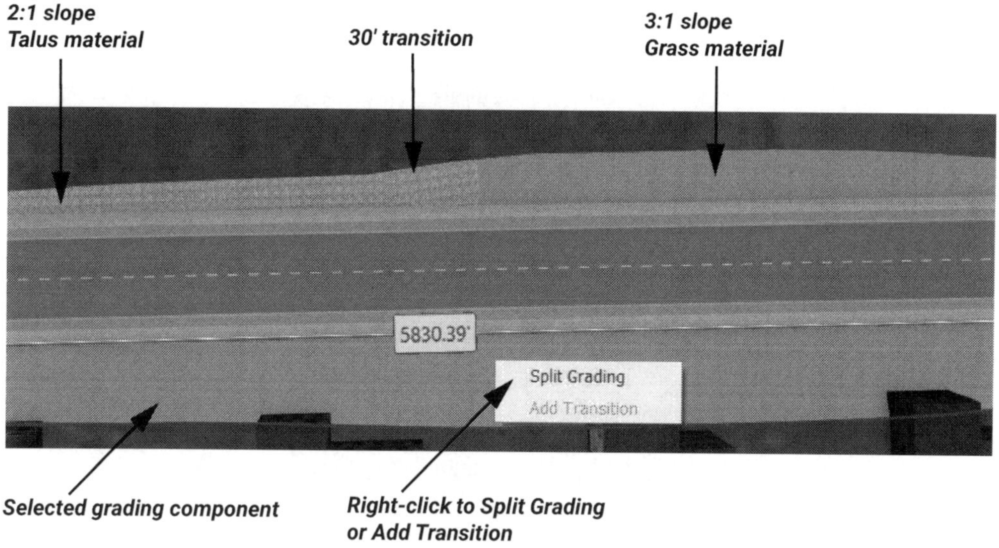

Figure 4–76

How To: Modify Roadside Grading Sections

1. In the model, select the component road.
2. In the *Road* asset card, under *Grading*, set the required material, grading method, grading limit, and cut/fill slopes, as shown in Figure 4–77.

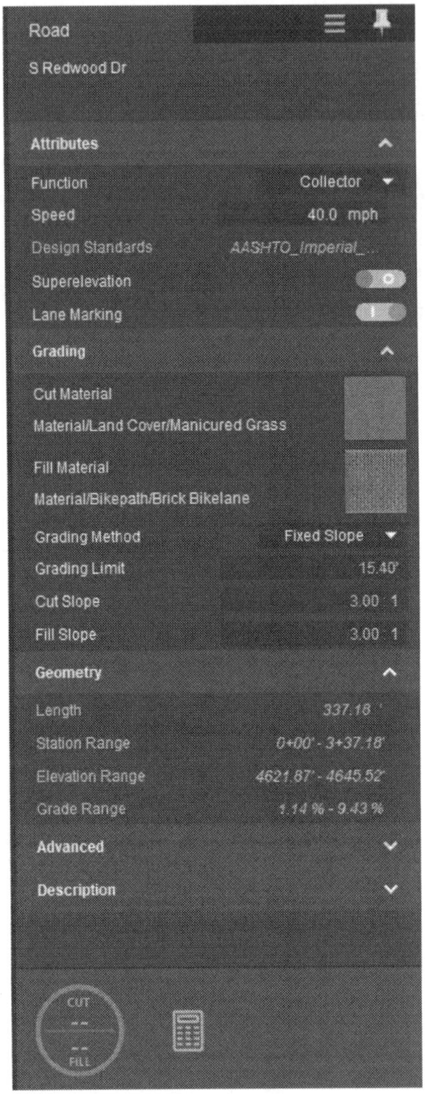

Figure 4–77

3. In the model, select a grading component on one side of the road to modify.

4. Right-click and select **Split Grading**, as shown in Figure 4–78.

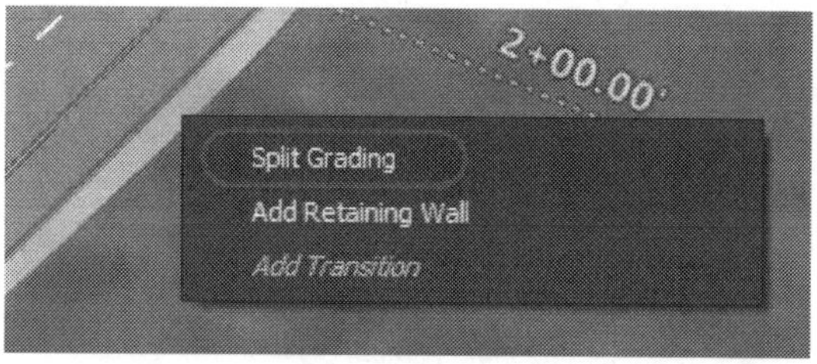

Figure 4–78

5. In the model, double-click to set the split point at the required station or type the station and press <Enter>, as shown in Figure 4–79.

Figure 4–79

6. In the model, click to select the grading slope on the side of the split that requires a different slope or material.
7. In the *Grading* stack, set the material and slope.
8. In the model, select the grading material on the side of the split that you wish to transition. Right-click and select **Add Transition**.

4.6 Modifying Vertical Layouts

Vertical Gizmos

When the model view is rotated more than 45° from plan view, a different set of gizmos display that enables you to change the vertical design of a component road. A full list of the available gizmos is shown in the table below.

Gizmo	Location	Description
	Point of Vertical Intersection (PVI)	Located at the endpoint of roads or at the point of vertical intersection (PVI). Changes the PVI station or elevation, but not both at the same time.
	High/Low Point of Curve	Located at the highest point of a crest curve, or at the lowest point of a sag curve. Changes cannot be made with this gizmo: it is for reference only.
	Point of Vertical Tangency	Located at the endpoint of a vertical curve where it meets the tangent. Changes the curve length, affecting the curve's start/end points and radius.
	Maintain Tangent Grade	Located at the point of vertical intersection when the PVI is selected. Changes the PVI location while keeping the grade of one tangent.

Additional tools display when you right-click. Depending on where you right-click, a different fly-out menu displays. Right-clicking on a tangent line displays the tools shown in Figure 4–80.

Right-clicking on the (PVI Gizmo) displays the tools shown in Figure 4–81.

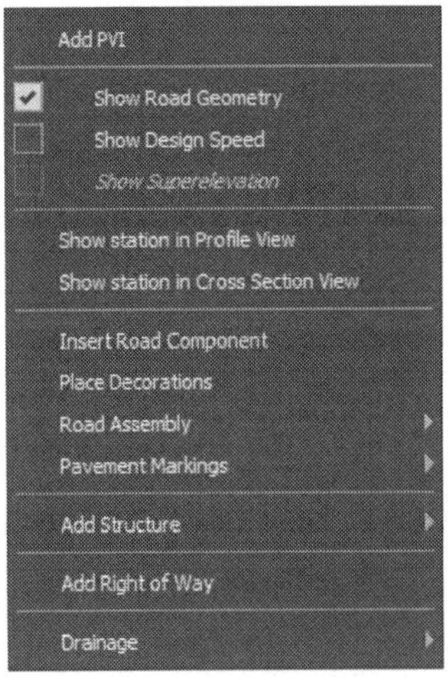

Figure 4–80

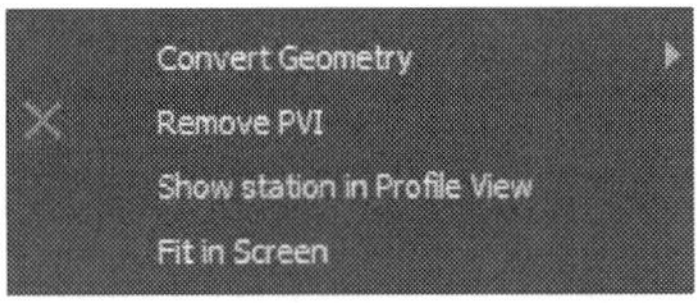

Figure 4–81

How To: Add and Adjust Points of Vertical Intersection in the Model View

1. In the model, select the component road.
2. Rotate the view more than 45° past plan view to display the vertical gizmos.
3. Right-click on the component road where you need to add a PVI. Select **Add PVI** from the fly-out menu.
4. In the model view, click the (PVI Gizmo). In the *Elevation* field, type a new elevation or type the station field to change its location, as shown in Figure 4–82. Alternatively, you can click and drag the (PVI Gizmo) up and down to change the elevation, or drag it left and right to change its station.

Figure 4–82

Profile View

When you right-click anywhere on the component road, the **Show station in Profile View** option displays in the fly-out menu. This opens a panel that shows the stations and elevations at the road centerline, as shown in Figure 4–83.

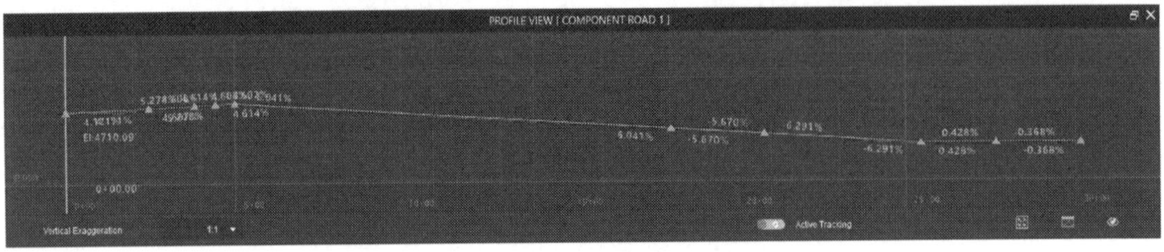

Figure 4–83

- You can control the vertical exaggeration and select which items display in the *Profile View* in the top-left corner of the panel. Items that can be displayed include:
  - Horizontal geometry
  - Existing ground
  - Drainage
  - Junctions
  - Structures
  - Surface layers
- The mouse wheel can be used to zoom in/out of the *Profile View*.
- Holding the left mouse button enables you to pan in the *Profile View*.
- Only two gizmos display in the *Profile View*, which are as follows:

Gizmo	Location	Description
	**Point of Vertical Intersection (PVI)**	Located at the endpoint of a road or at the vertical point of an intersection. Changes the endpoint or PVI station and elevation.
	**Point of Vertical Tangency**	Located at the endpoint of a vertical curve where it meets the tangent. This gizmo is for display purposes only and does not modify the profile.

Additional tools display when you right-click inside the *Profile View*. Depending on where you right-click, a different fly-out menu displays. Right-clicking on a tangent line provides the tools shown in Figure 4–84. Right-clicking on either of the *Profile View* gizmos provides the tools shown in Figure 4–85.

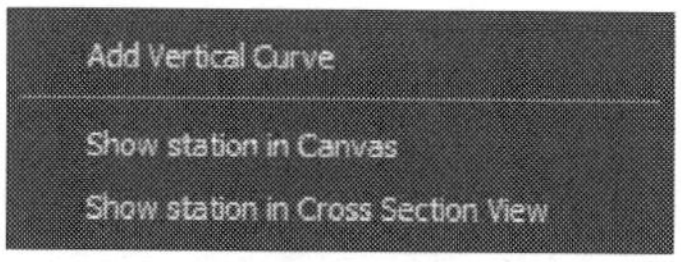

Figure 4–84

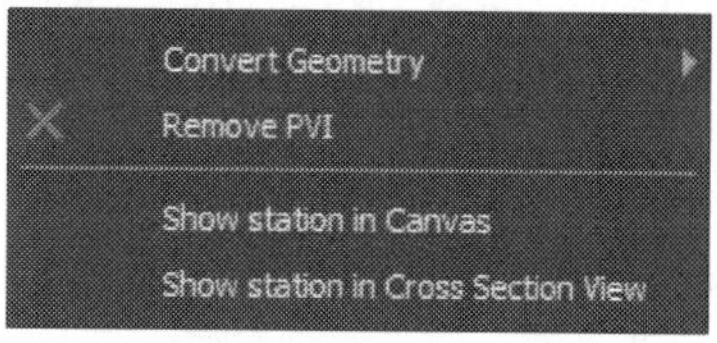

Figure 4–85

Curve Properties

Curve properties display directly on the curve in the *Profile View*, as shown in Figure 4–86. Changes can be made to any value not grayed out.

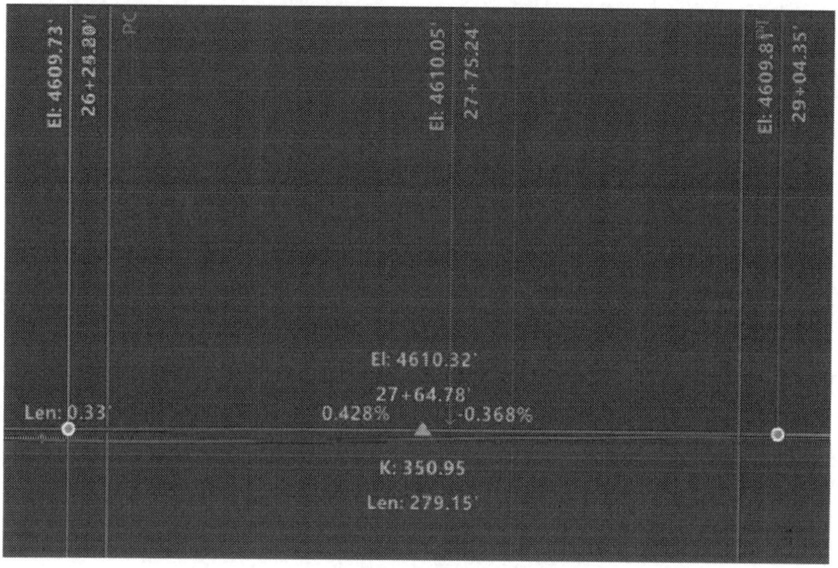

Figure 4–86

How To: Adjust Points of Vertical Intersection (PVI) in the Profile View

1. In the model, select the component road.
2. Ensure that the *Road* asset card is set to **Geometry** mode.
3. Right-click anywhere on the component road and select **Show station in Profile View** from the fly-out menu.

4. In the *Profile View*, click the  (PVI Gizmo) and drag the PVI to its new station and elevation, as shown in Figure 4–87.
   - If the **Active Tracking** option is enabled in the *Profile View* panel, the yellow bar, which tracks the stations both in canvas and in the *Profile View*, moves as you move your cursor in the *Profile View*.

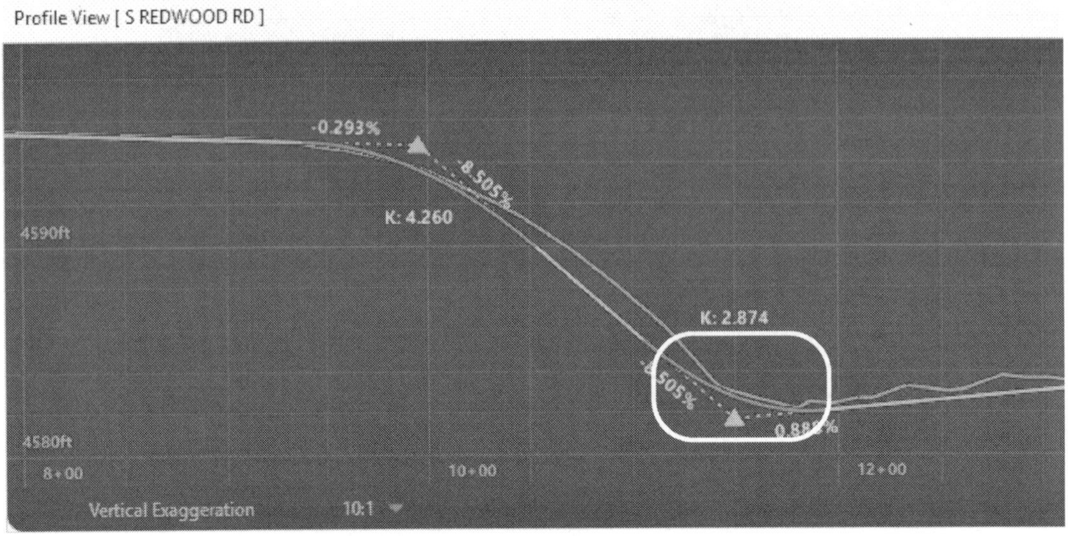

Figure 4–87

5. You can control the movement of PVIs in the *Profile View*, as noted in the Tip reproduced in Figure 4–88.
   - Holding <Shift> or <Ctrl> will lock the grades, so the PVI will only move right or left (in the profile view).
   - Holding <Alt> will lock the elevation, so the PVI will only move up or down (in the profile view).

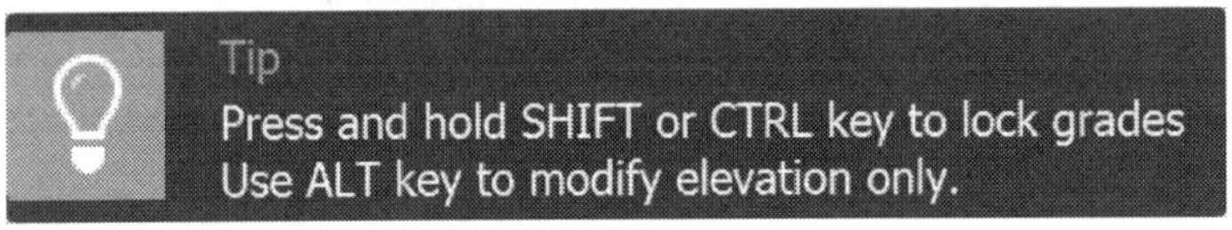

Figure 4–88

Practice 4e
Modify Component Roads

Practice Objective

- Modify the component road using the asset card and gizmos.

In this practice, you will modify the alignment of a component road by adjusting the horizontal curve radii and splitting the road into two different styles (typical cross sections). You will then set the daylight slopes for the road and adjust the vertical design by inserting PVIs and moving gizmos, as required (as shown in Figure 4–89).

Figure 4–89

Task 1: Modify the horizontal design.

In this task, you will modify the horizontal layout of the component road by modifying the curve radius, adding another style to a portion of the road, and adding daylight slopes.

1. Continue working in the same model as the last practice. If you closed the file, on the *Home* screen, click **Open**. In the *InfraWorks Practice Files\4-Roads* folder, select **CreateRoads.sqlite** and click **Open**.
2. If you did not complete the last task, select **D_Task1** in the (Proposals) drop-down list to make it current.

3. Click (Bookmarks) and select **Project Area**.

   Note: *Gizmos display in the model on the component road.*

4. In the model, select the **Church Loop** road shown in Figure 4–90.

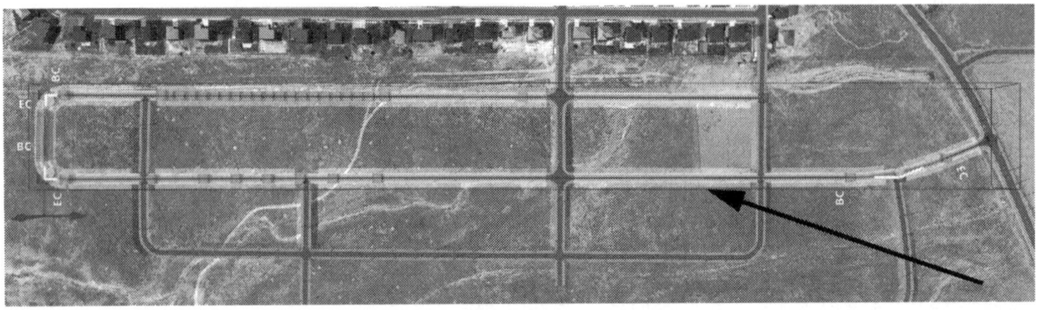

Figure 4–90

5. Zoom in on the west end of the road, as shown in Figure 4–91.

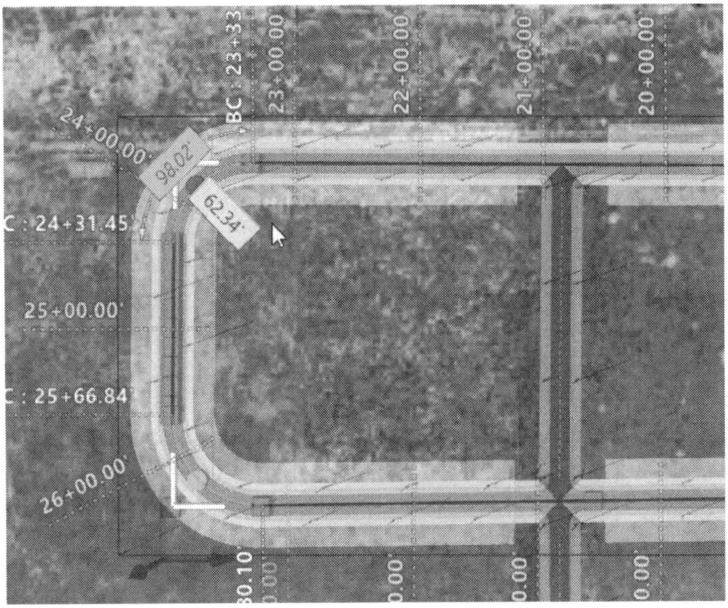

Figure 4–91

In the model, click on the (Curve Radius Gizmo) in the northwest corner, as shown previously in Figure 4–91. For the *Radius* measurement, type **60**. Press <Enter> to accept the radius. You can ignore the warnings about minimum curve radius requirements, as shown in Figure 4–92.

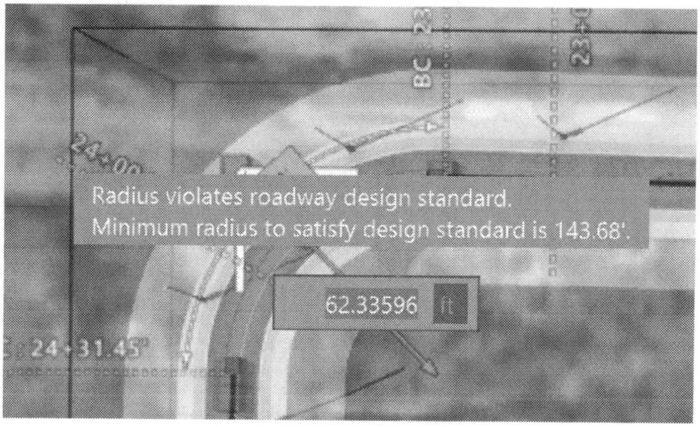

Figure 4–92

6. Repeat Step 6 for the curve in the southwest corner. Press <Enter> to release the curve radius gizmo.

7. Click (Bookmarks) and select **School Area**.

8. With the road still selected, right-click and hover over *Road Assembly* and select **Replace Assembly**.

9. In the *Select Draw Style* asset card, select the **Component>Custom>ASC-Collector** road assembly (at the bottom of the list), as shown in Figure 4–93. You had previously added this custom component to the library.

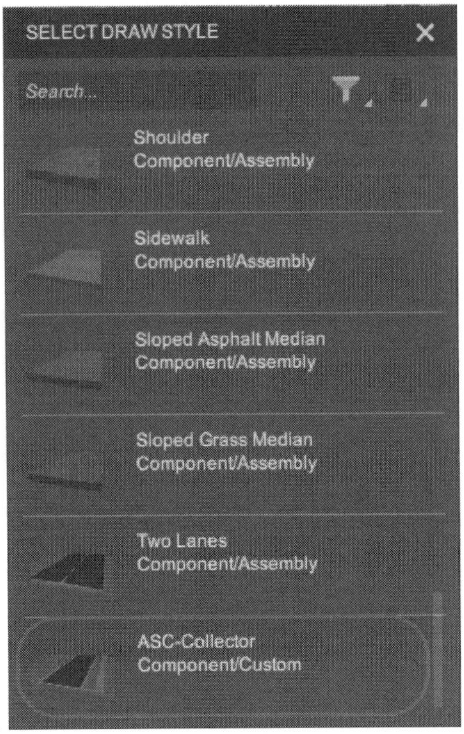

Figure 4–93

10. In the model, click a point near station **50+00** for the beginning of the assembly zone, as shown in Figure 4–94. Stretch the assembly zone to the end of the road where it meets S Redwood Rd, as shown in Figure 4–94. Press <Enter> to accept the change.

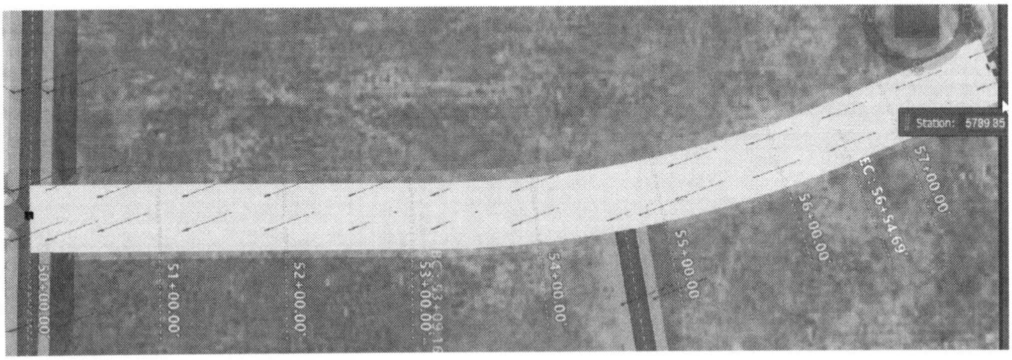

Figure 4–94

11. In the *Road* asset card, set the following options, as shown in Figure 4–95:
    - *Grading Method*: **Fixed Slope**
    - *Cut Material*: **Manicured Grass**
    - *Fill Material*: **Manicured Grass**
    - *Grading Limit*: **33'**
    - *Cut Slope*: **3.0:1**
    - *Fill Slope*: **3.0:1**

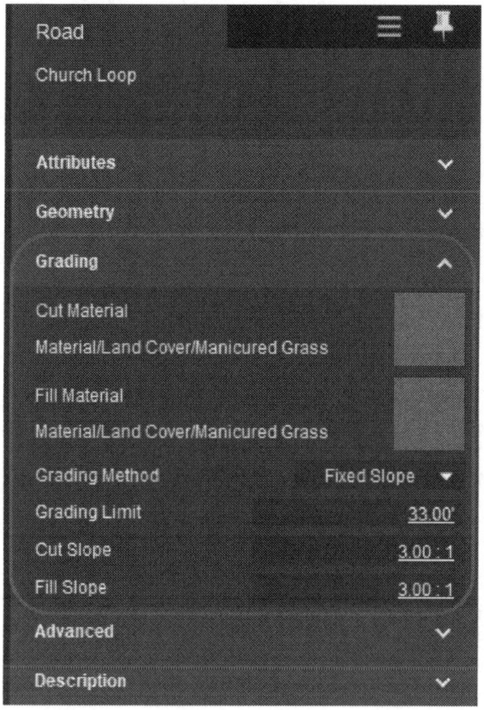

Figure 4–95

12. Press <Esc> to release the selected road.

Task 2: Adjust the vertical profile of the component road.

1. Continue working in the same model as the last task. If you did not complete the last task, select the **D_Task2** proposal to make it current.
2. Click (Bookmarks) and select **DesignElevations**.

Note that there are several locations where there is a lot of fill required along the new component road, as shown in Figure 4–96. This could cause flooding issues for the proposed homes. In this task, you will modify the vertical design of the new road to prevent flooding in the neighborhood.

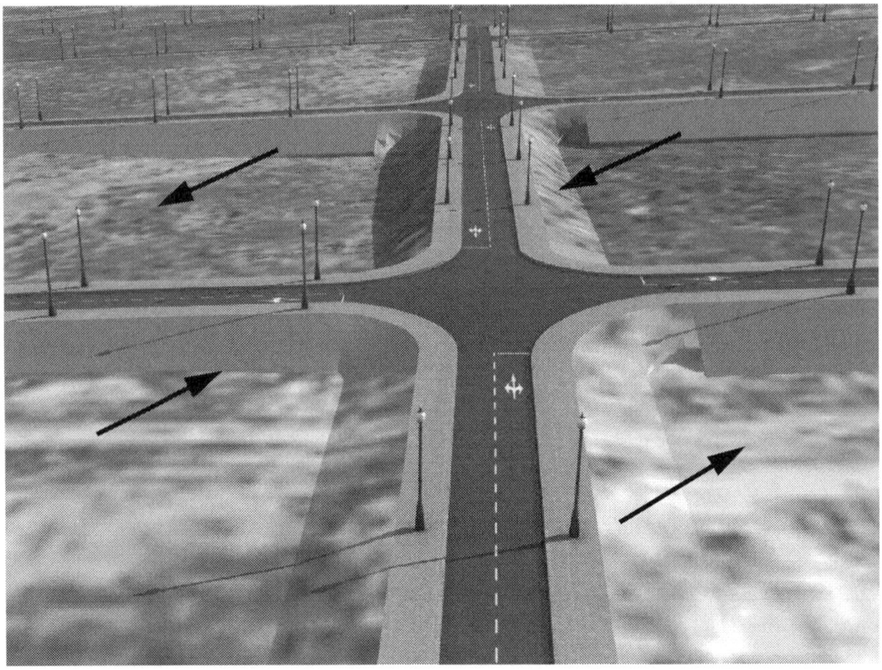

Figure 4–96

3. In the model, select the **Adams Ave** component road.
4. In the model, right-click and select **Show station in Profile View** from the fly-out menu.
5. In the *Profile View*, click  (Asset Toggle) and toggle on **Existing Ground**, as shown in Figure 4–97.

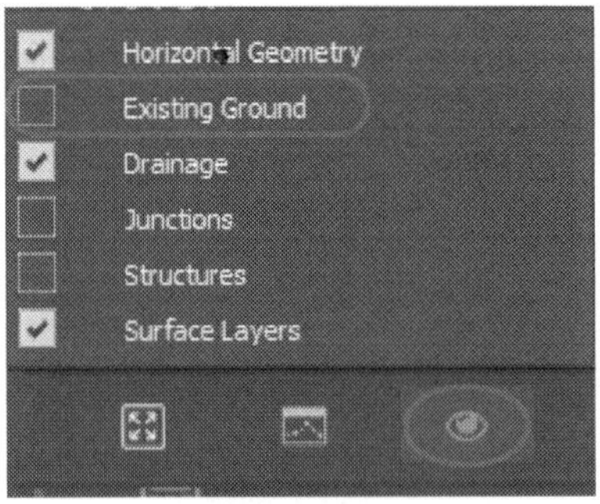

Figure 4–97

6. In the *Profile View*, drag the yellow vertical line (section view plane) to the intersection, as shown in Figure 4–98. Note in the model the thick yellow slice indicating the area.

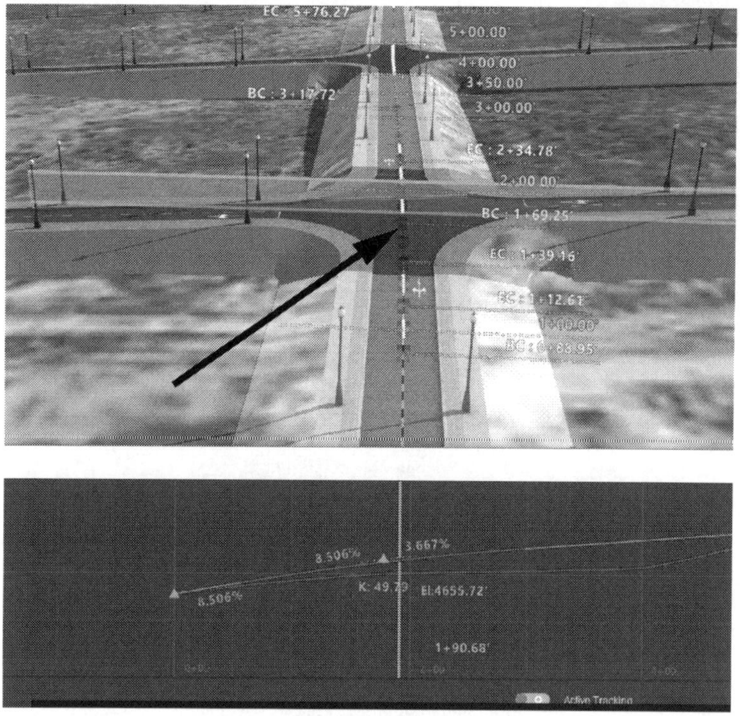

Figure 4–98

7. Click the (PVI Gizmo) to drag it to the intersection of the yellow line and the green existing ground profile (station **191.19**, elevation **4650**), as shown in Figure 4–99. Note that all *Profile View* changes regenerate simultaneously in the model as soon as you move the cursor into the model window.

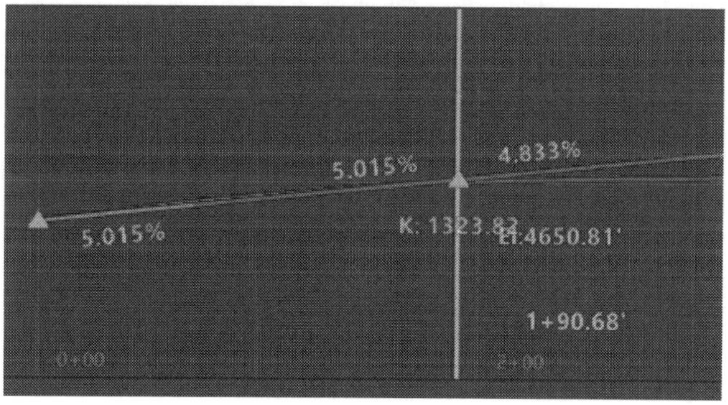

Figure 4–99

8. In the *Profile View*, hover near station 400, right-click, and add a vertical curve. Then, click the (PVI Gizmo) to drag it to the intersection of the yellow line and the green existing ground profile (station **400**, elevation **4652**). Click on the right PVI gizmo and lower that to the existing ground, as shown in Figure 4–100. You can also type in the values for the vertical curves in the *Profile View*.

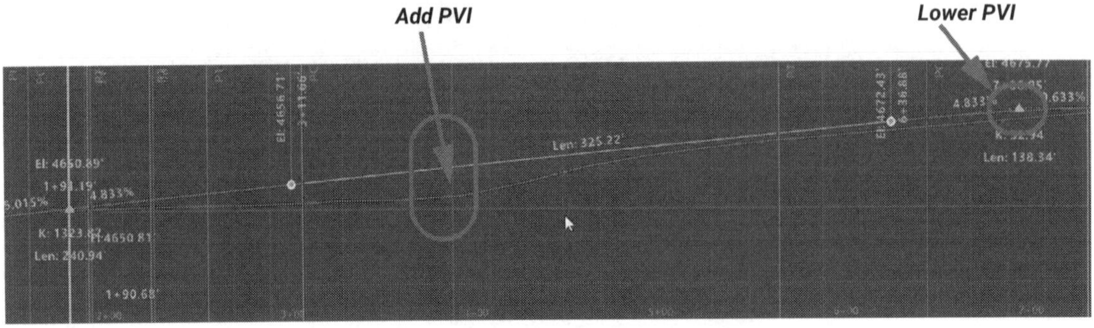

Figure 4–100

Note that in the model, an overpass has been created in the upper road and a heaped intersection has been created in the lower road. You need to correct this.

9. Select the **Church Loop** component road running north to south. In the *Profile View*, drag the yellow vertical line to the intersection, as shown in Figure 4–101.

Figure 4–101

10. Right-click in the *Profile View* to add a vertical curve, then click the (PVI Gizmo) to drag it to the intersection of the yellow line and just a bit above the green existing ground profile (station **689**, elevation **4649.3**). You can zoom in as required in the *Profile View*.
11. Drag the thick yellow line in the *Profile View* to the upper intersection (overpass), which is near station **4310**. Repeat Step 10 to add a PVI and adjust it (station **4311**, elevation **4658.0**).
12. Close the *Profile View* by clicking the red **X** in the upper-right corner.

Task 3: Adjust Morris Beach Blvd.

1. If you did not complete the last task, select the **D_Task3** proposal to make it current.
2. Click (Bookmarks) and select **Beach Access**. Zoom and pan to the end of the road near the beach, as shown in Figure 4–102.

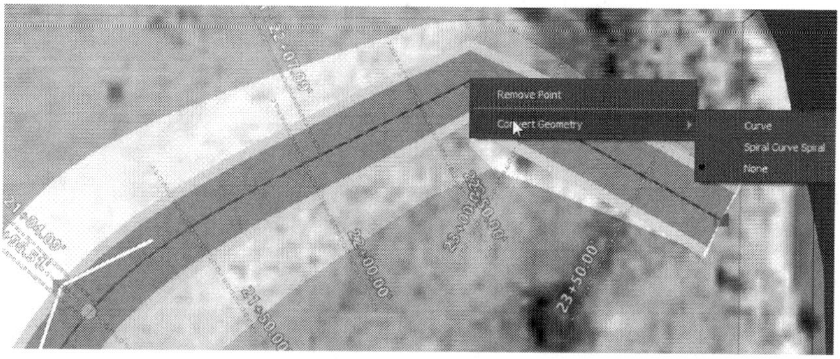

Figure 4–102

3. To adjust the vertical curve length, in the model, select **Morris Beach Blvd**. Select the PI designated by the blue square gizmo.
4. Right-click and select **Convert Geometry>Curve**.
5. Click on the new curve that has been inserted, then click on the beginning of the curve from the incoming tangent gizmo and note the tooltips that display, as shown in Figure 4–103.

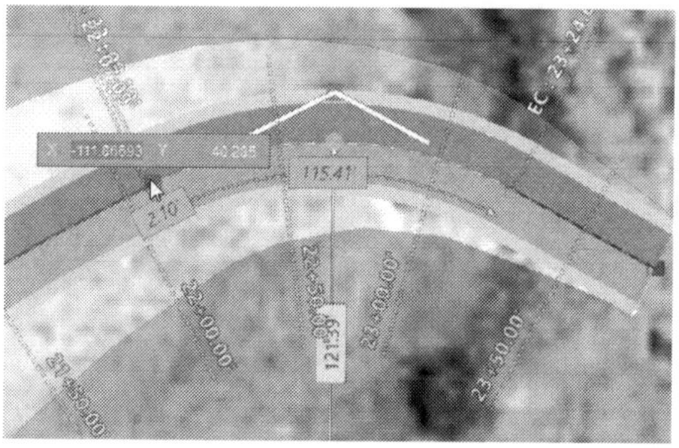

Figure 4–103

6. In the *Radius* tooltip, change the radius to **120.0'**. Again, you can ignore the curve radius warnings.
7. In the model, with the road still selected, right-click and select **Show station in Profile View** from the fly-out menu. You can also use the <Ctrl>+<0> (zero) keyboard shortcut.
8. Similarly to the previous task, insert and adjust PVIs where required. Three or four should suffice.
9. To adjust the vertical curve length, select one of the circular gizmos at the end of the curve and drag it, as shown in Figure 4–104.Since this is a symmetrical parabola curve, either gizmo will adjust the curve equally. The curve can be converted to an asymmetrical parabola curve, if needed.

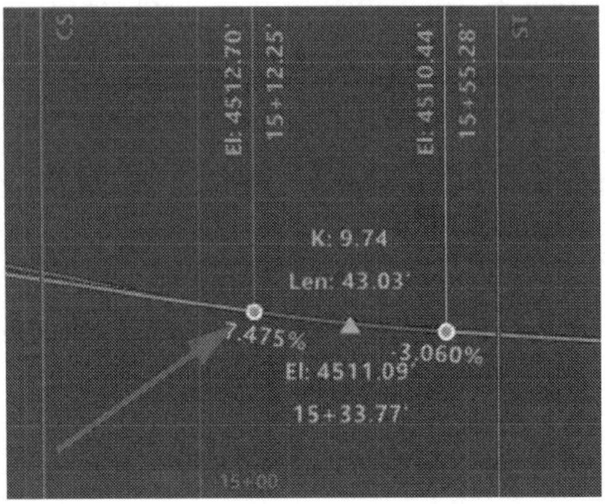

Figure 4–104

10. (Optional) For additional practice, you can adjust the PVIs for **Ascent Hotel Dr**. If you do not complete this step, you can select the next proposal in the following task.
11. Close the *Profile View* by clicking on the red **X** in the upper-right corner.

Task 4: Set roadside grading.

1. If you did not complete the last task, select the **D_Task4** proposal to make it current.
2. Click  (Bookmarks) and select **S Redwood Start**. Pan and zoom so you are near the intersection of **Pier Lane** and **S Redwood Rd**.
3. In the model, select **S Redwood Rd**.

4. In the *Road* asset card, under *Grading*, set the *Grading Method* to **Fixed Slope** and the *Material* (both cut and fill) to **Manicured Grass**, as shown in Figure 4–105. Note that you might not see a difference in the side slopes because the Grading Limit is too small.

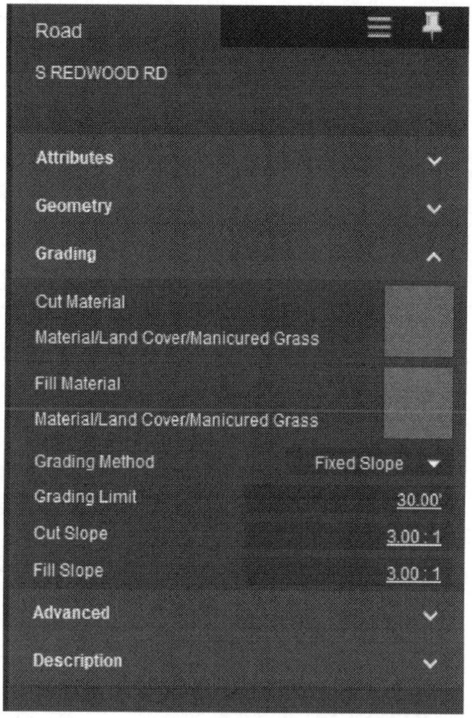

Figure 4–105

5. Leave the *Grading Limit* to **30** and the *Cut and Fill Slopes* to **3.00:1**.
6. Select the grading slope on the west side of **S Redwood Rd**.
7. Right-click and select **Split Grading**, as shown in Figure 4–106.

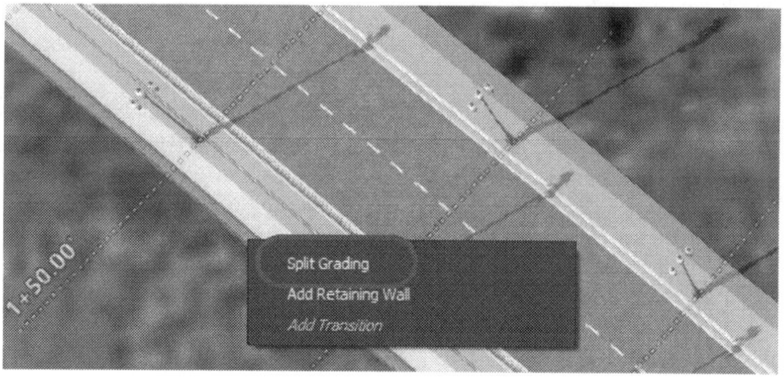

Figure 4–106

8. For the stations, type **200** and press <Enter>, then type **350** and press <Enter>. Press <Enter> again to complete the command.
9. In the model, select the section of grading between stations **200** and **350**.
10. In the *Grading* stack, change both the *Cut Slope* and the *Fill Slope* to **5.00:1**. The results are shown in Figure 4–107.

Figure 4–107

11. Click on the upper black square of the new grading region (it turns yellow when picked). Right-click and select **Add Transition**, as shown above in Figure 4–107.
12. Either drag to the south for about **20'** or type in **220** for the station. Press <Esc>. Repeat for the lower grading region limit and set that transition to **20'** (station **330.0'**) as well. Press <Esc>.
13. Press <Esc> to release the component and road selection.

14. Orbit about the road and study the difference in grading on that stretch of **S Redwood Rd**, as shown in Figure 4–108.

Figure 4–108

End of practice

4.7 Component Road Superelevation

You can apply superelevations to component roads. Once applied, you can inspect cross sections through critical stations of the road. Superelevation critical station gizmos display as blue slices along the road, as shown in Figure 4–109. In addition, yellow and red tracks display beside the roadway, representing runoff and runout areas, which are also shown in Figure 4–109.

Figure 4–109

How To: Apply Superelevations to Component Roads

1. In the model, select a component road.
2. In the *Road* asset card, under *Attributes*, toggle on the **Superelevation** option, as shown in Figure 4–110.
3. Once the **Superelevation** option is enabled, right-click on the road and toggle on **Show Superelevation**. This opens the *Superelevation Input* section in the asset card, where you can adjust the values, as shown in Figure 4–110.

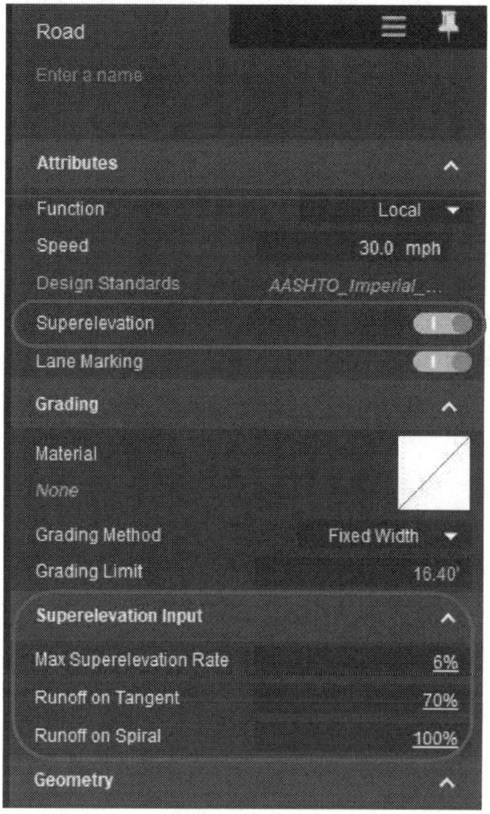

Figure 4–110

4. Press <Esc> to clear the selection of the road.

How To: View Road Cross Section Attributes in the Cross Section Viewer

1. Once superelevations are applied to a road, select the road in the model.
2. Click on a superelevation critical station gizmo. The *Cross Section Viewer* should display, as shown in Figure 4–111.

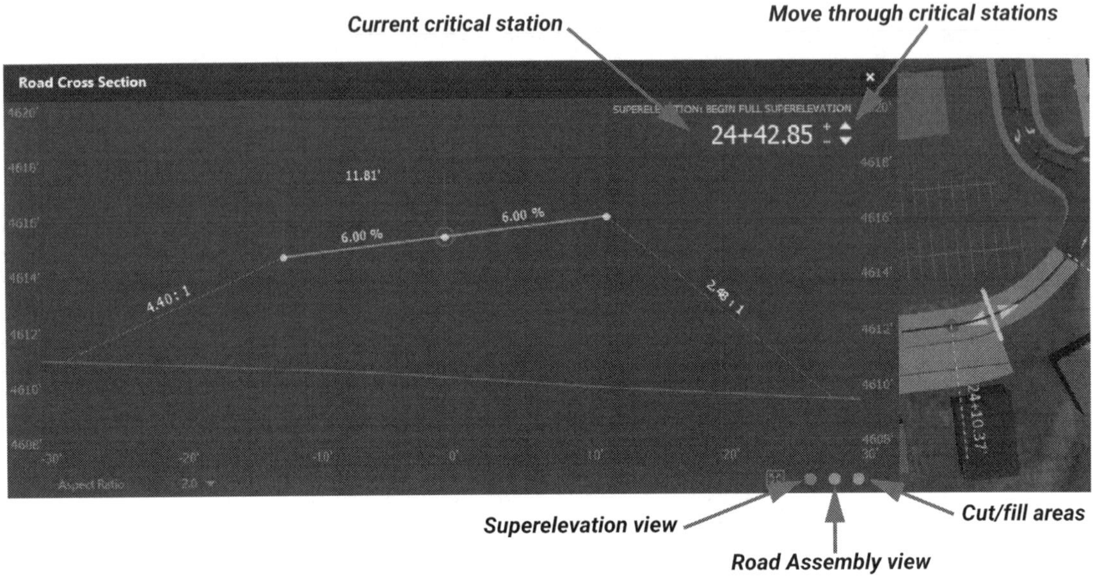

Figure 4–111

3. Click ▲/▼ (Next/Previous Critical Section) in the viewer to view other critical stations.

Practice 4f
Review Superelevations

Practice Objective

- Toggle on superelevations for review.

In this practice, you will display the superelevation data for a component road, and then review the superelevation critical stations, as shown in Figure 4–112.

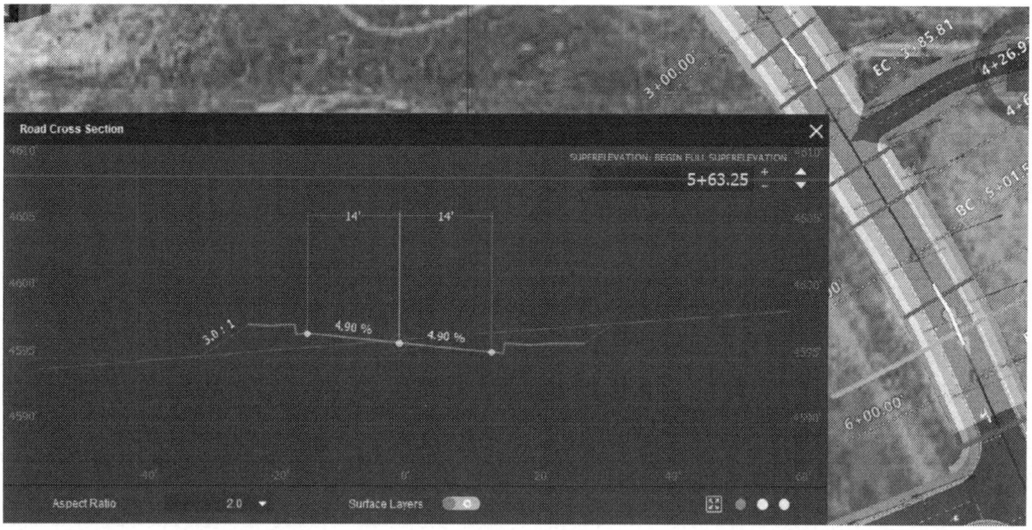

Figure 4–112

1. Continue working in the same model as the last practice. If you closed the file, on the *Home* screen, click **Open**. In the *InfraWorks Practice Files\4-Roads* folder, select **CreateRoads.sqlite** and click **Open**.
2. If you did not complete the last task, select **E_Task1** in the (Proposals) drop-down list to make it current.
3. Click (Bookmarks) and select **School Area**. Pan upwards towards the **Church Loop** and **S Redwood Rd** intersection.
4. In the model, select **S Redwood Rd** (the road running north to south).

5. In the *Road* asset card, under *Attributes*, toggle on the **Superelevation** option and press <Enter>, then right-click on the road and toggle on **Show Superelevation**. This opens the *Superelevation Input* section in the asset card, as shown in Figure 4–113.

6. Adjust the *Superelevation Input* values, as follows (shown in Figure 4–113):

   - *Max Superelevation Rate:* **6%**
   - *Runoff on Tangent:* **60%**
   - *Runoff on Spiral:* **100%**

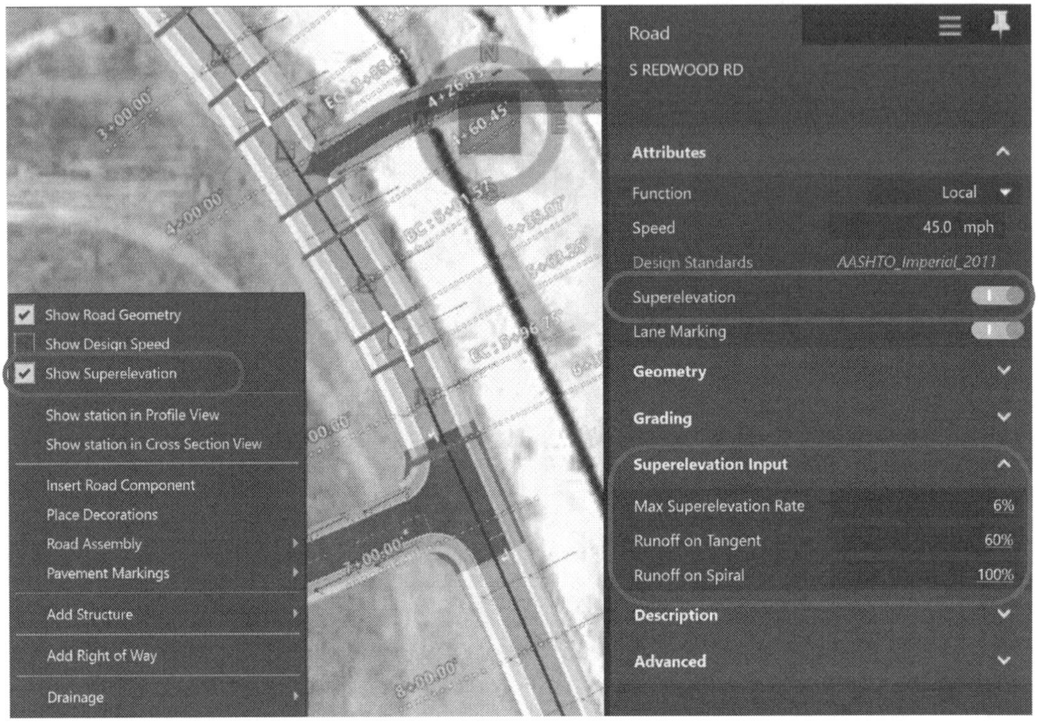

Figure 4–113

7. Click on a superelevation critical station gizmo (cyan cross-section line that turns yellow when picked), as shown in Figure 4–114. Review the superelevation data in the *Cross Section Viewer*.

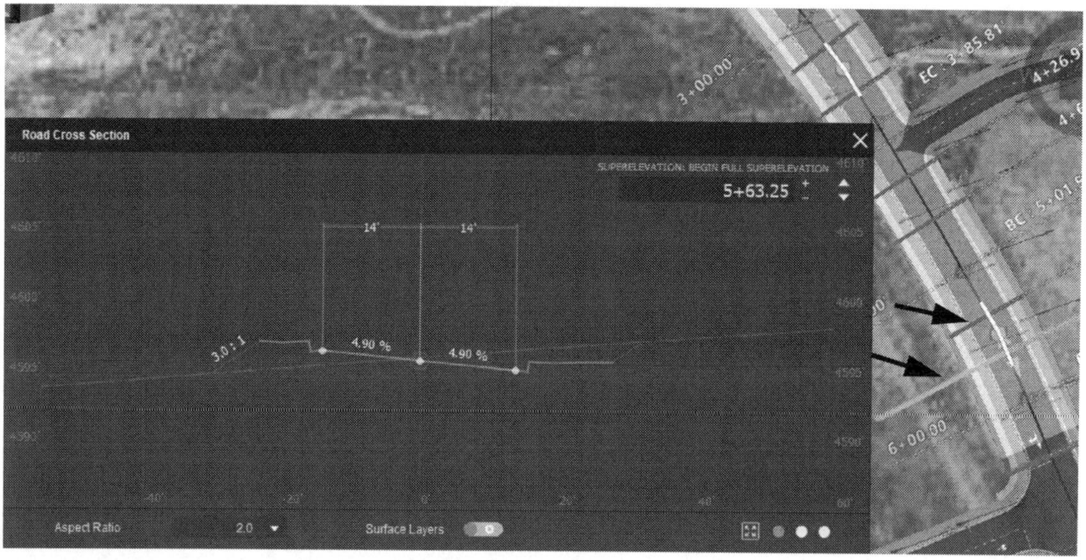

Figure 4–114

8. Click (Next Critical Section), (Previous Critical Section), or in the viewer to view other critical stations in the current view.
9. Press <Esc> twice to clear the selection of the road.

End of practice

4.8 Working with Intersections

When two component roads intersect each other, an intersection object is automatically created. Selecting an intersection in the model causes an *Intersection* asset card to display, as shown in Figure 4–115.

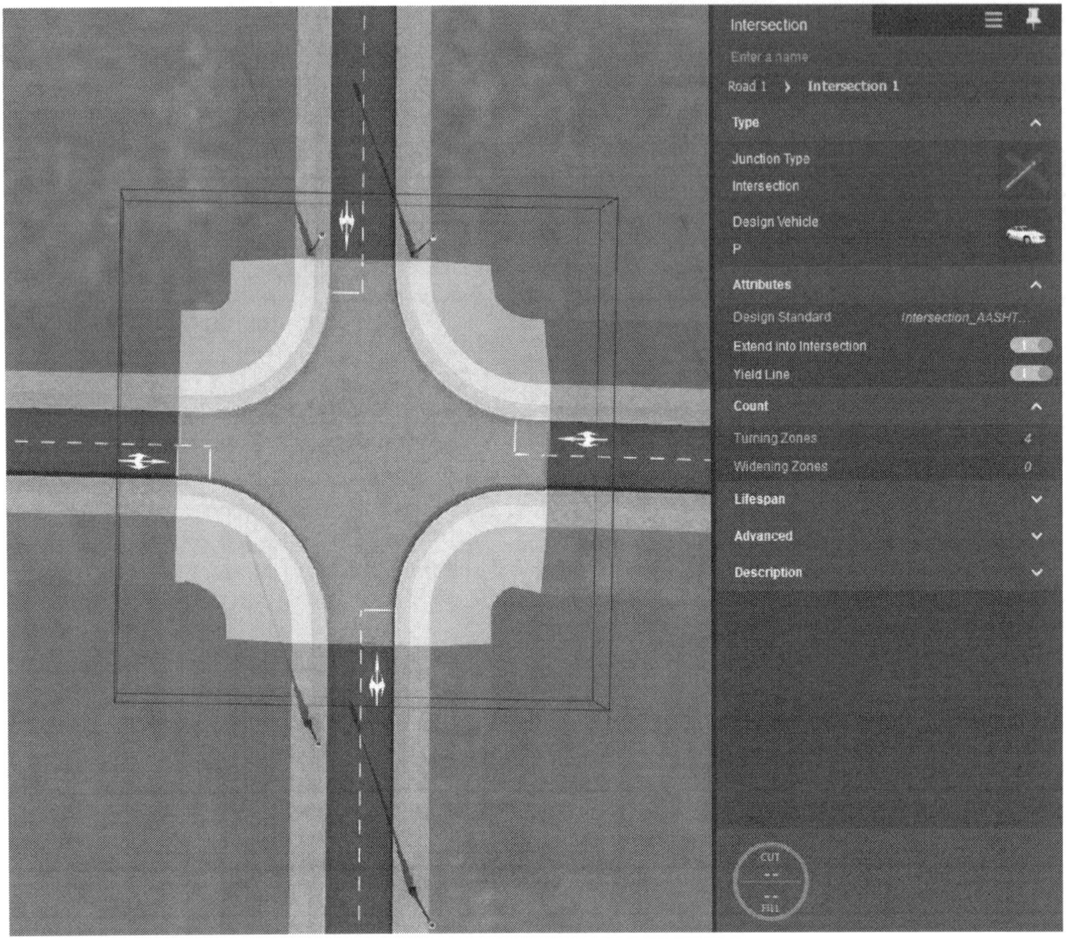

Figure 4–115

Similar to component roads, there are multiple edit modes for intersections. The edit modes that are available depend on what you have selected in the model. Clicking once on the intersection enables you to set the *Junction Type* and other settings in the Intersection stack. Clicking twice on the intersection enables you to edit specific parts of the intersection. Depending on where you click the second time, you can edit the **Turning Zone** or **Lane Group**, as shown in Figure 4–116.

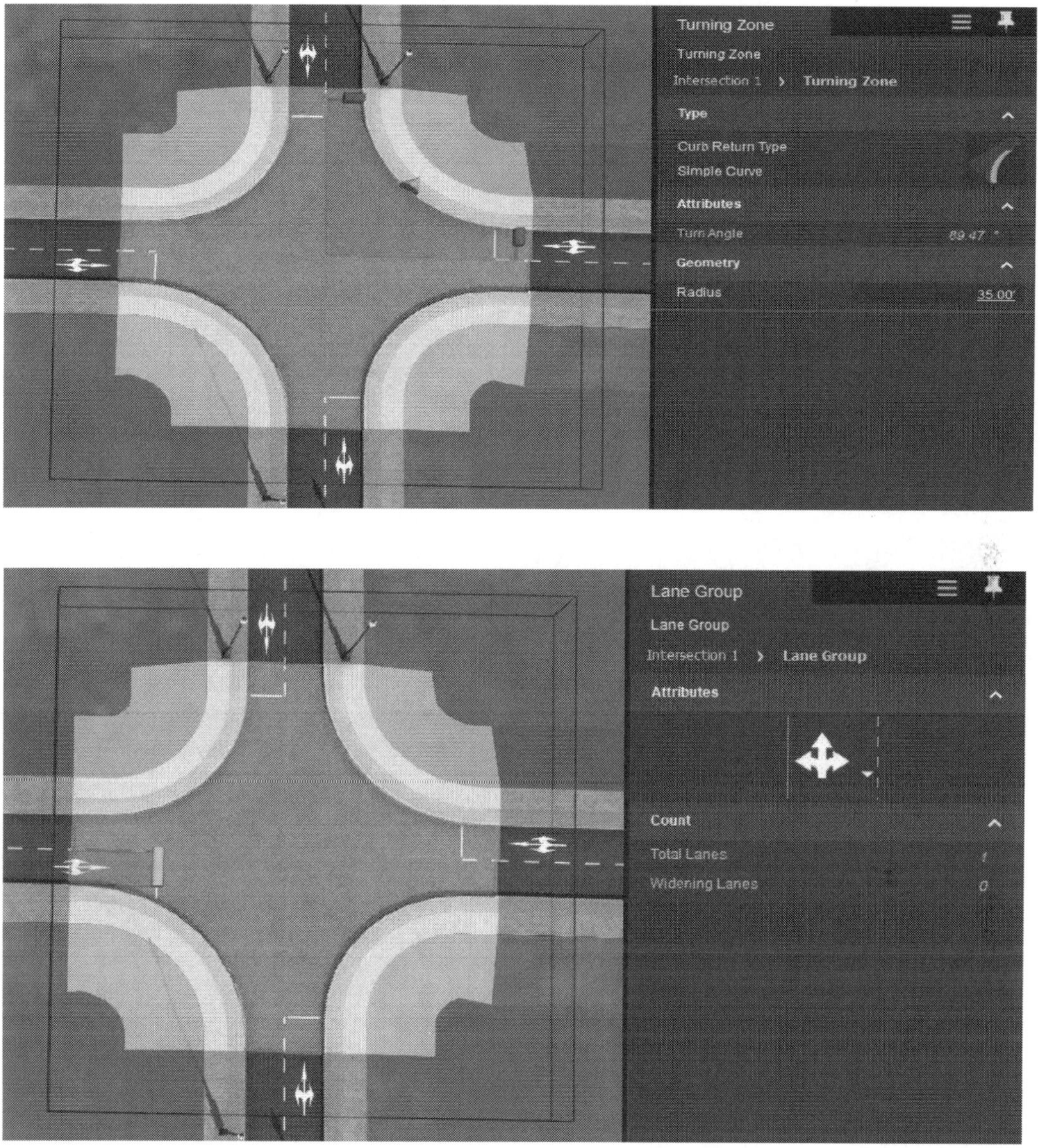

Figure 4–116

It is recommended that you name the intersection for easy identification.

Junction Type

When an intersection is selected, the *Type* area displays in the *Intersection* asset card. Two junction types, **standard intersection** and **roundabout**, are currently available, as shown in Figure 4–117. Roundabouts are discussed in the next section.

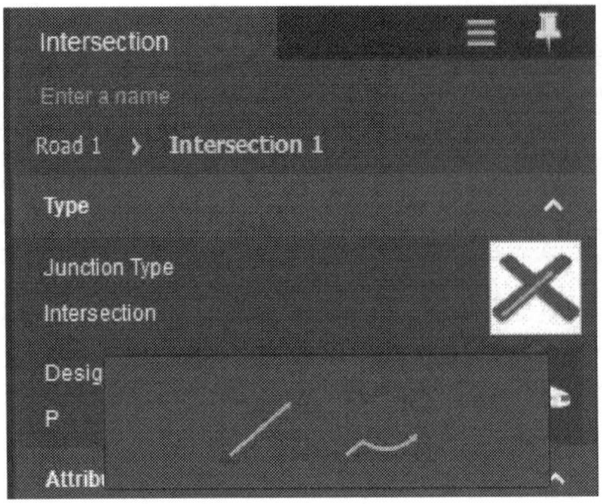

Figure 4–117

Standard Intersection

The *Standard Intersection* junction type is for three-way and four-way intersections. When a *Standard Intersection* junction type is selected, you can modify the vehicle class and turning zones. You can also create a traffic simulation.

Vehicle Class

Various design vehicle classes are available to set for the intersection rating, as shown in Figure 4–118. Changing the rating causes the intersection geometry to adjust in order to accommodate the design vehicle class.

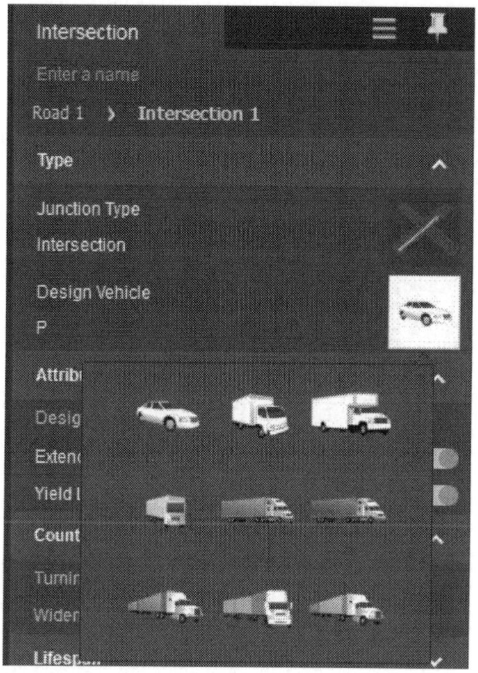

Figure 4–118

Turning Zone

Once an intersection is selected, you can select any of the turning zones within the intersection. This causes the *Turning Zone* stack to display, as shown in Figure 4–119. The curve type and curve radius for the curb return can be modified using the *Turning Zone* stack. If the **Simple Curve with Taper** option is selected, the *Radius*, *Offset*, and *Taper* parameters can all be set, as shown on the far right in Figure 4–119.

Figure 4–119

Lane Markings

In the *Intersection* stack, under *Attributes*, you can modify how lanes are painted through the intersection. Lane markings can extend into intersections and create a yield line, as shown in Figure 4–120.

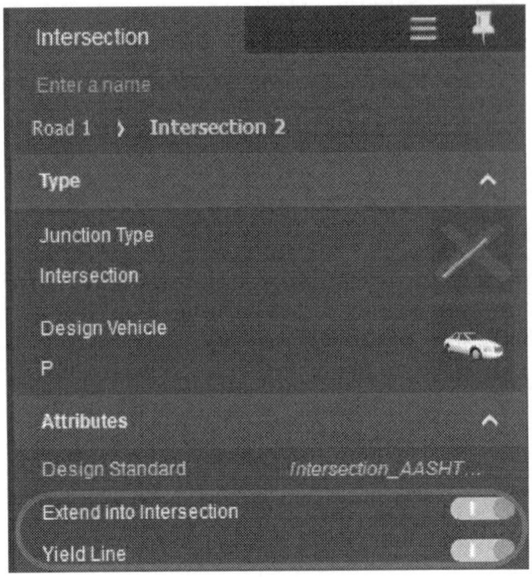

Figure 4–120

In order to set the directional arrows that indicate which way traffic can flow, you must select the lane group in the model. In the *Lane Group* stack, you can set the turn arrows under *Attributes*, as shown in Figure 4–121.

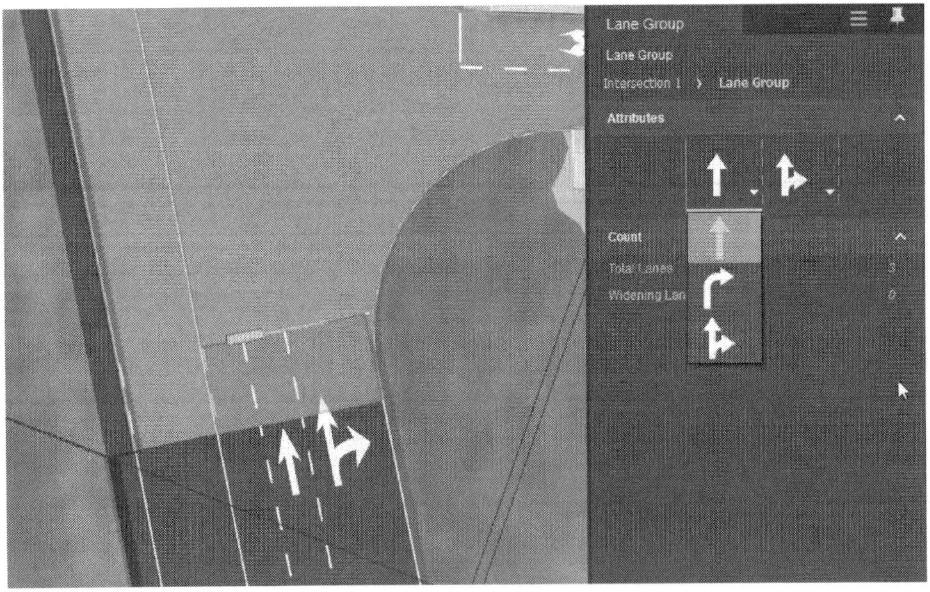

Figure 4–121

4.9 Roundabouts

The *Roundabout* junction type replaces the intersection geometry with a circular intersection for almost continuous traffic flow in one direction around a central island. There are several roundabout options to select from, as shown in Figure 4–122.

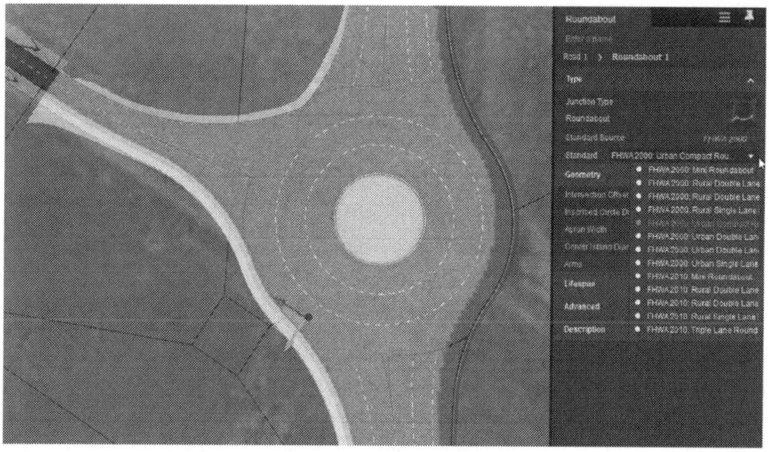

Figure 4–122

Once a roundabout is placed, you can use gizmos to modify it in both the horizontal and vertical directions, as shown in Figure 4–123. To see the vertical gizmos, the model must be orbited more than 45° from a plan view.

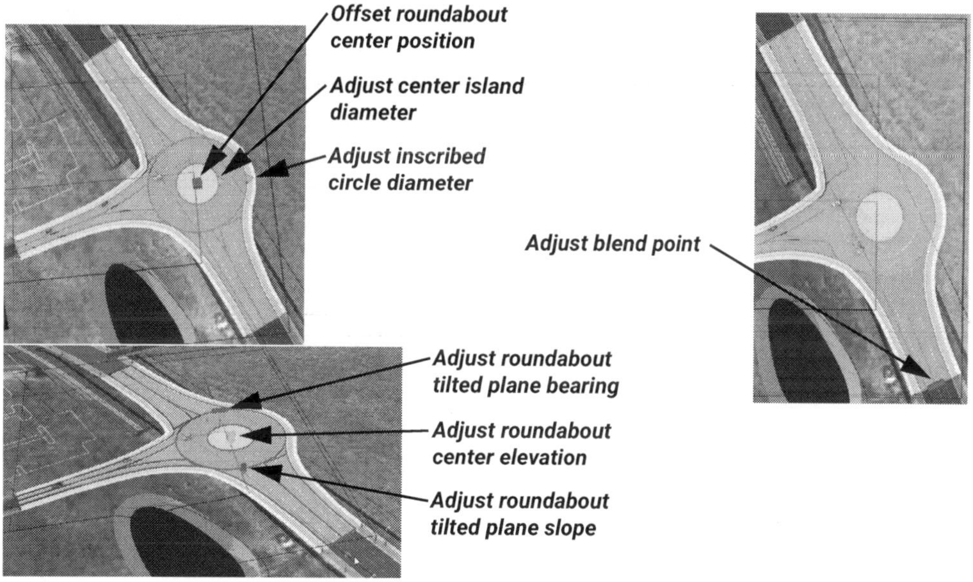

Figure 4–123

Practice 4g
Modify Intersections

Practice Objectives

- Modify a standard intersection.
- Create a roundabout where two component roads intersect.

In this practice, you will modify a standard intersection to increase the curb radius. You will then turn another standard intersection into a roundabout to create a more continuous traffic flow.

Task 1: Modify a standard intersection.

1. Continue working in the same model as the last practice. If you closed the file, on the *Home* screen, click **Open**. In the *InfraWorks Practice Files\4-Roads* folder, select **CreateRoads.sqlite** and click **Open**.
2. If you did not complete the last task, select **F_Task1** in the (Proposals) drop-down list to make it current.
3. Click (Bookmarks) and select **Hotel Intersection**. Zoom in to the intersection.
4. Select the intersection. In the *Intersection* stack, name the intersection **Ascent Hotel-Redwood**. Naming intersections will facilitate importing data into Civil 3D.
5. In the *Design Vehicle* field, select **WB-40**, as shown in Figure 4–124. Once it is selected, you will note the turning lane radii of the intersection increase to accommodate the truck.

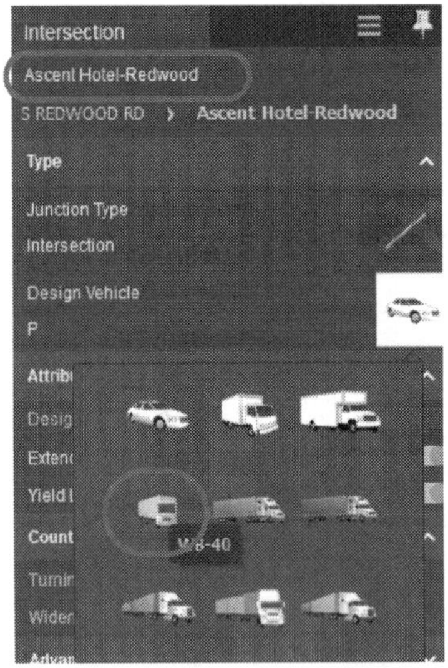

Figure 4–124

6. In the model, select the northeast turning zone of the intersection.
7. In the *Turning Zone* stack, change *Taper* to **20:1**, as shown in Figure 4–125.

Figure 4–125

8. In the model, select the west lane on the north side of the intersection. In the *Lane Group* stack, change the lane to a straight only lane, as shown in Figure 4–126.

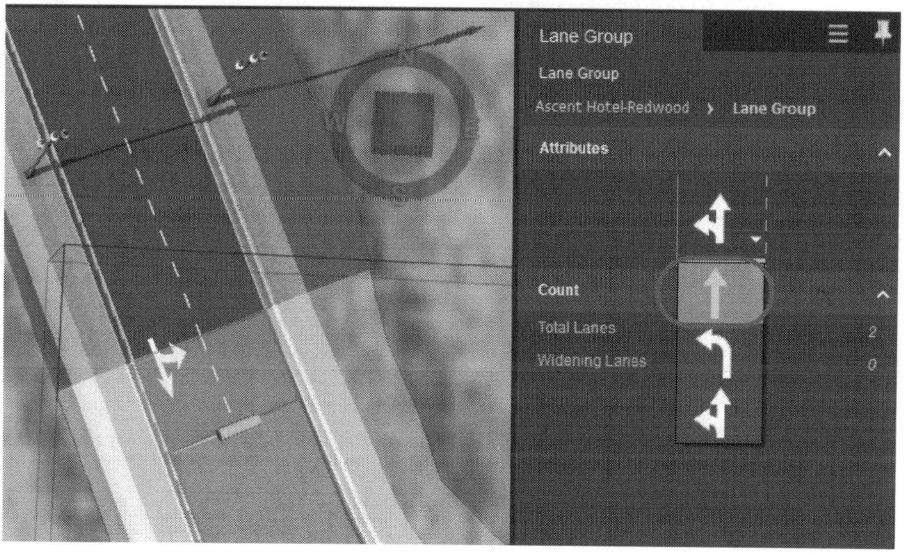

Figure 4–126

9. In the model, select the north lane of **Ascent Hotel Drive** of the intersection. In the *Lane Group* stack, change the lane to a right only lane, as shown in Figure 4–127.

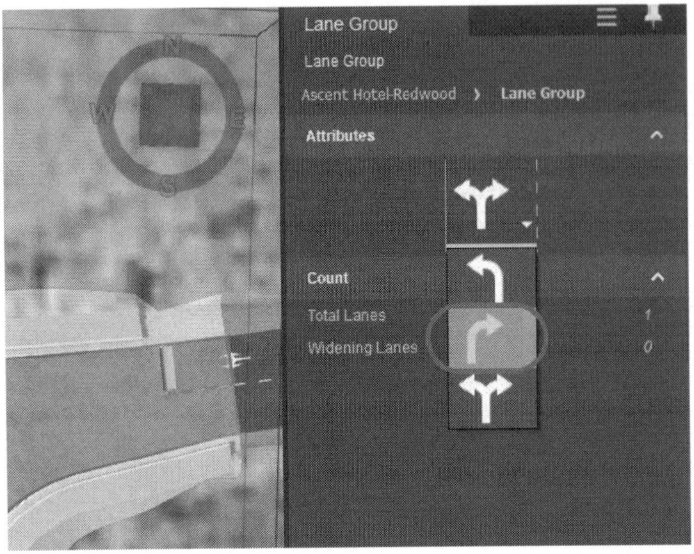

Figure 4–127

10. Note the difference in the centerline marking of **S Redwood Dr**. It is now continuous and not broken in the intersection, since no left turns are allowed, as shown in Figure 4–128.

Figure 4–128

11. Press <Esc> to clear the selection of the intersection.

Task 2: Turn a standard intersection into a roundabout.

The design team has decided to look at the option of replacing the intersection with a roundabout.

1. Continue working in the same model as the previous task. If you did not complete the previous task, select the **F_Task2** proposal to make it current.
2. Click (Bookmarks) and select **Hotel Intersection**. Zoom in to the intersection.
3. Select the intersection.
4. In the *Intersection* asset card, under *Type,* for the *Junction Type*, select **Roundabout**.
5. In the *Standard* drop-down list, select **FHWA 2000-Urban Compact Roundabout**, as shown in Figure 4–129.

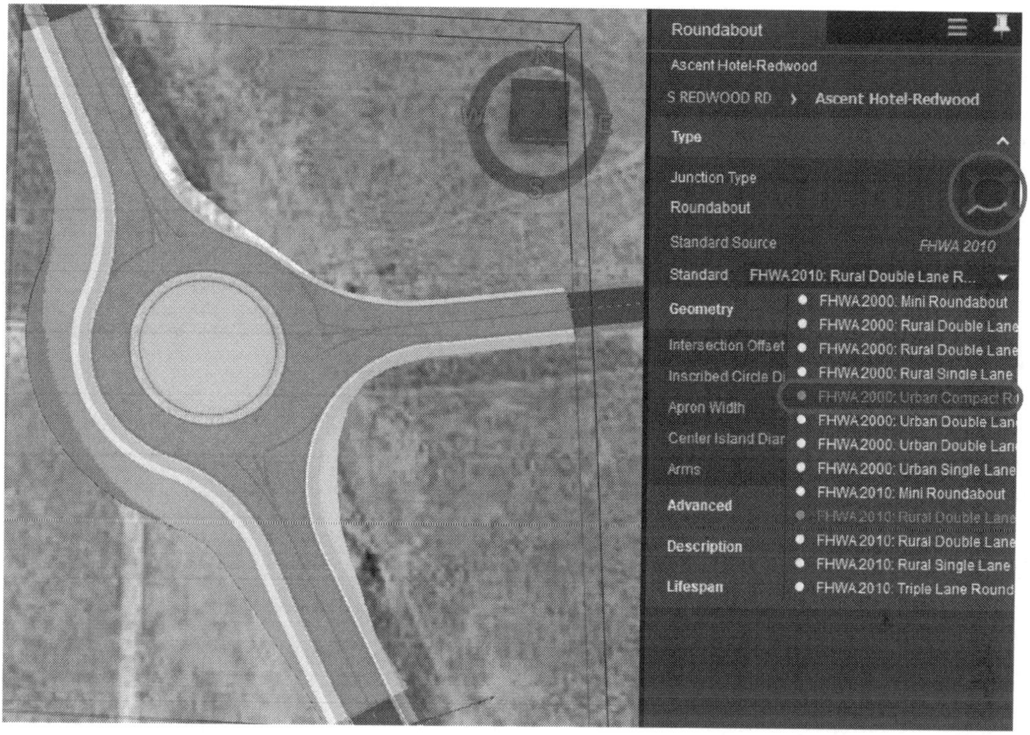

Figure 4–129

6. In the model, select the center island of the roundabout. Click the (Offset roundabout center position gizmo) and move the center about **40** feet to the east and **20** feet to the south, as shown in Figure 4–130.

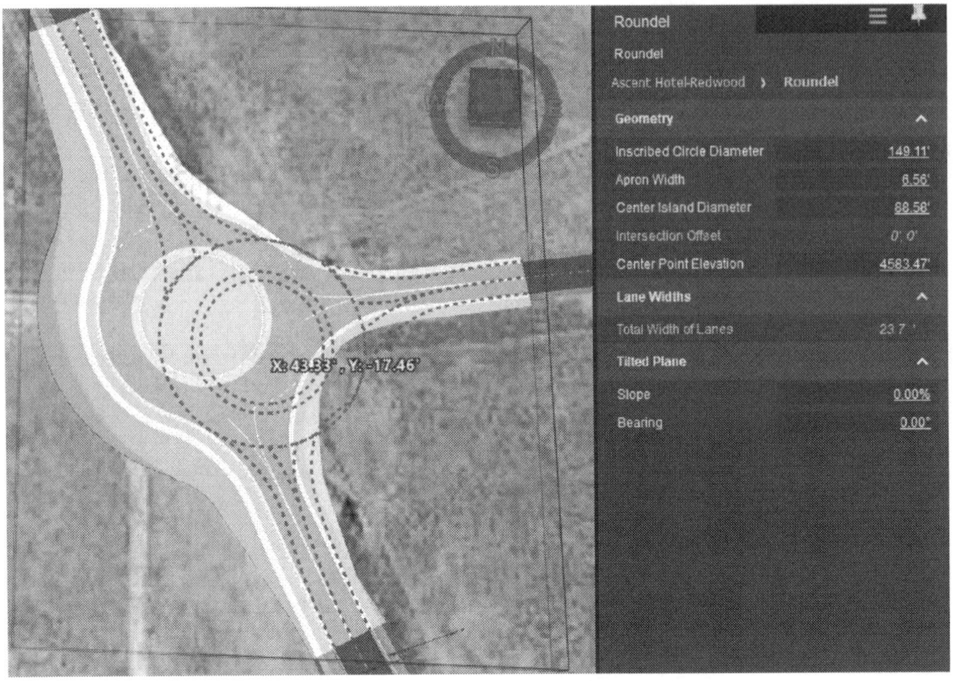

Figure 4–130

7. Orbit the model more than 45° from plan view. Click the (Adjust roundabout tilted plane bearing gizmo) and move it to align with **Ascent Hotel Drive**, then click the (Adjust roundabout tilted plane slope gizmo) and move it up about **4**%, as shown in Figure 4–131.

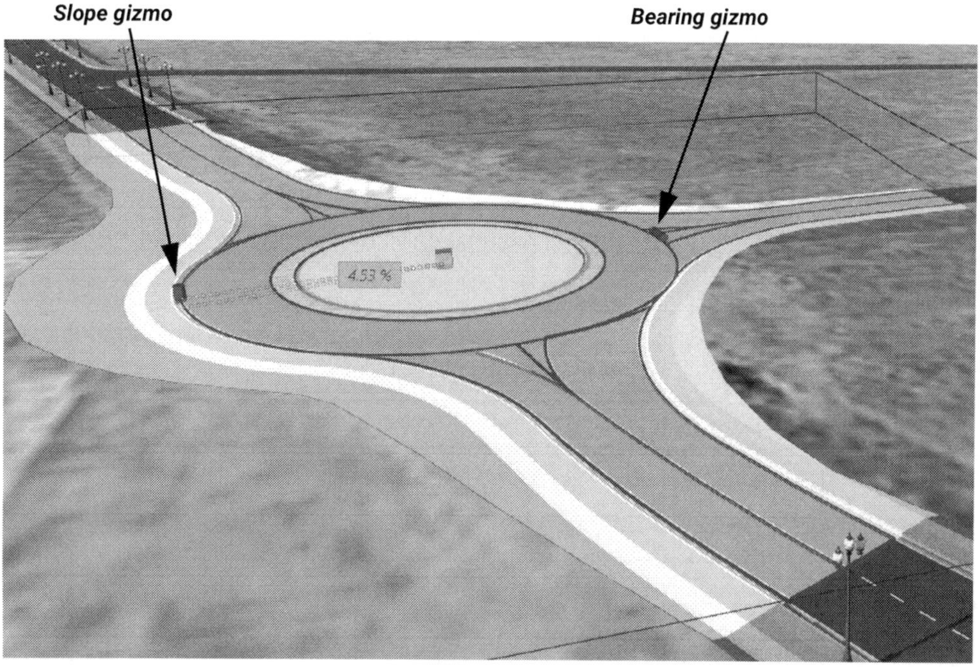

Figure 4–131

8. Press <Esc> to clear the selection of the roundabout.

End of practice

Chapter Review Questions

1. How does a right of way differ from a parcel or an easement?
    a. There is no difference.
    b. A right of way enables you to offset an existing feature parallel to its centerline, while parcels or easements must have each segment drawn in.
    c. Parcels or easements enable you to offset an existing feature parallel to its centerline, while a right of way must have each segment drawn in.

2. Which of the following road functions would be used to set a maximum design speed of 50 mph?
    a. Freeway
    b. Arterial
    c. Collector
    d. Local

3. Which of the following dialog boxes can be used to set the component road standards? (Select all that apply.)
    a. New Model
    b. Application Options
    c. Model Properties
    d. Model Explorer

4. You can modify road geometry annotations that display in the model window when the road is selected.
    a. True
    b. False

5. You can click on a specific grading on one side of the road to edit its parameters independent of the rest of the road.
    a. True
    b. False

6. Intersection objects are created automatically when two component roads cross each other.
   a. True
   b. False

7. Which of the following types can be used for intersections? (Select all that apply.)
   a. Single Point Urban Interchange (SPUI)
   b. 3-way Intersection
   c. 4-way Intersection
   d. Roundabout

Command Summary

Button	Command	Location
	**Component Road**	• **Toolbar:** *Create* tab>*Transportation* panel
	**Easements**	• **Toolbar:** *Create* tab>*Environment* drop-down list
	**Parcels**	• **Toolbar:** *Create* tab>*Environment* drop-down list
	**Planning Road**	• **Toolbar:** *Create* tab>*Transportation* panel
	**Profile View**	• **Toolbar** • Right-click menu when component road is selected
	**Right of Ways**	• **Toolbar:** *Create* tab>*Transportation* drop-down list

Chapter 5

Waterways and Drainage

The Drainage Design for InfraWorks® tools enable you to add drainage features to component roads. You can use the rule-based tool sets to lay out a drainage network and then follow a four-step process to identify and analyze watersheds and their stream flows, create and modify culverts, create pavement drainage networks, and review the quantities of materials for culverts or pavement drainage networks by road, type, and number. In this chapter, you will also learn how to work with the conceptual design tools for pipeline and pipeline connectors, as well as create conceptual water areas and rivers.

Learning Objectives

- Determine the extents of a watershed area.
- Create and modify culverts.
- Create water features in a model to represent lakes, ponds, rivers, or streams.
- Add pipelines and pipeline connectors to a model to indicate where utilities are to be located.
- Design pavement drainage along a component road.
- Calculate quantities for a drainage network.

5.1 Watershed Analysis

Determining the discharge of a stream is important for designing culverts and other structures used to protect transportation systems from ponding, freezing, and water runoff damage. With the Drainage Design for InfraWorks module, you can add drainage networks to the model. Before creating the drainage network, it is important to run a watershed analysis to determine the extents of a watershed area. By running a watershed analysis, the watershed extents and stream locations display in the model. Additionally, pins are placed where the streams cross a component road to indicate that either a culvert or bridge is required.

The analysis identifies the existing drainage patterns prior to road placement and design. Therefore, it uses the original terrain surface that was in the model before any component roads were created. A single analysis can identify multiple watersheds, each of which is a selectable feature. During the analysis process, square grids of terrain are sampled. The grid spacing and stream threshold can each be adjusted in the *Create Watersheds* asset card, as shown in Figure 5–1. Lowering the values finds smaller streams, but also requires more analysis. Raising the values finds larger streams and reduces the analysis.

- **Grid Spacing:** Controls the size of the square grids sampled for the terrain.
- **Stream Threshold:** Sets the number of grid cells used to define streams. For example, a stream threshold of 50 indicates that a stream is created once there are a minimum of 50 upstream grid squares flowing into a stream's starting point.

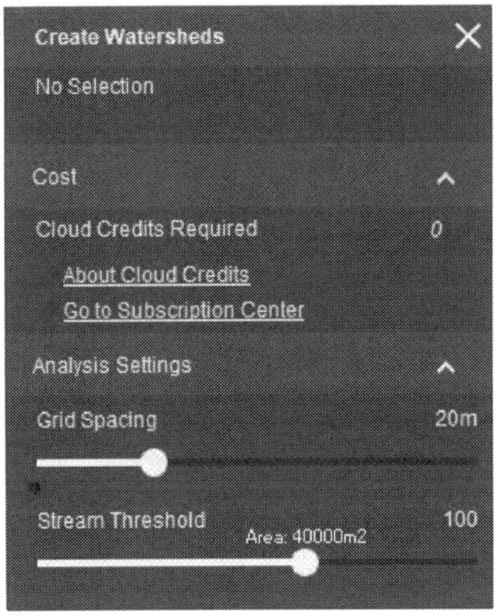

Figure 5–1

Modify Peak Flows

Once a watershed is created, it contains a *Watershed* asset card. Within the *Watershed* asset card, the peak flows can only be modified if the *Hydrology Method* is set to **User Defined**. However, two other methods are available that cause the *Peak Flow* fields to calculate automatically, as shown in Figure 5–2:

- **Regression** analysis is available for select areas. It enables you to set the state and region.
- **Rational** analysis enables you to enter a *Runoff Coefficient* and a *Rainfall Intensity* for 100-year storms.

Figure 5–2

How To: Run a Watershed Analysis to a Component Road

1. In the *Analyze* tab>*Drainage* panel, click (Watershed).
2. In the model, all of the component roads are highlighted, as shown in Figure 5–3.

Figure 5–3

3. Select how you want to calculate the watershed:

To calculate a watershed...	Start the analysis by...
Upstream from a point	Double-clicking on a point in a valley or low-lying area.
Along a component road	Select a component road and press <Enter>. The watershed is calculated upstream from the selected road.
Along a region of a component road	Selecting a component road, clicking to select the start and end points of the region, and then pressing <Enter>. The watershed is calculated upstream from the selected road.

4. In the *Create Watersheds* asset card, set the *Grid Spacing* and *Stream Threshold* sliders according to the terrain being analyzed, as shown in Figure 5–4.

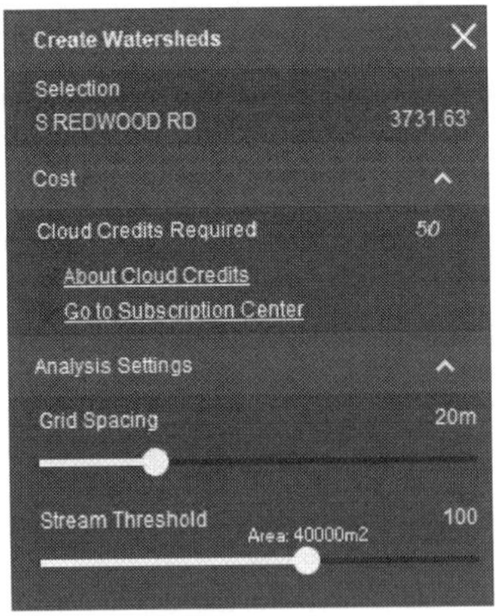

Figure 5–4

5. Once the analysis is complete, the watershed boundary and stream network display in the model, as shown in Figure 5–5. Additionally, a pin should display in the model at the point that a stream crosses the road.

Figure 5–5

6. In the model, select the watershed area.
7. In the *Watershed* asset card, do the following:
   - Set the *Hydrology Method*.
   - Set additional field values according to the hydrology method selected.
8. Press <Esc> to clear the selection of the watershed area.

9. To control the watershed area display, do the following, as shown in Figure 5–6:

   - In the *Manage* tab>*Model* panel, click (Model Explorer). In the *Model Explorer*, right-click on *Surface Layers* and select **Surface Layers**. Alternatively, in the *Manage* tab>*Display* panel, select (Surface Layers).
   - Under the *Watersheds & Streams* category, turn off the **Watershed** layer by clicking (Show/Hide data source contents).

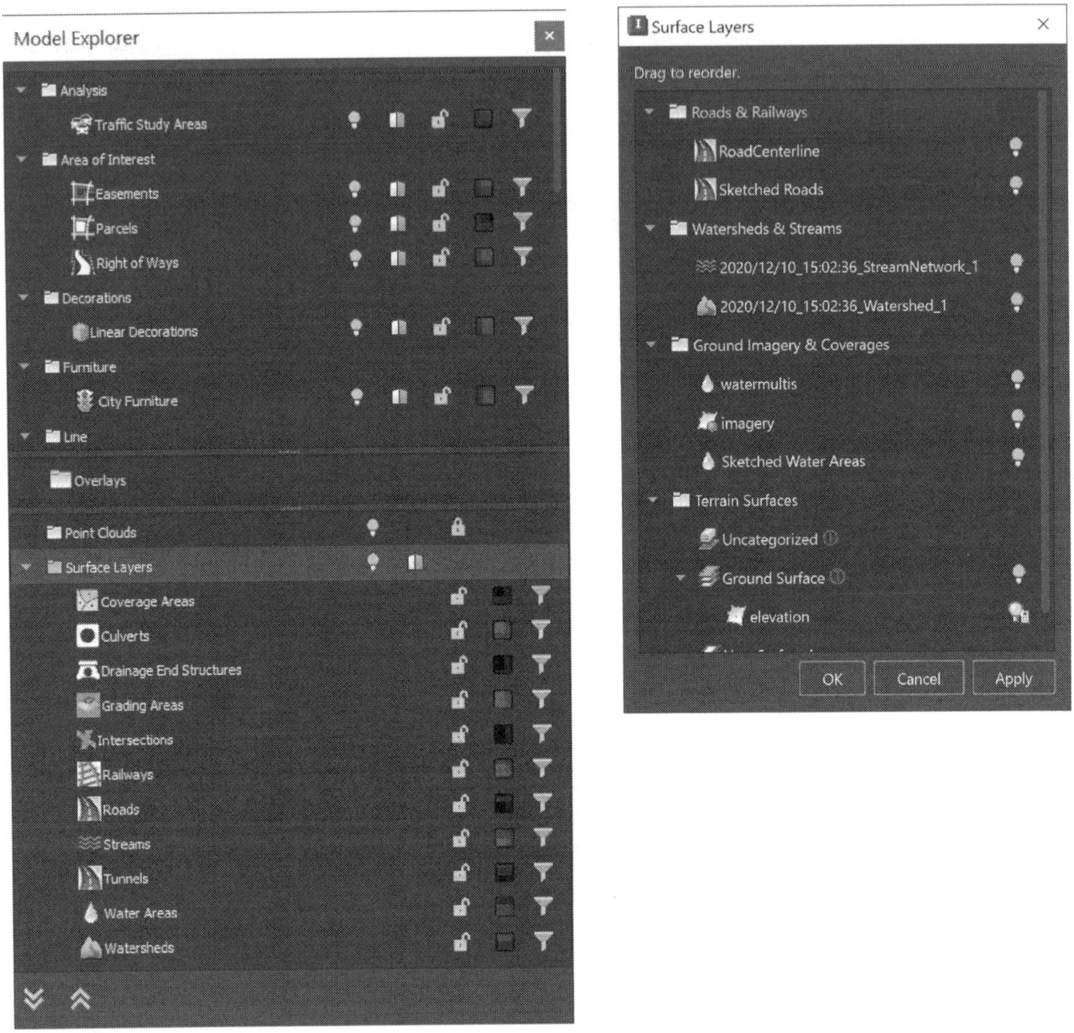

Figure 5–6

Practice 5a
Create a Watershed

Practice Objective

- Create a watershed upstream from a component road.

In this practice, you will create a watershed, as shown in Figure 5–7.

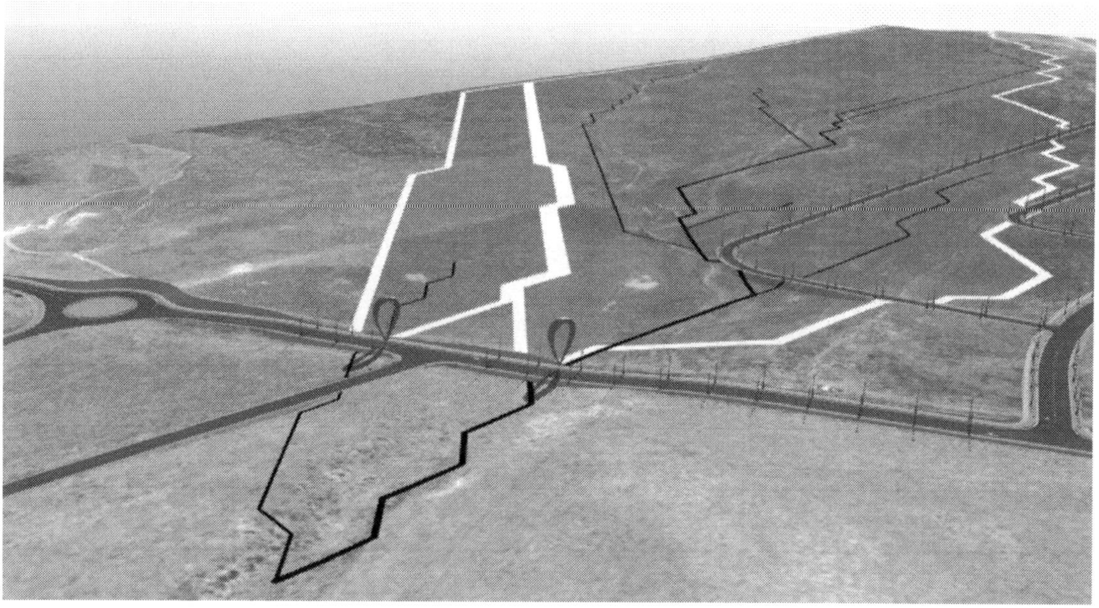

Figure 5–7

Note: *To use this feature, access to the Internet is required. If no access is available, the analysis will fail and display a message similar to Figure 5–8.*

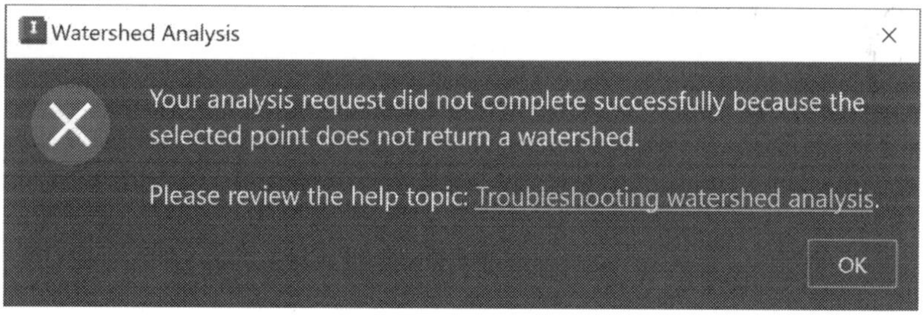

Figure 5–8

1. On the *Home* screen, click **Open**.
2. In the *InfraWorks Practice Files\5-Waterways-Drainage* folder, select **CreateDrainage.sqlite** and click **Open**.
3. Click  (Bookmarks) and select **River**. Ensure that **A_Task1** is the current proposal.
4. In the *Analyze* tab>*Drainage* panel, click  (Watershed).
5. In the *Create Watersheds* asset card, set the *Grid Spacing* to **15** and the *Stream Threshold* to **70**, as shown in Figure 5–9. The component roads are highlighted in the model.
6. Select the **S Redwood Rd** component road, then select the section shown in Figure 5–9, approximately from station **800** to station **1400**.

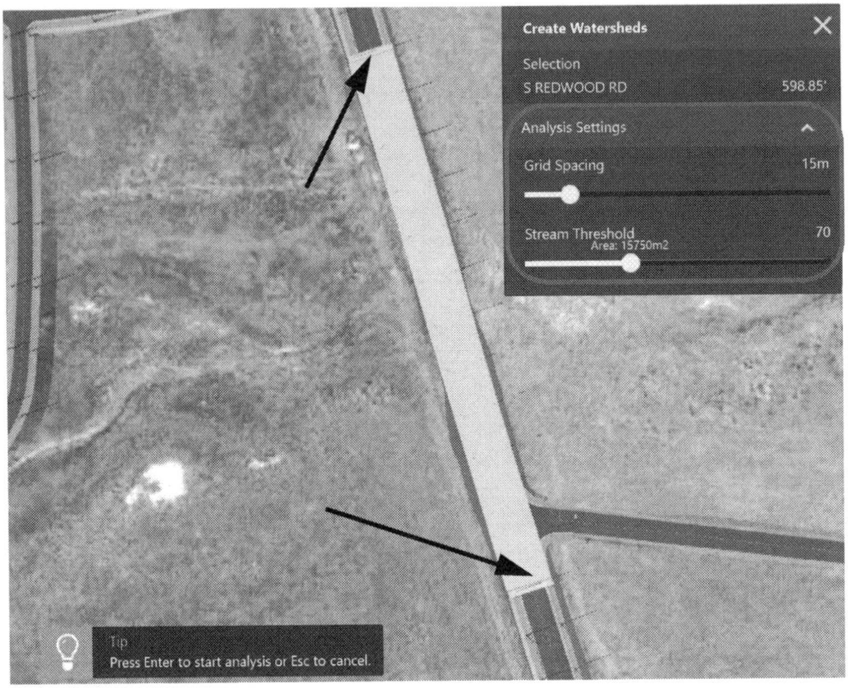

Figure 5–9

7. Press <Enter> to analyze the section of road.

8. Two watersheds have been created, along with two point of interest (POI) markers where the watershed drains across the road, designated by the black lines, as shown Figure 5–10. The southern (lower) watershed will eventually get diverted into the northern one and can be deleted along with its POI marker. Select the lower watershed and press <Delete>, then select the marker and press <Delete>.

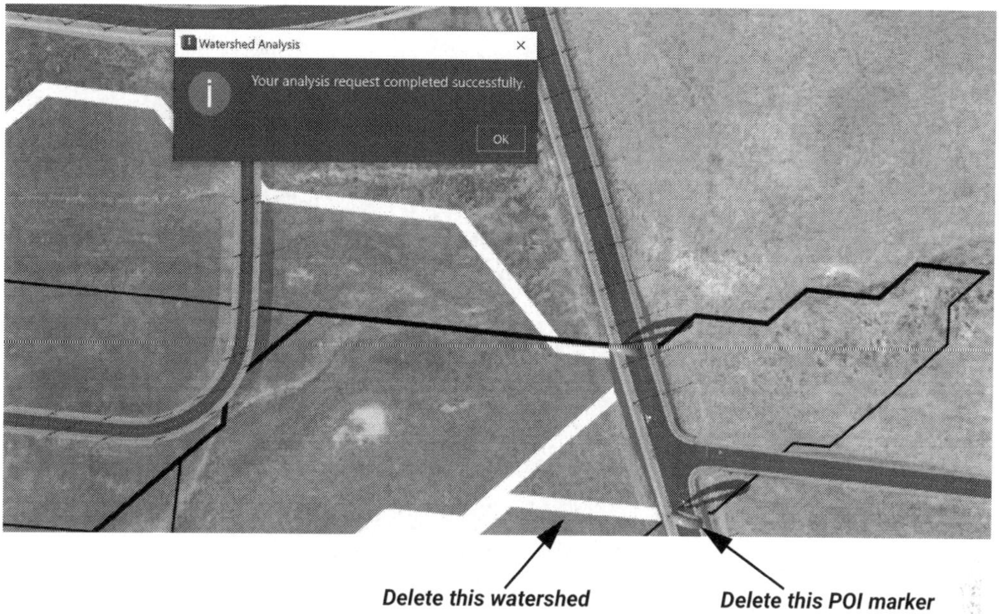

Figure 5–10

9. In the model, select the remaining watershed area.

10. In the *Watershed* asset card, set the following options, as shown in Figure 5–11:
    - *Name:* **Heather Run**
    - *Hydrology Method*: **Regression**
    - *State*: **Utah**
    - *Region:* **Region 3**

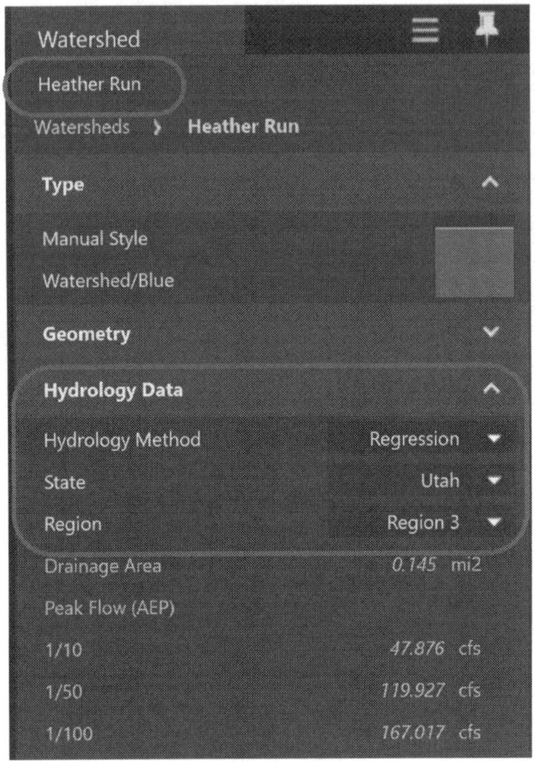

Figure 5–11

11. Press <Esc> to clear the selection of the watershed area.

End of practice

5.2 Create and Modify Culverts

Add Culverts Automatically

Once a watershed analysis has been run, one or more culverts can be added to the model anywhere that streams cross the component road. Once added, the culvert information displays in the model in the form of tooltips, as well as in the *Culvert* asset card, as shown in Figure 5–12.

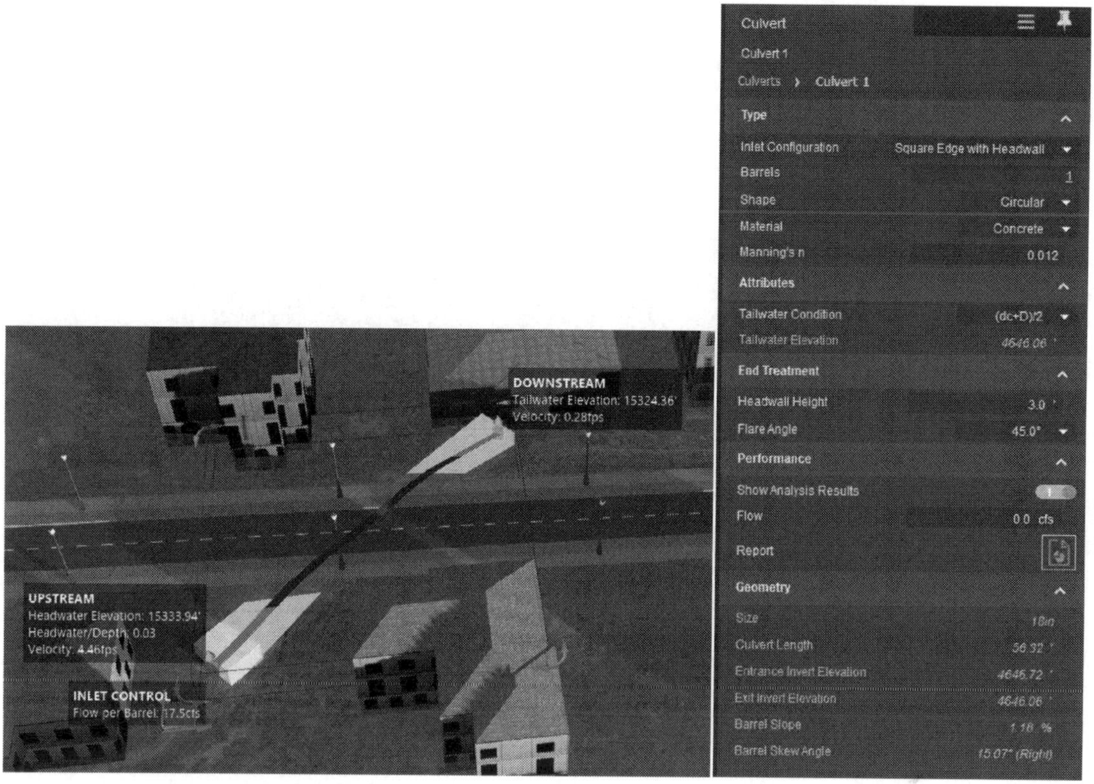

Figure 5–12

How To: Add Culverts at Stream Crossings Automatically

1. In the model, run a watershed analysis using the  (Watershed) tool.
2. In the model, select the component road.
3. Right-click on the component road and select **Drainage>Add Culverts**, as shown in Figure 5–13.

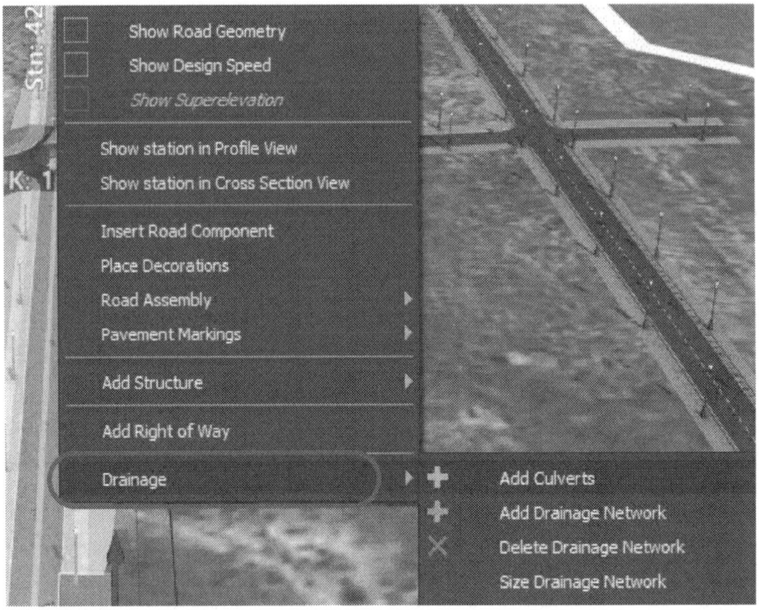

Figure 5–13

4. Culverts display in the model at each of the stream crossing pins that were placed during the watershed analysis. To clear the culvert selection, press <Esc>.

Create Culverts Manually

Culverts can be added automatically or manually. The benefit of adding a culvert manually is that it can be added to objects other than component roads.

How To: Create a Culvert Manually

1. In the *Create* tab>*Drainage* panel, click  (Culvert).
2. Click two points in the model to place the beginning and ending points for the culvert.
3. Press <Esc> to clear the culvert selection.

Modify a Culvert

Culverts can be modified using gizmos or the *Culvert* asset card. If the culverts were created automatically using the **Add Culverts** command, they can be updated automatically as well. If the road style or number of lanes are changed for a component road, the culvert length, slope, and invert elevations change to match the new design.

The gizmos available for editing culverts manually are described in the table below.

Gizmo	Transformation	Description
	**Elevation/ Control Point**	Stretches culverts horizontally and vertically, changing the elevation or beginning/ending point location.
	**Headwall Height**	Stretches the headwall height without changing its length or width.
	**Move**	Moves a culvert without changing its size or shape.
	**Rotate**	Rotates a culvert around its Z-axis.
	**Size**	Changes the size of the barrel.

The following features and options of a culvert can be modified using the *Culvert* asset card, shown in Figure 5–14:

- *Barrels:* **1** or **2**
- *Shape:* **Box** or **Circular**
- *Material:* **Concrete** or **Corrugate Metal**
- *Manning's n:* Coefficient values to triangles
- *Tailwater Condition:* **(dc+D)/2**, **Crown**, **Critical**, **Normal**, or **User Defined**
- *End Treatment: Headwall Height* and *Flare Angle*
- *Show Analysis Results:* Toggle on/off

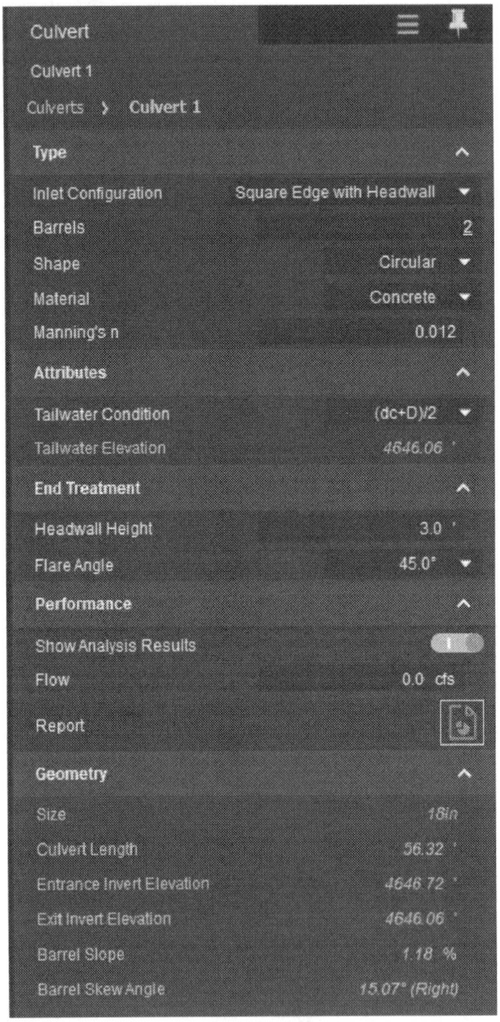

Figure 5–14

Practice 5b
Create a Culvert

Practice Objective

- Add a culvert to a component road.

In this practice, you will create a culvert, as shown in Figure 5–15. When the watershed was calculated, InfraWorks placed a marker at the discharge point at the component road. This is where you will place a culvert.

Figure 5–15

1. Continue working in the same model as the last practice. If you closed the file, on the *Home* screen, click **Open**. In the *InfraWorks Practice Files\5-Waterways-Drainage* folder, select **CreateDrainage.sqlite** and click **Open**.
2. If you did not complete the last task, select **B_Task1** in the (Proposals) drop-down list to make it current.
3. Click (Bookmarks) and select **Bridge Area.**

4. In the model, select **S Redwood Rd**. Right-click and select **Drainage>Add Culverts**, as shown in Figure 5–16.

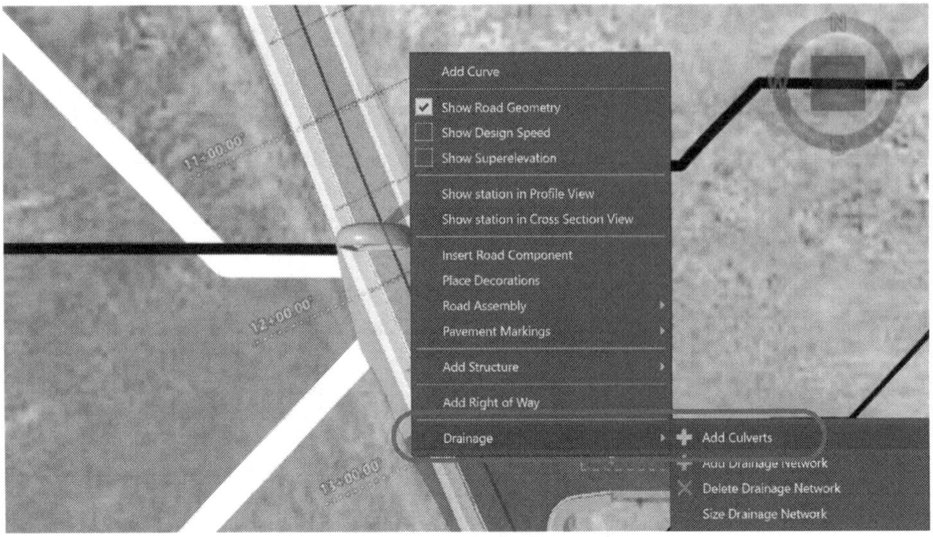

Figure 5–16

5. Two culverts have been created where the black watershed stream crosses **S Redwood Rd**, as shown in Figure 5–17. The lower one will not be necessary as the two watersheds are to be merged, so it can be deleted. In the model, select the lower culvert (you can find it by orbiting and zooming in on where the black watershed stream crosses **S Redwood Rd**) and press <Delete>.
6. Select the remaining culvert by the POI marker.
7. In the *Culvert* asset card, name the culvert **Redwood Rd - Heather Run**. Set *Barrels* to **2** and ensure that under *Performance*, **Show Analytical Results** is toggled on, as shown in Figure 5–17.
    - Note how the analytical results change as you increase the barrels to 2. If you did not see the changes, set *Barrels* back to 1 and then up to 2 again to see them.

8. In the *Culvert* asset card, set the *Shape* to **Box**. Note the changes, as shown in Figure 5–17.

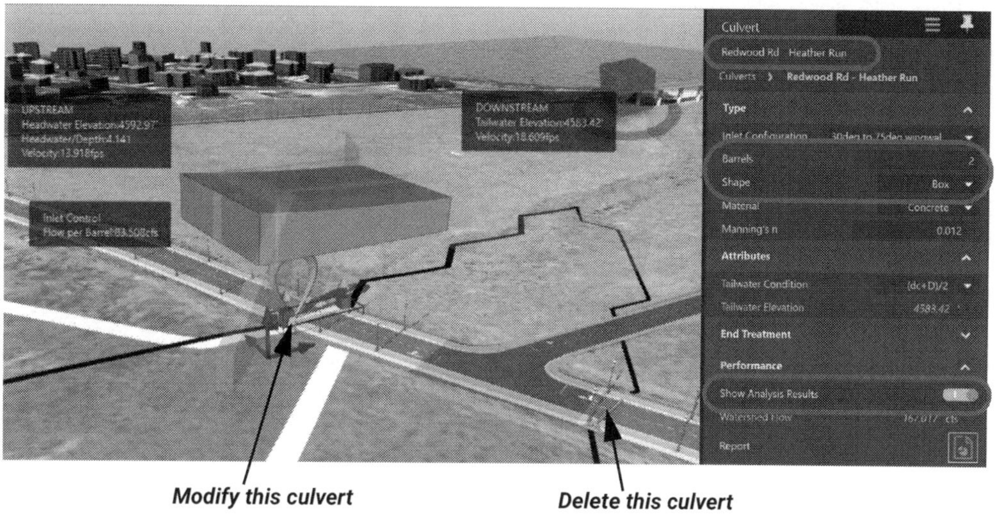

Figure 5–17

9. In the model, click the lower (Control gizmo) to extend the end of the culvert past the daylight line on each side of the road, as shown in Figure 5–18.

Figure 5–18

10. In the model, click the (Move in the Z axis gizmo) to move the culvert in the Z-direction down about 3.5 feet. The culvert will be better positioned when you put in the stream in the next task.

11. To clear the culvert selection, press <Esc>.

12. Since it is no longer needed, you can select the cyan POI marker and press <Delete>.

End of practice

5.3 Create Water Features in a Model

When designing a new community, water features are often required. Water features have a number of purposes. They can act as a water retention area that is used by local residents for drinking water, such as a reservoir. They can also be used to divert excess water away from homes and businesses to avoid flooding. This is often required when new hard surfaces prevent water from being absorbed into the ground as it did before the land was developed. Finally, water areas can be used to provide recreation and make an area more visually appealing.

Water areas are a surface layer in the *Model Explorer*. You can create the following two types of water features:

- **Water Areas:** Enables you to create bodies of water, such as ponds, lakes, and wetlands. To create a body of water, you click points that act as a boundary for the water area. Figure 5–19 shows a small pond water area.

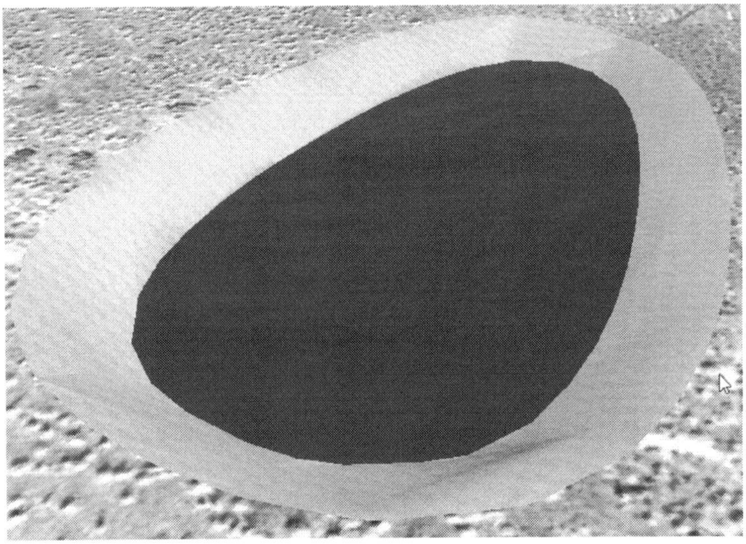

Figure 5–19

- **Rivers:** Enables you to create linear water features, such as canals, rivers, and streams. To create a river, you click points along a linear path. A buffer surrounds the water on either side. The buffer width is set in the *Water* asset card, as shown in Figure 5–20.

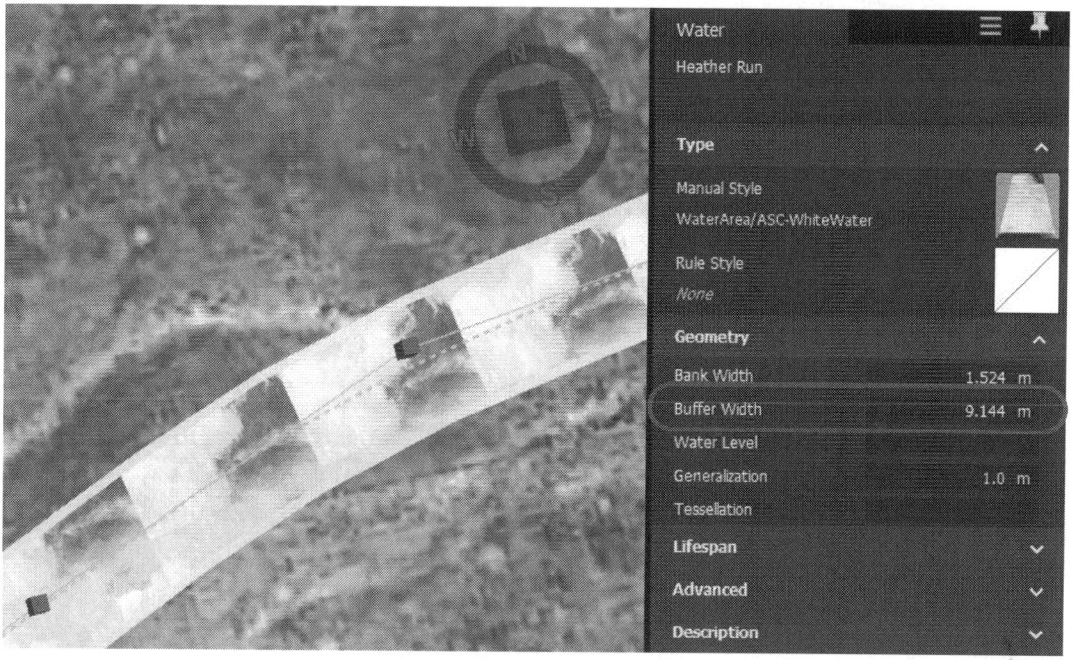

Figure 5–20

How To: Create Rivers or Streams

1. In the *Create* tab>*Environment* drop-down list, click (River).
2. In the *Select Draw Style* asset card, select the required water style, as shown in Figure 5–21.

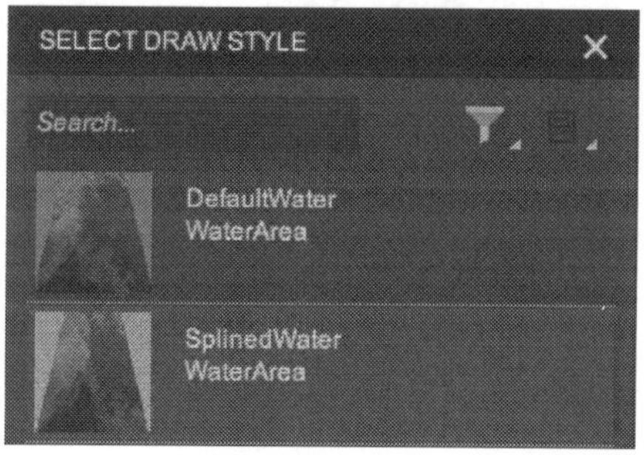

Figure 5–21

3. Click in the model to define the start location of the linear path for the water area.

4. Move the cursor in the direction in which you want the river or steam to run. Type a distance for the length to the next point of intersection (PI) and press <Enter> to set the distance. Click in the model to place the PI.
5. Continue clicking to place PIs until all of the lengths of the river or stream have been created for the water area.
6. Double-click to place the last point and end the command.
7. With the water area selected, in the *Water* asset card, do the following, as shown in Figure 5–22:
   - Set the required *Bank Width*.
   - Set the required *Buffer Width*.
   - Set the required *Water Level*.

   Note: *The Water Level is an absolute elevation for the entire river, causing a flat water surface.*

Figure 5–22

How To: Create Lakes or Ponds

1. In the *Create* tab>*Environment* drop-down list, click (Water Areas).
2. In the *Select Draw Style* asset card, select the required water style, as shown in Figure 5–23.

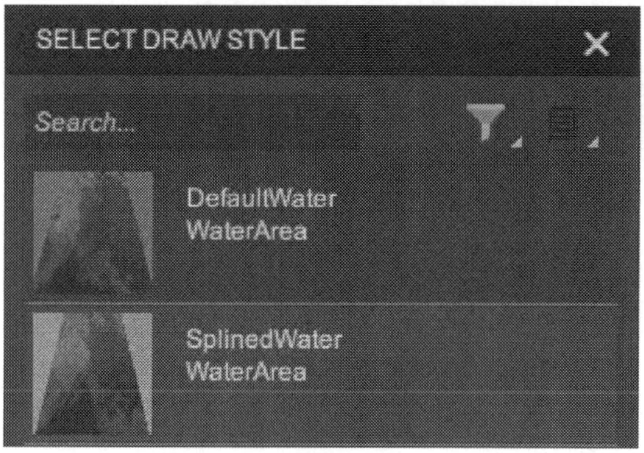

Figure 5–23

3. Click in the model to start the creation of the water boundary.
4. Move the cursor in the direction that you want the water boundary to follow. Type a distance for the length to the next point on the boundary and press <Enter> to set the distance. Click in the model to place the boundary point.
5. Continue clicking in the model until all of the boundary points have been created for the water area.
6. Double-click to place the last boundary point and end the command.

Practice 5c
Create Water Features in the Model

Practice Objective

- Create water features in the model to represent a retention pond.

In this practice, you will create a water area that represents a water retention pond for the new subdivision and a new stream to carry off the watershed.

Task 1: Create water areas.

1. Continue working in the same model as the last practice. If you closed the file, on the *Home* screen, click **Open**. In the *InfraWorks Practice Files\5-Waterways-Drainage* folder, select **CreateDrainage.sqlite** and click **Open**.
2. If you did not complete the last task, select **C_Task1** in the (Proposals) drop-down list to make it current.
3. Click (Bookmarks) and select **School Area**.
4. In the *Create* tab>*Environment* drop-down list, click (Water Areas).
5. In the *Select Draw Style* asset card, select **Splined Water**, as shown in Figure 5–24.

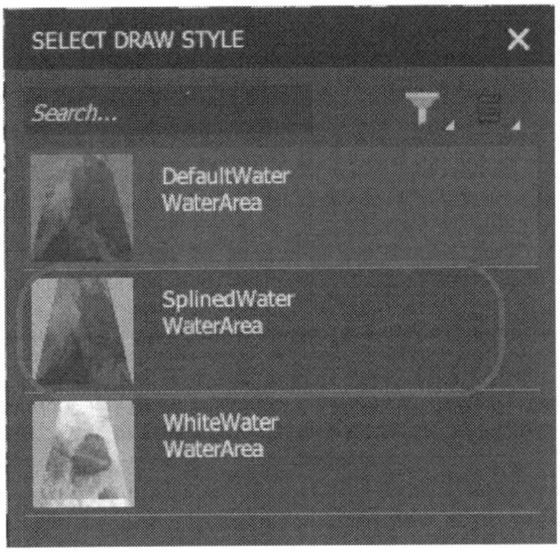

Figure 5–24

6. Click near the entrance to the new neighborhood to start the boundary, as shown in Figure 5–25. Ensure that you leave room for the new railway to be expanded in the future.

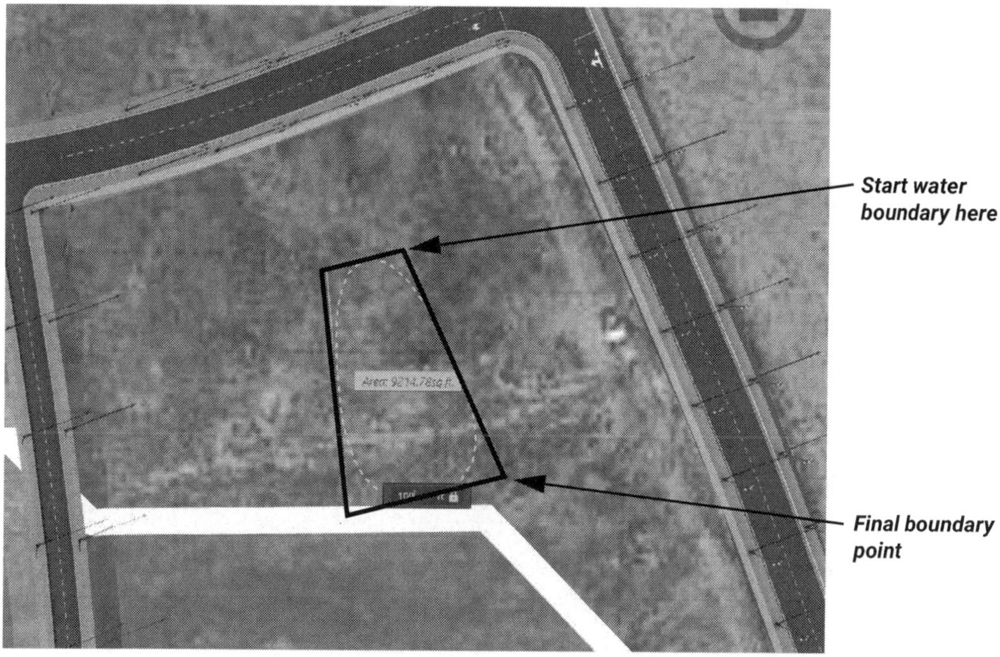

Figure 5–25

7. In the model, move the cursor to the west, parallel to the **Church Loop** road. Type **50** for the length to the next point on the boundary and press <Enter> to set the distance. Click in the model to place the boundary point.
8. Move the cursor due south, parallel to the road. Type **150** for the length to the next point on the boundary and press <Enter> to set the distance. Click in the model to place the boundary point.
9. Move the cursor to the east. Type **100** for the length to the next point on the boundary and press <Enter> to set the distance. Double-click to place the last boundary point and end the command.

10. In the *Water* asset card, enter the following, as shown in Figure 5–26:
    - *Name:* **School Pond**
    - *Bank Width:* **10.0'**
    - *Buffer Width:* **25.0'**
    - Leave the other values as their defaults.

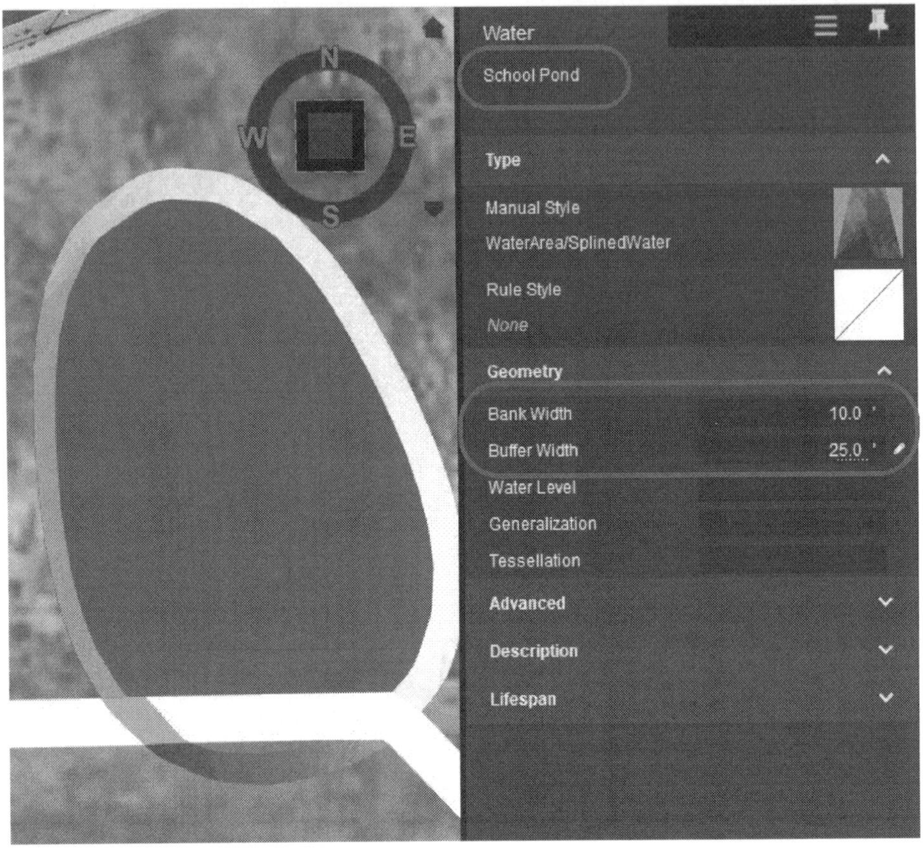

Figure 5–26

11. Press <Esc> twice to clear the selection of the new water area.

Task 2: Create a river.

The developers on the project are concerned about the watershed near their project site and are proposing that a river be created to control the runoff and manage flood waters. For practice, you will create a new material style and add it to a new water style. You will then use the new water style to create a river to the west of Redwood Rd, as shown in Figure 5–27.

Figure 5–27

1. If you did not complete the last task, select the **C_Task2** proposal to make it current.
2. Click (Bookmarks) and select **River**.
3. In the *Manage* tab>*Content* panel, click (*Style Palette*). In the *Style Palette*, use the down arrow in the lower-left area of the panel to select the *Material* tab.
4. At the top of the *Material* tab, click (Add new style catalog).
5. In the center pane, a new folder is created and is prompting you for a name. Type **ASC-Custom** as the new catalog name.
6. Double-click on the new **ASC-Custom** catalog to make it current.
7. At the bottom of the *Material* tab, click (Add new style to current catalog above).

8. Do the following to create the new material style, as shown in Figure 5–28:
   - Set the *Type* to **Texture**.
   - Browse for the **WhiteWater.png** image to use as the texture. (If needed, it can be found in the *InfraWorks Practice Files\References\Images* folder. Click **OK** to dismiss the notification message in the *Added Texture File to Model Resources* alert box).
   - Set both the *Width* and *Height* to **100** ft.
   - Click **OK**.
   - Name the new material **WhiteWater**. (If the material already exists, overwrite it.)

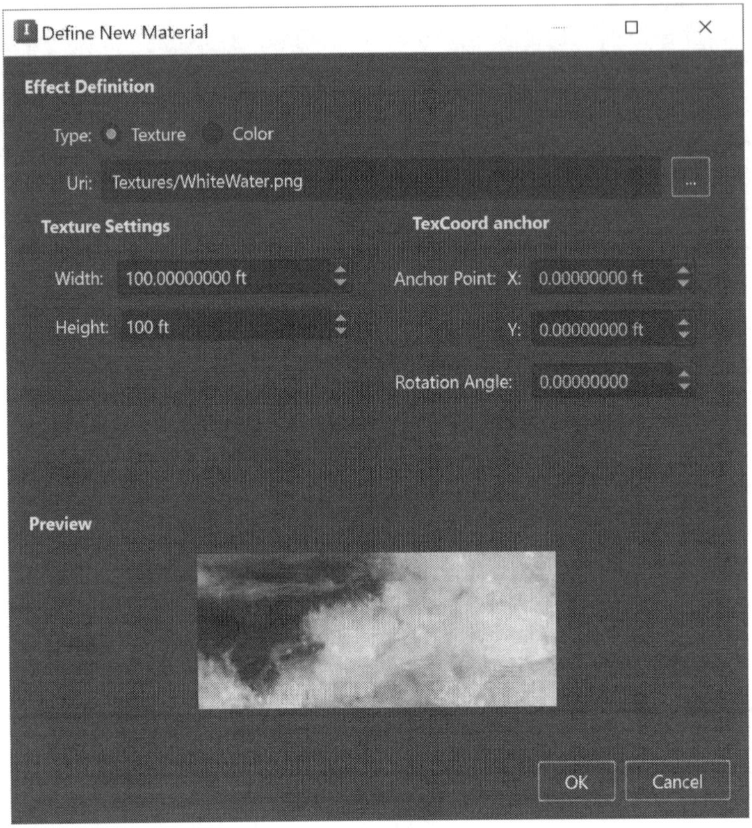

Figure 5–28

9. In the *Style Palette*, use the down arrow in the lower-left area of the panel to select the *Water* tab.
10. Select the **SplinedWater** style, then at the bottom of the *Water* tab, click (Make a local copy of the selected style to the current catalog).
11. Name the copied style **WhiteWater**.

12. Double-click on the **WhiteWater** style. Modify the new style as follows so that it matches Figure 5–29:
    - Set the *Bank width* to **30 ft**.
    - Set the *Water level offset* to (negative) **-5 ft**.
    - Set the *Water surface material* to ***Material/ASC-Custom/WhiteWater***. (Use the ellipsis (...) to browse to the *ASC-Custom* folder and the material you just created.)
    - Click **OK**.

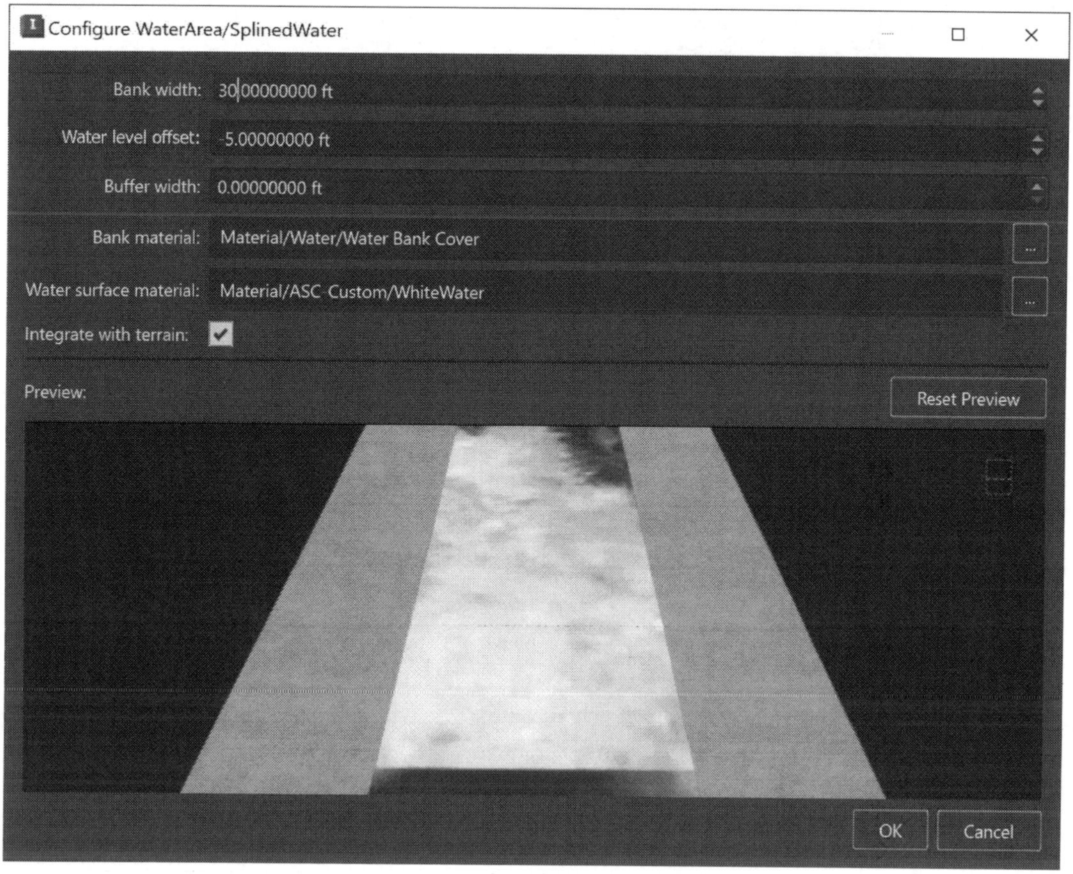

Figure 5–29

13. In the *Create* tab>*Environment* drop-down list, click  (River).
14. In the *Select Draw Style* asset card, select **WhiteWater**.

15. Create a river similar to the one shown in Figure 5–30.

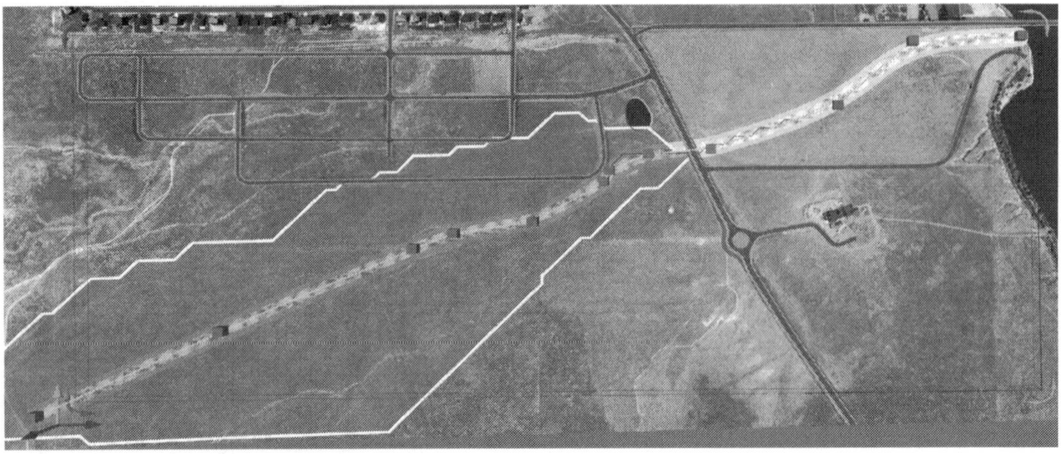

Figure 5–30

16. Press <Esc> to show the river gizmos.
17. In the *Water* asset card, set the following:
    - *Name:* **Heather Run**
    - *Geometry* area:
        - *Bank Width:* **5 ft**
        - *Buffer Width:* **30 ft**
        - *Water Elevation:* leave blank

    Note: *The Water Elevation is an absolute elevation for the entire river, causing a flat water surface. It is not suitable for a watercourse.*

18. Press <Esc> to release the river selection.

19. In the *Manage* tab>*Display* panel, select  (Surface Layers). Under the *Watersheds & Streams* category, turn off the **Watershed** layer (the lower one), as shown in Figure 5–31.

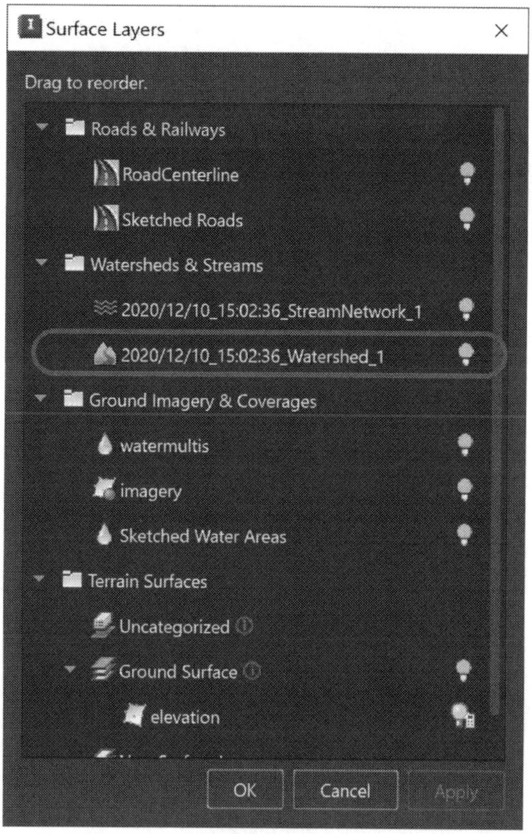

Figure 5–31

End of practice

5.4 Create Pipe Networks in a Model

Utilities are an important part of a project. They provide electricity, gas, water, etc., to a project site. They also provide a way to divert excess storm water.

Creating conceptual utilities in InfraWorks is a two-step process, as both pipelines and pipeline connectors must be created separately. Once created, they can be imported into the Autodesk® Civil 3D® software, where they become a pipe network. Pipelines become Civil 3D pipes, while pipeline connectors become Civil 3D structures. If you enter a name for the pipeline in the *Network Name* field in the *Pipeline* asset card (as shown in Figure 5–32), the name can be used in Civil 3D to identify the pipe network.

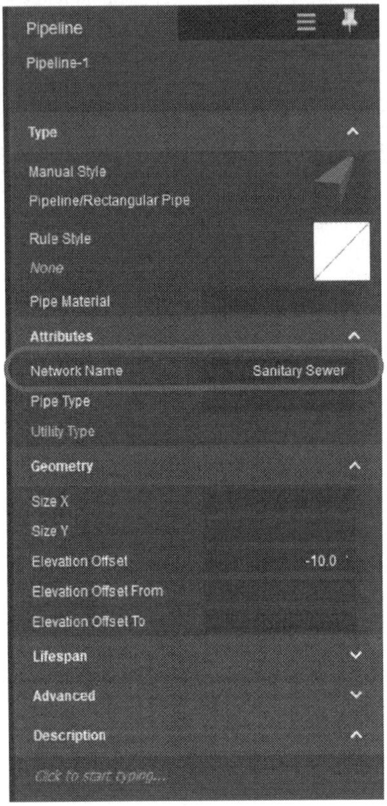

Figure 5–32

Hint: Order of Operations

It is easier to create the pipeline connectors first. Pipelines snap to existing pipeline connectors and stay connected. This enables you to control the location of any pipeline by moving the pipeline connectors to which it is connected.

Pipeline Connectors

Pipeline connectors are nodes that connect to pipe ends. They can represent pipeline structures (such as manholes and catch-basins) along a pipeline.

How To: Create Pipeline Connectors

1. In the *Create* tab>*Drainage* panel, click (Pipeline Connector). The *Select Draw Style* asset card displays.
2. In the *Select Draw Style* asset card, select a pipeline connector style, as shown in Figure 5–33.

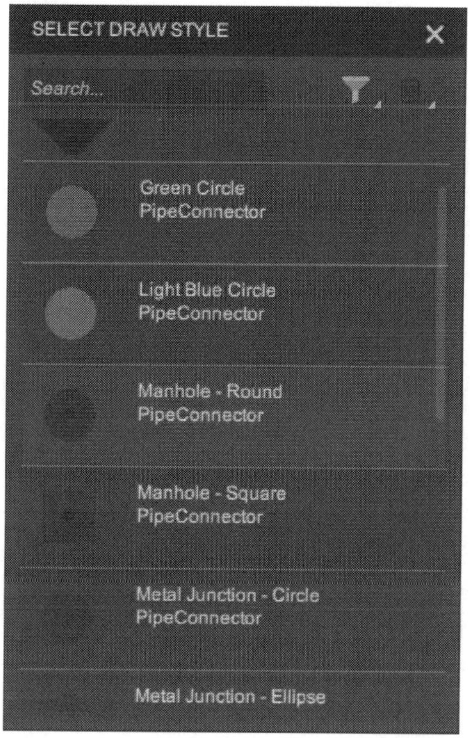

Figure 5–33

3. Double-click in the model to place the pipeline connector. Each pipeline connector is added separately, as required.
4. Connectors are merely conceptual and are not part of the pipe network as structures. Lowering the pipes will not elongate the conceptual connectors.

Create Pipelines

Pipelines represent various utility lines (e.g., gas, water, sanitary sewer, storm sewer, etc.). Pipelines can connect to pipeline connectors or other pipe ends.

How To: Create Pipelines

1. In the *Create* tab>*Drainage* panel, click  (Pipeline).
2. In the *Select Draw Style* asset card, select the required pipeline style, as shown in Figure 5–34.

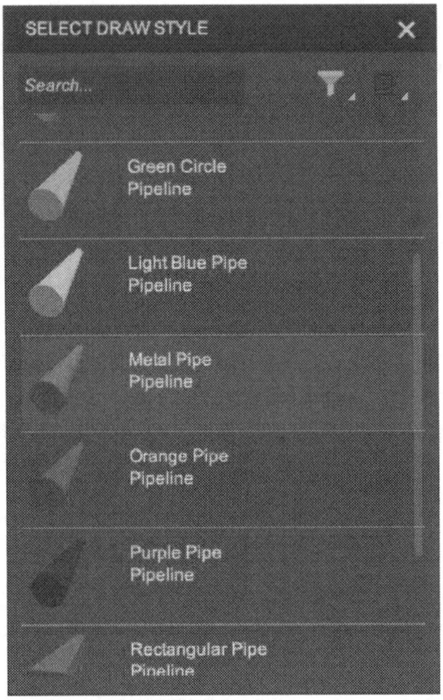

Figure 5–34

Note: *If you click in the model near a pipeline connector, the pipeline automatically snaps to the connector.*

3. Click in the model to place the first pipe end.
4. Move the cursor in the direction in which you want the pipeline to run. Type a distance for the pipe length and press <Enter> to set the distance. Click in the model to place a pipe bend.
5. Continue clicking in the model to place pipe bends until all of the lengths of pipe have been created for the pipeline.
6. Double-click to place the last pipe segment and end the command.

Edit Pipelines

Pipelines are created as 2D features that drape on the terrain surface. However, in the real world, most pipes are buried below the ground.Therefore, once you lay out the horizontal location of the pipelines, you must adjust the vertical layout by adding a negative value in the *Elevation Offset* field in the *Pipeline* asset card (as shown in Figure 5–35) or by using the cyan cone of the (Elevation Gizmo) in the model.

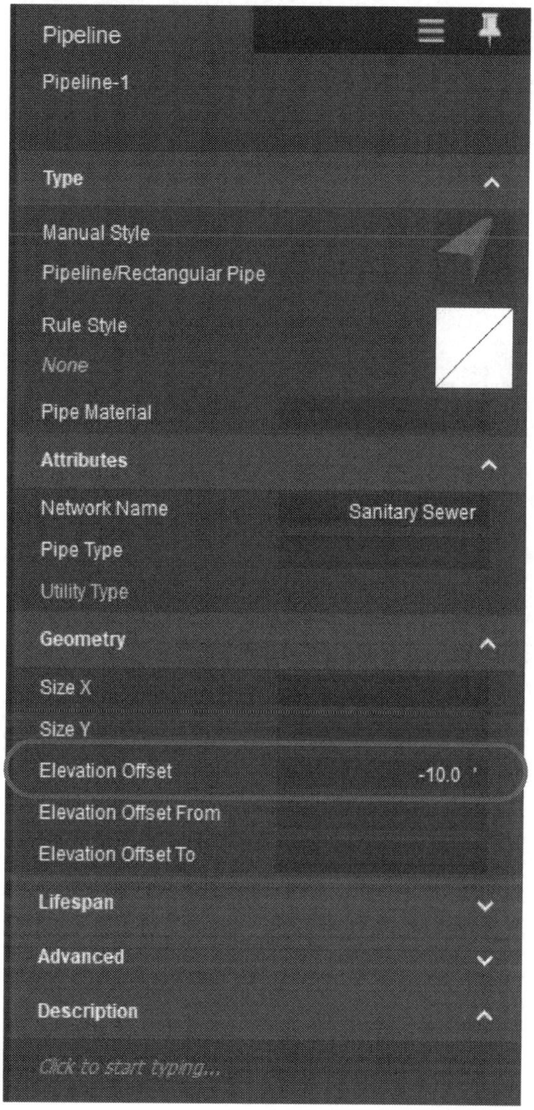

Figure 5–35

After a pipeline elevation has been adjusted below a surface, the pipeline gizmos continue to drape on the terrain surface, as shown in Figure 5–36.

Figure 5–36

How To: Adjust the Pipeline Elevations

1. Select the pipeline in the model and orbit the view to a side view. The pipes lie on the road surface, and a box displays indicating the orthogonal directions (also known as level lines), as shown in Figure 5–37.

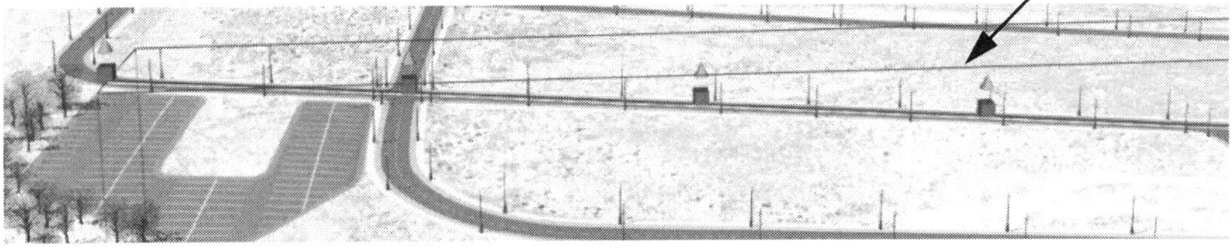

Figure 5–37

2. In the *Pipeline* asset card, type a negative value in the *Elevation Offset* field (as shown in Figure 5–38) to place the pipes below ground.

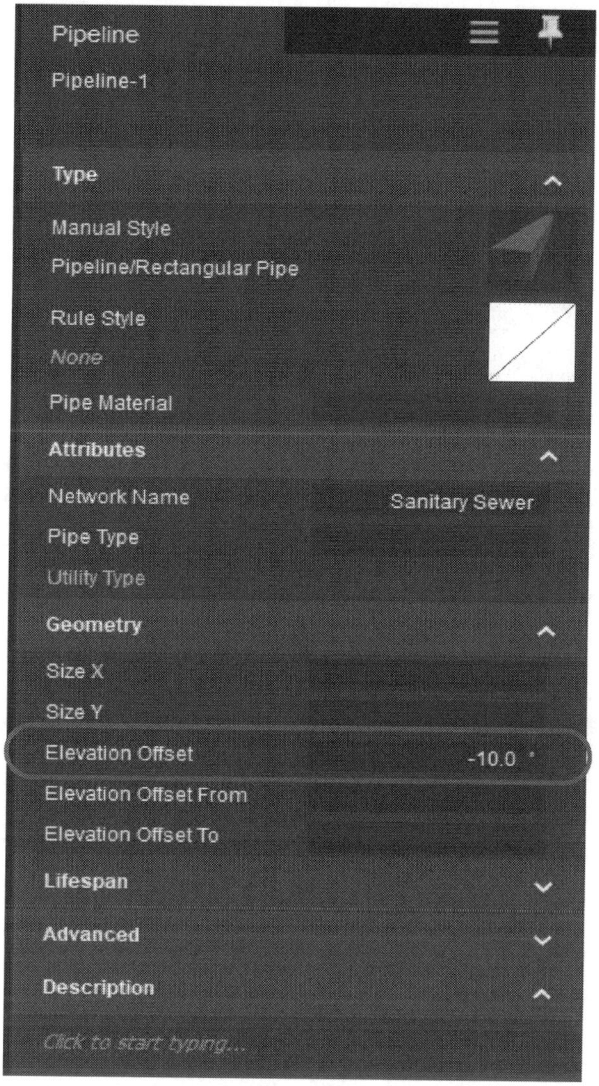

Figure 5–38

3. Use the cyan cone of the  (Elevation Gizmo) to make changes to individual pipe bend elevations.
4. Any connectors are merely conceptual and are not part of the pipe network as structures. Lowering the pipes will not elongate the conceptual connectors.

Practice 5d
Create Utilities in the Model

Practice Objective

- Create a sanitary sewer in the model to illustrate the design concept.

In this practice, you will create manholes and connect them with a pipeline that will act as a sanitary sewer for the project.

Task 1: Create manholes.

1. Continue working in the same model as the last practice. If you closed the file, on the *Home* screen, click **Open**. In the *InfraWorks Practice Files\5-Waterways-Drainage* folder, select **CreateDrainage.sqlite** and click **Open**.
2. If you did not complete the last task, select **D_Task1** in the (Proposals) drop-down list to make it current.
3. Click (Bookmarks) and select **Church Area**.
4. In the *Create* tab>*Drainage* panel, click (Pipeline Connector).
5. In the *Select Draw Style* asset card, select the **Manhole-Square** style, as shown in Figure 5–39.

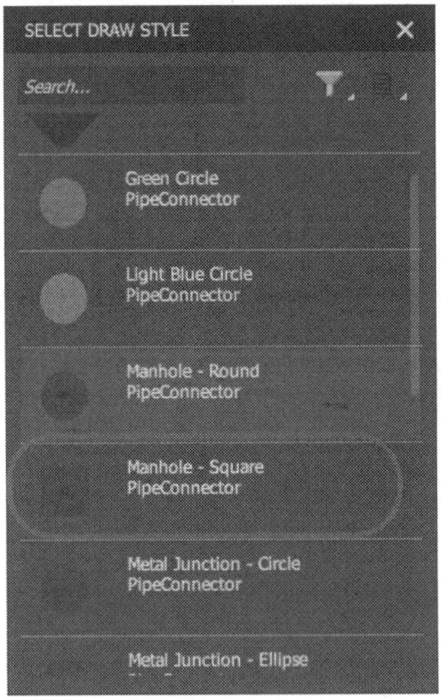

Figure 5–39

6. Double-click near the centerline of the road (as shown in Figure 5–40) to place the first pipeline connector (Point 1). Note that if you only single click to place the structure, you are prompted for a second point. You can simply press <Enter> to place the manhole.

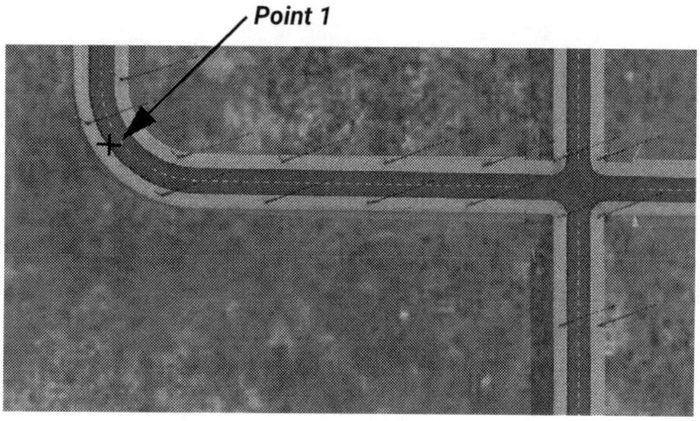

Figure 5–40

7. Pan the model and double-click to place a pipeline connector at the southwest corner of each intersection, as shown in Figure 5–41. You will place seven pipeline connectors in total.

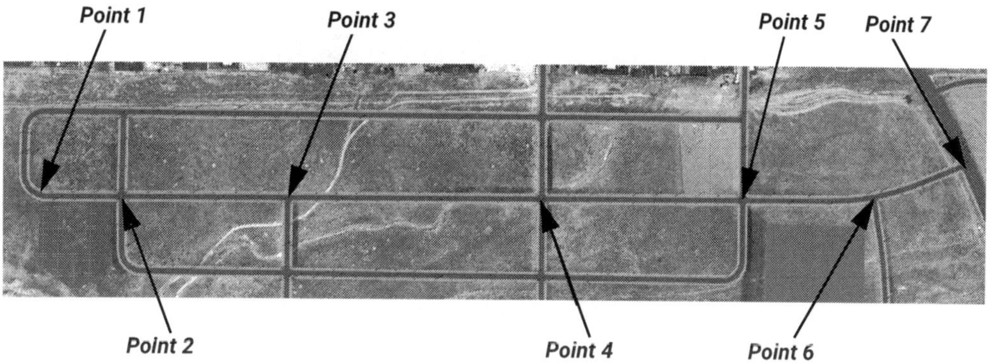

Figure 5–41

Task 2: Create the pipeline to connect the manholes.

1. Click (Bookmarks) and select **Church Area**. In the (Proposals) drop-down list, select **D_Task2**.

2. In the *Create* tab>*Drainage* panel, select (Pipeline). The *Select Draw Style* asset card displays.

3. In the *Select Draw Style* asset card, select the **Blue Pipe** pipeline style, as shown in Figure 5–42.

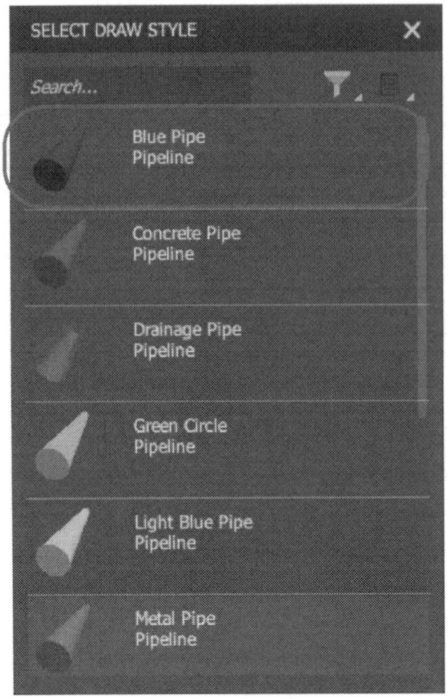

Figure 5–42

4. Close the *Select Draw Style* asset card.
5. Click near the *Point 1* pipeline connector to connect the pipe. Note how when you get in the vicinity of the pipe connector, the pipeline snaps to it.

6. Pan the model to the right and zoom in as required, then click in each intersection to connect the pipe to the pipeline connector located there (as shown in Figure 5–43). Note how the pipeline will snap to the structure as it gets close. Double-click when you connect the pipeline to Point 7 to end the command.

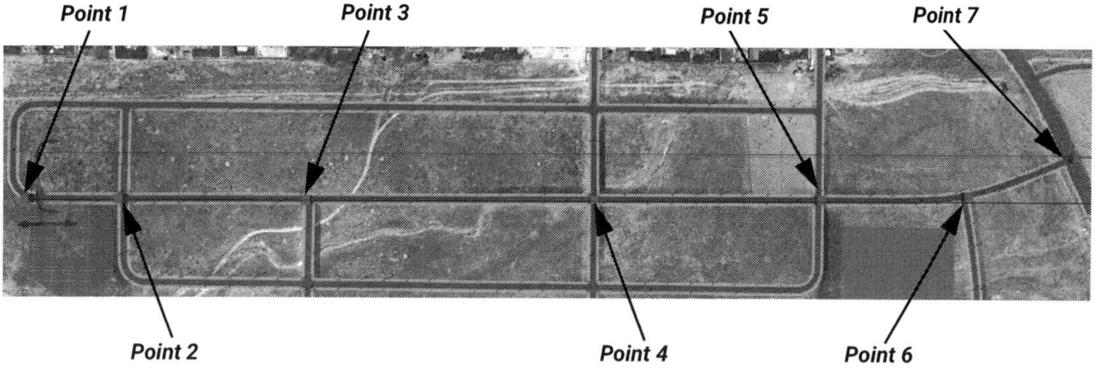

Figure 5–43

7. Orbit the view to a side view. The pipes lie on the road surface, and a box displays indicating the orthogonal directions (also known as level lines), as shown in Figure 5–44.

Figure 5–44

8. In the *Pipeline* asset card, enter the following (as shown in Figure 5–45):
   - *Name:* **Gasline - Church Loop**

   Note: *Naming pipelines will facilitate importing data into Civil 3D.*

   - *Pipe Material:* **PVC**
   - *Network Name:* **Gasmain**
   - *Elevation Offset*: (negative) **-3** (to place the pipes below ground)

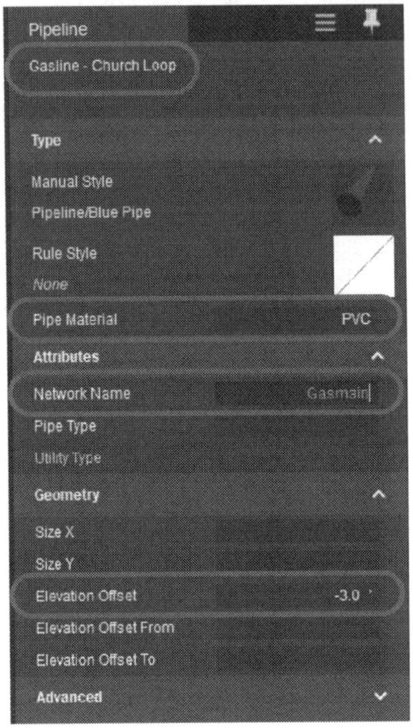

Figure 5–45

9. In the toolbar, expand the *View Style* drop-down list and click  (Configure current view).
10. In the *View Settings* asset card, click  (Change navigation and application feedback settings) to open the Interaction stack.
11. Under *Navigation*, click the **Lock Mouse Above Ground** slider to toggle it off, if it is on. Although the pipes are below the ground, the gizmos remain draped on the terrain surface.

The manholes placed earlier in the exercise are conceptual and are not part of the pipe network as structures. Lowering the pipes will not elongate these manholes. In order to get the structures to elongate, you have two options:

a. You can drag the existing vertex away from the structure and place it, then drag it back to the structure. Since the pipeline is set to -3' elevation, it will connect to the structure at that elevation and the structure will lengthen accordingly.

b. Place a pipeline away from the structures, then give the run the desired elevation in the *Pipeline* asset card and drag the endpoints and vertices to the structures. Insert vertices as needed using the right-click menu.

In the following steps, you will use the first method to elongate the structures.

12. Click (Bookmarks) and select **Gas Connector 3D**.
13. Select the pipeline, then restore the **Project Area** bookmark.
14. For each vertex, select the vertex and move it away from the structure. Release it, then select it again and connect it back to the structure. This will elongate the structure, as shown in Figure 5–46.

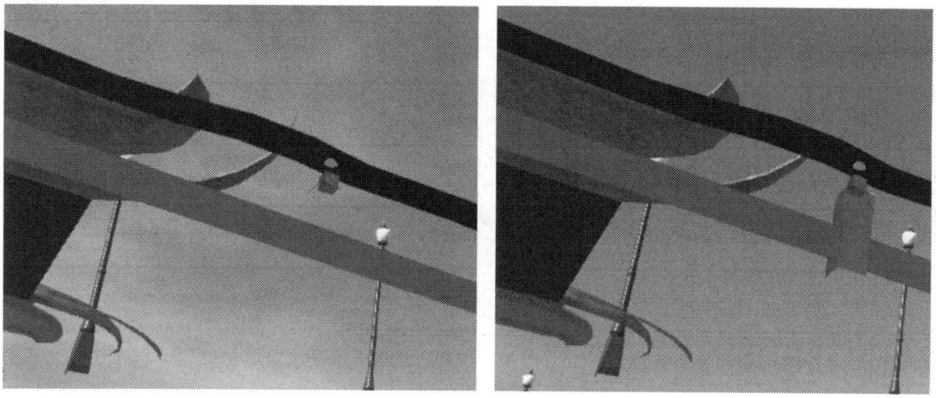

Figure 5–46

15. Orbit the model to display the pipes below ground. Note how they are connected to the structures.
16. Press <Esc> to clear the selection of the pipeline.

End of practice

5.5 Pavement Drainage

Industry standard rules and calculations inside the Drainage Design for InfraWorks module provide analysis-driven design for pavement drainage networks. By inputting various coefficients and varying the Annual Exceedance Probability (AEP) setting, you can examine pipe runs in different storm-level conditions. The data displays in the model or in the drainage structure's asset card, as shown in Figure 5–47.

> **Note:** *In this guide, a structure refers to either an inlet or a manhole that is at the end of a pipe in the drainage network.*

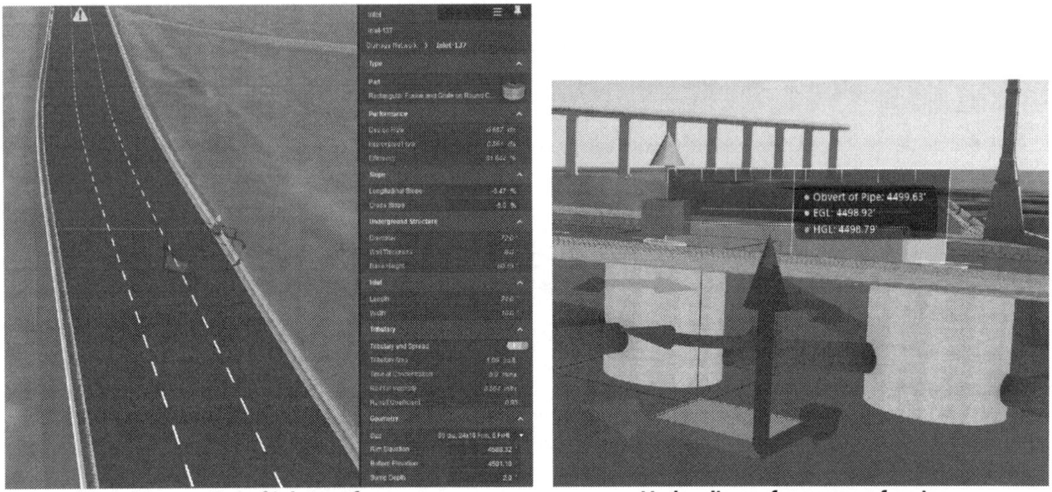

Visual inspection of inlet performance ***Hydraulic performance of a pipe***

Figure 5–47

General Workflow

The order in which commands are used for setting up the pavement drainage network is important. Certain commands do not work if specific steps are not completed first. For example, you cannot analyze the surface drainage unless you have already sized the pavement drainage. The steps should be completed in the following order.

1. Create the conceptual design by adding pavement drainage to a component road.
2. Modify the design by moving, adding, and removing pipes and structures, as required.
3. Fine-tune the changes that have been made by sizing pavement drainage.
4. Analyze the surface drainage between inlets to verify performance of pipe runs.

Input Rainfall Quantities

A rainfall editor enables you to customize the rainfall content for a model.

How To: Customize Rainfall Content

1. In the *Analyze* tab>*Drainage* drop-down list, click (Rainfall Content).
2. In the *Rainfall Content* panel, double-click on any of the existing tables to open it for editing.
   - Alternatively, click (Add a new empty rainfall content of the current rainfall type) to create a new table.
3. In the *Rainfall Editor* panel, click in any of the fields that require editing and type in the new values, as shown in Figure 5–48.

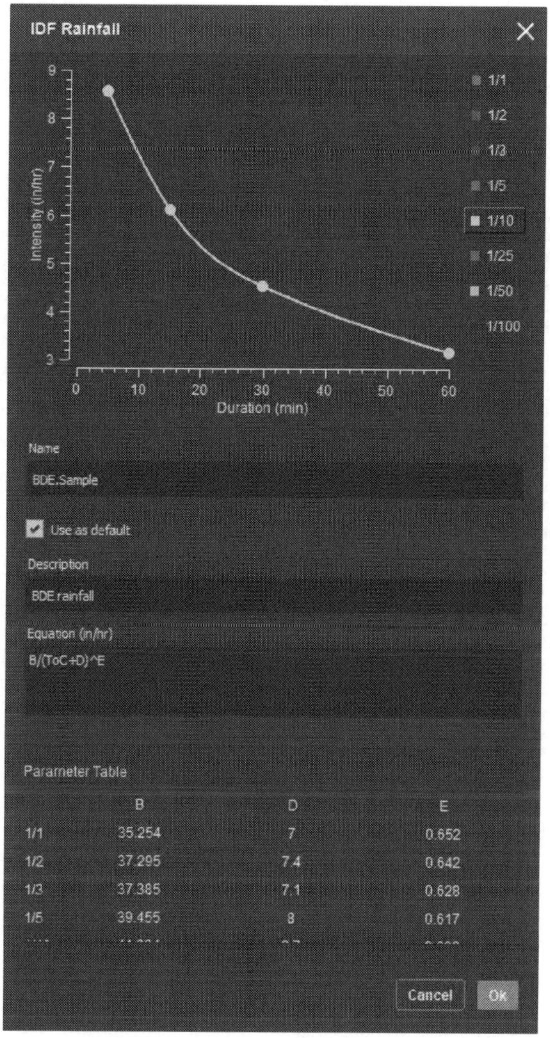

Figure 5–48

Create a Network

A component road must exist before a pavement drainage network can be added to the model. To add a network, simply edit the component road.

How To: Create a Pavement Drainage Network

1. In the model, select a component road.
2. Right-click on the component road and select **Drainage>Add Drainage Network**, as shown in Figure 5–49.

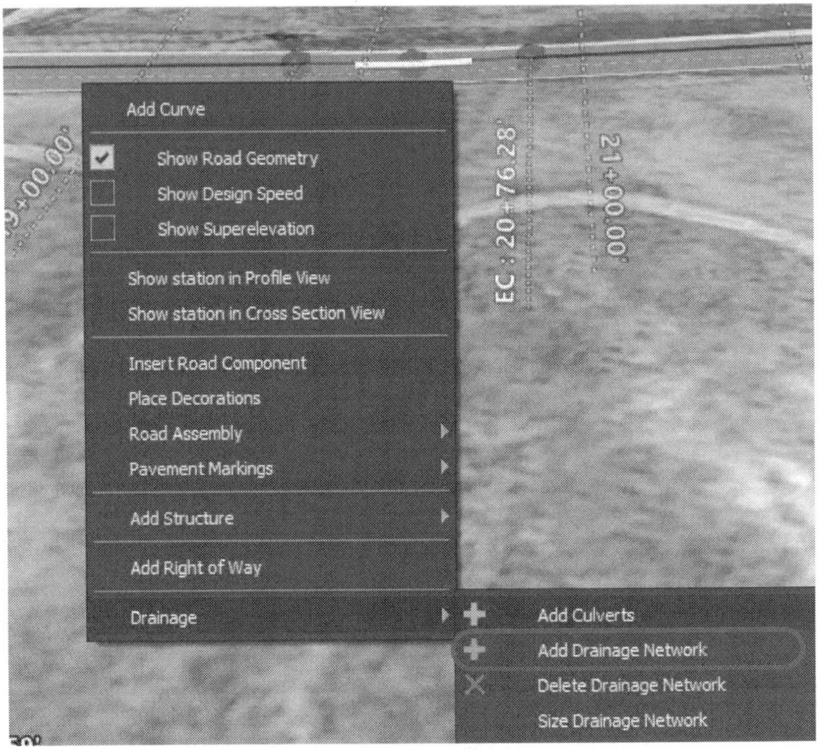

Figure 5–49

3. Press <Enter> to accept the selection and create the drainage.

Modify Drainage Networks

Similar to the other features in the Autodesk InfraWorks software, drainage networks can be modified using gizmos.

Gizmo	Transformation	Description
	**Elevation/ Control Point**	Displays at each point of intersection along a pipe or at the center of each structure. In a 3D view, it can stretch features horizontally or vertically by changing the elevation of the vertex. In plan view, it becomes a control point.
	**Rotate**	Rotates a feature around the Z-axis.
	**Control Point**	Displays at each point of intersection of pipes or at the center of structures. Stretches pipes by moving the selected vertex of the pipe. Moves the location of structures. Note: Additional control points can be added by holding <Alt> and selecting the new control point location.
	**Move**	Moves the selected feature or vertex.

When a pipe is selected in the model, the *Pipeline* asset card displays. This asset card enables you to change the material, size, and invert elevations of the pipe, as shown in Figure 5–50. The length and slope are calculated values.

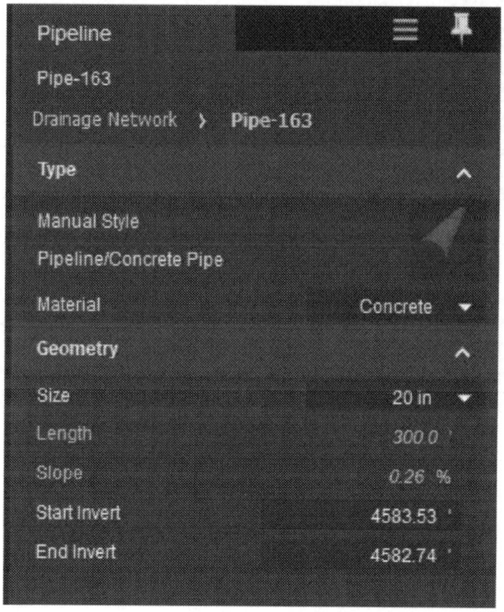

Figure 5–50

When a structure is selected in the model, the appropriate asset card displays, enabling you to change the type and the size of structure, as shown in Figure 5–51. If the *Type* field is selected, the *Select Component* asset card displays, which enables you to select from a number of predefined structure types.

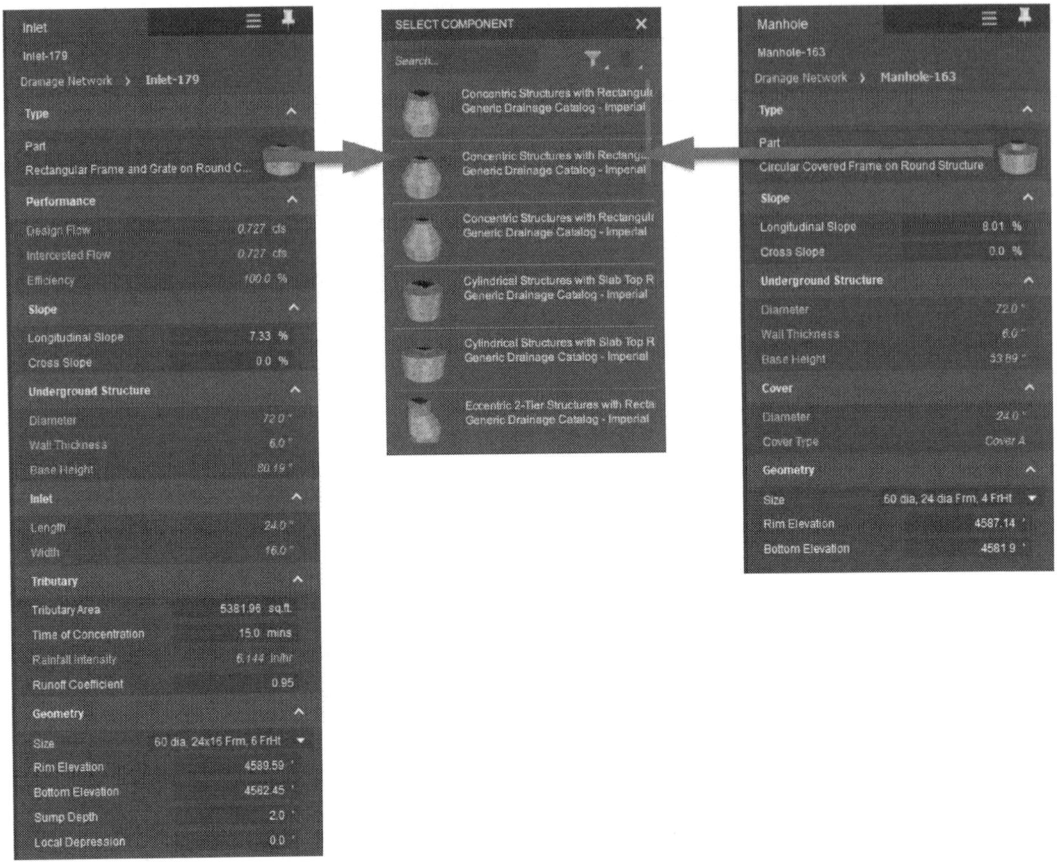

Figure 5–51

Hint: Component Road Changes

If you want to change a component road that already has pavement drainage added to it, do not modify the drainage network. It is best to delete the drainage network and add a new drainage network to any revised component roads.

How To: Add Drainage Features to an Existing Network

1. In the *Create* tab>*Drainage* drop-down list, click (Drainage Network).

2. In the *Create Drainage Network* asset card, set the appropriate *Inlets, Manholes*, and *Pipelines* types, sizes, and other parameters, as shown in Figure 5–52.

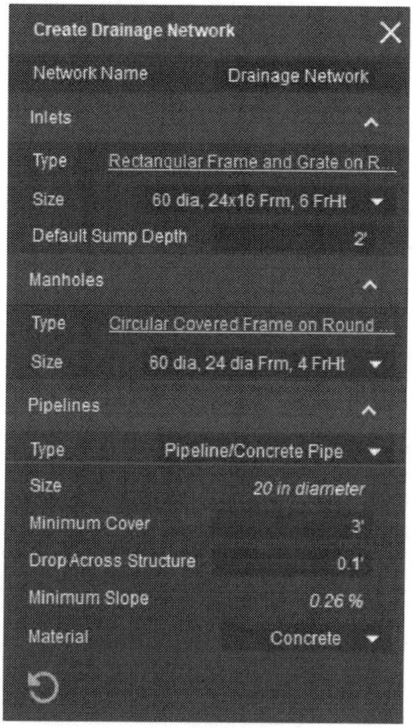

Figure 5–52

3. In the model, click to place the features. Right-click to change the features being placed or to enable the **Show high and low points** option, as shown in Figure 5–53.

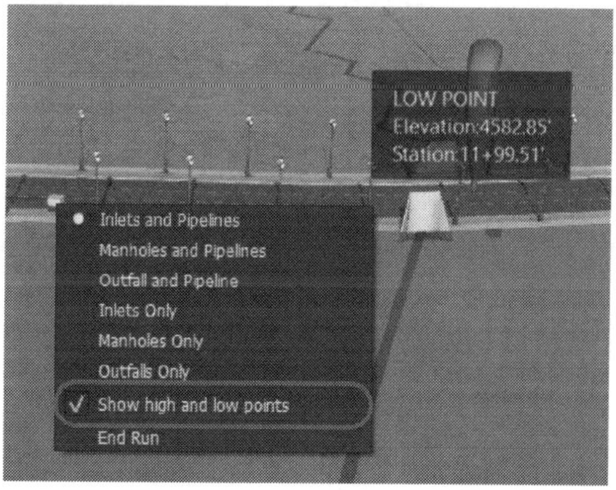

Figure 5–53

4. Double-click to place the last feature or right-click and select **End Run**.

Size Drainage Network

After moving structures or adding additional structures to a design, it is necessary to fine-tune the placement and sizing of the structures. You can do this by running the **Size Drainage Network** command. This recalculates the pipe diameters, adjusts pipe slopes, and resizes connectors as required to accommodate any changes.

How To: Size Drainage Network

1. In the model, select the component road.
2. Right-click and select **Drainage>Size Drainage Network**, as shown in Figure 5–54.

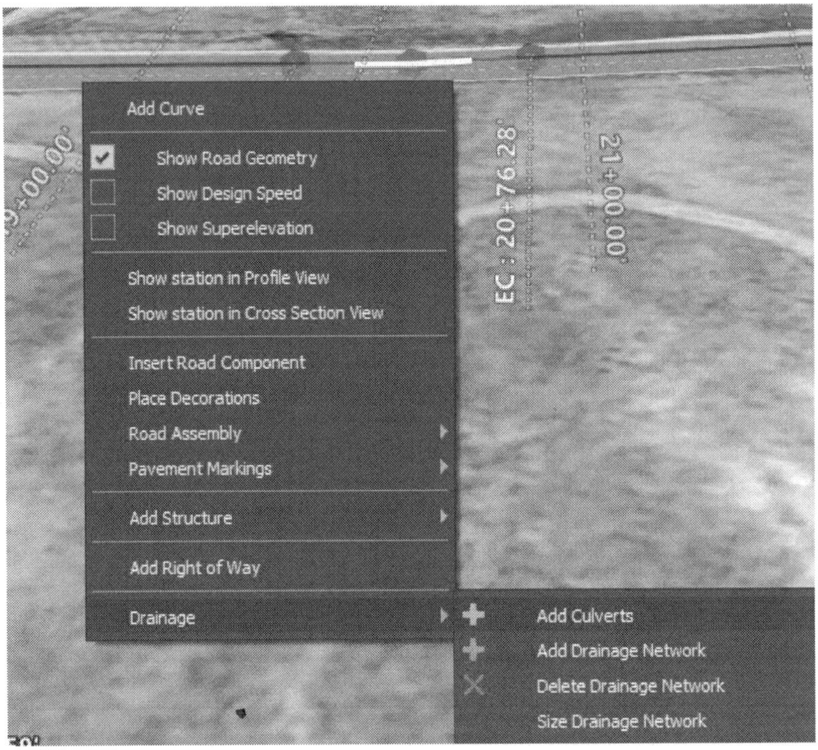

Figure 5–54

Analyze Pavement Drainage

Visual Inspection of Inlet Performance

Inlets are analyzed in real-time by the Autodesk InfraWorks software. By selecting an inlet, you can visually inspect it to ensure that its performance meets the design parameters. When selected, the *Inlet* asset card displays along with the water capture, spread, and bypass, as shown in Figure 5–55.

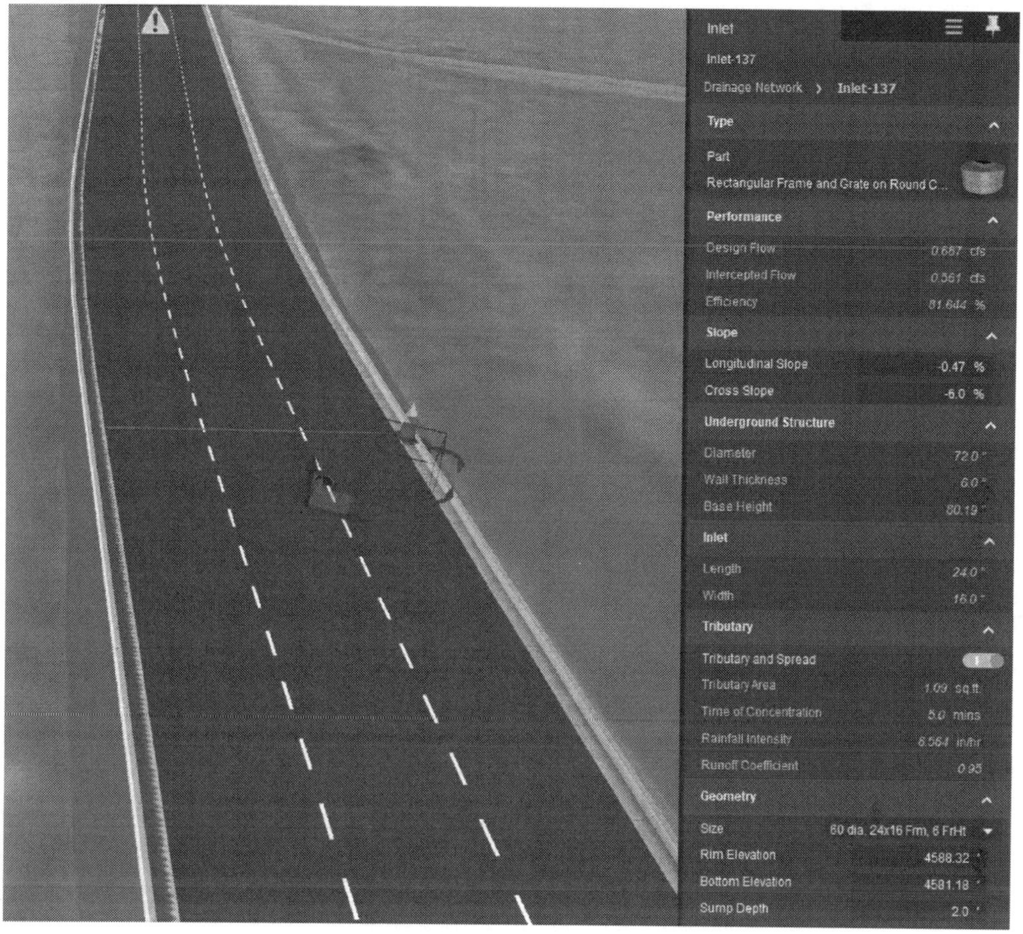

Figure 5–55

Hydraulic Performance of a Pipe

Flooded manholes and surcharged pipes can be identified visually in the model. After running an analysis, the EGL, HGL, and Obvert of pipe elevations can be viewed by moving the cursor over the hatched area over the analyzed pipes.

How To: Analyze Pavement Drainage

1. Navigate the view below the terrain surface so that underground pipes and structures are displayed and selectable.
   - Alternatively, you can decrease the opacity of the surface to see below the ground.
2. In the *Analyze* tab>*Drainage* drop-down list, click (Inspect Performance).
3. Adjust the *AEP* and *Tailwater Condition* values as required in the *Analysis Settings* asset card.
4. In the model, select one of the pipe connectors that is connected to the pipe you want to analyze, then select the pipe connector on the opposite side of the pipe.
5. Press <Enter> to analyze the pipe.
6. Move the cursor over the vertical bar along the hatched bounding box to view analysis results, as shown in Figure 5–56.

Figure 5–56

- The blue bar indicates the hydraulic gradeline (water depth in the pipe).
- The green line represents the obvert (inside) of the pipe.
- The yellow line represents the energy gradeline.

Practice 5e
Create a Pavement Drainage Network

Practice Objectives

- Add a pavement drainage network to a component road.
- Add inlets, pipes, and manholes to a drainage network.
- Size a pavement drainage network.
- Analyze a pavement drainage network.
- Calculate quantities for a drainage network.

In this practice, you will create a pavement drainage network. You will then analyze it for performance, as shown in Figure 5–57.

Figure 5–57

Task 1: Add a pavement drainage network to a component road.

1. Continue working in the same model as the last practice. If you closed the file, on the *Home* screen, click **Open**. In the *InfraWorks Practice Files\5-Waterways-Drainage* folder, select **CreateDrainage.sqlite** and click **Open**.
2. If you did not complete the last task, select **E_Task1** in the (Proposals) drop-down list to make it current.
3. Click (Bookmarks) and select **School Area**. Zoom out a bit and pan to the west to center **S Redwood Rd** in the view.

4. In the model, select **S Redwood Rd**, right-click, and select **Drainage>Add Drainage Network**, as shown in Figure 5–58.

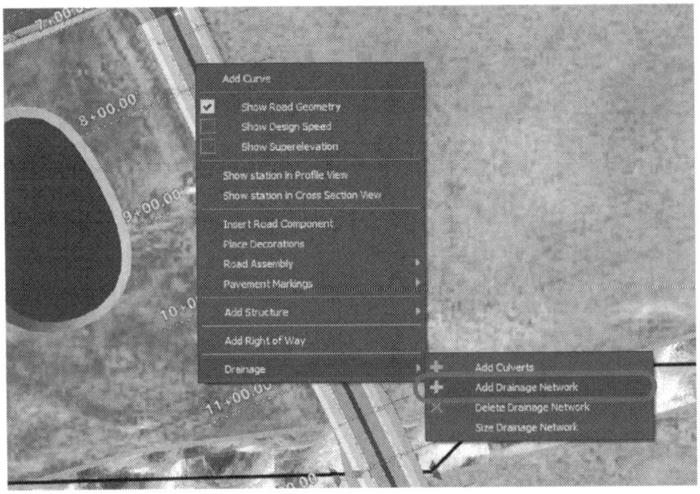

Figure 5–58

5. In the *Add Drainage Network* asset card, enter **Storm Network** for the *Network Name* and leave the rest as the default values, as shown in Figure 5–59.

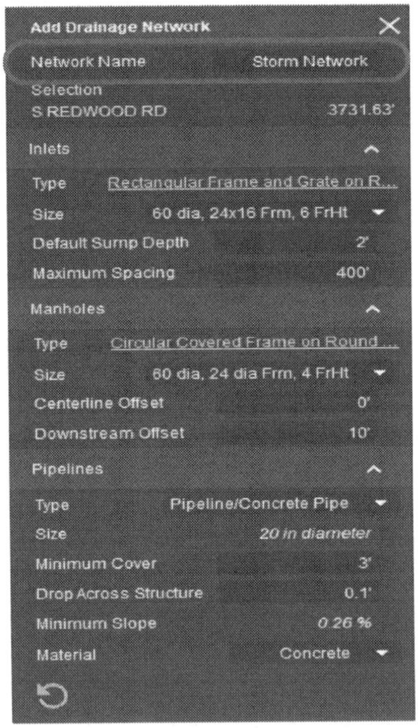

Figure 5–59

6. Note the message in the lower part of the screen (shown in Figure 5–60). Press <Enter> to build the network.

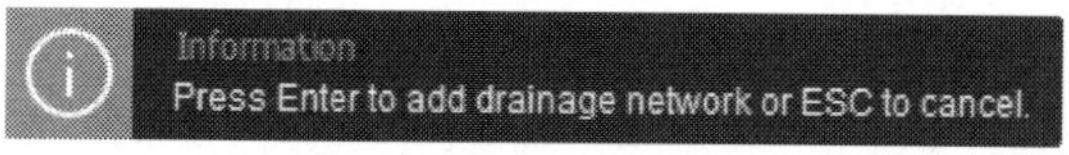

Figure 5–60

7. Read the message about generating the drainage network (shown in Figure 5–61). After a while, the message will close and the network will be built.

Figure 5–61

Due to the lowering of the roundabout in a previous practice, InfraWorks is having trouble maintaining a proper slope of the drainage. It zooms in to the problem area and displays an informative message, as shown in Figure 5–62. For now, you can click **OK** to dismiss the notice. (The issue will be dealt with in a later practice.)

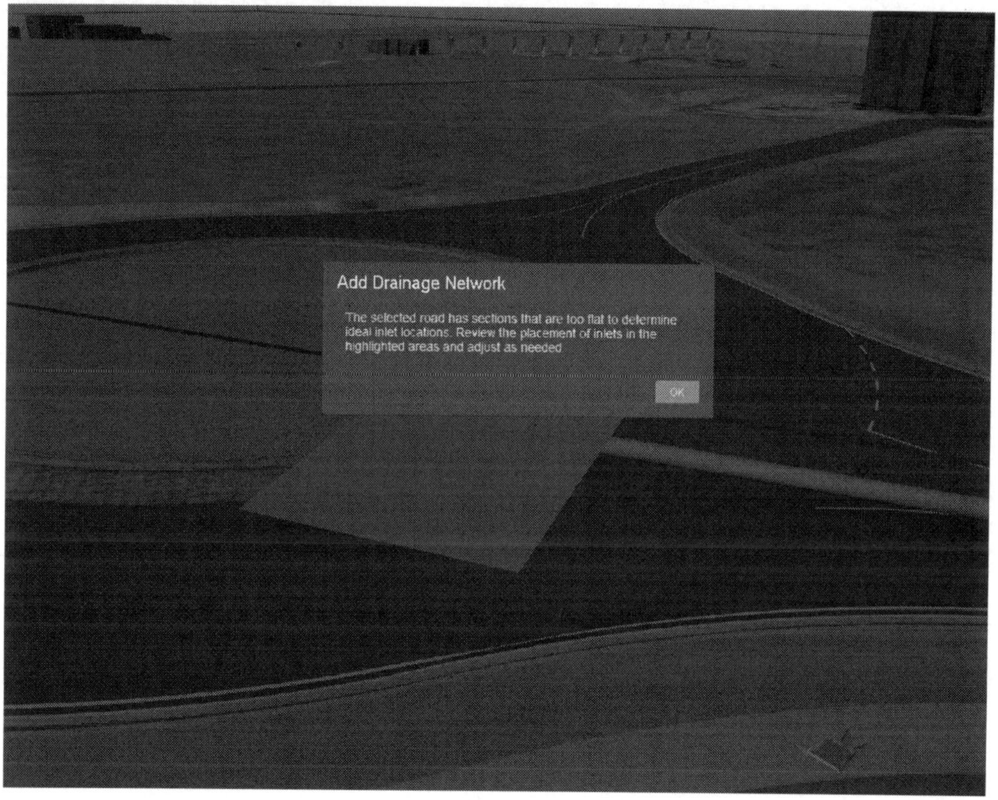

Figure 5–62

8. To get another view of the problem area, go to the *Profile View* using the <Ctrl>+<0> (zero) shortcut. Zoom in around station 1870, where you can see the existing ground is below the pipes, as shown Figure 5–63.

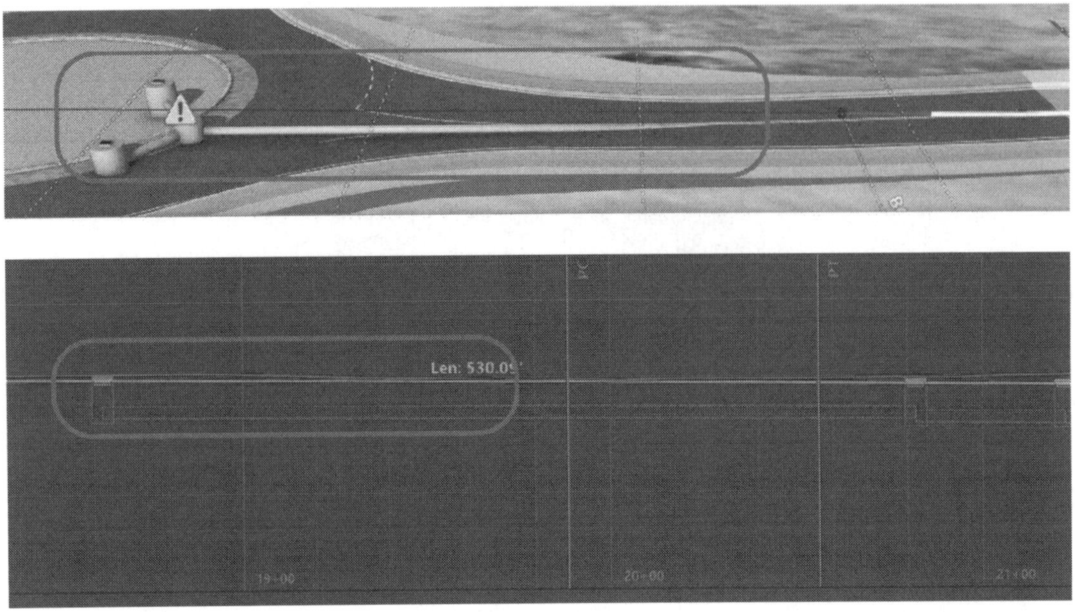

Figure 5–63

Task 2: Modify pavement drainage.

1. In the toolbar, expand the *View Style* drop-down list and click (Configure current view).
2. In the *View Settings* asset card, click (Change navigation and application feedback settings) to open the *Interaction* stack.

3. Under *Navigation*, ensure that the **Lock Mouse Above Ground** slider is toggled off, as shown in Figure 5–64, so that you can see below the ground.

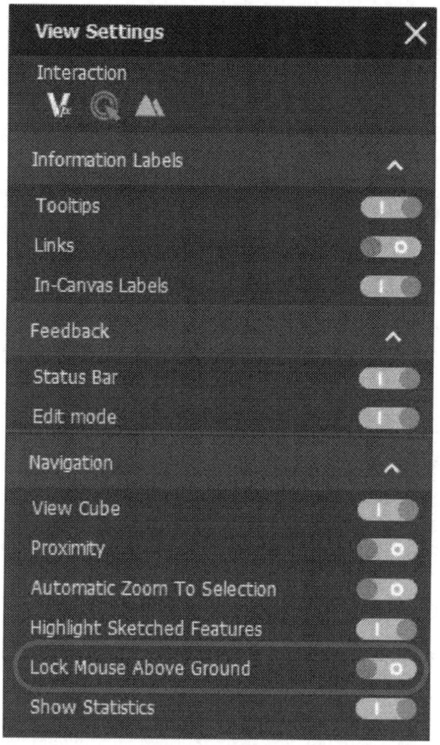

Figure 5–64

4. Close the *View Settings* asset card.
5. Click  (Bookmarks) and select **Missing Drainage 3D**.

Even though there are outlets on each network, the approving agency wants the two networks to be connected and one more manhole and two more inlets to be added.

6. Click  (Bookmarks) and select **Missing Drainage**.
7. In the *Create* tab>*Drainage* drop-down list, click  (Drainage Network).
8. In the *Create Drainage Network* asset card, accept the default inlet, manhole, and pipe types, sizes, and other parameters. Note that the *Network Name* is the same as before.
9. Note the message in the lower part of the screen (shown in Figure 5–65).

Figure 5–65

10. In the model, right-click and select **Manholes and Pipelines**, then click on the existing manhole in the **S Redwood Rd / Pier Lane** intersection, as shown in Figure 5–66.

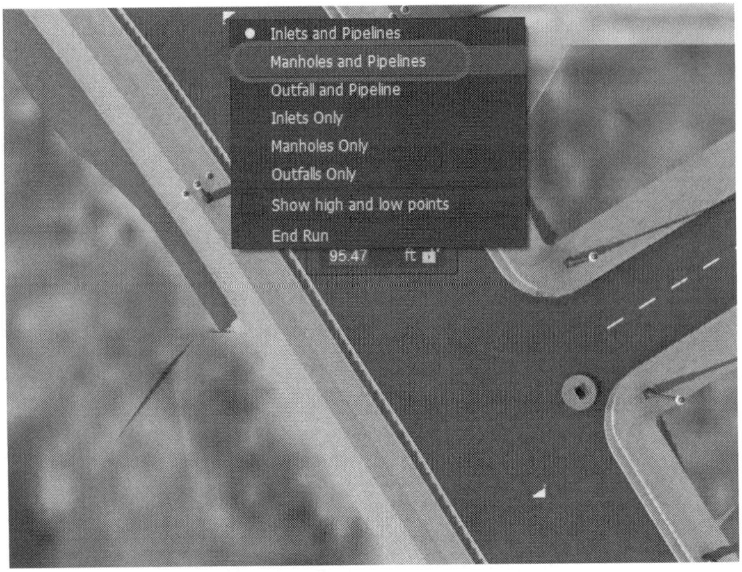

Figure 5–66

11. In the model, move the cursor north and type **200'** for the distance, press <Enter> to lock the distance into place, then click near the centerline of the road, as shown Figure 5–67.

Figure 5–67

12. For the endpoint, double-click on the manhole at the end of the **S Redwood Rd** component road.
13. Now you need to add inlets at the new manhole you created. Click (Bookmarks) and select **Add Inlet 3D** to inspect the situation underneath, then select the **Add Inlet** bookmark to add the inlets.
14. In the *Create* tab>*Drainage* drop-down list, click (Drainage Network).
15. In the model, right-click and select **Inlets and Pipelines.** Click on the new manhole, as shown in Figure 5–68. For the location of the inlet (Point A), veer out at about a 45° angle and double-click in the gutter (Point B). You can orbit the view around to ensure you select the proper manhole.

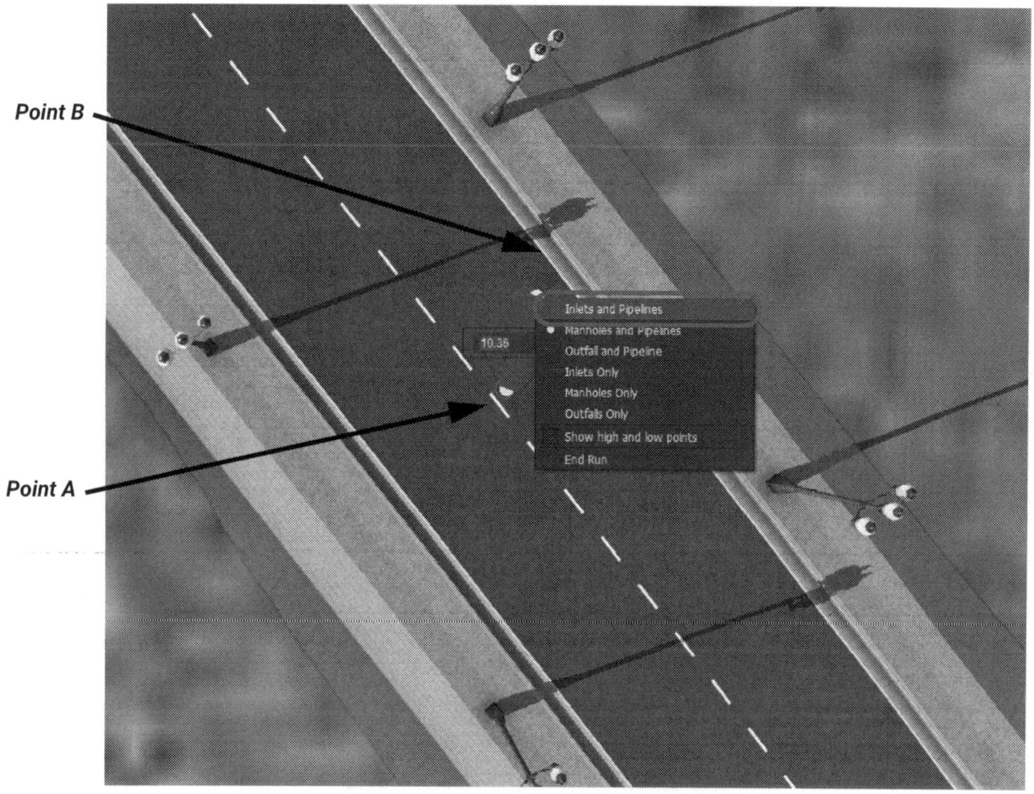

Figure 5–68

16. Repeat the same steps to add an inlet on the opposite side.

17. As before, click (Bookmarks) and select **Add Inlet 3D** to inspect the situation underneath, as shown in Figure 5–69.

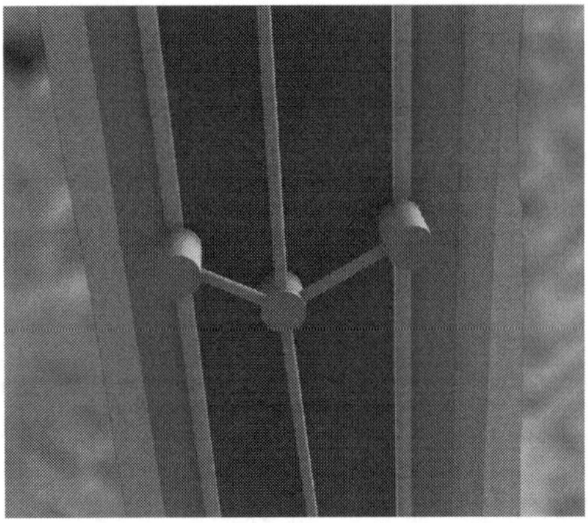

Figure 5–69

18. Press <Esc> twice to exit the command.
19. Orbit, zoom and pan around the area to check for irregularities.

Hint: Unsolvable Terrain

At times, when placing drainage networks, the roadside grading can become unsolvable and the terrain shoots vertically up and/or down, as shown in Figure 5–70.

You can go to the *Profile View* and adjust the vertical curves radii or elevation. This in turn can affect the culvert elevation placed earlier in the practices, which will need readjusting, since there are pipes and structures running underneath and pushing the culvert up.

Figure 5–70

Task 3: Size pavement drainage.

1. Continue working in the same model as the previous task. If you did not complete the previous task, set **E_Task2** as the current proposal.
2. Click (Bookmarks) and select **Add Inlet 3D**, then zoom out a bit.
3. In the model, select **S Redwood Rd**. Take care not to select a pipe or a structure.
4. In the *Road* asset card, click on (Material Quantities) at the bottom of the card to produce material quantities.
5. Note that there is only one size of circular pipe (20") and one type of manhole, as shown in Figure 5–71.

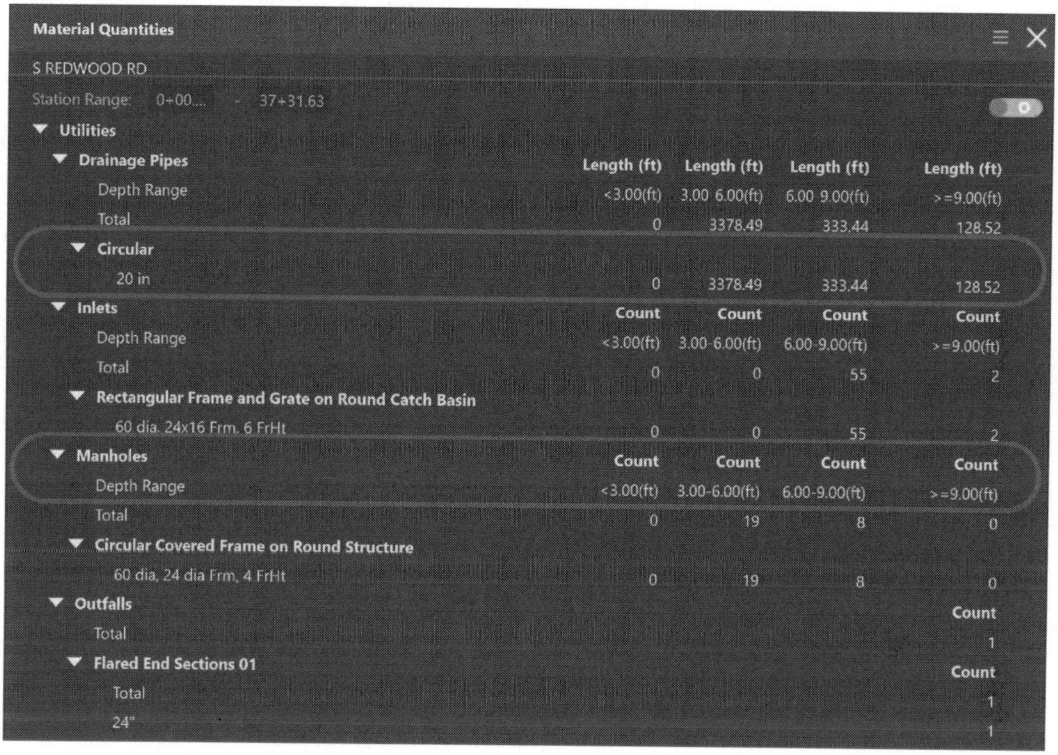

Figure 5–71

6. Close the *Material Quantities* panel.

7. Right-click and select **Drainage>Size Drainage Network**, as shown in Figure 5–72. If you get the message *Missing Outfall in sub-network, skipping relevant calculations. Do you want to continue?*, click **Yes**.

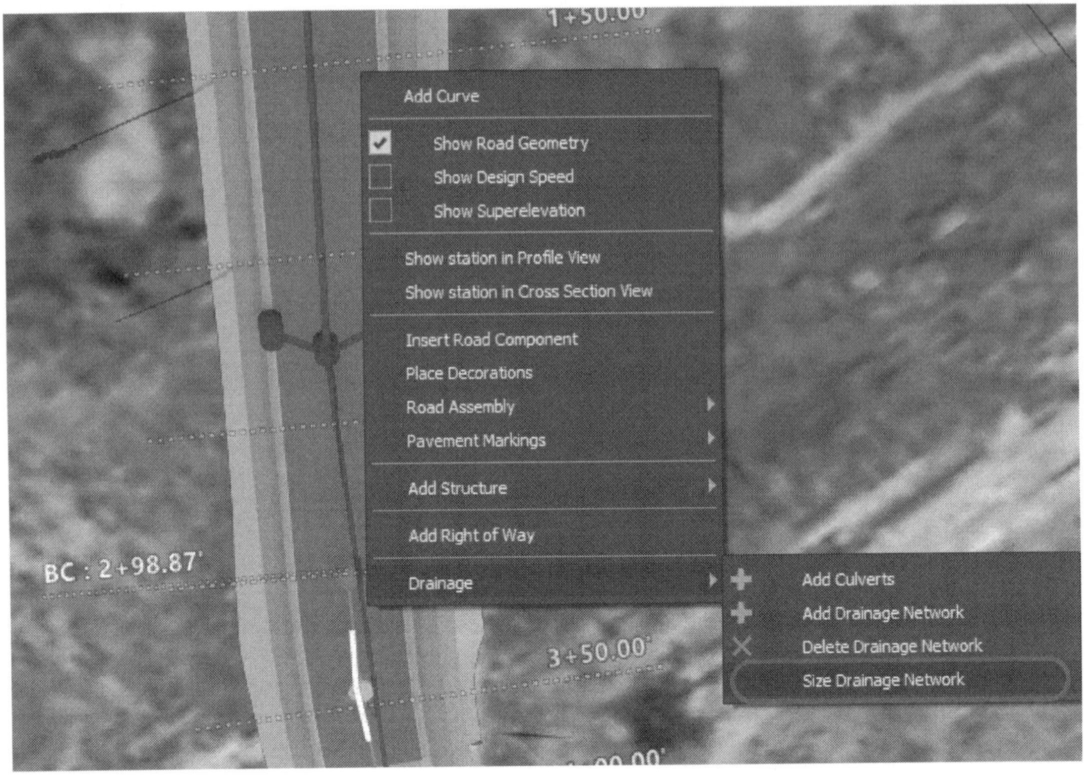

Figure 5–72

8. Press <Enter> to accept the default values in the *Size Drainage Network* asset card.
9. Read the message about sizing the drainage network (shown in Figure 5–73). After a while, the message will close and the network will be properly sized.

Figure 5–73

10. In the *Road* asset card, click on  (Material Quantities) at the bottom of the card to produce material quantities.

11. The quantities and types have changed since InfraWorks has sized the drainage network according to the values given. Note that there are now three sizes of circular pipes (18", 20", and 21") and two types of manholes, as shown in Figure 5–74.

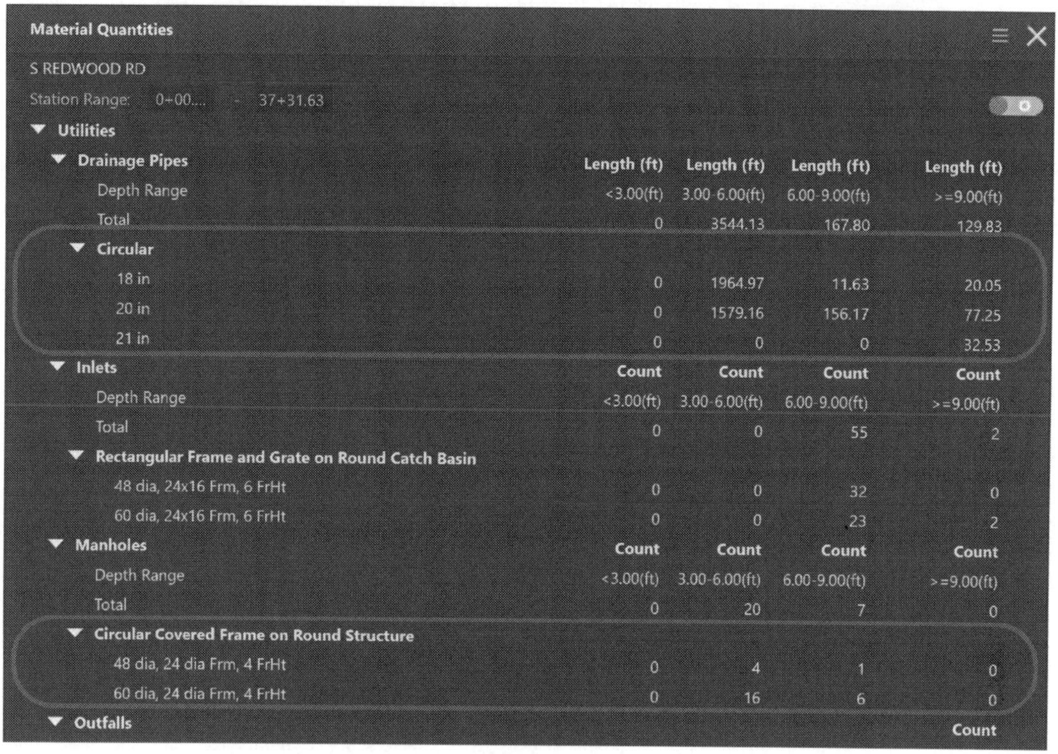

Figure 5–74

12. Close the *Material Quantities* panel.

Task 4: Analyze pavement drainage.

1. Continue working in the same model as the previous task. If you did not complete the previous task, set **E_Task3** as the current proposal.
2. Click (Bookmarks) and select **Drain Analysis 3D**.

3. Select one of the inlet structures to view its asset card, the water capture, spread, and bypass measurements, and the warning in the model, as shown in Figure 5–75.

Figure 5–75

4. Press <Esc> when finished.
5. In the *Analyze* tab>*Drainage* drop-down list, click  (Inspect Performance).
6. In the *Analysis Settings* asset card, change *AEP* to **1/5**.
7. In the model, select the lower manhole in the view. Note that now many inlets and manholes turn pink in color, indicating that these can be selected as the second pipe connector. Select the manhole further up, as shown in Figure 5–76.

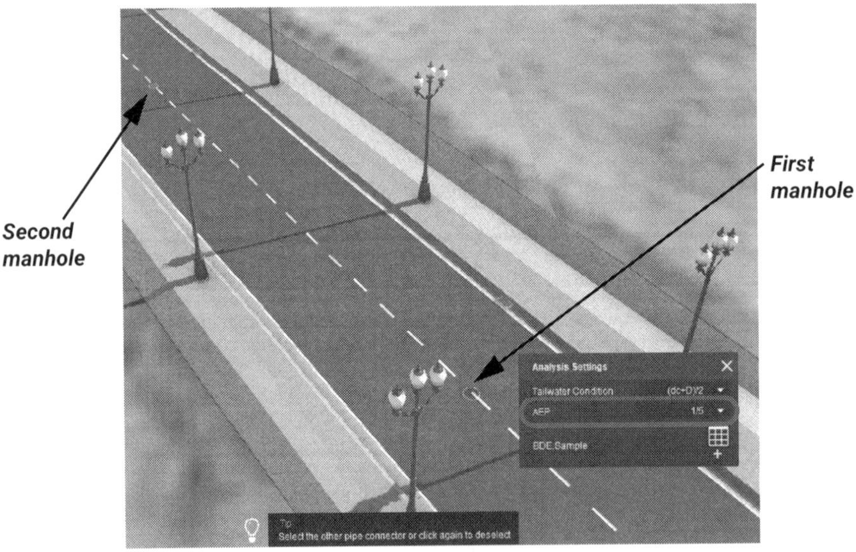

Figure 5–76

8. Press <Enter> to analyze the pipe.

9. Read the message about analyzing the drainage network (shown in Figure 5–77). After a while, the message will close and the network will be analyzed.

Figure 5–77

10. Pivot the view to see above ground. Move the cursor over the vertical bar along the hatched bounding box to view analysis results, as shown in Figure 5–78.

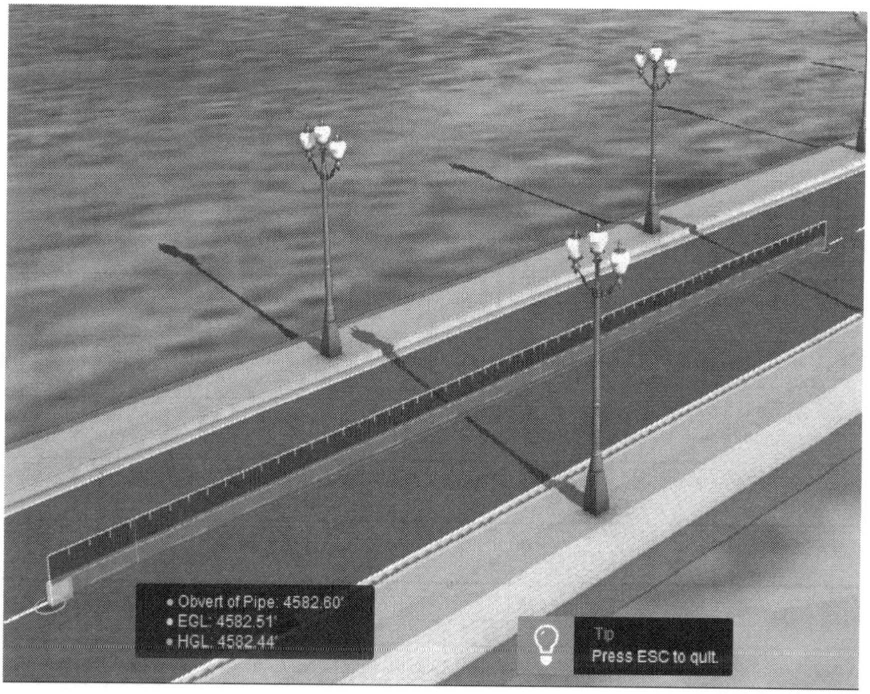

Figure 5–78

11. Press <Esc> when done.

End of practice

Chapter Review Questions

1. For which of the following can watershed areas can be calculated? (Select all that apply.)
    a. A single low-lying point.
    b. A single high point.
    c. An entire component road.
    d. A select station range of a component road.

2. Culverts can be added to component roads automatically.
    a. True
    b. False

3. Which of the following must you do before you can analyze the surface drainage between inlets to verify the performance of pipe runs?
    a. Create the conceptual design by adding pavement drainage to a component road.
    b. Modify the design by moving, adding, and removing, pipes and structures, as required.
    c. Run the  (Watershed) command.
    d. Fine-tune the changes that have been made by sizing pavement drainage.

4. How do you find the obvert value of a pipe?
    a. Run the  (Watershed) command.
    b. Run the  (Drainage Network) command.
    c. Run the  (Inspect Performance) command.
    d. Select the pipe to open the *Pipe* asset card.

5. How do you size pavement drainage?
   a. Select the component road and right-click.
   b. Select a network feature and right-click.
   c. Run the  (Drainage Network) command.
   d. Run the  (Inspect Performance) command.

Command Summary

Button	Command	Location
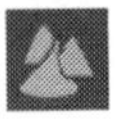	**Watershed**	• **Toolbar:** *Analyze* tab>*Drainage* panel
	**Culvert**	• **Toolbar:** *Create* tab>*Drainage* panel
	**Drainage Network**	• **Toolbar:** *Create* tab>*Drainage* drop-down list
	**Inspect Performance**	• **Toolbar:** *Analyze* tab>*Drainage* drop-down list
	**Pipeline**	• **Toolbar:** *Create* tab>*Drainage* panel
	**Pipeline Connector**	• **Toolbar:** *Create* tab>*Drainage* panel
	**Rainfall Content**	• **Toolbar:** *Analyze* tab>*Drainage* drop-down list
	**River**	• **Toolbar:** *Create* tab>*Environment* drop-down list
	**Water Areas**	• **Toolbar:** *Create* tab>*Environment* drop-down list

Chapter 6

Bridges, Railways, and Tunnels

There are specific transportation design tools available in Autodesk® InfraWorks® for bridges, railways, and tunnels. Bridge Design tools enable you to add bridges to component roads and the rule-based tool sets enable you to lay out bridges. During the creation process, you can instantly visualize the designed bridge in context with its surroundings. In this chapter, you will also review creating parametric tunnels and railways.

Learning Objectives

- Describe many of the bridge components that are inserted when a bridge is added to a component road.
- Add bridges to a component road over waterways, railways, or other roadways.
- Edit bridges using gizmos and the *Bridge* asset cards.
- Send design bridges to other software for the detailed design phase.
- Create railways in a model to indicate the locations of the mass transit lines or freight lines.
- Lay out a tunnel as an underpass.

6.1 Bridge Components

The Bridge Design tools in Autodesk InfraWorks enable you to add bridge structures to any component road. Bridges can be used for overpasses, for roads crossing a river or ravine, or for roads intersecting a railway without interfering with traffic. Bridges are very complex structures that contain multiple sub-components. Figure 6–1 illustrates many of these components.

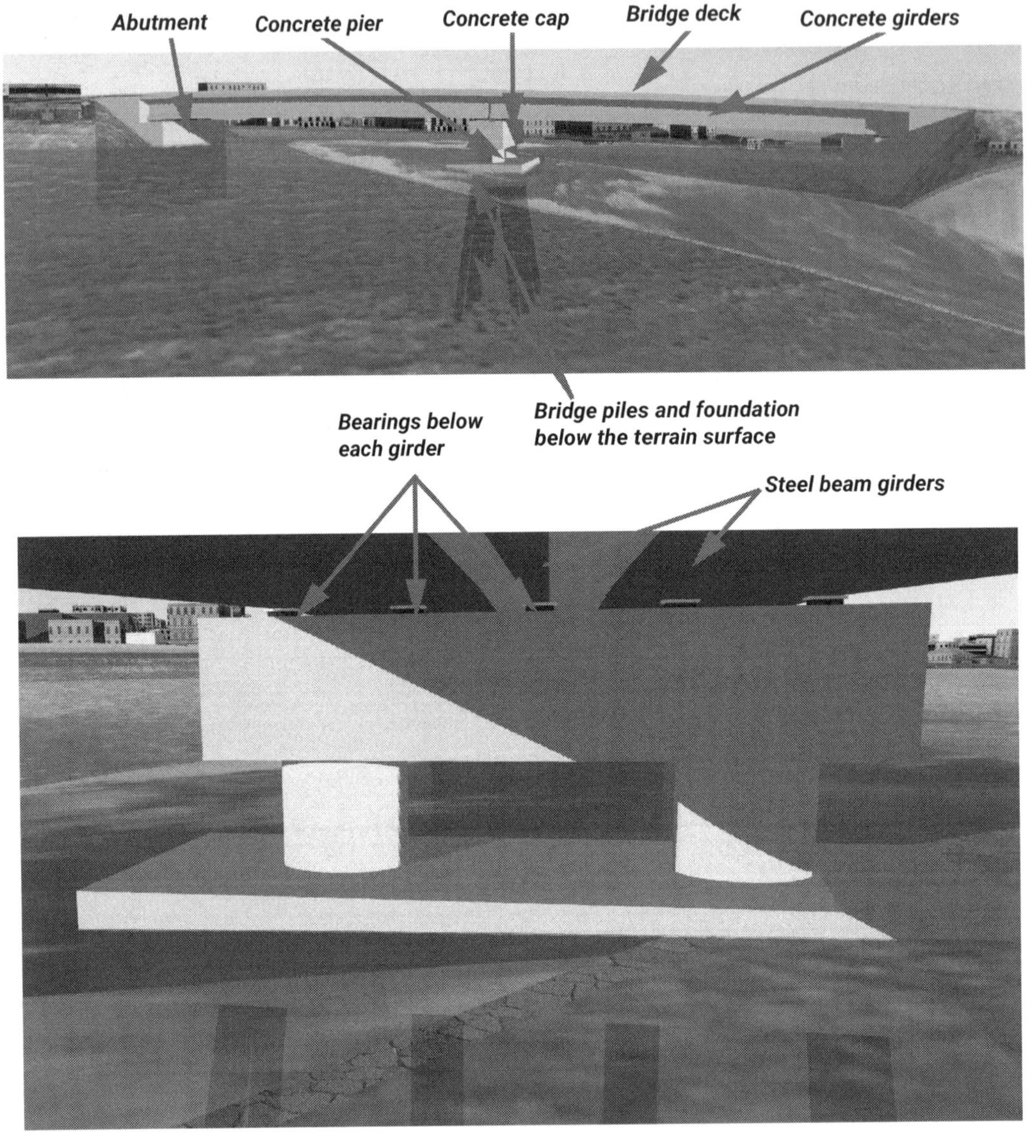

Figure 6–1

Before you can add a bridge to the model, you must have a component road.

How To: Add a Bridge to a Component Road

1. In the model, draw a component road.
2. In the *Create* tab>*Transportation* panel, click  (Bridge).
3. In the model, click on the component road that you want to add a bridge to.
4. Move your cursor to the desired location of the start of the bridge and click to place the start station, or type the starting station and press <Enter>.
5. In the model, click on the component road at the station where you want the bridge to end. Alternatively, you can press <Tab> and type the bridge length, or you can press <Tab> twice to type the ending station, then press <Enter>, as shown in Figure 6–2.

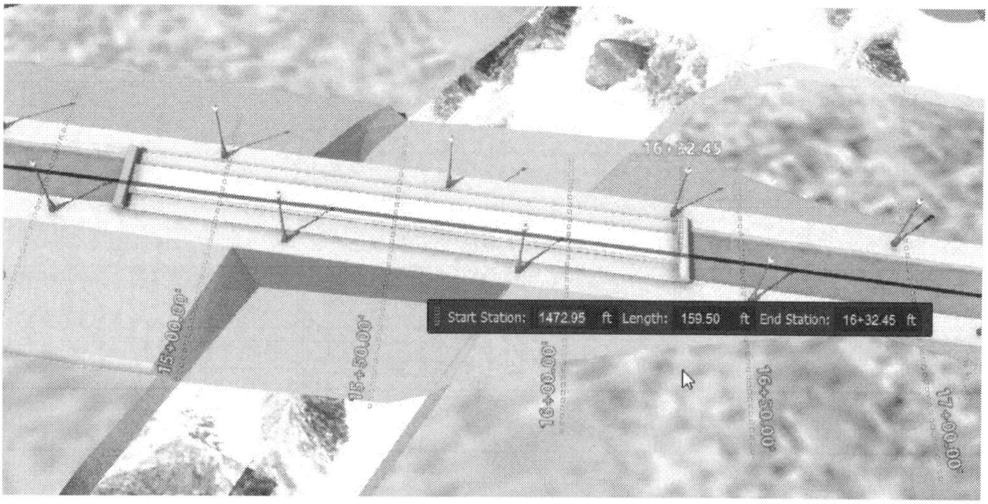

Figure 6–2

6.2 Modify Bridges

Once a bridge has been created, it can be modified using the *Bridge* asset card, various stacks of selected components, or gizmos.

Bridge Asset Card

The *Bridge* asset card enables you to change the type of bridge being modeled, the number of piers used to support the bridge, the clearance below the bridge, or the deck and bearing attributes, as shown in Figure 6–3.

> **Note:** *When any part of the bridge is selected by clicking once, it is referred to as a Bridge asset card. When anything else on the bridge is selected by clicking twice, it is referred to as the (selected component) stack.*

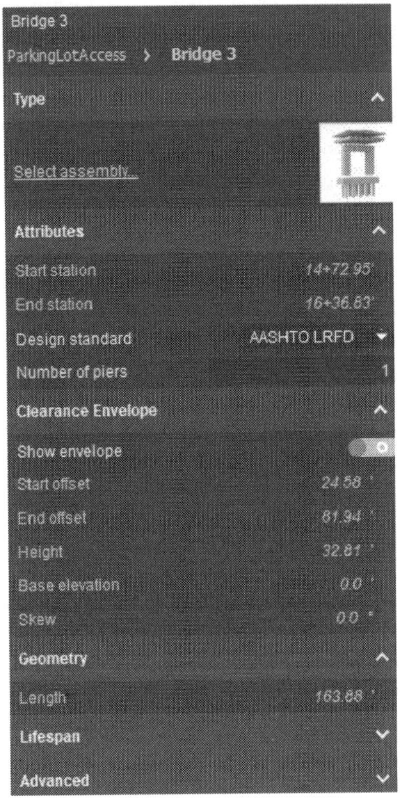

Figure 6–3

Bridge Clearance

To ensure that the bridge has the correct clearance for traffic below it, the clearance envelope can be displayed in the model. The clearance envelope is a purple box that indicates the clearance height required for the bridge. The **Show envelope** option is found in the *Bridge* asset card, as shown in Figure 6–4.

Figure 6–4

Once the **Show envelope** option is toggled on, all of the values within the *Clearance* area can be modified. Changing the *Height* value changes the height of the clearance envelope only. To change the height of the bridge, you must right-click on the bridge deck in the model and select **Update Vertical Profile**, as shown in Figure 6–5. This causes the profile of the road to adjust to accommodate the clearance envelope.

Figure 6–5

How To: Modify the Number of Bridge Piers Using the Bridge Asset Card

1. In the model, select the design bridge. The *Bridge* asset card displays.
2. In the *Bridge* asset card, change the *Number of piers*, as shown in Figure 6–6.

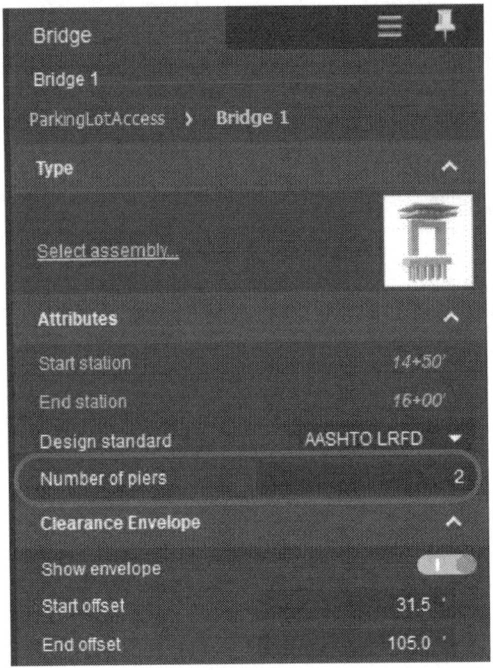

Figure 6–6

3. Press <Esc> to clear the bridge selection.

Bridge Grading

When a bridge is selected, additional parameters are displayed for grading. Both ends of the bridge structures have separate parameters to control their grading for offsets start, transitions and the offset ending, as shown in Figure 6–7.

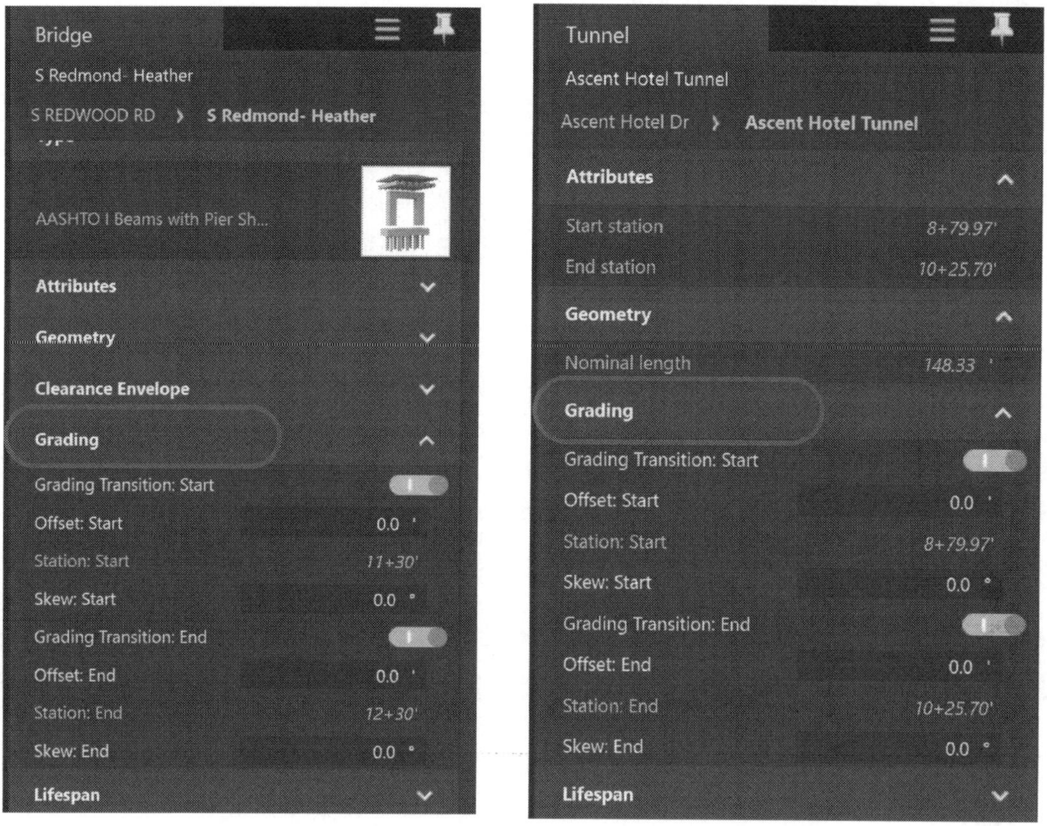

Figure 6–7

Note: *The same technique is used for controlling the grading for tunnels.*

Bridge Gizmos

When the bridge is selected, gizmos display at the beginning and ending stations of the bridge. Selecting either gizmo enables you to change the station for that specific gizmo, as shown in Figure 6–8.

Figure 6–8

If both the beginning and ending stations require changing, the space between the two gizmos can be selected. This enables you to change both stations at the same time, as shown in Figure 6–9.

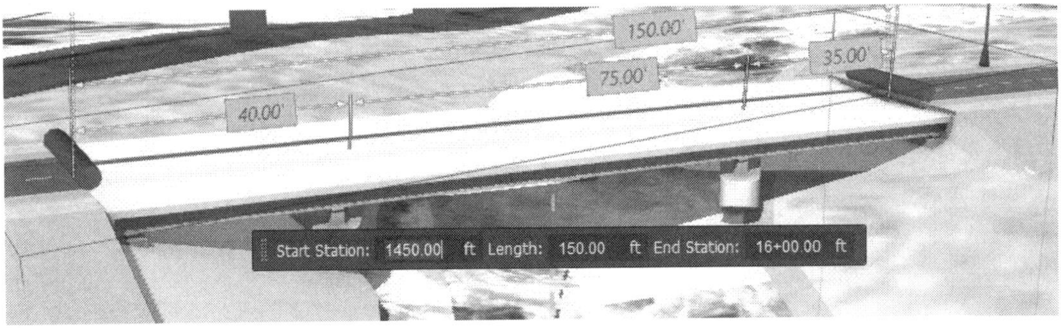

Figure 6–9

Selecting a pier causes a control gizmo to display. Clicking the (Control Gizmo) for the pier enables you to change the location of the pier. Additionally, you can rotate each pier with the (Rotate Gizmo), as shown in Figure 6–10.

Figure 6–10

How To: Modify the Bridge Using Gizmos

1. In the model, select the **design bridge**, then click on the bridge's beginning or ending station gizmo.
2. Drag the bridge gizmo to a new location to change the length of the bridge. Alternatively, you can type a new station value for the beginning or ending station and press <Enter>, as shown in Figure 6–11.

Figure 6–11

3. Press <Esc> to clear the bridge selection.

Bridge Properties

Properties for each component of a bridge can be modified using the component stack (asset card). Select the bridge component that needs to be modified to display its stack. Different properties are available depending upon which component of the bridge is selected in the model, as shown in Figure 6–12.

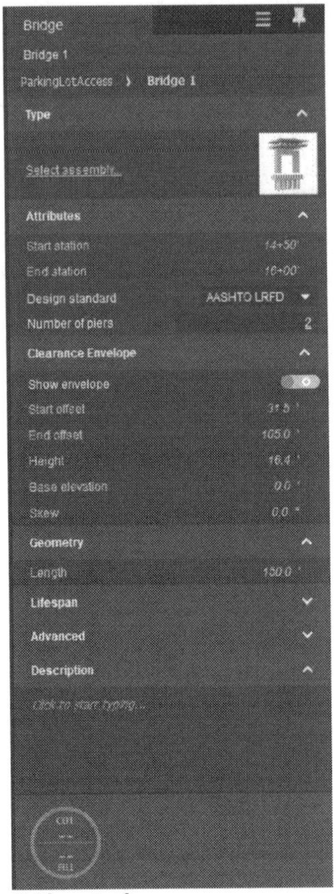

Bridge stack

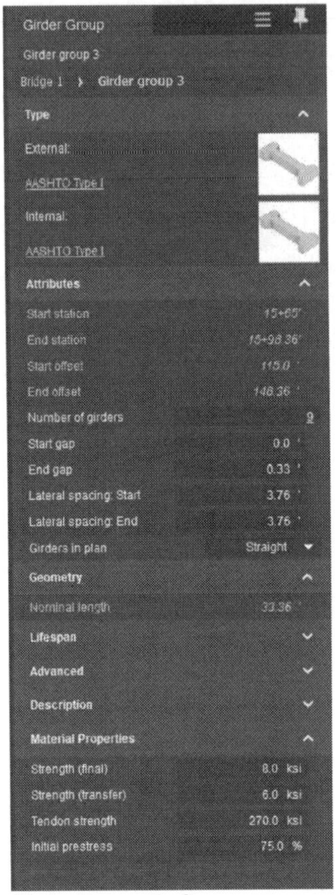

Girder Group stack

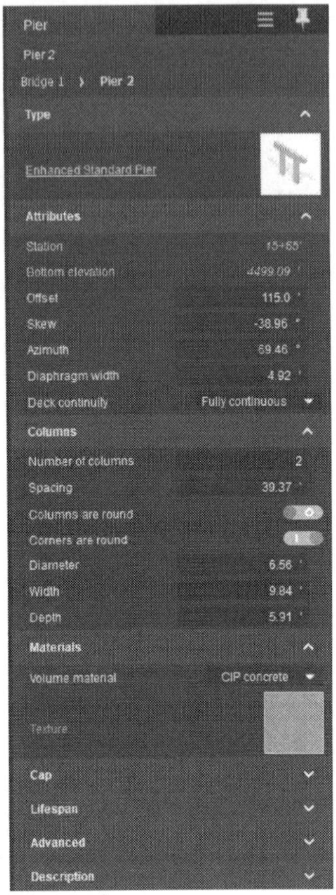

Pier stack

Figure 6–12

Bridge Templates Styles

In the *Style Palette*, the *Bridge Template* tabs enable you to create a library of bridge templates for reuse. The *Bridge Template* tab houses different parts for bridges that follow specific standards. To add items to the *Bridge Template*, you cannot use the traditional methods of adding or modifying items within the *Style Palette*. Instead, you select the bridge on screen and through the right-click menu, select **Add to Library...**, as shown in Figure 6–13.

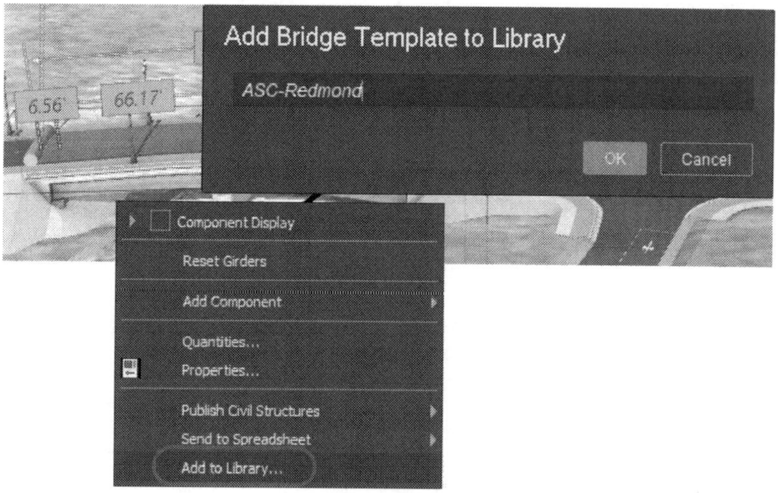

Figure 6–13

The template will go into a **Custom** folder within the *Bridge Component* tab of the *Style Palette*. You can create additional folders and rename the folders in the *Style Palette*.

Parametric Models

Parametric bridge model components can be created for use in Autodesk InfraWorks. The advantage of using parametric models is that you can use the same component part for multiple sizes of the same component, as shown in Figure 6–14. This is similar to a dynamic block in AutoCAD.

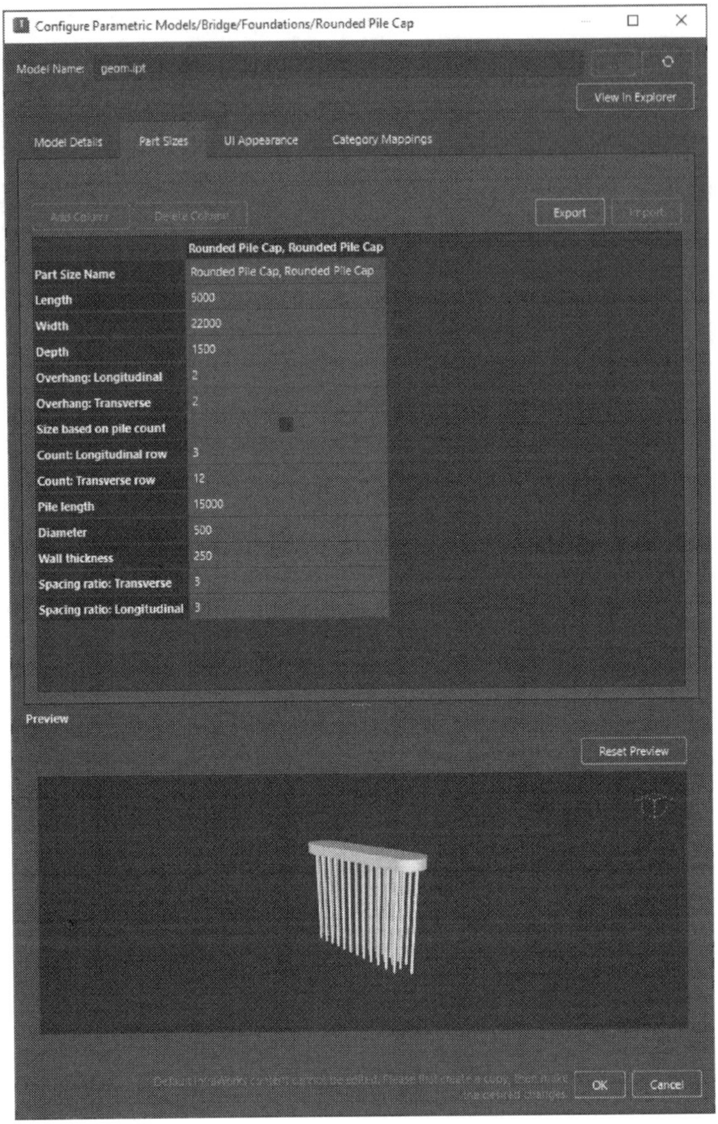

Figure 6–14

Note that within the preview area, you can zoom, pan, and orbit to inspect the item.

> ***Note:** See the Autodesk InfraWorks Online Help for information on installing the Infrastructure Part Shape Utilities plug-in.*

- Autodesk® Inventor® is used to create and configure parametric models in the form of .IPT files. You must use the Infrastructure Part Shape Utilities plug-in for Autodesk Inventor to make these files usable in InfraWorks.

  Note: *Only Autodesk Inventor Pro supports workflows for creating assemblies; Autodesk Inventor LT does not.*

How To: Add Parametric Bridge Components to the Style Palette

1. Open **Autodesk Inventor**.
2. Create a parametric model that fits your needs using Inventor.
3. Use the *Infrastructure Part Shape Utilities* plug-in for Inventor to specify key dimensions that can be viewed and edited in the InfraWorks software.
4. Use the *Infrastructure Part Shape Utilities* plug-in for Inventor to export the parametric bridge component model to an .IPT file format.
5. Open **Autodesk InfraWorks**.
6. In the *Manage* tab>*Content* drop-down list, click  (*Style Palette*).
7. Select the *Parametric Models* tab and double-click on **Bridge**. From here, you can modify several parametric bridge components, as shown in Figure 6–15.

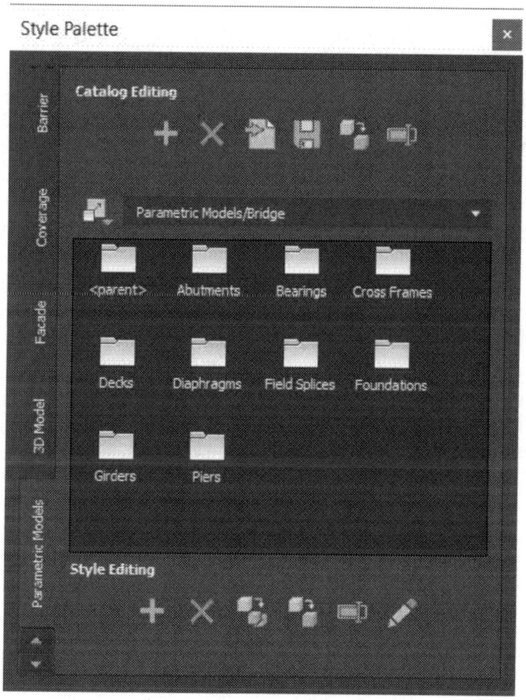

Figure 6–15

8. Double-click on the type of bridge component (*Abutments, Bearings, Cross Frames, Decks, Diaphragms, Field Splices, Foundations, Girders,* or *Piers*) for which you plan to create a parametric style.
9. At the bottom of the *Style Palette*, click (Add new style) in the *Style Editing* area.
10. In the *Configure Parametric Models* dialog box, click the ellipsis (...) and select an .IPT file that has been exported from Inventor using the *Infrastructure Part Shape Utilities* plug-in.
11. In the *Model Details* tab, fill in the *Name*, *Description*, *Domain*, and *Component type*, as shown in Figure 6–16.

    Note: *The Units field is not editable. You can orbit and navigate in the preview for a better view of the component.*

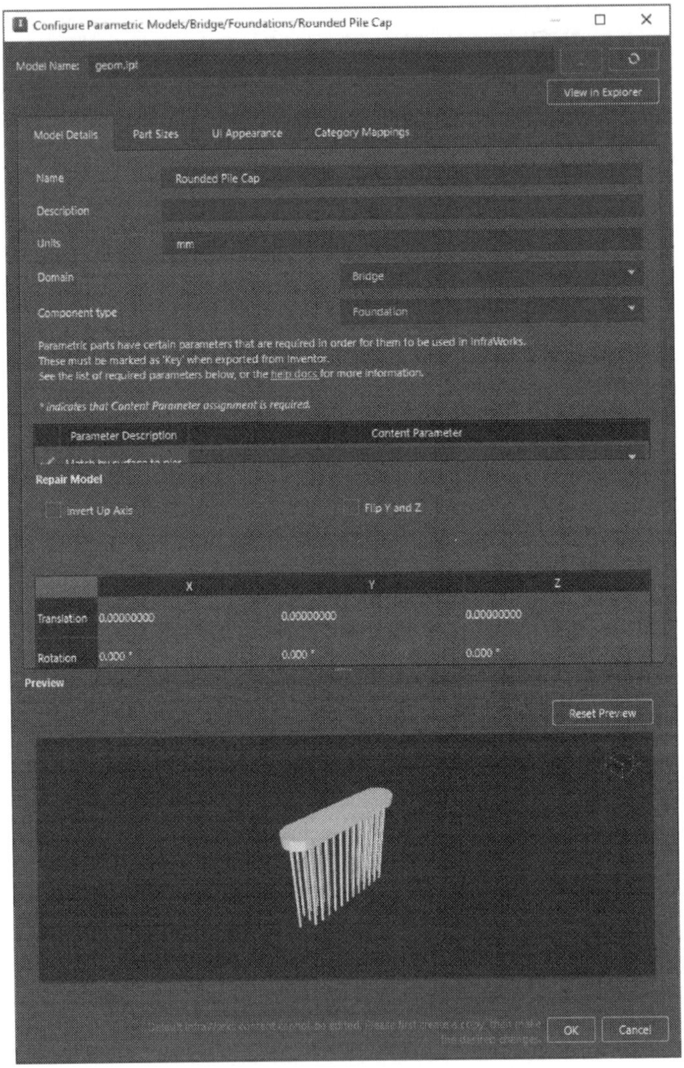

Figure 6–16

12. In the *Configure Parametric Models* dialog box, click the *Part Sizes* tab.
13. In the *Part Sizes* tab, do the following:
    - Click **Add Row** to add a new part size.
    - Each column represents a key dimension. Fill in each of the measurements across the row.
    - Continue adding rows for each part size.
14. In the *Configure Parametric Models* dialog box, click the *UI Appearance* tab.
15. In the *UI Appearance* tab, customize how attributes display in the component panel.
16. Click **OK**.

6.3 Clipping Planes

Clipping planes can provide better visualization and design of your bridges (and other civil structures such as tunnels) by clipping away content and displaying the cross section of the structure.They have the following characteristics:

- You can have multiple clipping planes on a structure and enable or disable any of them for effective design / visualization tools.
- You can reverse the direction of the clip of a clipping plane.
- You can display or hide the terrain and surfaces crossing the clipping plane.
- You can align your view perpendicular to the clipping plane.
- You can adjust the angle of the clip from the default perpendicular.
- You can delete clipping planes.
- Gizmos represent clipping planes for easy selection when the clips are disabled.

You can use clipping planes to temporarily expose the interior of a structure.

Clipping planes are managed through a floating menu when enabled, as shown in Figure 6–17.

Figure 6–17

How To: Enable and View Clipping Planes

1. Select the structure.
2. In the right-click menu, select **Show Clipping Planes**.

3. To disable or hide clipping planes, deselect the option in the right-click menu of the selected structure, as shown in Figure 6–18.

Figure 6–18

4. For the first clipping plane, you will be prompted to create the plane when they get enabled. Move your cursor to the desired location along the structure and press <Enter>.

The clipping plane displays as a flag above its location and has two states: unclipped ( ) and clipped ( ). You can change the state of clipped or unclipped by clicking on the flag. When enabled, you can manually reposition the clipping plane location by clicking and dragging the red arrow ( ) along the structure, as shown in Figure 6–19.

Figure 6–19

When clipping planes are enabled, the *Clipping Plane* toolbar displays, which can be used for tighter control over the positioning of the planes, as shown in Figure 6–20.

Figure 6–20

Icon	Description
	**Reverse Direction** - Swaps the clipped geometry to the opposite side of the plane.
	**Align Camera** - Aligns the camera to view the clip plane perpendicularly.
	**Clip Terrain** - Allows the terrain and surfaces to be clipped by the plane along with the civil structure.
	**Offset** - The location of the clip plane from the Start Station of the structure.
	**Skew** - The horizontal rotation in degrees of the plane relative to the perpendicular.
	**Create Plane** - Adds a new clipping plane. Move cursor to the desired location and press <Enter>.
	**Delete Plane** - Removes the currently selected clipping plane.

When the terrain is clipped, everything in the model is clipped and hidden beyond the clipping edge. When the terrain is unclipped, all surfaces are revealed (ponds, road subsurfaces, coverage and grading areas), but everything else in the model is hidden, as shown in Figure 6–21.

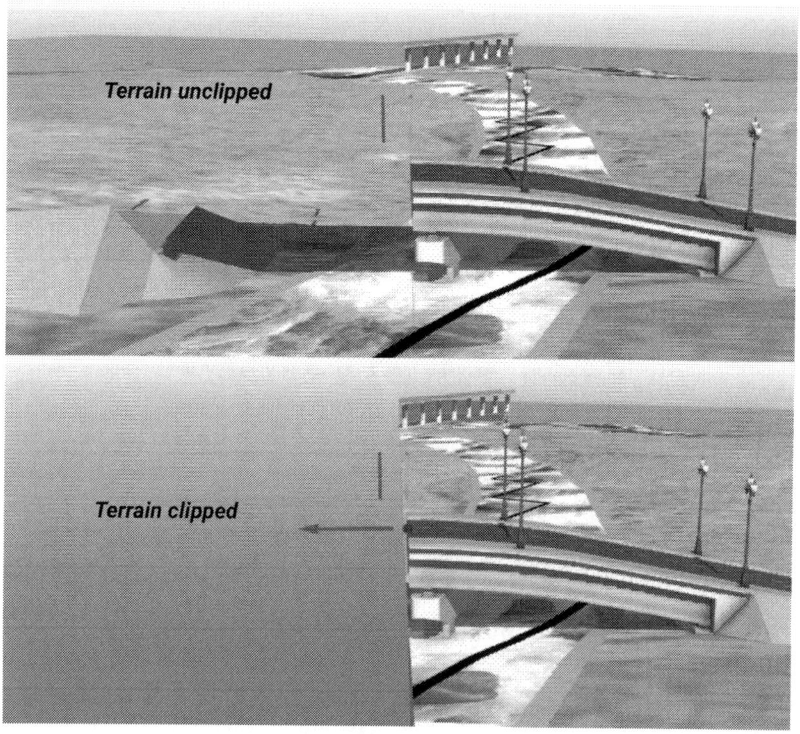

Figure 6–21

Aligning the camera with the clipping plane allow for detailed dimensioning within the civil structure. For example, one can measure and dimension the clear span between girders, as shown in Figure 6–22.

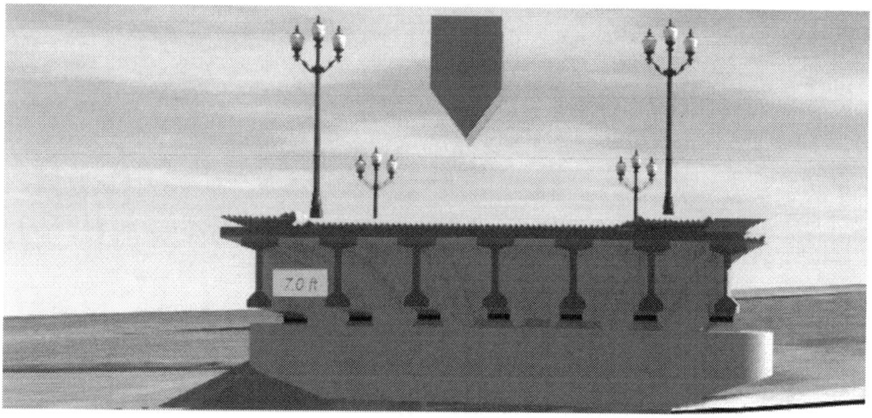

Figure 6–22

Practice 6a
Work with Bridges

Practice Objectives

- Add a bridge to the component road to provide passage over the river.
- Modify the design bridge to change the starting and ending stations and number of piers.

In this practice, you will add a bridge to the component road where it crosses the Heather Run river, as shown in Figure 6–23.

Figure 6–23

Please note that the road designs in these practices are meant as a learning exercise rather than proper road design. Therefore, the engineering and layout may not be optimal or appropriate for real-world use.

Task 1: Create a design bridge.

1. On the *Home* screen, click **Open**.
2. In the *InfraWorks Practice Files\6-Rails-Bridge-Tunnel* folder, select **CreateTransport.sqlite** and click **Open**.
3. Click (Bookmarks) and select **Add Transport**. Also ensure that **A_Task1** is the current proposal.
4. In the *Create* tab>*Structures* panel, click (Bridge).
5. In the model, click on the **S Redwood Rd** component road near where it crosses the **Heather Run** river.

6. In the *Start Station* field, type **1130**. Press <Tab> twice, then in the *Length* field, type **100**, as shown in Figure 6–24. Press <Enter>. It takes a while to construct the bridge.

Figure 6–24

7. In the *Bridge* asset card, name the bridge **S Redwood-Heather**.
8. Under *Type*, click **Select assembly**.
9. In the *Select Template* asset card, click **BridgeTemplate>AASHTO I Beams with Pier Shafts**, as shown in Figure 6–25. Click **OK**.

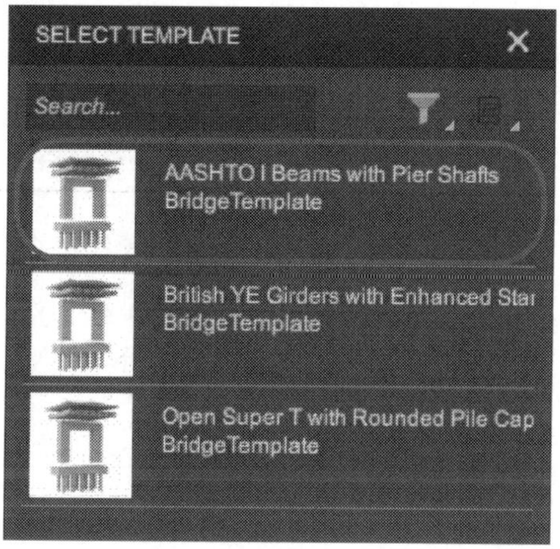

Figure 6–25

10. Press <Esc> to clear the selection of the bridge.

Note that the bridge deck remains the same as the rest of the road and the culvert is poking out. All that changed is the supporting structure below the road.

11. Click (Bookmarks) and select **Add Transport 3D**. Pan below the surface to see that the bridge is actually submerged below the road, as shown in Figure 6–26. This will get rectified in the next task. Pan back up.

Figure 6–26

12. Select the culvert, as shown in Figure 6–27, and delete it since it is no longer needed. If there are two culverts, delete both of them.

Figure 6–27

Task 2: Modify the bridge and road elevations.

In this task, you will raise the bridge and road elevations.

1. Continue working in the same model as the last task. If you did not complete the last task, select the **A_Task2** proposal to make it current.
2. In the model, click on the **S Redwood Rd** component road, then press <Ctrl>+<0> (zero) or use the right-click menu to open the *Profile View*.
3. In the *Profile View*, in the lower-right corner, click (Asset Toggle) to toggle on **Structures** if it is off. Note the tunnel icon and the white line indicating the length and vertical curvature of the tunnel, as shown in Figure 6–28.

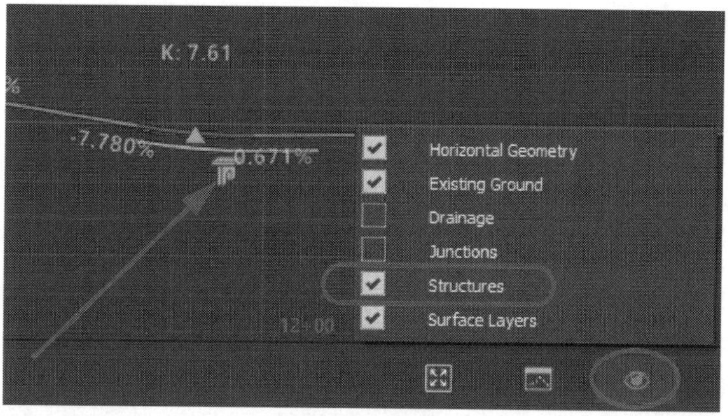

Figure 6–28

4. Zoom and pan in the *Profile View* to center around station **11+00**, as shown in Figure 6–29.

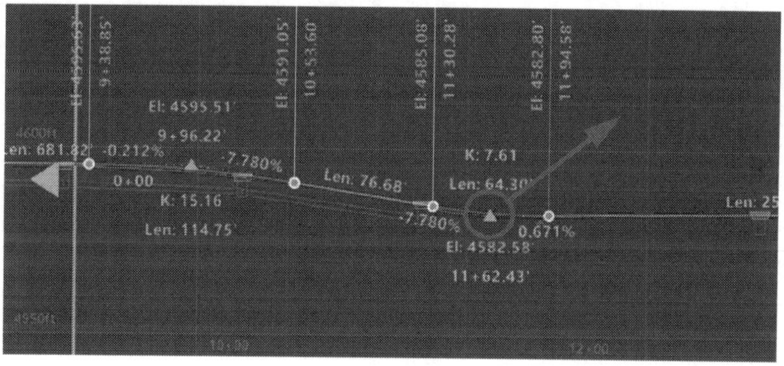

Figure 6–29

5. In the *Profile View*, slide the yellow section marker so it is located near the center of the bridge (near station **11+90**). As you move it, keep an eye on the 3D model to see where it is being positioned.

6. Move the PVI shown previously in Figure 6–29 to the section marker at an elevation of about **4606'**, as shown in Figure 6–30. If required, you can also type in the elevation by clicking on the elevation text.

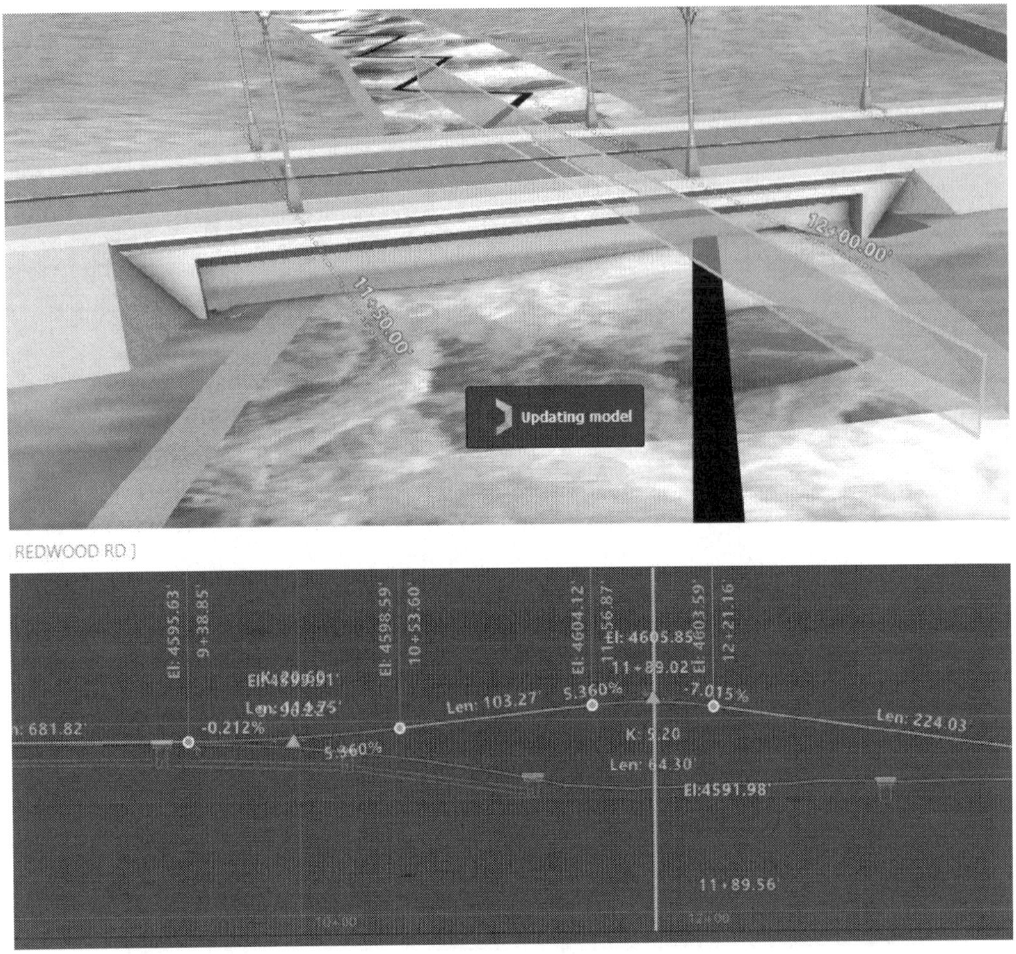

Figure 6–30

Raising the road elevation causes the next intersection to get disconnected and this needs to be corrected.

7. In the *Profile View*, slide the yellow section marker so it is located near the center of the intersection of *Morris Beach Blvd* (near station 13+20). Orbit and pan in the model to get a better view of the intersection.

8. Move the next PVI as noted in Figure 6–29 from station 14+89.40' to the section marker at an elevation of about **4583'**, as shown in Figure 6–31.

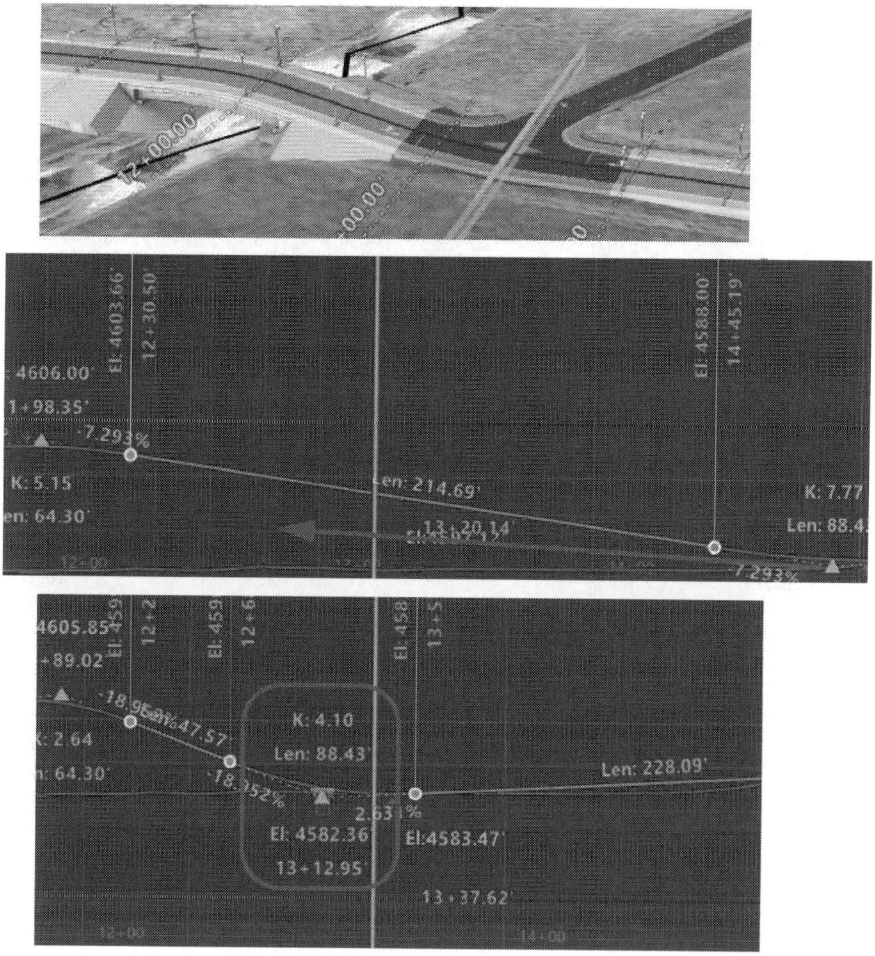

Figure 6–31

9. Close the *Profile View* either by pressing <Ctrl>+<0> (zero) or by clicking on the **X** in the upper-right corner.

10. Click (Bookmarks) and select **Bridge-Grading 3D**.

11. Note that the roadside grading of **S Redwood Road** falls short. Select the grading components on both sides (one at a time) and set the *Fill Slope* to **2.00:1** and the *Grading Limit* to **50.00'**, as shown in Figure 6–32.

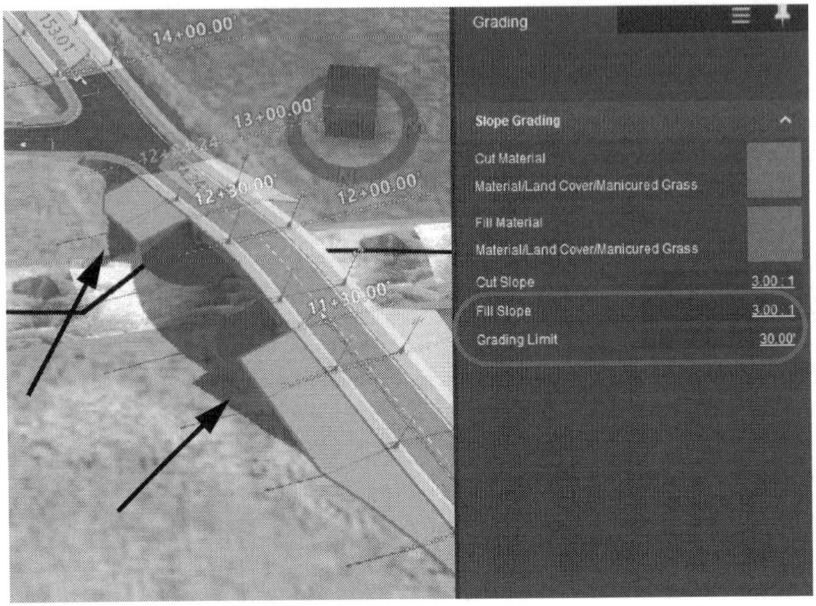

Figure 6–32

12. The bridge converges into the river and must be adjusted. Select the bridge by picking on a girder, then select the oncoming yellow tube. Type **1115** for the *Start Station* and press <Enter>.
13. Pick the outgoing cyan tube, type **1250** for the *End Station*, and press <Enter>.
14. Press <Esc> to release the bridge.

Task 3: Modify the S Redwood Rd drainage network.

Note: *The recommended workflow is to complete a component road with all its components, bridges, tunnels, and interchanges (roundabouts) before adding a drainage network, which would avoid this task.*

With the addition of the bridge to **S Redwood Road**, you need to check and adjust the drainage network.

1. Do not continue working in the last task. Rather, select the **A_Task3** proposal to make it current.
2. Click (Bookmarks) and select **Bridge-Drainage 3D**, which shows the road and river from the underside.

3. Select the manhole (A) shown in Figure 6–33. Use the purple cube gizmo to move it onto the pavement. In a similar fashion, move the two inlets (B) and (C) onto the gutters.
4. Finally, select and delete the manhole, two inlets, and pipes (D) on the other side of the bridge, since they have become superfluous.

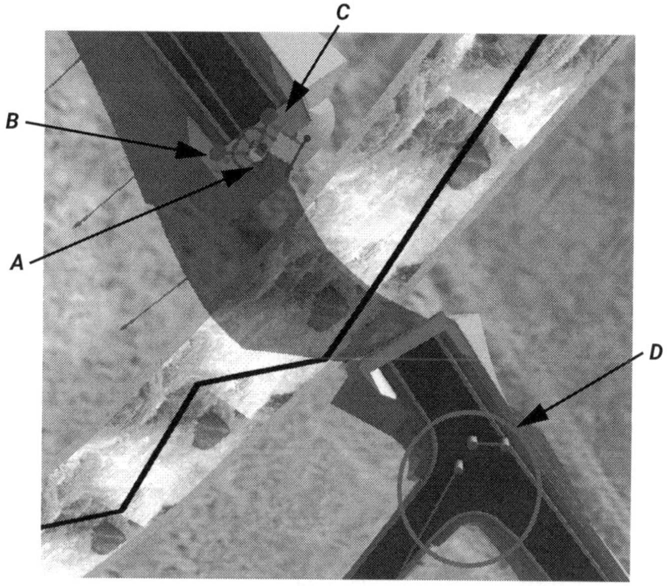

Figure 6–33

5. The final result should be similar to Figure 6–34.

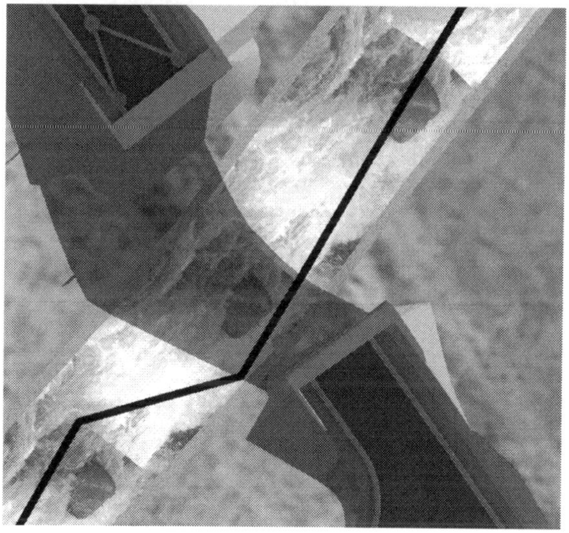

Figure 6–34

Task 4: Modify the bridge to remove the pier.

In this task, you will modify the bridge to remove the pier using the *Bridge* asset card.

1. Continue working in the same model as the last task. If you did not complete the last task, select the **A_Task4** proposal to make it current.
2. Click (Bookmarks) and select **Add Transport 3D**.
3. In the model, click on the design bridge pier to display the *Bridge* asset card.

   Note: *If you click on the bridge deck, the Road asset card displays instead. To avoid this, ensure you click on part of the supporting structure.*

4. In the *Bridge* asset card, change the *Number of piers* to **1**, as shown in Figure 6–35. Press <Enter> to accept the change.

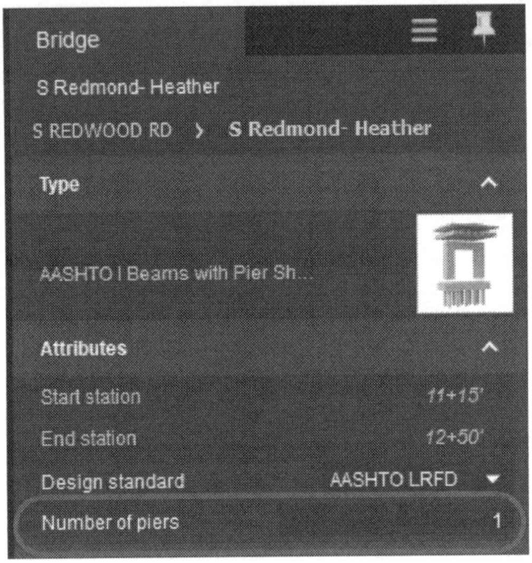

Figure 6–35

- Alternatively, once the bridge is selected, you can right-click and select **Add Component>Pier**, as shown in Figure 6–36.

Figure 6–36

5. Press <Esc> to release the bridge selection.

6. Select the newly added pier. Use the (Control Gizmo) to move the pier into the center of the river and the (Rotate Gizmo) to align the pier with the river, as shown in Figure 6–37.

Figure 6–37

7. Press <Esc> to release the bridge.

Task 5: Create clipping planes.

In this task, you will create a clipping plane on the bridge and make a detailed dimension between the girders.

1. Continue working in the same model as the last task.
2. Click (Bookmarks) and select **Add Transport-3D.**
3. Zoom in closer to the **S Redmond-Heather** bridge.
4. Select the bridge. Ensure you have the bridge selected, and not a component of the bridge.
5. In the right-click menu, toggle on **Show Clipping Planes**, as shown in Figure 6–38.

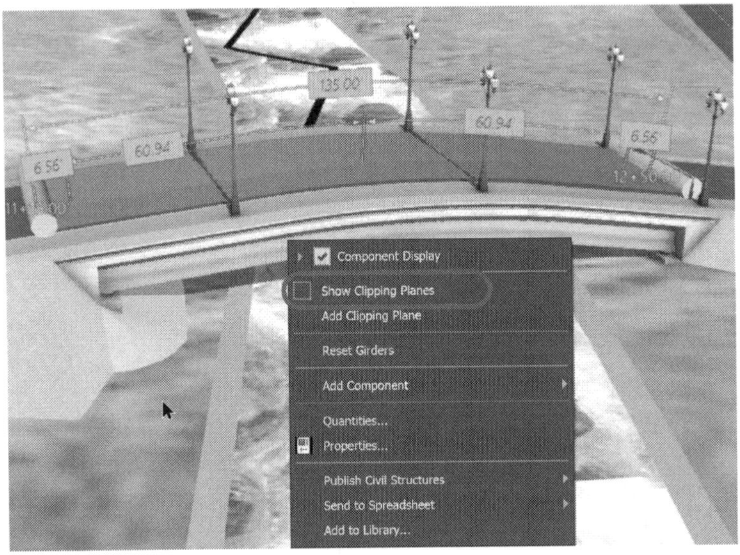

Figure 6–38

6. The *Clipping Plane* toolbar is displayed near the bridge, as shown in Figure 6–39.

Figure 6–39

7. As you move your cursor back and forth, the model is clipped on a plane perpendicular to the bridge. The *Offset* value in the toolbar updates relative to the starting station of the bridge.

8. Select a point near the 40' station and press <Enter>. The entire model is clipped at that point and a cyan marker appears above the clipping plane, as shown in Figure 6–40.

Figure 6–40

9. Click on (Toggle Terrain) to see all the surfaces in the model, while the bridge and roads remain clipped, as shown in Figure 6–41.

Figure 6–41

10. Click on (red arrow) to adjust the clipping plane.
11. Click on (Cyan marker) to disable the clipping. The marker turns red, indicating it is not active.
12. Click anywhere in the model and the toolbar and red arrow vanish, but the red marker remains.
13. Click on (Red marker) to enable the clipping plane and its toolbar.
14. Click on (Align Camera) to orient the view perpendicular to the clipping plane.

    Note: *Measuring tools will be covered in more detail later in this guide.*

15. In the *Measure* drop-down menu, click on (Point to Point Distance) and click the two points on either side of two girders, as shown in Figure 6–42. You may have to reposition the *Clipping Plane* menu.

Figure 6–42

16. In the toolbar, expand the (Measure) drop-down list and click (Point Elevation). Select any point on the top deck to see what the elevation of the bridge is. Optionally, you can select a second point to position the elevation readout.
17. Press <Esc> to remove the measurement.
18. In the toolbar, click on (Delete clipping plane) to erase the clipping plane. The clipping plane is deleted, the marker disappears and the toolbar closes.
19. Click (Bookmarks) and select **Add Transport**.

End of practice

6.4 Bridge Line Girder Analysis

Girders

Girders can be edited individually or in groups (interior and exterior). Autodesk InfraWorks contains multiple precast girder styles. You can assign different girder styles to each girder in a bridge, or assign styles to a group of girders.

- Clicking on a bridge girder once selects the bridge and displays the *Bridge* asset card.
- Clicking on a bridge girder a second time selects a bridge girder group and displays the *Girder Group* stack.
- Clicking on a specific girder displays the *Girder* stack.

The *Girder Group* stack and the *Girder* stack are shown in Figure 6–43.

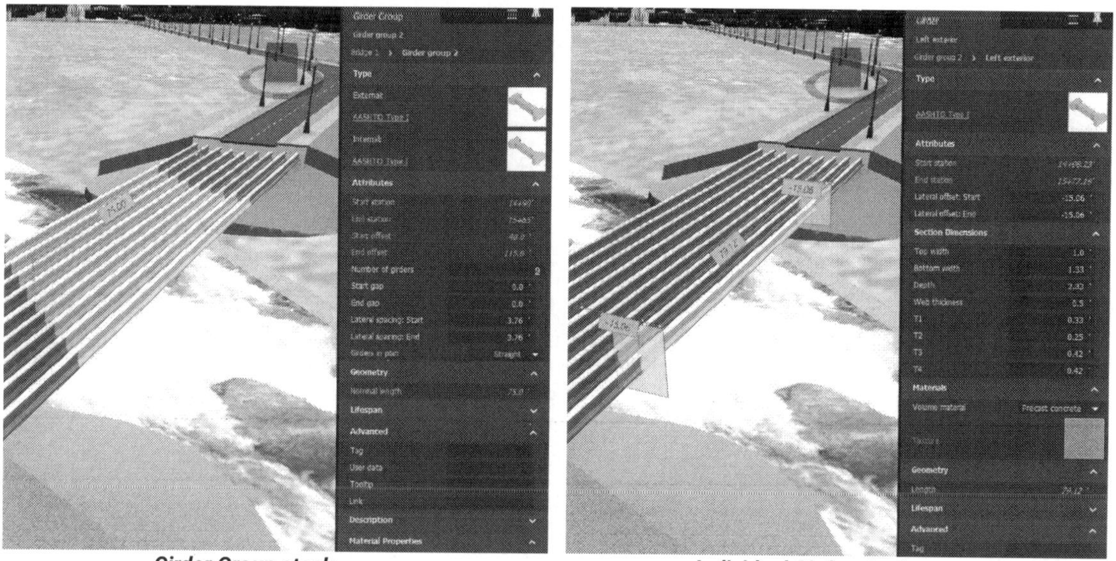

Girder Group stack ***Individual Girder stack***

Figure 6–43

In the *Girder* stack, in the *Type* area, when you click inside the girder image, a girder schematic panel displays, as shown in Figure 6–44.

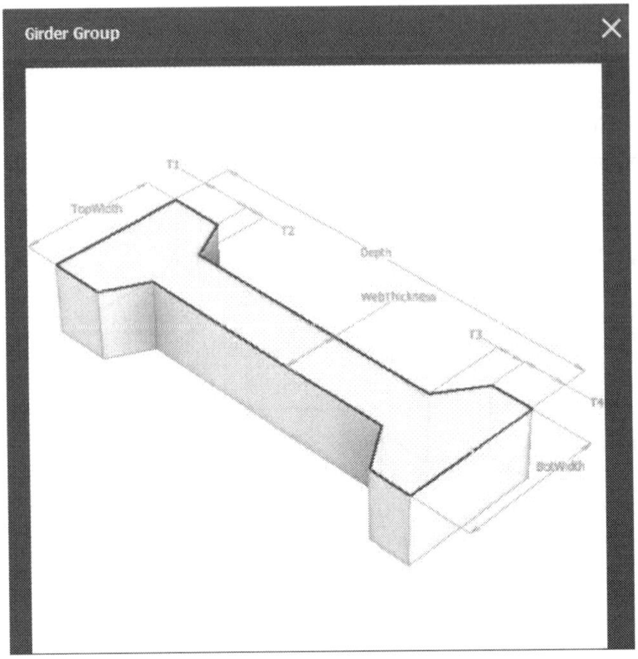

Figure 6–44

Girder Analysis

The structural strength of pre-stressed concrete bridge girders can be verified using the *Autodesk InfraWorks* cloud service. Initial results can be viewed in the model. The design optimization is computed using the *Autodesk Structural Bridge Design* software.

You can also update your InfraWorks model with design changes made directly in *Autodesk Structural Bridge Design*, as shown in Figure 6–45.

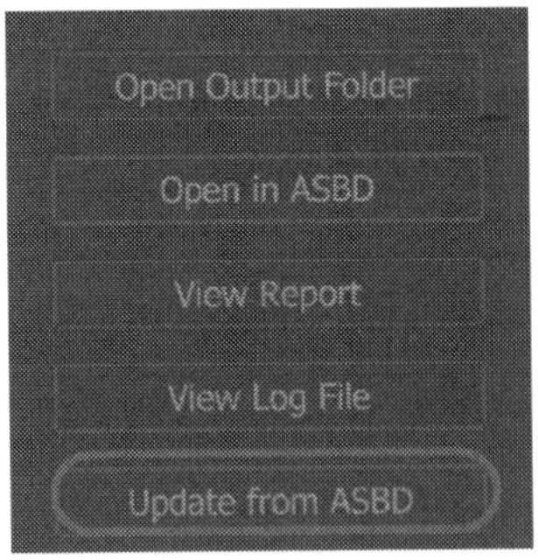

Figure 6–45

Project Information

Information provided during the analysis displays in the final PDF report. By completing as much information as possible, others reading the report can identify the project it belongs to and the company that created the report. The following information can be added to the report, as shown in Figure 6–46:

- Project name
- Job name
- Job reference
- Company information
  - Company name
  - Address
  - Logo file
  - User initials

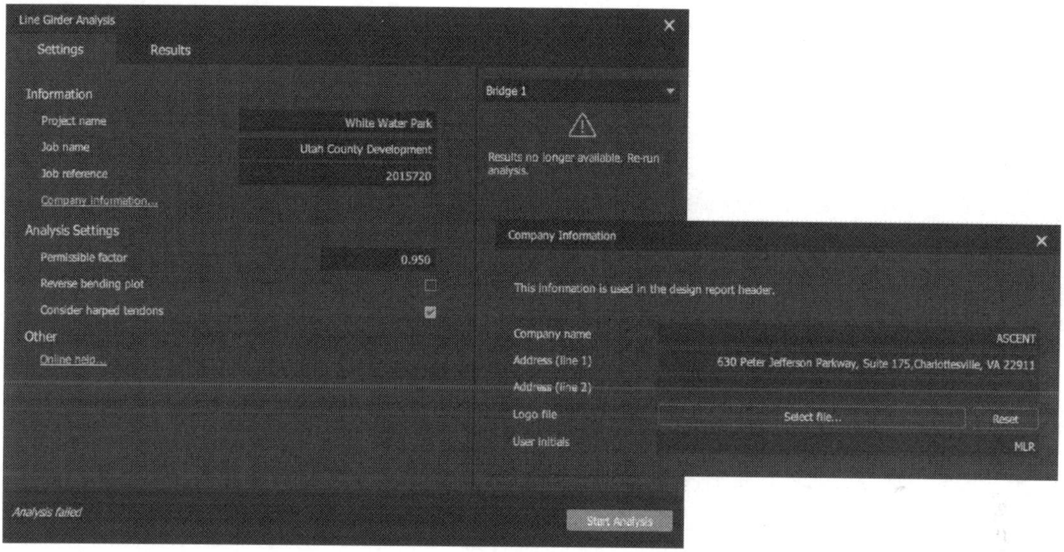

Figure 6–46

Once an analysis is complete, selecting any girder displays the results of the analysis in the *Line Girder Analysis* panel. Additional analysis information can be viewed by clicking **View Report**. A sample report is shown in Figure 6–47.

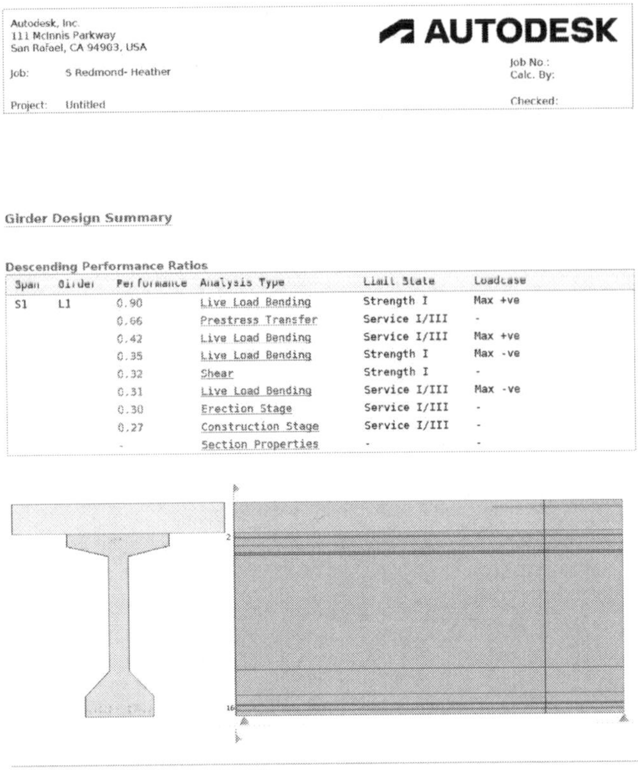

Autodesk, Inc.
111 McInnis Parkway
San Rafael, CA 94903, USA

AUTODESK

Job: S Redmond- Heather

Job No :
Calc. By:

Project: Untitled

Checked:

Girder Design Summary

Descending Performance Ratios

Span	Girder	Performance	Analysis Type	Limit State	Loadcase
S1	L1	0.90	Live Load Bending	Strength I	Max +ve
		0.66	Prestress Transfer	Service I/III	-
		0.42	Live Load Bending	Service I/III	Max +ve
		0.35	Live Load Bending	Strength I	Max -ve
		0.32	Shear	Strength I	-
		0.31	Live Load Bending	Service I/III	Max -ve
		0.30	Erection Stage	Service I/III	-
		0.27	Construction Stage	Service I/III	-
		-	Section Properties	-	-

Figure 6–47

How To: Run a Bridge Line Girder Analysis

1. In the *Analyze* tab>*Structures* panel, click (Line Girder Analysis).

   Note: *To use this feature, access to the Internet is required.*

2. In the *Line Girder Analysis* panel, verify the *Project name*, and enter the *Job name* and *Job reference*.
3. In the *Line Girder Analysis* panel, click **Company information...**.
4. In the *Company Information* panel, enter all of the available project information. Close the panel.
5. In the *Line Girder Analysis* panel, enter a *Permissible Factor*. This factor is applied to the permissible values during the tendon design.

6. Check or clear **Reverse bending plot**.
    - This affects the graphic representations that are received in the detailed girder documentation (full report). It changes the direction of bending moments but not the direction of torsion moments.
7. Check or clear **Consider harped tendons**. This sets whether harping is considered in the tendon design.
8. Click **Start Analysis.**
9. The status of the analysis is displayed and updated in the lower portion of the panel, as shown in Figure 6–48.

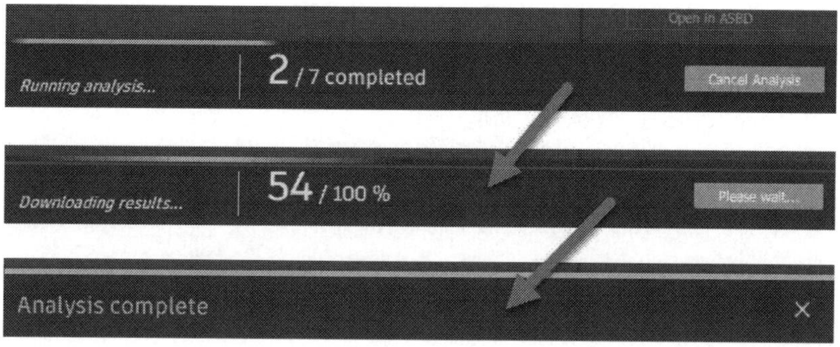

Figure 6–48

10. Once complete, select a girder to view the results in the *Line Girder Analysis* panel.
11. Click **Open Output Folder**, then go to the *Report* folder, where all the PDF reports are stored.

Practice 6b
Run a Girder Analysis

Practice Objective

- Analyze the bridge girders for structural strength.

> **Note:** *To complete this project, access to the Internet is required. Traffic load in the cloud may cause delays in the analysis and results.*

In this practice, you will analyze the bridge girders for structural strength.

1. Continue working in the same model as the last practice. If you closed the file, on the *Home* screen, click **Open**. In the *InfraWorks Practice Files\6-Rails-Bridge-Tunnel* folder, select **CreateTransport.sqlite** and click **Open**.
2. If you did not complete the last practice, select the **B_Task1** proposal to make it current.
3. Click (Bookmarks) and select **Add Transport 3D**.
4. In the model, select the design bridge. Right-click, then click on *Component Display* and expand *Component Display*. Clear the selection of **Road, Deck**, **Generic Features**, and **Decorations** (as shown in Figure 6–49) to make it easier to see the girders.

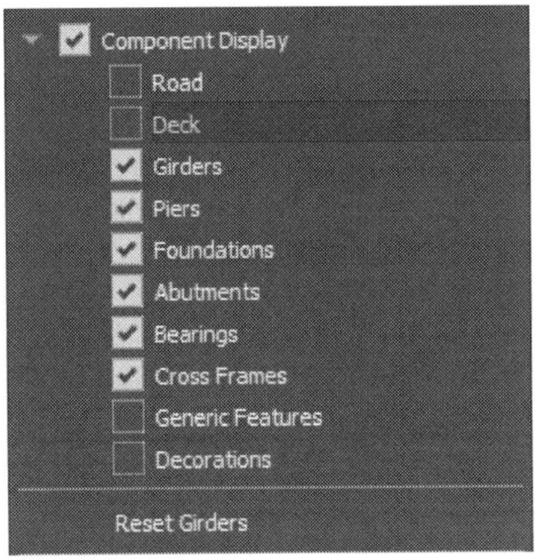

Figure 6–49

5. With the bridge still selected, in the *Analyze* tab>*Structures* panel, select (Line Girder Analysis).

> **Note:** *If this information is already present, it is because the last person to use your computer already filled it in. The information remains on the system for convenience.*

6. In the *Line Girder Analysis* panel, select the *Settings* tab and set the following, as shown in Figure 6–50:
    - *Project name:* **Ascent Fundamentals**
    - *Job name*: **Heather Run Bridge**
    - *Job reference:* **123456**
7. Click on **Company information...**. In the *Company Information* panel, fill in your company information and initials, as shown in Figure 6–50.
8. Close the *Company Information* panel by clicking on the **X** in the upper-right corner.
9. In the *Line Girder Analysis* panel, leave the default values for the remaining fields and click **Start Analysis**, as shown in Figure 6–50. Once you start the analysis, it will take some time to process.

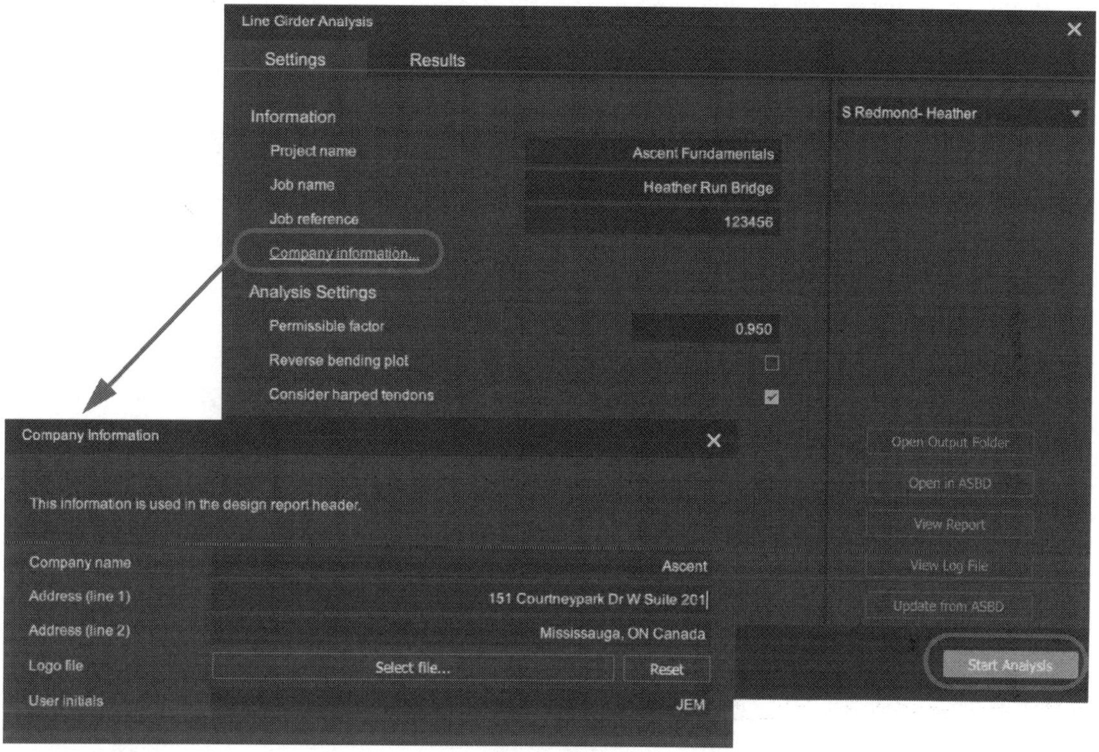

Figure 6–50

Hint: Analysis Time Requirements

If the analysis is taking too long, you can cancel the analysis and browse to the *InfraWorks Practice Files\References\Reports\S Redmond- Heather\Report* folder to see the results.

10. When the analysis is complete, it should return **14 Girders analyzed, 14 Girders satisfy design requirements**. Click **Open Output Folder**, as shown Figure 6–51.

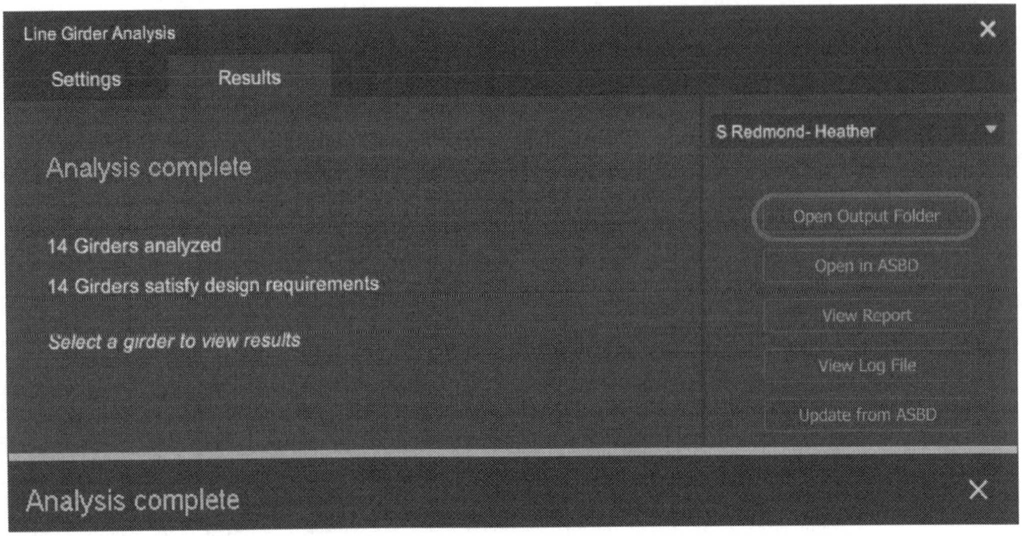

Figure 6–51

11. InfraWorks has created the following folder in your practice files folder: *InfraWorks Practice Files\Autodesk Bridge Analysis\CreateTransport\<Current Task>\S Redwood- Heather\Report*. Windows File Explorer opens to that folder.
12. Select one of the PDF reports and double-click to open it and see the results.
13. Return to the InfraWorks application and exit the *Line Girder Analysis* panel by clicking on the **X** in the upper-right corner.
14. Press <Esc> to clear the selection of the bridge.
15. In the model, select the design bridge. Right-click and uncheck **Component Display**. This will make all components of the bridge visible.

End of practice

6.5 Detail Design for Bridges

A key benefit to designing the bridge in the InfraWorks software is the ability to view the bridge in the context of its surroundings without losing any time on the design. When you are ready to proceed into the detailed design phase for the bridge, you can move the design easily into the Autodesk Revit or Autodesk Navisworks software.

Preparing a Bridge for Autodesk Revit

The Autodesk Revit software provides many more tools for designing bridges than InfraWorks. Fortunately, you can send the bridge from InfraWorks to Revit with a simple right-click command. When doing so, you have three options on how it is included in Revit:

- You can use Revit families as parametric content in InfraWorks.
- You can use Revit to create and configure .RFA parametric model files for use in InfraWorks.
- As a direct shape.

Note: *Only Revit supports workflows for creating families; Revit LT does not.*

How To: Publish a Bridge for Autodesk Revit

1. Click to select any part of the bridge.
2. Right-click on the bridge and select **Publish Civil Structures>Create New**, as shown in Figure 6–52.

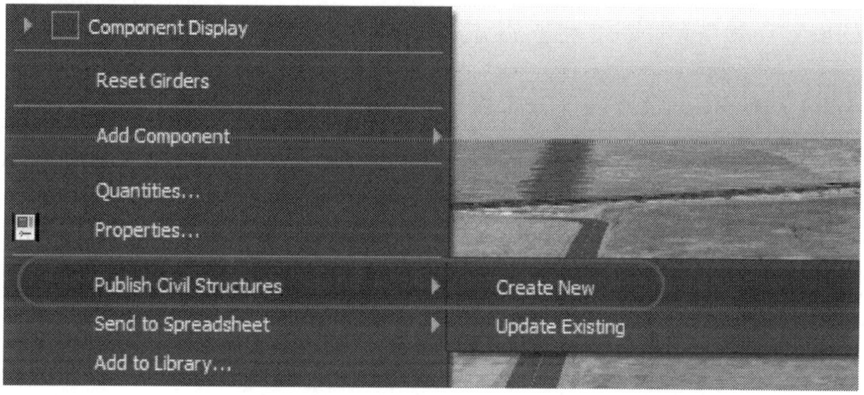

Figure 6–52

3. The *Publish Civil Structures* dialog box opens.

4. Next to the *Location* field, click the ellipsis (...) for browsing to navigate to the folder you want to store the export files, as shown in Figure 6–53.
5. Choose a *Backup proposal name* for the backup proposal that will be generated, as shown in Figure 6–53.

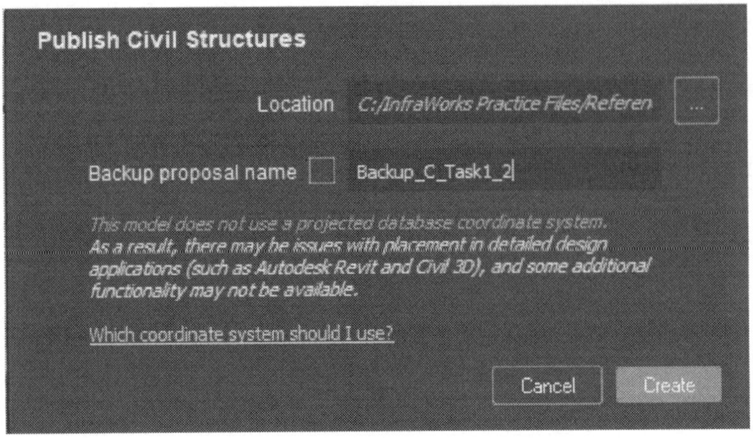

Figure 6–53

6. Click **Create**.

Open a Bridge in Autodesk Navisworks

The design can be opened directly in the Autodesk Navisworks software to uncover design problems and constructibility issues more effectively and plan the construction sequencing. There are two options when porting an InfraWorks model to Navisworks.

- **Option 1:** First, open the bridge in Autodesk Civil 3D, then open the .DWG file in Navisworks.
- **Option 2:** From InfraWorks, export a 3D model, which you can append to the Navisworks file.

If a 3D model is used to import a design into Navisworks, you can export the model as a single file or multiple files. The benefit of using multiple files is that you can select which features in the model to export.

How To: Export an InfraWorks Model to Autodesk Navisworks

1. In the *Present/Share* tab>*Share* panel, click (Export 3D Model).
2. In the *Export to 3D Model File* dialog box, do the following, as shown in Figure 6–54:
   - Define the area to export.
   - Set the *Target Coordinate System*.
   - Determine if you want a single file or multiple files.
   - Click **Export**.

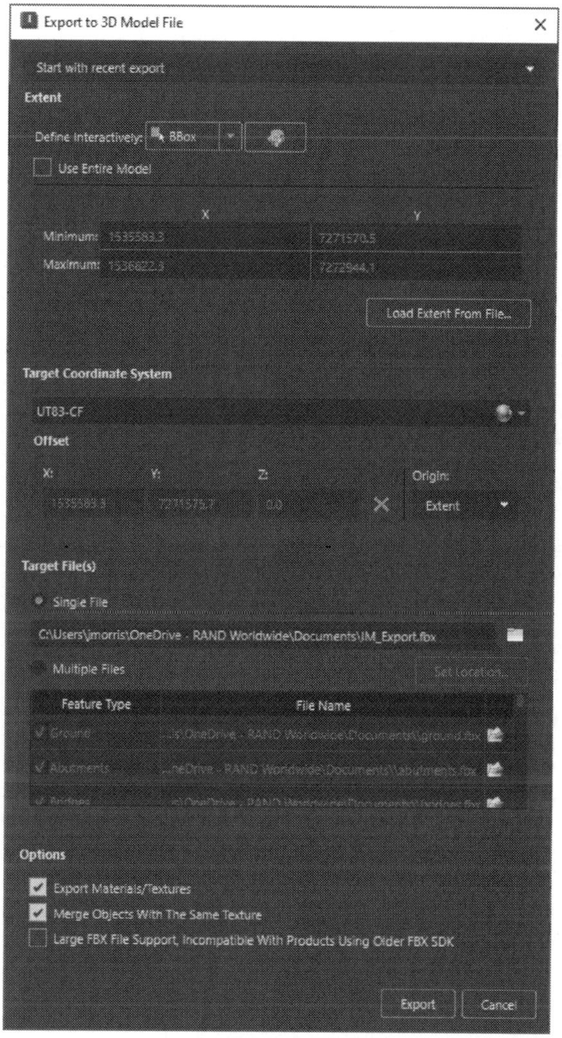

Figure 6–54

Practice 6c
Send the Bridge to the Detailed Design Phase

Practice Objectives

- Prepare a bridge for use within the Autodesk Revit software.
- Create a 3D model of the bridge for the Autodesk Navisworks software.

In this practice, you will prepare a bridge for use within the Autodesk Revit software, then export the bridge to create a 3D model for the Autodesk Navisworks software.

Task 1: Publish a bridge for Autodesk Revit.

1. Continue working in the same model as the last practice. If you closed the file, on the *Home* screen, click **Open**. In the *InfraWorks Practice Files\6-Rails-Bridge-Tunnel* folder, select **CreateTransport.sqlite** and click **Open**.
2. If you did not complete either of the previous practices, select the **B_Task1** proposal to make it current.
3. Click (Bookmarks) and select **Add Transport 3D**.
4. In the model, select the **S Redmond- Heather** bridge. Right-click on the bridge and select **Publish Civil Structures>Create New**, as shown in Figure 6–55.

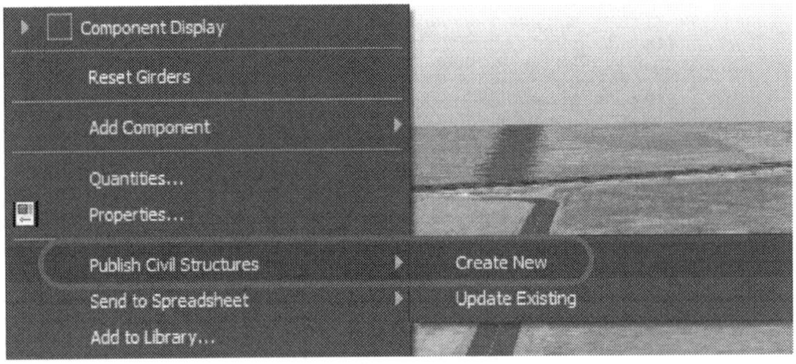

Figure 6–55

5. In the *Publish Civil Structures* dialog box, click the ellipsis (...) for browsing, next to the *Location* field and navigate to the *InfraWorks Practice Files\References\RVT* folder. Accept the default for the *Backup proposal name* and click **Create**, as shown in Figure 6–56.

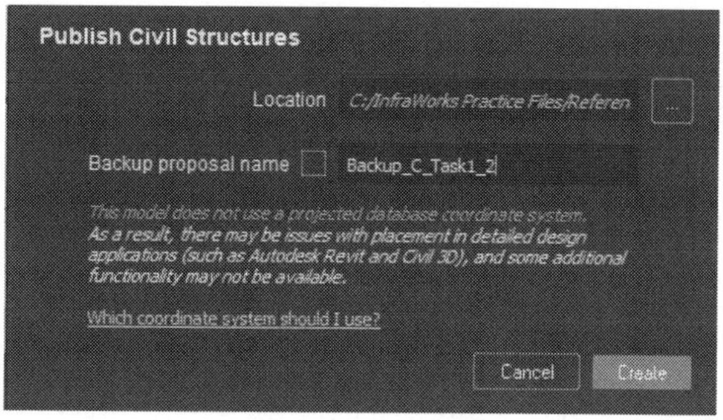

Figure 6–56

6. The message shown in Figure 6–57 will display as the export is processing. It may take some time to export the files, so be patient.

Figure 6–57

***Note:** The Revit Civil Structures tools are not covered in this guide. In Revit, in the Add-Ins tab>Civil Structures panel, there are tools to continue the detailed design of the bridge, as shown in Figure 6–58.*

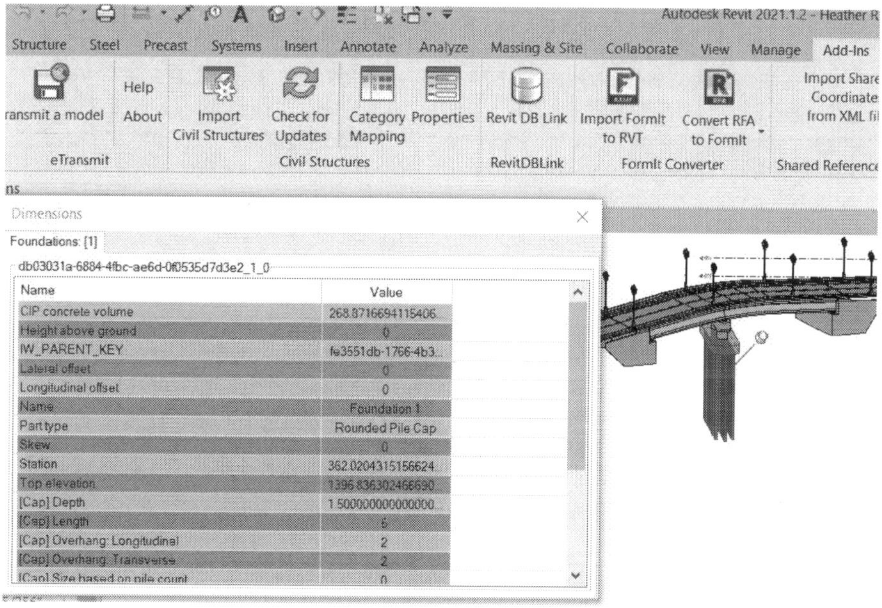

Figure 6–58

Task 2: Send a model to multiple Autodesk FBX files.

1. Click (Bookmarks) and select **Add Transport**.
2. In the *Present/Share* tab>*Share* panel, select (Export 3D Model).
3. Next to *Define Interactively*, select **Polygon**. Define the polygon, as shown in Figure 6–59, and double-click at the last vertex to finish.

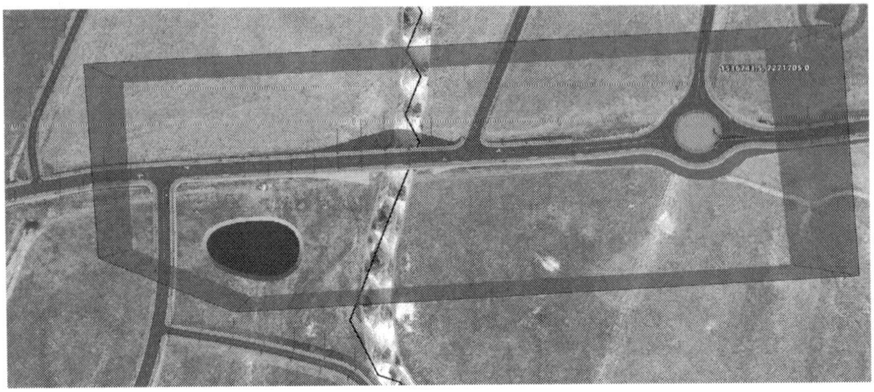

Figure 6–59

4. Ensure that the *Target Coordinate System* is set to **UT83-CF**, as shown in Figure 6–60.

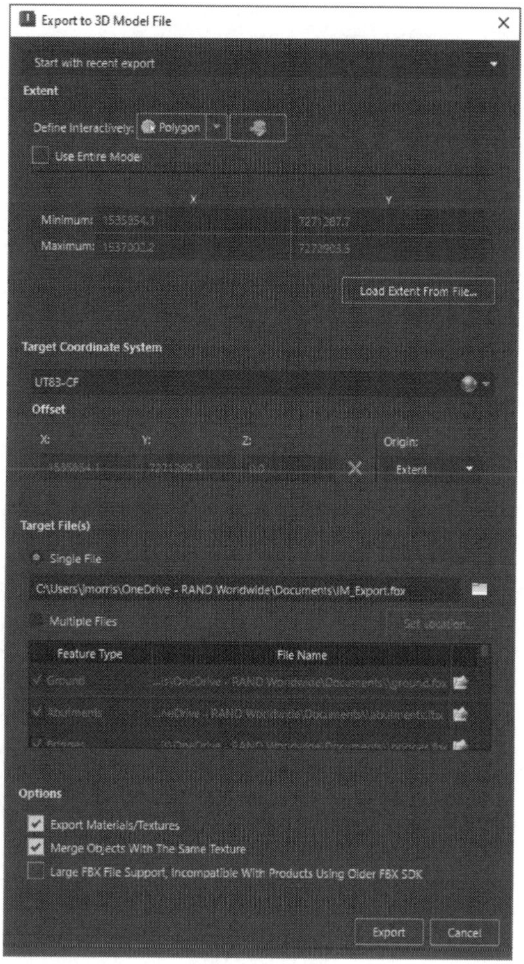

Figure 6–60

5. In the *Target File(s)* area, select **Multiple Files**. Set the location to the *InfraWorks Practice Files\References\FBX* folder.
6. Click **Export**.
7. Using Windows File Explorer, open the *InfraWorks Practice Files\References\FBX* folder and note all the .FBX files created for each category of models in your model. Now the files can be imported into the Autodesk Navisworks or Autodesk 3ds Max software.

End of practice

6.6 Create Railways in a Model

Many cities are searching for cost-effective, environmentally sensitive, and socially responsible ways to provide public transportation systems. At the same time, freight trains are still used for transporting goods from one location to another. Both freight and commuter rail projects can be modeled in the Autodesk InfraWorks software.

Create Railways

It does not matter if you are creating a freight railway line or a commuter railway line. Both use the same command. The style for a railway determines how the rail, tracks, sleepers, rail bed, ground below, and daylighting display in the model. By default, a gravel, rip-rap, and grass look is provided, as shown in Figure 6–61. Additional styles can be created using the Railway material group provided with the software.

Figure 6–61

Regardless of the style that is used, the railway and road are automatically cleaned up where they intersect. This ensures that the rails display flush with the road surface, as they would in the real world. An example is shown in Figure 6–62.

Figure 6–62

How To: Create Railways

1. In the *Create* tab>*Transportation* drop-down list, click (Railways).
2. In the *Select Draw Style* asset card, select the railway style, as shown in Figure 6–63.

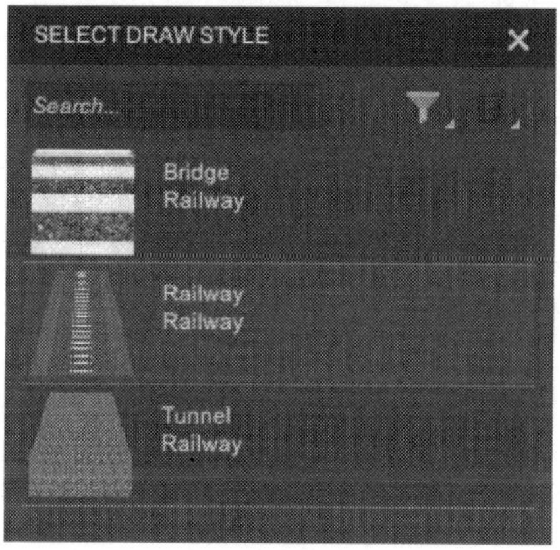

Figure 6–63

3. Click in the location at which you want the railway to start.
4. Move the cursor in the direction in which you want the railway to run. Type a distance for the length to the next point of intersection (PI) and press <Enter> to set the distance. Click in the model to place the PI.

5. Continue clicking in the model to place PIs until all of the lengths of rail have been created for the railway.
6. Double-click to place the last railway point and end the command.

Edit Railways

Once a railway has been created, it can be reshaped using the (Control Point Gizmo), which displays at each PI when the railway is selected in the model. If you orbit the model more than 45°, the (Elevation Gizmo) displays and can be used to adjust the elevation of each PI.

Additional vertices can be added anywhere along the railway to add additional control and elevation points. To add a vertex, select the railway, right-click in the location where you want the additional control, and select **Add Vertex**, as shown in Figure 6–64.

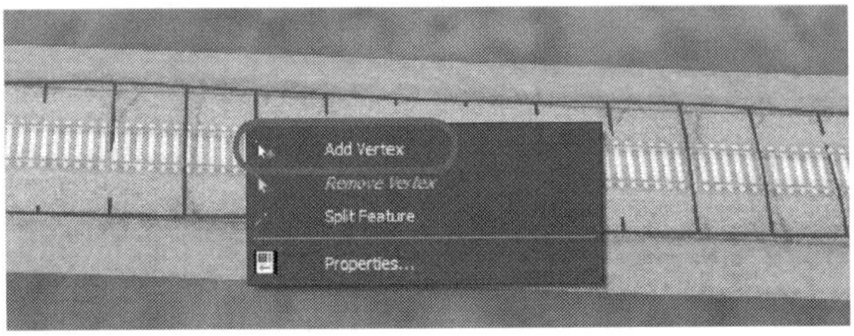

Figure 6–64

Similar to planning roads, conceptual railways must be split where bridges are required, and then the style must be changed where a section of the railway goes over a bridge. This can be accomplished by dragging the **Railway>Bridge** style from the *Style Palette* or by using the *Manual Style* field in the *Railway* asset card, as shown in Figure 6–65.

Figure 6–65

Practice 6d
Create a Passenger Railway in the Model

Practice Objective

- Create a passenger railway in the model.

In this practice, you will create a light rail system for commuter passengers that provides transportation options for the new community.

1. Continue working in the same model as the last practice. If you closed the file, on the *Home* screen, click **Open**. In the *InfraWorks Practice Files\6-Rails-Bridge-Tunnel* folder, select **CreateTransport.sqlite** and click **Open**.
2. If you did not complete any of the previous practices, select the **C_Task1** proposal to make it current.
3. Click (Bookmarks) and select **Railway**.
4. In the *Create* tab>*Transportation* drop-down list, click (Railways).
5. In the *Select Draw Style* asset card, select the **Railway** style, as shown in Figure 6–66.

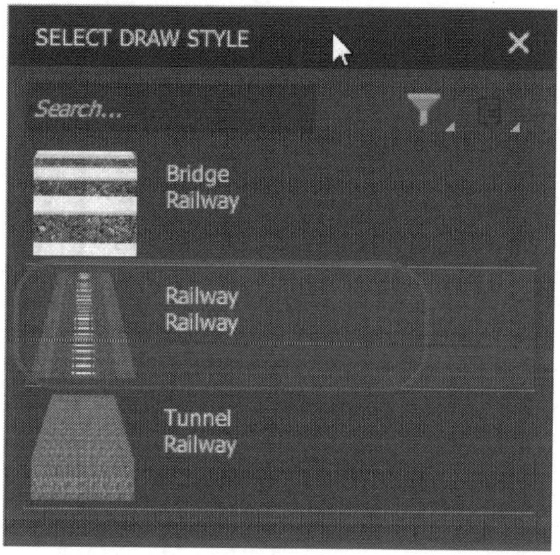

Figure 6–66

6. In the model, click points on the west side of **Redwood Rd** to place the railway, similar to that shown in Figure 6–67. Note the location of the three vertices.

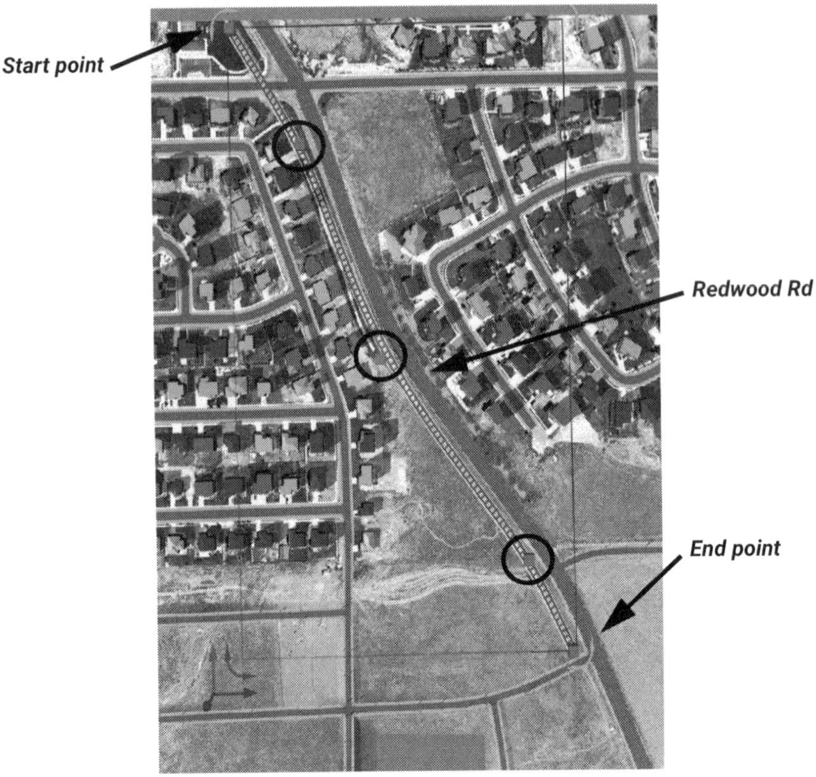

Figure 6–67

7. Double-click north of the road that runs into the new neighborhood to place the last point and end the command.

8. Click (Bookmarks) and select **Railway 3D**.

   Note that the intersection at the road automatically adjusted where the railway crosses the road (the road elevation was modified). It would need to be fine-tuned due to the proximity to the road intersection.

End of practice

6.7 Create Tunnels in a Model

In many ways, a tunnel can be thought of as the antithesis of a bridge. Whereas a bridge spans over structures, waterways, or topological depressions, a tunnel bores under such obstacles or topological elevations.

Similar to bridges, tunnels often are a structural challenge. InfraWorks offers tools to assist in the design and layout of a tunnel. The tunnels are parametric, consisting of components available in the *Style Palette*. If these prove inadequate, additional components can be created in Autodesk® Inventor® and then added and customized in the *Style Palette*.

Tunnels can be constructed with detailed parametric tunnel ring components to simulate bored tunnels. These rings will be automatically placed to follow the alignment without gaps or overlaps. Bored tunnels will also adjust if the reference alignment is changed. You can also specify portals to the start and end of the tunnel. It is even possible to disallow segment seams in successive rings to avoid points of structural weakness.

As with bridges, you must have a component road in place to add a tunnel, as shown in Figure 6–68.

Figure 6–68

How To: Add a Tunnel to a Component Road

1. In the model, draw a component road.
2. In the *Create* tab>*Structures* panel, click  (Tunnel).
   - Alternatively, you can select the component road, right-click, and select **Add Structure>Tunnel**.
3. Move your cursor and click the start station, or type the start station and press <Enter>.
4. In the model, click on the component road at the station where you want the tunnel to end, as shown in Figure 6–69.
   - Alternatively, you can press <Tab> and type the tunnel length, or you can press <Tab> twice to type the end station, then press <Enter>.

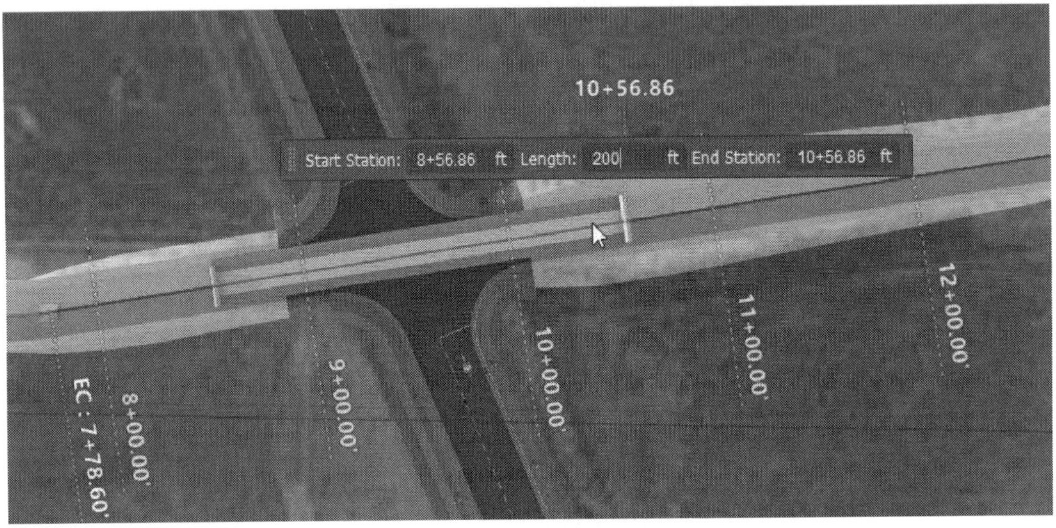

Figure 6–69

Tunnel Gizmos

Again, as with bridges, when a tunnel is selected, gizmos display at the beginning and ending stations of the tunnel. Selecting either gizmo enables you to change the station for that specific gizmo, as shown in Figure 6–70.

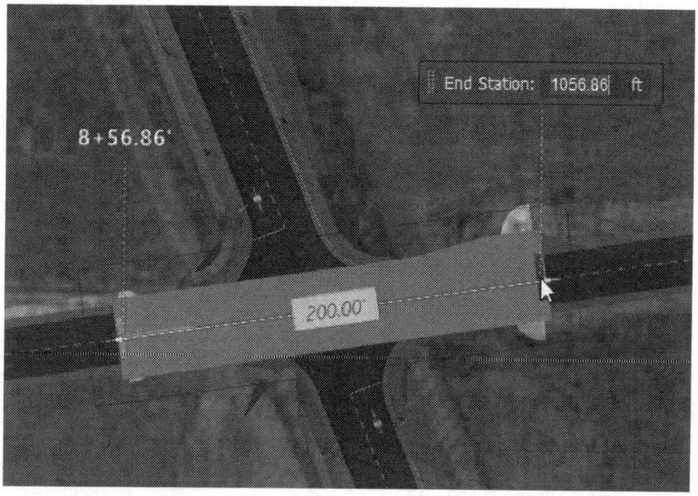

Figure 6–70

If both the beginning and ending stations require changing, the space between the two gizmos can be selected. This enables you to change both stations at the same time, as shown in Figure 6–71.

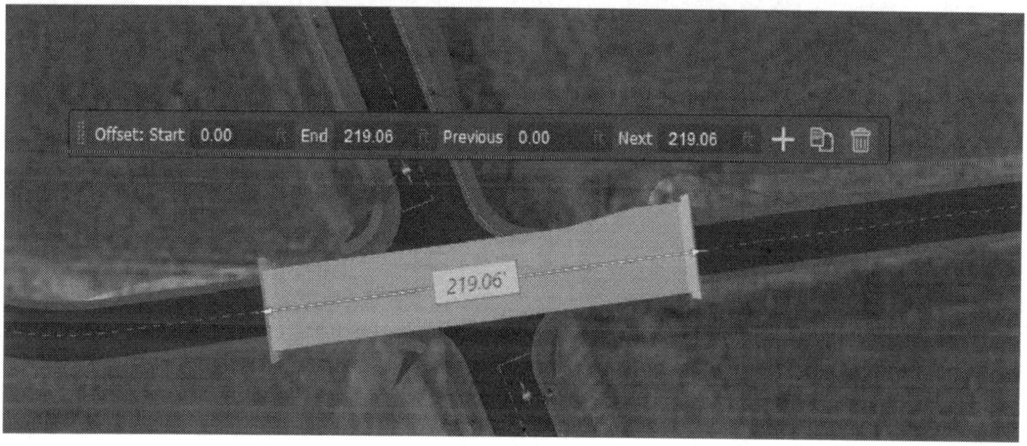

Figure 6–71

Tunnel Asset Card

Clicking the tunnel once will display a summary of the stationing and length in the asset card. You can also assign a name to the tunnel, as shown on the left in Figure 6–72.

Clicking a second time on the tunnel will display more detail in the new asset card. Here you can adjust the *Type* and *Material* for the tunnel, as well as adjust various properties related to sidewalks, centering with corridor, and more, as shown on the right in Figure 6–72.

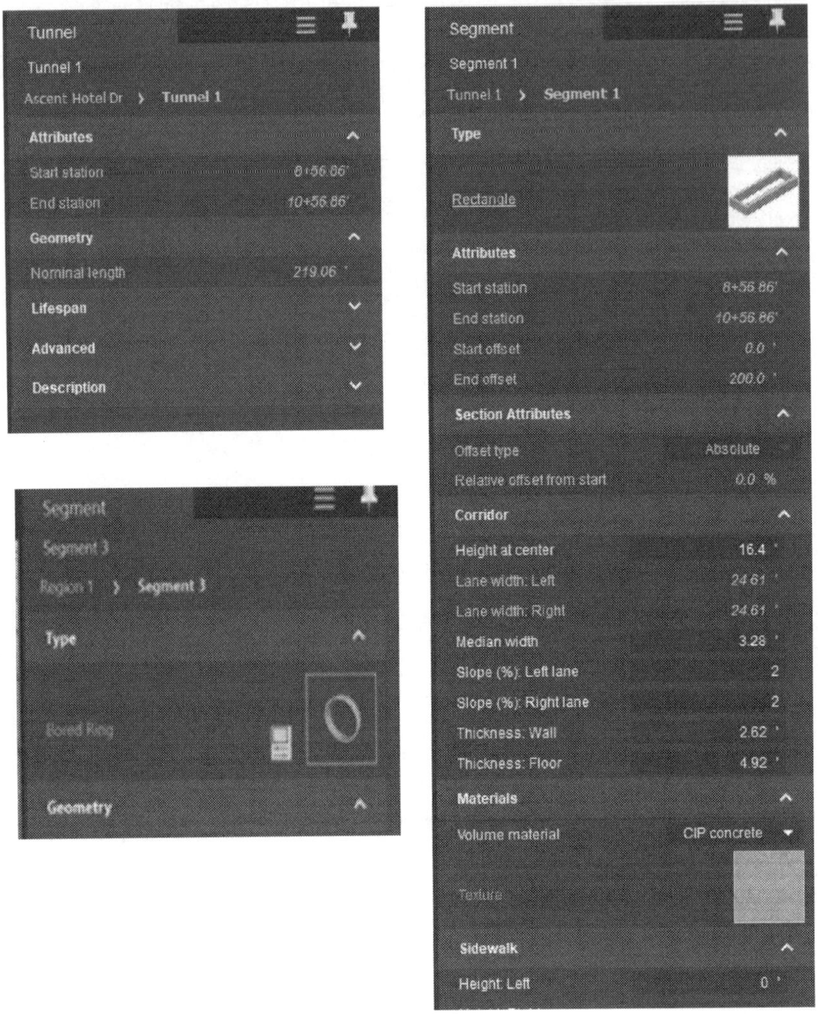

Figure 6–72

Note: *Tunnel structures can use parametric ring components for bored tunnels, as shown on the left in Figure 6–72. This will place and precisely follow the parenting alignment without and gaps or overlaps. Bored tunnels will update if the reference alignment is altered.*

Portals

When tunnels are added to component roads, portals are placed automatically at the beginning and end of the tunnel. The properties for these portals can be changed in a similar fashion to InfraWorks components, as shown in Figure 6–73.

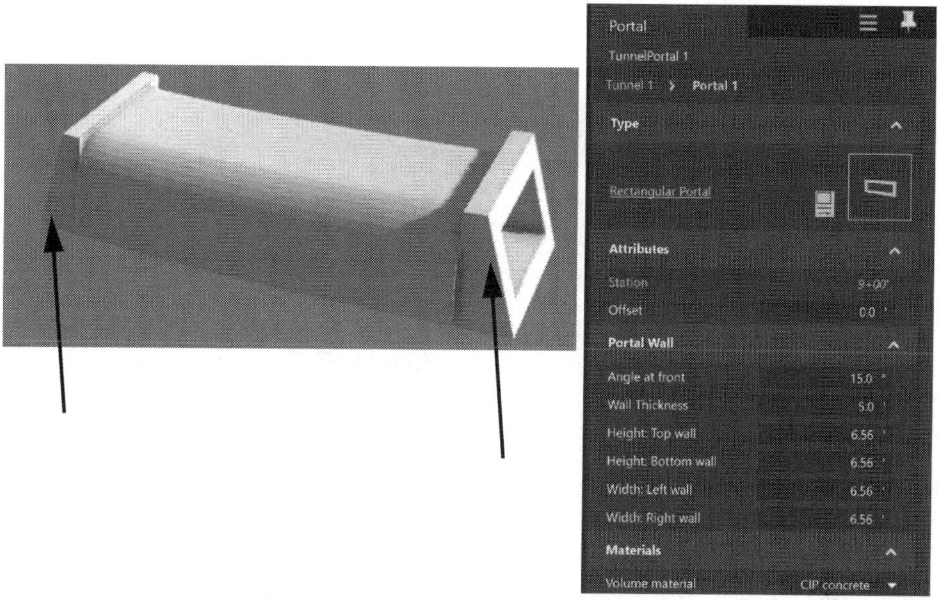

Figure 6–73

Stock portals included in the software are circular or rectangular portal components at the tunnel ends. They are parametric and will adapt to align to the surrounding terrain.

Adjusting Elevations

To fine-tune the design and layout of the tunnel, you can add both horizontal points of intersection (PIs) and points of vertical intersection (PVIs) to the component road at necessary locations to shift the road horizontally or down below the ground. You can also adjust the tunnel to display through the ground.

How To: Adjust the Tunnel to Display Below Ground

Note: *The Clipping planes described in the Bridge section also work on Tunnels.*

1. Select the component road.
2. Right-click on the component road and select **Show station in Profile View**, as shown in Figure 6–74.

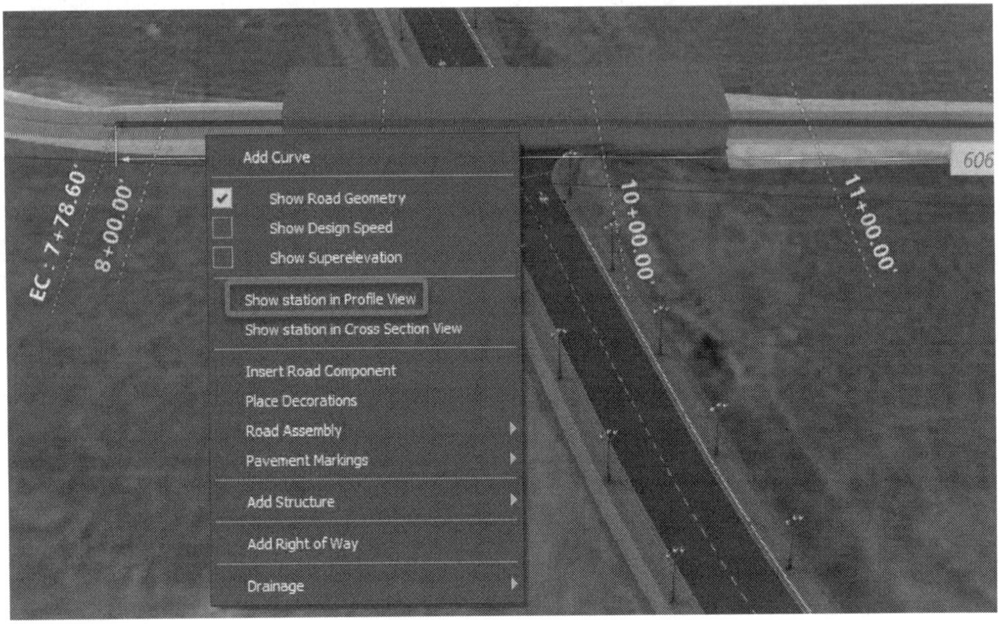

Figure 6–74

3. In the *Profile View*, turn on **Active Tracking** and move the yellow line near the intersection of both roads, as shown in Figure 6–75.

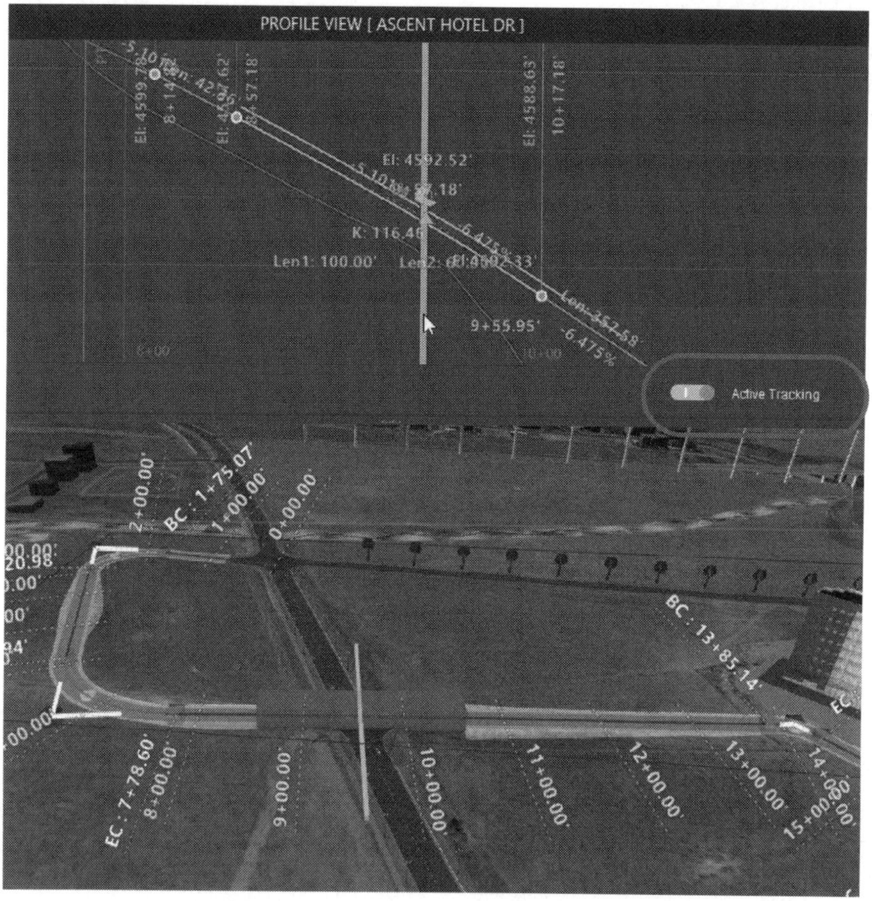

Figure 6–75

4. In the *Profile View*, you can click  (Asset Toggle) to toggle on **Structures, Drainage, Existing Ground**, and other markers to assist in the design and layout. This will cause various icons of linework to be displayed; for example, the tunnel icon and the white line indicate the length and vertical curvature of the tunnel in the *Profile View*, as shown in Figure 6–76.

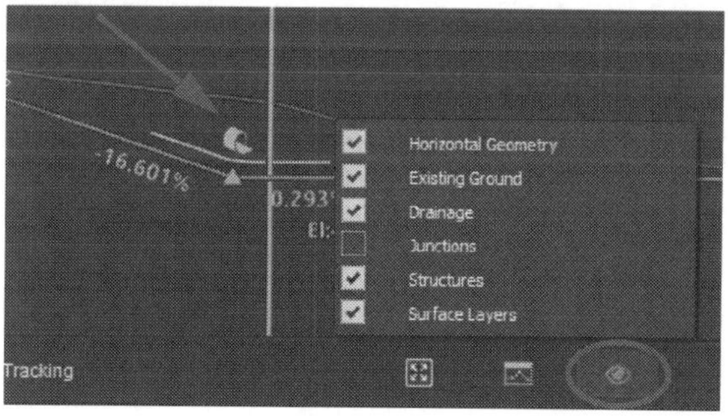

Figure 6–76

5. Add a PVI and adjust the height to below ground, as shown in Figure 6–77. (You may also choose to add PVIs in different locations of the component road to make a smoother transition to enter the tunnel.)

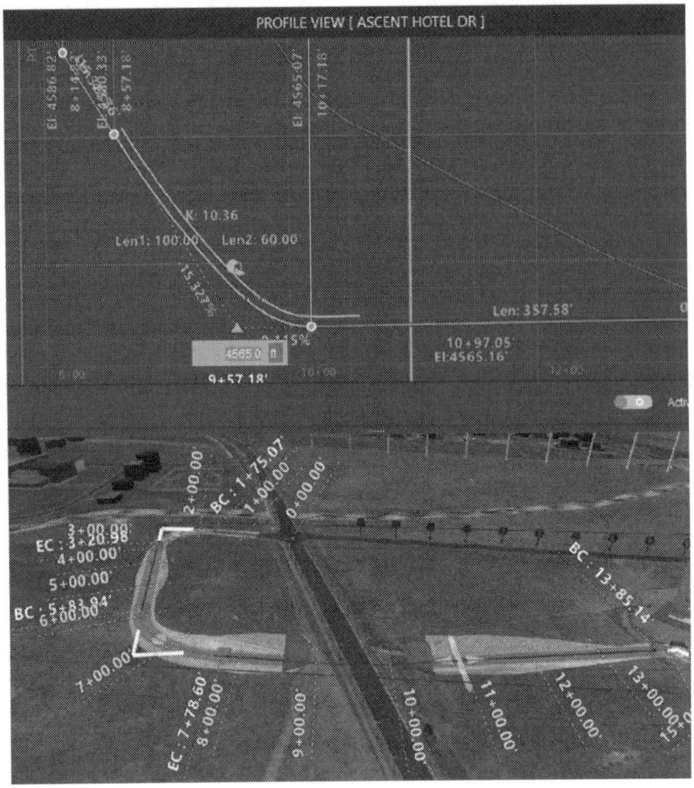

Figure 6–77

6. When finished, press <Esc> twice to release the tunnel. Close the *Profile View*.

Practice 6e
Create a Tunnel in the Model

Practice Objective

- Create a tunnel in the model.

In this practice, you will create a small tunnel in lieu of the roundabout created earlier.

Task 1: Change the roundabout and reroute Ascent Hotel Dr.

In order to add a tunnel, you need to have the crossing of **S Redwood Rd** and **Ascent Hotel Dr** occur on different elevations to remove their intersection. You will also elongate **Ascent Hotel Dr** and connect it to the previous intersection of **Morris Beach Blvd**.

1. Continue working in the same model as the last practice. If you closed the file, on the *Home* screen, click **Open**. In the *InfraWorks Practice Files\6-Rails-Bridge-Tunnel* folder, select **CreateTransport.sqlite** and click **Open**.
2. If you did not complete any of the previous practices, select the **D_Task1** proposal to make it current.
3. Click (Bookmarks) and select **Add Transport**.
4. Select the roundabout. In the *Roundabout* asset card, change the *Junction Type* to **Intersection**, as shown in Figure 6–78.

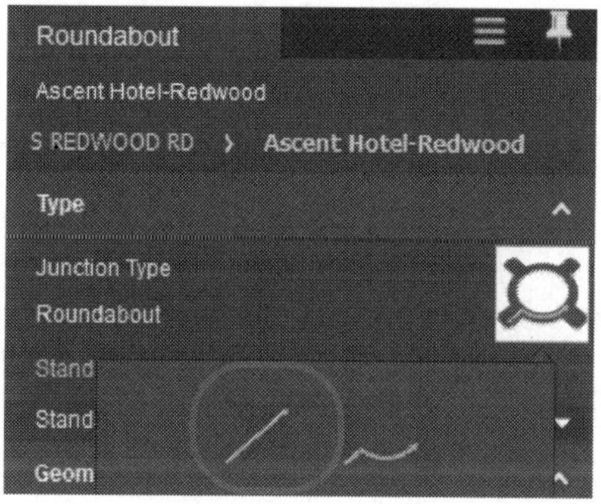

Figure 6–78

5. Pan upwards so you have room to extend the **Ascent Hotel Dr** component road in the next steps.

6. Select the **Ascent Hotel Dr** component road. Click on the cube endpoint gizmo (in the intersection) and drag it westward so the total length is about **650'**, as shown Figure 6–79. Hold <Shift> as you are dragging the gizmo to keep the direction of the road the same.
7. Select the shoulder component of **Ascent Hotel Dr,** click on the endpoint gizmo, and drag it westward to the end of the road, as shown Figure 6–79.

Figure 6–79

8. Repeat for the shoulder component on the other side.
9. Press <Esc> to release your current selection.
10. Select the **Ascent Hotel Dr** component road once again. Click on the cube endpoint gizmo and drag it further down so the total length is about **1000'**. Once again, hold <Shift> down.
11. With the component road still highlighted, right-click near station 400 (near the point you had previously dragged the road to) and select **Add Curve**, as shown in Figure 6–80.

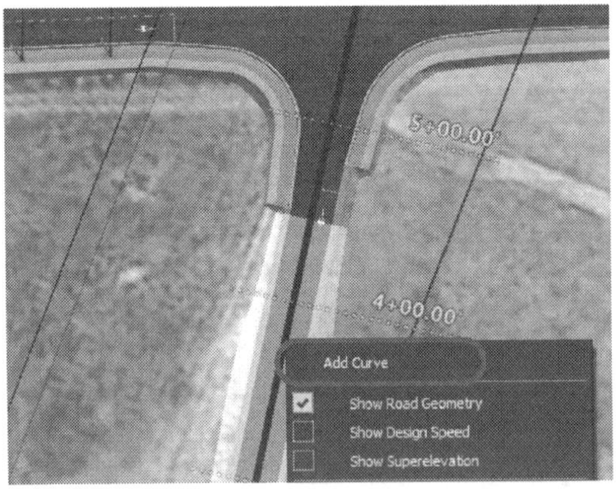

Figure 6–80

12. Click on the cube endpoint gizmo and drag it northward so that it runs parallel to **S Redwood Rd** and cumulates near the **Heather Run** river's edge, as shown in Figure 6–81.

Figure 6–81

13. With the component road still highlighted, right-click near station 250 and select **Add Curve**.
14. Click on the cube endpoint gizmo and drag it eastward so that it goes to the center of the **S Redwood Rd/Morris Beach Blvd** intersection, as shown in Figure 6–82.

Figure 6–82

15. Select the round cyan radius gizmo of the newly created curve and change the radius to **75.0'**, as shown in Figure 6–83.

Figure 6–83

Task 2: Change the elevations of both roads to make a quasi overpass.

In order to remove the intersection, you need to lower the elevation of **Ascent Hotel Rd** to pass underneath **S Redwood Rd**.

1. If you did not complete the last task, select the **D_Task2** proposal to make it current.
2. Click (Bookmarks) and select **Add Transport 3D**. Zoom and orbit toward the **Ascent Hotel Dr** intersection.
3. Select the **Ascent Hotel Dr** component road and press <Ctrl>+<0> (zero) (or use the right-click menu) to open the *Profile View*.
4. In the *Profile View*, slide the yellow section marker so it is located near the center of the intersection (near station 9+77).

5. Move the PVI shown in Figure 6–84 to the section marker and to an elevation of about **4575'**.

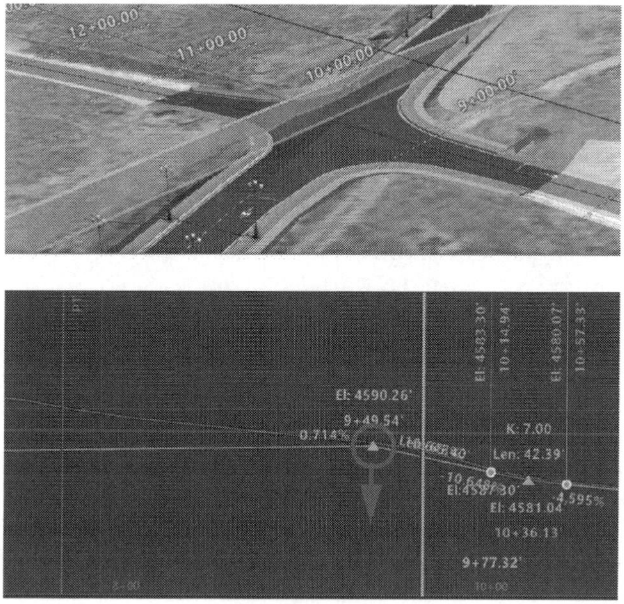

Figure 6–84

6. In the *Profile View*, select the next PVI, right-click, and select **Remove PVI**, as shown in Figure 6–85.

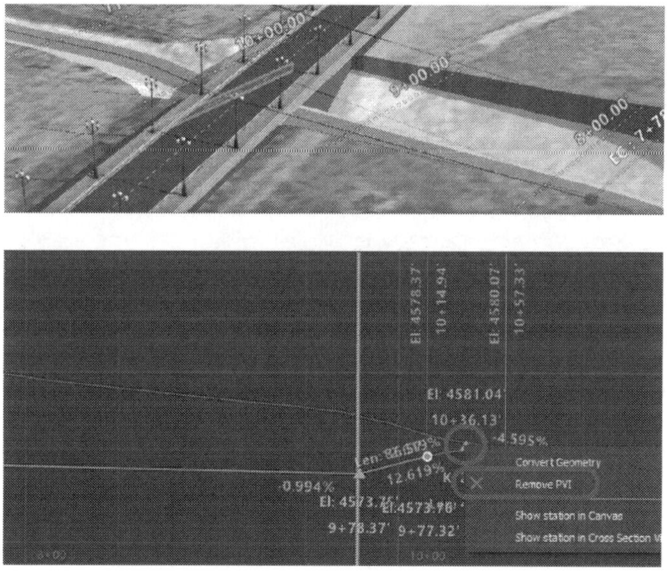

Figure 6–85

7. In the *Profile View*, right-click near station 6+90 and select **Add Vertical Curve**.
8. Raise the new vertical curve so it is slightly above the green existing ground line. Increase the vertical curve length to about **253'** by sliding either the PC or PT white circle grips to hug the existing ground, as shown in Figure 6–86.

   Note: *If you do not see the green existing ground line, click (Asset Toggle) to toggle on **Existing Ground**.*

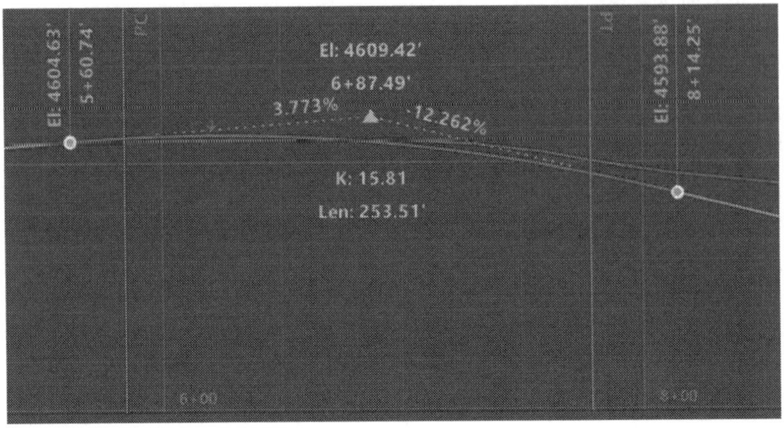

Figure 6–86

9. Repeat Steps 7 and 8 to add and adjust a vertical curve around station 2+50.
10. Close the *Profile View* by clicking the red **X** in the upper-right corner.

Task 3: Create the tunnel.

1. If you did not complete the last task, select the **D_Task3** proposal to make it current.
2. Click (Bookmarks) and select **Add Transport 3D**. Zoom and orbit toward the **Ascent Hotel Dr** intersection.
3. In the *Create* tab>*Structures* panel, click (Tunnel).
4. Select the **Ascent Hotel Dr** component road near the underpass.

5. In the *Start Station* field, type **880**. Press <Tab> twice, and in the *Length* field, type **130**, as shown in Figure 6–87. Press <Enter>.

Figure 6–87

6. In the *Bridge* asset card, name the tunnel **Ascent Hotel Tunnel**.
7. Click on a component of the new tunnel. In the *Segment* asset card, under *Type*, click **Rectangle** to open the *Select Component* asset card.
8. Select the **D Shape - sidewalks** component, as shown in Figure 6–88.

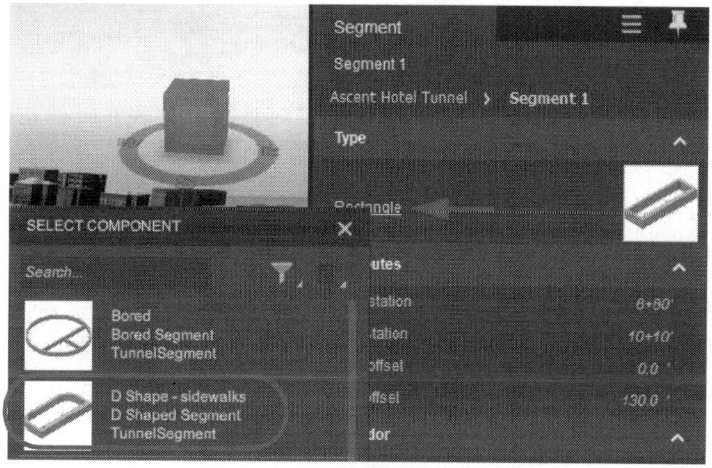

Figure 6–88

9. In the *Segment* asset card, under *Corridor*, set the *Height at center* to **17.50**.
10. Press <Esc> to release your current selection.
11. Select the front portal.

12. In the *Portal* asset card, set the *Angle at front* to **15.0°** and the *Wall Thickness* to **5.0'**, as shown in Figure 6–89.

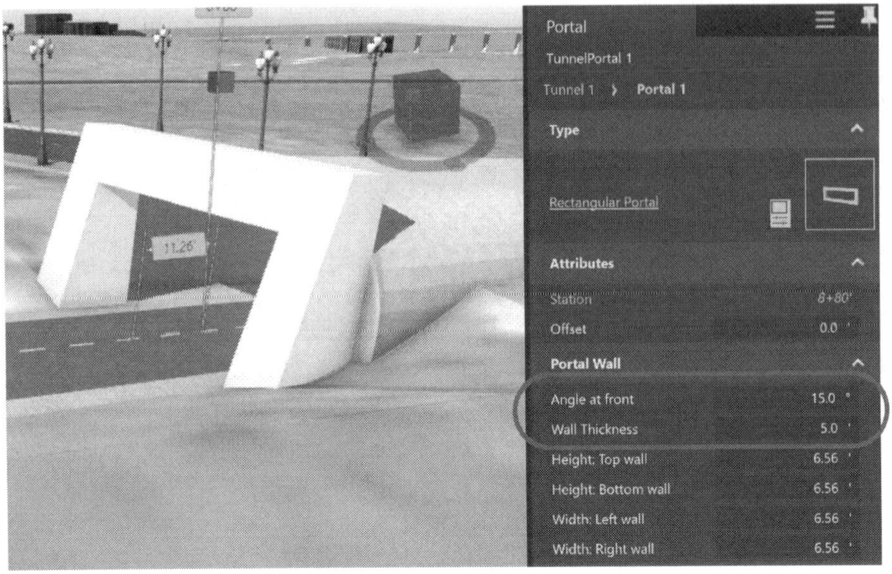

Figure 6–89

13. Press <Esc> to release your current selection.
14. Repeat the procedure for the rear portal.
15. Select the **Ascent Hotel Dr** component road and press <Ctrl>+<0> (zero) (or use the right-click menu) to open the *Profile View*.
16. In the *Profile View*, slide the yellow section marker so it is located near the center of the intersection (near station 9+65).
17. In the *Profile View*, in the lower-right corner, click (Asset Toggle) to toggle on **Structures** if it is off. Note the tunnel icon and the white line indicating the length and vertical curvature of the tunnel in the *Profile View*, as shown in Figure 6–90.

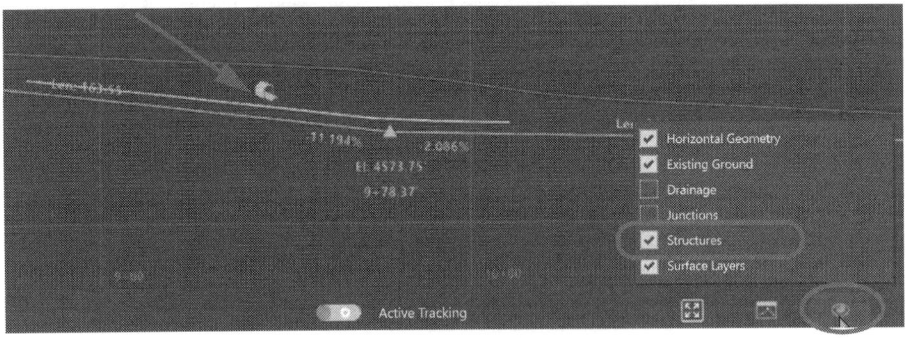

Figure 6–90

18. Move the tunnel PVI so it coincides with the yellow section line (around station 9+66).
19. Right-click on the tunnel PVI and select **Convert Geometry>Asymmetric Parabola Curve**, as shown in Figure 6–91.

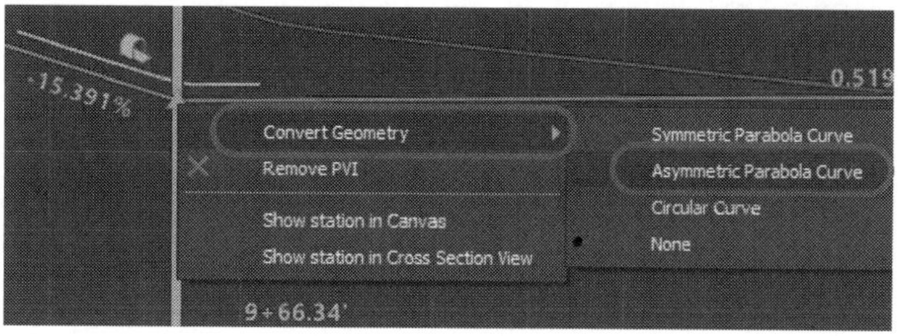

Figure 6–91

20. Increase the vertical curve length by sliding the PC white circle grip (on the left side) to a length of about **100'**, and the PT white circle grip (on the right side) to a length of about **60'**.
21. Visually check in the model view to ensure there is still enough coverage under **S Redwood Rd** and that the tunnel does not protrude into the road. Lower the tunnel PVI in the *Profile View* to adjust (to about elevation **4560.0**). If you press and hold <Alt> when moving the PVI, it locks the PVI so only the elevation will change.
22. Press <Esc> to deselct the road.
23. In the model view, select the tunnel's oncoming yellow tube, which turns red when selected, as shown in Figure 6–92. Type **900** for the *Start Station* and press <Enter>.

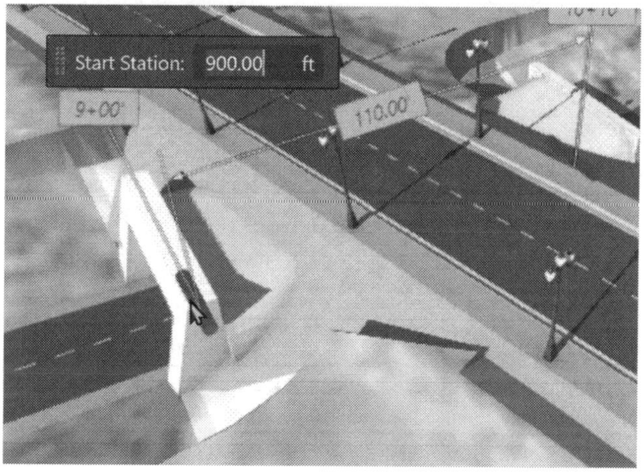

Figure 6–92

24. Set the *End Station* to **1000 ft**.
25. Close the *Profile View* by clicking the **X** in the upper-right corner.

Task 4: Create clipping planes.

In this task, you will hide the existing ground to be able to inspect the tunnel more easily, then create a clipping plane in the tunnel to inspect it.

1. If required, navigate the view to get a bird's eye view of the tunnel.
2. In the *Manage* tab>*Display* panel, select  (Surface Layers).
3. Under the *Terrain Surfaces* category, turn off the **Ground Surface** layers by clicking  (Show/Hide data source contents) and clicking **Apply**. Now the tunnel (and the bridges) can be viewed more clearly, as shown in Figure 6–93.

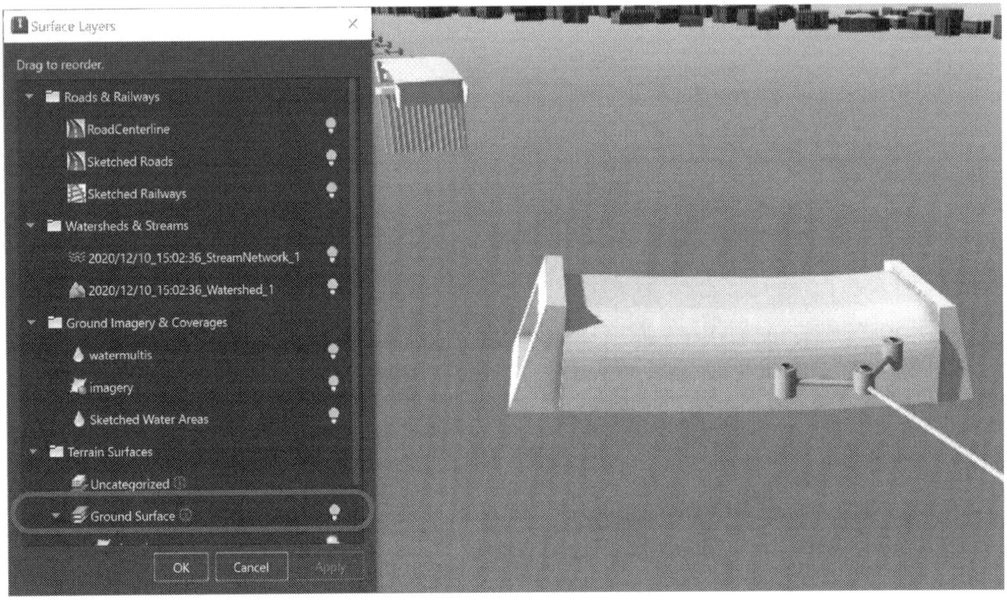

Figure 6–93

4. Under the *Terrain Surfaces* category, turn on the **Ground Surface** layers again by clicking  (Show/Hide data source contents) and clicking **OK**.
5. Select the tunnel.

6. In the right-click menu, toggle on **Show Clipping Planes**, as shown in Figure 6–94.

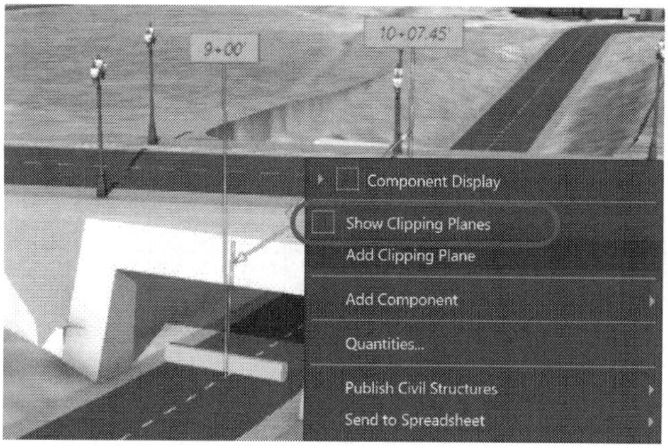

Figure 6–94

7. The *Clipping Plane* toolbar is displayed near the tunnel, as shown in Figure 6–95.

Figure 6–95

8. As you move your cursor back and forth, the model is clipped on a plane perpendicular to the tunnel. Select a point near the 90' station and press <Enter>. The entire model is clipped at that point and a cyan marker appears above the clipping plane.
9. In the *Clipping Plane* toolbar, for the Offset value, type in **50** and press <Enter>. For the *Skew* value, type in **45** and press <Enter>. The clipping plane moves slightly and changes its angle according to the entered values, as shown in Figure 6–96.

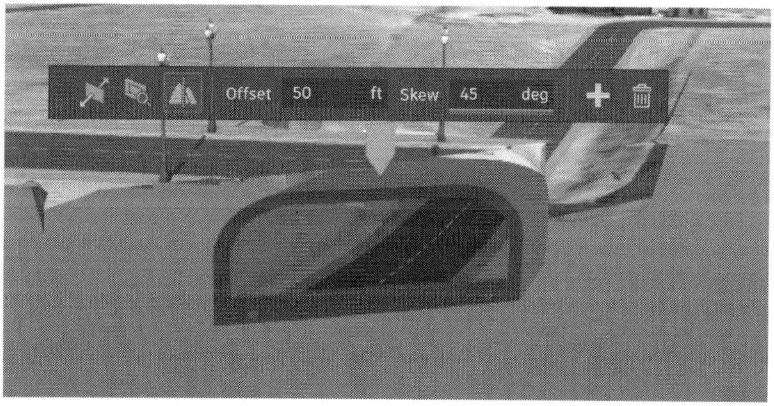

Figure 6–96

10. Click on (Toggle Terrain) to see all the surfaces in the model, while the tunnel and roads remain clipped. Toggle the terrain off again.

11. Click on (Align Camera) to orient the view perpendicular to the clipping plane. The view reorients itself to see the tunnel at the skewed angle, as shown in Figure 6–97.

Figure 6–97

12. In the toolbar, click on (Delete clipping plane) to erase the clipping plane. The clipping plane is deleted, the marker disappears and the toolbar closes.

13. Click (Bookmarks) and select **Add Transport**.

14. Close the InfraWorks model.

End of practice

Chapter Review Questions

1. What key component do you need in the model before you can create a bridge?
    a. Component road
    b. River
    c. Railway
    d. None of the above

2. Which bridge component do you select in the model in order to change the bridge beginning station?
    a. Girder
    b. Pier
    c. Bridge deck
    d. Abutment at the beginning of the bridge

3. How would you change the number of piers that support the bridge?
    a. Select the pier and make copies to add more piers or press <Delete> to remove piers.
    b. Select the bridge deck. In the *Bridge* asset card, change the value in the *Number of piers* field.
    c. Modify the bridge style in the *Style Palette*.
    d. You cannot change the number of piers.

4. How would you change the type of bridge in the model once it has been added to a component road? (Select all that apply.)
    a. Right-click on the bridge deck and select **Properties**. In the *Properties* palette, change the *Manual Style*.
    b. You cannot change the bridge type once it has been created.
    c. Drag and drop a different style from the *Bridge* tab of the *Style Palette*.
    d. Select the bridge deck. In the *Bridge* asset card, change the value in the *Type* field.

5. What type of bridge girders can you run a Line Girder Analysis on?
   a. Concrete
   b. Steel

6. When you run a Line Girder Analysis, the design optimization is computed using the Autodesk Structural Bridge Design software.
   a. True
   b. False

7. To make a railway flush with a road (as shown in Figure 6–98), you must split the railway into multiple segments and apply different styles at the road intersection.

Figure 6–98

   a. True
   b. False

Command Summary

Button	Command	Location
	**Align Camera**	• Pop-up Clipping Plane Menu
	**Asset Toggle**	• **Profile View**
	**Bridge**	• **Toolbar:** *Create* tab>*Transportation* panel
	**Clip Terrain**	• Pop-up Clipping Plane Menu
	**Create Plane**	• Pop-up Clipping Plane Menu
	**Delete Plane**	• Pop-up Clipping Plane Menu
	**Export 3D Model**	• **Toolbar:** *Present/Share* tab>*Share* panel
	**Line Girder Analysis**	• **Toolbar:** *Analyze* tab>*Structures* panel
	**Offset**	• Pop-up Clipping Plane Menu
	Publish Civil Structures	• Right-click menu of selected bridge
	**Railways**	• **Toolbar:** *Create* tab>*Transportation* drop-down list
	**Reverse Direction**	• Pop-up Clipping Plane Menu
	**Skew**	• Pop-up Clipping Plane Menu
	**Tunnel**	• **Toolbar:** *Create* tab>*Structures* panel

Chapter 7

Add Model Details

Using conceptual design tools, you can add additional details to a model, including buildings, landscaping, common urban elements known as "city furniture", and points of interest. In this chapter, you will learn how to add many of these model elements and how to edit the elements once they have been created. You will also learn how to input Autodesk Revit models.

Learning Objectives

- Create buildings in a model using the draw tools.
- Add predefined 3D buildings to a model.
- Import an Autodesk Revit model.
- Create city furniture to add 3D models to a model.
- Add landscaping details to a model using vegetation.
- Create barriers to add fences and traffic control to a model.

7.1 Create Coverages in a Model

Coverages are used to shape the terrain and change the way the ground displays. Coverages can be used to add ground cover in a landscape design, set the elevation of a building pad, or create a park areas and green spaces for a site design. Additionally, *Terrain Hole* material can be used on a coverage to create openings in a surface with a clean edge. This enables you to display what is going on underground. If you just need to reshape the terrain surface without changing how it displays, a transparent material style can be used.

How To: Shape and Style the Terrain Surface

1. In the *Create* tab>*Environment* panel, click (Coverage).
2. Select the style for the surface you are creating from the *Select Draw Style* asset card that displays, as shown in Figure 7–1.

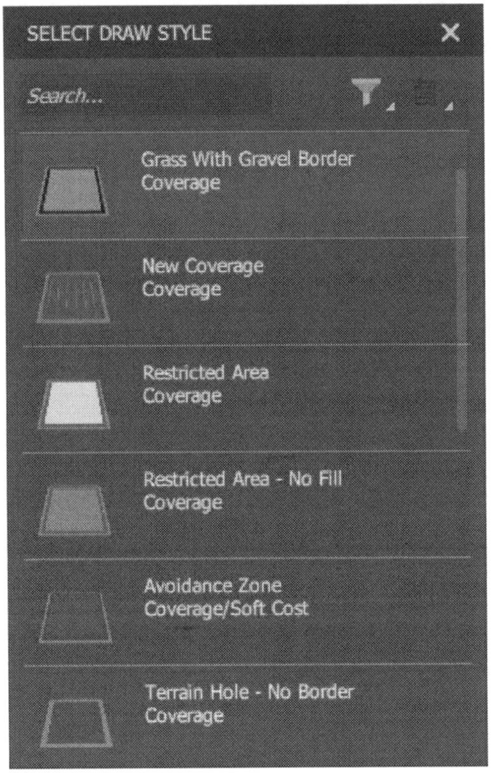

Figure 7–1

3. In the model, click to place the corners of the coverage footprint. After the first corner has been placed, move the cursor in the direction in which you want the next corner to be placed. Note the dimensions that display, as shown in Figure 7–2.

Figure 7–2

Note: *Locking a length means that even if you drag the cursor, the dimension value does not change.*

4. Type the required length for that side of the coverage and press <Enter> to lock the length. Move the cursor as required to set the correct angle and click to place the vertex.
5. Continue clicking in the model until all but the last vertex have been set.
6. Double-click on the location at which you want to place the final vertex. Doing so ends the command.
7. Press <Esc> to clear the selection of the newly created coverage.

Edit Coverages

Once a coverage has been created, it can be reshaped using the (Control Point Gizmo). The gizmo displays at each vertex when the coverage is selected in the model and Edit mode is toggled on in the View Settings Interaction stack. If you orbit the model more than 45°, the (Elevation Gizmo) displays and can be used to adjust the elevation of each corner.

As you adjust the elevation of a coverage, the surrounding terrain updates to gradually slope toward the new elevation, as shown in Figure 7–3.

Figure 7–3

How gradual the slope is depends upon the *Smooth Radius* value for the coverage, as shown in Figure 7–4. This value is changed by selecting the coverage and changing the *Smooth Radius* value in the asset card or the Properties palette.

Smooth Radius value = 20'

Smooth Radius value = 100'

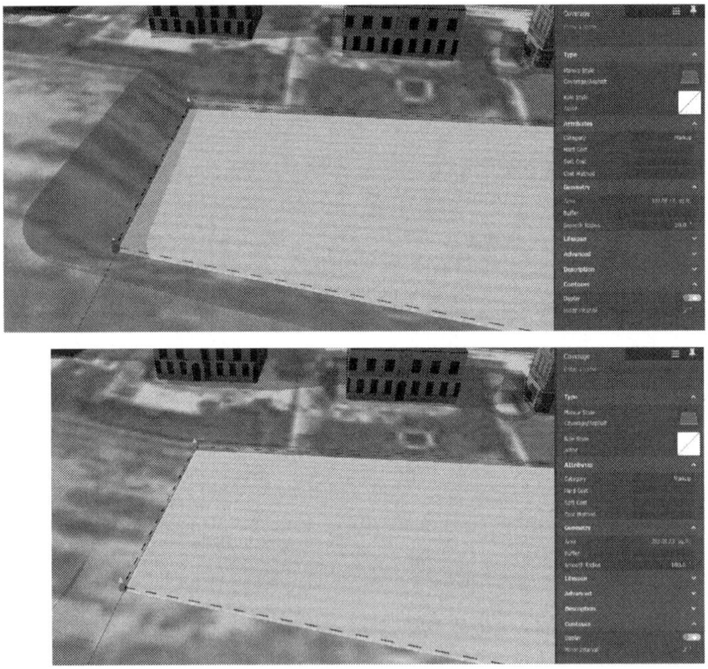

Figure 7–4

If a flat coverage (i.e., with all vertices having the same elevation) is desired, right-click on the selected coverage and select **Shape Terrain**. Then, use the ⬆ (Elevation Gizmo) at the center of the coverage to adjust the elevation of all vertices at once, as shown in Figure 7–5.

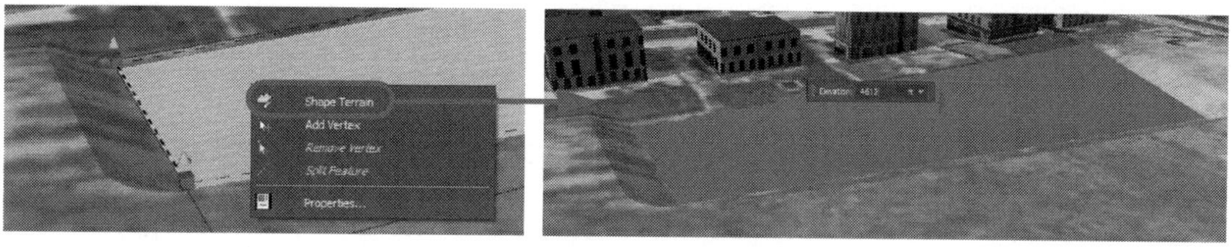

Figure 7–5

Vertices can be added anywhere along a side to add additional control and elevation points. To add a vertex, select the coverage, right-click on the side where you want to have additional control, and select **Add Vertex**, as shown in Figure 7–6.

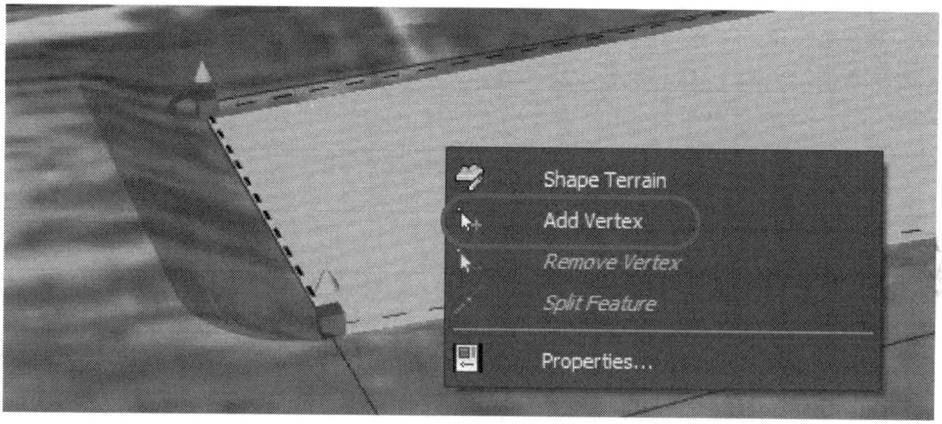

Figure 7–6

Practice 7a
Create Coverages in the Model

Practice Objectives

- Change the look of the terrain surface using coverages to display parking lots and other surface materials.
- Shape the terrain surface using coverages to change the elevations.

In this practice, you will create coverages to change the display settings and elevations associated with a terrain surface.

Task 1: Create a parking lot.

1. On the *Home* screen, click **Open**. In the *InfraWorks Practice Files\7-Model-Details* folder, select **CreateFeatures.sqlite** and click **Open**.
2. In the toolbar, expand the (Proposals) drop-down list and select **A_Task1** to make it current.
3. Click (Bookmarks) and select **Church Area**.
4. In the *Create* tab>*Environment* panel, click (Coverage).
5. In the *Select Draw Style* asset card, select the **ParkingLot** style that was created in an earlier practice, as shown in Figure 7–7.

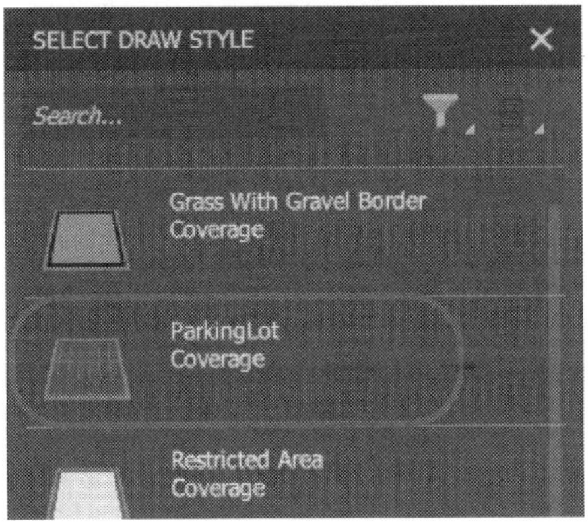

Figure 7–7

6. Click in the model to place the vertices of the parking lot, similar to that shown in Figure 7–8. Ensure that you double-click on the last corner to place it and end the command.

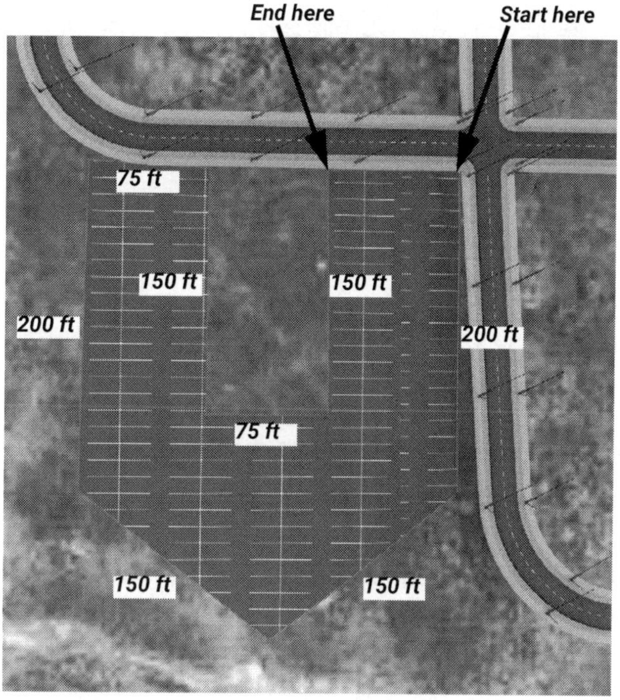

Figure 7–8

7. Press <Esc> twice to clear the selection of the newly created parking lot. A building will be added later which sits in the middle of the parking lot.
8. This method of creating a parking lot should be considered only as a schematic solution. The parking markings are only representational and not meant for actual parking. Creating a parking lot with specific parking tools is covered later in this chapter.

Task 2: Shape the terrain using a coverage.

In this task, you will shape the ground surface in preparation for a school. You will create another coverage and adjust its elevations.

1. Click (Bookmarks) and select **School Area**.
2. In the toolbar, expand the (Proposals) drop-down list and select **A_Task2** if you did not complete the previous task.
3. In the *Create* tab>*Environment* panel, click (Coverage).
4. In the *Select Draw Style* asset card, select **Asphalt**.

5. In the model, click to place the corners of the asphalt slab in the field reserved for the school, as shown in Figure 7–9. Make the measurement **350' x 300'** with the long side running east to west. Double-click on the last corner to place it and end the command.

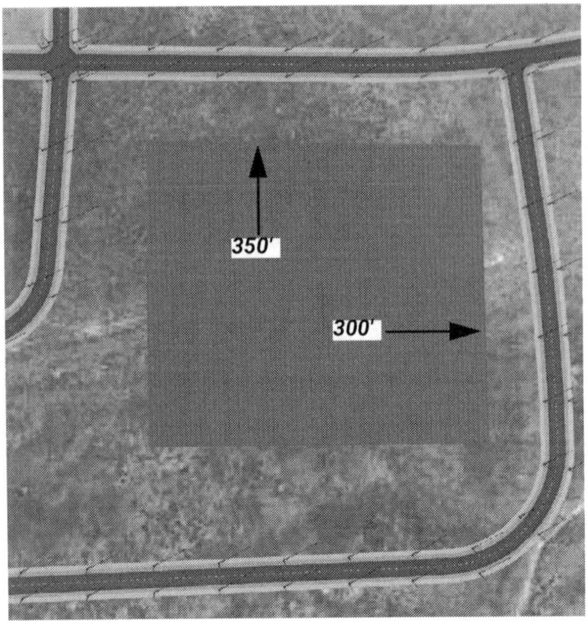

Figure 7–9

6. Press <Esc> to show the coverage's gizmos.
7. With the new asphalt coverage selected, orbit the view so that the elevation of the south side displays, as shown in Figure 7–10.

Figure 7–10

8. Right-click and select **Shape Terrain**. A box displays indicating orthogonal directions, otherwise known as level lines. The level line in the view can help you to level the pad if you are shaping it manually.

9. With the new asphalt coverage selected, click the ↑ (Elevation Gizmo), type **4620** in the *Elevation* field (as shown in Figure 7–11), and press <Enter>.

Figure 7–11

10. With the coverage still selected, in the *Coverage* asset card, *Geometry* section, change the *Smooth Radius* value to **20**. The surrounding ground gradually slopes into the school pad based on the change in elevation and the Smooth Radius value in the *Coverage* asset card.
11. Change the *Smooth Radius* value to **80** and press <Enter>. Note the change in the surrounding grade.
12. In the *Coverage* asset card, change the name to **School Pad**.
13. With the coverage area still selected, right-click and select **Edit Vertices**.
14. Right-click again and select **Add Vertex**. Add one vertex along the northern edge and two along the western edge, as shown in Figure 7–12.

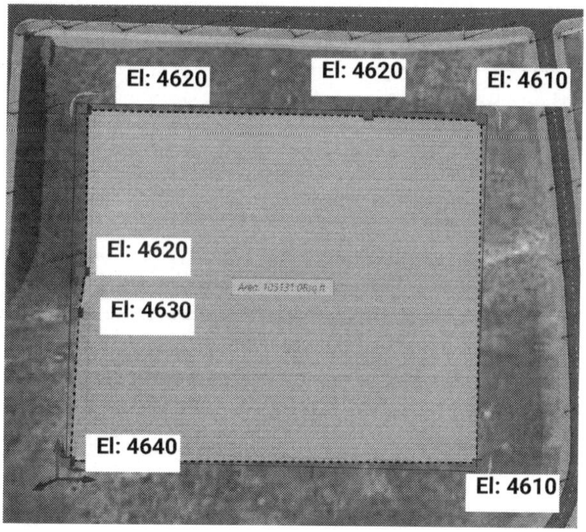

Figure 7–12

15. Orbit around so you can get a clear view of the cyan cones at the vertices, as shown Figure 7–13. Click on the cyan cone (which turns red when selected) and type the elevations shown earlier in Figure 7–12 for each vertex.

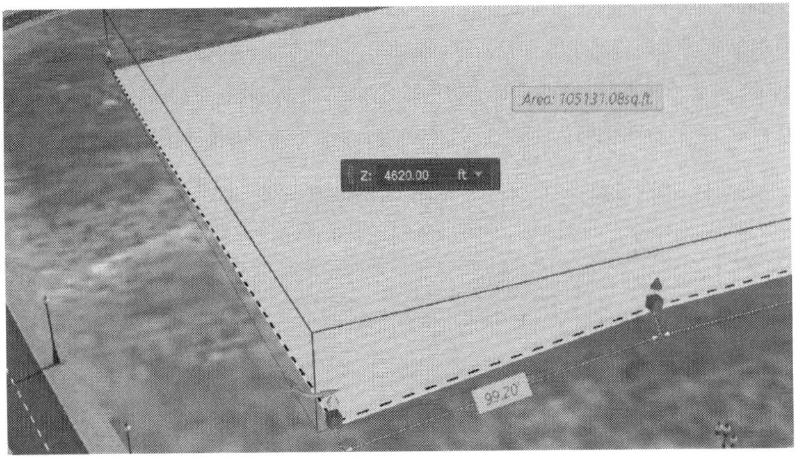

Figure 7–13

16. Press <Esc> to clear the selection of the school pad.

End of practice

7.2 Grading Areas

Similar to coverages, grading areas provide a way for you to grade areas and change how the terrain displays. There are two key differences that grading areas have over coverages:

- The top surface of a grading area is automatically flattened, as shown in Figure 7–14. A coverage drapes on the surface until the terrain is manually shaped.
- Grading areas enable you to control the display of cut and fill areas separately. Figure 7–14 shows an area with a 3:1 grass material for the fill and a 1:1 stone wall material for the cut.

Figure 7–14

How To: Create a Grading Area

1. In the *Create* tab>*Environment* drop-down list, click (Grading Area).
2. Select the material style for the top surface you are creating from the *Select Draw Style* asset card that displays, as shown in Figure 7–15. This style is used for the grading area top surface only, not the cut and fill slopes. The cut and fill styles are set later.

Figure 7–15

3. In the model, click to place the vertices of the grading area footprint. After the first vertex has been placed, move the cursor in the direction in which you want the next vertex to be placed.
4. Type the required length for the side of the grading area and press <Enter> to lock the length. Locking a length means that even if you move the cursor, the dimension value does not change. Move the cursor as required to set the correct angle and click to place the vertex.
5. Continue adding vertices in the model until all but the last vertex has been set.
6. Double-click on the location at which you want to place the final vertex. Doing so ends the command.
7. Press <Esc> to clear the selection of the newly created grading area.

Grading Styles

Grading styles control how the cut and fill slopes display. Several grading styles are provided in the Autodesk InfraWorks software (as shown in Figure 7–16) and additional styles can be created as required. The thumbnails in the *Style Palette* display a preview of the materials and slopes that are used in each style. If the cut and fill slopes use the same material, only one material is shown in the thumbnail. If the cut and fill slopes use different materials, both materials display in the thumbnail with their slope values, as shown in Figure 7–17.

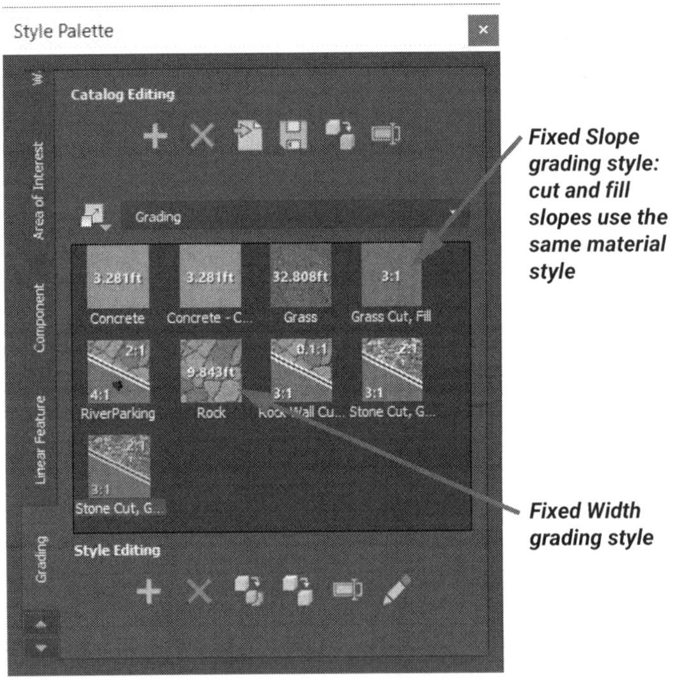

Figure 7–16

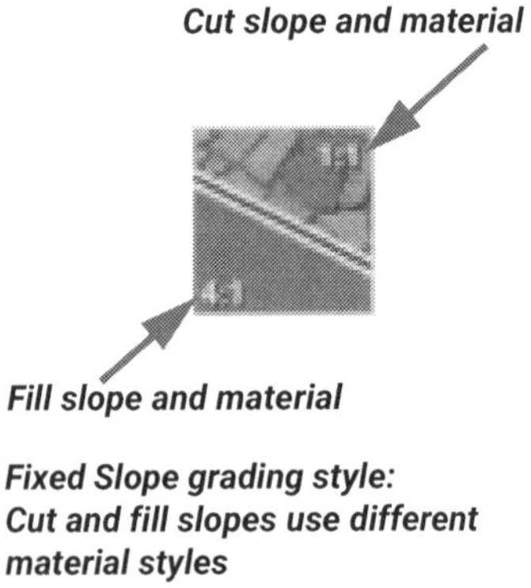

Figure 7–17

How To: Create a New Grading Style

1. Open the *Style Palette* and select the *Grading* tab.
2. In the *Style Editing* area at the bottom of the *Style Palette*, click  (Add new style to the current catalog above).
3. In the *Configure Grading* dialog box, set the *Grading Method* to either **Fixed Width** or **Fixed Slope**.
4. If **Fixed Slope** is selected, set the following options, as shown in Figure 7–18, and click **OK**. Otherwise, continue to the next step.
   - Set the *Cut Slope* (Run:Rise).
   - Set the *Fill Slope* (Run:Rise).
   - If the cut and fill materials use different styles, clear the **Cut and Fill Material use the same Style** checkbox.
   - Select the appropriate *Cut Material* and *Fill Material* styles.
   - Set the *Grading Limit*, if required. Otherwise, clear the **Set Limit for Grading** checkbox.

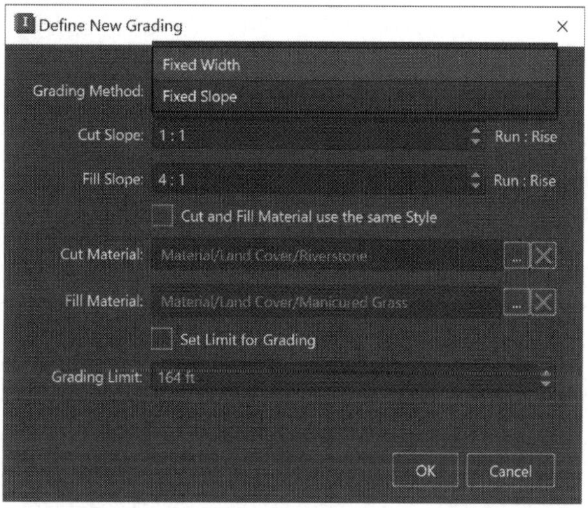

Figure 7–18

5. If **Fixed Width** is selected, set the following options, as shown in Figure 7–19.
   - Set the *Grading Width.*
   - Select a *Grading Material*.

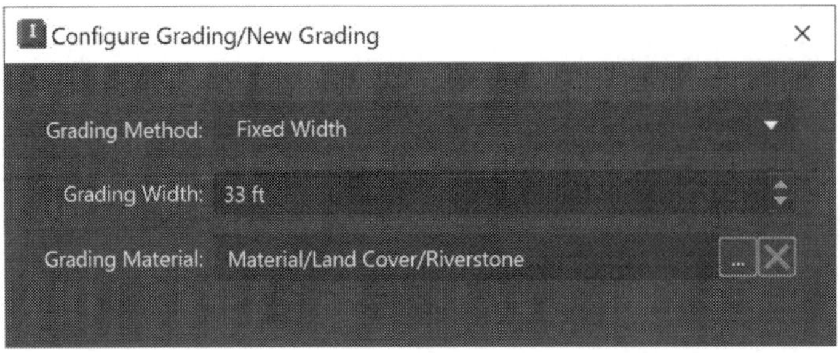

Figure 7–19

6. Click **OK**.

Edit Grading Areas

Once a grading area has been created, it can be reshaped using the (Control Point Gizmo). The gizmos display at each vertex when the grading area is selected in the model. By default, the grading area top surfaces are flat with all of the footprint vertices sharing the same elevation. If the model is orbited more than 45°, the (Elevation Gizmo) displays and can be used to adjust the elevation of each vertex independently.

Vertices can be added anywhere along a side to add additional control and elevation points. To add a vertex, select the grading area, right-click on the point at which you want to have additional control, and select **Add Vertex**, as shown in Figure 7–20.

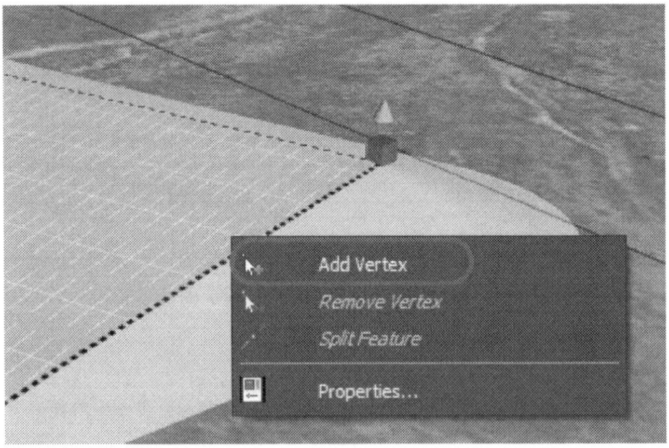

Figure 7–20

Set Cut/Fill Slopes

The graduation of a slope that extends from a grading area footprint depends upon the grading style selected for the grading area. This value is changed by setting the *Rule Grading* value for the grading area.

How To: Apply Cut/Fill Slopes to a Grading Area

1. Create a grading area.
2. With the grading area still selected, in the *Grading Area* asset card, change the *Rule Grading* style, as shown in Figure 7–21.

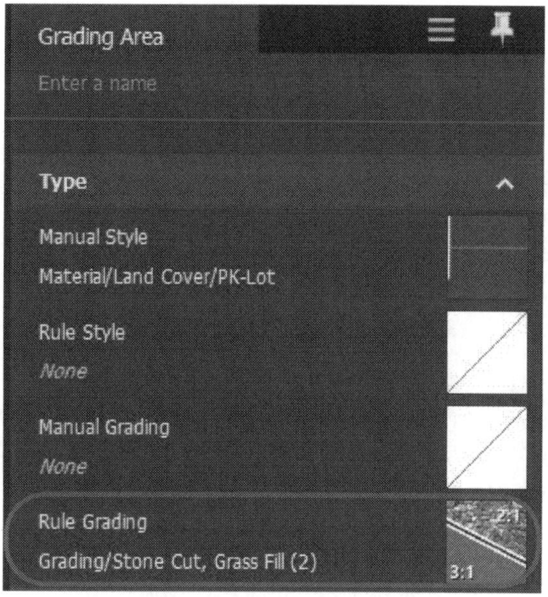

Figure 7–21

7.3 Parking Tools

InfraWorks has three dedicated tools for parking:

- Parking Area
- Parking Layout
- Parking Row

Before these tools were introduced, the standard approach to creating parking lots was to create customized materials for parking stalls and customized coverage areas for parking lots. This method has been discussed earlier in this guide.

How To: Create Parking Lots

1. Create a parking area.
2. Apply parking layouts to the parking area.
3. Make adjustments and apply styles.
4. If needed, add parking rows.

Parking Areas

Parking areas are similar to Grading Areas. They identify areas for parking layouts. It is only in parking areas and coverage areas that parking layouts can be applied. However, Parking Rows can be applied on any surface.

When the **Parking Area** command is launched, you can set the style and the standards in the Asset Card, as shown in Figure 7–22.

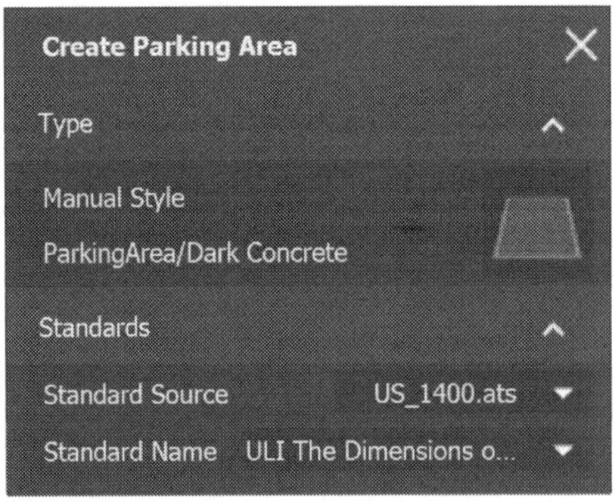

Figure 7–22

Sketching the parking area and modifying it are identical to creating and modifying grading areas. As with grading areas, a parking area can either drape over a surface or it can be flattened through the right-click menu, as shown in Figure 7–23.

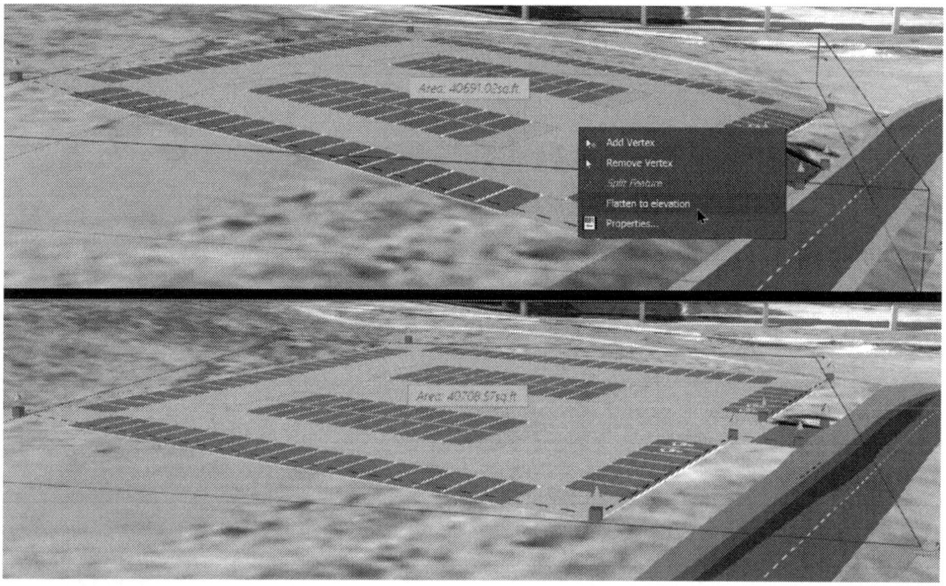

Figure 7–23

Hint: Parking Layout

The first point defined in a parking area becomes the start point of the perimeter parking stalls when the parking layout is applied to the parking area.

Parking Layouts

Parking layouts can be created once a parking area (or a coverage area) has been defined. If the defined parking area encloses buildings, the parking layout is also added around the perimeter of the building, as shown in Figure 7–24.

Figure 7–24

To add a parking layout, invoke the command and select an existing parking area (or coverage area). A preview of the proposed layout appears. The layout is in accordance to the standards set when the parking area was created.

In the Tip box, it states how many parking spaces can be created and to type **B** to cycle through bay angles or type **O** to cycle through orientations within the parking area, as shown in Figure 7–25.

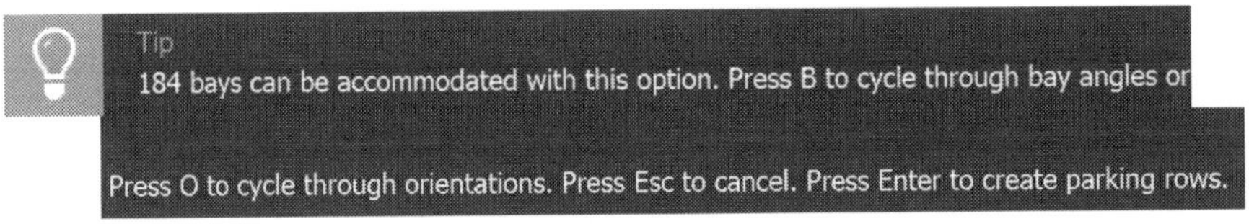

Figure 7–25

- Pressing <B> will alternate between the angle of the parking stalls within the parking bays.
- Pressing <O> will alternate between the orientation of all the parking bays.

Once an acceptable layout is established, pressing <Enter> will finalize the layout and the preview layout is erased.

The perimeter parking and the individual parking bays are all independent linear objects can be modified and deleted separately. As with other linear objects in InfraWorks, vertices can be inserted or deleted through the right-click menu. Linear objects can also be split, which allows for parking rows to be separated for the creation of driving lanes.

If parking layouts are applied to a parking area, and the parking area is deleted, the parking layout is also deleted. However if a parking layout is applied to a coverage area, it will remain if the coverage area is deleted.

If the geometry of parking area or coverage area which contains parking layouts is modified, the parking layout is NOT updated accordingly.

Parking Rows

Parking rows can added to parking areas or any other surface area in InfraWorks. The rows are linear objects and are created by picking points on the surfaces. Double-clicking will finish the linear object. To finish the command, press <Esc>.

In the *Create Parking Row* asset card, select the *Type*, *Standards*, *Attributes* and *Bay Detail Settings* for the row, as shown in Figure 7–26.

Figure 7–26

Note that you can choose if the parking row contains stalls on both sides or either the left or right side.

Vertices can be inserted or deleted through the right-click menu. Linear objects can also be split, which allows for parking rows to be separated for the creation of driving lanes.

Once parking bays are created, their properties can be modified in the *Parking Row* asset card, as shown in Figure 7–27.

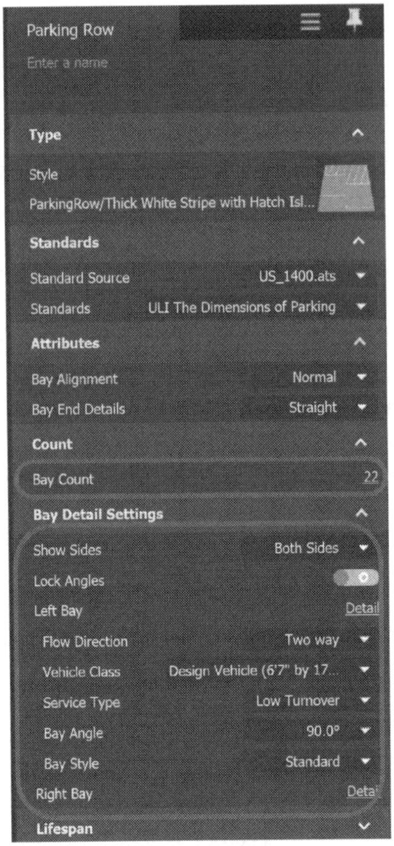

Figure 7–27

A count of stalls is available. Each side of the bay can be individually modified.

An individual stall can also be modified in terms of accessibility. First select the parking bay, then select the stall. In its asset card, you can choose either **Standard** or **Accessible**, as shown in Figure 7–28.

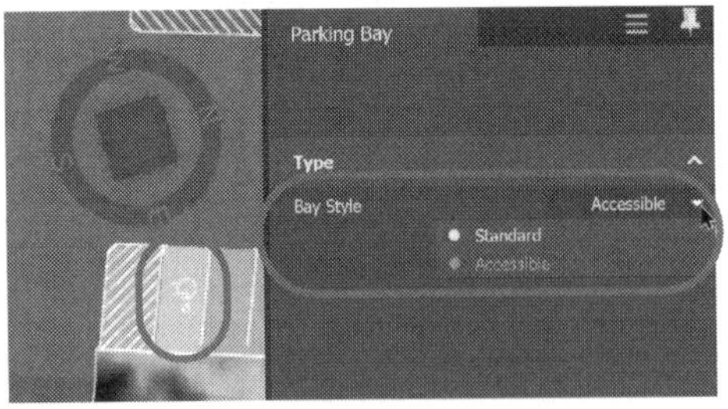

Figure 7–28

Practice 7b
Create Parking Lots

Practice Objectives

- Create parking lots with specific parking tools
- Create grading areas in the model to represent a park area.
- Create a building pad area for a hotel.

In this practice, you will use the parking tools in InfraWorks to create a parking lot for **Morris Beach**. Then you will create a custom grading style, setting the cut and fill slope displays separately. You will add a grading area with a gradual slope covered in grass for the patrons to access the beach area. Finally, you will create a parking area and a building pad for the **Ascent Hotel**.

Task 1: Create a parking lot and grass area for beach access.

In this task, you will create a parking lot for access to **Morris Beach** and a grass area to provide a more gradual slope to the beach area.

1. Continue working in the same model as the last practice. If you closed the file, on the *Home* screen, click **Open**. In the *InfraWorks Practice Files\7-Model-Details* folder, select **CreateFeatures.sqlite** and click **Open**.
2. If you did not complete the last practice, select the **B_Task1** proposal to make it current.
3. Click  (Bookmarks) and select **Beach Access**.
4. Zoom in to the northeast end of the road prior to the last curves.
5. In the *Create* tab>*Environment* drop-down list, click  (Parking Area).
6. In the *Create Parking Area* asset card that displays, change the *Manual Style* to **Parking/ Dark Grey Asphalt** and ensure that the *Standard Source* is set to **US_1400.ats**, as shown in Figure 7–29.

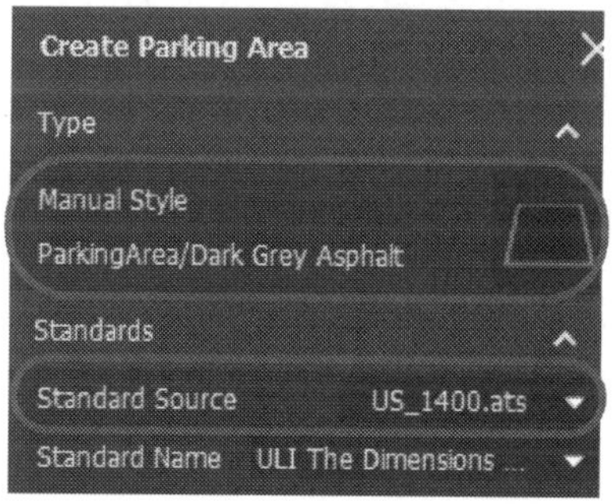

Figure 7–29

7. The starting point of the parking area will be the access point, so consider this when placing the first point. In the model, click to place the first vertex of the grading area footprint, as shown in Figure 7–30.

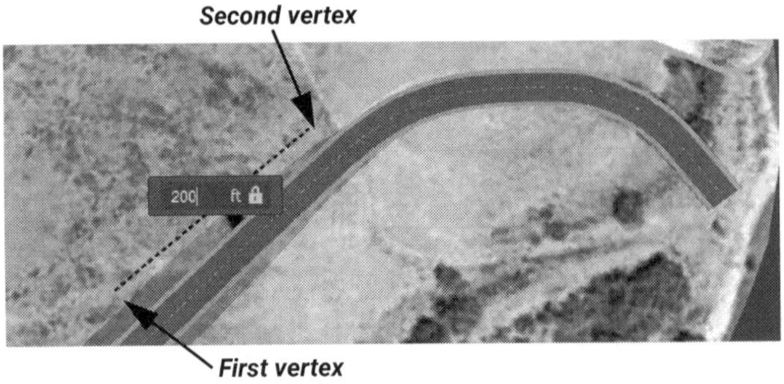

Figure 7–30

8. Move the cursor in the northwest direction, type **200**, and press <Enter> to lock in the distance. Click to place the second vertex, as shown above in Figure 7–30.
9. Move the cursor in the northeast direction, type **100**, and press <Enter> to lock in the distance. Click to place the third vertex, as shown in Figure 7–31.
10. Move the cursor in the southeast direction, type **200**, and press <Enter> to lock in the distance. Double-click to place the final vertex and end the command, as shown in Figure 7–31.

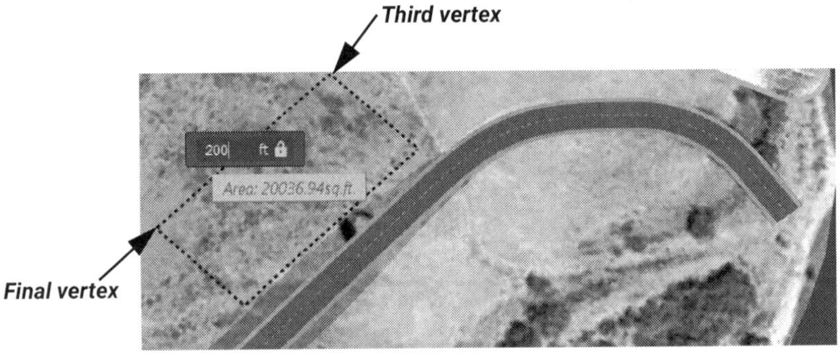

Figure 7–31

11. Select the newly created parking area and click on the last vertex you created (lower-left corner).Temporary dimensions show the length of the last segment.

12. If it needs adjusting, click and drag on the vertex, as shown in Figure 7–32.

Figure 7–32

13. In the *Parking Area* asset card, name the grading area **Morris Beach Parking**. Naming the grading area will facilitate importing data into Civil 3D.
14. Now that the area has been defined, you can place parking areas on it. In the *Create* tab>*Environment* drop-down list, click (Parking Layout).
15. In the model, select the parking area you have just created. A preview of the proposed parking layout appears, as shown in Figure 7–33. Depending on your parking area, the results may be different than illustrated.

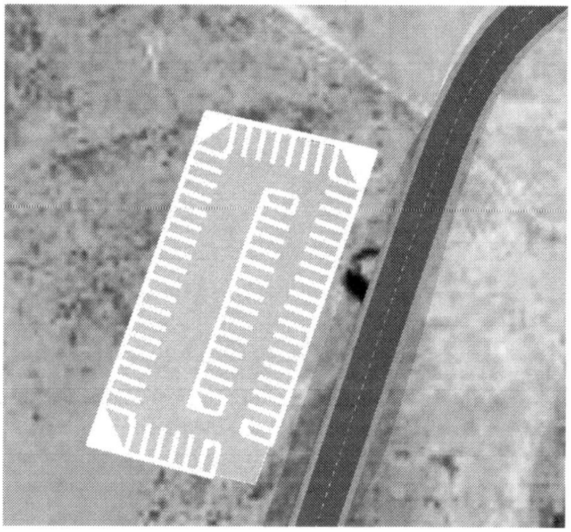

Figure 7–33

16. Press <B> to cycle through bay options. InfraWorks displays all options available and repeats these options. Go through all the options until you reach the one shown in Figure 7–34.

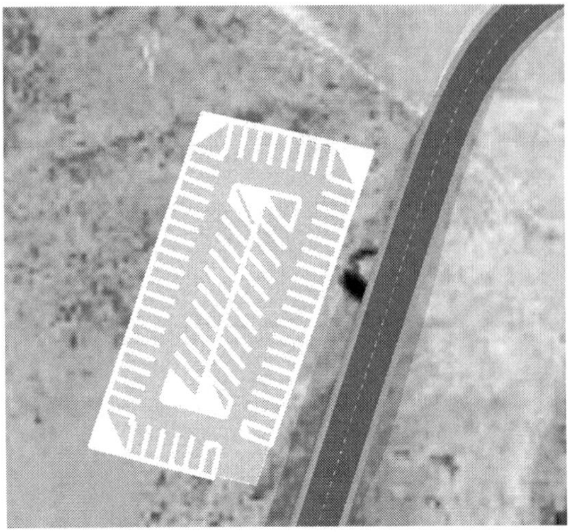

Figure 7–34

17. Press <O> to examine the orientation options. The bays will flip their orientation each time you press <O>. Keep the orientation as shown in Figure 7–34.
18. Press <Enter> to accept the layout. The preview is replaced with permanent parking markings.
19. The center bay may not be centered properly. Select the bay and move it by clicking and dragging the *Move* gizmo, as shown in Figure 7–35. You can also elongate or shorten the bay by clicking on the square endpoint grips, if required. Experiment with this as you wish.

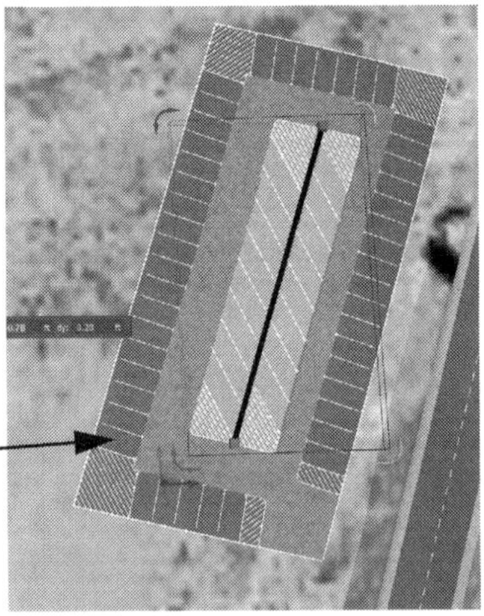

Figure 7–35

20. You will be rearranging the parking lot in the next task and the bay will be superfluous, so it can be deleted. With the bay still selected, press <Delete> to remove the bay.

Task 2: Redesigning the parking lot.

In this task, you will widen the parking area and then realign the parking layout.

1. Continue working in the same model. If you did not complete the last task, set **B_Task2** as the current proposal.
2. Click (Bookmarks) and select **Beach-Parking**.
3. Select the parking area. Be sure you do not select the parking layout instead.
4. Click and drag the upper-left corner grip and extend it **200 feet**. Repeat for the upper-right corner grip and extend **200 feet**, as shown in Figure 7–36. Press <Esc> to clear the selection.

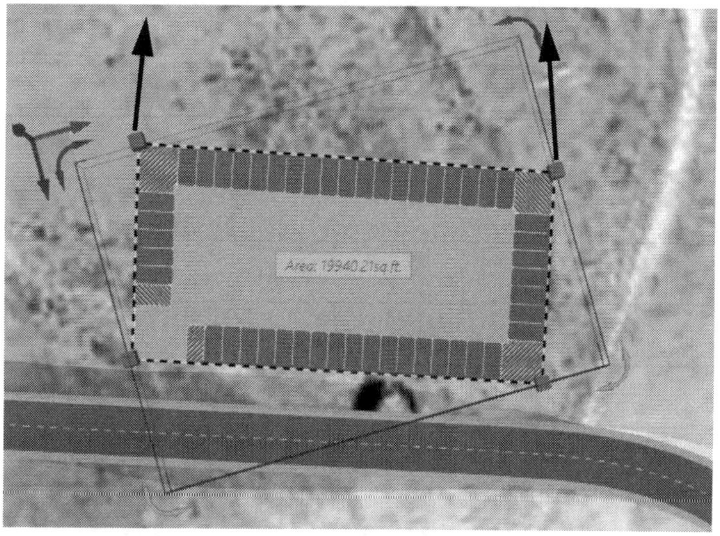

Figure 7–36

5. Select the parking layout this time. Be sure you do not select the parking area instead.

6. Click and drag the grips, as shown in Figure 7–37.

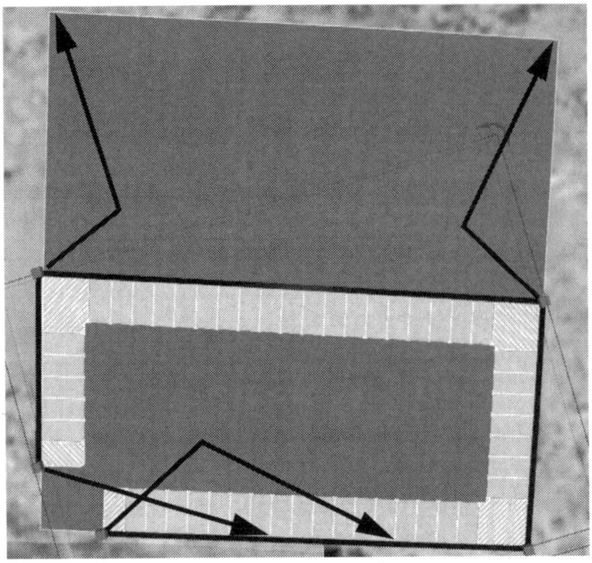

Figure 7–37

7. Right-click on the left edge and select **Add Vertex**, as shown Figure 7–38. Now drag the new vertex down to the lower-left corner of the parking area. Press <Esc> to clear the selection.

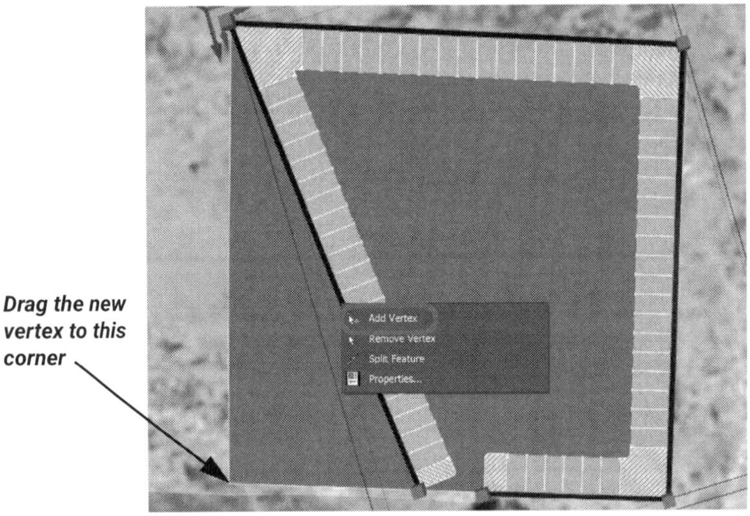

Figure 7–38

8. Select the parking area, again. Be sure you do not select the parking layout instead.

9. Right-click on the lower edge by one side of the entrance bay and select **Add Vertex**. Repeat for the other side, and then add two more vertices in between, as shown in Figure 7–39. Press <Esc> to clear the selection.

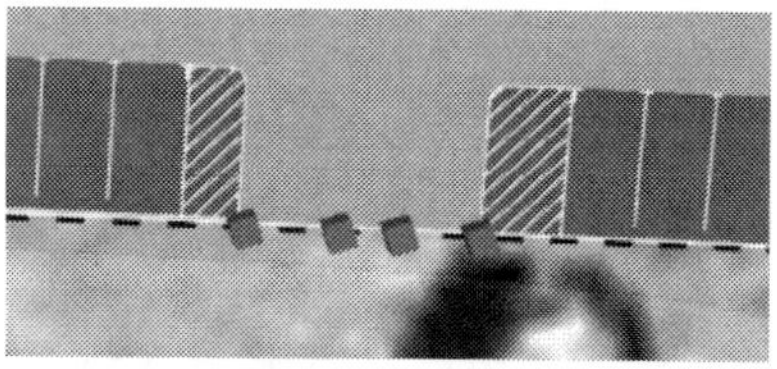

Figure 7–39

10. Click and drag the inner two grips to the edge of the shoulder of the road to create an entrance, as shown in Figure 7–40. Press <Esc> to clear the selection.

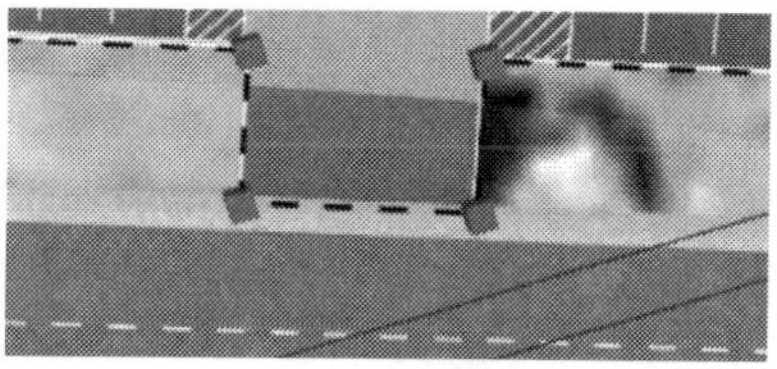

Figure 7–40

11. Now that the perimeter has been defined, you can place parking rows in between. In the *Create* tab>*Environment* drop-down list, click  (Parking Rows). For the first row, click in the upper-left area, then drag the line down and double-click to finish. Repeat for the second row. Press <Esc> to clear the selection. The final result is shown in Figure 7–41.

Figure 7–41

12. Select the parking rows and in its asset card, change the style to **Thick White Stripe with Grass Islands**. Repeat the style change for the perimeter.

13. Select the perimeter parking row, then select the stall next to the entrance. In the asset card, change the *Bay Style* to **Accessible**, as shown in Figure 7–42. Repeat for additional stalls you deem to be accessible. Press <Esc> to clear the selection.

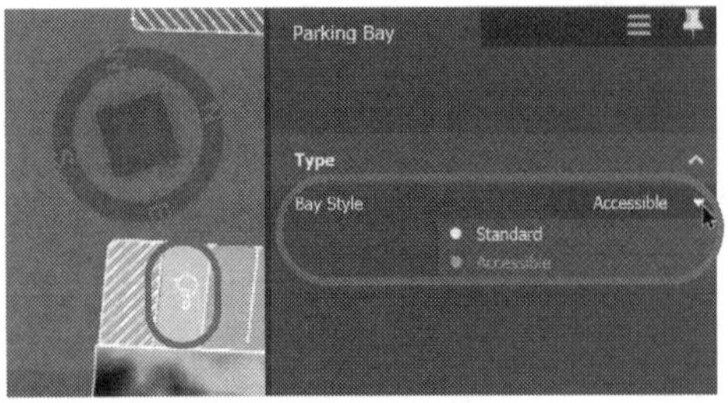

Figure 7–42

14. Orbit the view to see the parking area in 3D. Select the parking area. In the right-click menu, select **Flatten Elevation**, as shown in Figure 7–43. The parking area flattens, dragging the surrounding area to it, as shown in the lower part of Figure 7–43. Use the *Move* gizmo to lower the parking area by a few feet. Press <Esc> to clear the selection.

Figure 7–43

15. The road is lowered accordingly and must be adjusted through the *Profile View*. If you are pressed for time and are unable to complete this task, use the adjusted road available in the proposal for the next task.

Task 3: Create a new grading style.

In this task, you will create a new grading style that uses river stone for the cut and grass for the fill of the proposed park area.

1. If you did not complete the last practice, select the **B_Task3** proposal to make it current. In this proposal, the **Morris Beach road** profile has been adjusted to accommodate the flattened and lower parking area.
2. Click (Bookmarks) and select **Beach-Parking**. Pan up a bit so see the shoreline.
3. In the *Manage* tab>*Content* panel, select (*Style Palette*). In the *Style Palette*, use the down arrow in the lower-left area of the panel to select the *Grading* tab at the very bottom.
4. In the *Style Editing* area at the bottom of the *Style Palette*, click (Add new style to the current catalog above).
5. In the *Define New Grading* dialog box, set the following options, as shown in Figure 7–44:
    - *Grading Method:* **Fixed Slope**
    - *Cut Slope*: **1:1**
    - *Fill Slope*: **4:1**
    - Clear the **Cut and Fill Material use the same Style** checkbox.
    - *Cut Material*: **Material/Land Cover/Riverstone**
    - *Fill Material:* **Material/Land Cover/Manicured Grass**
    - Ensure that the **Set Limit for Grading** checkbox is not selected.

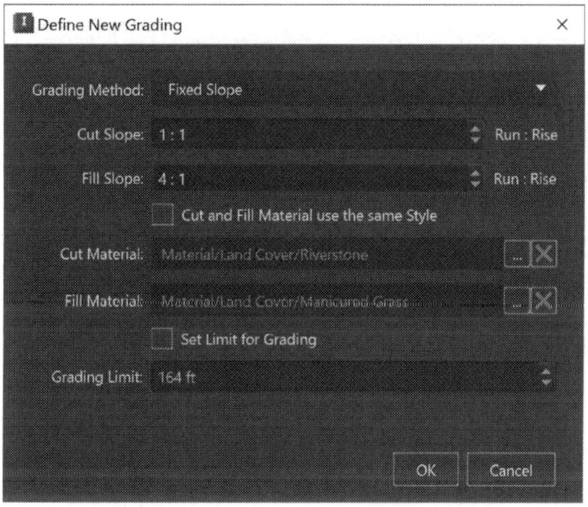

Figure 7–44

6. Click **OK**.
7. Type **XXX-RiverPark** for the name (substituting XXX with your initials).
8. In the *Create* tab>*Environment* drop-down list, click (Grading Area).
9. Select **ManicuredGrass** for the style.

10. Set the points for the vertices, similar to those shown in Figure 7–45.

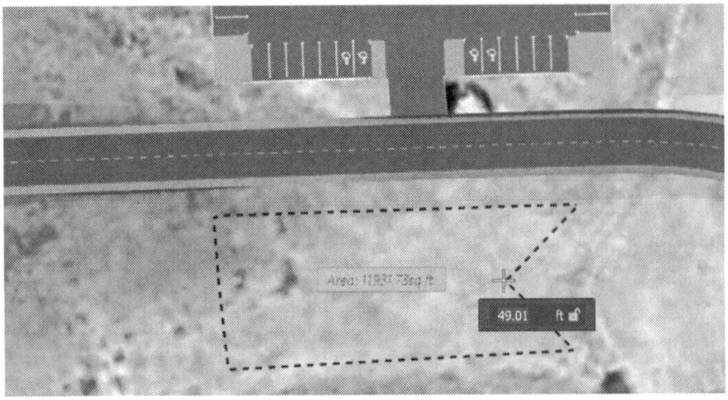

Figure 7–45

11. Ensure that you double-click the last point to end the command.
12. Press <Esc> twice to end the command.
13. In the *Grading Area* asset card, name the grading area **Morris Beach Lawn**.
14. In the *Grading Area* asset card, change the *Rule Grading* style to the new **XXX-RiverPark** grading style created earlier, as shown in Figure 7–46. Click on **More Styles** to find it.

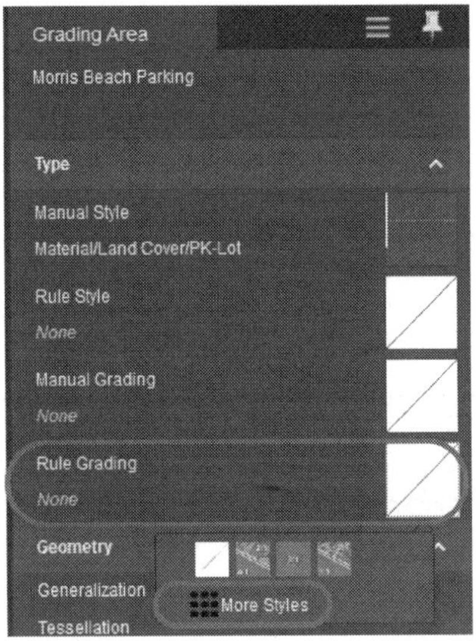

Figure 7–46

15. Orbit the view to see the area in 3D.

16. Raise and lower the grading area with the move gizmo and note how the cut area is updated with a near vertical slope and stone material, as shown in Figure 7–47. Settle on an elevation where only the upper-left corner has a bit of a retaining wall, as shown in the upper part of the figure.

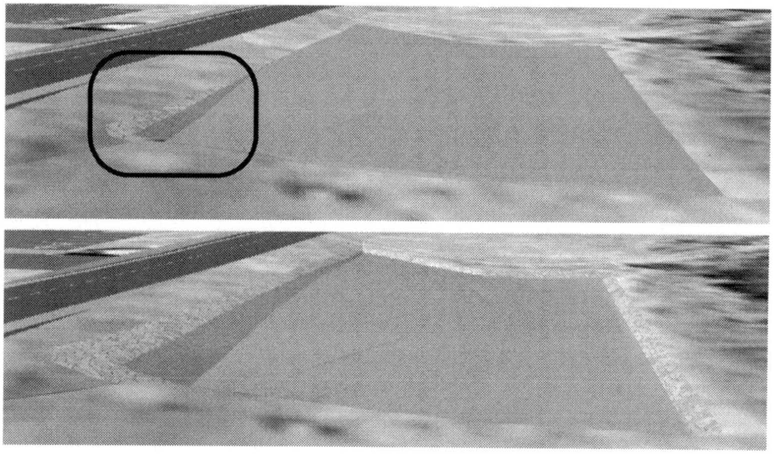

Figure 7–47

17. The results are shown in Figure 7–48.

Figure 7–48

Task 4: Create a parking lot and grass area for hotel patrons.

In this task, you will create a parking lot and a level building pad for the **Ascent Hotel**.

1. Continue working in the same model. If you did not complete the last task, set **B_Task4** as the current proposal.
2. Click (Bookmarks) and select **Hotel**.
3. Delete the two existing buildings at the end of **Ascent Hotel Drive** (shown in Figure 7–49) by selecting them and pressing <Delete>.
4. In the *Create* tab>*Environment* drop-down list, click (Parking Area).
5. In the *Select Draw Style* asset card that displays, type **PK** in the *Search* field and select **PK-Lot**.
6. In the model, click to place the first vertex of the parking area at the northern side of the end of **Ascent Hotel Drive**, as shown in Figure 7–49.

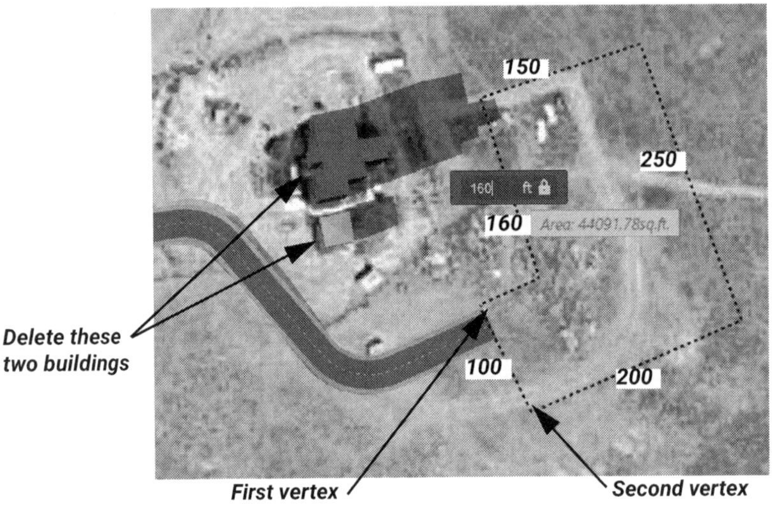

Figure 7–49

7. Move the cursor in the southeast direction (perpendicular to the road), type **100**, and press <Enter> to lock in the distance. Click to place the second vertex, as shown in Figure 7–49.
8. Move the cursor in the northeast direction, type **200**, and press <Enter> to lock in the distance. Click to place the vertex.
9. Move the cursor in the northwest direction, type **250**, and press <Enter> to lock in the distance. Click to place the vertex.
10. Move the cursor in the southwest direction, type **150**, and press <Enter> to lock in the distance. Click to place the vertex.

11. Move the cursor in the southeast direction, type **160**, and press <Enter> to lock in the distance. Move the vertex so the bearing is perpendicular to the previous segment and double-click to place the final vertex and end the command.
12. In the *Parking Area* asset card, name the grading area as **Hotel Parking**.
13. If time permits, use the parking layout and parking row tools to lay out the parking area and change the style as you had done earlier, as shown on the left in Figure 7–50. The access road's profile will also need adjusting.

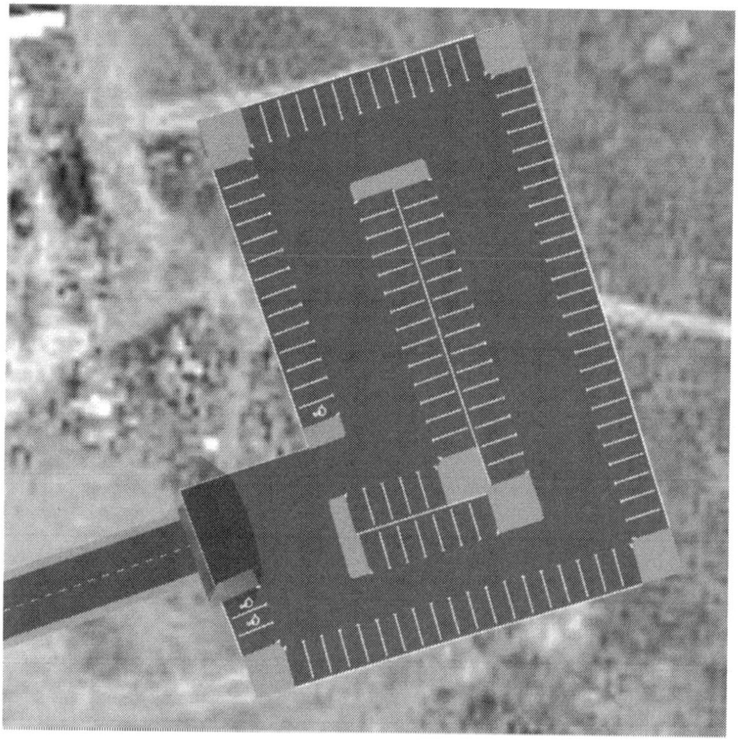

Figure 7–50

14. In the *Create* tab>*Environment* drop-down list, click  (Grading Area).
15. Select **MSE Block** for the style.

16. In the model, click to place the first vertex offset from the L-corner of the parking lot, as shown in Figure 7–51.

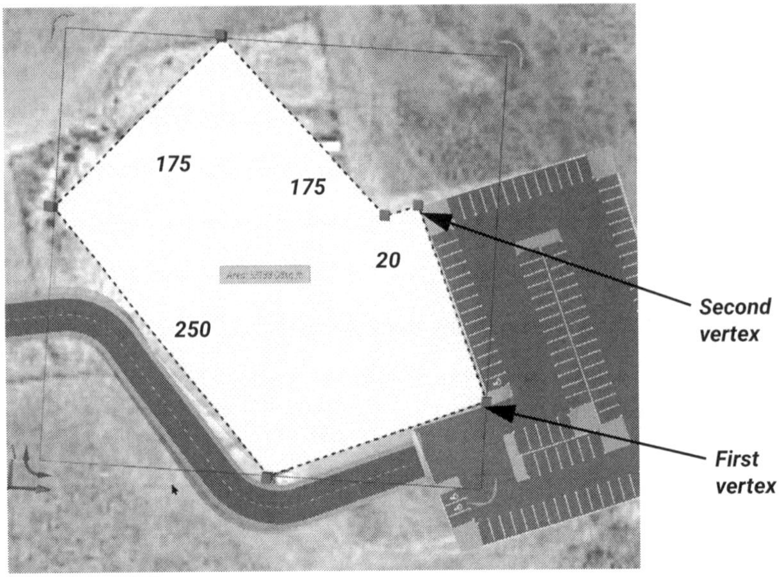

Figure 7–51

17. Move the cursor in the northwest direction, parallel to the parking area, to the northwest corner of the parking area, as shown in Figure 7–51. Click to place the second vertex.
18. Follow the outline shown in Figure 7–51, with the following distances:
    - **20'**
    - **175'**
    - **175'**
    - **250'**
19. Ensure that you double-click the last point to end the command.
20. Press <Esc> twice to end the command.
21. In the *Grading Area* asset card, name the grading area **Hotel Pad**.
22. Click (Bookmarks) and select **Hotel 3D**.
23. Select the **Hotel Pad** grading area.

    Note: *Once the blue Z-axis arrow is selected, it turns red.*

24. Click on the blue Z-axis arrow and type **0.5** to raise the pad 6 inches, as shown in Figure 7–52.

Figure 7–52

25. Select the **Ascent Hotel Drive** component road and press <Ctrl>+<0> (zero) to open the *Profile View*.
26. Zoom and pan to the right end of the profile and select the last PVI. Change the elevation to **4555.18**, as shown in Figure 7–53.

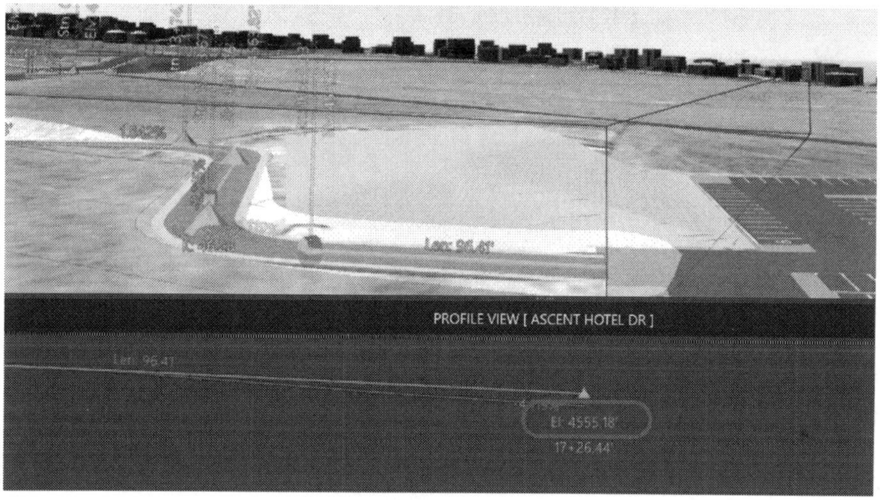

Figure 7–53

27. Press <Esc> to clear the selection of the road.
28. Close the *Profile View*.

End of practice

7.4 Create Buildings in a Model

Custom buildings can be added to a model to add additional detail to the design. When creating a custom building, the look of the outside of the building is defined using a **Facade** style in the *Select Draw Style* asset card.

How To: Create Custom Buildings

1. In the *Create* tab>*Structures* panel, click (Building).
2. The *Select Draw Style* asset card opens, as shown in Figure 7–54. Select the style for the exterior of the building. Note that the asset card has the option to filter by building material types, such as bricks, marble, concrete, etc.

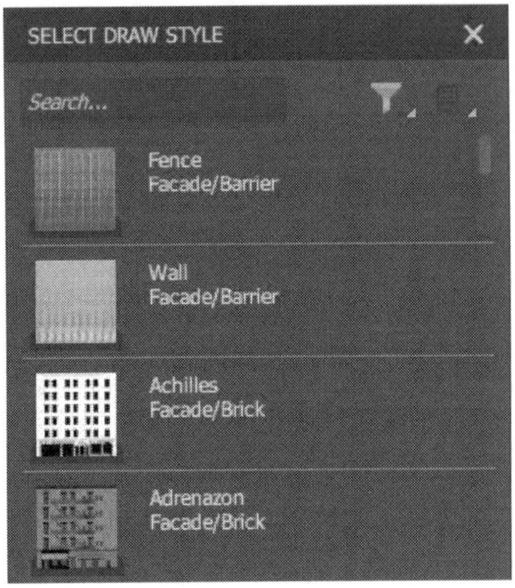

Figure 7–54

3. In the model, click to place the first corner of the building footprint.

4. After the first corner has been placed, move the cursor to where you want the next corner to be placed. The dimensions for that side of the building display, as shown in Figure 7–55.

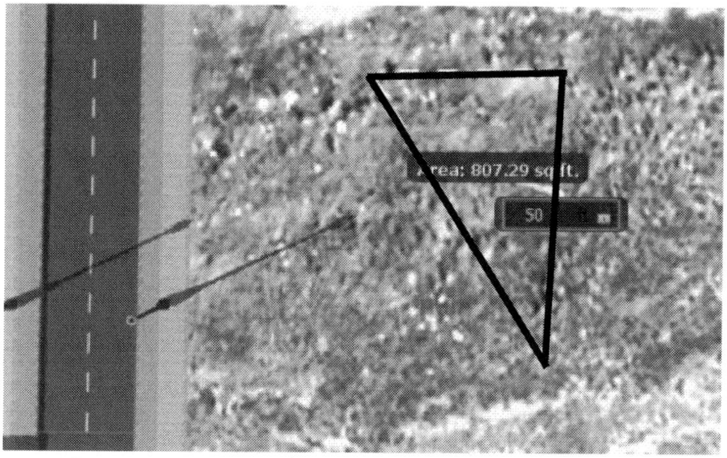

Figure 7–55

5. Type the required length for that side of the building and press <Enter> to lock the length. Move the cursor as required to set the correct angle and click to place the corner.

   Note: *If you start drawing a building and enter a distance for the first side (for example, 100'), you can hold <Shift> to snap to a right angle.*

6. Repeat Steps 4 to 5 until all but the last corner have been set.
7. Double-click on the location at which you want to place the final corner to end the command.
8. Press <Esc> to clear the selection of the newly created building.

Edit Buildings

Once a building has been created, the height should be adjusted by using the *Building* asset card or by using the (Height Gizmo) while the building is selected. Clicking and dragging the (Control Point Gizmo) enables you to reshape the building footprint.

Hint: Changing Building Attributes

The roof material, slope, height, and other attributes can be set in the *Building* asset card (shown in Figure 7–56).

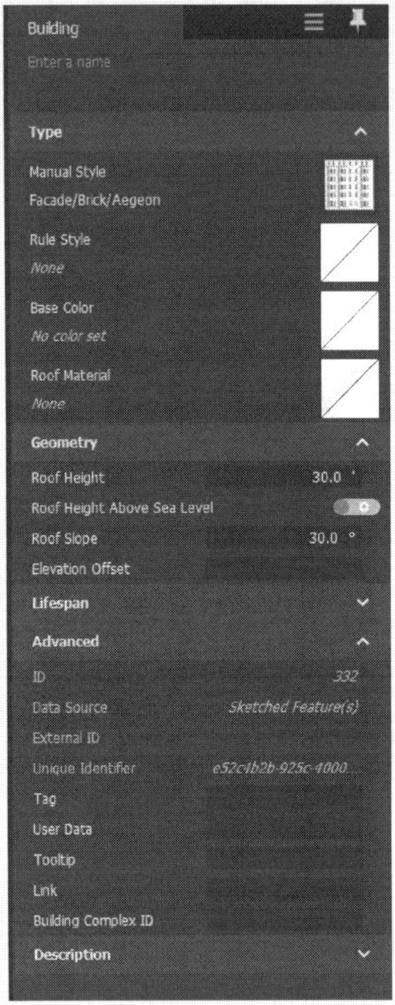

Figure 7–56

Practice 7c
Create Buildings in the Model

Practice Objective

- Create buildings in the model.

In this practice, you will create buildings using exact measurements to populate the new subdivision.

1. Continue working in the same model as the last practice. If you closed the file, on the *Home* screen, click **Open**. In the *InfraWorks Practice Files\7-Model-Details* folder, select **CreateFeatures.sqlite** and click **Open**.
2. Set the proposal to **C_Task1** if you did not complete the previous practices.
3. Click  (Bookmarks) and select **Add Homes**.
4. In the *Create* tab>*Structures* panel, click  (Building).
5. In the *Select Draw Style* asset card, type **Brick** in the *Search* field, then select **Servillius**.
6. In the model, click to place the first corner of the building footprint, as shown in Figure 7–57.

Figure 7–57

7. After the first corner has been placed, move the cursor due east, type **40** for the length of the first side, as shown in Figure 7–58, and press <Enter>. Click to place the second corner.

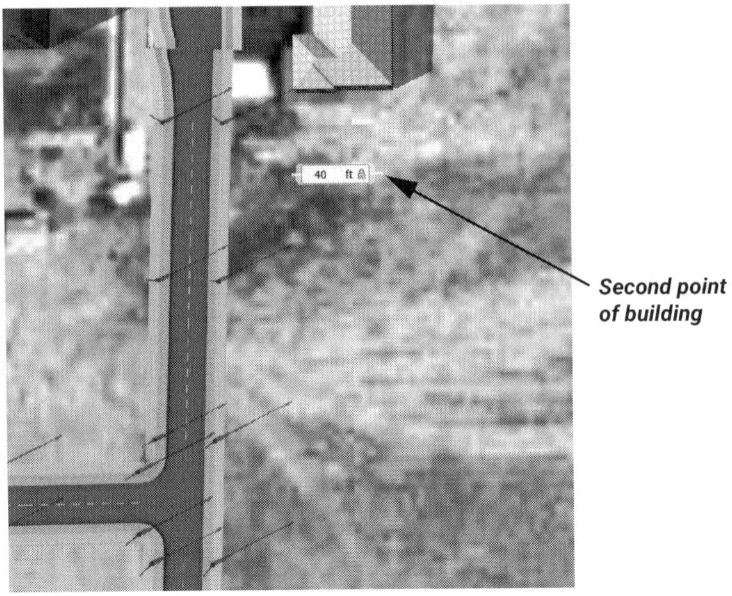

Figure 7–58

8. In the model, move the cursor due south, type **40** for the length of the second side, and press <Enter>. Hold <Shift> to snap to a right angle and click to place the third corner.
9. Move the cursor due west, type **30** for the length, and press <Enter>. Hold <Shift> to snap to a right angle and click to place the fourth corner.
10. Move the cursor due north, type **15** for the length, and press <Enter>. Hold <Shift> to snap to a right angle and click to place the fifth corner.
11. Move the cursor due west, type **10** for the length, and press <Enter>. Hold <Shift> to snap to a right angle. Double-click to place the sixth corner and end the command.

12. Press <Esc> twice to clear the selection of the newly created building. The last corner lines up with the first corner, as shown in Figure 7–59.

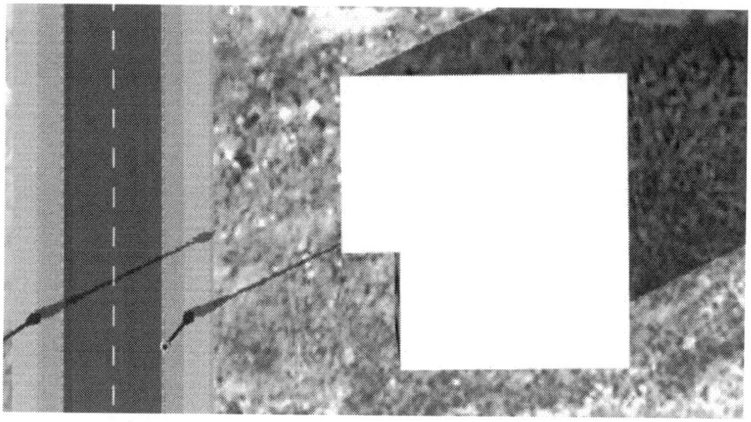

Figure 7–59

13. Create a similar building to the south of the one you just created. Use the measurements shown in Figure 7–60.

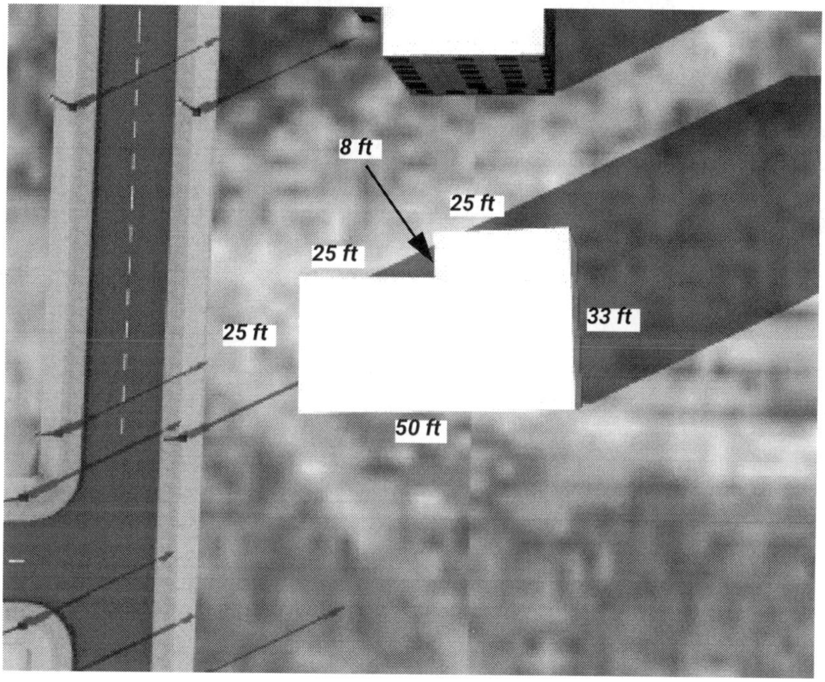

Figure 7–60

14. Press <Esc> to show the second building's gizmos. Hold <Ctrl> and click on the first building to select it as well.

15. In the *Building* asset card, set both the *Roof Height* and *Roof Slope* to **30**, as shown in Figure 7–61. Both buildings should update.

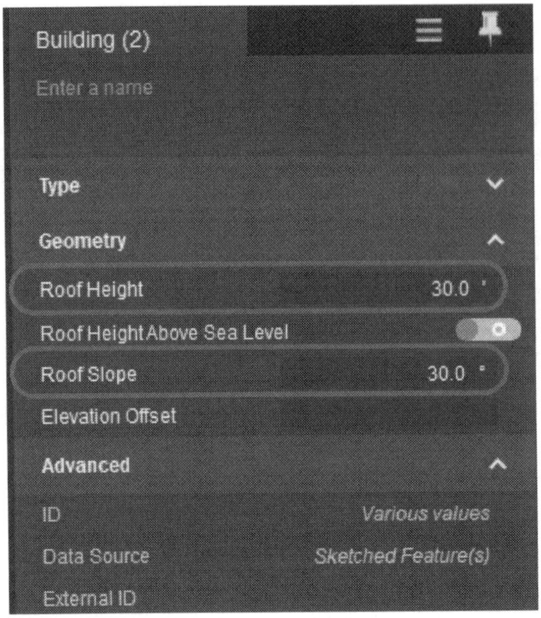

Figure 7–61

16. Press <Esc> to clear the selection.

End of practice

7.5 Create City Furniture in a Model

InfraWorks has a comprehensive library of predefined objects, shapes, and symbols that simplify creating a realistic model. These are all grouped together as "city furniture".

If you need to create multiple predefined 3D buildings or other 3D models in your model, it is recommended that you use  (City Furniture). This command enables you to create multiple 3D models spaced along a path, or a single feature at the location specified. Any type of 3D model style can be selected as city furniture, including trees and railway models. However, these models display in the *Furniture* category in the *Model Explorer* and are furniture features in the database.

The following 3D models can be added as city furniture to a model:

- **Bridge Components:** There are several 3D models of various barriers and other components you would find on a bridge. Figure 7–62 shows a list of what is available in the software out of the box. Others can be added as required.

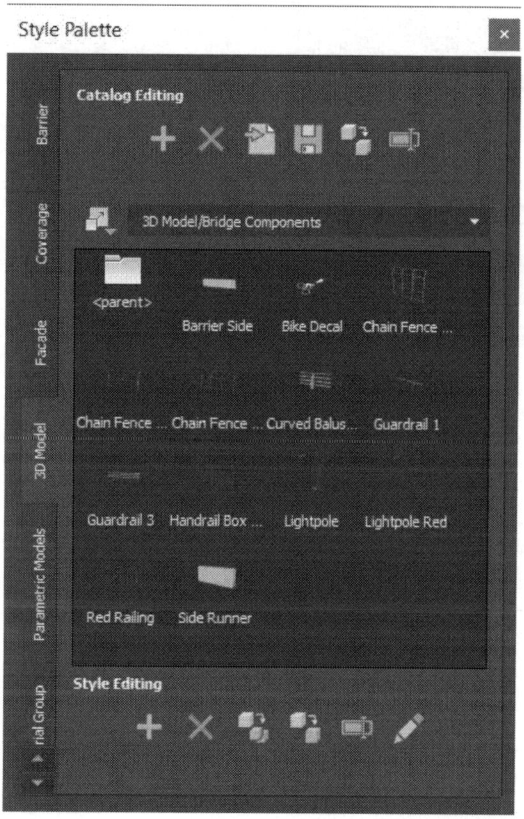

Figure 7–62

- **Buildings:** There are a number of predefined 3D building models. They fall into three categories that you can select from:
  - **Furniture:** 3D models of rooftop items, such as solar panels and HVAC units.
  - **Neighborhood:** A few common building types that are found in a typical city, such as gas stations, churches, and post offices.
  - **Residential:** Multiple single-family home models.

  These 3D model options are located on the *3D Model* tab of the *Style Palette*. The **Neighborhood** and **Residential** style options are shown in Figure 7–63.

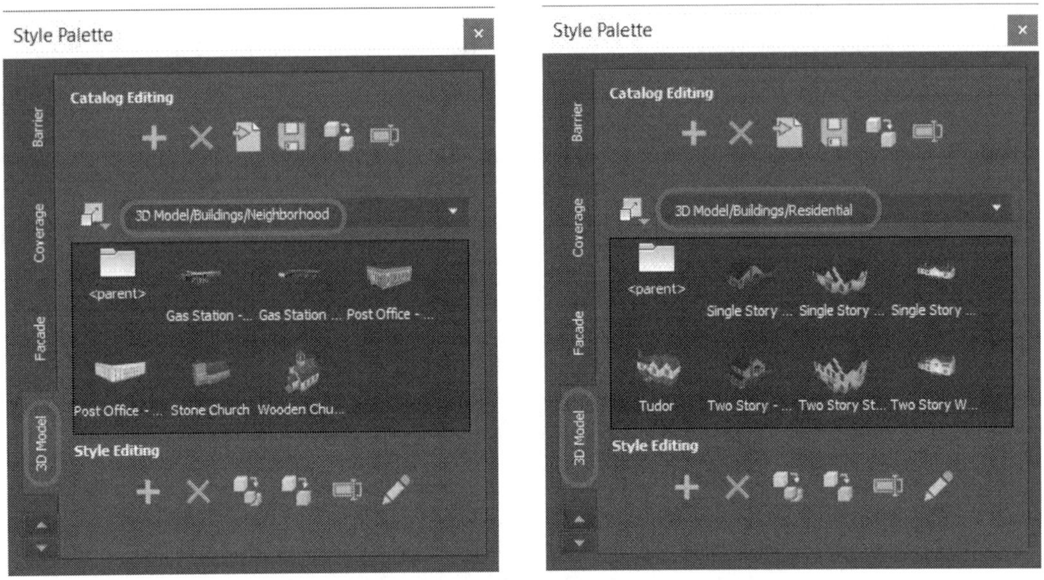

Figure 7–63

- **City Furniture:** Objects found in a city, including signs, fences, bike stands, parking meters, and dumpsters, as shown in Figure 7–64.

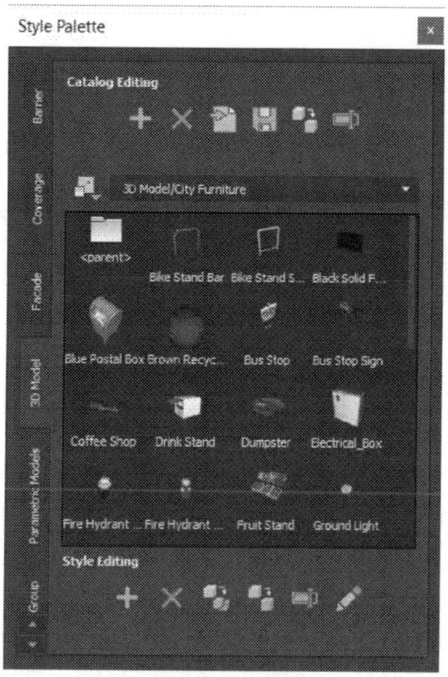

Figure 7–64

- **Construction:** Objects found on a construction site, including piles of dirt or sand, various pieces of equipment, and Porta Potties, as shown in Figure 7–65.

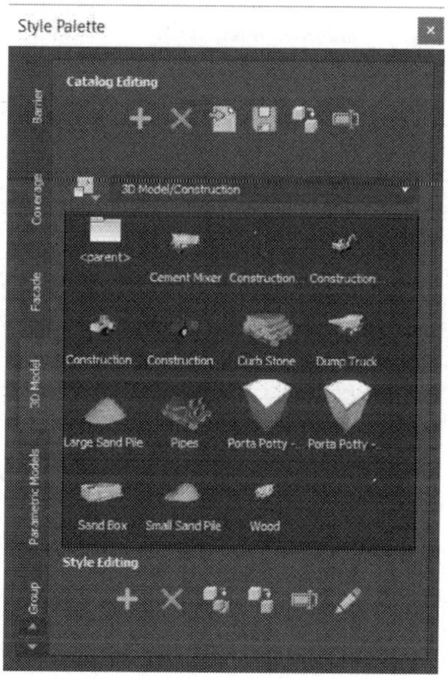

Figure 7–65

- **Energy:** Objects used to deliver energy to specific areas, including distribution pylons, solar panels, oil pumps, oil rigs, transmission poles, and wind turbines, as shown in Figure 7–66.

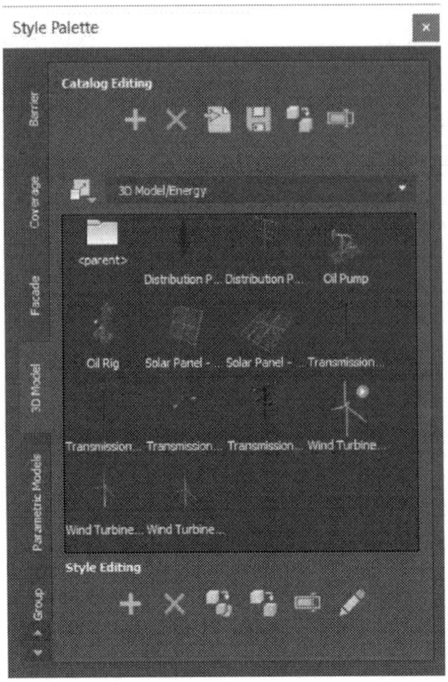

Figure 7–66

- **Highway:** Safety features used in road design, including guard rails and noise barriers, as shown in Figure 7–67.

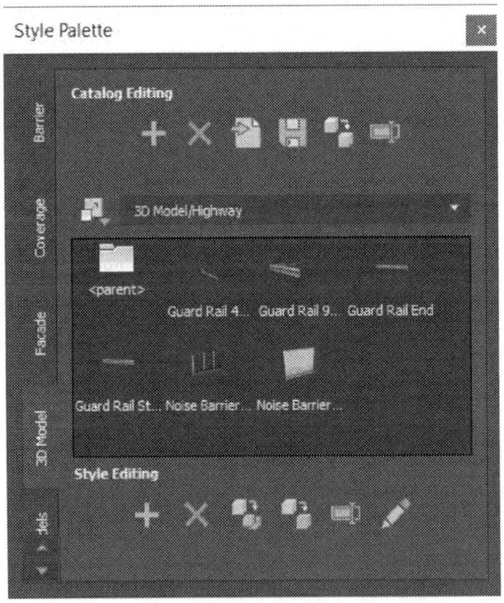

Figure 7–67

- **POI (Points of Interest):** Markers and flag pins that can be used to draw attention to specific areas of the model, as shown in Figure 7–68.

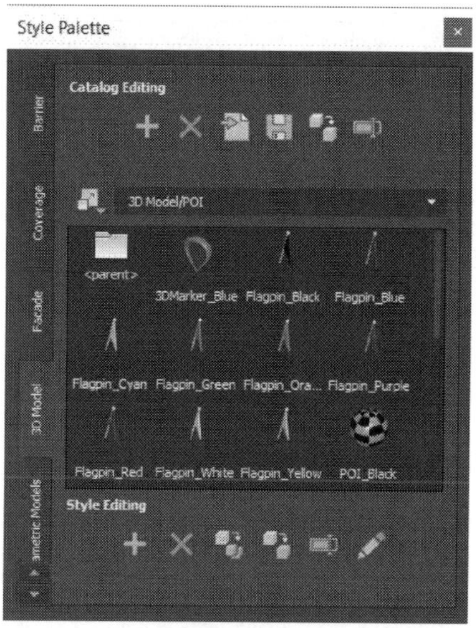

Figure 7–68

- **People:** One or more people walking or standing, as shown in Figure 7–69.

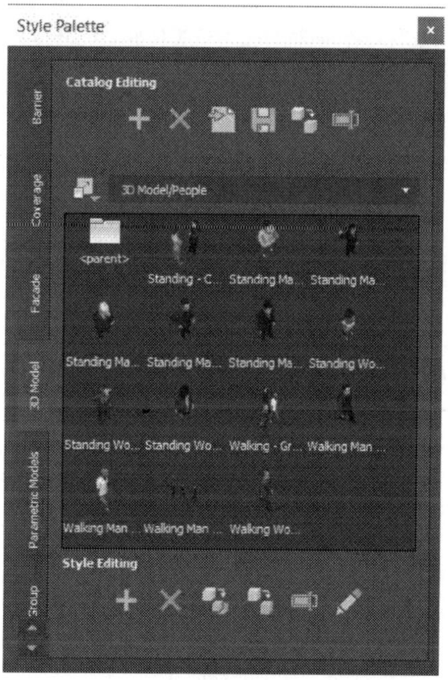

Figure 7–69

- **Planes & Ships:** Planes, helicopters, and water vessels, as shown in Figure 7–70.

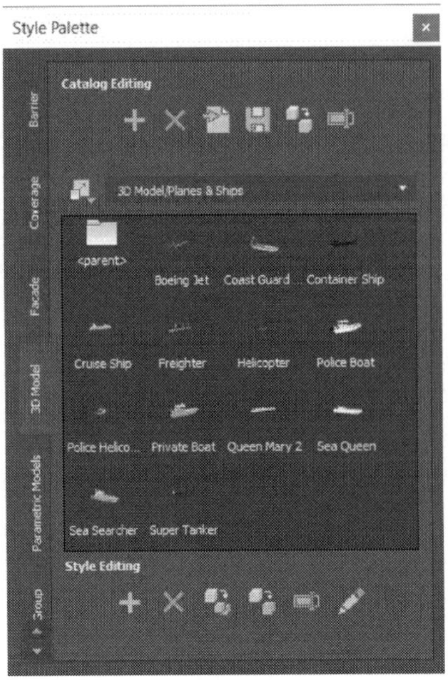

Figure 7–70

- **Railway:** Passenger cars, freight cars, and railway furniture, as shown in Figure 7–71.

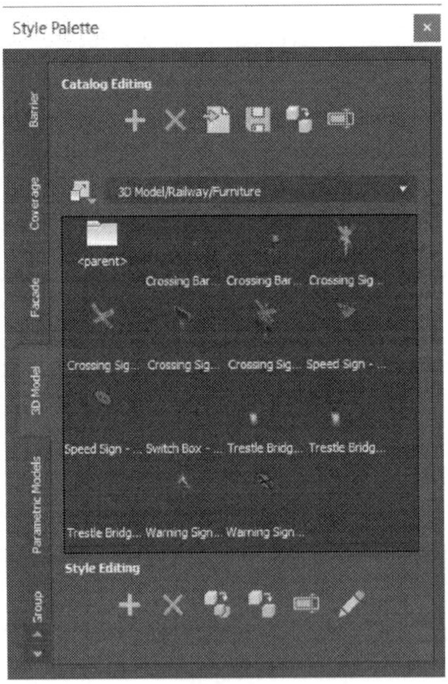

Figure 7–71

- **Shapes:** Shapes in multiple colors that can be used to draw attention to specific areas of the model, as shown in Figure 7–72.

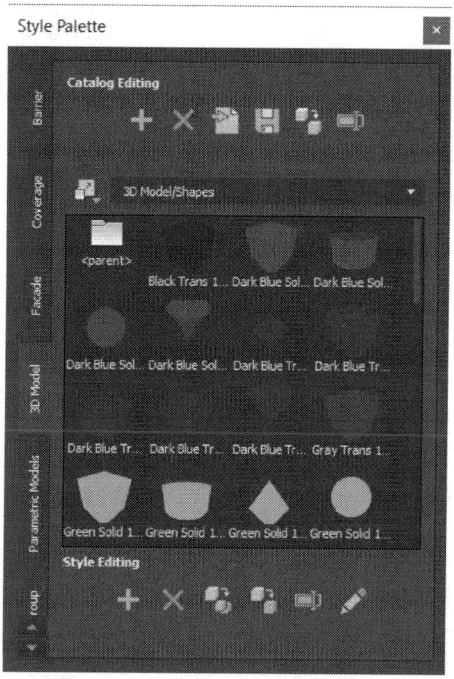

Figure 7–72

- **Stones:** Objects used in landscaping, as shown in Figure 7–73.

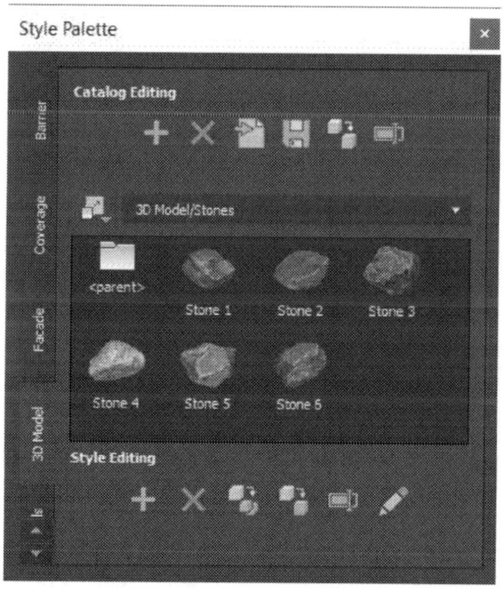

Figure 7–73

- **Traffic & Barriers:** Objects used to control traffic, including traffic lights, construction cones, metal fences, and barriers, as shown in Figure 7–74.

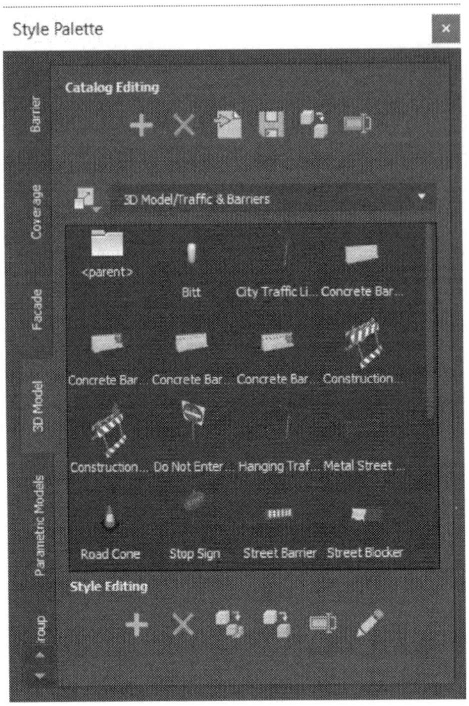

Figure 7–74

- **Vegetation:** Objects used in landscaping, including trees and bushes, as shown in Figure 7–75. Even though vegetation is available in the City Furniture collection, there are better tools for placing vegetation that are covered later in this chapter.

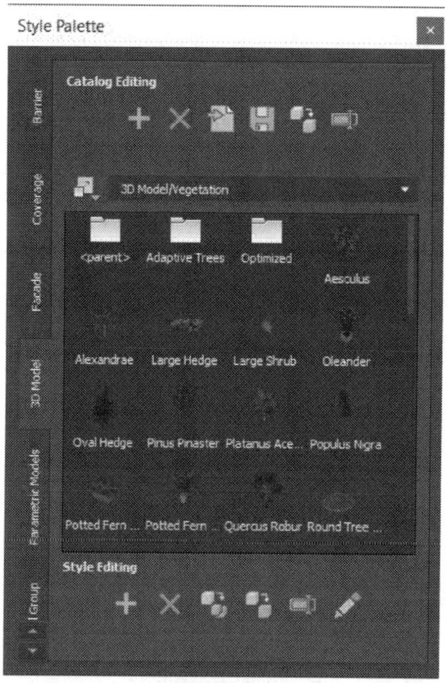

Figure 7–75

- **Vehicles:** Cars, trucks, vans, buses, and bicycles, as shown in Figure 7–76.

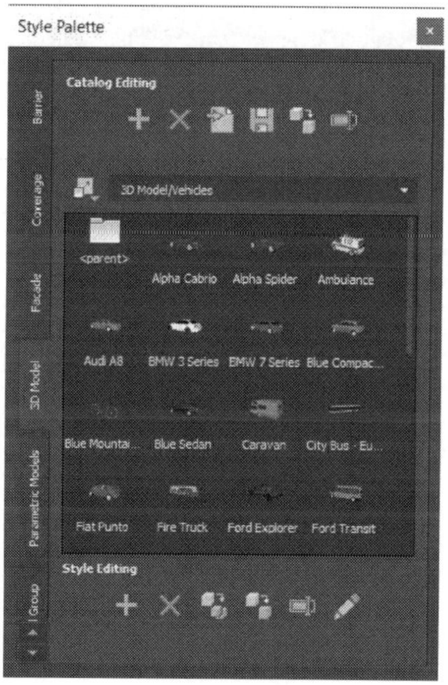

Figure 7–76

How To: Add a Predefined 3D Building or Another Single Piece of City Furniture

1. In the *Create* tab>*Environment* panel, click  (City Furniture).
2. The *Select Draw Style* asset card displays, as shown in Figure 7–77. Select the 3D model, or use the filter area to narrow down the selection options.

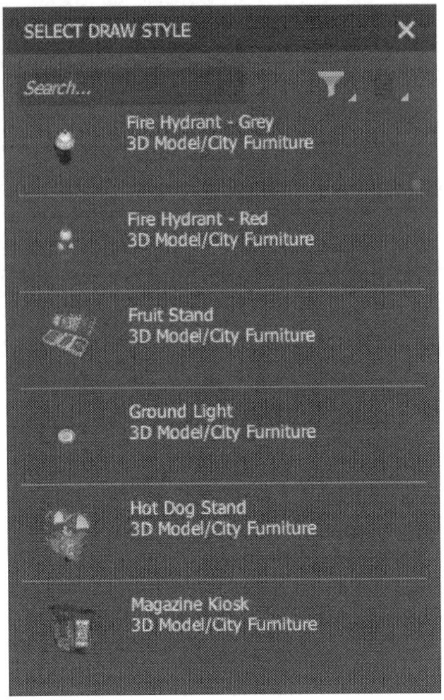

Figure 7–77

3. In the model, double-click to place the model and end the command. The size is not important because the 3D model size and shape are predetermined.
4. Press <Esc> to clear the selection.

Hint: Model Size/Shape

You cannot reshape a building created from a 3D model. The height and shape are predetermined by the model style. However, you can change the scale of the building using the (Height Gizmo) or the *Properties* panel. Using the height gizmo causes the building to change scale while keeping the same ratio in the X, Y, and Z planes. However, changing the scale in the *Properties* panel enables the model to be stretched in one or more directions, as shown in Figure 7–78.

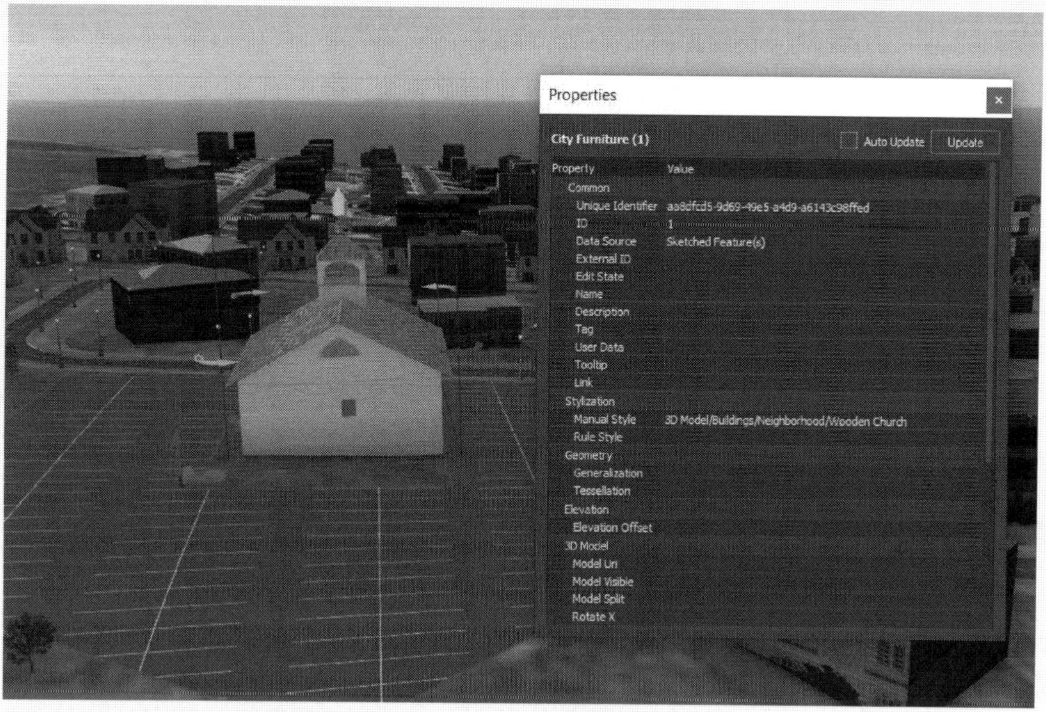

Figure 7–78

How To: Add Multiple Predefined 3D Buildings or Other City Furniture

1. In the *Create* tab>*Environment* panel, click  (City Furniture).
2. The *Select Draw Style* asset card displays, as shown in Figure 7–79. Select the 3D model, or use the filter area to narrow down the selection options.

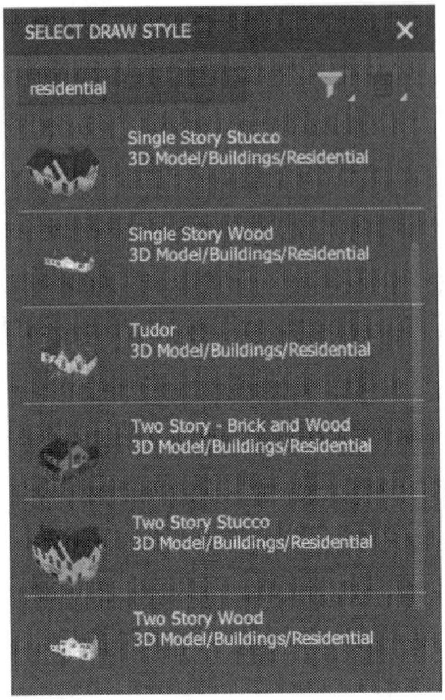

Figure 7–79

3. In the model, single-click to start the path to be followed by the 3D models.
4. Move the cursor in the direction in which you want the 3D model path to follow. Type a distance for the length to the next point of intersection (PI) and press <Enter> to set the distance. Click in the model to place the PI.
5. Continue clicking in the model until the full path has been created.
6. Double-click to place the last point and end the command.
7. To change the number of items that display along the path, slide the **Adjust Density** slider (shown in Figure 7–80) until the model density is set as required.

Figure 7–80

8. Press <Esc> to clear the selection of the newly created 3D models.

9. Move and rotate each 3D model by selecting it and using the (Rotate Gizmo), (Height Gizmo), and (Move Gizmo), as required.
10. If you need to change which 3D model displays at a specific location, you can drag and drop another 3D model in its place from the *Style Palette*, as shown in Figure 7–81.

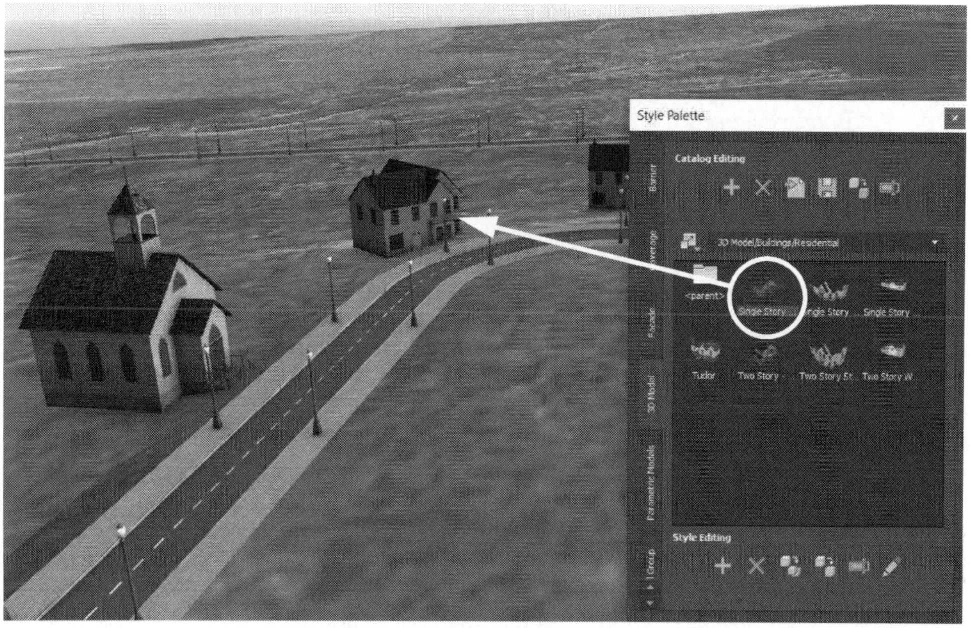

Figure 7–81

Practice 7d
Add Buildings and City Furniture to the Model

Practice Objective

- Add buildings and other 3D models to the model.

In this practice, you will create buildings to populate the new subdivision. First, you will use predefined 3D models to place a church and a row of houses. Next, you will create copies of existing buildings to make populating the subdivision more efficient. Finally, you will add vehicles and a traffic light to the roads and a crossing barrier to the railway.

Task 1: Add predefined buildings.

1. Continue working in the same model as the last practice. If you closed the file, on the *Home* screen, click **Open**. In the *InfraWorks Practice Files\7-Model-Details* folder, select **CreateFeatures.sqlite** and click **Open**.
2. In the toolbar, expand the (Proposals) drop-down list and select **D_Task1** if you did not complete the previous practices.
3. Click (Bookmarks) and select **Church Area**.
4. In the *Create* tab>*Environment* panel, click (City Furniture). <Ctrl> G is the keyboard shortcut.
5. In the *Select Draw Style* asset card that displays, type **church** in the *Search* field. Select the **Wooden Church**, as shown in Figure 7–82.

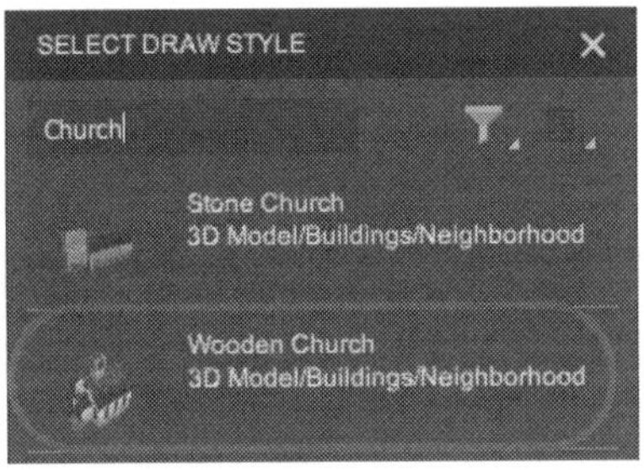

Figure 7–82

6. In the model, double-click in the open area at the center of the parking lot to place the church and end the command, as shown in Figure 7–83.

Figure 7–83

7. Press <Esc> to display the building gizmos.

8. With the church still selected, use the  (Rotate Gizmo),  (Height Gizmo), and  (Move Gizmo), as required, to relocate it (as shown in Figure 7–84).

Figure 7–84

9. Press <Esc> to clear the selection of the church.

10. Click (Bookmarks) and select **Project Area**.
11. In the *Create* tab>*Environment* panel, click (City Furniture).
12. In the *Select Draw Style* asset card, type **stucco** in the *Search* field. Select the **Two Story Stucco** building, as shown in Figure 7–85.

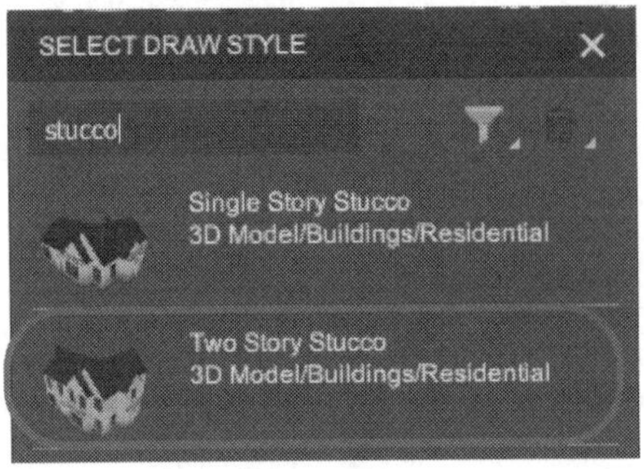

Figure 7–85

13. In the model, click to start a path, and then continue clicking to add PIs for the path the buildings should follow, as shown in Figure 7–86. Double-click to place the last point of the path and end the command.

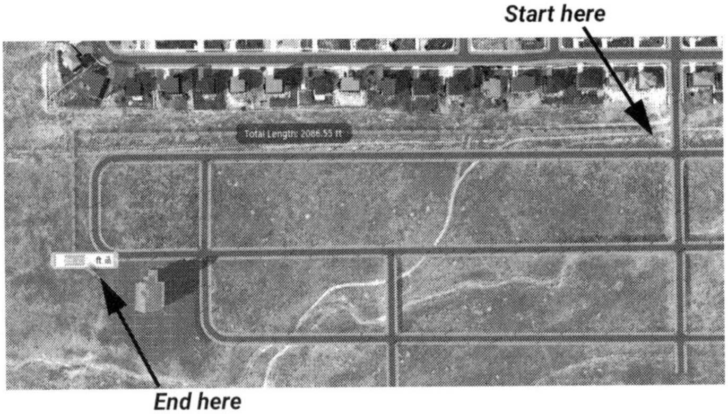

Figure 7–86

14. Press <Esc> to display the gizmos and the **Adjust Density** slider.
15. Slide the **Adjust Density** slider to the left to thin out the homes (set to approximately 40%), as shown in Figure 7–87.

    Note: *To bring the slider back up, you can click on a single item in the group, then click again (do not double-click).*

Figure 7–87

16. With the homes still selected as a group, right-click and select **Properties.**
17. In the *Properties* panel, change *Scale X*, *Scale Y*, and *Scale Z* to **1.5**, as shown in Figure 7–88. Click **Update**.

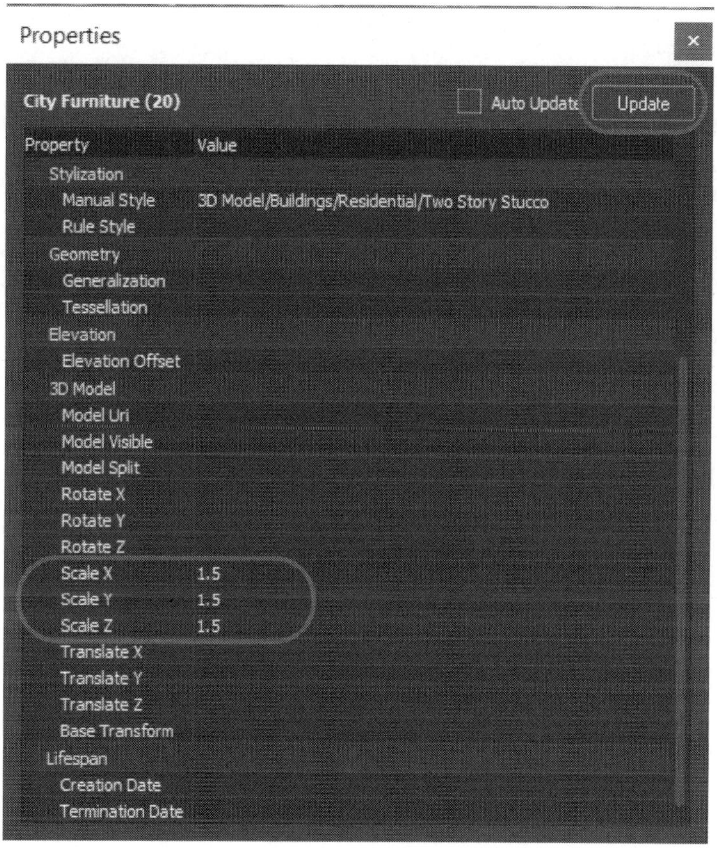

Figure 7–88

18. Press <Esc> to clear the selection. Close the *Properties* panel.

19. Click (Bookmarks) and select **Church 3D.**

20. In the *Manage* tab>*Content* panel, select (*Style Palette*).

21. In the *Style Palette*, select the *3D Model* tab and double-click **Buildings>Residential**. Select the **Single Story Brick** style and drag it to the house closest to the church, as shown in Figure 7–89.

Figure 7–89

22. In the model, select the single story home and use gizmos to move and rotate it appropriately, then adjust the height to **30 ft**, as shown in Figure 7–90.

Figure 7–90

23. Press <Esc> to clear the selection.

Task 2: Create copies of existing buildings.

1. Continue working in the same model. If you did not complete the last task, set the proposal to **D_Task2**.

2. Click (Bookmarks) and select **Project Area**. Pan the model to the north to display the yellow highlighted homes shown in Figure 7–91. (The traced enclosure is for reference only.)

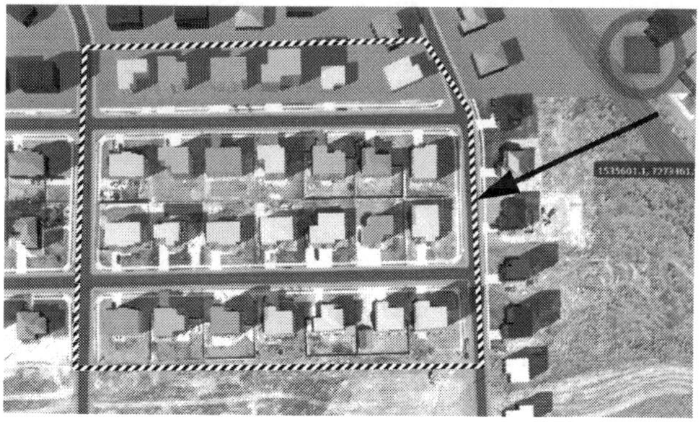

Figure 7–91

3. In the toolbar, expand (Select) and select (Rectangle Select).
4. In the model, create the selection rectangle shown in Figure 7–92. Remember to double-click on the third point to end the selection.

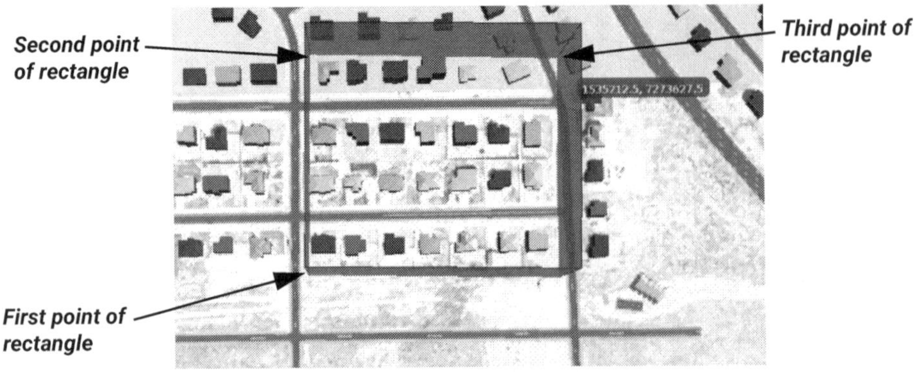

Figure 7–92

5. Press <Ctrl>+<C> to copy the selected homes to the clipboard.
6. Press <Ctrl>+<V> and double-click in the model to place the homes as shown in Figure 7–93.

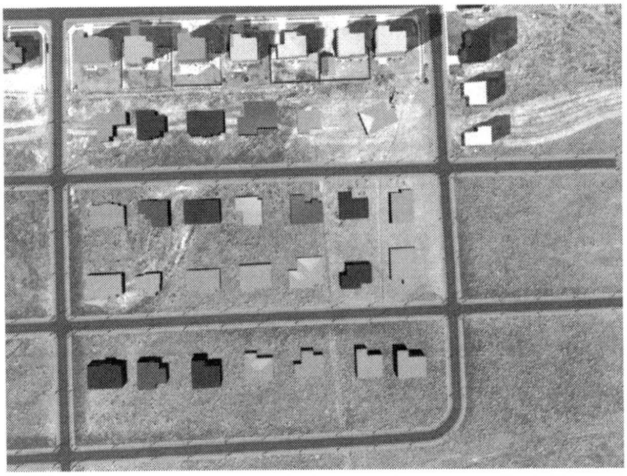

Figure 7–93

7. Continue to create or copy homes to fill in the new neighborhood using any of the tools discussed so far. Ensure that you leave an area open for the proposed green space, as shown in Figure 7–94.

Figure 7–94

Task 3: Create city furniture.

In this task, you will place a traffic light at the three-way intersection for the new neighborhood. You will then place cars on the roads to indicate how traffic should look as it enters the new neighborhood.

1. Continue working in the same model. If you did not complete the last task, set the proposal to **D_Task3**.
2. Click (Bookmarks) and select **School Area**. Pan to the right to the intersection
3. In the *Create* tab>*Environment* panel, click (City Furniture).
4. The *Select Draw Style* asset card displays. Type **traffic** in the *Search* field and select the **City Traffic Light**, as shown in Figure 7–95.

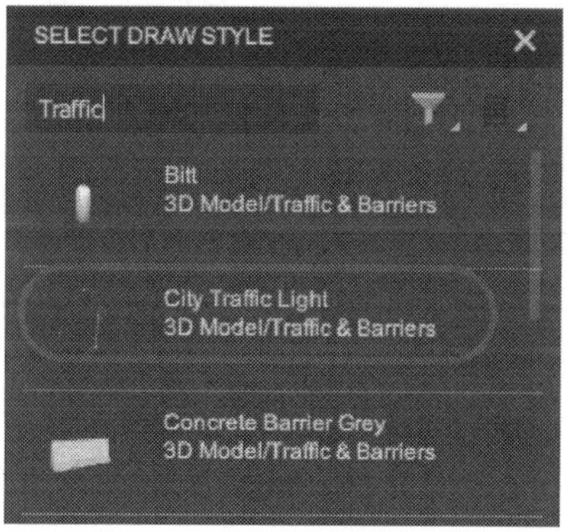

Figure 7–95

5. Double-click in the model to place a traffic light on the east side of the intersection, as shown in Figure 7–96.

Figure 7–96

6. Press <Esc> to display the gizmos, then move and rotate the light using the (Rotate Gizmo) and (Move Gizmo), as required, to line it up as shown in Figure 7–97.

Figure 7–97

7. Press <Esc> to clear the selection of the traffic light.
8. Click (Bookmarks), select **School Area**, and pan to the right to the intersection, if required.
9. In the *Create* tab>*Environment* panel, click (City Furniture).
10. The *Select Draw Style* asset card displays. Type **vehicle** in the *Search* field and select the **Alpha Spider**, as shown in Figure 7–98.

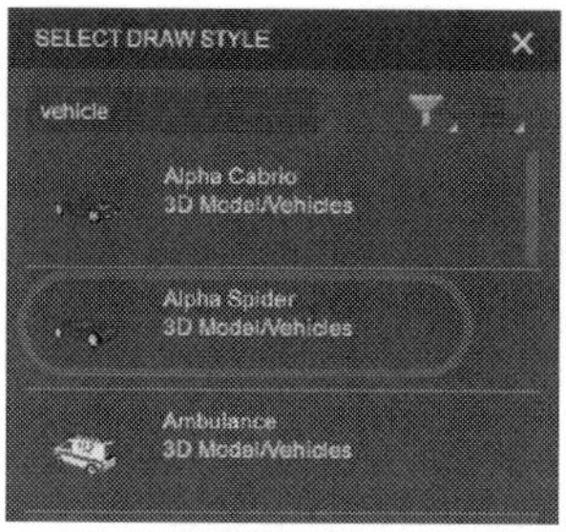

Figure 7–98

11. Create the path shown in Figure 7–99. Remember to double-click to place the last point along the path.

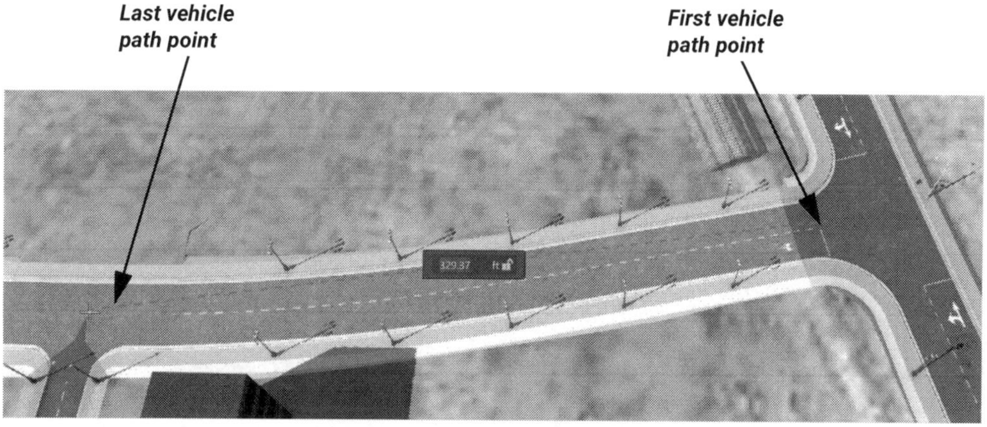

Figure 7–99

12. Press <Esc> to display the gizmos and the **Adjust Density** slider. Slide the **Adjust Density** slider until the density is set close to **55%** so that there are 5 cars (as shown in Figure 7–100).

Figure 7–100

13. Press <Esc> to clear the selection of the newly created vehicles.

14. Move and rotate each vehicle using the (Rotate Gizmo) and (Move Gizmo), as required, to make them parallel to the road.
15. In the *Manage* tab>*Content* panel, select (*Style Palette*)
16. In the *Style Palette*, in the *3D Model* tab, double-click on **Vehicles**.
17. Drag and drop various vehicle styles or colors onto the existing vehicles in the model. Figure 7–101 shows that different vehicle styles have been applied.

Figure 7–101

18. Press <Esc> to clear the selection of all of the features.

Hint: Add City Furniture to Styles

Multiple styles can incorporate city furniture to make populating the model much easier. In ***Chapter 3 Stylize Data Sources***, you learned how to add vehicles to a road style to quickly populate the roadway. Other items that you might want to incorporate include fire hydrants and light poles. Just keep in mind that adding 3D models to a style does cause the model size to increase. Therefore, it is recommended that you only add a few vehicles to the road styles that will be used for the proposed roads, then add vehicles sparsely to an existing roadway only where required for visualization purposes.

Task 4: Add railway 3D models.

1. Continue working in the same model. If you did not complete the previous task, set the proposal to **D_Task4**; a few adjustments to the rail crossing have been made in this proposal.
2. Click (Bookmarks) and select **Railway 3D**.
3. In the *Create* tab>*Environment* panel, click (City Furniture).

4. In the *Select Draw Style* asset card, type **railway** in the *Search* field and scroll down to select the **Crossing Barrier - US** style, as shown in Figure 7–102.

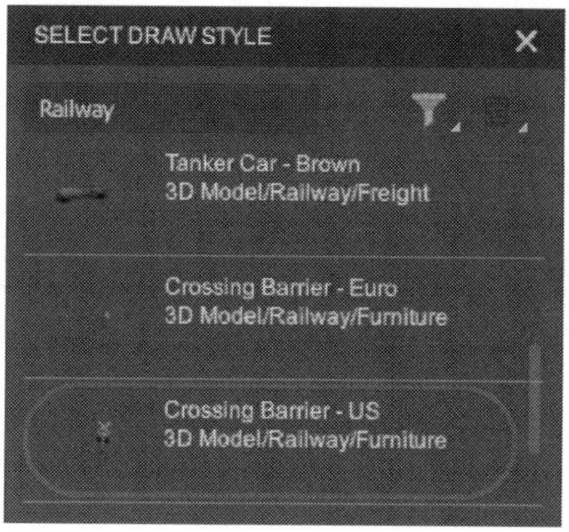

Figure 7–102

5. Double-click in the model to place the 3D model, as shown in Figure 7–103.

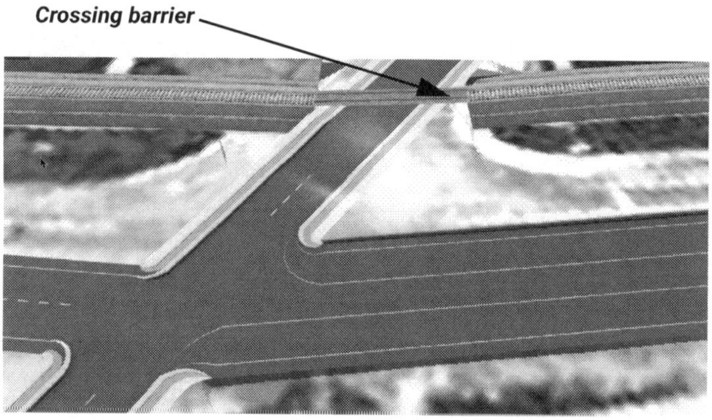

Figure 7–103

6. Press <Esc> to display the gizmos.

7. Use the (Rotate Gizmo) to rotate the crossing barrier arm to make it parallel to the tracks. Use the (Move Gizmo) to move the model to the park strip on the right side of the road, as shown in Figure 7–104.

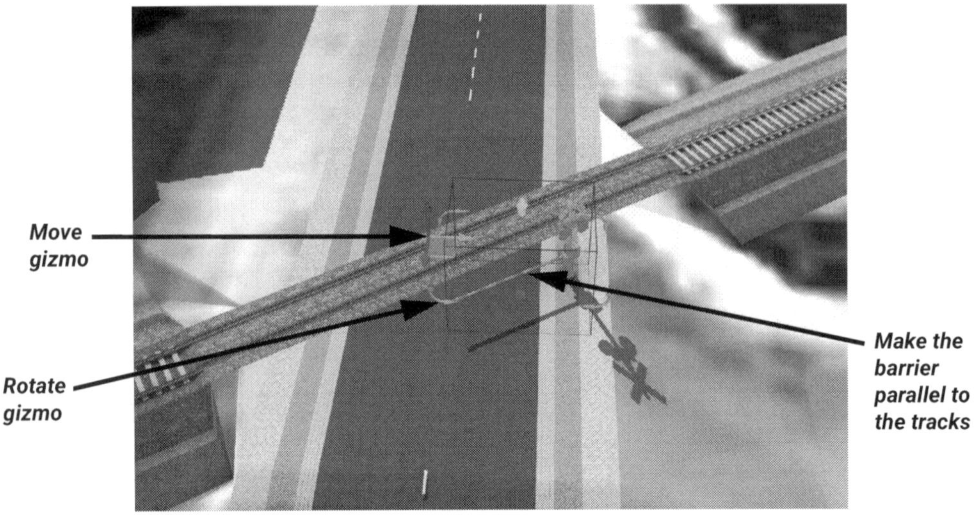

Figure 7–104

8. With the crossing barrier still selected, press <Ctrl>+<C> to copy the model to the clipboard.
9. Press <Ctrl>+<V> to paste a second crossing barrier in the model. Double-click in the model to place it on the other side of the tracks from the first one.
10. With the second crossing barrier still selected, use the (Rotate Gizmo) and (Move Gizmo) to place and orient the 3D model similar to that shown in Figure 7–105.

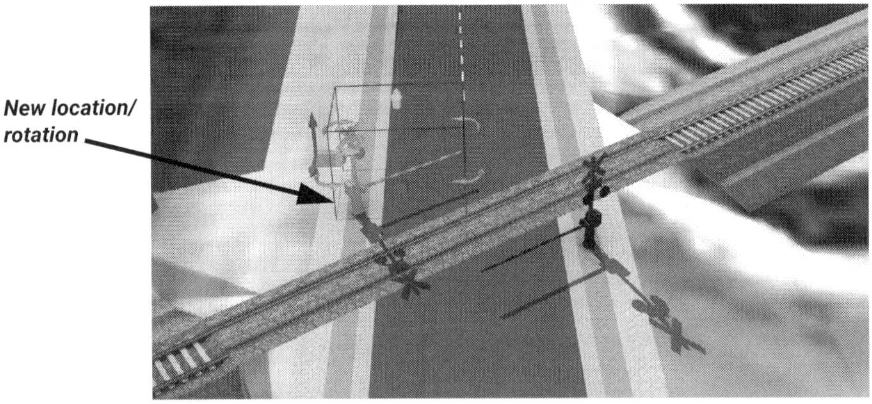

Figure 7–105

11. Press <Esc> to clear the selection of the crossing barrier.
12. Click (Bookmarks) and select **Railway 3D**. Orbit to a plan view, looking straight down on the crossing.
13. In the *Create* tab>*Environment* panel, click (City Furniture).
14. In the *Select Draw Style* asset card, type **passenger** in the *Search* field. Select the **Light Rail - US Midwest** style, as shown in Figure 7–106.

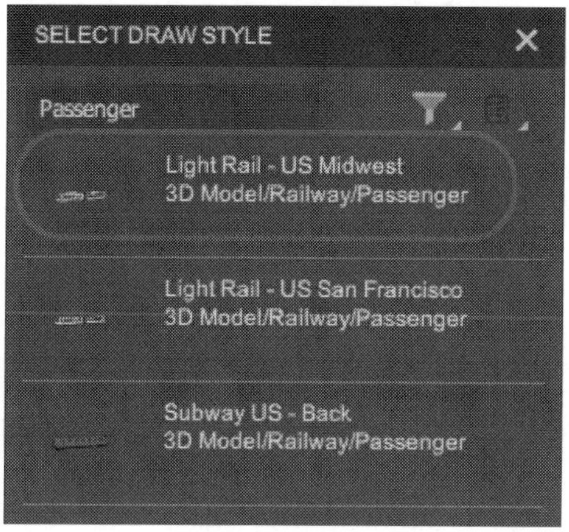

Figure 7–106

15. Double-click to place the 3D model just north of the road crossing, as shown in Figure 7–107.

Figure 7–107

16. Press <Esc> and use the (Rotate Gizmo) to rotate the model and make it parallel to the tracks, as shown in Figure 7–108.

Figure 7–108

17. Press <Esc> to clear the selection of the railway car.

End of practice

7.6 Add Vegetation to a Model

> ***Note:*** *Even though vegetation is available in the City Furniture collection, the tools covered in this section are better for placing vegetation.*

Adding vegetation can add privacy, shade, noise barriers, and landscape appeal to a project. Trees and other vegetation can also help stakeholders to better understand how the project could look when completed. You can add vegetation in three different ways:

- **Single Plant:** A single plant is placed in the model when you double-click on an insertion point, no matter which vegetation tool is used. Figure 7–109 shows a single tree.

Figure 7–109

- **Row of Trees:** A group of plants are placed in the model along a line, with differing scales and rotations, as shown in Figure 7–110.

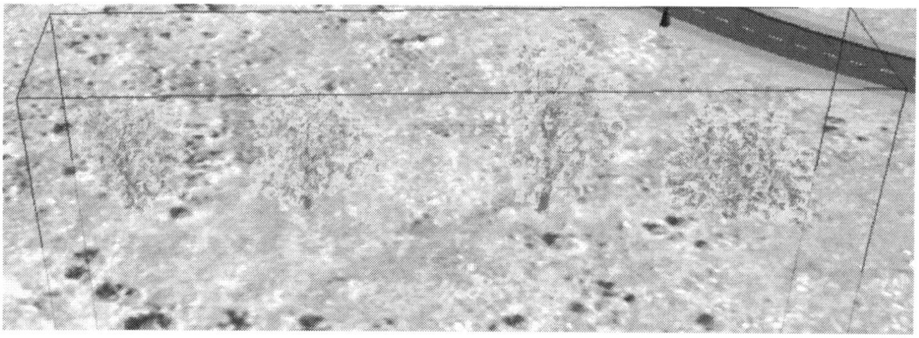

Figure 7–110

- **Stand of Trees:** A group of randomly spaced plants, with differing scales and rotations, are placed in the model inside a polygon, as shown in Figure 7–111.

Figure 7–111

If you create vegetation along a line or in a polygon, you can increase or decrease the number of plants that display using the **Adjust Density** slider, as shown in Figure 7–112. The higher the density (slider moved to the right), the more plants that display.

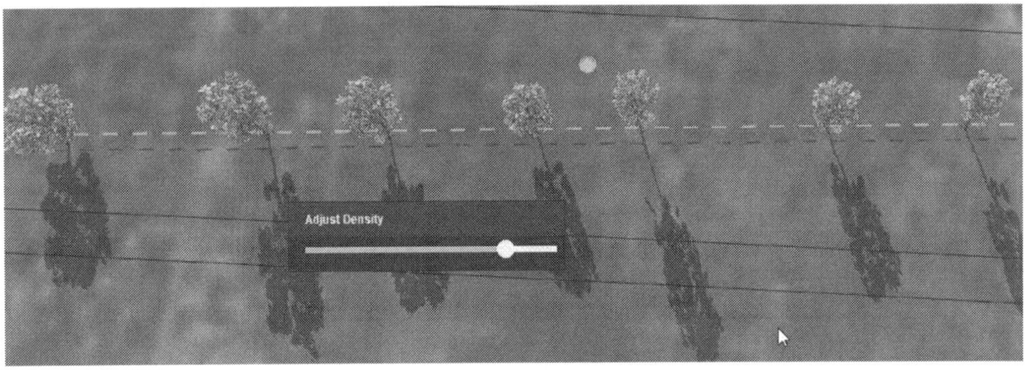

Figure 7–112

How To: Create Vegetation in a Group

1. In the *Create* tab>*Environment* drop-down list, click  (Stand of Trees).

2. In the *Select Draw Style* asset card, select the type of plant required, as shown in Figure 7–113.

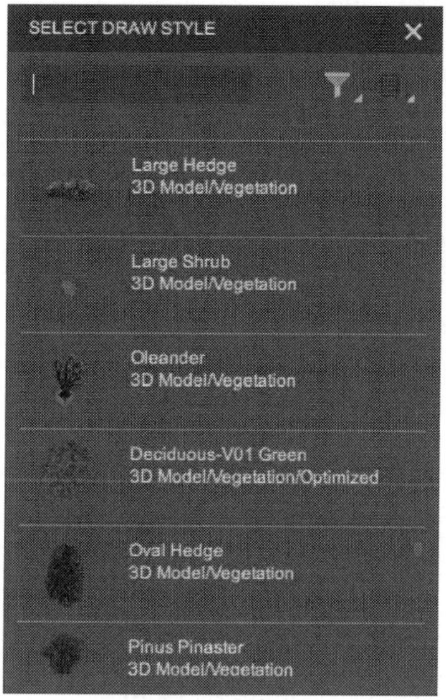

Figure 7–113

3. In the model, click the corners of a polygon for the vegetation group area, as shown in Figure 7–114. Remember to double-click on the final corner to finish the polygon.

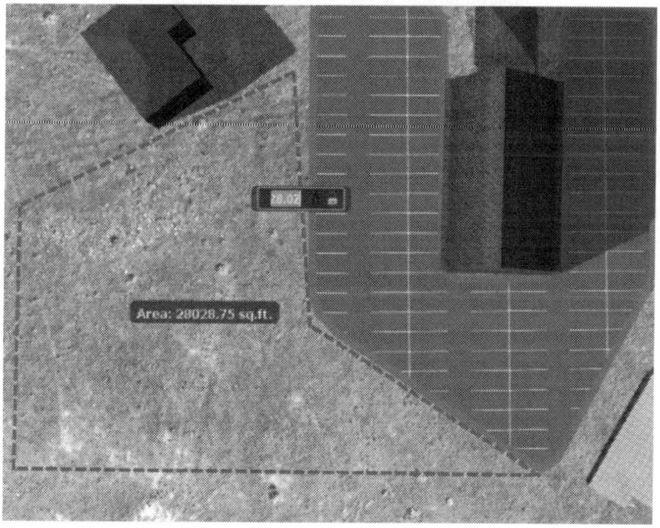

Figure 7–114

4. Press <Esc> to make the **Adjust Density** slider display, then slide it until the required number of plants displays in the model, as shown in Figure 7–115.

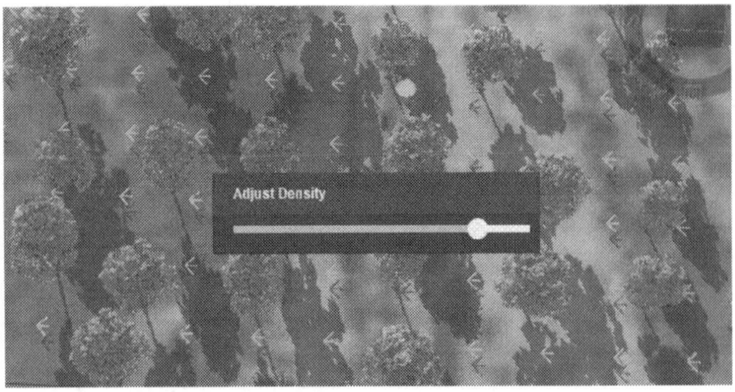

Figure 7–115

5. Press <Esc> to clear the selection of the newly created trees.

How To: Create Vegetation Along a Line

1. In the *Create* tab>*Environment* drop-down list, click (Row of Trees).
2. In the *Select Draw Style* asset card, type **vegetation** in the *Search* field. Select the type of plant required, as shown in Figure 7–116.

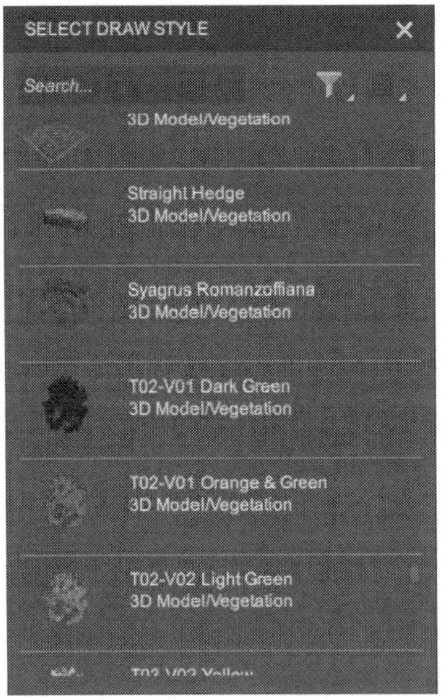

Figure 7–116

3. In the model, click the vertices of a polyline for the vegetation to follow, as shown in Figure 7–117. Remember to double-click on the final vertex to finish the polyline.

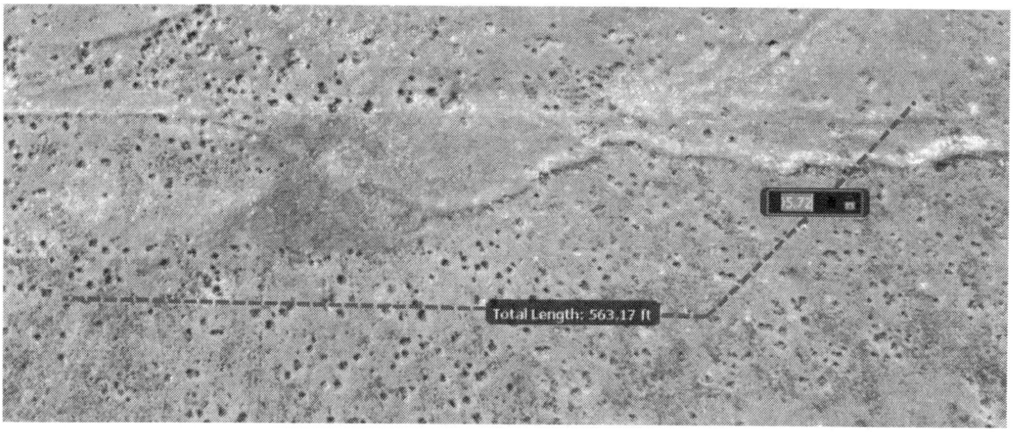

Figure 7–117

4. Press <Esc> to make the **Adjust Density** slider display, then slide it until the required number of plants displays in the model, as shown in Figure 7–118.

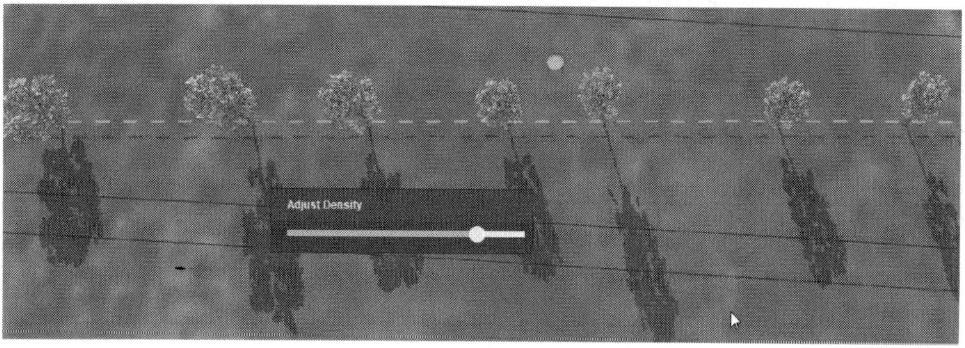

Figure 7–118

5. Press <Esc> to clear the selection of the newly created trees.

Edit Vegetation

When you select vegetation, gizmos display to enable you to modify the plants. The (Elevation Gizmo) enables you to adjust the height of the plants, while the (Height Gizmo) enables you to change the size and scale of the plants.

If you select a vegetation group (row or stand of trees), the **Adjust Density** slider displays, enabling you to change the number of plants that display in the group. Move the slider left or right until the required number of plants displays in the model. If the slider is not displayed, orbit the view to a plan view to make it display, as shown in Figure 7–119.

> ***Note:*** *To bring the slider back up, you can click on a single item in the group, then click again (do not double-click).*

Figure 7–119

Hint: Using Other City Furniture for Stands or Rows

Even though these tools are labeled **Stand of *Trees*** and **Row of *Trees***, they can be used for any objects in the City Furniture collection. Of course, the tools are ideal for vegetation; however, with a bit of imagination, they can be used successfully for other city furniture items.

Caution: Since these tools place the items with differing scales and rotations, the results might be unexpected.

To swap an individual item, you can drag and drop another 3D model in its place from the *Style Palette*, as shown in Figure 7–120.

Figure 7–120

Practice 7e
Add Trees to the Model

Practice Objective

- Add trees to the model to add landscaping details.

In this practice, you will create vegetation that represents a small orchard to illustrate how the final design will look in a new development.

The church owns a piece of land next to the parking lot, which they want to turn into a small orchard to help with fundraising. You will create trees using the **Stand of Trees** command to create an orchard in the model.

1. Continue working in the same model as the last practice. If you closed the file, on the *Home* screen, click **Open**. In the *InfraWorks Practice Files\7-Model-Details* folder, select **CreateFeatures.sqlite** and click **Open**.
2. In the toolbar, expand the (Proposals) drop-down list and select **E_Task1** if you did not complete the previous practices.
3. Click (Bookmarks) and select **Church Area**.
4. In the *Create* tab>*Environment* drop-down list, click (Stand of Trees).
5. In the *Select Draw Style* asset card, type **vegetation** in the *Search* field and select **T16-V05 Dark Green**, as shown in Figure 7–121.

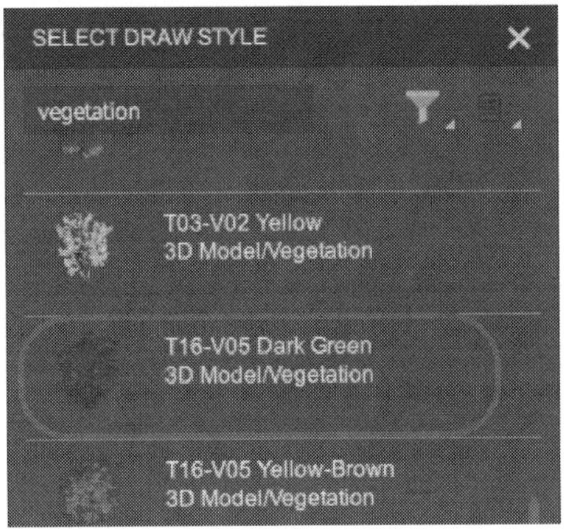

Figure 7–121

6. Click the corners of a polygon for the orchard area, as shown in Figure 7–122.

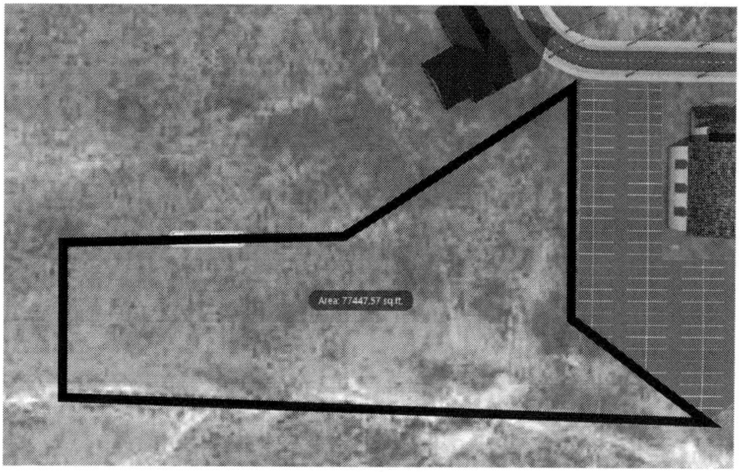

Figure 7–122

7. Double-click on the final corner to finish the polygon.
8. Press <Esc> to display the **Adjust Density** slider.
9. Use the **Adjust Density** slider to set the density close to **90%**, as shown in Figure 7–123.

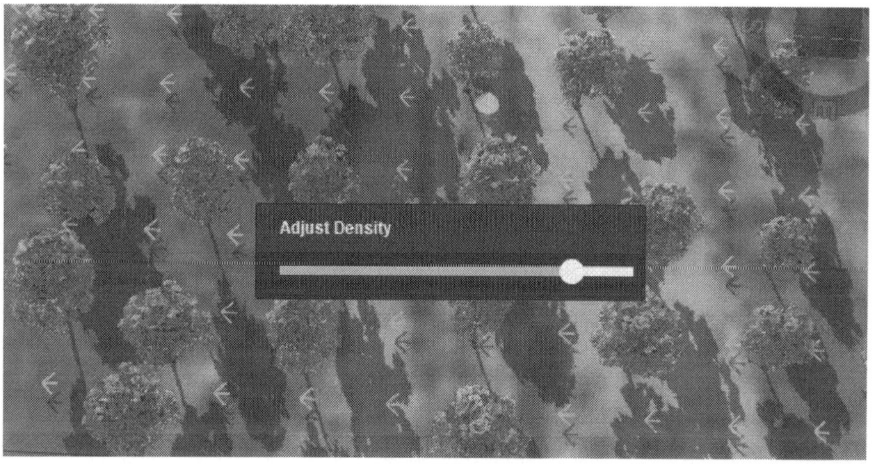

Figure 7–123

10. Press <Esc> to clear the selection of the newly created trees.

End of practice

7.7 Add Miscellaneous Details to a Model

You can enhance the overall visualization of the final design by indicating to stakeholders where sound barriers, signs, bike stands, etc. can be placed in the project.

Barriers

Barriers are useful items to add to any project. Sound barriers are placed along transportation corridors to muffle the sound of traffic experienced by neighboring residents. To control how traffic is to be handled during construction, barriers can be used to temporarily or permanently block off an area. You might need to create a construction proposal and indicate any barriers, alternative routes, and temporary roads that are to be used during the construction process. All of these uses and more can be added to an Autodesk InfraWorks project to communicate design concepts.

Barriers can be linear features that are added using the **Barrier** command, or 3D models that are added using the **City Furniture** command. Multiple 3D model style catalogs are available (as shown in Figure 7–124) and different barrier styles can be found in many of these catalogs.

Barriers can also be added to road or railway styles by adding decorations.

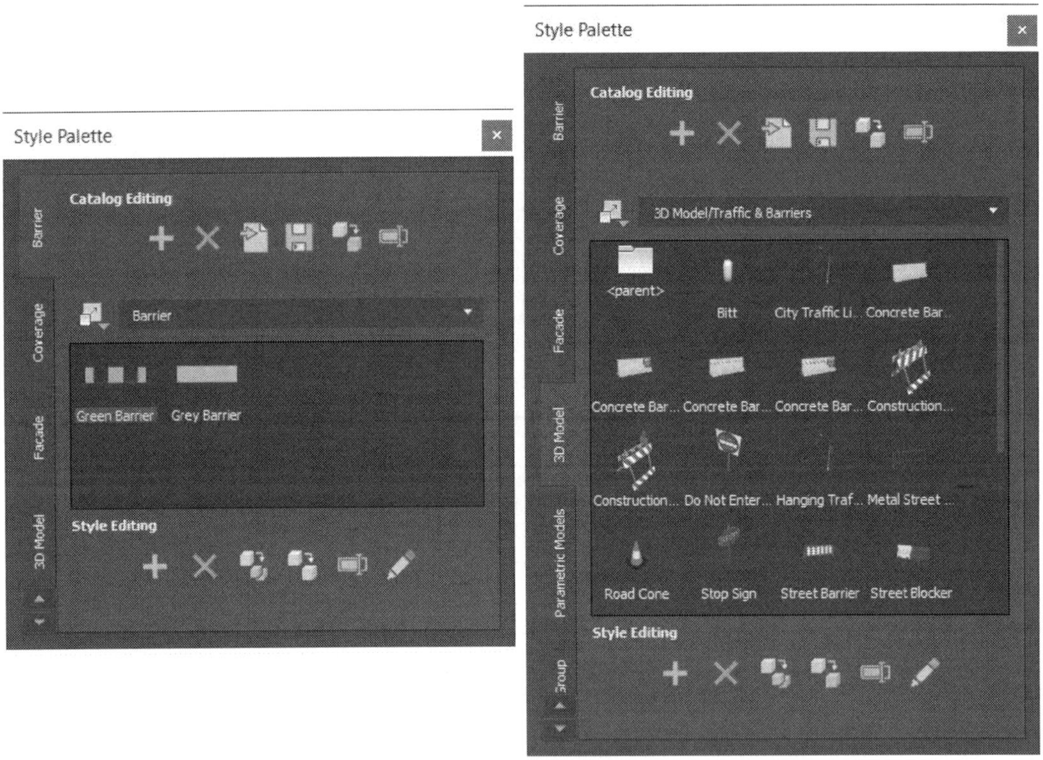

Figure 7–124

How To: Create Barriers

1. In the *Create* tab>*Transportation* panel, click (Barriers).
2. In the *Select Draw Style* asset card, select the required barrier style, as shown in Figure 7–125.

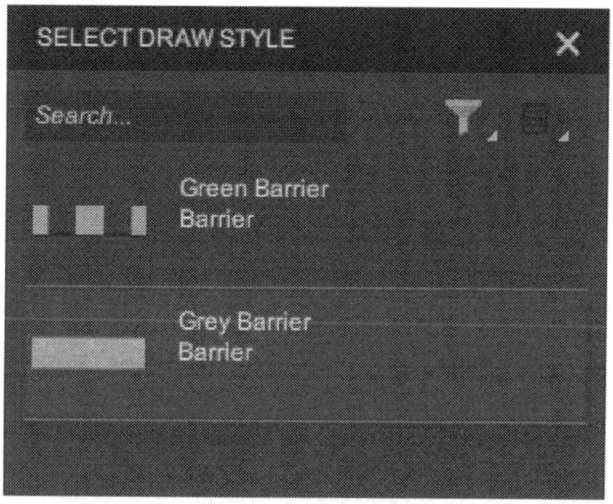

Figure 7–125

3. Click in the model to start the linear path for the barrier to follow.
4. Move the cursor in the direction in which you want the barrier to run. Type a distance for the length to the next point of intersection (PI) and press <Enter> to set the distance. Click in the model to place the next PI.
5. Continue clicking in the model to place PIs until all of the lengths of barrier have been created.
6. Double-click to place the last point and end the command.

Edit Barriers

If you have created a linear barrier, it can be modified using the (Control Point Gizmo). Once you have placed a 3D model, use the (Rotate Gizmo) and (Move Gizmo) to rotate and move the model as required.

Points of Interest

You might need to draw attention to a specific area of your model. You can do so by adding points of interest (POI). In addition to drawing attention to an area, POI can be used to add text, HTML tooltips, or hyperlinks that automatically open a web page, image, or other file when you move the cursor within a specified distance of the POI. This is done using the *Proximity Distance* field in the *Point of Interest* asset card (shown in Figure 7–126).

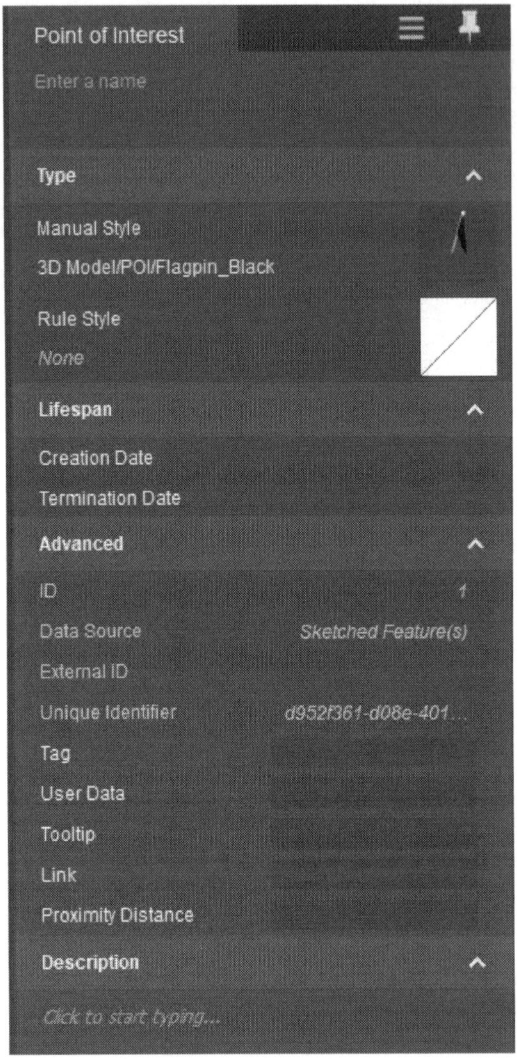

Figure 7–126

How To: Create Points of Interest

1. In the *Create* tab>*Environment* panel, click  (Points of Interest).
2. In the *Select Draw Style* asset card, select the required 3D model style, as shown in Figure 7–127. You can select any 3D model that is listed in the *City Furniture* section of this chapter.

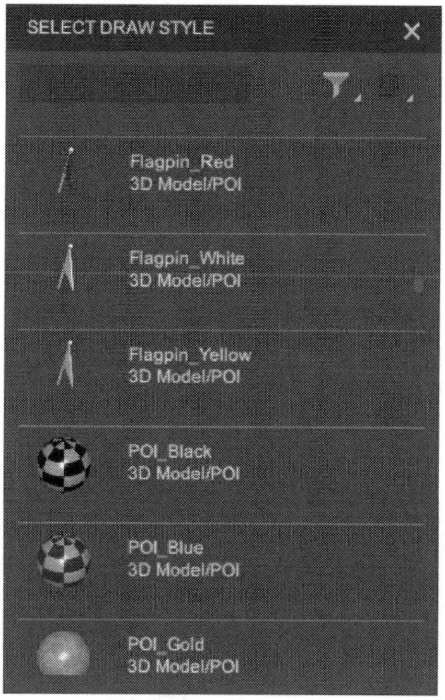

Figure 7–127

3. Depending on the model, either double-click in the model to place a single POI or single-click in the model to start the linear path that the POIs should follow.
4. Move the cursor in the direction that you want the POIs to run. Type a distance for the length to the next point of intersection and press <Enter> to set the distance. Click in the model to place the next point of intersection.
5. Continue clicking in the model as required until all of the lengths of POI path have been created.
6. Double-click to place the last point and end the command.

How To: Create Tooltips for Points of Interest

1. In the model, select the POI.
2. In the *Point of Interest* asset card, expand *Advanced*, select the *Tooltips* field, and click (Edit Tooltip).
3. In the *Edit Tooltip* dialog box, either enter the text you want to display in the *Visual* tab (as shown in Figure 7–128) or use HTML code to create a link in the *Html* tab. Click **OK**.

Figure 7–128

4. In the *Point of Interest* asset card, type a value in the *Proximity Distance* field (shown in Figure 7–129) to specify how close the cursor needs to be to the POI to activate the tooltip.

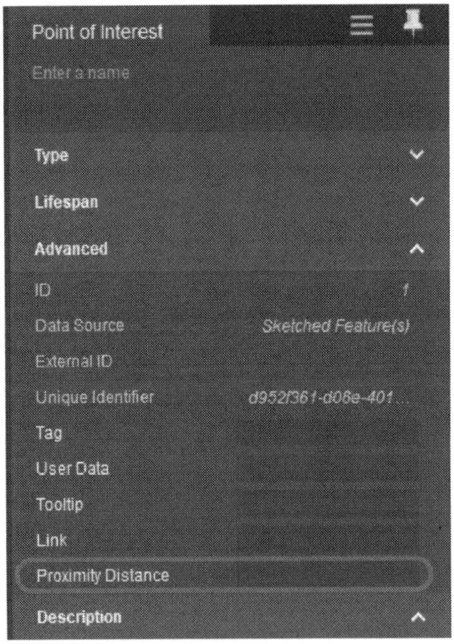

Figure 7–129

Edit Points of Interest

If you have placed a 3D model from any category other than POI, you can select it and use the (Move Gizmo) and (Rotate Gizmo) to move and rotate the model as required.

Practice 7f
Add Miscellaneous Details to the Model

Practice Objective

- Add miscellaneous details to the model to better communicate the design concept.

In this practice, you will create a barrier around the pond to prevent children from falling in it. You will then add city furniture to the model to help communicate the final design to stakeholders.

Task 1: Create a barrier.

In this task, you will create a barrier around the pond.

1. Continue working in the same model as the last practice. If you closed the file, on the *Home* screen, click **Open**. In the *InfraWorks Practice Files\7-Model-Details* folder, select **CreateFeatures.sqlite** and click **Open**.
2. In the toolbar, expand the (Proposals) drop-down list and select **F_Task1** if you did not complete the previous practices.
3. Click (Bookmarks) and select **School Area**. Pan to the East so the entire pond is in view.
4. In the *Create* tab>*Transportation* panel, click (Barriers).
5. In the *Select Draw Style* asset card, select the **Grey Barrier** style, as shown in Figure 7–130.

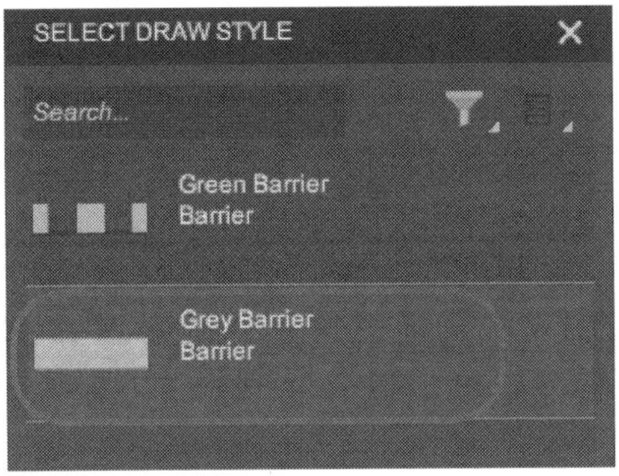

Figure 7–130

6. Click in the model to start the linear path that the barrier should follow, as shown in Figure 7–131.

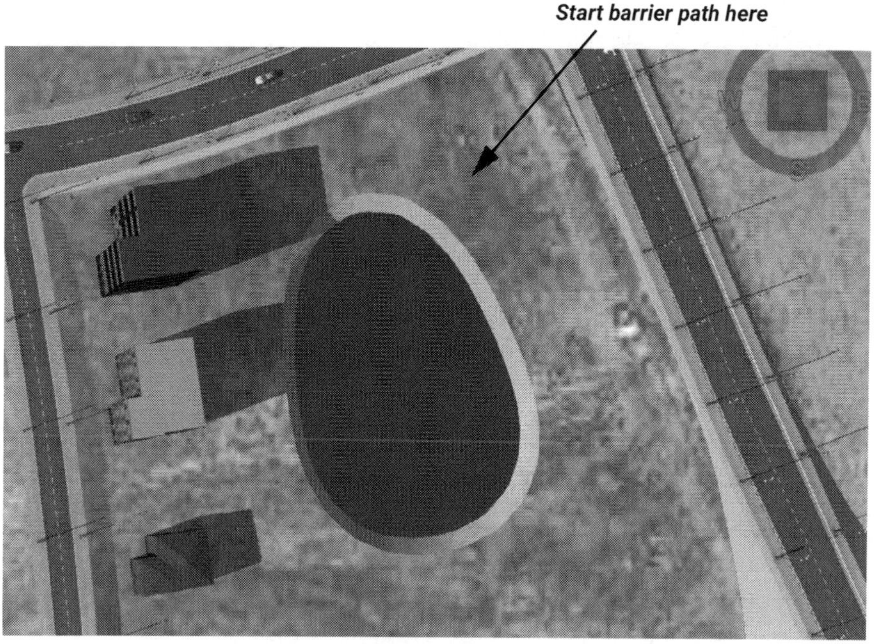

Figure 7–131

7. Move the cursor to the west. Type **140** for the length to the next point on the boundary and press <Enter> to set the distance. Click in the model to place the barrier point parallel to the road.
8. Move the cursor south by approximately the same distance to the west of the pond as the PI placed in Step 7, as shown in Figure 7–132 that follows. Type **250** for the length to the next point on the barrier path and press <Enter> to set the distance. Click in the model to place the boundary point.
9. Move the cursor to the east. Type **180** for the length to the next point on the boundary and press <Enter> to set the distance. Click to place the barrier path point parallel to the upper portion of the fence.

10. Move the cursor back to the first barrier point and double-click to place the last barrier path point and end the command. Figure 7–132 shows the complete barrier path.

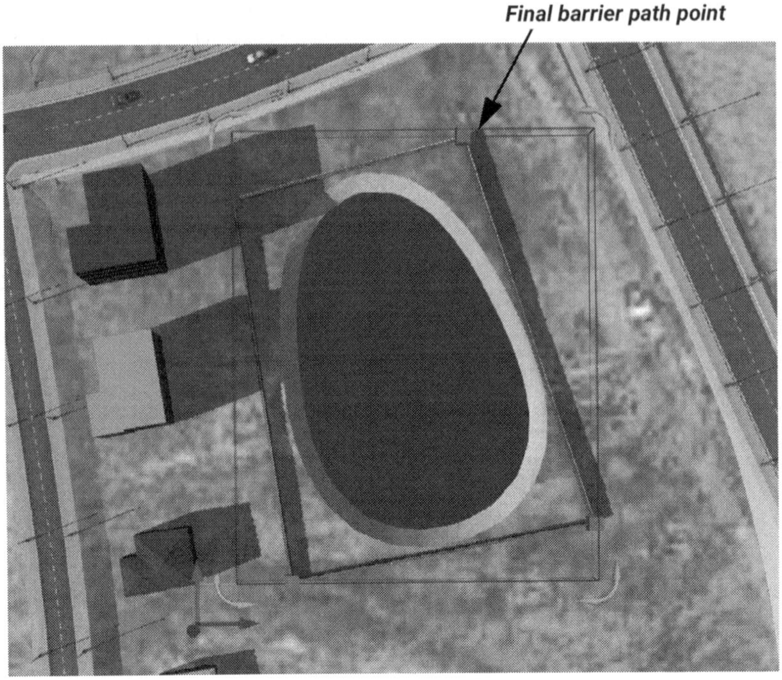

Figure 7–132

11. Press <Esc> to clear the selection of the barrier.

Task 2: Add pier components.

In this task, you will add components to the pier so that it is only available to foot and bike traffic.

> **Note:** *In order to challenge you to remember the steps and make them more automatic, not every step of the process is listed in this task.*

1. Continue working in the same model. If you did not complete the previous task, set the proposal to **F_Task2**.
2. Click (Bookmarks) and select **Pier 3D**. Orbit and zoom to the endpoint of the pier.
3. In the *Create* tab>*Environment* panel, click (City Furniture).

4. In the *Select Draw Style* asset card, type **bridge** and select the **Barrier Side** style, as shown in Figure 7–133.

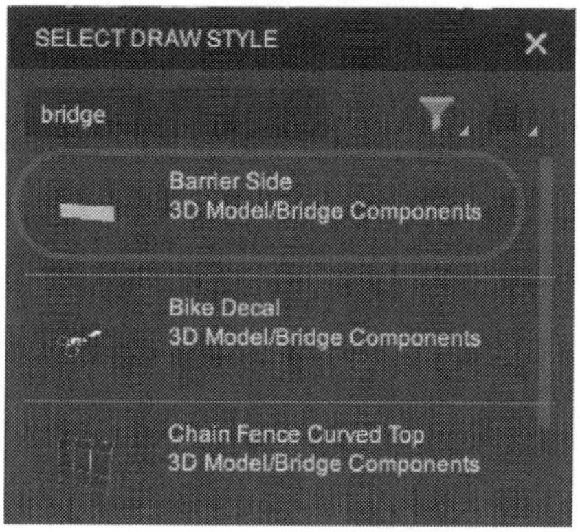

Figure 7–133

5. Double-click in the model to place the barrier at the end of the pier. Add two more barriers. You can either copy and paste the first one or go through the *City Furniture* panel.

   Note: *The barrier is likely placed on top of the water by default. You must move it vertically and horizontally, and then rotate it as required.*

6. Press <Esc> and use the (Move Gizmo) and (Rotate Gizmo) as required to correctly position the barriers side by side, as shown in Figure 7–134, so that foot and bike traffic cannot go off the end of the pier.

Figure 7–134

End of practice

7.8 Working with Autodesk Revit Models

> ***Note:*** *To use this feature, access to the Internet and an Autodesk® 360 account are required.*

Determining how a building interacts with its surrounding environment is valuable for gaining stakeholder buy-in. Until recently, the best an architect could do was to approximate the ground surface using basic tools in the Autodesk Revit software. At the same time, civil professionals could only create basic 2D line work or a basic 3D model of the building in the Autodesk Civil 3D software to simulate where the building was to be located. Using the Autodesk InfraWorks software, architects, engineers, and civil professionals can bring their models together into one model to better demonstrate the entire project upon completion. Figure 7–135 shows a Revit model of a building that has been imported into an InfraWorks model.

Figure 7–135

The tools used to import a Revit model are the same as those used to import existing conditions data sources. The difference in the importing process is that a coordinate system has not been assigned to most Revit models. Therefore, you either have to know the exact coordinates of where to place the building, or you have to interactively place the building in the model.

When importing a Revit model, you can preview the model being imported and make any required corrections before placing it in the model. The *Data Source Configuration* dialog box is shown in Figure 7–136.

> ***Note:*** *Models larger than 100 megabytes in size can negatively affect performance. It is recommended that you simplify large 3D models in their source applications before importing them. The import fails if the 3D model is larger than a gigabyte in size.*

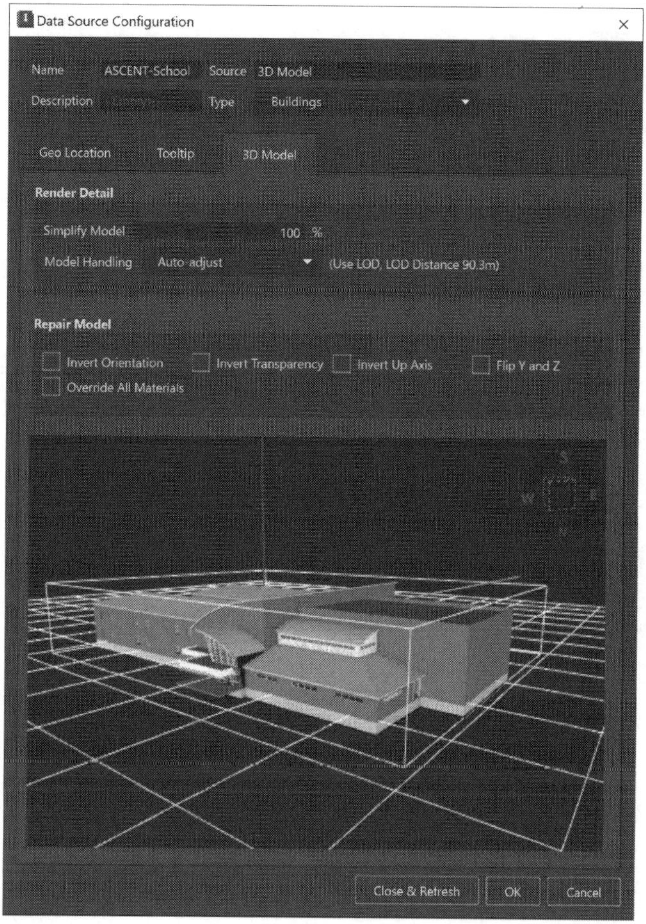

Figure 7–136

Hint: Sharing Coordinates Between Civil 3D and Revit

There is a product extension for both Revit and Civil 3D known as the **Autodesk Shared Reference Point** tool. This extension allows for the Civil 3D coordinates to be imported (shared) into Revit so that the Revit model will be geolocated properly.

Render Detail

How the model renders in the InfraWorks model can be controlled using the *Model Handling* drop-down list in the *3D Model* tab of the *Data Source Configuration* dialog box. The options used to adjust the model are as follows:

- **Auto-adjust:** InfraWorks determines the settings for the 3D model. If the automatic setting applies a level of detail (LOD), you can change the *LOD Distance* setting by selecting the **Use LOD** option and adjusting the *LOD Distance*.
- **Direct Display:** The *Repair Model* options and settings for *Simplify Model* are applied to the 3D model, but they do not adjust how the model is rendered. Use this setting if the model uses a small number of triangles to define its shape (for example, a house with little detail).
- **Use LOD:** LOD settings generate a series of simplifications, assigning the best one based on viewing distance. If you select this option, ensure that you also set the *LOD Distance*. The LOD Distance setting is found in the *Model Explorer*. Higher LOD settings enable you to see greater detail from a greater distance
- **Tile:** Permanently attaches the 3D model to multiple display tiles. When a single object spans multiple tiles, its display can be erratic. If the object is on the periphery of the displayed area of the model, it might not display at all, or might only display when you zoom in closer to the object. Permanently attaching the 3D model to multiple display tiles helps avoid these issues. This is especially helpful if the model is large or spans several model units (such as a bridge).
- **Use Dynamic LOD:** Sets the LOD dynamically.

Repair Model

When a model does not display as expected in the model, you might need to make slight adjustments to it. The following five adjustment options can be used to repair the imported model.

- **Invert Orientation:** Inverts the direction of the *Face Normals* that form each surface of the model.
- **Invert Transparency:** Makes the transparent areas of the model solid and the solid areas transparent.
- **Invert Up Axis:** Flips the model upside down.
- **Flip Y and Z:** Controls whether the *up* axis runs along the Y- or Z-axis since some applications use the Y-axis as the *up* direction, rather than the Z-axis.
- **Override All Materials:** Use this option if you want to replace all material from the Revit model with a constant color. When enabled, you need to select the color for the override.

How To: Import an Autodesk Revit Model

1. In the *Manage* tab>*Content* panel, click (Data Sources).
2. In the *Data Sources* panel, click (Add file data source) and select **Autodesk Revit**.
3. In the *Select Files* dialog box, browse to the required Revit file and click **Open**.
   - If the *Data Import* dialog box opens (as shown in Figure 7–137), click **Send**.

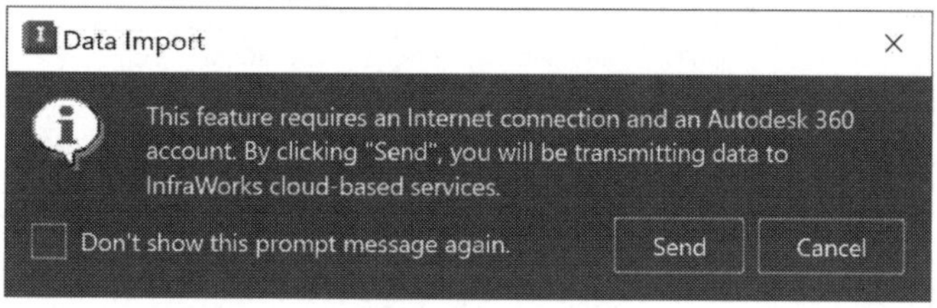

Figure 7–137

   - A *Data Import* alert box (shown in Figure 7–138) may open stating limitations of importing Revit files and that linked files and custom textures will not be included in the import. You can avoid this message by checking **Don't show this prompt message again.** Click **OK.**

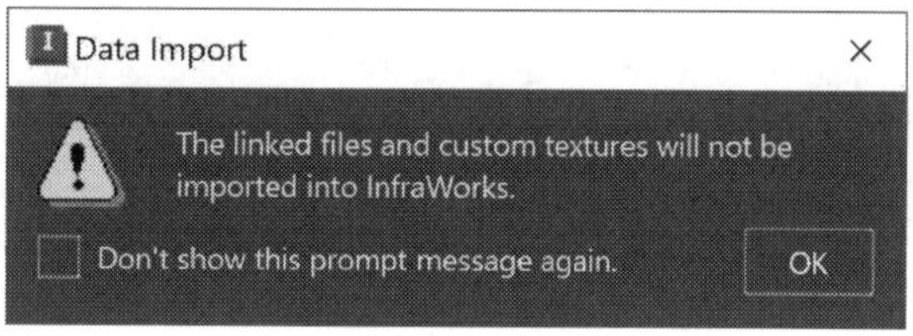

Figure 7–138

   - If the *Transfer Navisworks Files* message displays (as shown in Figure 7–139), click **Transfer**.

***Note:** This message displays because you need a Navisworks Manage license to import Revit files unless you clear the selection of the application option **Navisworks based Local Import** on the Data Import page.*

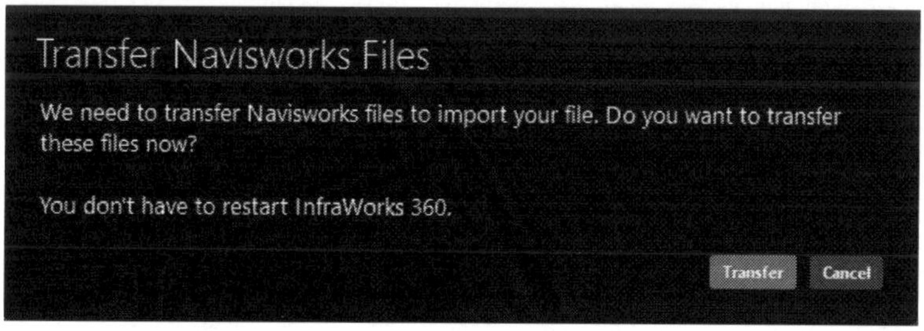

Figure 7–139

4. In the *Data Sources* panel, double-click on the Revit model data source that you just imported to open the *Data Source Configuration* dialog box.
5. In the common area, the *Type* can be set, as shown in Figure 7–140. By default, the *Type* is set to **Buildings**. Only change the type if the imported model is not a building.

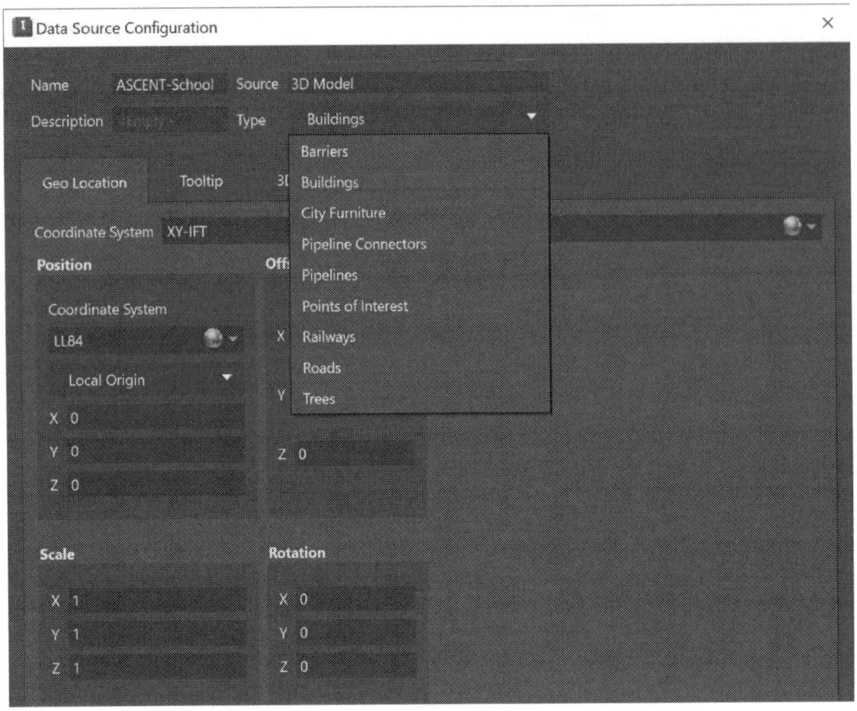

Figure 7–140

6. On the *Geo Location* tab, set the *X*, *Y*, and *Z* values under *Position* or click **Interactive Placing**, as shown in Figure 7–141. If provided, InfraWorks can automatically read the location data from the Revit file.

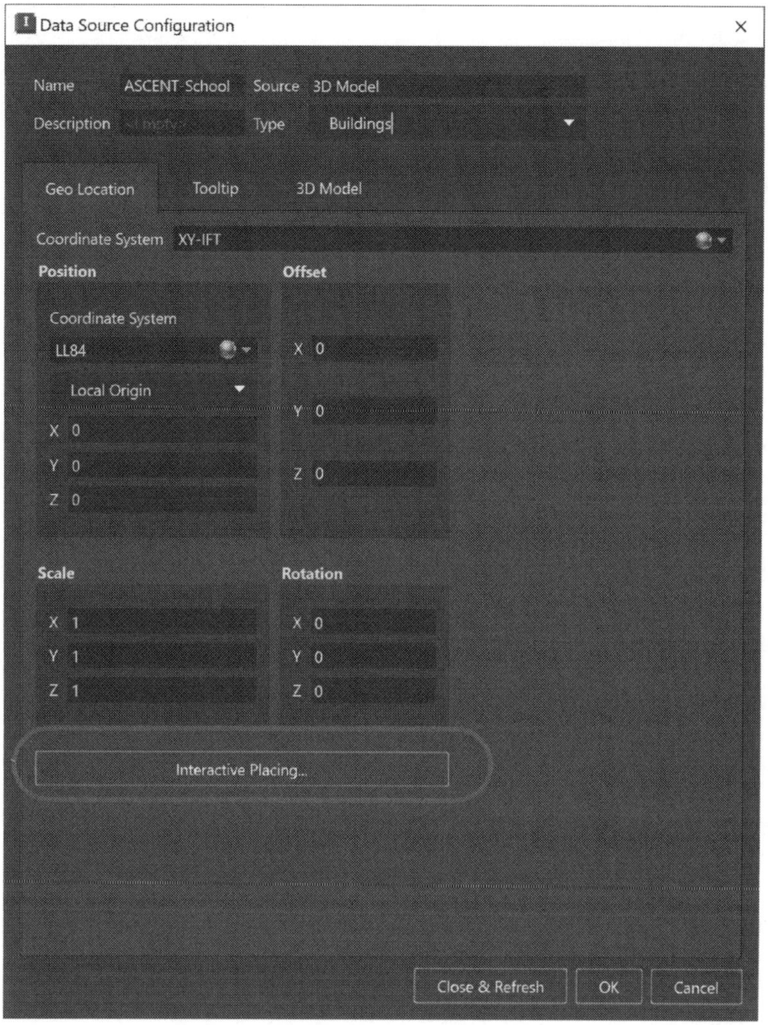

Figure 7–141

7. Preview the model on the *3D Model* tab, as shown in Figure 7–142.
    - Select an appropriate *Model Handling* option to set the level of detail (LOD).
    - Make any necessary adjustments to the model under the *Repair Model* area.

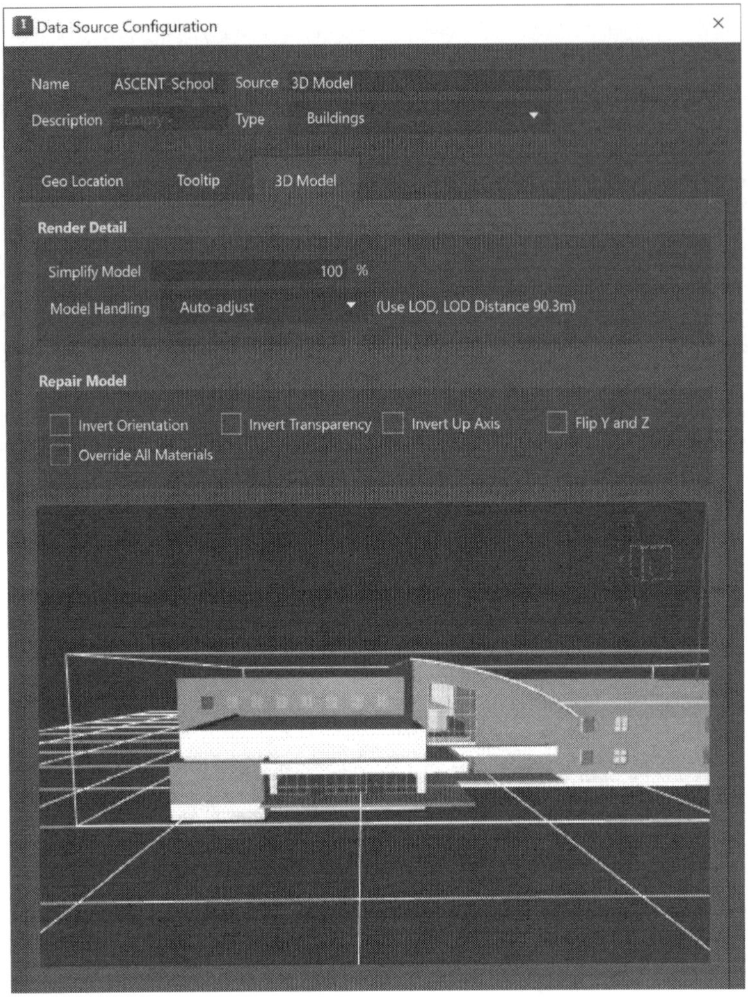

Figure 7–142

8. Click **Close & Refresh** to complete the import process and display the imported model in the model.

Practice 7g
Import an Autodesk Revit File

Practice Objective

- Import a Revit model and note how it fits with other design elements.

In this practice, you will import a school model and a hotel model that were created using the Autodesk Revit software.

> ***Note:*** *To use this feature, access to the Internet and an Autodesk® 360 account are required.*

Task 1: Import the school building.

1. Continue working in the same model as the last practice. If you closed the file, on the *Home* screen, click **Open**. In the *InfraWorks Practice Files\7-Model-Details* folder, select **CreateFeatures.sqlite** and click **Open**.
2. Click (Bookmarks) and select **School Area**.
3. In the toolbar, expand the (Proposals) drop-down list and select **G_Task1**if you did not complete the previous practices.
4. In the *Manage* tab>*Content* panel, click (Data Sources).
5. In the *Data Sources* panel, click (Add file data source) and select **Autodesk Revit**.
6. In the *Select Files* dialog box, browse to the *InfraWorks Practice Files\References\RVT* folder, select **ASCENT-School.rvt**, and click **Open**.
7. When the **Connecting to Data Sources** twirl box disappears, in the *Data Sources* panel, in the *Building* folder, double-click on the **ASCENT-School** model data source that you just imported.
8. In the *Data Source Configuration* dialog box, ensure that the *Type* is set to **Buildings**.
9. In the *Geo Location* tab, click **Interactive Placing**.

10. In the model, double-click to place the school model on the coverage, as shown in Figure 7–143. You can fine-tune its placement later with the appropriate gizmos.

Note: *If changes are made to the original Revit model, you will need to import the updated model.*

Figure 7–143

11. Click on the *3D Model* tab.

12. Pan and orbit around the model preview.

13. Experiment with checking and unchecking the options under *Repair Model*, then ensure that they are all unchecked. Set the *Simplify Model* value to **80%**, as shown in Figure 7–144.

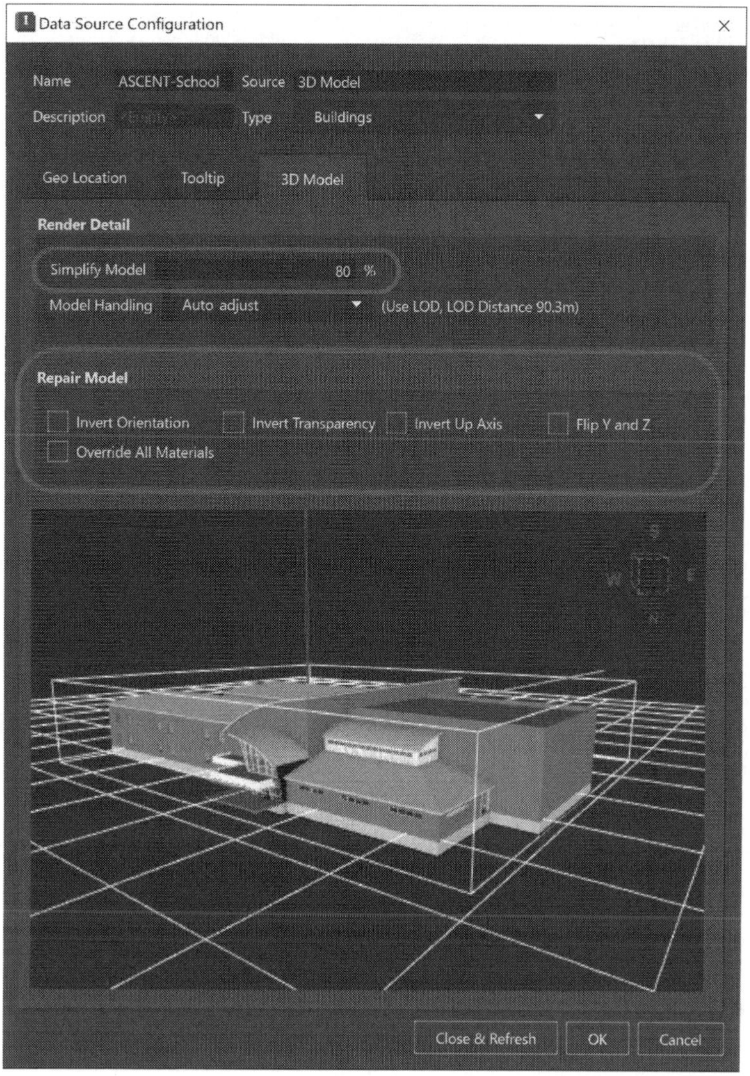

Figure 7–144

14. In the *Data Source Configuration* dialog box, click **Close & Refresh** to update the model. The Revit model now displays in the InfraWorks model.

15. In the model, select the school. Use the  (Move Gizmo) to reposition the model as required.

Task 2: Import the hotel.

1. Continue working in the same model. If you did not complete the previous task, set the proposal to **G_Task2**.
2. Click (Bookmarks) and select **Hotel**.
3. Repeat Steps 4 to 11 from Task 1 to import the **ASCENT-Hotel.rvt** file found in the *InfraWorks Practice Files\References\RVT* folder.
4. In the model, double-click to place the hotel model on the grading area, as shown in Figure 7–145.

Figure 7–145

5. In the *Data Source Configuration* dialog box, click **Close & Refresh** to update the model.
6. In the model, select the building and use the (Move Gizmo) to reposition and rotate the model, as required.
7. Click (Bookmarks) and select **Hotel-Interior**.
8. Use the navigation tools to explore both the interior and the exterior of the hotel.

End of practice

Practice 7h
(Optional) Add More Detail to the Model for a Presentation

Practice Objective

- Spruce up the model with additional details to prepare for using the presentation tools available in InfraWorks.

In this practice, you will add more detail to the model to add realism and items to which your clients can relate. In the following chapters, you will learn about a variety of presentation tools and this optional exercise will prepare your model for using those presentation tools.

Task 1: Add city furniture.

1. Continue working in the same model as the last practice. If you closed the file, on the *Home* screen, click **Open**. In the *InfraWorks Practice Files\7-Model-Details* folder, select **CreateFeatures.sqlite** and click **Open**.
2. In the toolbar, expand the  (Proposals) drop-down list and select **H_Task1** if you did not complete the previous practices.
3. Click  (Bookmarks) and select **Beach Access**. Zoom in to the parking/grass area
4. In the *Create* tab>*Environment* panel, click  (City Furniture).
5. In the *Select Draw Style* asset card, type **hot** in the *Search* field. Select the **Hot Dog Stand**, as show in Figure 7–146.

Figure 7–146

6. Double-click in the **Morris Beach** lawn area. Use the gizmos to adjust the rotation and position.
    - Repeat this procedure for other city furniture items of your choosing. Here are some suggestions:
        - Fruit stand
        - People (a variety of them)
        - Cars and buses in the parking lot
        - Bike stand (recommend to place in a row and adjust density)
        - Coffee shop
        - Street lights

    Note: *You can either place these individually or in a row, or copy and paste items.*

7. In the *Create* tab>*Environment* panel, click  (City Furniture).
8. In the *Select Draw Style* asset card, type **turbine** in the *Search* field. Select **Wind Turbine - Animated**, as shown in Figure 7–147. Note the blue circle icon next to the image, indicating that it is animated.

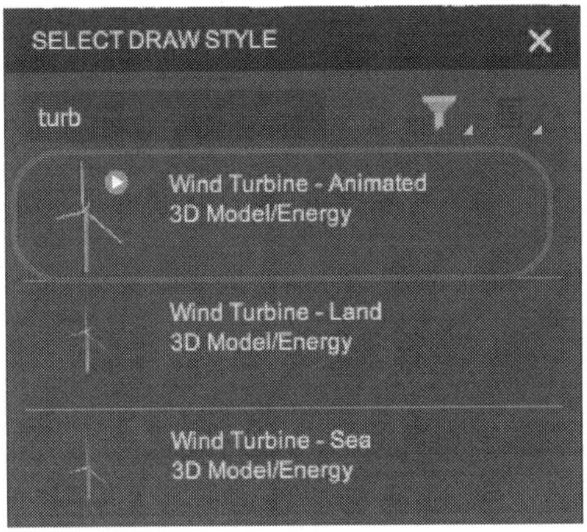

Figure 7–147

9. Place a row of turbines between **Pier Access Road** and the river. Adjust the density and height as required.

10. Add some vegetation using the (Stand of Trees) and (Row of Trees) commands from the *Create* tab>*Environment* drop-down list. Select any type of vegetation you deem appropriate. Adjust the density and height as required.

    Figure 7–148 is an example of what your model could look like.

Figure 7–148

Task 2: Add decorations to a component road.

1. Continue working in the same model. If you did not complete the previous task, set the proposal to **H_Task2**.
2. Click (Bookmarks) and select **Beach Access**, then zoom in to the intersection with **S Redwood Rd**.
3. Select the **Morris Beach Blvd** component road.
4. Right-click and select **Place Decoration**.

5. In the *Select Draw Style* asset card, type **light** in the *Search* field. Select **Lightpole Red**. Ensure that the yellow line on the component road is at the southernmost edge, as shown in Figure 7–149, then click on the yellow line. Press <Enter> to place the decorations.

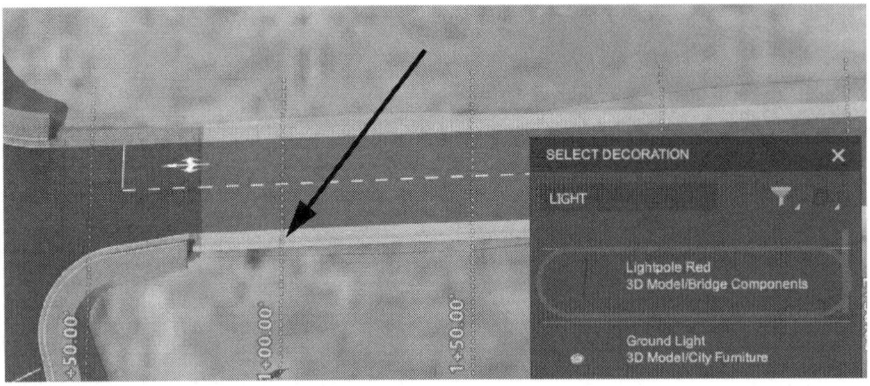

Figure 7–149

6. In the *Decoration* asset card, set the *Spacing* to **100.0'** and the *Rotation* to **180**. Press <Esc> to finish the command.
7. Select the **Morris Beach Blvd** component road once again and right-click and select **Place Decoration**.
8. In the *Select Draw Style* asset card, type **palm** in the *Search* field. Select the only choice available. Ensure that the yellow line on the component road is the northernmost edge, then click on the yellow line. Press <Enter> to place the decorations.
9. In the *Decoration* asset card, set the *Spacing* to **75.0'**, the *Scale* to **1.2**, and the *Horizontal Offset* to (negative) **-10** to place the trees away from the road.
10. Press <Esc> to release the selection.
11. Orbit pan and zoom to inspect the road, as shown in Figure 7–150.

Figure 7–150

End of practice

Chapter Review Questions

1. Which selection tool would you use to select multiple model elements completely inside a specified area?

   a. (Window Select)

   b. (Rectangle Select)

   c. (Polygon Select)

2. Which of the following gizmos would not change the height or elevation of a model element?

   a. (Elevation Gizmo)

   b. (Height Gizmo)

   c. (Control Gizmo)

   d. (Move Gizmo)

3. How do you change the elevation of a road at a point at which a point of intersection does not exist?

   a. Select the road, right-click, and select **Add Vertex**. Use the (Elevation Gizmo) to adjust the elevation.

   b. Select the road, right-click, and select **Add Vertex**. Use the (Control Gizmo) to adjust the elevation.

   c. Select the road, right-click, and select **Split Feature**. Use the (Elevation Gizmo) to adjust the elevation.

   d. You cannot adjust the elevation of roads.

4. How do you change the appearance or elevation of a terrain surface?
   a. Apply a different terrain style to it to change the appearance and right-click to add elevation points.
   b. Create a coverage or grading area and adjust the elevations at each vertex along the boundary of the coverage.
   c. You cannot change the appearance or elevation of surfaces.
   d. Import a new surface from external data sources.

5. Where are pipeline gizmos located?
   a. At the end of each pipe length, draped on the terrain surface.
   b. At the end of each pipe length and at the elevation of the pipe ends.
   c. Only at the beginning and end of the entire pipe network, draped on the terrain surface.
   d. Only at the beginning and end of the entire pipe network and at the elevation of the pipe ends.

6. How do you set the width of a river?
   a. Create a polyline area manually that sets where each bank ends.
   b. Select the river and change the buffer width in the *Water Area* asset card.
   c. After creating the centerline of the river, click a point to set the width.
   d. The width cannot be changed.

7. How are grading areas different than coverages? (Select all that apply.)
   a. Grading area top surfaces start out flat while coverages drape on the terrain surface.
   b. Grading areas are used to create piles of rock and dirt.
   c. Grading areas enable you to control the cut slope separate from the fill slope.
   d. There are no differences between grading areas and coverages.

8. Which of the following is not a category for a predefined 3D building model?
   a. Furniture
   b. Residential
   c. Neighborhood
   d. Commercial

9. Once placed, you can change the shape of a building that has been created from a 3D model.
    a. True
    b. False

10. Which of the following commands would you use to create a grouping of multiple trees in a specified area?
    a.  (Row of Trees)
    b.  (Stand of Trees)

11. Which of the following commands should you use if you want to add tooltips that are activated within a specified distance from the location of the 3D model?
    a.  (City Furniture)
    b.  (Barriers)
    c.  (Points of Interest)
    d.  (Coverage)

Command Summary

Button	Command	Location
	**Barriers**	• **Toolbar:** *Create* tab>*Transportation* panel
	**Building**	• **Toolbar:** *Create* tab>*Structures* panel
	**City Furniture**	• **Toolbar:** *Create* tab>*Environment* panel
	**Coverage**	• **Toolbar:** *Create* tab>*Environment* panel
	**Grading Area**	• **Toolbar:** *Create* tab>*Environment* panel
	**Parking Area**	• **Toolbar:** *Create* tab>*Environment* panel
	**Parking Layout**	• **Toolbar:** *Create* tab>*Environment* panel
	**Parking Rows**	• **Toolbar:** *Create* tab>*Environment* panel
	**Points of Interest**	• **Toolbar:** *Create* tab>*Environment* panel
	**Row of Trees**	• **Toolbar:** *Create* tab>*Environment* drop-down list
	**Stand of Trees**	• **Toolbar:** *Create* tab>*Environment* drop-down list

Chapter

8

Analyzing the Model

Before progressing too far into the design process, it is important to ensure that the proposed area meets the project needs. You can repeatedly analyze the model to ensure the critical design criteria are being met and make adjustments as necessary or address any issues that arise along the way. In this chapter, you will learn how to analyze the model using spatial and numerical analysis tools to determine the feasibility of the project.

Learning Objectives

- Analyze features in a model using underlying data using themes.
- Select a subset of features in a layer.
- Graphically indicate avoidance zones in the model.
- Select features that are in the line of sight from a specified viewpoint and angle.
- Measure a model to determine the length, area, or volume of specific features.
- Analyze a model to determine whether the project receives the appropriate amount of sunlight.

8.1 Theme a Data Source

The display of a feature class can be modified by creating a theme. Themes use underlying data found in the database to highlight sets of values using various colors. Figure 8–1 shows coverages themed by the current market value, which was pulled from a parcel database.

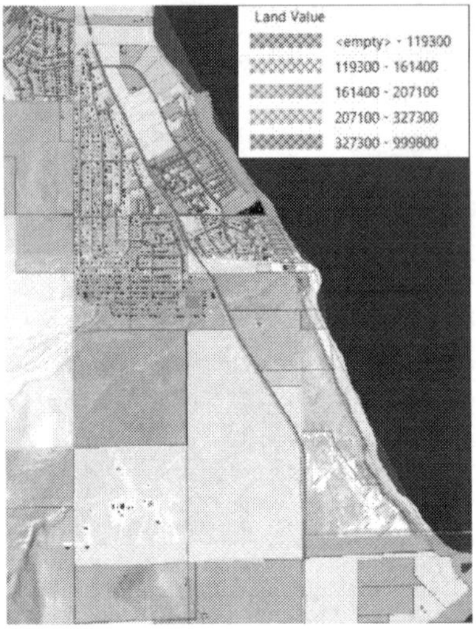

Figure 8–1

The *Themes* panel is used to create new themes, modify existing themes, delete themes, and change the display settings and priority of themes. Additionally, you can share themes with other models to ensure consistency across models that use similar data sources. The icons used in the *Feature Themes* panel (shown in Figure 8–2) are consistent for all theme types.

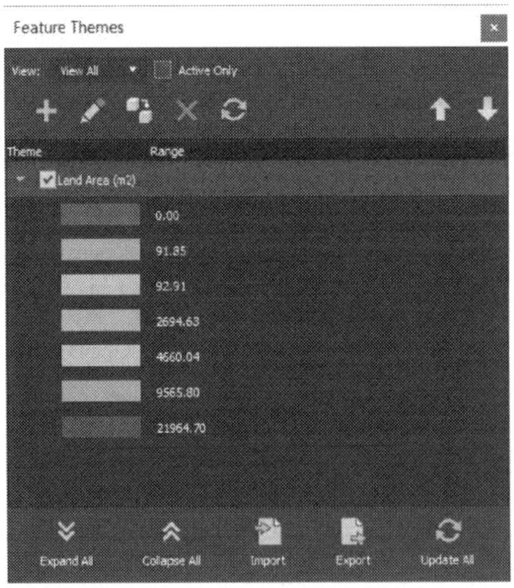

Figure 8–2

The icons in the *Feature*, *Terrain*, and *Point Cloud Themes* panels are as follows:

Icon	Purpose
(Add a New Theme)	Adds a new theme for a feature class.
(Edit Selected Theme)	Enables you to edit the properties of a selected theme.
(Duplicate Selected Theme)	Enables you to copy a selected theme.
(Delete Selected Themes)	Deletes any selected themes.
(Refresh Selected Themes)	Refreshes the display of selected themes.
/ (Move Selected Theme Up/ Down)	Changes the priority of the themes by moving the selected theme up or down in the list.
/ (Expand/Collapse All)	Shows/hides the details of the themes in the current model.
(Import Themes)	Used to import one or more theme properties from an external file created in another model.
(Export Themes)	Used to export one or more theme properties to an external file for use in other models.
(Update All)	Refreshes the display of all themes in the current model.

Feature Themes

Creating a feature theme helps you visualize specific aspects of data sources. For example, if you want to display the location of various soil types in the model, you can display each category as a different color using the individual values that are associated with a soil data source. Additionally, you can display parcels according to their market value to ensure that the project location is appropriate and fits in the project budget.

Nearly any data source can be themed and associated with features in the model, according to data found in the database. Using a variety of distribution methods, values are divided into ranges. The distribution methods available for feature themes include:

- **Equal:** The difference between the high and low values is the same for every range.
- **Standard Deviation:** Ranges are based on how much the value varies from the mean value. The mean value is calculated first, and then the standard deviation is added or subtracted from the mean to calculate the ranges.
- **Quantile:** An equal number of features are included in each range.
- **Jenks:** Ranges are based on natural groupings of the data values. This is the same as a natural breaks method, because features with similar values use the same display properties.
- **Individual Values:** Ranges look at values that are most often used when the values represent categories.
- **Logarithm:** Uses a logarithmic scale to distribute values after evaluating the highest and lowest values from the source.

The *Feature Themes* panel is shown in Figure 8–3.

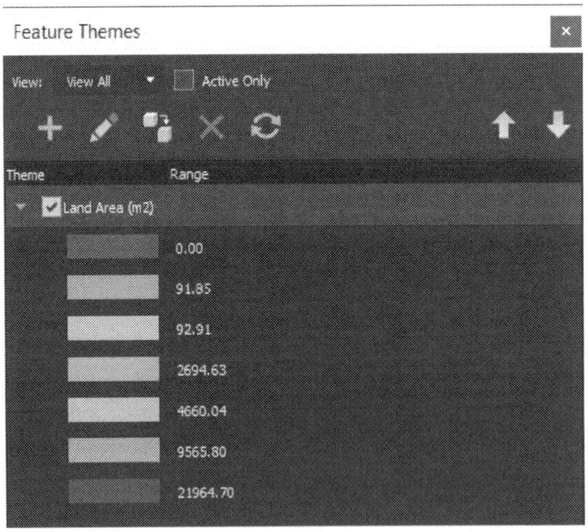

Figure 8–3

How To: Create a Feature Theme

1. In the *Manage* tab>*Display* panel, click (Feature Themes).
2. In the *Feature Themes* panel, click (Add a New Theme).
3. In the *Theme Properties* dialog box (shown in Figure 8–4), set the following properties and click **OK**:
   - *Name:* Enter a name for the theme.
   - *Feature Class:* Select the feature class to theme.
   - *Property:* Select the property in the database, which holds the values to be used for the theme.
   - *Distribution:* Select the distribution method to use.
   - *Number of Rules:* Set the number of rules.
   - *Color Range:* Select the color range and transparency.

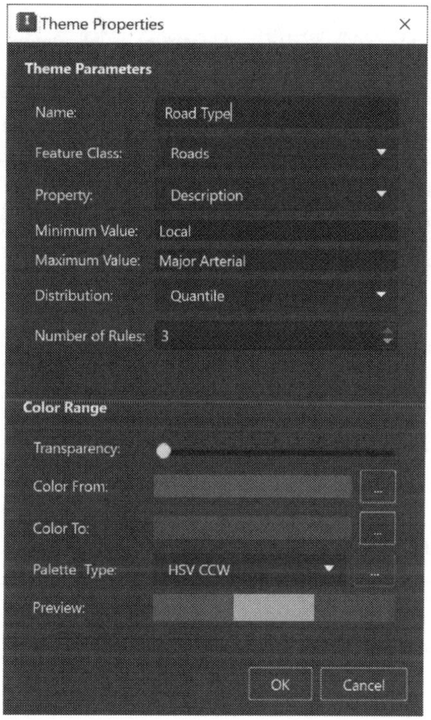

Figure 8–4

Terrain Themes

Terrain themes enable you to display surfaces according to their elevation, slope, or aspect. When creating a terrain theme, you can set the number of rules, colors, and degree of transparency of the surface. Terrain themes only use the equal distribution method for creating ranges. There are a few predefined palettes that automatically set the number of rules and the color for each range according to the type of analysis being run. For example, the *Land Cover* panel sets up 13 ranges with colors starting with light cyan and ending with brown. The *Slope* panel sets up five ranges with colors starting with gray and ending with red, as shown in Figure 8–5.

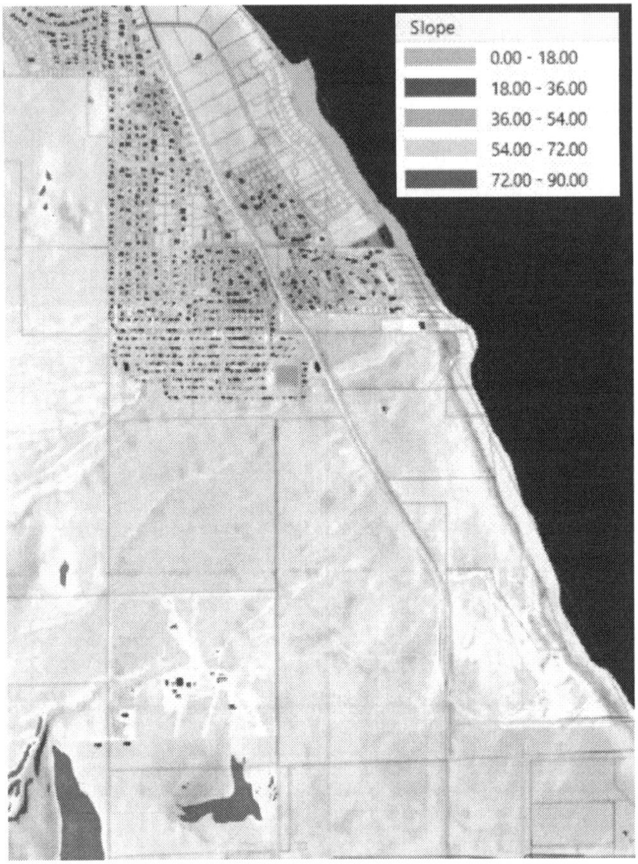

Figure 8–5

How To: Create a Terrain Theme

1. In the *Manage* tab>*Display* panel, click (Terrain Themes).
2. In the *Terrain Themes* panel, click (Add a New Theme).
3. In the *Theme Properties* dialog box (shown in Figure 8–6), set the following parameters and click **OK**:
   - *Name:* Type a name for the theme.
   - *Analysis Type:* Select the analysis type.
   - *Number of Rules:* If the palette type was not set, set the number of rules.
   - *Color Range:* Select the color range and transparency.
   - *Palette Type:* Select the palette type.

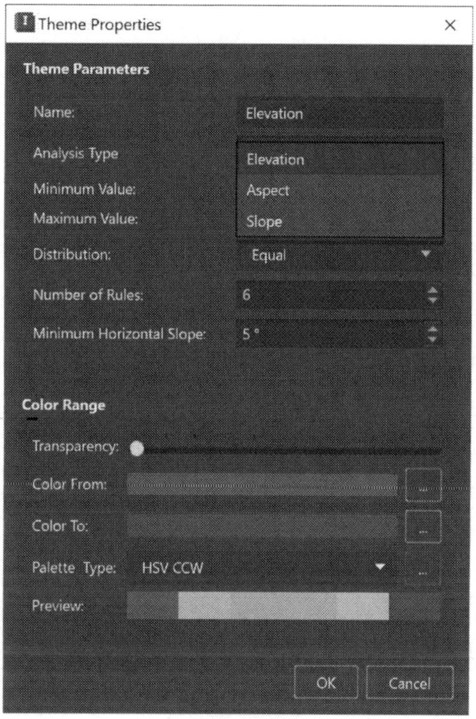

Figure 8–6

Practice 8a
Create Themes in the Model

Practice Objective

- Create themes that will be used to analyze data.

In this practice, you will change the colors in the model according to underlying data to determine whether the project falls within parcels that fit the project budget. You will then perform a slope analysis to determine whether there are any unbuildable areas in the project.

Task 1: Create a feature theme.

1. On the *Home* Screen, click **Open**.
2. In the *InfraWorks Practice Files\8-Analyze-Model* folder, select **Analyze.sqlite** and click **Open**.
3. In the toolbar, expand the  (Proposals) drop-down list and select **A_Task1**.
4. Click  (Bookmarks) and select **Project Area**. Zoom out to see most of the model.
5. In the *Manage* tab>*Model* panel, click  (Model Explorer).
6. In the *Model Explorer* panel, click on the light bulb next to **Parcels** to turn it on and make the parcels visible, as shown in Figure 8–7. The light bulb will turn yellow ().

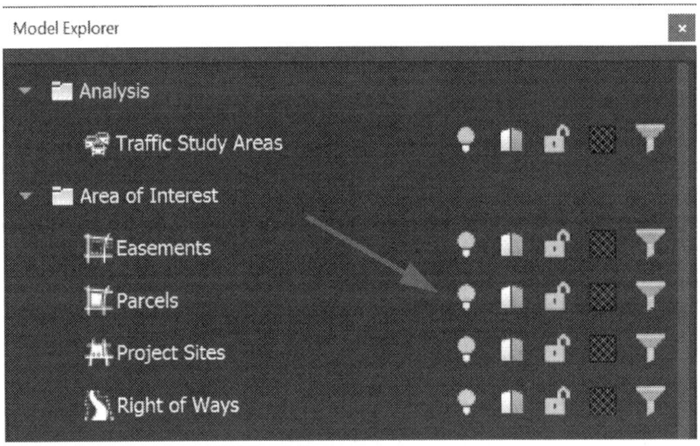

Figure 8–7

7. Close the *Model Explorer* panel.
8. In the *Manage* tab>*Display* panel, click  (Feature Themes).

9. In the *Feature Themes* panel, click  (Add a New Theme).
10. In the *Theme Properties* dialog box, set the following parameters (as shown in Figure 8–8) and click **OK**:
    - *Name:* **Land Values**
    - *Feature Class:* **Parcels**
    - *Property:* **User Data** (the current market value is already mapped to the *User Data* field)
    - *Distribution:* **Quantile**
    - *Number of Rules:* **5**
    - *Transparency:* approximately **50%** (midpoint)
    - *Palette Type:* **HSV CCW**

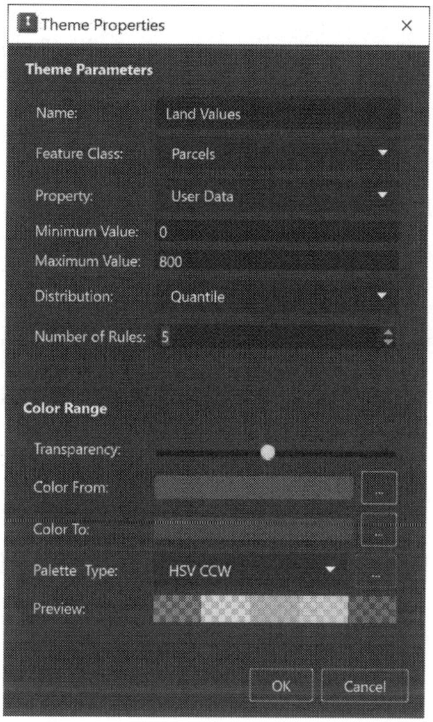

Figure 8–8

- Your model should look similar to that shown in Figure 8–9.

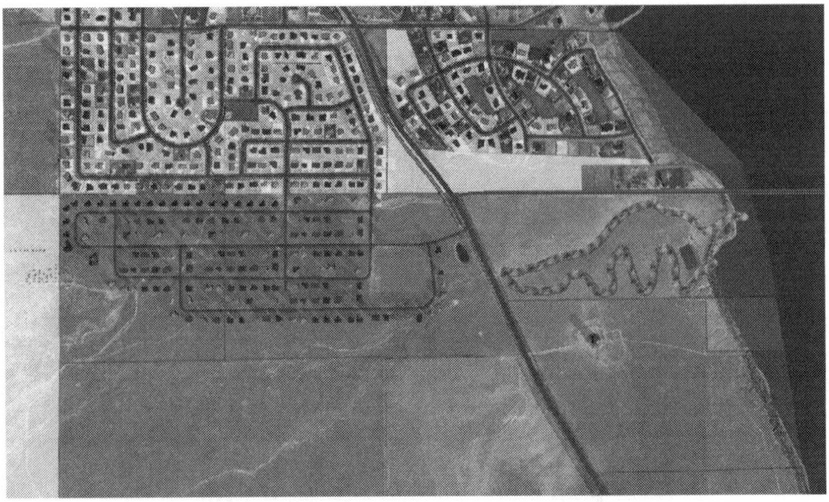

Figure 8–9

Note: *If all of the colors do not display, open the Data Sources panel and double-click on the* ***TaxParcel*** *layer. In the Table tab, ensure that* ***MKT_CNTVAL*** *is selected for the User Data property. Click* ***Close & Refresh****. The theme should automatically recognize the values and update the model display.*

11. In the *Feature Themes* panel, clear the checkmark next to **Land Values** to toggle off the display of the theme.
12. Close the *Feature Themes* panel by clicking on the **X** in the upper-right corner.

Task 2: Create a terrain theme.

1. In the *Manage* tab>*Display* panel, click  (Terrain Themes).
2. In the *Terrain Themes* panel, click  (Add a New Theme).
3. In the *Theme Properties* dialog box, set the following parameters (as shown in Figure 8–10), leaving the rest of the parameters at their defaults, and click **OK**:
   - *Name:* **Slope**
   - *Analysis Type:* **Slope**
   - *Transparency:* approximately **50%** (midpoint)
   - *Palette Type:* **Slope palette**

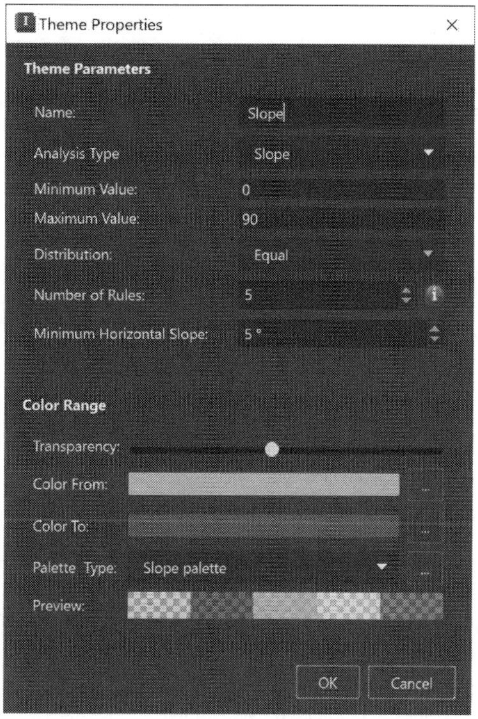

Figure 8–10

- Your model should look similar to that shown in Figure 8–11.

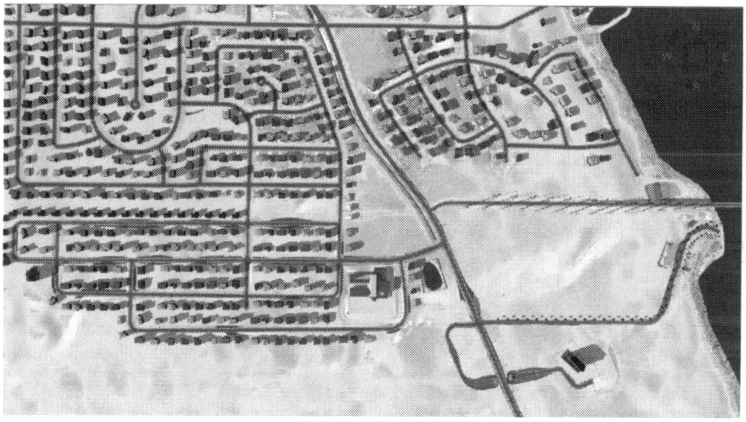

Figure 8–11

4. The client wants to see the slope of the site in 5% increments. In the *Terrain Themes* panel, double-click on the *Slope* theme to open the *Theme Properties* dialog box. Position the box so that you can see the model as you make changes.

5. In the *Theme Properties* dialog box, do the following:
   - Change the *Palette Type* to **User Defined**.
   - Slowly click **Increase** to change the *Number of Rules* to **18**. Watch the model as you do so.
   - Click **OK**.

   Your model should look similar to that shown in Figure 8–12.

Figure 8–12

6. In the *Terrain Themes* panel, note that the ranges are now in 5% slope increments. Clear the checkmark next to **Slope** to toggle off the display of the theme.
7. Close the *Terrain Themes* panel by clicking the **X** in the upper-right corner.
8. In the *Manage* tab>*Model* panel, click  (Model Explorer).
9. In the *Model Explorer* panel, click on the light bulb next to **Parcels** to turn it off again and make the parcels invisible.
10. Close the *Model Explorer* panel.

End of practice

8.2 Suitability Maps

Infrastructure projects can become difficult to manage and sustain if the location or soil types are not suitable for the project. Suitability maps enable you to input your own data to help determine the most cost-effective location for an infrastructure project. This data can come from a layer in the *Model Explorer* or a subset of a layer in the *Model Explorer*, as shown in Figure 8–13. Layer settings enable you to set a gradient width or an offset around the feature.

> ***Note:*** *To use this feature, access to the Internet is required.*

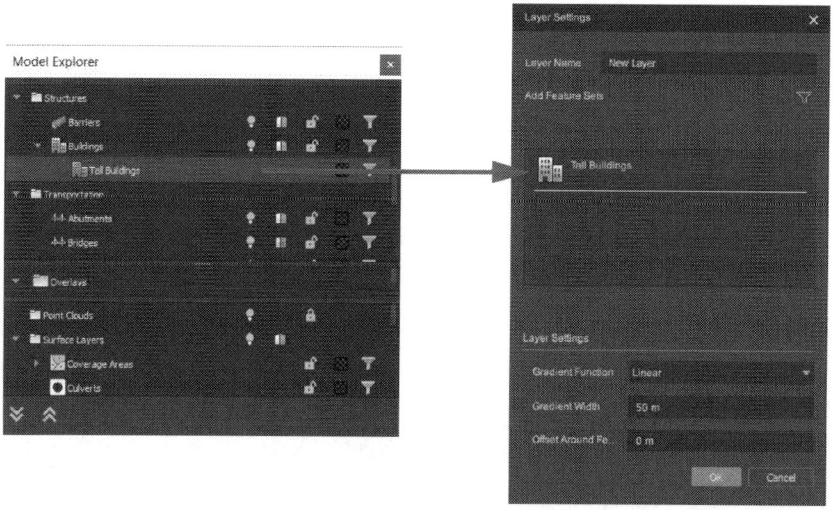

Figure 8–13

Multiple avoidance zone layers can be added to the suitability map. Weights can be adjusted to indicate that one avoidance zone has a higher or lower impact on the project cost over another, as shown in Figure 8–14.

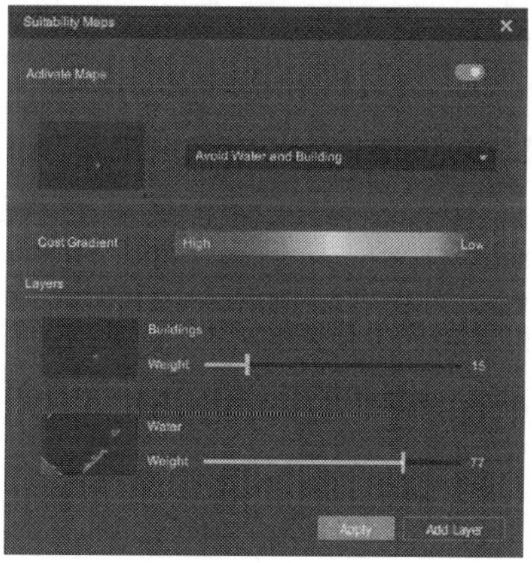

Figure 8–14

Layer Subsets

Many of the GIS layers that are used to create suitability maps require filtering to correctly create avoidance zones.

For example, placing buildings or roads in liquefaction zones near fault lines should be avoided. To address this, a soil map data source could be attached to the model. Then, a layer subset could be created for specific soil types to indicate where liquefaction zones are expected. Finally, the layer subset(s) could be added to the suitability map with weights to indicate which soils to avoid building upon.

How To: Create a Layer Subset

1. In the *Manage* tab>*Model* panel, click (Model Explorer).
2. In the *Model Explorer*, click (Create subset) next to the layer to create any layer subset(s) that might be required.
3. In the *Create New Subset* dialog box, create the necessary filter expression, as shown in Figure 8–15. Click **OK**.

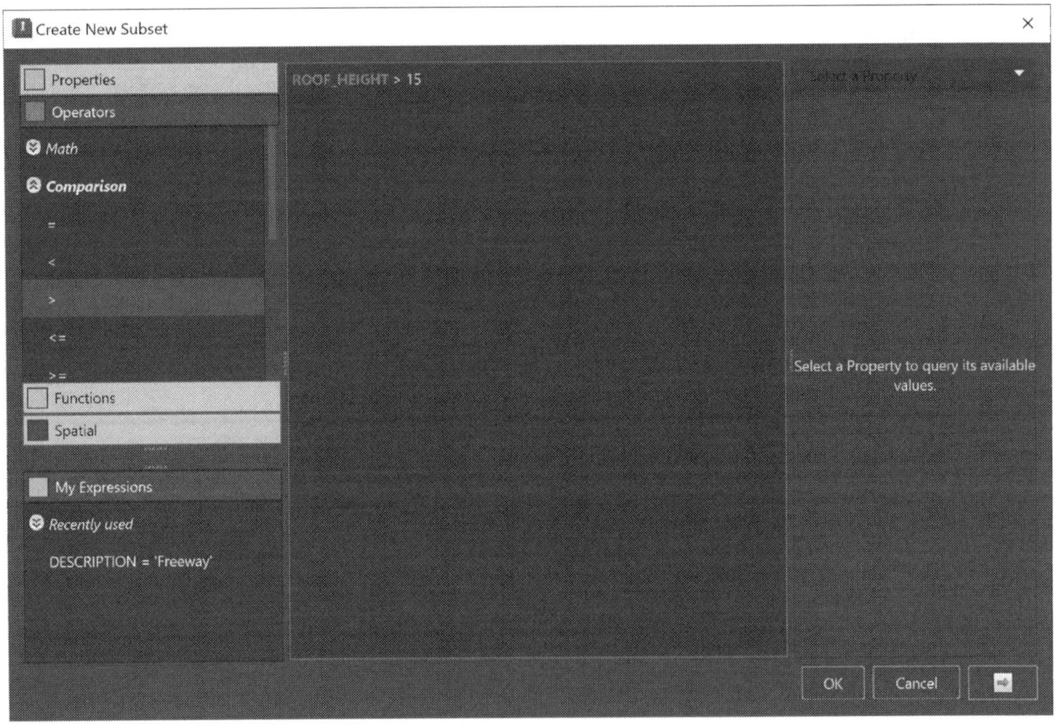

Figure 8–15

How To: Create a Suitability Map

1. In the *Model Explorer*, create any layer subset(s) that might be required.
2. In the *Create* tab>*Environment* drop-down list, click (Suitability Maps).
3. In the *Suitability Maps* panel, toggle on the **Activate Maps** option and select **Create new map...** from the drop-down list, as shown in Figure 8–16.

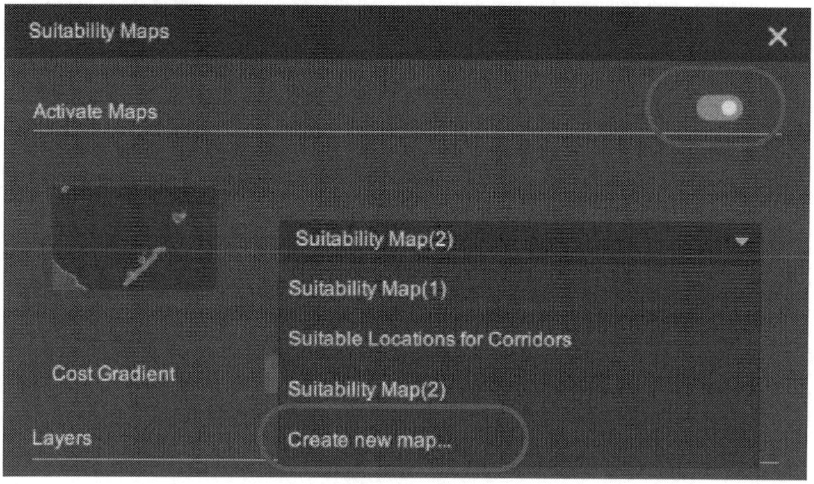

Figure 8–16

4. In the *Layer Settings* panel, click (Select features through Model Explorer).

5. In the *Feature Selection* dialog box, select the layer(s) to apply a buffer to, as shown in Figure 8–17.

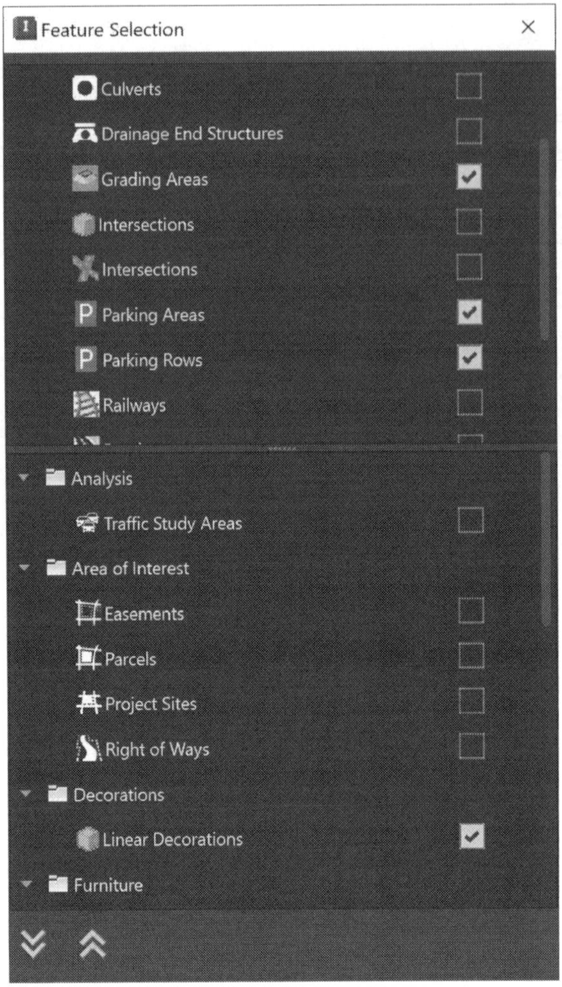

Figure 8–17

6. In the *Layer Settings* panel, type a value in the *Gradient Width* and/or *Offset Around Feature* fields, as shown in Figure 8–18. Click **OK**.

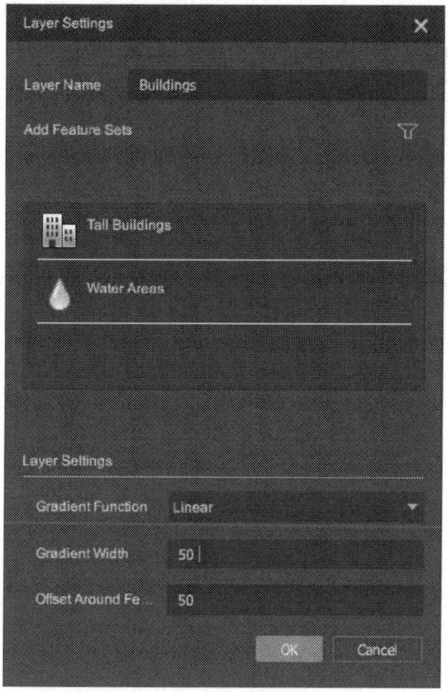

Figure 8–18

7. *In the Suitability Maps* panel, add any additional layers, as required, and then set their weights using the sliders next to each layer, as shown in Figure 8–19. **Note:** You have to use the sliders; you cannot type in the value.

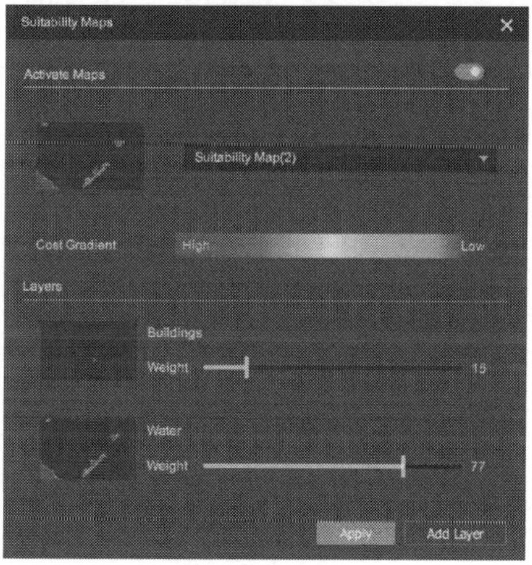

Figure 8–19

8. Click **Apply** to display the results in the model.

Practice 8b
Create a Suitability Map

Practice Objective

- Determine the most cost-effective location for an infrastructure project using avoidance zones.

In this practice, you will create avoidance zones and analyze existing features to ensure that you have selected the best location for a new infrastructure project. First, you will create a layer subset to avoid building a road too close to the taller buildings, which will help reduce the number of car accidents that might occur due to icy roads that are constantly in the shadows of the buildings. Next, you will use the water areas and streams to ensure that the road is not built within 50 meters of the water's edge.

1. Continue working in the same model as the last practice. If you closed the file, on the *Home* screen, click **Open**. In the *InfraWorks Practice Files\8-Analyze-Model* folder, select **CreateFeatures.sqlite** and click **Open**.
2. If you did not complete the last practice, select the **B_Task1** proposal to make it current.
3. In the *Manage* tab>*Model* panel, click (Model Explorer).
4. In *Model Explorer*, in the *Structures* branch, next to the **Buildings** layer, click (Create subset).
5. In the *Create New Subset* dialog box, do the following to create the expression shown in Figure 8–20:
    - Under *Properties*, expand *Building* and double-click on **ROOF_HEIGHT**.
    - Under *Operators*, expand *Comparison* and double-click on **>**.
    - Select the value in the *Expression* area (by double-clicking on *[value]*) and type **15**.
    - Click **OK**.

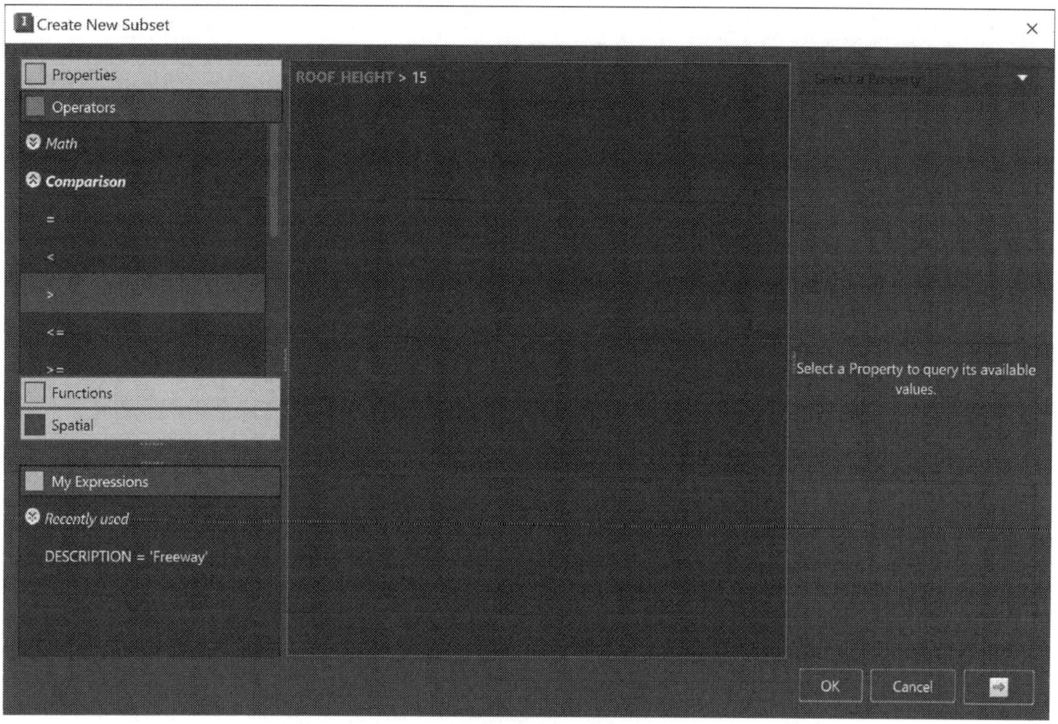

Figure 8–20

6. In the *Model Explorer*, click on the newly created subset to rename it. For the subset name, type **Tall Buildings**.
7. Close the *Model Explorer*.
8. In the *Create* tab>*Environment* drop-down list, select  (Suitability Maps).
9. In the *Suitability Maps* panel, expand ***Select a Map*** and select **Create new map...**, as shown in Figure 8–21.

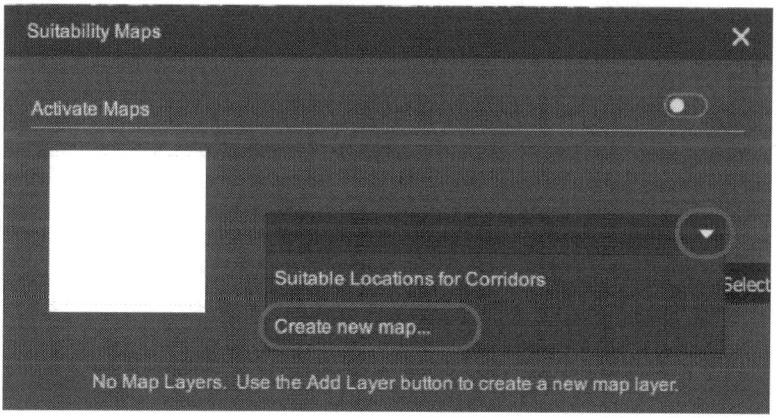

Figure 8–21

10. In the *Suitability Maps* panel, highlight the existing default name to rename the map. In the *Map Name* field, type **Avoid Water & Buildings**.
11. In the *Suitability Maps* panel, click **Add Layer** in the lower-right corner.
12. In the *Layer Settings* panel, type **Water** for the name and press <Enter>, then click (Select features through Model Explorer).
13. In the *Feature Selection* dialog box, under *Feature Selection*, select the **Streams** and **Water Areas** layers, as shown in Figure 8–22.
14. Close the *Feature Selection* dialog box by clicking the **X** in the upper-right corner.

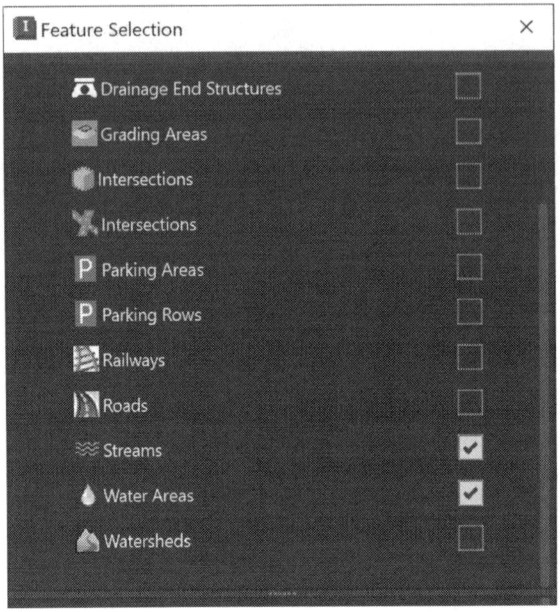

Figure 8–22

15. In the *Layer Settings* panel, set both the *Gradient Width* and *Offset Around Feature* to **50**, as shown in Figure 8–23. Click **OK**.

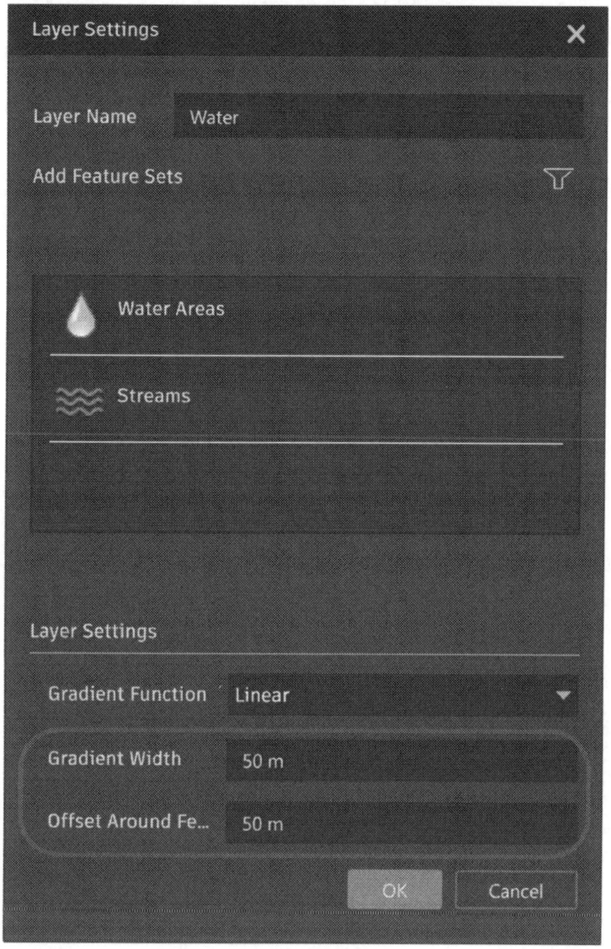

Figure 8–23

16. In the *Suitability Maps* panel, toggle on the **Activate Maps** option, if necessary. Click **Apply** to see the results in the model.

17. In the *Suitability Maps* panel, click **Add Layer**, as shown in Figure 8–24.

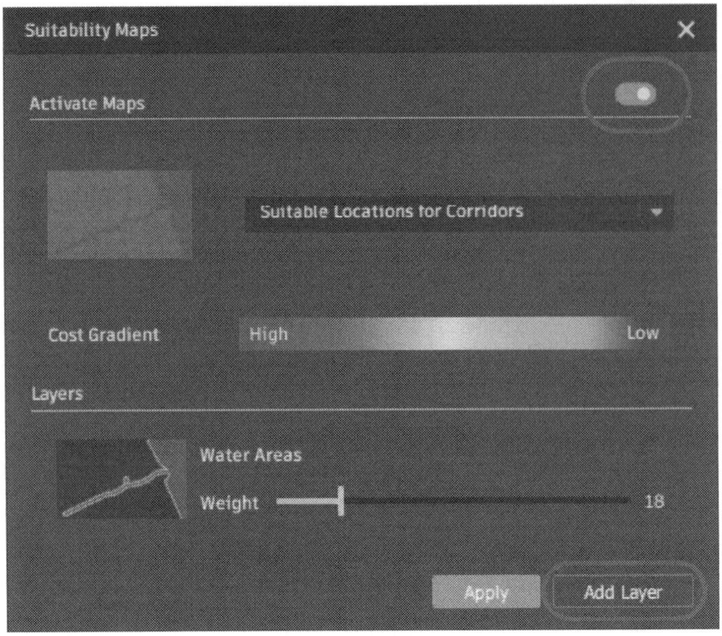

Figure 8–24

18. In the *Layer Settings* panel, type **Buildings** for the name and click  (Select features through Model Explorer).
19. In the *Feature Selection* dialog box, under the *Structures* folder, expand the *Buildings* layer and select the **Tall Buildings** subset that you created earlier.
20. Close the *Feature Selection* dialog box.
21. In the *Layer Settings* panel, in the *Gradient Width* and *Offset Around Feature* fields, type **10**. Click **OK**.
22. In the *Suitability Maps* panel, click **Apply** to display the results in the model.
23. In the *Suitability Maps* panel, adjust the layer weights using the sliders next to each layer. Set the *Water* weight to **65** and the *Building* weight to **25**, as shown in Figure 8–25.

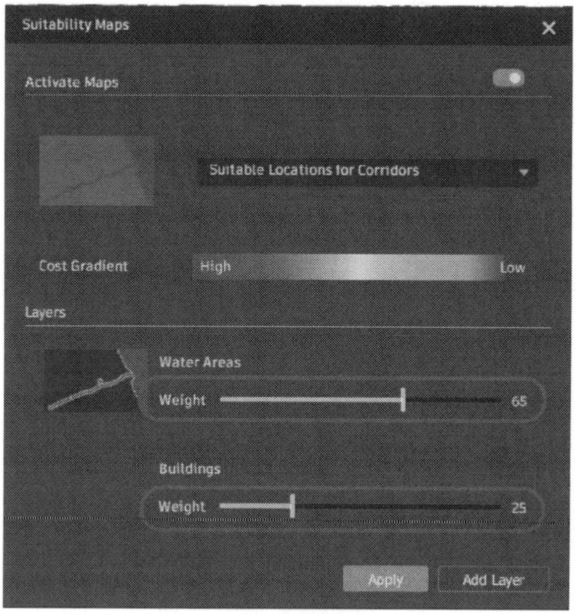

Figure 8–25

24. Click **Apply** to display the results in the model. The result should be similar to that shown in Figure 8–26.

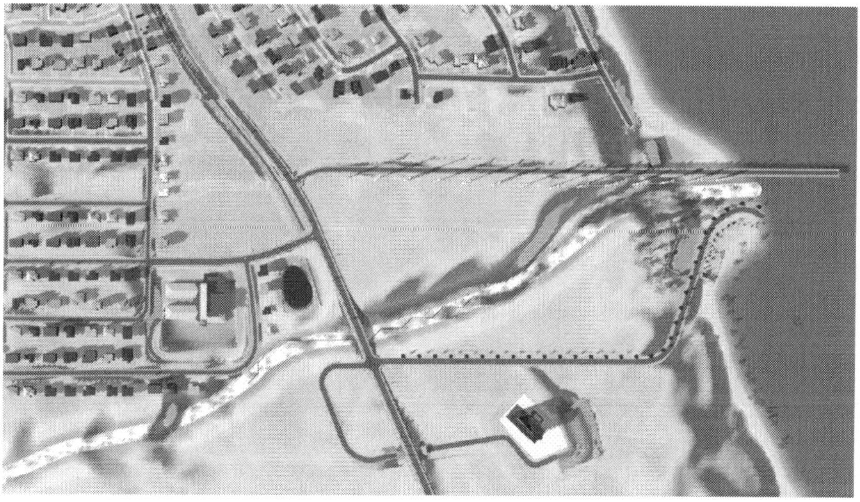

Figure 8–26

25. Toggle off the **Activate Maps** option, then close the *Suitability Maps* panel by clicking the **X** in the upper-right corner.

End of practice

8.3 Line of Sight Analysis

Stakeholders are justifiably concerned about how a project is expected to look from a specific vantage point. They also want to know what they can or cannot see from a specific point of view. Residents from the surrounding community will want to know that passing traffic cannot see into their backyards. Stakeholders may also want to know that views of the surrounding landscape are not going to be lost because of the proposed project. In these cases, a line of sight study can be conducted to better understand what can be seen from a specific location.

A line of sight analysis is conducted by orienting the view to the angle and direction to be analyzed. Anything in the line of sight becomes selected in the model when you run the analysis, as shown in Figure 8–27. These objects remain selected even when the view changes, enabling you to see what is selected after moving the camera.

Figure 8–27

How To: Conduct a Line of Sight Analysis

1. In the toolbar, expand the (Select) drop-down list and click (Select Visible).
2. The visible objects are selected and remain selected as you navigate around the model.
3. When finished studying the model for the sight analysis, press <Esc> to clear all of the selected features.

8.4 Measure the Model

To meet project constraints, correct measurements must be taken. It is recommended to continually check the model and ensure that features are the correct distance from each other and have the correct area and volumes. These checks help you to avoid having to recreate and edit objects later. Measurement tools are found in the toolbar in the (Measure) drop-down list. The available tools are as follows:

Icon	Purpose
(Point to Point Distance)	Measures length, width, and height from one point to another along a straight line. Distance displays in the model similar to a dimension.
(Point Elevation)	Measures the elevation of a point along geometry.
(2D Distance & Slope)	Measures the slope between two points. Distance displays in the model similar to a triangle showing the 2D horizontal distance, vertical distance, and grade between two points.
(Path Distance)	Measures length, width, and height along a polyline path. Distance displays in the model similar to a series of dimensions with individual values displayed for each segment, as well as the total distance. It can be used to display measurements across a terrain.
(Range Finder)	Measures the distance of a target point from your current position. Distance displays in the model similar to a single point with a label indicating the distance, altitude, heading, and inclination from your position. You can set multiple target points in a session.
(Terrain Statistics)	Measures the area and volume of a terrain by specifying the perimeter points.

How To: Measure Single Distances

1. In the toolbar, expand the (Measure) drop-down list and click (Point to Point Distance).
2. Click the first point to start the measurement.

3. Click the second point where the measurement ends. The measured value displays, similar to the one shown in Figure 8–28.

Figure 8–28

4. Press <Esc> to remove the temporary dimension.

How To: Measure 2D Distance and Slope

1. In the toolbar, expand the (Measure) drop-down list and click (2D Distance & Slope).
2. Click the first point to start the measurement.
3. Click the second point where the measurement ends. The measured value displays, similar to those shown in Figure 8–29.

Figure 8–29

4. Press <Esc> to remove the temporary dimension.

How To: Measure a Series of Distances

1. In the toolbar, expand the (Measure) drop-down list and click (Path Distance).
2. Click the first point to start the measurement.

3. Click all of the subsequent points along the path, as required. Double-click on the last point where the measurement ends. The measured values display, similar to those shown in Figure 8–30.

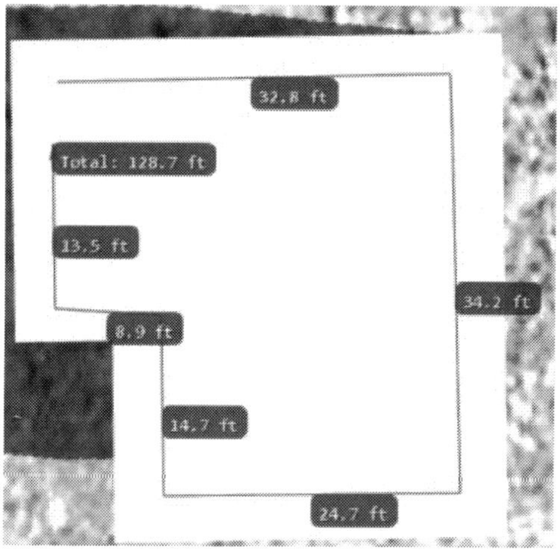

Figure 8–30

4. Press <Esc> to remove the temporary dimensions.

How To: Measure Elevations

1. In the toolbar, expand the (Measure) drop-down list and select (Point Elevation).
2. In the model, click a point of which you want to determine the elevation. When you move the mouse, a leader appears. Click a point and the elevation is displayed as a tooltip appears as shown in Figure 8–31.

Figure 8–31

3. Press <Esc> to remove the temporary dimensions.

How To: Measure Ranges

1. In the toolbar, expand the (Measure) drop-down list and click (Range Finder).
2. Click a point in the model. The range values display, similar to those shown in Figure 8–32.

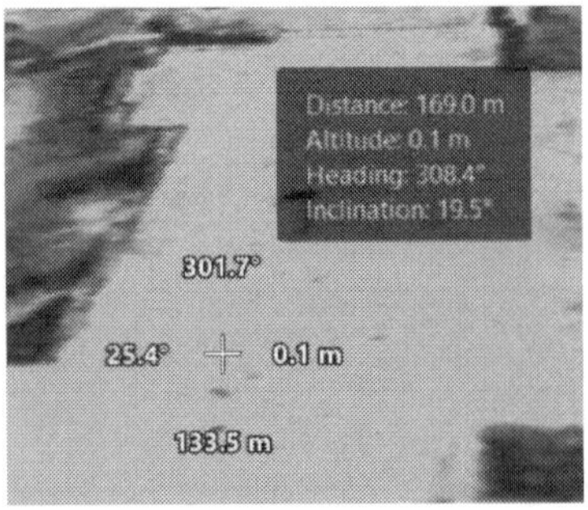

Figure 8–32

3. Press <Esc> to remove the temporary dimensions.

How To: Measure Terrain Statistics

1. In the toolbar, expand the (Measure) drop-down list and click (Terrain Statistics).
2. Click the first point to start a boundary. The boundary defines the area to measure.
3. Click all of the subsequent points along the required boundary. Double-click on the point where the boundary should end. A boundary and its measure values display, similar to that shown in Figure 8–33.

Figure 8–33

4. Press <Esc> to remove the temporary dimensions.

8.5 Analyze Shadows

Conducting a shadow study can demonstrate whether the project will be obscured or will cause obscuring of sunlight at specific times of day or throughout the year. During a shadow study, you can toggle shadows on or off, and set various sun and sky settings.

Visual Effects

To adjust the lighting and appearance of your model, change the *View Style* settings. In the toolbar, expand the *View Style* drop-down list and click (Configure current view). Change the settings on the *Visualization* stack of the *View Settings* asset card, as shown in Figure 8–34.

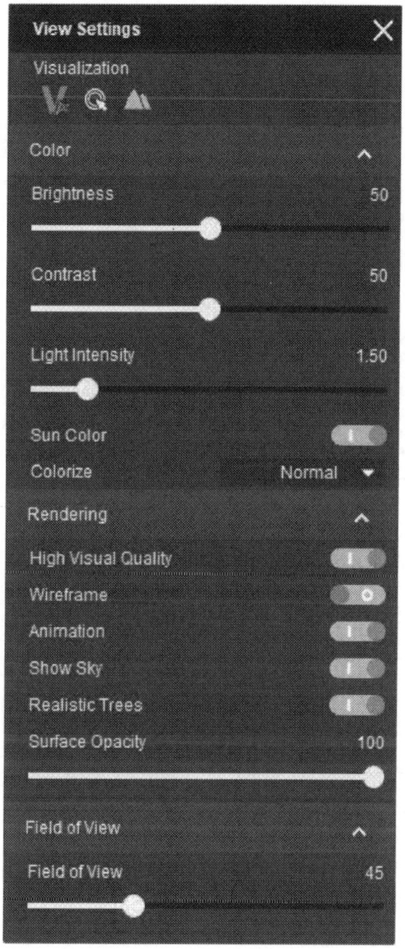

Figure 8–34

Toggle Shadows On/Off

Studying how shadows are cast in a model helps you to determine whether solar panels can be used to power a building or whether there will be excessive solar gain for heating/ventilation concerns. It can also help you to determine whether horizontal and vertical curves need to be modified along a transportation corridor to reduce the effects of shadows. For instance, too much shade on a road that is prone to snow and ice can create dangerous conditions for commuters.

In the *View Settings* asset card, you can toggle on shadows by toggling the **High Visual Quality** setting to **On**, as shown in Figure 8–35. Changing this setting to **Off** toggles the shadows off.

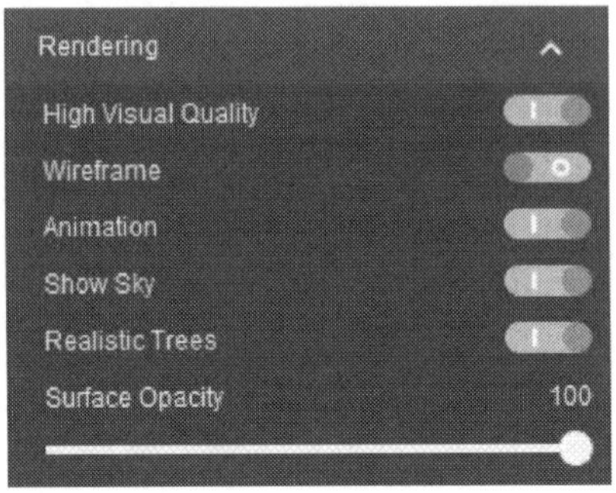

Figure 8–35

Brightness and Contrast

Both the brightness of the model and the contrast between light and dark can be controlled in the *View Settings* asset card, as shown previously in Figure 8–34. Additionally, you can change the color palette used by the model, selecting the **Normal**, **Grayscale**, or **Sepia** palettes found in the *Colorize* drop-down list, as shown in Figure 8–36.

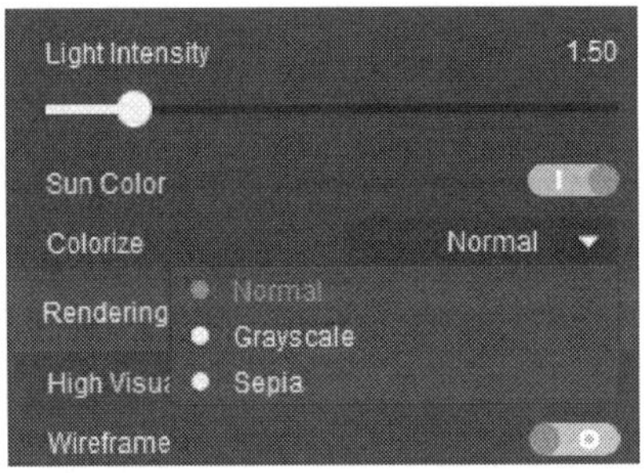

Figure 8–36

Field of View

The *Field of View* slider, found in the *View Settings* asset card, enables you to control how much of the model displays in the view as you zoom in and out.

Sun & Sky Settings

The time of year and time of day can both be set using the *Date* and *Time* sliders in the *Sun & Sky* asset card, as shown in Figure 8–37. Additionally, you can set the wind speed/direction and amount of cloud cover in the model. To open the *Sun & Sky* asset card, in the

Manage tab>*Display* drop-down list, click (Sun & Sky).

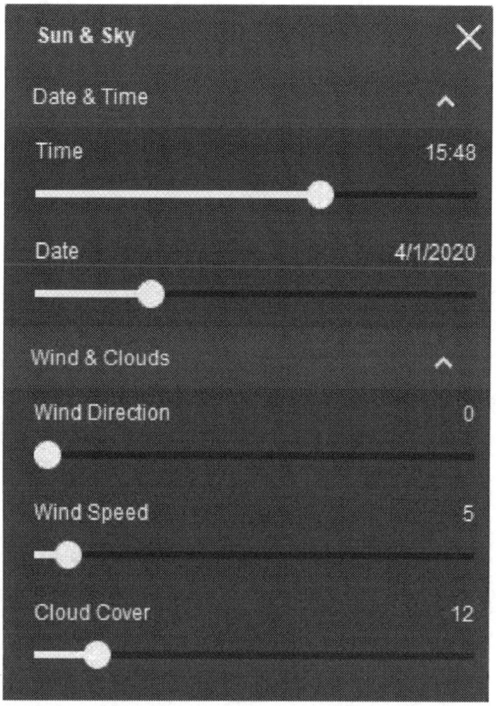

Figure 8–37

Practice 8c
Analyze the Model

Practice Objectives

- Analyze the model graphically by conducting a line of sight analysis and a shadow study.
- Analyze the model numerically by measuring the model.

In this practice, you will conduct a line of sight analysis and measure the model to ensure that it meets the project requirements. You will then conduct a shadow study to ensure that the project receives enough sunlight and that shadows do not create any unforeseen issues.

Task 1: Conduct a line of sight analysis.

In this task, you will conduct a line of sight analysis to determine whether certain features can be seen from a specific point from a proposed hotel location.

1. Continue working in the same model as the last practice. If you closed the file, on the *Home* screen, click **Open**. In the *InfraWorks Practice Files\8-Analyze-Model* folder, select **Analyze.sqlite** and click **Open**.
2. If you did not complete the previous practices, select the **C_Task1** proposal to make it current.
3. Click (Bookmarks) and select **Hotel Interior**. Hold the mouse button down to move your vantage point upward by a couple levels, then use the right mouse button to pan leftward outside the hotel, similar to the vantage point shown in Figure 8–38.

Figure 8–38

4. In the toolbar, expand the (Select) drop-down list and click (Select Visible). All of the objects displayed in this line of sight are selected and highlighted in light blue to display them clearly.

5. Click (Bookmarks) and select **Project Area**. *Homes* and roads will be selected, as shown in Figure 8–39. **Note:** After changing the view orientation, the selected objects remain selected and can be reviewed more easily.

Figure 8–39

6. Press <Esc> to clear the selection.

Task 2: Measure the model.

In this task, you will measure the church building to ensure that it meets the project requirements for capacity. You will then measure the length of road to a specific cul-de-sac to ensure that it meets emergency evacuation codes.

1. Click (Bookmarks) and select **Church Area**.

2. In the toolbar, expand the (Measure) drop-down list and click (Point to Point Distance).

3. Measure the length and width of the main chapel of the church, as shown in Figure 8–40.

   ***Note:** The actual measurements may vary in your model.*

Figure 8–40

4. Press <Esc> to remove the temporary dimensions, then press <Esc> again to clear your selection.
5. Click (Bookmarks) and select **Pier 3D**. Zoom and pan toward the end of the pier.
6. In the toolbar, expand the (Measure) drop-down list and click (2D Distance & Slope).
7. Click the first point to start the measurement near the start of the bridge, as shown in Figure 8–41.
8. Click the second point near the edge of the water. The measured value displays, as shown in Figure 8–41.

Figure 8–41

9. Press <Esc> to remove the temporary dimensions, then press <Esc> again to clear your selection.

10. In the toolbar, expand the (Measure) drop-down list and click (Point Elevation).
11. In the model, click a point on tone of the turbine shafts (not a blade). When you move the mouse, a leader displays. Click a point and the elevation is displayed as a tooltip appears as shown in Figure 8–42.

Figure 8–42

12. Press <Esc> to clear all measurements.
13. Click (Bookmarks) and select **Project Area**.
14. In the toolbar, expand the (Measure) drop-down list and click (Path Distance).
15. Click the series of points shown in Figure 8–43 to measure the new roads from where they intersect **Redwood Rd** to where they end at the future cul-de-sac.

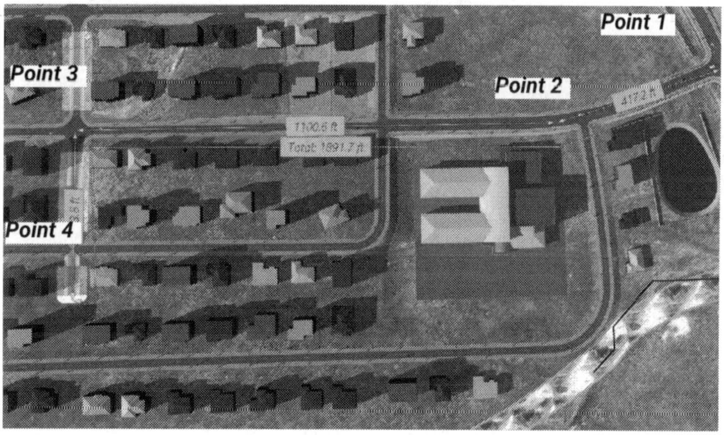

Figure 8–43

16. Press <Esc> to remove the temporary dimensions.

Task 3: Conduct a shadow study.

In this task, you will conduct a shadow analysis to ensure that the new roads will not have increased numbers of accidents due to ice buildup on the roads that is caused by shadows.

1. In the toolbar, expand the *View Style* drop-down list and click (Configure current view).
2. In the *View Settings* asset card, click (Change rendering and lighting settings).
3. Under *Rendering*, toggle on **High Visual Quality**, if it is not already set.
4. Close the *View Settings* asset card by clicking the **X** in the upper-right corner.
5. Click (Bookmarks) and select **Hotel 3D**.
6. In the *Manage* tab>*Display* drop-down list, select (Sun & Sky).
7. In the *Sun & Sky* asset card, set the *Date* slider to **April 30** of the current year and set the *Time* slider to **7:00 am**.
8. Set the *Time* slider to **18:15 (6:15pm)** and note that the sun in the sky is beginning to set, as shown in Figure 8–44.

Figure 8–44

9. Continue moving the sliders to analyze the shadows over time.
10. Close the *Sun & Sky* asset card by clicking the **X** in the upper-right corner.

End of practice

Chapter Review Questions

1. Which of the following is not a theme that you can create in the model?
   a. Feature theme
   b. Terrain theme
   c. Point cloud theme
   d. Sky theme

2. When conducting a line of sight analysis, the selected objects in the line of sight change when the view changes.
   a. True
   b. False

3. Which measurement tool would you use to determine the distance, altitude, or inclination of a point from the current camera viewpoint?
   a. 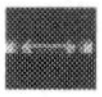 (Point to Point)
   b.  (Path Distance)
   c.  (Range Finder)
   d. 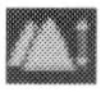 (Terrain Statistics)

4. How do you toggle shadows on in the model?
   a. In the *View Settings* asset card.
   b. In the *Sun & Sky* asset card.

5. How do you filter a data source in preparation for adding it to a suitability map?
   a. Select the features in the model first.
   b. Create a terrain theme.
   c. Create a feature theme.
   d. Create a subset of the data source in the *Model Explorer*.

Command Summary

Button	Command	Location
	**2D Distance & Slope**	• **Toolbar:** *Measure* drop-down list
	**Change rendering and lighting settings**	• ***View Settings* asset card**
	**Create Subset**	• ***Model Explorer***
	**Feature Themes**	• **Toolbar:** *Manage* tab>*Display* panel
	**Measure**	• **Toolbar**
	**Path Distance**	• **Toolbar:** *Measure* drop-down list
	**Point Elevation**	• **Toolbar:** *Measure* drop-down list
	**Point to Point Distance**	• **Toolbar:** *Measure* drop-down list
	**Range Finder**	• **Toolbar:** *Measure* drop-down list
	**Select Visible**	• **Toolbar:** *Select* drop-down list
	**Sky & Sun**	• **Toolbar:** *Manage* tab>*Display* drop-down list
	**Suitability Maps**	• **Toolbar:** *Create* tab>*Environment* drop-down list
	**Terrain Statistics**	• **Toolbar:** *Measure* drop-down list
	**Terrain Themes**	• **Toolbar:** *Manage* tab>*Display* panel

Chapter 9

Communicate the Design to Stakeholders

An important part of any project is the approval process. Without buy-in from the stakeholders or authorities, a project can be delayed, which can impact the project's timeline and budget. To ensure buy-in from all of the stakeholders and reviewing agencies, proper communication tools are vital. You need to ensure that everyone involved understands how the intended project fits in its environment and neighborhood.

In this chapter, you will learn how to create high-end visualizations to help communicate the design intent. Images and storyboards will be created to make this possible.

Learning Objectives

- Present a simple image of the model using a snapshot.
- Create a visual style for viewing the model in various ways.
- Present a slideshow of the design to stakeholders by creating storyboards.
- Share views for others to review through the *Autodesk Viewer* browser.

9.1 Creating Images

The Autodesk InfraWorks software enables you to create images of varying quality. You can create quick snapshots or realistic renderings of the model to communicate to stakeholders exactly how a project is expected to look when construction is finished.

Snapshots

A snapshot is a quick, lower-resolution image of the current model view. Figure 9–1 shows an example of a snapshot. The image reflects the current view and uses the current visual effects settings. Therefore, if shadows are toggled off in the model, they do not display in the snapshot. The quality of the image can be adjusted using various settings, such as the level of detail (LOD), style, and snapshot resolution settings.

Figure 9–1

How To: Create a Snapshot

1. In the *Present/Share* tab>*Present* drop-down list, click  (Create Snapshot).
2. In the *Camera Snapshot* dialog box, set the required resolution for the image, as shown in Figure 9–2. Click the ellipsis (...) for browsing to set the path and file name for the image.

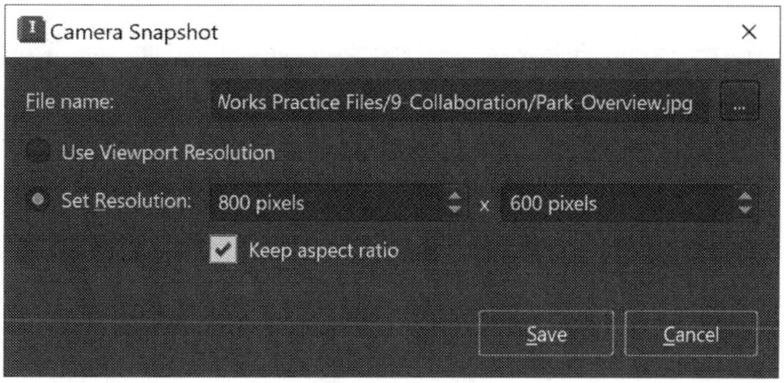

Figure 9–2

3. In the *Select image file* dialog box, in the *Save as type* drop-down list, select the image type that you want to create, as shown in Figure 9–3. Snapshot images can be saved as **JPG**, **PNG**, or **TIFF images**. Enter the required file name and location and click **Save**.

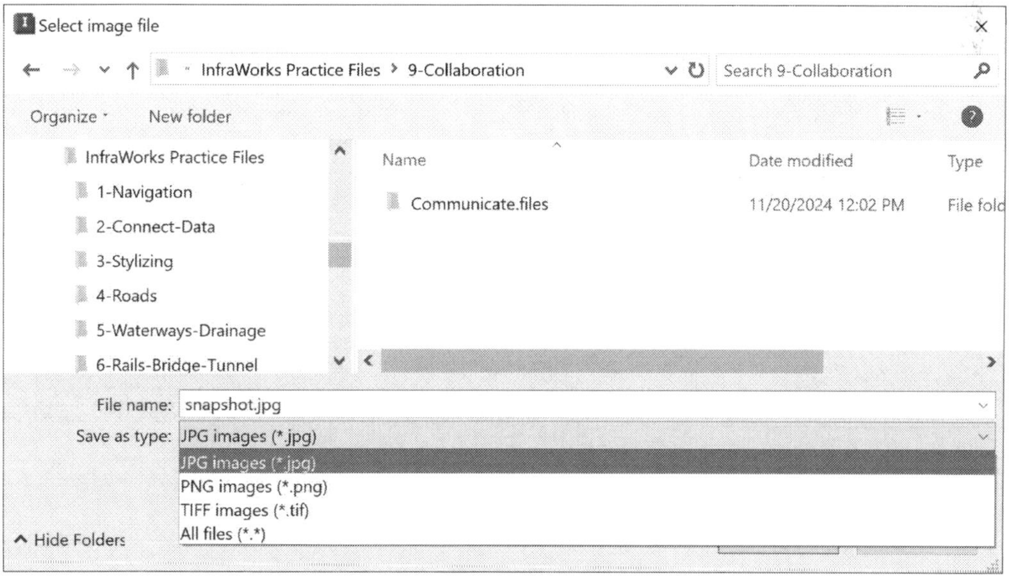

Figure 9–3

4. In the *Camera Snapshot* dialog box, click **Save**.
5. To display the image, use File Explorer to open it from the saved location.

View Settings

When working with snapshots, what you see in the model when you save the image is how the image will be stored. This is controlled by the visual style. Change the current view setting in the toolbar. New visual styles can be created to highlight various aspects of the model, as shown in Figure 9–4.

Wireframe toggled on in the View Settings asset card>Visualization stack

Wireframe toggled off in the View Settings asset card>Visualization stack

Figure 9–4

Different view settings can be assigned to each visual style. Visual styles and view configurations are saved locally, so that they are available in every model that you open. All of the view settings options can be found in one of three stacks in the *View Settings* asset card.

Visualization Stack

The *Visualization* stack controls a range of lighting effects.

- *Color*
  - **Brightness:** Adjusts the amount of black in the model's colors.
  - **Contrast:** Adjusts the definition between areas of differing values to provide more image depth.
  - **Light Intensity:** Adjusts the overall brightness and intensity of colors uniformly.
  - **Sun Color:** Adds a tint to simulate sun position.
  - **Colorize:** Select between **Normal**, **Grayscale**, or **Sepia** color schemes.
- *Rendering*
  - **High Visual Quality:** Toggles shadows for high or rough resolution model display.
  - **Wireframe:** When on, reduces features to 3D skeletons, displaying only lines and vertices.
  - **Animation:** Toggles water wave and cloud movement.
  - **Show Sky:** Toggles the display of the sky background.
  - **Realistic Trees:** Toggles from detailed, realistic trees to more simplistic "lollipop" tree styles.
  - **Surface Opacity:** Adjusts the transparency of the ground surface.
- *Field of View*
  - **Field of View:** Adjusts feature flatness, similar to a wide-angle lens on a camera.

Interaction Stack

The *Interaction* stack controls the visibility of certain tools and other interaction settings.

- *Information Labels*
  - **Tooltips:** Toggles the text, images, links, or model property values that display when you hover over a command or feature.
  - **Links:** Toggles the display of feature links to external data stores, tooltips, or maps.
  - **In-Canvas Labels:** For roadways, rail, etc., toggles label visibility (stationing, alignment geometry, etc.).
- *Feedback*
  - **Status Bar:** Toggles the cursor's coordinates on the bottom left of the model window.
  - **Edit mode:** Toggles the ability to make changes to model features.

- *Navigation*
  - **View Cube:** Toggles the display of the ViewCube.
  - **Proximity:** Toggles the display of tooltips when the proximity distance is reached.
  - **Automatic Zoom To Selection:** Toggles the automatic zoom on selected features.
  - **Highlight Sketched Features:** Toggles the linework that highlights sketched features when in drawing mode.
  - **Lock Mouse Above Ground:** Toggles the ability to view features below the surface.
  - **Show Statistics:** Toggles the display of feature statistics while in edit or draw mode.

Terrain Stack

In the *Terrain* stack, the *Contours* section controls the visibility and display of surface contour lines and their labels. Settings enable you to control the line color and thickness, as well as the label size, color, and thickness, as shown in Figure 9–5.

> **Note:** *The Terrain Themes section is another way of accessing terrain themes as described in Chapter 8: Analyzing the Model.*

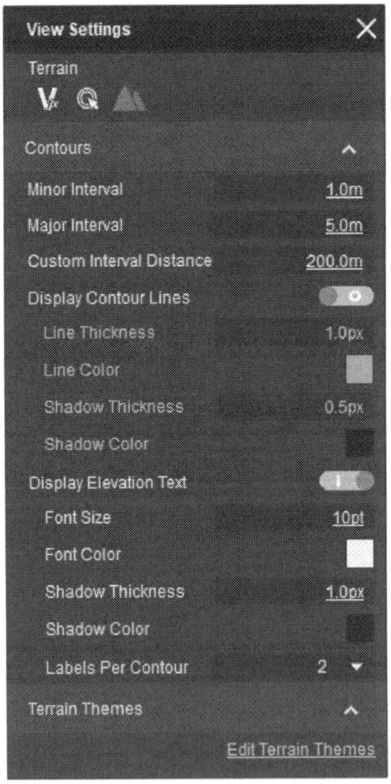

Figure 9–5

How To: Create a New Visual Style

1. In the toolbar, expand the *View Style* drop-down list and click **Add**.
2. In the *View Settings* asset card, in the *Visualization* stack, make the required changes to adjust the model display, as shown in Figure 9–6.

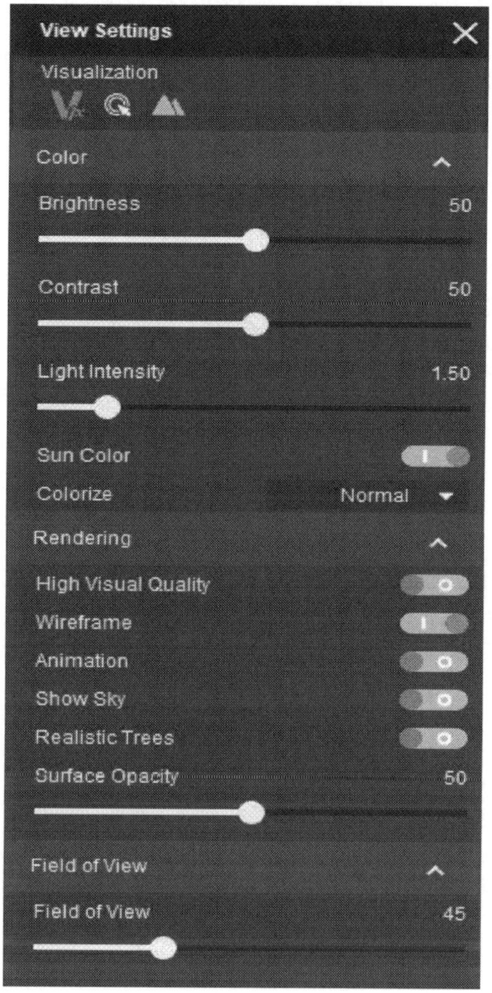

Figure 9–6

3. In the *View Settings* asset card, click (Change navigation and application feedback settings) to open the *Interaction* stack.

4. Set the required toggles to the right to toggle them on or to the left to toggle them off, as shown in Figure 9–7.

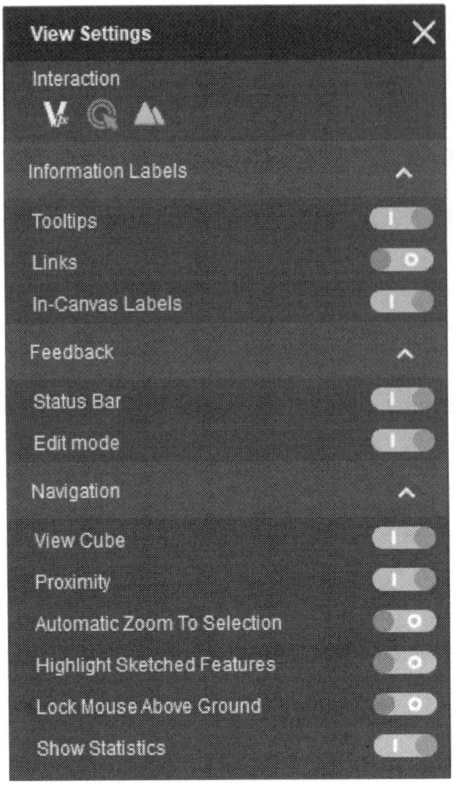

Figure 9–7

5. In the *View Settings* asset card, click  (Change terrain view settings) to open the *Terrain* stack.

6. In the *Contours* section, set the required toggles to the right to toggle them on or to the left to toggle them off, and click to set values and colors, as shown in Figure 9–8.

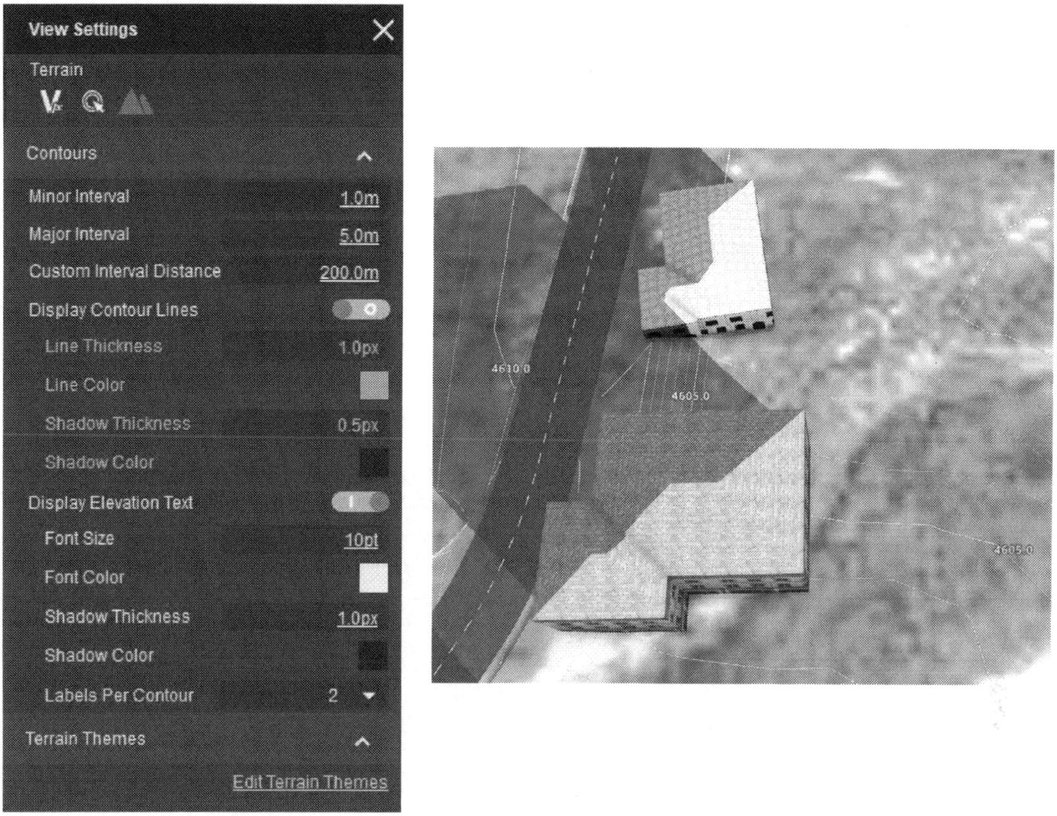

Figure 9–8

9.2 Shared Views

Shared views are stored in the cloud and can be viewed and commented on by any web-enabled desktop, tablet, or mobile device. The links created for sharing views expire after thirty days but can be extended or terminated at any time.

Shared Views Panel

A history of the published shared views display in the *Shared Views* panel, as shown in Figure 9–9. Click on the ellipsis next to the shared view to see a list of available commands.

How To: Create a Shared View

1. In the toolbar, click (Shared Views) to display the *Shared Views* panel, then click **New Shared View**, as shown in Figure 9–9.

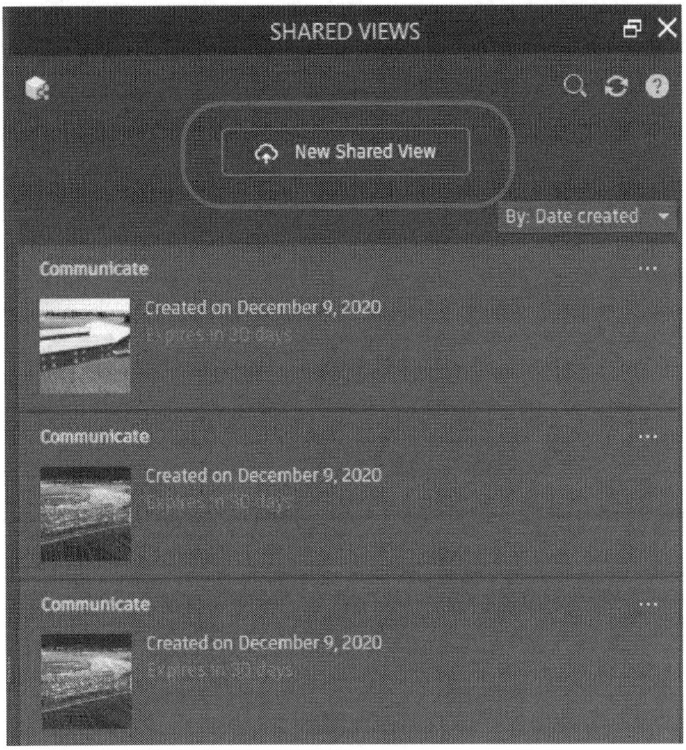

Figure 9–9

2. In the *Create a Shared View* dialog box, type a name and set the view extents, as shown in Figure 9–10. Click **Share**.

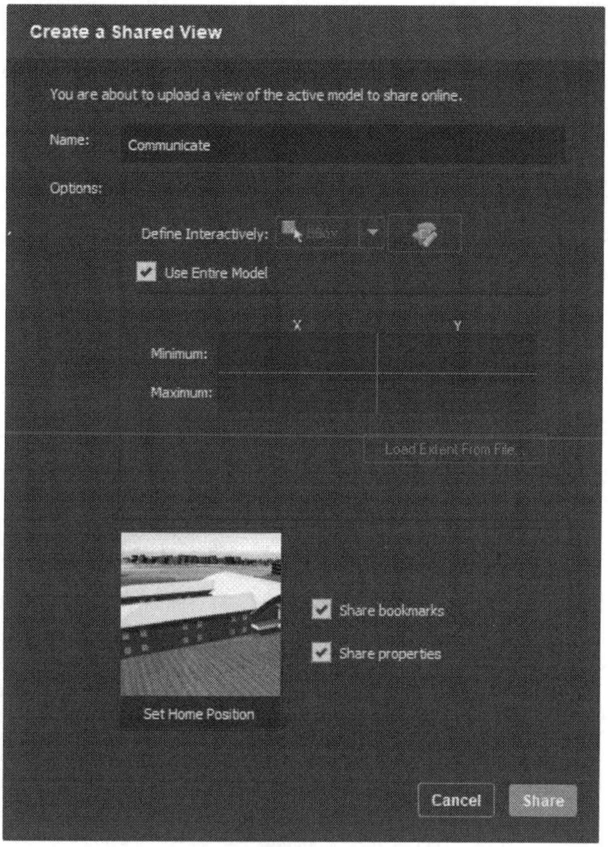

Figure 9–10

3. When the *Create a Shared View* dialog box indicates *Communicate successfully uploaded* (as shown in Figure 9–11), click **Copy** to share the link, click **View in browser** to view the model yourself, or click **Close**.

Figure 9–11

Autodesk Viewer

The *Autodesk Viewer* opens the saved view link in an Internet browser on your desktop, tablet, or other mobile device. This enables you to share the view with stakeholders who do not have the InfraWorks software, without having to email files back and forth or install other viewing software. Using a browser, they can review and mark up the design for better communication. Figure 9–12 shows the *Autodesk Viewer* interface for models created in InfraWorks.

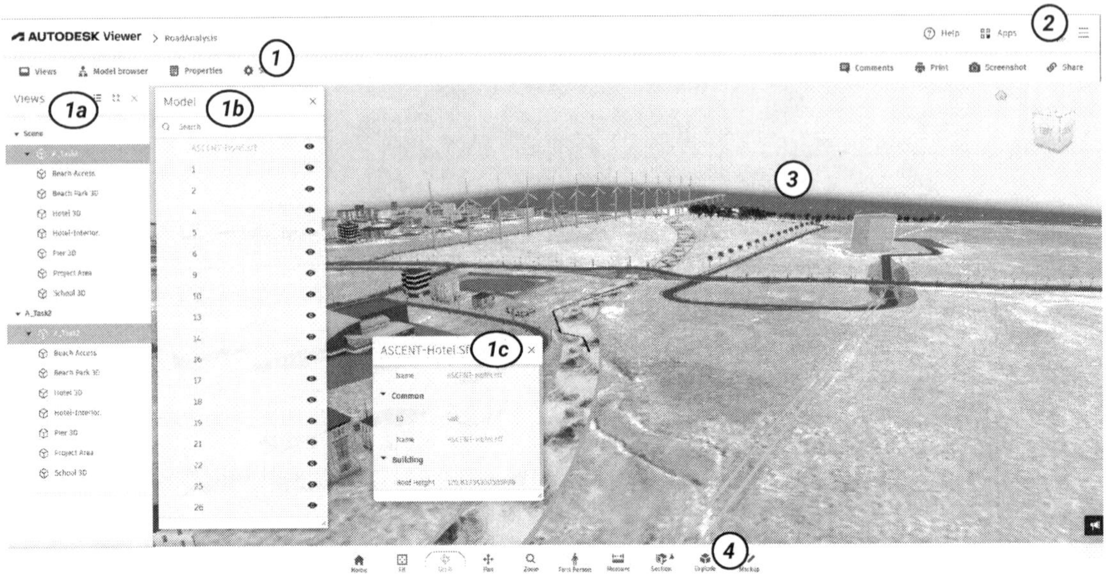

Figure 9–12

1. Panels

Multiple panels are available to help navigate, share, and analyze the model. The available panels are *Views*, *Model* browser, *Properties*, *Settings*, *Comments*, *Print*, *Screenshot*, and *Share*, and they can be accessed by selecting the tabs in the top toolbar.

1a - Views panel: Lists all the model and sheet views shared when the view link was created.

1b - Model panel: Provides control over the visibility of layers. Select the eye to toggle the layers on and off in the active view.

1c - Properties panel: Lists the properties of the currently selected object in the active view. Properties can include color, layer, linetype, material, length, and more.

2. Autodesk 360 Sign In

Sign in to your Autodesk 360 account to be able to open views and save markups.

3. Active View

The active view displays the model and proposal shared from InfraWorks.

4. Toolbar

The lower toolbar contains navigation and communication tools, as shown in Figure 9–13. The **Fit**, **Pan**, and **Zoom** tools help you quickly navigate the active view. The **Measure** and **Markup** tools help you communicate with other team members about the design.

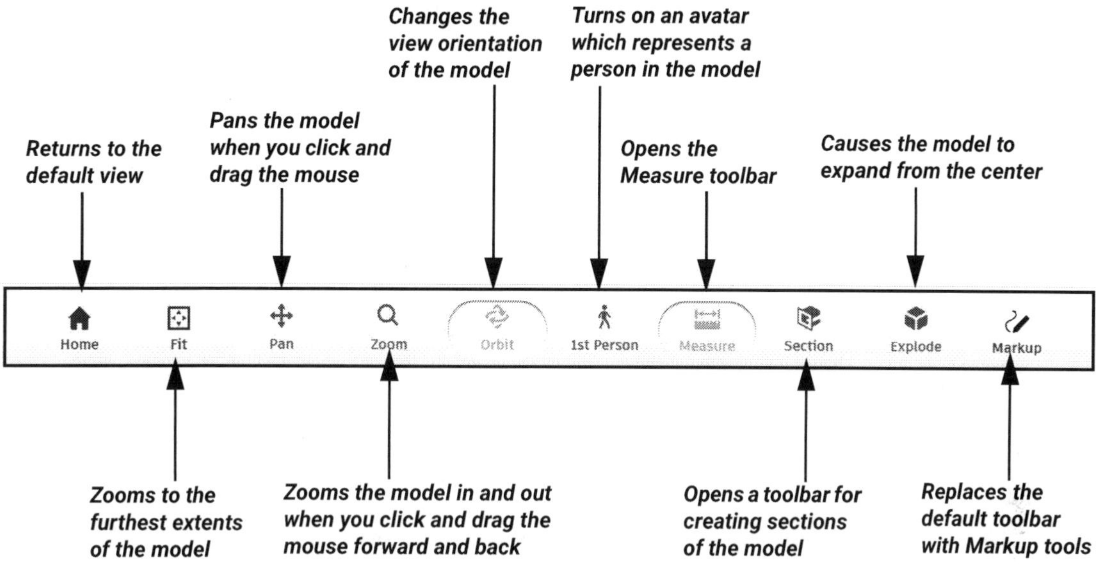

Figure 9–13

Measure and Markup

Measure

The Measure tool contains additional tools for measuring shared view objects, including distance and angle. You can also calibrate distances by placing a distance measurement and defining the distance you measured, as shown in Figure 9–14.

The following object snap options are available for more accurate measurements:

Tooltip	Osnap	Tooltip	Osnap
	Endpoint		Nearest
	Midpoint		Perpendicular

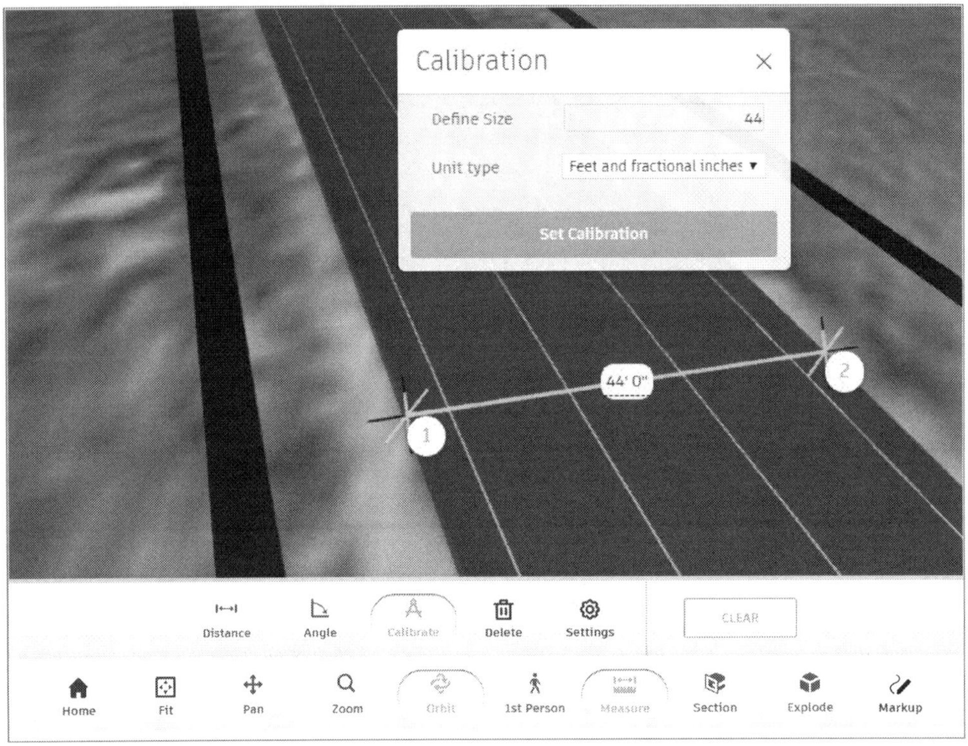

Figure 9–14

How To: Set Which Units Display

1. In the toolbar, click (Measure).
2. In the *Measure* toolbar, click (Settings).
3. In the *Settings* dialog box, select the unit type and precision, as shown in Figure 9–15.

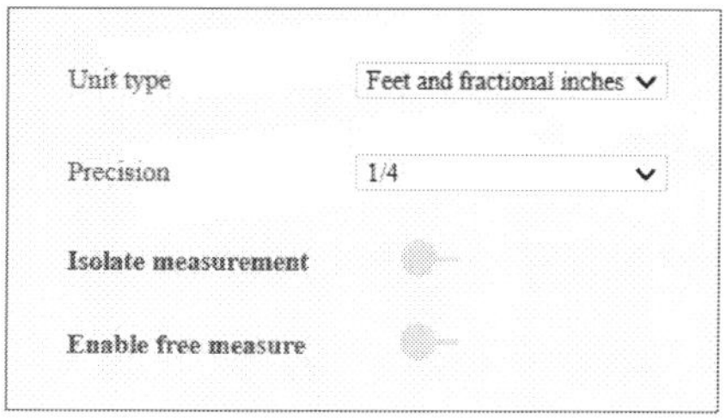

Figure 9–15

How To: Measure Objects

1. In the toolbar, click (Measure).
2. In the *Measure* toolbar, select the type of measurement you want to make: (Distance) or (Angle).
3. Click on the points you wish to measure. Note that object snaps are enabled automatically, as shown in Figure 9–16.

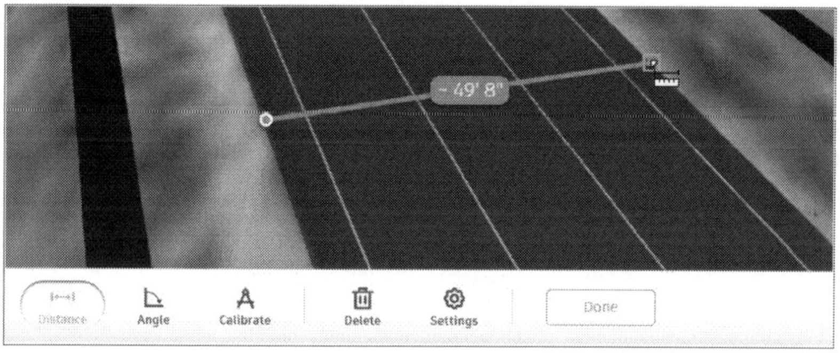

Figure 9–16

How To: Calibrate Measurements

1. In the toolbar, click (Measure).
2. In the *Measure* toolbar, click (Calibrate).

3. Click on the points you want to measure. In the *Calibration* dialog box, define the size and set the unit type, as shown in Figure 9–17. Click **Set Calibration**.

Figure 9–17

Markup

The *Markup* tools only become available when you sign into your Autodesk 360 account, as shown in Figure 9–18.

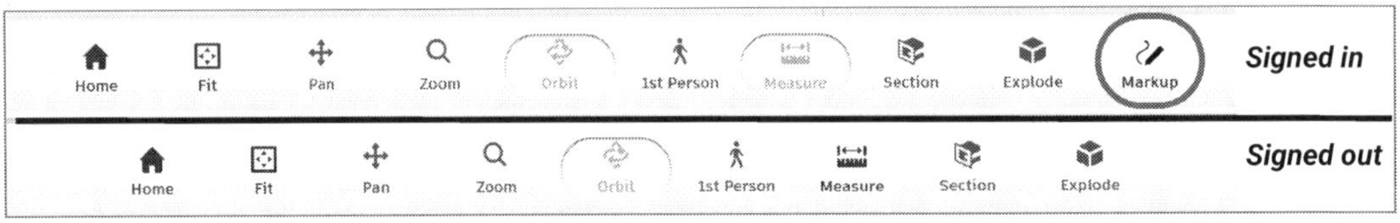

Figure 9–18

The *Markup* tools contain tools for redlining and marking up shared views, including text, arrows, clouds, etc., as shown in Figure 9–19. When you click  (Markup), the *Markup* toolbar replaces the original toolbar. Markups must be saved or canceled before the original toolbar can reappear. In order to save a markup, you must be signed in to your ***Autodesk 360*** account.

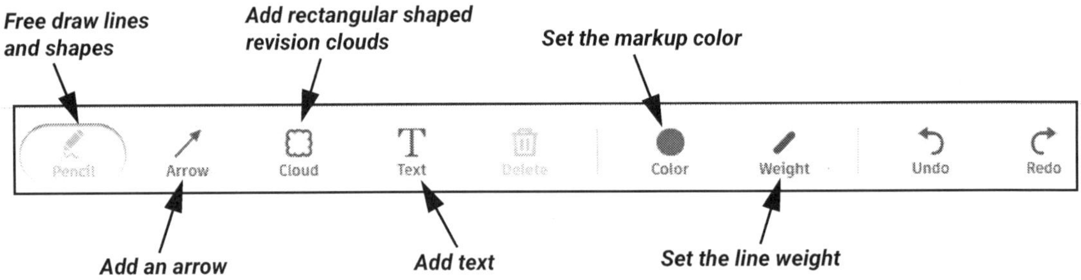

Figure 9–19

Practice 9a
Communicate the Design Using Images and Shared Views

Practice Objectives

- Communicate the design intent to stakeholders using images.
- Create shared views for stakeholders to measure and mark up.

In this practice, you will create a snapshot using a bookmark orientation. You will also render an image of the same view. The *Sun & Sky* settings were set to sunset in a previous exercise.

Task 1: Create a snapshot.

1. On the *Home* screen, click **Open**.
2. In the *InfraWorks Practice Files\9-Collaboration* folder, select **Communicate.sqlite** and click **Open**.
3. Click (Bookmarks) and select **Beach Park 3D**. Ensure that **A_Task1** is the current proposal.
4. In the toolbar, expand the *View Style* drop-down list and select **Engineering View**. Switch the view style back to **Conceptual View** and note the differences.
5. In the *Present/Share* tab>*Present* drop-down list, select (Create Snapshot).
6. In the *Camera Snapshot* dialog box, ensure that the resolution is set to the default, as shown in Figure 9–20. Click the ellipsis (...) for browsing to set the path to the *InfraWorks Practice Files\References\Images* folder and the file name for the image to **XXX-Park Entrance** (substituting **XXX** with your initials).

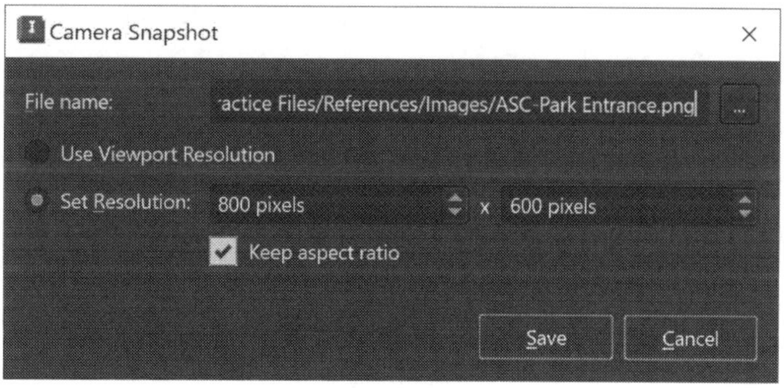

Figure 9–20

7. In the *Select image file* dialog box, expand the *Save as type* drop-down list and select the image format you require, as shown in Figure 9–21. Enter the required file name and location and click **Save**.

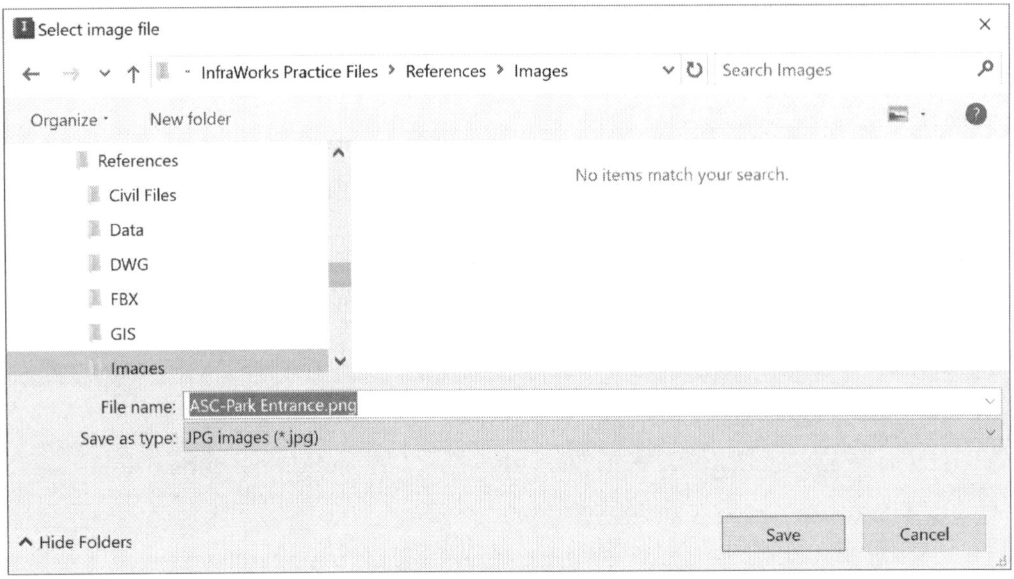

Figure 9–21

8. In the *Camera Snapshot* dialog box, click **Save**.
9. To display the image, use File Explorer to open it from the *InfraWorks Practice Files\References\Images* folder.

Task 2: Create a visual style.

1. In the toolbar, expand the *View Style* drop-down list and click **Add**.
2. Rename the new view style from *Custom View* to **Analytical View**, as shown in Figure 9–22.

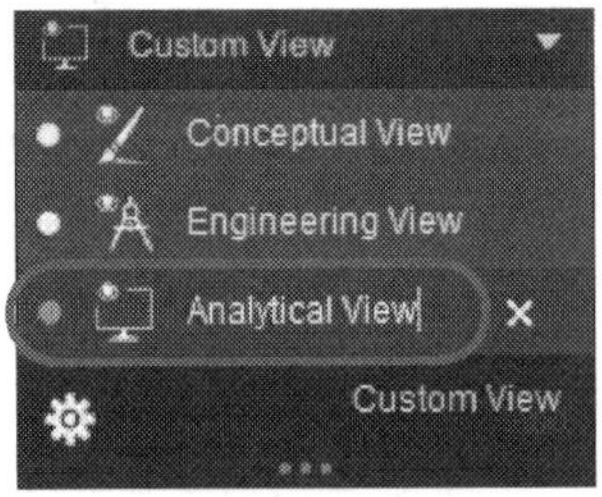

Figure 9–22

3. In the toolbar, expand the *View Style* drop-down list and click  (Configure current view).

4. In the *View Settings* asset card, in the *Visualization* stack, make the following changes, as shown in Figure 9–23:
    - Set both the *Brightness* and *Contrast* to **50**.
    - Set the *Light Intensity* to approximately **3**.
    - Toggle off **High Visual Quality**, **Animation**, and **Show Sky**.
    - Toggle on **Wireframe**.
    - Set the *Surface Opacity* to approximately **50**.

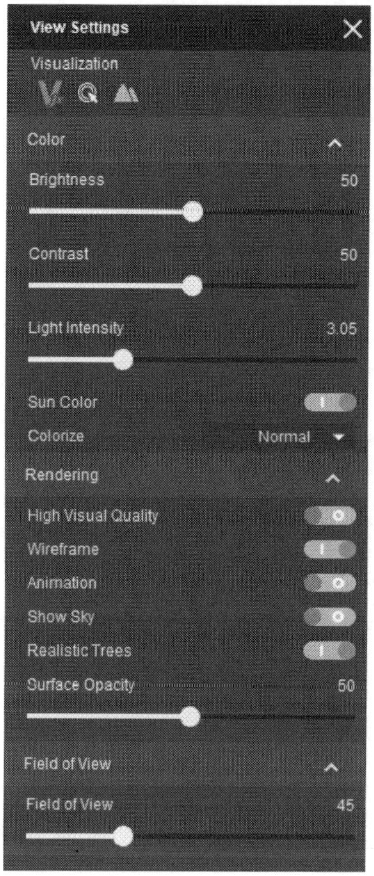

Figure 9–23

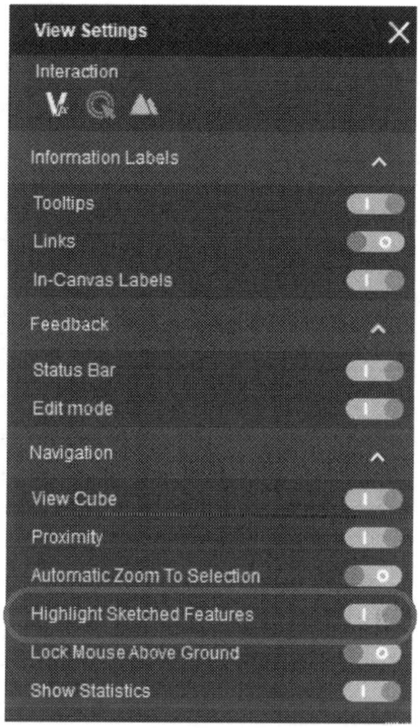

Figure 9–24

5. In the *View Settings* asset card, click  (Change navigation and application feedback settings) to open the *Interaction* stack.
6. Toggle on **Highlight Sketched Features**, as shown above in Figure 9–24.
7. In the *View Settings* asset card, click  (Change terrain view settings) to open the *Terrain* stack.

8. Ensure that **Display Contour Lines** is toggled off, as shown in Figure 9–25.

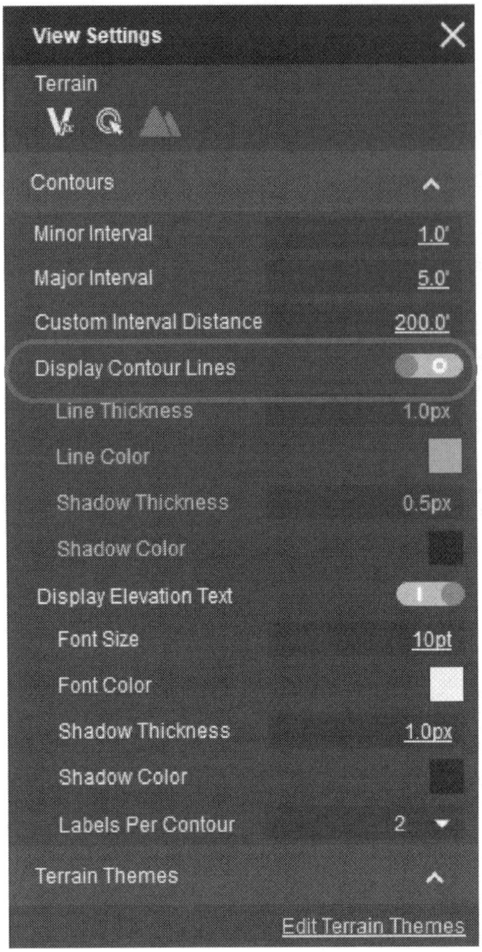

Figure 9–25

9. Close the *View Settings* asset card.
10. In the toolbar, use the *View Style* drop-down list to set the current view style back to **Conceptual View**.

Task 3: Create a shared view.

1. Click  (Shared Views) in the top-right corner of the screen to display the *Shared Views* panel.
2. Click **New Shared View**, as shown in Figure 9–26.

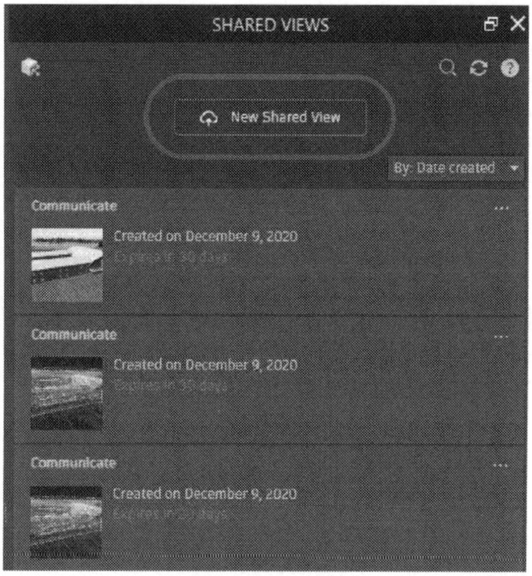

Figure 9–26

3. In the *Create a Shared View* dialog box, type **Communicate** for the name and select **Use Entire Model** for the view extents, as shown in Figure 9–27. Click **Share**.

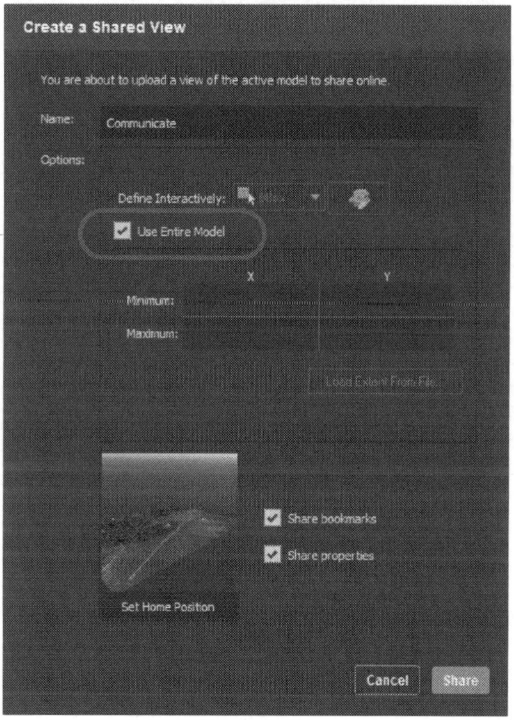

Figure 9–27

4. When the *Generating shared view...* message changes to *Uploading shared view...*, the *Create a Shared View* dialog box is displayed, as shown in Figure 9–28. Click **View in browser** to view to the model in the browser.

Figure 9–28

- Alternatively, if you closed the *Create a Shared View* dialog box, you can click  (Shared Views) again to display the *Shared View* panel. Next, click on the **Communicate** shared view that you just created, as shown in Figure 9–29.

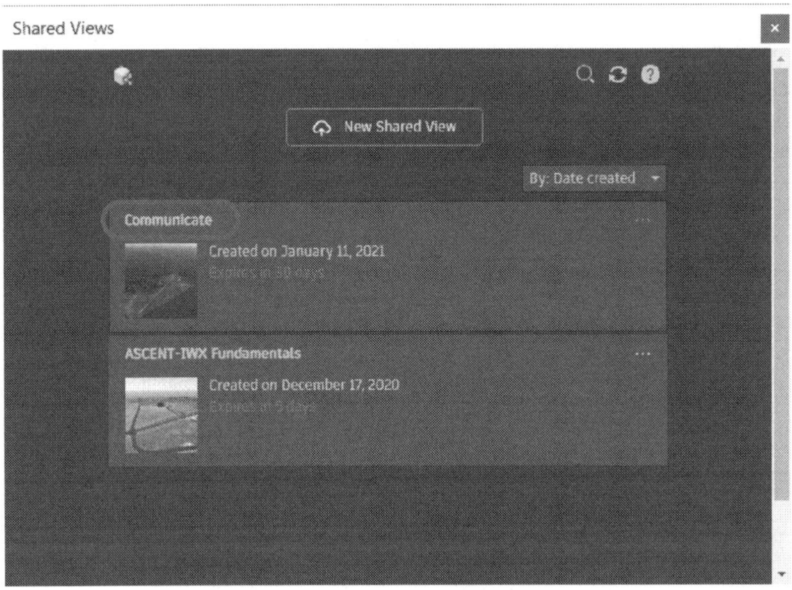

Figure 9–29

5. Click on the **Add a comment** hyperlink (the blue text), as shown in Figure 9–30, to launch the *Autodesk Viewer*.

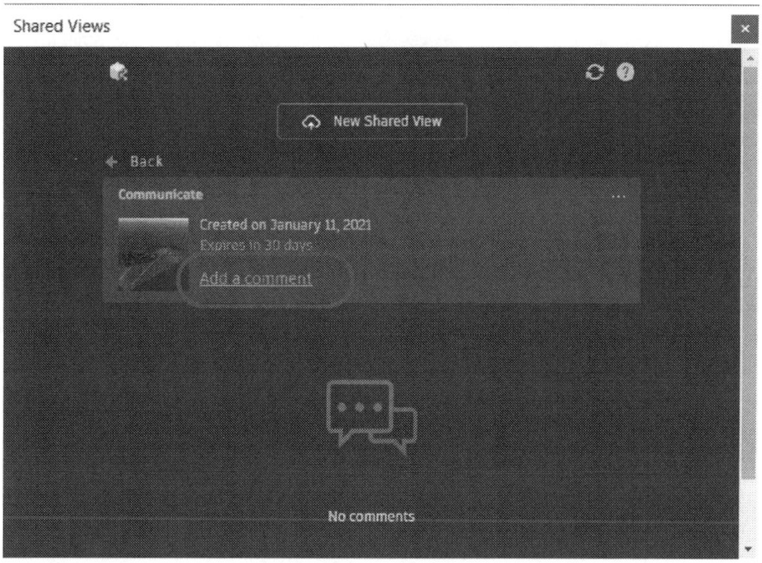

Figure 9–30

Task 4: Create a markup.

Note: *In the Autodesk Viewer, the InfraWorks bookmarks are converted to views.*

1. In the *Autodesk Viewer* toolbar, go to the *Views* tab in the upper-left corner to open the *Views* panel. Expand *Scene>A_Task1* and select the **Beach Access** view, as shown in Figure 9–31.

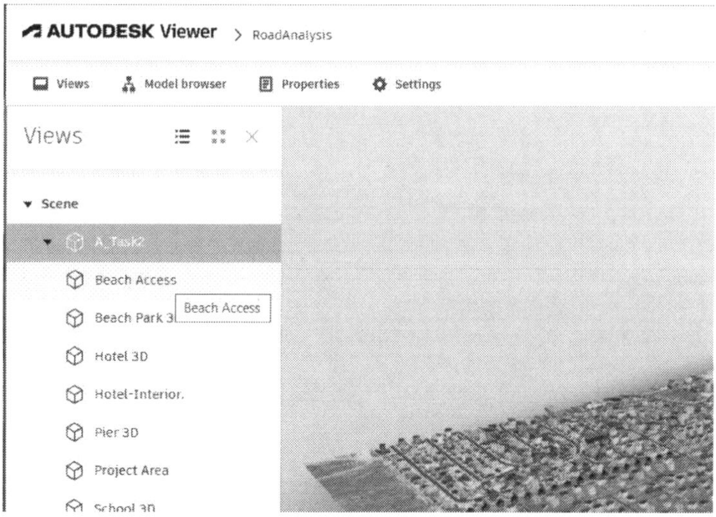

Figure 9–31

2. Using your mouse wheel, zoom in to the parking area.
3. Select **Morris Beach Blvd**. Note that the entire component road is selected, even its decorations (trees and street lights).
4. With the road still highlighted, select the *Properties* tab to open the *Properties* panel. Review the information, as shown in Figure 9–32, noting that it is all read-only. You may have to scroll to see all the information.

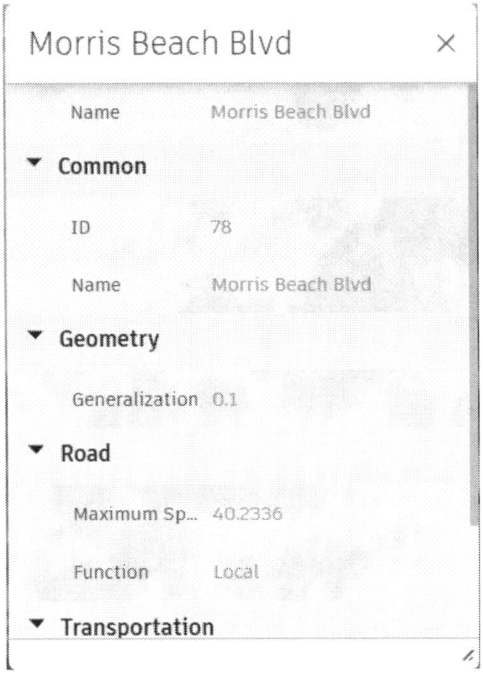

Figure 9–32

5. Close the *Properties* panel by either clicking the **X** in the upper-right corner or clicking on the *Properties* tab again.
6. Press <Esc> to deselect the road.
7. Sign in to your *Autodesk Viewer* account, if necessary. This is to be able to make markups and store them in your account.
8. Click Markup (Markup) in the lower-right corner of the screen. The interface changes to the *Create Markup* interface.
9. In the *Markup* toolbar, click T (Text).

10. Click a point to the lower right of the coffee shop, as shown in Figure 9–33. Type **Permit required for Coffee Shop?.** Adjust the text box as required to see all the text.

Figure 9–33

11. In the *Markup* toolbar, click ↗ (Arrow) and add an arrow pointing from the text box to the coffee shop, as shown in Figure 9–34.

Figure 9–34

12. In the *Markup* toolbar, click (Cloud) and add a cloud, as shown in Figure 9–35.

Figure 9–35

13. Click **Save** in the upper-right corner to make your markups available to others with the view link.
14. Close the *Autodesk Viewer*.
15. Back in InfraWorks, close the *Shared Views* panel.

End of practice

9.3 Working with Storyboards

Storyboards are a collection of views or keyframes that are combined together in a slide show to tell a compelling story about the design. The keyframes in a storyboard are generated from animations. These animations are either Path or Camera animations. Still images can also be incorporated using a Still Motion Camera animation.

Using storyboards, you can simulate driving through the model, get a birds-eye view of the model, or explore the model. Figure 9–36 shows the Storyboard palette.

Figure 9–36

- **Storyboard Name:** Displays the name of the current storyboard and enables you to edit the name as required.
- **Timeline:** Indicates when specific elements display and how long they remain in the view before changing to the next element.
- **Storyboard Tools:** Contains tools for creating elements and managing the storyboard.
- **Keyframe Settings:** Provides settings that can be specified for the active (selected) keyframe element.

Working with the Timeline

The Timeline identifies the sequence of the keyframes and details approximately how long each keyframe displays in the presentation. Keyframes can be an image, camera animation, or path animation.

Figure 9–37 shows a storyboard timeline and describes its contents. You can drag and drop keyframes to new locations in the timeline to change the order in which they display. You can also drag the right side of a keyframe to change its duration.

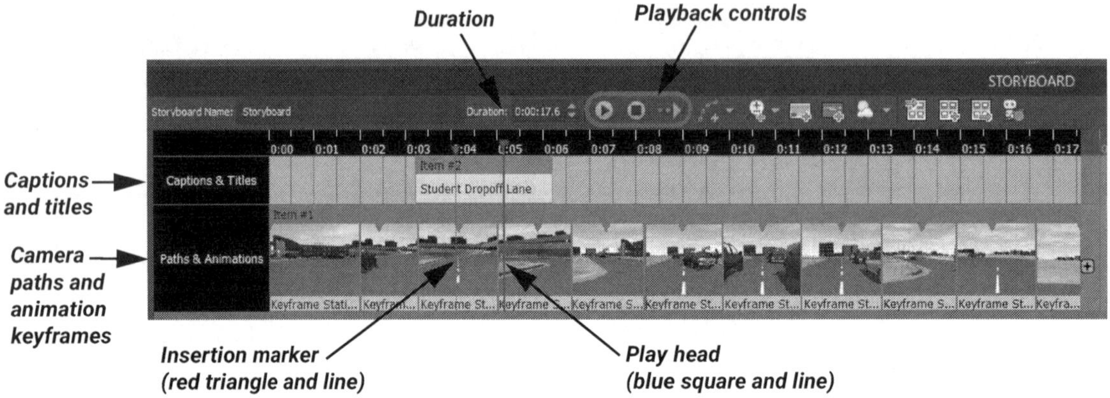

Figure 9–37

- **Play head (blue square and line):** Indicates where play stops and resumes during playback. Double-click on the timeline to move the play head to a specific location.
- **Duration:** Lists the total time (i.e., from start to finish) of the storyboard.
- **Playback controls:** Starts and stops the presentation at the play head location. It also enables you to control whether the model view follows the storyboard position.
- **Captions and titles:** Enables you to label specific views in the model to draw attention to points of interest.
- **Camera paths and animation keyframes:** Thumbnails used to indicate what is presented at specific times along the timeline. You can drag and drop the thumbnails to change their order or duration.
- **Insertion marker (red triangle and line):** Indicates where new elements display in the model when you add them. Click and drag the insertion marker to a location in the timeline to insert the next storyboard feature.

Playback Controls

The following playback controls can help you to view and navigate through the presentation.

Icon	Description
 (Play/Pause)	Starts playing the storyboard from the location of the play head. Once in Play mode, the button displays as a pause button, which enables you to stop the animation without moving the play head from its current position in the timeline.
 (Stop)	Stops playing the storyboard and causes the play head to return to its original position in the timeline.
 (Story Follow)	Causes the model view to change according to the current keyframe being played in the storyboard.

Adding Keyframes

The keyframes in a storyboard are generated from animations, which are either Path or Camera animations. In each animation category, there are multiple animation types. All of the path and camera animation types are added from the *Storyboard* palette, as shown in Figure 9–38.

Path animations

Camera animations

Figure 9–38

Path Animations

Path animations can be used to automatically create a series of camera positions/angles along a path. There are three path animation options:

- **Add Camera Path Animation:** Creates a series of views starting at one view, which is manually set, and ending at another view, which is also manually set.
- **Import a Camera Path:** Imports a saved path, which is found in a point feature file (e.g., .DB, .SHP, .SDF, or .SQLITE files).
- **Create from Component Road:** Creates a path along the centerline of a component road.

Hint: Create from Component Road

When you create a path animation from a component road, you can set the horizontal and vertical offsets for both the camera and the target. You can also set the speed, direction of travel, and keyframe density, as shown in Figure 9–39.

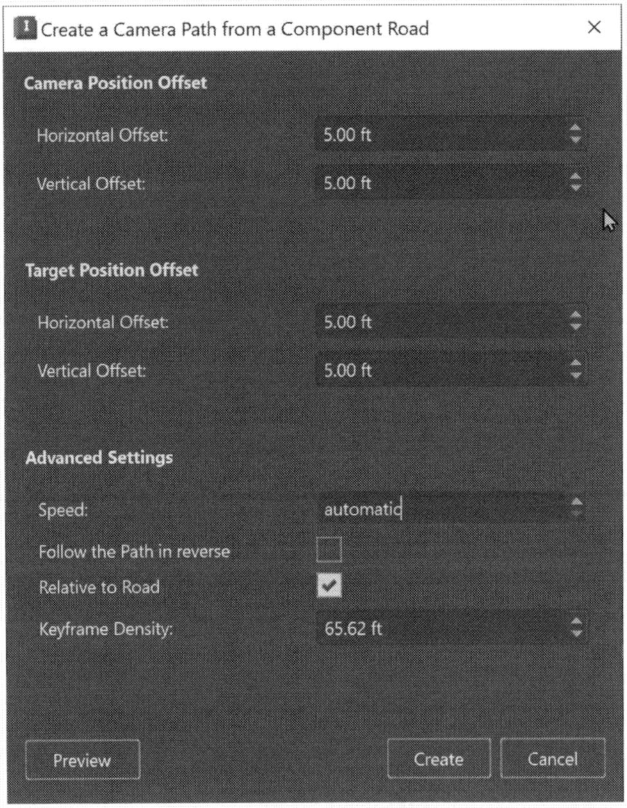

Figure 9–39

Camera Animations

Camera animations start the transition from a specific camera view and end at another camera view, which is determined by the storyboard keyframe settings. There are eight camera animation options:

- **Crane Animation:** Moves the camera up and away from or down and towards the camera view.
- **Look Around Animation:** Rotates the view while the camera remains in a fixed position.
- **Orbit Animation:** The camera rotates around a fixed focal point in the shape of a sphere.
- **Pan and Zoom Animation:** The camera pans and zooms simultaneously. The effect is a zooming motion along a path that is determined by distance values and zoom percentages.
- **Recorded Walk:** The camera jumps directly to a shot and then plays a recording that you create. It highlights specific design elements from set angles, rather than by panning or zooming.
- **Still Motion:** Transitions the camera to a still motion shot. The camera does not move for the duration of this shot.
- **Track Animation:** Moves the camera to the left or right of the original camera view.
- **Zoom Animation:** The camera moves closer to or further away from the original focal point of the camera view.

Keyframe Settings

Each keyframe that you add to a storyboard has its own set of properties that can be set to control how the camera moves in the model. Figure 9–40 shows the settings for a Look Around camera animation keyframe.

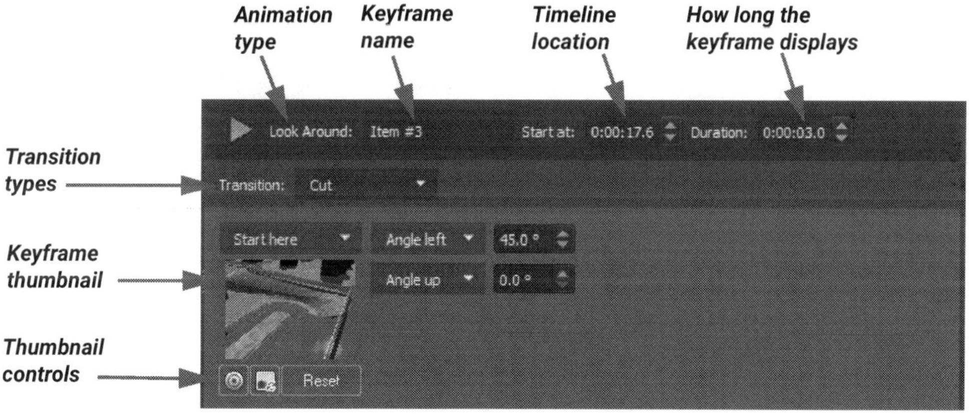

Figure 9–40

The following are areas of the keyframe settings that are used in multiple animation types.

- **Animation Type:** Lists the type of animation that was used to create the keyframe.
- **Transition Types:** Enables you to set the transition type when entering and exiting the keyframe. There are three transition types:
  - **Cut:** Moves directly to the current keyframe view.
  - **Fade from black:** After the previous keyframe, the view displays as black. It then fades into the current keyframe over a duration that you set using the setting to the right of the *Transition* drop-down list, as shown in Figure 9–41.

Figure 9–41

  - **Fade from white:** After the previous keyframe, the view displays as white. It then fades into the current keyframe over a duration that you set using the setting to the right of the *Transition* drop-down list.
- **Thumbnail Controls:** Enables you to change the model view or thumbnail view. The following options are available for all of the animation types:
  -  **(Go To Location):** Quickly sets the model view to be the location of the thumbnail.
  -  **(Refresh):** Refreshes the thumbnail of the keyframe from the current scene content.
  - **Reset:** Changes the keyframe view to the current model view.

How To: Add a Path Animation

> ***Note:*** *This procedure uses the Camera Path animation as an example. The process is similar for the other path animations.*

1. In the *Storyboard* palette, move the insertion marker (red triangle and line) to the location on the timeline where you want to insert the new path animation.
2. Navigate to the view that you want to use as the starting point of the animation.

3. In the *Storyboard* palette, expand the *Camera Animations* drop-down list and click 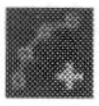 (Add Camera Path Animation), as shown in Figure 9–42.

Figure 9–42

- Note that the first keyframe displays as a thumbnail in the timeline, as shown in Figure 9–43.

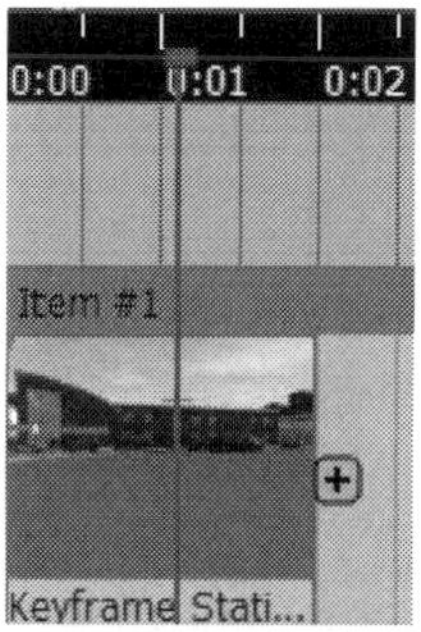

Figure 9–43

4. In the *Keyframe* settings, in the *Transition* and *Camera Focal Point* drop-down lists and for *Camera speed control*, set the options as shown in Figure 9–44. The settings displayed are applied to the currently selected keyframe.

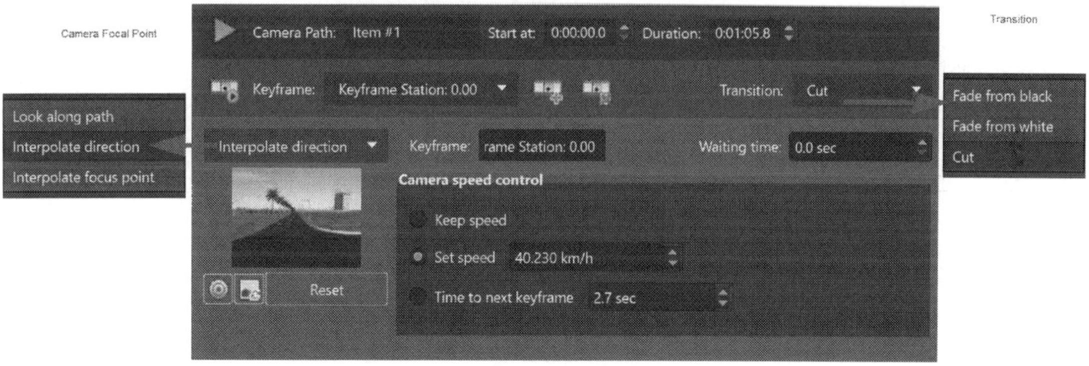

Figure 9–44

> **Hint: Camera Path Settings**
>
> You can select one of three focal points for the camera view, set the camera speed, and determine the type of transition. The *Camera Focal Point* drop-down list contains options for setting the camera to **Look Along Path**, **Interpolate Direction**, or **Interpolate Focus Point**. The *Camera speed control* options enable you to keep the camera speed as it is set by the current start time and duration, set a specific speed, or set the time until the next keyframe.

5. In the model, navigate to the required view to prepare the next keyframe in the camera path.
6. In the storyboard timeline, click (Add Keyframe) to the right of the first keyframe's thumbnail.
7. Repeat Steps 4 to 6 to add additional camera positions to extend the path, as required.

How To: Create a Camera Animation

> **Note:** *This procedure uses the Pan and Zoom animation as an example. The process is similar for the other camera animations.*

1. In the *Storyboard* palette, move the insertion marker (red triangle and line) to the location on the timeline where you want to insert the new camera animation.
2. Navigate to the view that you want to use as the starting point of the animation.
3. In the *Storyboard* palette, expand the *Camera Animations* drop-down list and click (Add Pan and Zoom Animation), as shown in Figure 9–45.

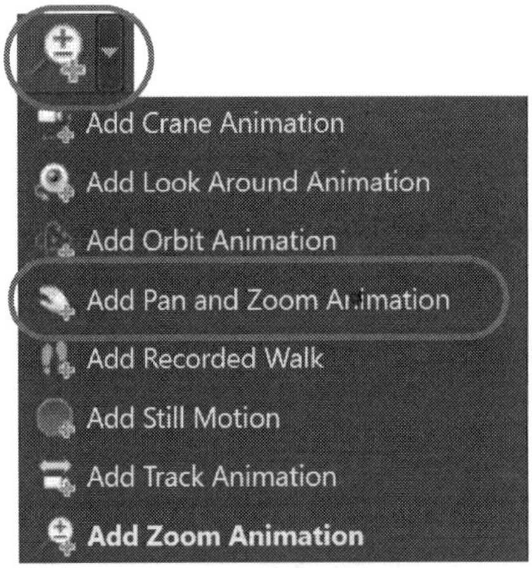

Figure 9–45

4. In the keyframe settings, set the options in the *Transition*, *Distance*, and *Zoom* drop-down lists, as shown in Figure 9–46. The settings apply to the currently selected keyframe.

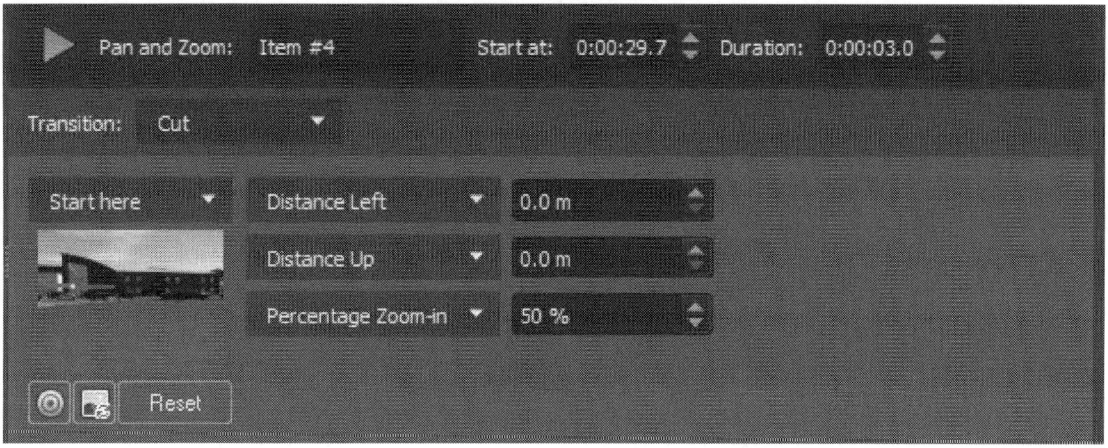

Figure 9–46

Add Captions and Titles

Captions and titles are located in the *Storyboard* palette. These tools enable you to place labels, text, and images into multiple keyframes in the storyboard. An example of a caption is shown in Figure 9–47.

Figure 9–47

Captions

Captions are labels that overlay keyframes in the storyboard presentation. You can add multiple captions, which become stacked vertically based on their assigned location. Click  (Add a new Caption) to create a caption in the model view. Use the caption settings to edit the caption's text, font, size, and transition settings.

Titles

Titles can include text and images to introduce the entire story or individual chapters of the story, or to display credits and acknowledgments. Click (Add a new Title) to create a caption in the model view. Use the caption settings to edit the title's text, font, size, and transition settings.

Reusing Storyboards

If a storyboard is created in another model, you can reuse it by importing it into the current model. All of the camera positions and transitions from the previous model remain the same, but the current model's elements display in the keyframes.

- **(Export Current Storyboard):** Creates a .JSON file for sharing storyboards between Autodesk InfraWorks models.
- **(Import Existing Storyboards):** Imports a .JSON file from another model.

Create and Share Storyboard Videos

Storyboards are most useful when you can share them with others. Unfortunately, most stakeholders do not have the Autodesk InfraWorks software. Exporting a storyboard to a video enables anyone to display the presentation. Storyboards can be exported to a number of different encoders. You can also use any DirectShow compatible encoders that are installed on your computer. The encoders that can be used when creating a video are as follows:

Format	Properties
Uncompressed Video	A generic .AVI format that does not have any properties that can be specified.
Windows Media® Video	Video compression format developed by Microsoft. You can select Windows Video Media 9 or Windows Video Media 9 Advanced Profile in Properties and set the bit rate (kilobits per second).
DV Video Encoder	An .AVI format that encodes an uncompressed video stream into digital video (DV). You can set the video format, DV format, and resolution in Properties. Video formats include: • NTSC (National Television System Committee standard) • PAL (Phase Alternating Line)
MJPEG Compressor	An .AVI format that compresses an uncompressed video stream using motion JPEG compression. It does not have any properties that can be specified.

How To: Record a Video

1. To create a video from a storyboard, in the *Storyboard* palette, click  (Export Storyboard to Video).
2. In the *Export Storyboard* dialog box (shown in Figure 9–48), select the required encoder, file name, frame rate, and resolution.

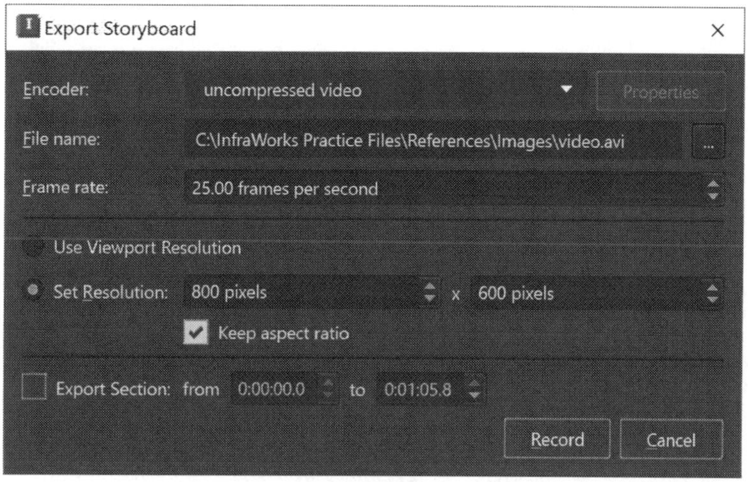

Figure 9–48

3. Click **Record**.

Additional Storyboard Tools

Additional storyboard tools are used to create and manage storyboards and control the display of the timeline. The following tools are available:

Icon	Description
 (Add New Storyboard)	Creates a new, empty storyboard.
 (Zoom Out/In)	Zooms the timeline to display a longer or shorter presentation duration in the timeline viewing area.
 (Zoom Resolution)	Sets the amount of time by which the timeline zooms in and out.
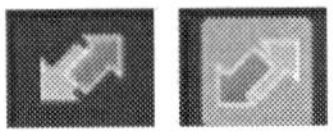 (Hide/Show Item Detail)	Displays or hides details connected to the currently selected item in the timeline viewing area.
 (Hide/Show Storyboard Library)	Displays a list of storyboards associated with the current model and their duration.

Practice 9b
Communicate the Design Using a Storyboard

Practice Objective

- Communicate the design intent to stakeholders using a storyboard.

In this practice, you will add path and camera animations to create a storyboard.

Task 1: Create a storyboard.

In this task, you will create a presentation to show how people can access **Morris Beach** in the proposed parking area and lawn area. You will use a camera path animation to simulate driving up to the drop-off location. You will then add camera path animations to get a bird's eye view of the area. If you do not have enough time, you can see the end result called **ASC-Beach Access** in the storyboard library.

1. On the *Home* screen, click **Open**.
2. In the *InfraWorks Practice Files\9-Collaboration* folder, select **Communicate.sqlite** and click **Open**.
3. Click (Bookmarks) and select **Beach Access**.
4. In the toolbar, ensure that **A_Task1** is the current proposal and **Conceptual View** is the current view style.
5. In the *Present/Share* tab>*Present* panel, select (Storyboard Creator).
6. If a blank storyboard is not available, in the *Storyboard* palette, click (Add New Storyboard).
7. In the *Storyboard* palette, in the top-left corner, rename the new storyboard as **XXX-Beach Access** (substituting **XXX** with your initials).
8. Click (Bookmarks) and select **Beach-1**.

9. In the *Storyboard* palette, click  (Add Camera Path Animation). The first view displays as a thumbnail in the timeline, as shown in Figure 9–49. The default duration is 3 seconds.

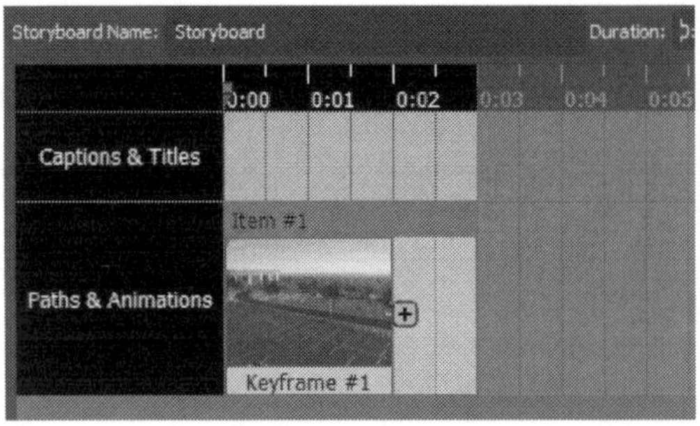

Figure 9–49

10. In the *Keyframe* settings, do the following, as shown in Figure 9–50:
    - Expand the *Transition* drop-down list and select **Cut**.
    - Expand the *Camera Focal Point* drop-down list and select **Interpolate direction**.
    - Set the *Camera speed control* to **Time to next keyframe** and set it to **8.0 sec** (this determines the speed for the whole path animation).

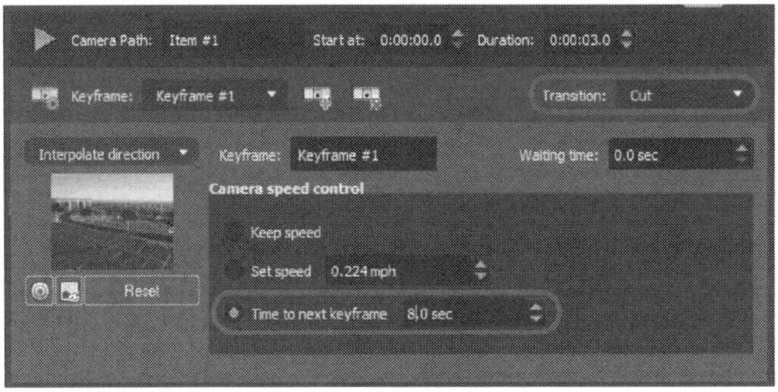

Figure 9–50

11. Click  (Bookmarks) and select **Beach-2**.

12. In the *Storyboard* timeline, click (Add Keyframe), as shown in Figure 9–51.

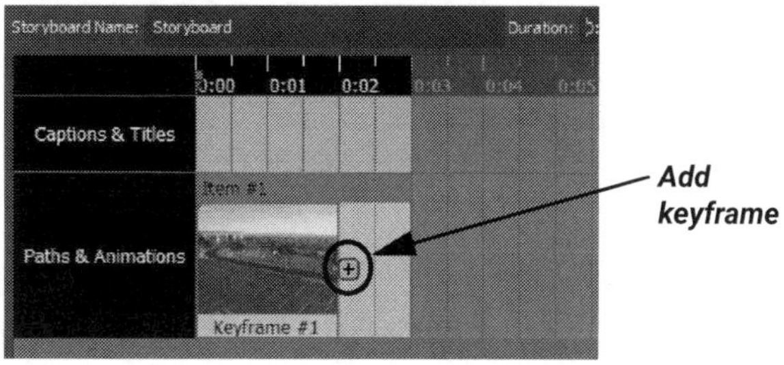

Figure 9–51

13. Repeat Steps 11 and 12 to add more camera positions and extend the path. Bookmarks have been created that will enable you to quickly move from one view to another along the path a car should follow to pick up students. Use the bookmarks in sequential order (Beach-3, Beach-4, etc.,). Note that the time interval changes because the speed remains constant.

14. When you have finished, the last keyframe view and the timeline should display as shown in Figure 9–52. The camera path animation (Item #1) consists of these seven keyframes.

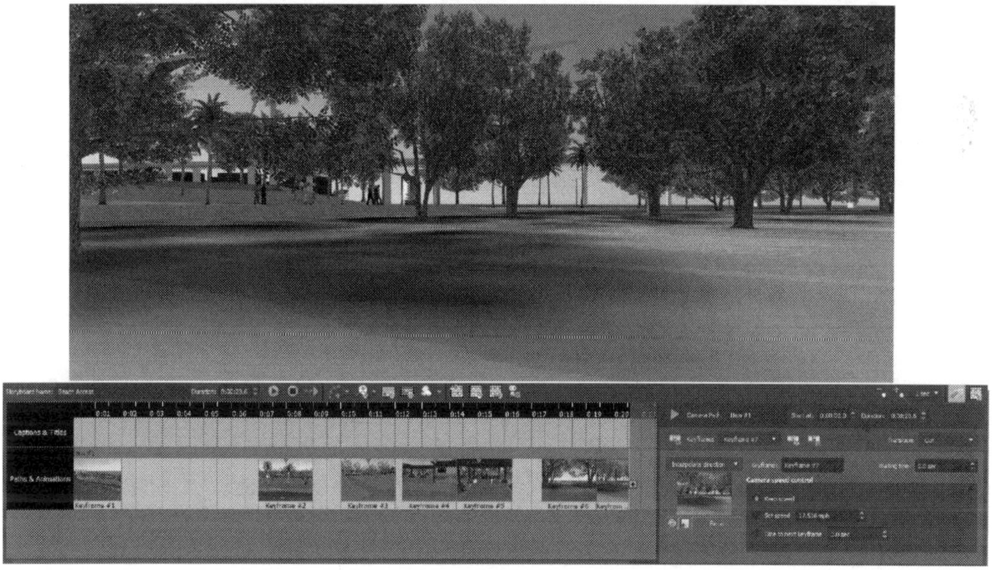

Figure 9–52

15. Move the insertion marker (red line) to the end of the storyboard. You may have to use the sliders at the bottom to move to the beginning to select the red line.

16. In the *Storyboard* palette, expand the *Camera Animations* drop-down list and click (Add Pan and Zoom Animation). The timeline displays as shown in Figure 9–53. This keyframe sets the camera to pan and zoom simultaneously.

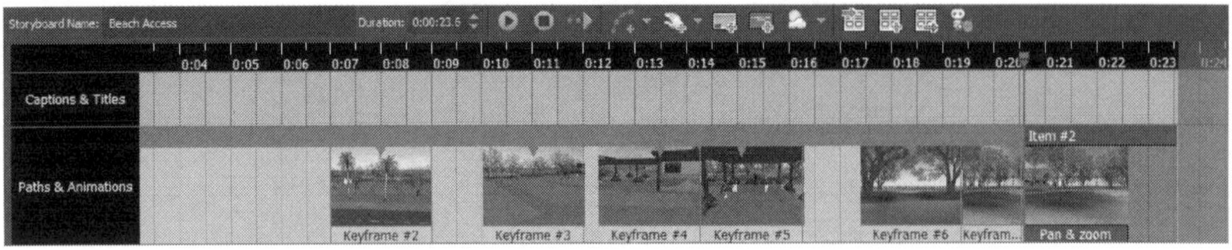

Figure 9–53

17. Ensure that the last keyframe is selected. In the *Keyframe* settings, do the following (as shown in Figure 9–54):
    - Select **Distance Right** and type **55** for the distance measurement.
    - Select **Distance Up** and type **55** for the distance measurement.
    - Select **Percentage Zoom-out** and set it to **50%**.

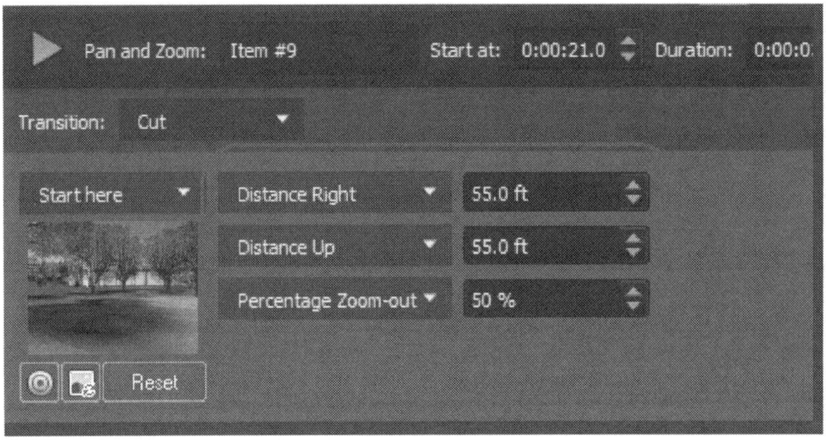

Figure 9–54

18. In the *Keyframe* settings, click to preview the keyframe. Make any changes you deem necessary and continue preview the changes until you are satisfied.

19. In the *Storyboard* palette, click (Play the current storyboard) to play the entire storyboard.

20. Move the insertion marker (red line) to the end of the storyboard.

21. In the *Storyboard* palette, expand the *Camera Animations* drop-down list and click  (Add Crane Animation). The timeline displays as shown in Figure 9–55.

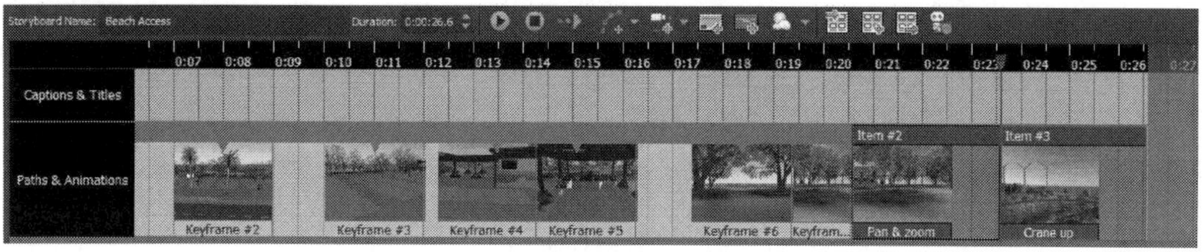

Figure 9–55

22. In the *Keyframe* settings, do the following (as shown in Figure 9–56):

- Set the *Duration* to **8.0** sec.
- Set the *Distance Up* to **50**.
- Set the *Distance Back* to **100**.
- Select **Distance Left** and type **400** for the distance measurement.
- Select the **Lock camera on center-of-interest** option.

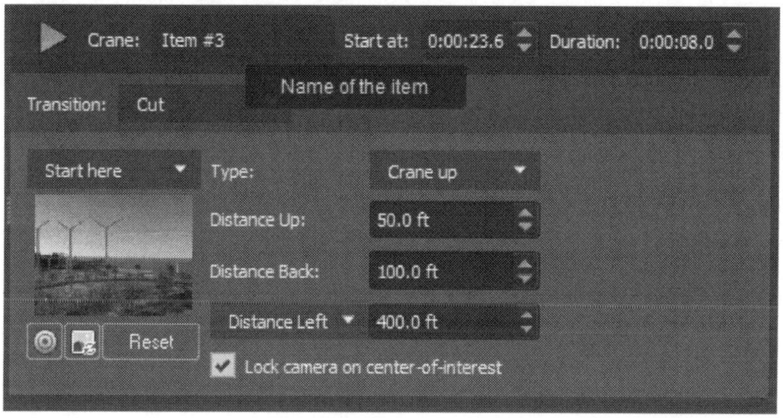

Figure 9–56

23. Move the insertion marker (red line) to the end of the storyboard.

24. In the *Storyboard* palette, expand the *Camera Animations* drop-down list and click 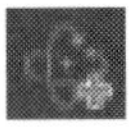 (Add Orbit Animation). The timeline displays as shown in Figure 9–57.

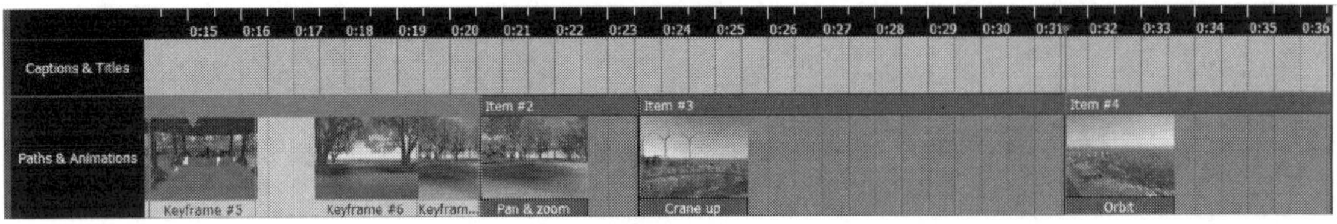

Figure 9–57

25. In the *Keyframe* settings, do the following (as shown in Figure 9–58):
    - Set the *Duration* to **5.0** sec.
    - Select **Angle left** and type **120** for the angle measurement.
    - Select **Ange up** and type **0** for the angle measurement.

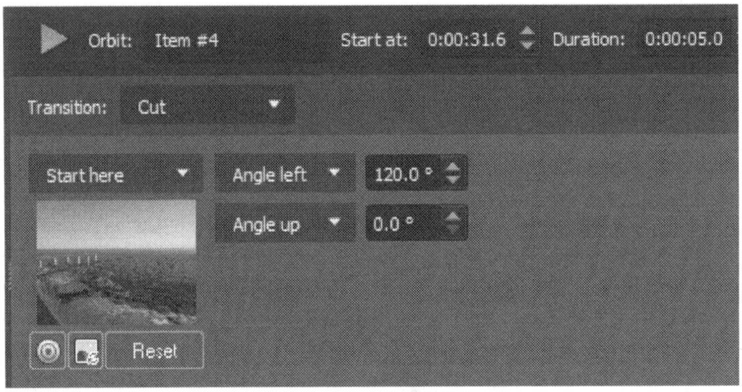

Figure 9–58

26. Move the insertion marker (red line) to the beginning of the storyboard.
27. In the *Storyboard* palette, click  (Play the current storyboard).
28. Move the insertion marker (red line) to the end of **Item #2** (Pan & zoom).
29. In the *Storyboard* palette, click  (Add Caption).
30. In the *Caption* settings, do the following (as shown in Figure 9–59):
    - Set the *Duration* to **8.0** sec.
    - Set the font size to **32.0 pt**.
    - Replace the *Your Caption* text with **Morris Beach Park**.
    - Slide the caption to start around **27** sec.

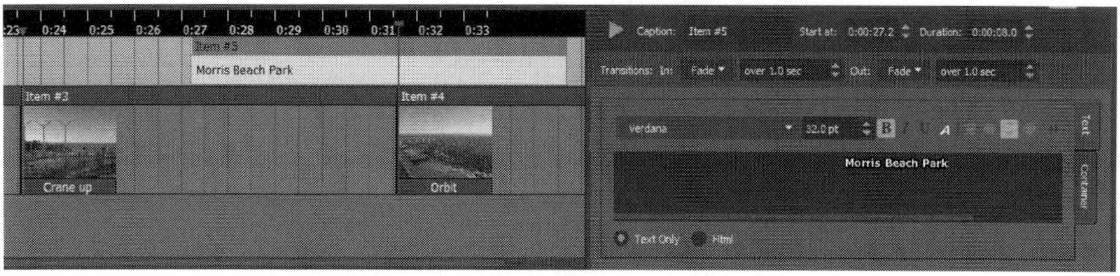

Figure 9–59

31. Move the insertion marker (red line) to the beginning of the storyboard.

32. In the *Storyboard* palette, click (Play the current storyboard).

Task 2: Export the storyboard to video.

1. In the *Storyboard* palette, click (Export Storyboard to Video).
2. In the *Export Storyboard* dialog box, next to the *File name* field, click the ellipsis (...) for browsing.
3. In the *Select Video File* dialog box, browse to the *InfraWorks Practice Files\References\Images* folder and enter **XXX-MorrisBeach** as the file name (substituting **XXX** with your initials).
4. Click **Save**.
5. In the *Export Storyboard* dialog box, click **Record**.
6. Using Windows® Media Player®, open and play the video you just created.

Task 3: Create a storyboard from a component road.

If you have component roads in your model, you can create a storyboard much quicker than the process used in the first task. In this task, you will create a new storyboard and use the **Morris Beach Blvd** component road to create a path animation.

> ***Note:*** *If you do not have enough time, you can see the end result called* ***ASC-Morris Beach Blvd*** *in the storyboard library.*

1. Click (Bookmarks) and select **Beach Access**.
2. In the *Storyboard* palette, in the top-right corner, click (Show Storyboard Library).

3. In the *Storyboard Library* pane, right-click and select **Add new Storyboard**, as shown in Figure 9–60.

Figure 9–60

4. In the *Storyboard* palette, rename the new storyboard as **XXX-Morris Beach Blvd** (substituting **XXX** with your initials).
5. In the *Storyboard* palette, expand 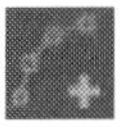 (Add Camera Path Animation) and select **Create from Component Road**.
6. In the model, select the **Morris Beach Blvd** component road, as shown in Figure 9–61.

Figure 9–61

7. In the *Create a Camera Path from a Component Road* dialog box, set the following (as shown in Figure 9–62):
   - *Camera Position Offset, Horizontal Offset*: **5**
   - *Camera Position Offset, Vertical Offset*: **5**
   - *Target Position Offset, Horizontal Offset*: **5**

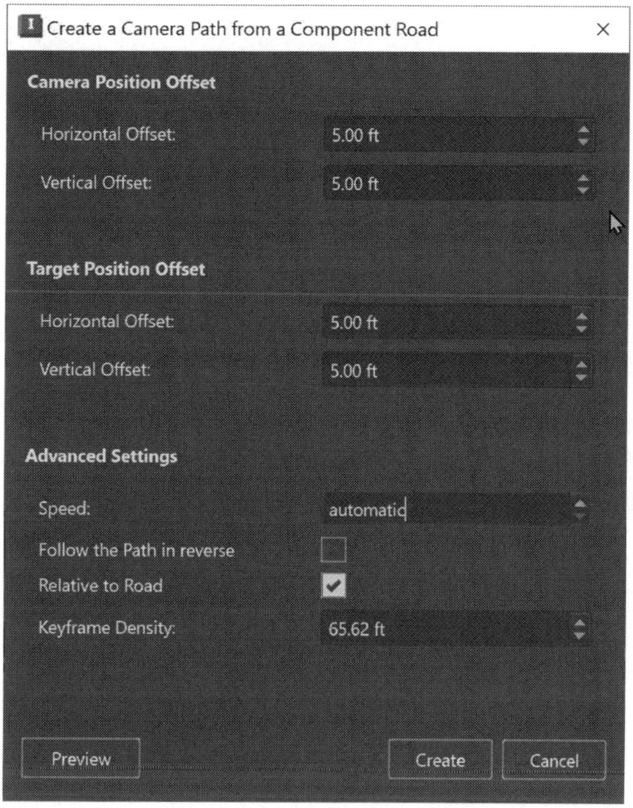

Figure 9–62

8. Click **Create**.

9. In the *Storyboard* palette, click (Play the current storyboard). The storyboard should look similar to the one shown in Figure 9–63.

Figure 9–63

End of practice

Chapter Review Questions

1. When creating snapshots, in which file format can the images be saved?
   a. JPG images (*.JPG)
   b. PNG images (*.PNG)
   c. TIFF images (*.TIF)
   d. All of the above

2. How do you share your design with someone who does not have InfraWorks and enable them to measure it, mark it up, and send back valuable electronic feedback?
   a. This is not possible without installing InfraWorks.
   b. Print a .DWF and have them use Autodesk Design Review.
   c. Share views and have them provide feedback in the *Autodesk Viewer* browser.
   d. Take screen shots of the design and email them.

3. When adding a title to a storyboard, which of the following can be included?
   a. Text only
   b. Text and an image
   c. An image only

4. Which camera animation would you use to move the camera up and away from the current view?
   a. Look Around Animation
   b. Still Motion
   c. Crane Animation
   d. Zoom Animation

5. Which of the following is not a transition option?
    a. Fade from Center
    b. Cut
    c. Fade to Black
    d. Fade to White

6. Which of the following can be used as keyframes in a storyboard? (Select all that apply.)
    a. Snapshots
    b. Rendered images
    c. Path animations
    d. Camera animations

Command Summary

Button	Command	Location
	**Change terrain view settings**	• ***View Settings*** **asset card**
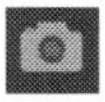	**Create Snapshot**	• **Toolbar:** *Present/Share* tab>*Present* drop-down list
	**Shared Views**	• **Toolbar**
	**Storyboard Creator**	• **Toolbar:** *Present/Share* tab>*Present* panel
	**Storyboard Player**	• **Toolbar:** *Present/Share* tab>*Present* panel

Appendix A

Road Tools

Once you have created a component road, it is important to analyze it to ensure that it meets the design criteria. In this appendix, you will learn how to analyze sight distances and improve traffic flows through detailed interchanges. You will also learn how to calculate quantities and eventually balance cut and fill quantities for the design using cloud-based optimization tools.

Learning Objectives

- Add traffic movement to your project by running a traffic simulation.
- Import a Civil 3D corridor.
- Identify the best horizontal location for a new roadway by running a corridor optimization.
- Calculate earthwork and material quantities for a roadway.
- Balance a component road's cut and fill values by running a vertical optimization.
- Analyze a roadway and intersection for sight distance obstructions.

A.1 Traffic Simulation

The *Traffic Simulation* module provides a way to run a traffic study of the project using a cloud-based traffic engine. Since it is cloud-based, the model must be published to the cloud before a simulation can be run.

Once a model is published, the *Traffic Simulation* module can generate an animation file based on traffic demand. Traffic can include all modes of transportation, not just private vehicles. During the traffic study, the following can be defined:

- Demand matrices
- Profiles
- Vehicle types
- Driver types

The animation files that are created can be played in the model, adding traffic movement to your project. Additionally, traffic analysis results can be displayed as infographics in the model, as shown in Figure A–1. Color coded queue lengths, which are based on demand, display in the traffic study area for each component road intersection.

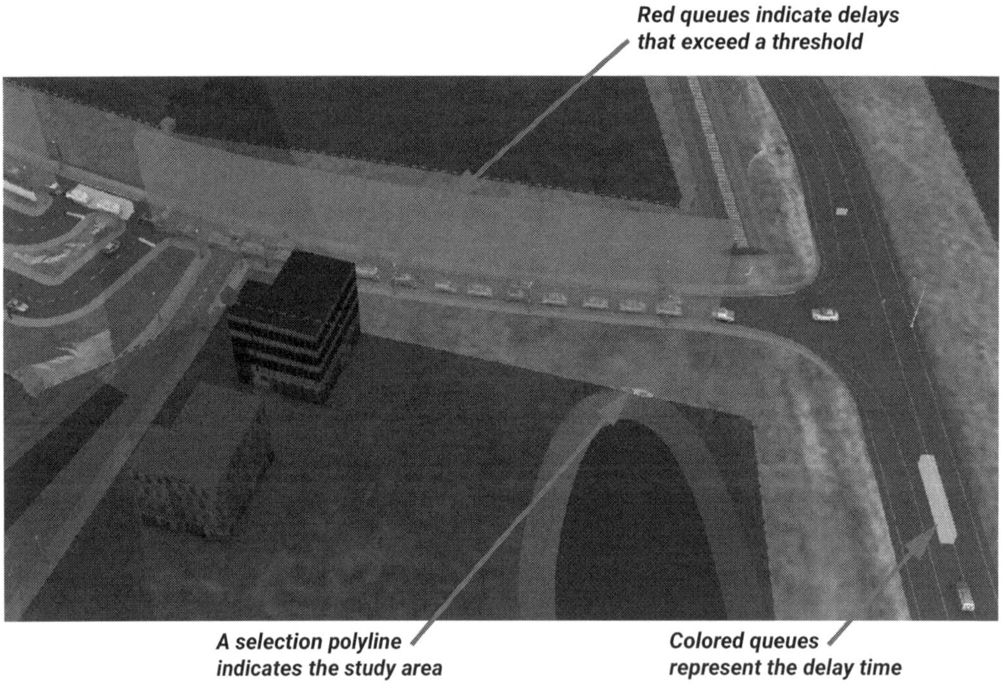

Figure A–1

Hint: Java Runtime Environment

The **Traffic Simulation Analysis** tool requires that a suppoted Java Runtime Environment be installed on your system. If you receive a message that the Java Runtime is not found, as shown in Figure A–2, you will need to install a supported Java Runtime Environment.

For more information, click the link provided in the alert box or search for **Java Requirements for Autodesk InfraWorks** in the InfraWorks Help documentation.

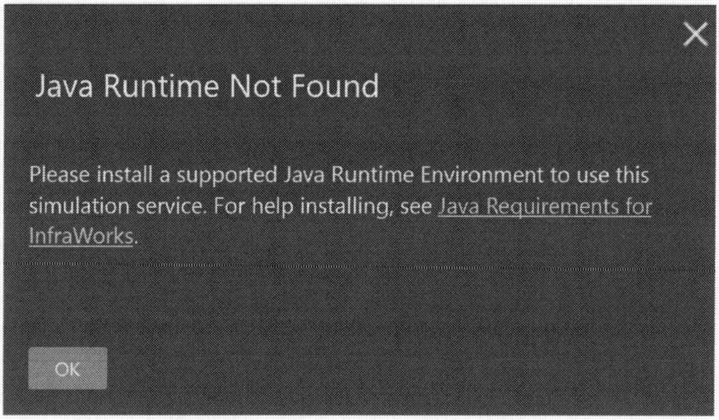

Figure A–2

General Steps

The following are the general steps for performing a traffic analysis in your model:

1. Define the traffic study area.
2. Add zones for traffic origin/destination/parking.
3. Define traffic demand.
4. Generate trips from demand.
5. Run a simulation, collecting the results.
6. Analyze the results.

How To: Define a Traffic Study Area

1. In the *Analyze* tab>*Transportation* drop-down list, click  (Traffic Simulation).The component roads are highlighted to indicate which roads can be analyzed using a traffic study.
2. In the model, define a polyline to indicate the traffic study area boundary.

3. If planning roads are included in the boundary, a message displays (as shown in Figure A–3) indicating that you have the option to turn them into component roads so that they can be analyzed during the traffic simulation. Click **Yes** or **No**, as required.

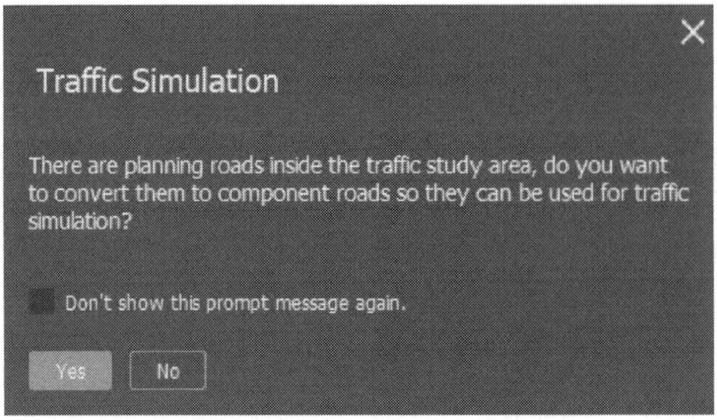

Figure A–3

4. In the *Traffic Study Area* asset card, select the *Result Volumes* option that suits your needs, as shown in Figure A–4.

Figure A–4

5. In the *Simulations* drop-down list, select the simulation length you wish to run, as shown in Figure A–5.

   Note: *The* ***Quick Simulation*** option *runs for 10 minutes. The other simulations require more time to process.*

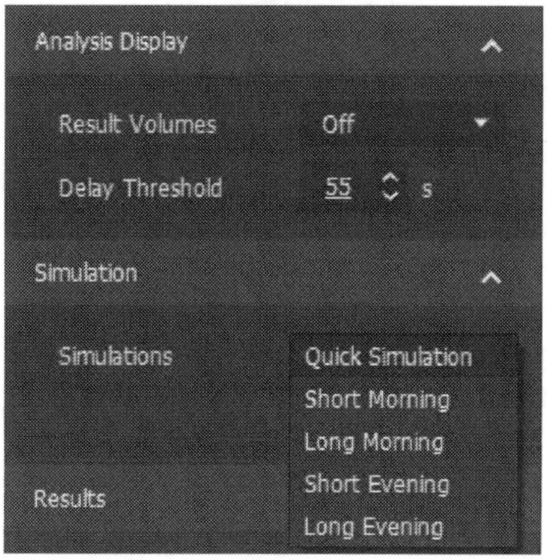

Figure A–5

6. Click **Run Simulation**.

Traffic Analyst Panel

The *Traffic Analyst* panel is where advanced parameters and multiple simulation variants are added to the traffic analysis. Figure A–6 shows the *Traffic Analyst* panel with the *Intersections* control panel open. Changing parameters and variables helps you to better predict traffic flow. For the best results, run the simulation a few times and analyze the distribution of results.

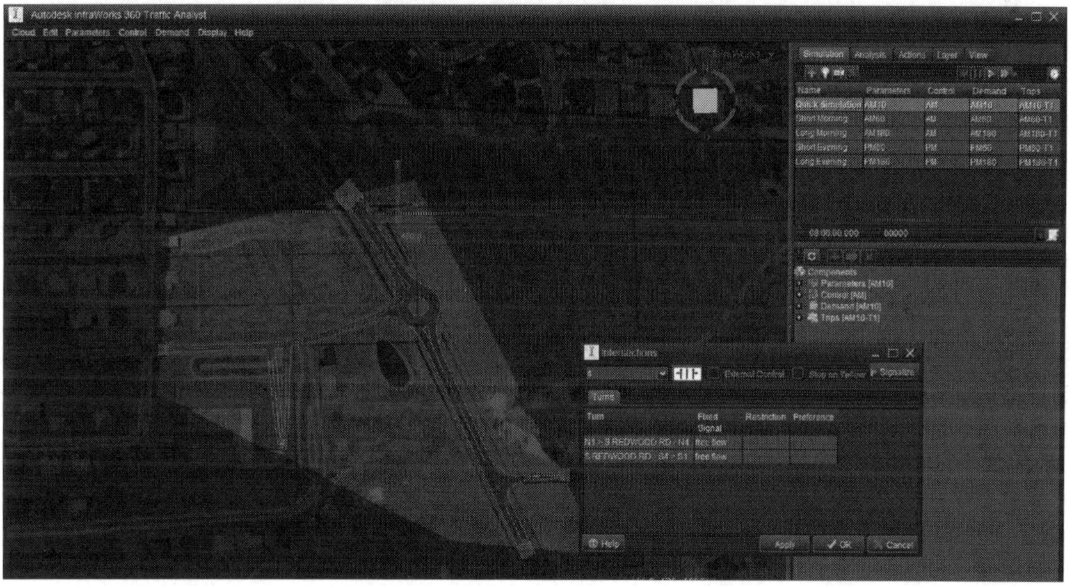

Figure A–6

Parameters

Several parameters can be set during a traffic analysis, including:

- **Terms:** Windows of time during the day, specified as HH:MM. An unlimited number of terms can be defined for a network. Terms can overlap or be sequential, and can also specify the day of the week (weekday, weekend, or a specific day).
- **Behaviors and MOBs:** Behaviors are assigned to either person types or vehicle types. They control decisions made by each person. A group of behaviors is a Mix of Behaviors (MOB). You can access the MOBs window by using a button at the bottom of the Behaviors window.
- **Restrictions and Speed Controls:** Restrictions are applied to surfaces to control the types of people or vehicles that can move on the surface. A MOB must be created before restrictions can be added.
- **Vehicle Types:** Controls the size, movement, and display of a vehicle in the model. A group of vehicle types is called a fleet. Behaviors are applied to vehicle types.

Controllers

The *Intersections* panel enables you to control conflicts between different streams of traffic. Each lane of an intersection can have a different control signal or no signal at all. When a lane is selected in the controller, an arrow displays in the *Traffic Analyst* panel indicating the direction of traffic, as shown in Figure A–7.

Figure A–7

The *Fixed Signal* options below are listed in order of increasing priority:

- **Barred:** The turn is closed to all traffic.
- **Stop Sign:** The approaching traffic has a stop sign and must stop before proceeding through the intersection.
- **Give Way:** Approaching traffic has a Give Way sign and slows down accordingly.
- **Yield:** Approaching traffic is on the main road, but must cross an opposing stream and must slow down on approach.
- **Free Flow:** Approaching traffic is on the main road, has priority, and does not need to check for conflicting traffic.

Demand

The *Demand Editor* enables you to modify the traffic counts for various times of day and origin points. Two or three tabs exist in the *Demand Editor*:

- **Directed Demand:** Uses origin-destination matrices where demand between all origin-destination pairs is known. When an origin point is selected in the *Demand Editor*, arrows display in the *Traffic Analyst* panel indicating the destination of traffic, as shown in Figure A–8.

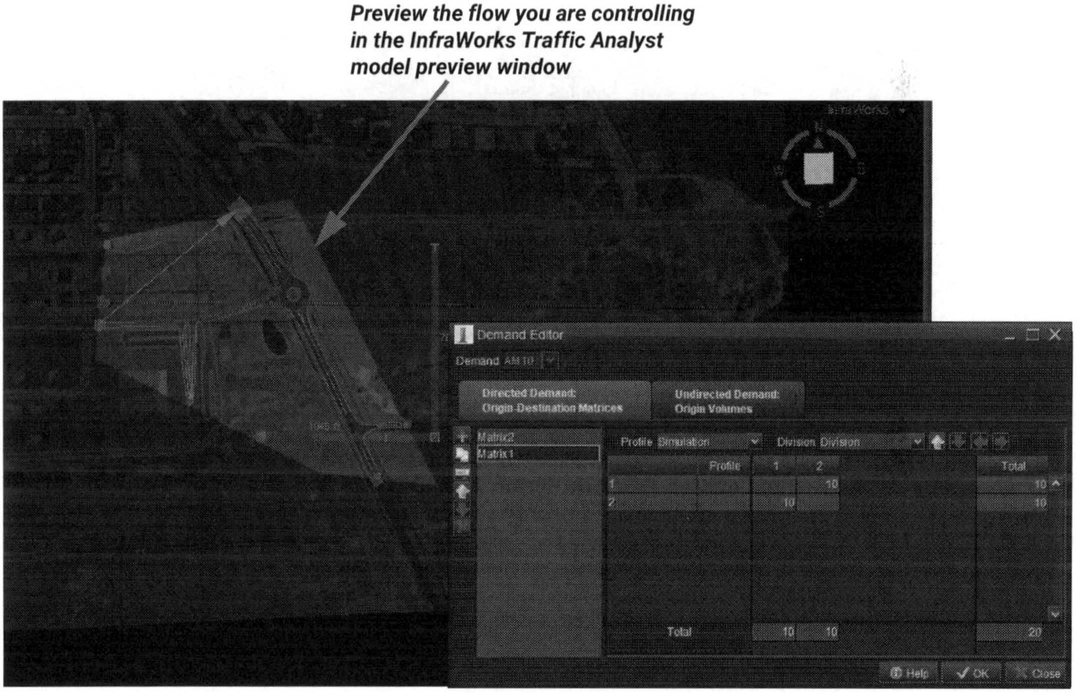

Figure A–8

- **Undirected Demand:** Uses traffic volumes from an origin zone, along with turning counts.
- **Transport Demand:** Lists all public transport services, departure times, and associated vehicle types, if any such vehicles are defined and included in the study.

How To: Control Traffic Flow per Intersection

1. Create a traffic simulation.
2. In the model, select the traffic study area boundary.
3. Right-click and select *Traffic Analyst* panel.
4. Click **OK** in the two *Traffic Simulation* dialog boxes that display.
5. In the **Control** menu, select **Intersections**.
6. In the *Intersections* panel, select the intersection or roundabout to work with from the *Intersection* drop-down list.
7. Select a control in the *Fixed Signal* column for each turn, as shown in Figure A–9.

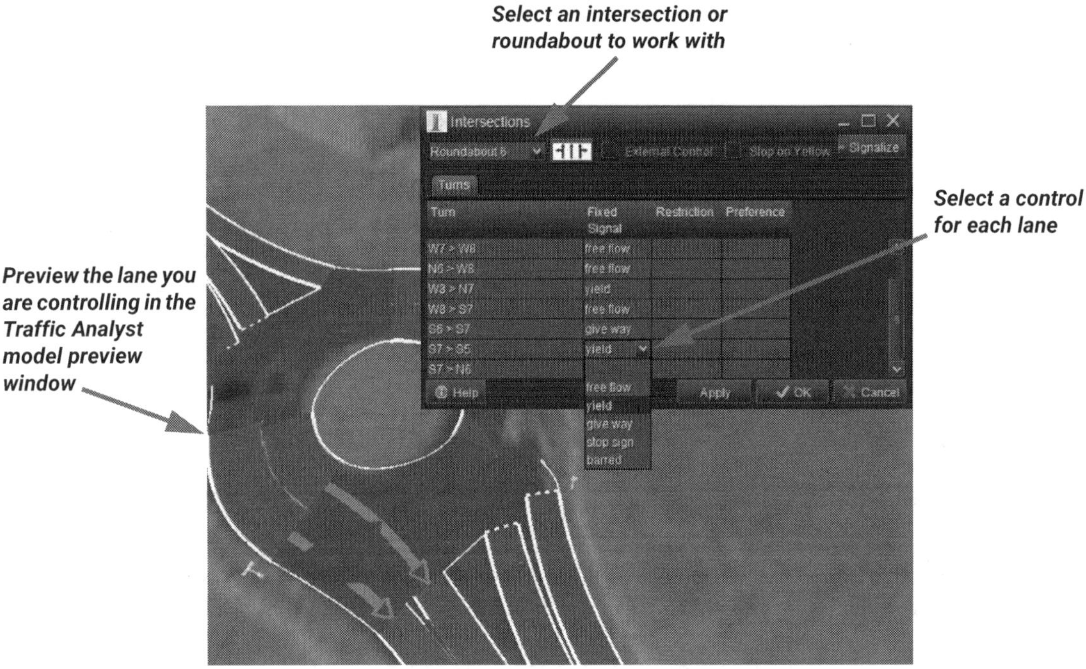

Figure A–9

8. Click **OK**.
9. In the **Demand** menu, select **Demand**.

10. In the *Demand Editor*, select the appropriate tab for the type of matrices required for the project:
    - Directed Demand
    - Undirected Demand
    - Transport Demand
11. Click  (Add) to add an additional matrix, origin, or destination.
12. Input the traffic count for each profile.
13. Click **OK**.

Hint: Mobility Simulation

A mobility simulation is launched in the same manner as the traffic simulation, from the right-click menu after the traffic study area has been defined (as shown in Figure A–10).

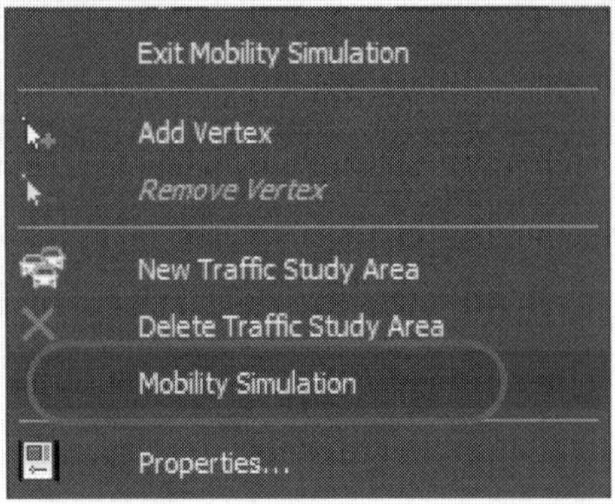

Figure A–10

-  (Mobility Simulation) is also available in the *Analyze* tab>*Transportation* drop-down list.

You would use the mobility simulation to estimate:

- Door-to-door journeys
- Pedestrian traffic in high volume areas, such as stadiums, public attractions, etc.
- Crowd flow control in secure areas, such as airports
- Crowd simulation for subways, trains, and ferries for queuing, embarking, and disembarking
- Foot traffic, bicycles, and other random traffic situations

Practice A1
Run a Traffic Study

Practice Objective

- Generate an animation file based on the default traffic demand.

In this practice, you will create a traffic study to analyze traffic flow along the component roads using default traffic counts. You will also set control signals for each lane at the signalized intersection.

1. On the *Home* Screen, click **Open**.
2. In the *InfraWorks Practice Files\AppA-Tools* folder, select **RoadAnalysis.sqlite** and click **Open**.
3. In the toolbar, expand the (Proposals) drop-down list and select **A_Task1** to make it current.
4. Click (Bookmarks) and select **Project Area**. Pan to the left so the school is centered on the screen.
5. In the *Analyze* tab>*Transportation* panel, click (Traffic Simulation).

Hint: Java Runtime Environment

If you receive a message about having a proper Java Runtime Environment, search for **Java Requirements for Autodesk InfraWorks** in the InfraWorks Help documentation for information on installing a supported version.

6. The component roads are highlighted to indicate which roads can be analyzed using a traffic study, and you are prompted to define the new Traffic Study Area boundary at the bottom of the screen, as shown in Figure A–11.

Figure A–11

7. In the model, define a polyline to indicate the traffic study area boundary, as shown in Figure A–12. Ensure that you double-click on the last point to finish the boundary.

Figure A–12

8. In the message box that displays, click **Yes**, as shown in Figure A–13.

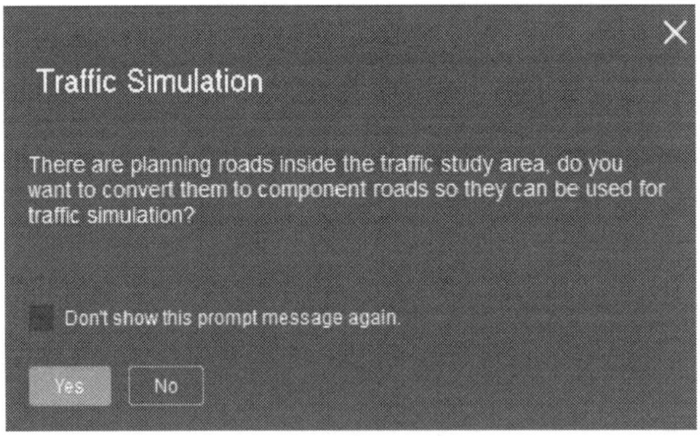

Figure A–13

9. After the three planning roads are successfully converted to component roads, the *Traffic Study Area* asset card is displayed. Set the following options, as shown in Figure A–14:
   - *Result Volumes*: **Per Lane**
   - *Simulations*: **Quick Simulation**

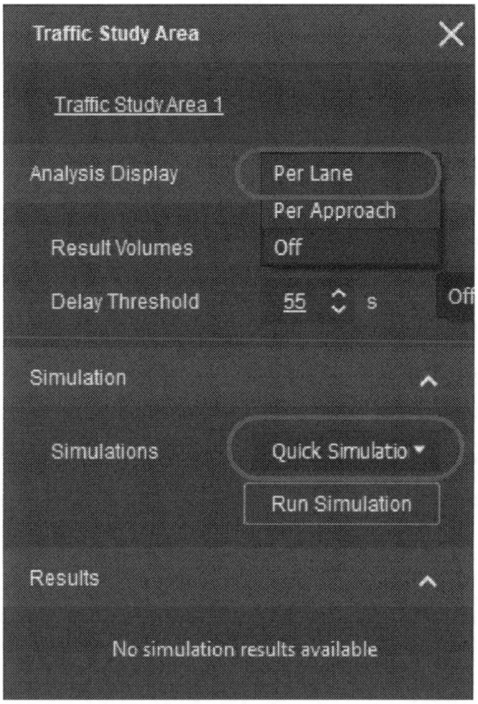

Figure A–14

10. Click **Run Simulation**.

11. In the *Animation Player* asset card, set the player speed to **x10** and click (Play).

    Note: *You will need to zoom in to an intersection to see the cars moving, as shown in Figure A–15.*

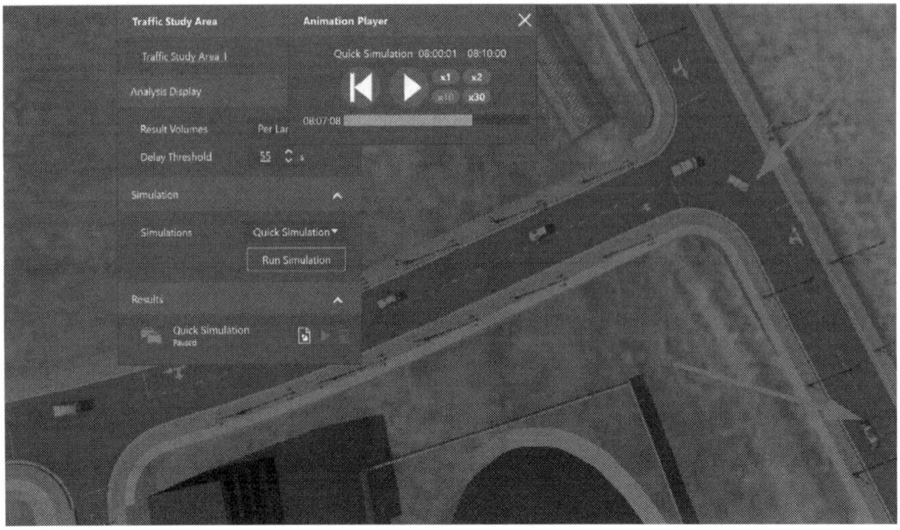

Figure A–15

12. Close the *Animation Player* asset card by clicking the **X** in the top-right corner.
13. The traffic study area boundary is still selected. Right-click in the boundary area and select **Traffic Analyst Panel**, as shown in Figure A–16.

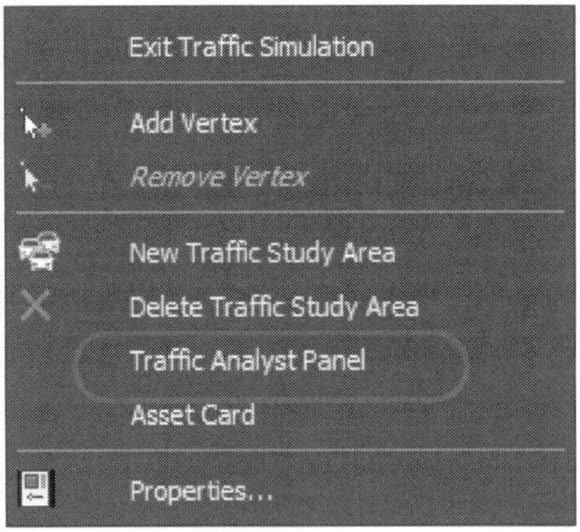

Figure A–16

14. Click **OK** in the *Traffic Simulation* dialog box that displays. The Autodesk InfraWorks Traffic Analyst program now launches, as shown in Figure A–17.

Figure A–17

15. In the **Control** menu, select **Intersections**, as shown in Figure A–18.

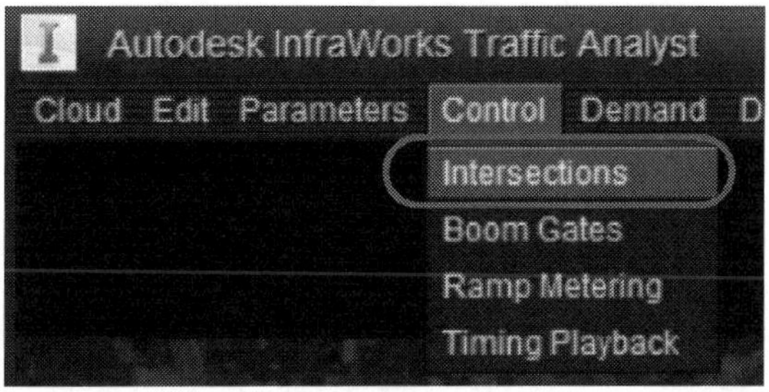

Figure A–18

16. In the *Intersections* panel, do the following:

- In the *Intersection* drop-down list, select **Redwood-Church**. The canvas pans to center on the intersection. You can zoom in to see the intersection better. As you click on a row in the table, the turn is annotated within the canvas.

Note: *Most intersections were given logical names in this InfraWorks model. Ideally, intersections should be given logical names when they are created.*

- Confirm that the following for each lane are set (as shown in Figure A–19); if not, make appropriate changes to make it match the figure.

Note: *Arrows display for the currently selected lane in the InfraWorks Traffic Analyst model preview window, as shown in Figure A–19.*

a. *S REDWOOD RD > Church Loop:* **free flow**
b. *S REDWOOD RD > S REDWOOD RD:* **free flow**
c. *Church Loop > S REDWOOD RD:* **stop sign**
d. *Church Loop > S REDWOOD RD:* **stop sign**
e. *S REDWOOD RD > S REDWOOD RD:* **free flow**
f. *S REDWOOD RD > Church Loop:* **yield**

- Click **Apply**.

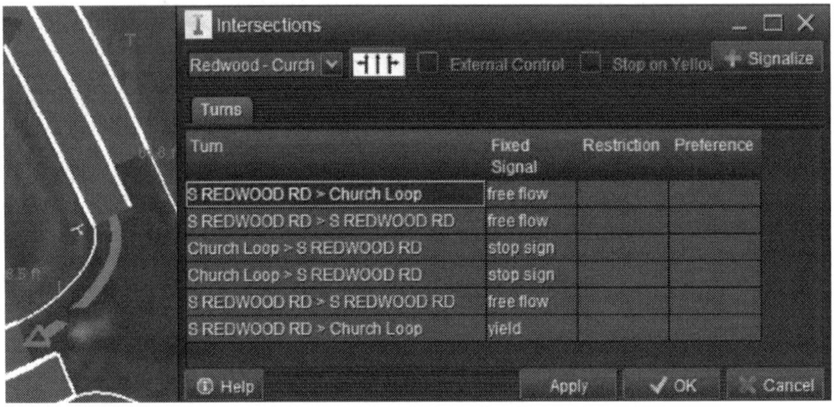

Figure A–19

17. In the *Intersections* panel, do the following:

- In the *Intersection* drop-down list, select **Redwood-Pier**.
- Ensure the following is set for each lane (as shown in Figure A–20). The *Fixed Signal* column should already be defaulted to the following values:

a. *S REDWOOD RD > Pier Lane:* **yield**
b. *S REDWOOD RD > S REDWOOD RD:* **free flow**
c. *S REDWOOD RD > S REDWOOD RD:* **free flow**
d. *S REDWOOD RD > Pier Lane:* **free flow**
e. *Pier Lane > S REDWOOD RD:* **stop sign**
f. *Pier Lane > S REDWOOD RD:* **stop sign**

- Click **Apply**.

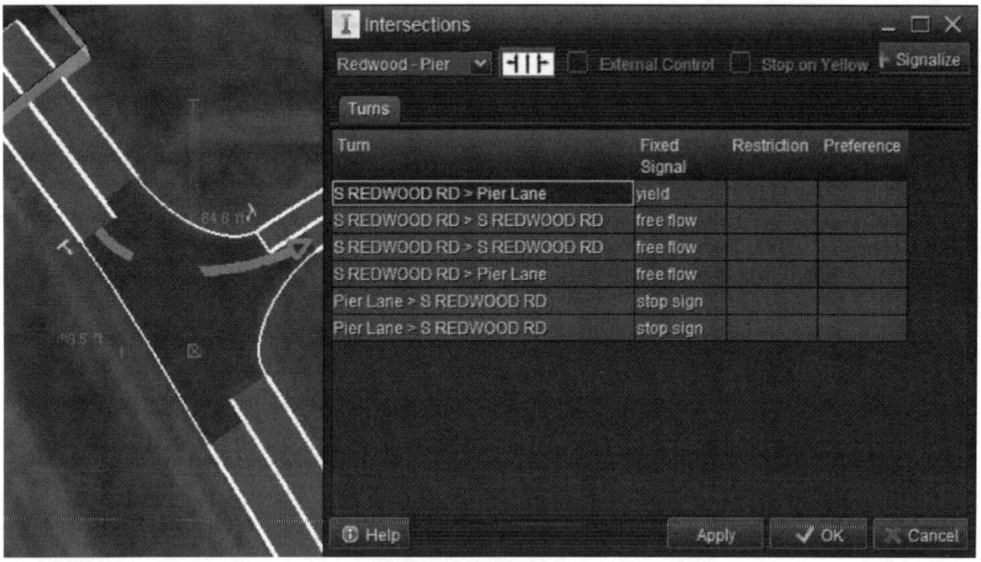

Figure A–20

18. Click **OK** to dismiss the *Intersections* panel.
19. In the **Demand** menu, select **Demands**.
20. In the *Demand Editor*, set the *Directed Demand* matrix for the project so that it matches the one shown in Figure A–21.

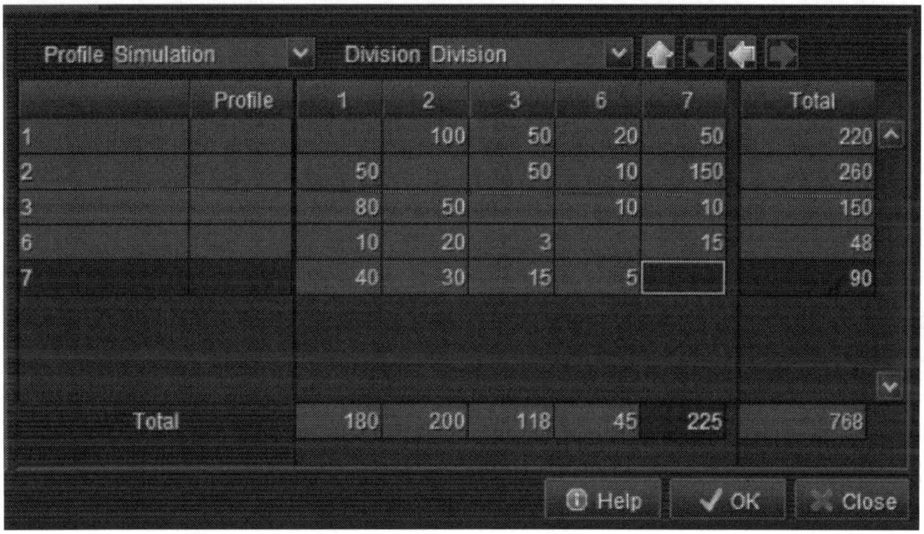

Figure A–21

21. Click **OK** to dismiss the *Demand Editor* panel.

22. In the *Traffic Analyst* panel, in the *Simulation* tab, click (Play). Zoom and pan around durig the playback and note how the cars bunch up at the intersections, as shown in Figure A–22.

Figure A–22

23. Watch the traffic start to back up. After a short while, click (Pause).
24. In the **Control** menu, select **Intersections**.
25. In the *Intersections* panel, do the following:
    - In the *Intersection* drop-down list, select **Redwood-Morris**.
    - Click (Edit Turn Lanes).
    - Click on each row and note how the view in the canvas reorients itself to show the flow direction of the selected lane.
    - Use the *Lane 1* drop-down list to select the type of flow, as shown in Figure A–23.
    - Click **Refresh**, then click **Close**.

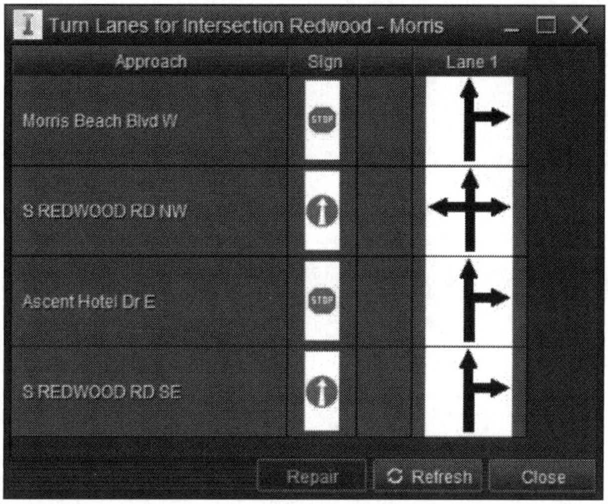

Figure A–23

26. Click **OK** to close the *Intersections* panel.
27. In the *Traffic Analyst* panel, zoom out to see the entire traffic analysis area. In the *Simulation* tab, click (Rewind) and then click (Play). Note how the cars now flow differently.
28. Click (Pause).
29. Note that there is still a bottleneck at the **S Redwood Rd > Church Loop** intersection, as shown in Figure A–24.

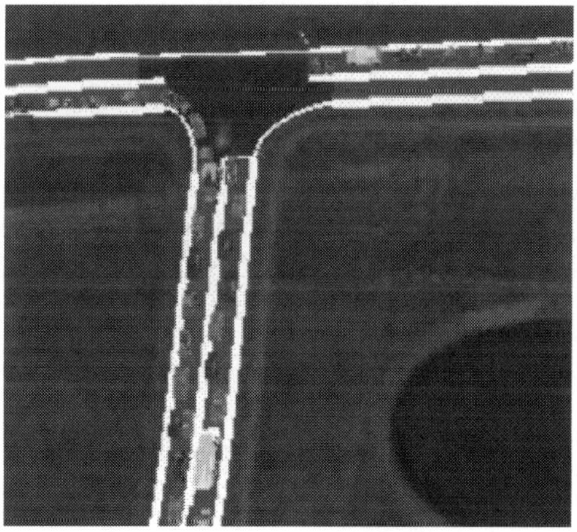

Figure A–24

30. In order to fix that, first try editing the demands. In the **Demand** menu, select **Demands**.
31. In the *Demand Editor*, select row 2 / column 7, as shown in Figure A–25. Note that the value is **150**, meaning 150 cars will attempt to make a left-hand turn, which is a bit excessive. Change the value to **35**. Also change the value in row 1 / column 2 from 100 to **50**.

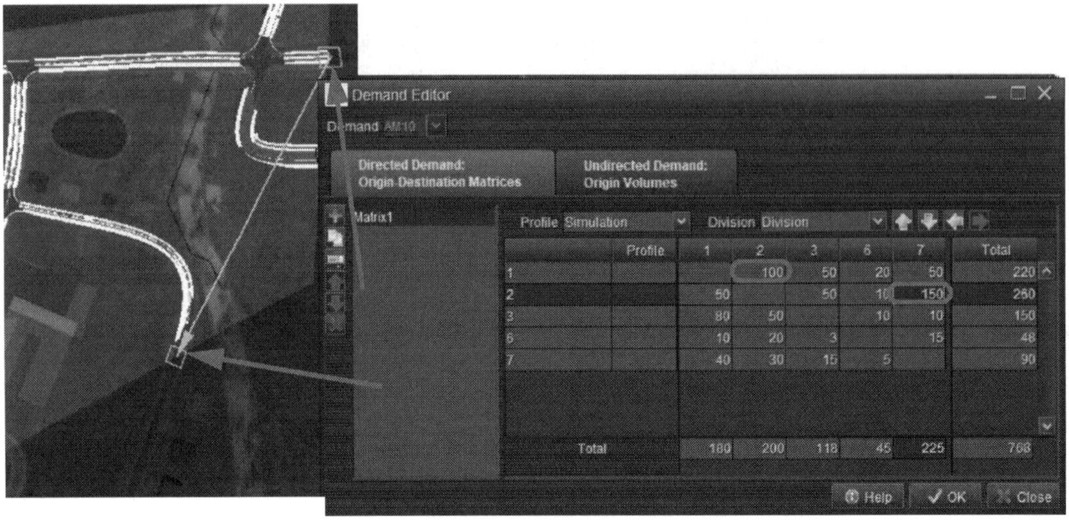

Figure A–25

32. Click **OK**.
33. In the *Simulation* tab, click  (Rewind) to clear all the bottlenecks, then click  (Play). Note how the cars now flow differently. Let it run for a while to see if a bottleneck still occurs at the intersection, then click  (Pause).
34. Close the *Traffic Analyst* panel by clicking the **X** in the upper-right corner.
35. In the *Traffic Study Area* asset card, click **Run Simulation**.
36. Click **OK** in the *Traffic Simulation* message that displays.

Note: *You must give the simulation time to complete before you can play the animation.*

37. In the *Animation Player* asset card, click (Play).

Note that if there are any red queues, as shown in Figure A–26, they indicate delays that exceed a threshold. Your model should not have any red queues.

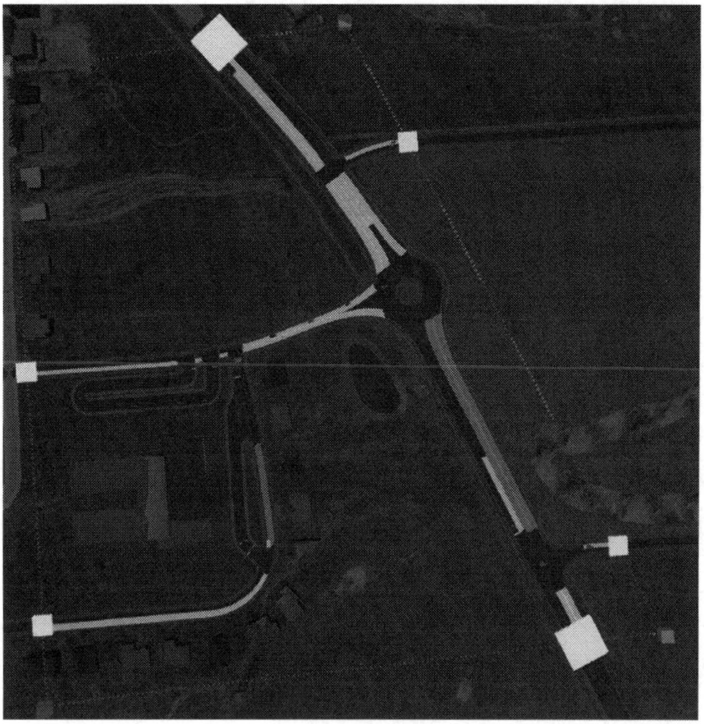

Figure A–26

38. In the *Analyze* tab>*Transportation* panel, click (Traffic Simulation), or right-click and select **Exit Traffic Simulation** to toggle off the traffic simulation boundary.

End of practice

A.2 Calculating Quantities

When a component road is selected, the *Road* asset card displays two options at the bottom for calculating quantities, as shown in Figure A–27.

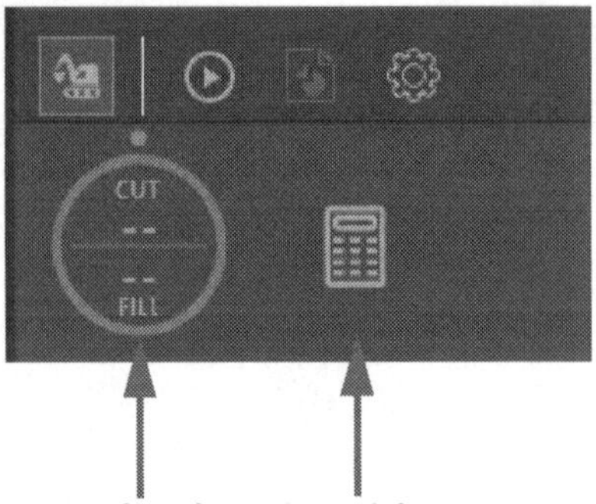

Figure A–27

The types of materials that can be calculated include:

- Earthwork cut and fill quantities at each sampled station, along with its cumulative volume.
- The road components' (assemblies') total length and area.
- Bridge materials.
- Drainage components, which include total length of pipe and counts of structures.
- 3D models that are used as decorations.
    - For objects spaced along an alignment, the calculations are based on the 2D length.
    - For objects at the beginning and end of the alignment, the calculations vary due to a difference in how items are placed and how the calculation handles a remainder in spacing.
    - Objects placed before the start or after the end of the alignment are not counted.

Note: *Road components within intersections or roundabouts are ignored.*

How To: Compute Earthwork Quantities

1. In the model, select the component road.
2. In the *Road* asset card, select  (Earthwork Quantities), then click  (Specify settings).

3. In the *Earthwork Setting* panel, set the *Station Increment* value and toggle on which geometry you want to sample, as shown in Figure A–28. Close the *Earthwork Setting* panel.

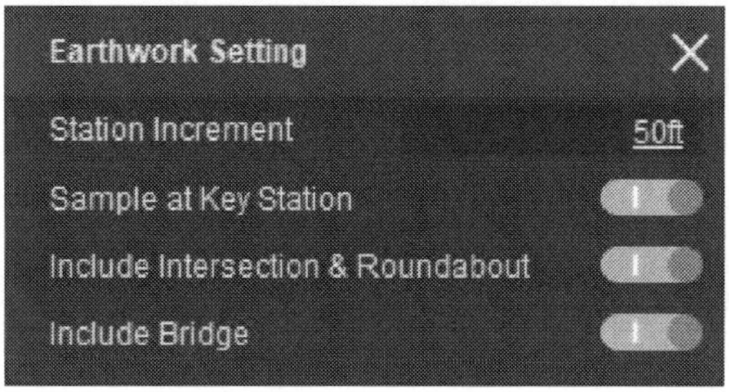

Figure A–28

4. In the *Road* asset card, click  (Compute earthwork quantities). Wait for it to process.

5. To see the results, click  (View detail values). The *Earthwork Quantities* panel displays, as shown in Figure A–29.

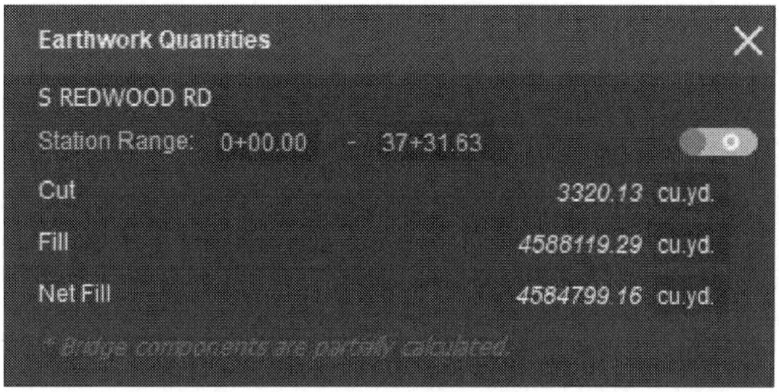

Figure A–29

6. To create a report, in the *Road* asset card, click 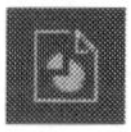 (Generate report).
7. In the *Save Quantities* dialog box, type a file name, browse to the folder where you want to save the file, and click **Save**.
8. When the file is done saving, File Explorer automatically opens to the location where you saved the file. Double-click on the file to open it in ***Microsoft Excel***, or right-click on it and select **Open with...** to open it in a different program.

9. When opened in ***Microsoft Excel***, the report displays similarly to the one shown in Figure A–30.

	A	B	C	D	E	F	G	H	I	J
1	Station (ft)	Cut (cu.yd.	Cut area (ɛ	Fill (cu.yd.)	Fill area (a	Cumulativ	Cumulativ	Cumulativ	Note	
2	0	0	0.002	0	0	0	0	0		
3	66	185.7	0.002	27.31	0	185.7	27.31	158.39		
4	109.05	124.58	0.002	16.55	0	310.27	43.86	266.41		
5	132	62.01	0.002	9.43	0	372.28	53.3	318.98		
6	174.67	109.22	0.002	22.77	0	481.5	76.06	405.43		
7	198	57.15	0.001	16.48	0	538.65	92.55	446.1		
8	240.28	102.66	0.002	37.54	0.001	641.31	130.08	511.23		
9	264	59.9	0.002	24.76	0.001	701.21	154.84	546.37		
10	310.11	129.79	0.002	73.86	0.001	831	228.7	602.3		
11	330	59.03	0.002	42.95	0.001	890.03	271.65	618.38		
12	371.52	123.33	0.002	88.21	0.001	1013.36	359.86	653.5		
13	396	73.74	0.002	49.54	0.001	1087.1	409.4	677.7		
14	462	198.48	0.002	130.84	0.001	1285.59	540.24	745.35		
15	518.92	175.08	0.002	106.44	0.001	1460.67	646.68	813.98		
16	528	28.76	0.002	16.13	0.001	1489.43	662.82	826.62		
17	584.34	174.92	0.002	83.86	0.001	1664.35	746.67	917.68		
18	594	29.34	0.002	11.05	0.001	1693.69	757.73	935.97		
19	650.15	177.71	0.002	47.2	0	1871.41	804.92	1066.48		
20	660	32.46	0.002	5.65	0	1903.87	810.58	1093.29		
21	715.77	195.65	0.002	26.36	0	2099.52	836.94	1262.59		
22	726	37.45	0.002	4.02	0	2136.97	840.96	1296.01		
23	781.38	179.64	0.002	17.32	0	2316.6	858.29	1458.32		
24	792	29.88	0.002	2.54	0	2346.49	860.83	1485.66		
25	858	178.2	0.002	16.26	0	2524.69	877.09	1647.6		
26	924	170.77	0.002	19.44	0	2695.45	896.53	1798.93		
27	990	151.17	0.001	21.51	0	2846.62	918.03	1928.59		
28	1056	169.09	0.002	13.36	0	3015.71	931.4	2084.32		
29	1122	160.41	0.001	17	0	3176.13	948.39	2227.73		
30	1188	155.78	0.002	47.45	0.001	3331.91	995.85	2336.06		
31	1235.57	168.4	0.003	40.37	0	3500.31	1036.22	2464.09		
32	1243.51	32.18	0.002	5.25	0	3532.49	1041.47	2491.02		
33	1246.28	10.82	0.002	1.76	0	3543.3	1043.23	2500.08	Start - intersection	
34	1397.67	286.32	0.001	119.14	0.001	3829.63	1162.36	2667.26	End - intersection	
35	1400	4.37	0.001	1.56	0	3834	1163.92	2670.07		

Figure A–30

How To: Compute Material Quantities

1. In the model, select the component road.
2. In the *Road* asset card, select (Material Quantities)

3. Once done processing, review the quantities that display in the *Material Quantities* panel, as shown in Figure A–31.

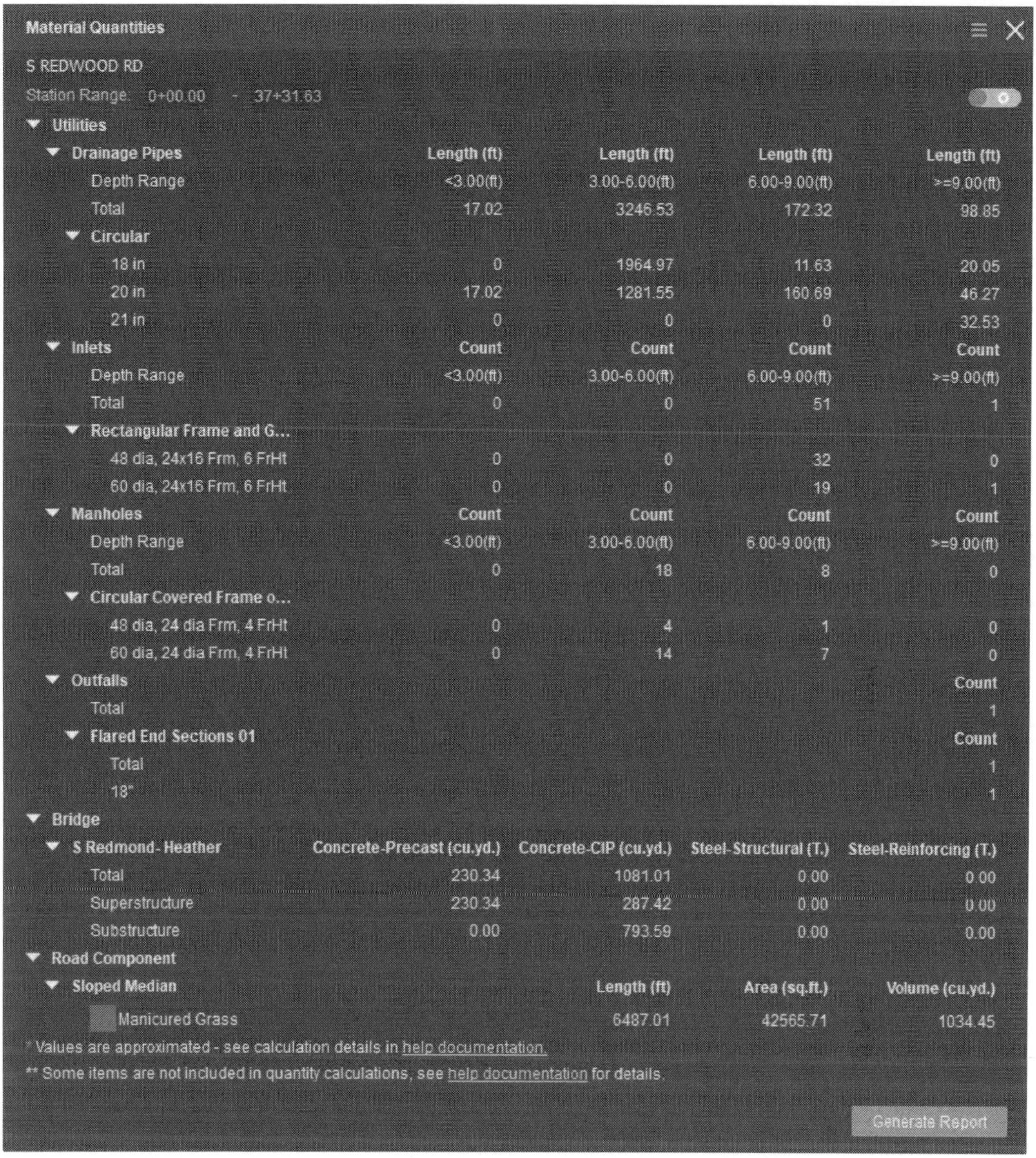

Figure A–31

4. In the *Material Quantities* dialog box, click **Generate Report** to send the calculations to a .CSV file, similar to the one shown in Figure A–32.

	A	B	C	D	E	F	G	H	I
1	Asset Type	Group	Name	Count	Count is Approximate	Length (ft)	Area (ac)	Volume (cu.yd.)	
2	Road Component	Sidewalk	Grey Patterned Sidewalk			3118.85	0.352	186.51	
3	Road Component	Sloped Median	Manicured Grass			3218.85	0.485	513.29	
4	Road Component	Curb & Gutter	surface light grey concrete 3w 3h			6038.85	0.3	469.87	
5	Road Component	Lane	Surface Dark Grey Asphalt 1w 1h			11143.32	3.069	3248.72	
6	Road Component	Lane	Gray80			14564.39	0.084	88.49	
7	3D Model	Traffic & Barriers	City Traffic Light	1					
8	3D Model	City Furniture	Street Light w_3 Bulbs	98	Approximated				
9	3D Model	Vehicles	BMW 3 Series	1					
10	3D Model	POI	Pushpin_Blue	1					

Figure A–32

5. Close the *Material Quantities* panel by clicking the **X** in the top right corner.

6. To display the *Material Quantities* panel again, click (Show Road Quantities).

Practice A2
Calculate Quantities

Practice Objective

- Calculate how much material is required to build the road.

In this practice, you will run two calculations to figure out how much material is required to build the road. First, you will calculate the earthwork quantities. You will then calculate the concrete, asphalt, and other materials according to what is designed in the assemblies used in the road.

Task 1: Calculate earthwork quantities.

1. In the *InfraWorks Practice Files\AppA-Tools* folder, select **RoadAnalysis.sqlite** and click **Open**.
2. In the toolbar, expand the (Proposals) drop-down list and select **B_Task1** to make it current.
3. Click (Bookmarks) and select **Project Area**.
4. In the model, select **S Redwood Rd**, running north to south to the left of the pond.
5. In the *Road* asset card, click (Earthwork Quantities).
6. Near the bottom right of the *Road* asset card, click (Specify settings).
7. In the *Earthwork Setting* panel, set the *Station Increment* value to **50** and toggle on all of the geometry options to sample them, as shown in Figure A–33. Close the *Earthwork Setting* panel.

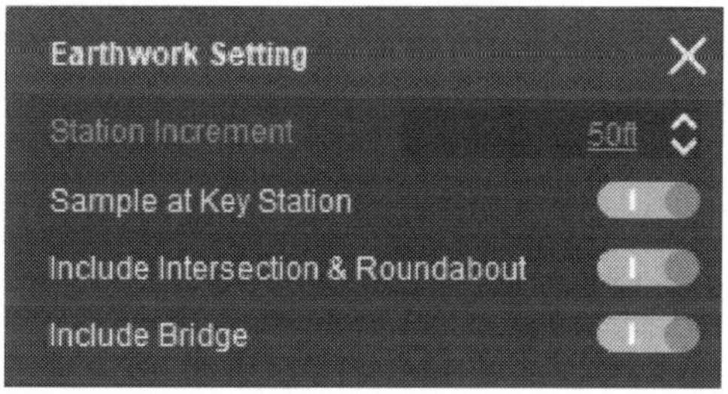

Figure A–33

8. Near the bottom of the *Road* asset card, click (Compute earthwork quantities). Wait for it to process.

9. If the results are not showing by default, in the *Road* asset card, click  (View detail values). The *Earthwork Quantities* panel displays, as shown in Figure A–34.

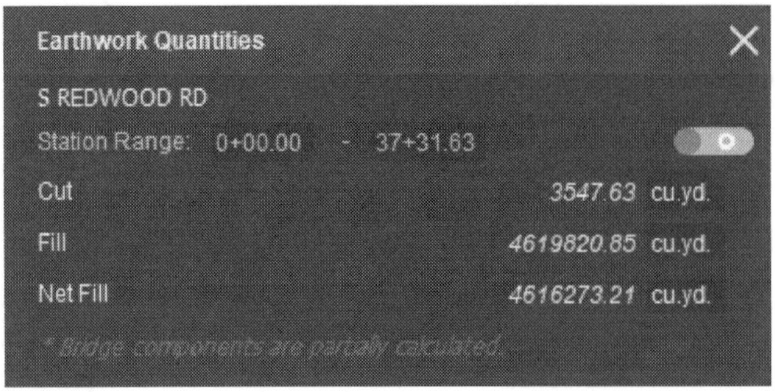

Figure A–34

Note: *Your quantities might be slightly different than those shown above.*

10. These quantities are also displayed in real-time at the bottom of the *Road* asset card, as shown in Figure A–35.

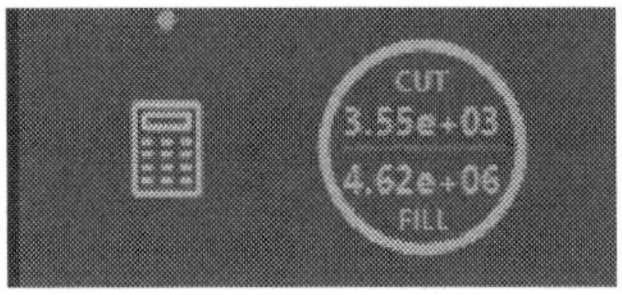

Figure A–35

11. To create a report, in the *Road* asset card, click 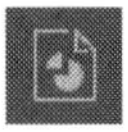 (Generate report).
12. In the *Save Quantities* dialog box, browse to the *InfraWorks Practice Files\References\Reports* folder, type **XXX-RoadAnalysis-S REDWOOD RD.csv** as the file name (substituting **XXX** with your initials), and click **Save**.

Note: *If File Explorer does not open automatically, open Microsoft Excel and open the .CSV file.*

13. When the file has finished saving, File Explorer automatically opens to the location where you saved the file. Double-click on the **.CSV** file to open it in ***Microsoft Excel***. The report displays similar to the one shown in Figure A–36.

	A	B	C	D	E	F	G	H	I	J	K
1	Station (ft)	Cut (cu.yd.	Cut area (s	Fill (cu.yd.)	Fill area (s	Cumulativ	Cumulativ	Cumulativ	Note		
2	0	0	34.07	0	8.64	0	0	0			
3	50	68.01	39.39	14.49	7.01	68.01	14.49	53.53			
4	100	71.61	37.95	13.42	7.49	139.62	27.91	111.71			
5	150	67.33	34.76	13.28	6.85	206.95	41.19	165.76			
6	200	64.21	34.58	13.24	7.44	271.16	54.42	216.73			
7	200	0	34.58	0	7.44	271.16	54.42	216.73			
8	220	25.73	34.88	5.5	7.39	296.88	59.92	236.96			
9	242.33	31.31	40.85	7.31	10.28	328.2	67.23	260.97			
10	250	11.79	42.18	2.99	10.78	339.99	70.22	269.77			
11	300	78.43	42.52	28.07	19.54	418.42	98.29	320.13			
12	330	46.27	40.77	26.22	27.65	464.69	124.51	340.18			
13	339.55	14.49	41.2	10.04	29.14	479.18	134.55	344.64			
14	345.13	8.38	39.83	5.9	27.96	487.56	140.45	347.11			
15	350	7.13	39.22	4.94	26.82	494.69	145.39	349.3			
16	363.42	19.15	37.83	12.79	24.64	513.83	158.18	355.65	Start - intersection Redwood - Pier		
17	450.07	7.96	27.36	192.68	16.65	521.79	350.86	170.93	End - intersection Redwood - Pier		

Figure A–36

14. Close the report in ***Microsoft Excel*** without saving the file.
15. In InfraWorks, close the *Earthworks Quantities* panel.

Task 2: Calculate material quantities.

1. In the model, select **S Redwood Rd**, if not already selected.
2. At the bottom of the *Road* asset card, click  (Material Quantities).
3. In the *Road* asset card, click  (Show Road Quantities) if the *Material Quantities* panel does not display.

4. Review the quantities that display in the *Material Quantities* panel, as shown in Figure A–37.

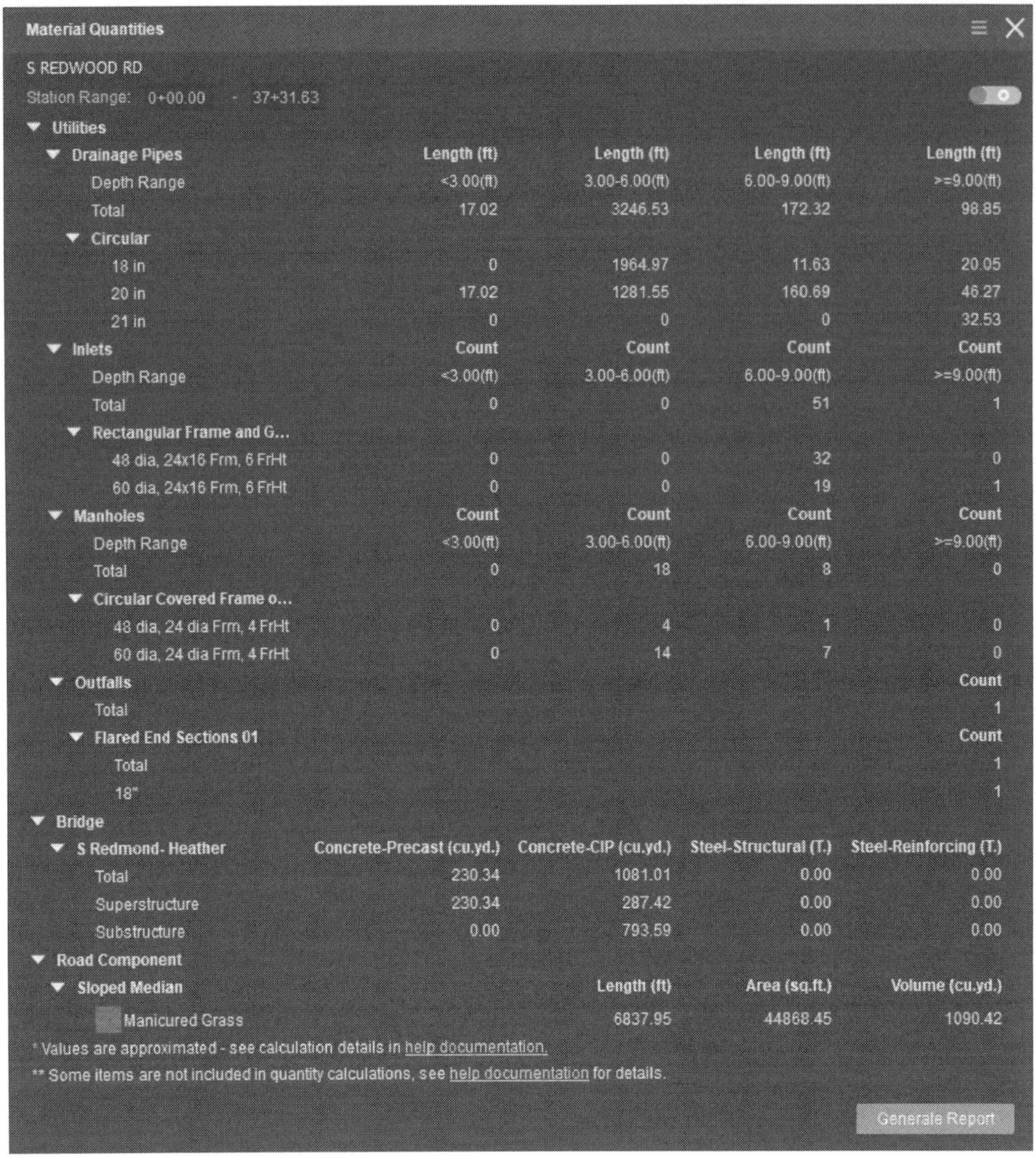

Figure A–37

Note: *Your quantities might be slightly different than those shown above.*

5. In the *Material Quantities* panel, click **Generate Report** to send the calculations to a .CSV file.

6. In the *Save Quantities* dialog box, browse to the *InfraWorks Practice Files\References\Reports* folder, type **XXX-RoadAnalysis-S REDWOOD RD-Quantities.csv** as the file name (substituting **XXX** with your initials), and click **Save**.

7. When the file has finished saving, a File Explorer window automatically opens to the location where you saved the file. Double-click on the **.CSV** file to open it in Microsoft Excel. The report displays similar to the one shown in Figure A–38.

	A	B	C	D	E
1	Asset Type	Group	Sub Group	Name	Length (ft
2	Utilities	Drainage Pipes	Circular	18 in	
3	Utilities	Drainage Pipes	Circular	20 in	
4	Utilities	Drainage Pipes	Circular	21 in	
5	Utilities	Inlets	Rectangular Frame and Grate on R	48 dia, 24x16 Frm, 6 FrHt	
6	Utilities	Inlets	Rectangular Frame and Grate on R	60 dia, 24x16 Frm, 6 FrHt	
7	Utilities	Manholes	Circular Covered Frame on Round	48 dia, 24 dia Frm, 4 FrHt	
8	Utilities	Manholes	Circular Covered Frame on Round	60 dia, 24 dia Frm, 4 FrHt	
9	Utilities	Outfalls	Flared End Sections 01	18",",",",",",",",1"	
10	Bridge	S Redmond- Heather		Total	
11	Bridge	S Redmond- Heather		Superstructure	
12	Bridge	S Redmond- Heather		Substructure	
13	Road Component	Sloped Median		Manicured Grass	6837.95
14	Road Component	Curb & Gutter		Surface Light Grey	6837.95
15	Road Component	Lane		Surface Dark Grey	6837.95
16	Road Component	Generic Shape		Gray80	6837.95
17	Road Component	Sidewalk		Grey Patterned Sid	3418.98
18	3D Model	Traffic & Barriers		City Traffic Light	
19	3D Model	City Furniture		Street Light w_3 Bulbs	

Figure A–38

8. Close the report in Microsoft Excel without saving the file.

9. In InfraWorks, close the *Material Quantities* panel.

End of practice

A.3 Civil 3D Objects

Civil engineers and surveyors work on the detailed design phase using the Autodesk® Civil 3D® software. InfraWorks can communicate with other Autodesk software types, which enables you to take advantage of models created by other departments.

InfraWorks models can be opened directly in the Civil 3D software. Therefore, you do not have to recreate these design elements for the design development and detailed design phase of the modeling process.

Additionally, Civil 3D drawing files can be imported into an InfraWorks model to help communicate the final design to stakeholders by taking advantage of the high definition graphics. When you add a Civil 3D DWG data source, the following Civil 3D data objects are imported:

- Corridors
- Surfaces
- Pipes (Note: This does not include pressure pipes at the time of publication.)
- Pipe Networks

When importing Autodesk Civil 3D DWG files into an Autodesk InfraWorks model, it is recommended to create a new proposal from the Master Proposal and remove any roads that might end up duplicated before starting the import process. If you do not do this, your roads might display similar to that shown in Figure A–39. The problem occurs when the software cannot determine which alignment to use, and tries to use both.

Figure A–39

How To: Open an InfraWorks Model in Civil 3D

1. Open the **Autodesk Civil 3D** software.
2. Start a new drawing or open the model you want to work in.
3. Ensure that a coordinate system is set in the drawing settings, as shown in Figure A–40.

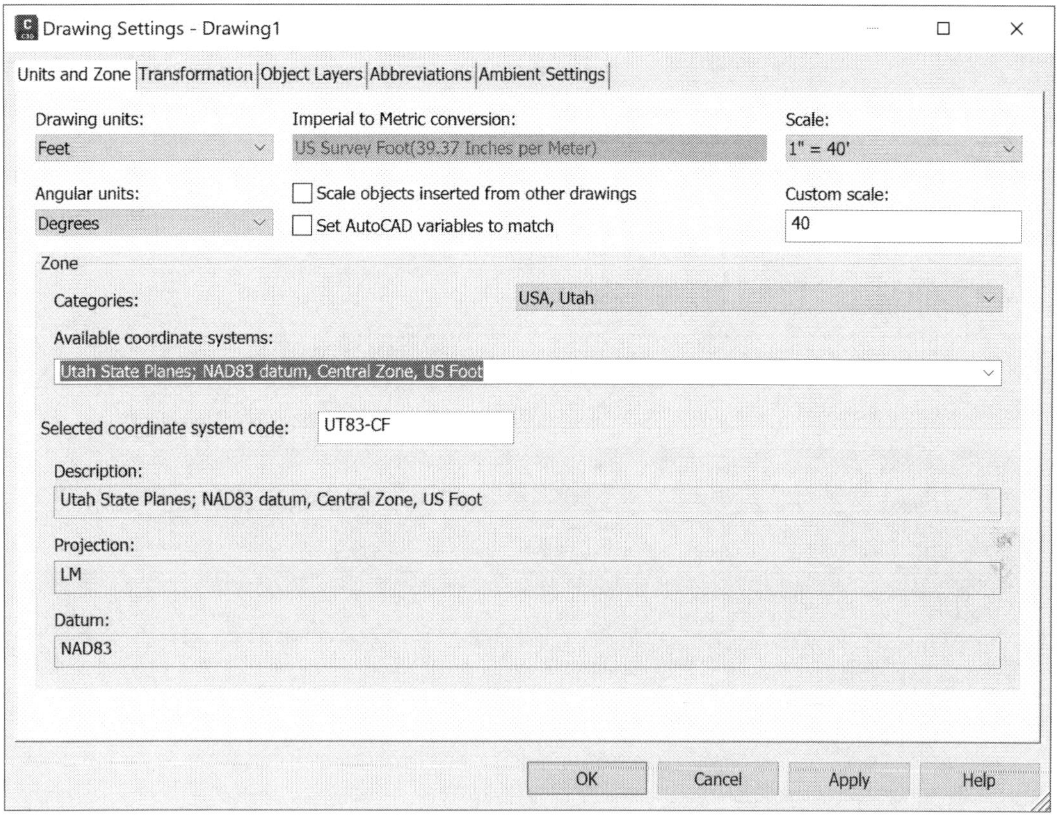

Figure A–40

4. In the *Insert* tab>*InfraWorks* panel, select **Open Model**, as shown in Figure A–41.

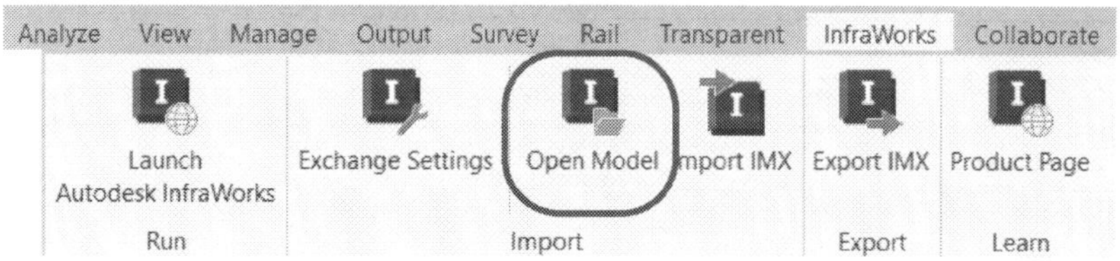

Figure A–41

5. In the *Open InfraWorks* Model dialog box, do the following, as shown in Figure A–42:
   - Select the model.
   - Determine the model's area in interest to view. Choose to use the Online Maps to orient yourself properly.
   - Set the proper coordinate system (if in doubt, use the InfraWorks model coordinate system).
   - Refine the *Selection Set* (selecting which features to include), as shown in Figure A–43.

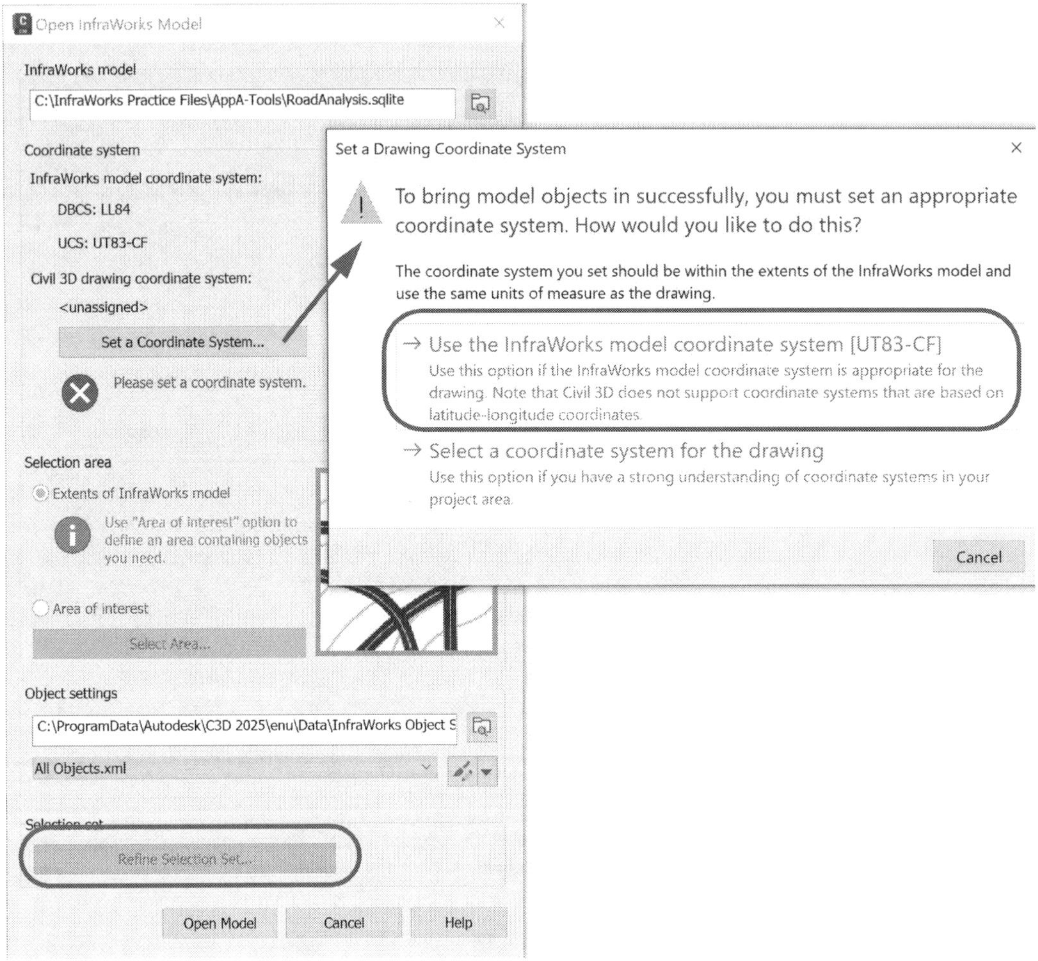

Figure A–42

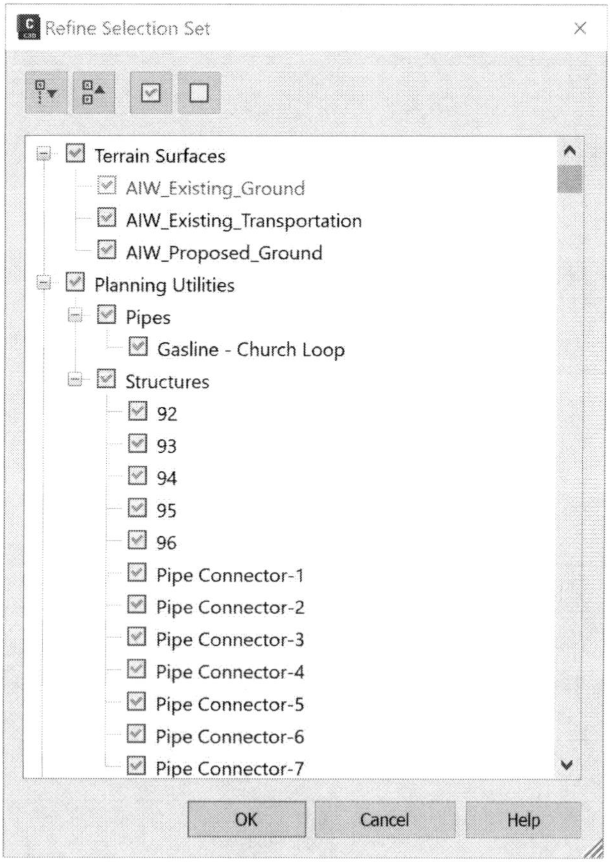
Refine Selection Set
Terrain Surfaces
AIW_Existing_Ground
AIW_Existing_Transportation
AIW_Proposed_Ground
Planning Utilities
Pipes
Gasline - Church Loop
Structures
92
93
94
95
96
Pipe Connector-1
Pipe Connector-2
Pipe Connector-3
Pipe Connector-4
Pipe Connector-5
Pipe Connector-6
Pipe Connector-7
OK
Cancel
Help

Figure A–43

The drawing opens in Civil 3D. The InfraWorks objects are converted as follows:

InfraWorks	Civil 3D
Terrain	TIN surface
Planning utilities	Pipe networks
Planning roads	Alignments
Component roads	Alignments, ground profiles, corridors assemblies (no profile view)
Intersections	Intersections with curb return alignments
Roundabouts	Roundabouts with alignments and ground profiles
Tunnels	AutoCAD 3D solids and meshes (see right panel in Figure A–44)
Bridges	Civil bridge girders and decks (see left panel in Figure A–44)
Drainage networks	Pipe networks
Coverage areas	AutoCAD 3D polylines
Water areas	AutoCAD 3D polylines

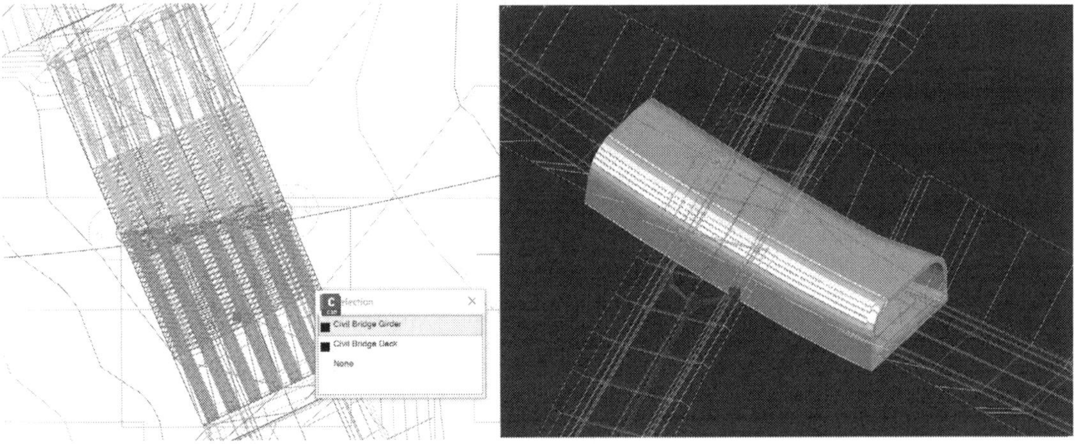

Figure A–44

All Civil 3D objects are displayed in the *Prospector* tab of the *Toolspace* as regular Civil 3D objects, as shown in Figure A–45.

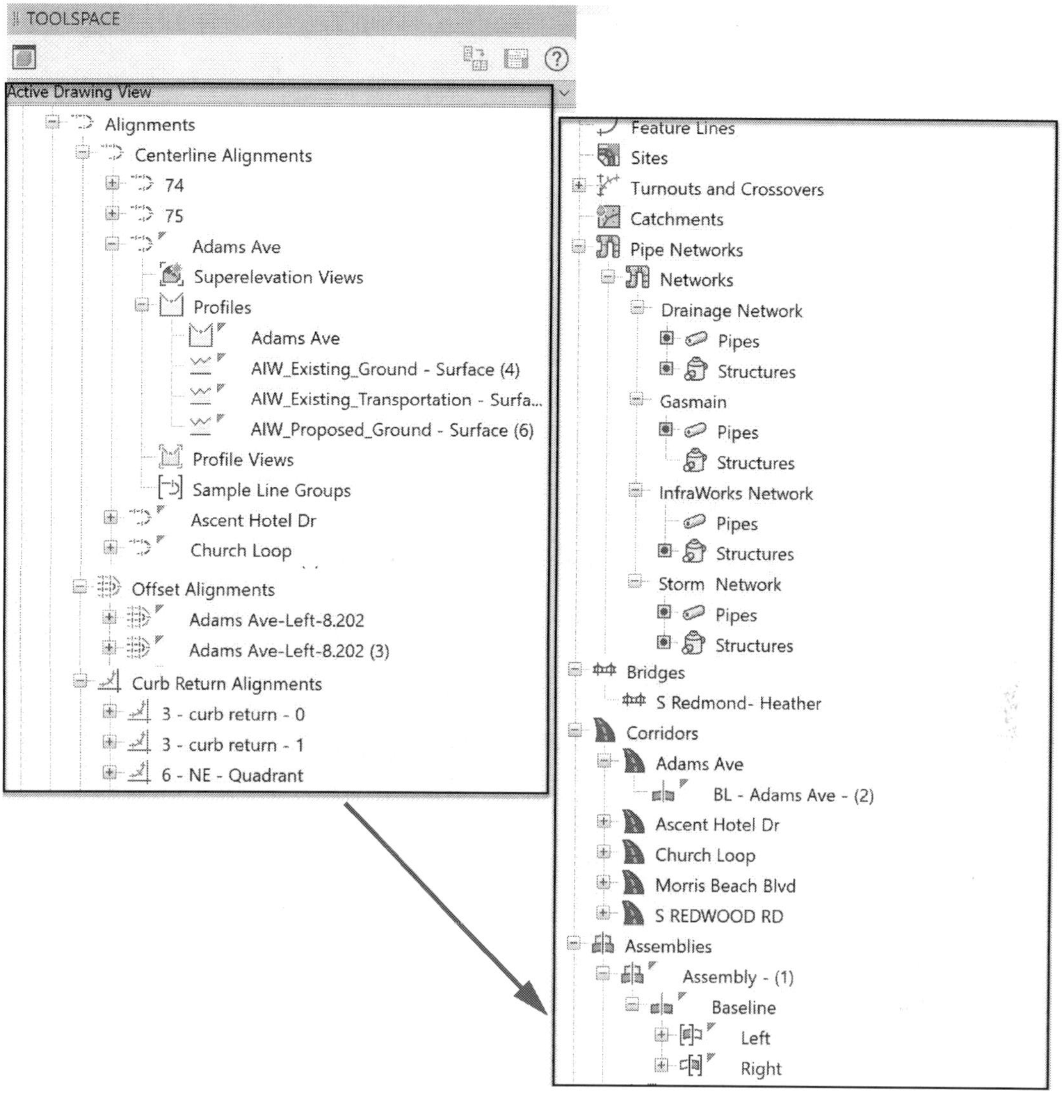

Figure A–45

How To: Import Civil 3D AEC Objects from DWG Files

Note: *In order to import a Civil 3D DWG file directly, you must have the current Civil 3D version installed on your computer.*

1. In the *Manage* tab>*Content* panel, click  (Data Sources) to open the *Data Sources* panel.
2. In the *Data Sources* panel, expand  (Add file data source) and select **Autodesk Civil 3D DWG**, as shown in Figure A–46.

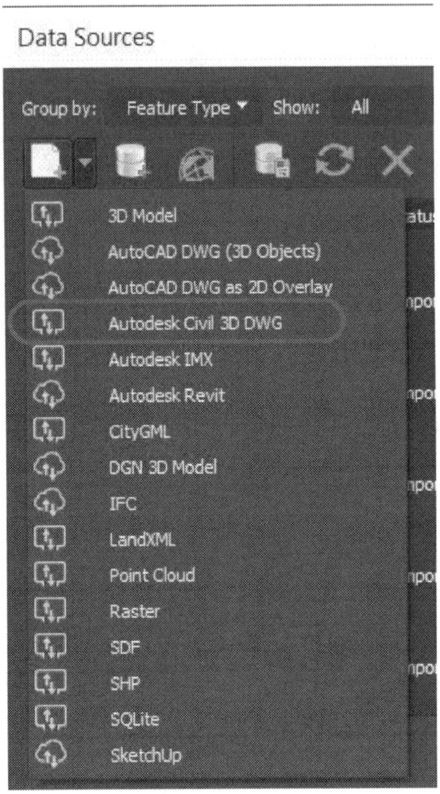

Figure A–46

- Alternatively, you can drag and drop .DWG files into the InfraWorks model from File Explorer. When you do, a *DWG File Import* dialog box displays that enables you to select what type of data source to use for the file, as shown in Figure A–47. Select the **Autodesk Civil 3D DWG** option and click **OK**.

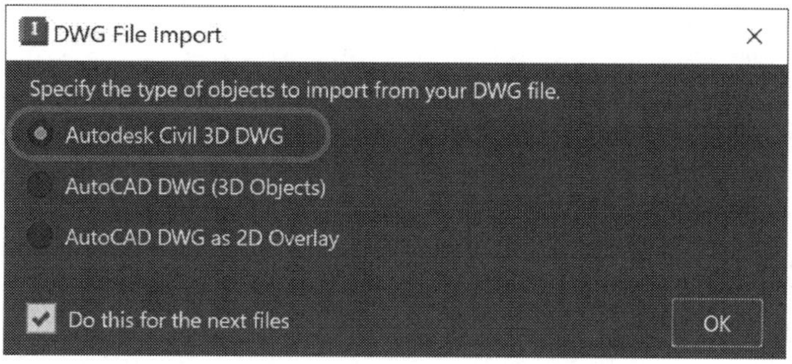

Figure A–47

3. In the *Choose Data Sources* dialog box, select all of the AEC objects you want in the InfraWorks model, as shown in Figure A–48. Click **OK**.

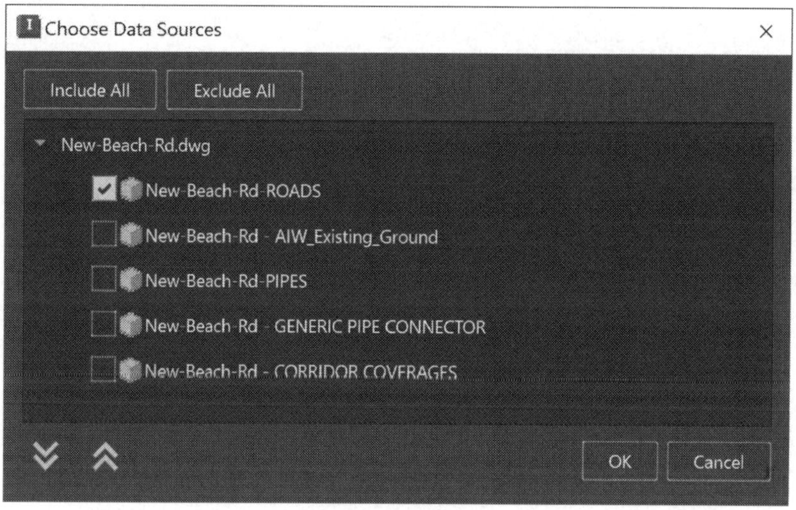

Figure A–48

4. In the *Data Sources* panel, note that all of the imported AEC objects display under their appropriate source type and are selected, as shown in Figure A–49. Click (Refresh data source).

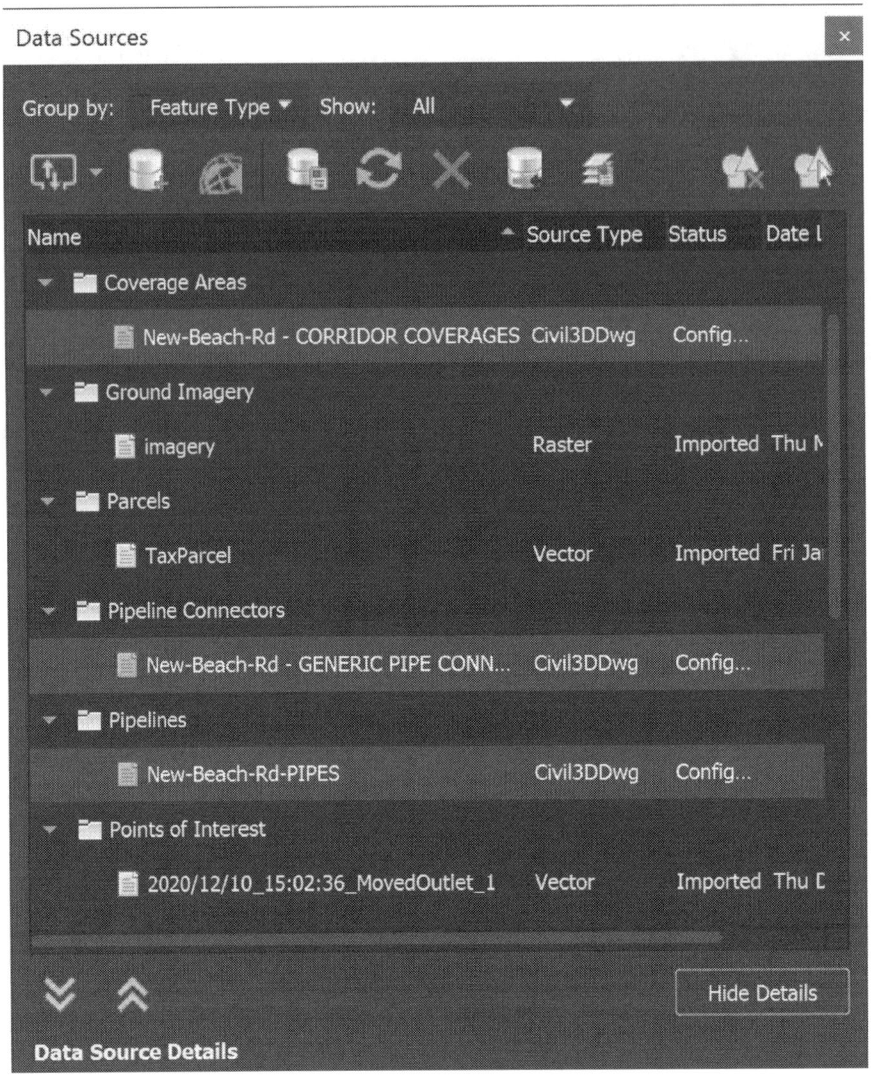

Figure A–49

When configuring the imported roads from Civil 3D, by default alignments will convert to component roads and corridors will convert to corridor component roads. There is a special tab (*Civil 3D DWG*) in the *Data Source Configuration* dialog box to control which option is preferred, as shown in Figure A–50.

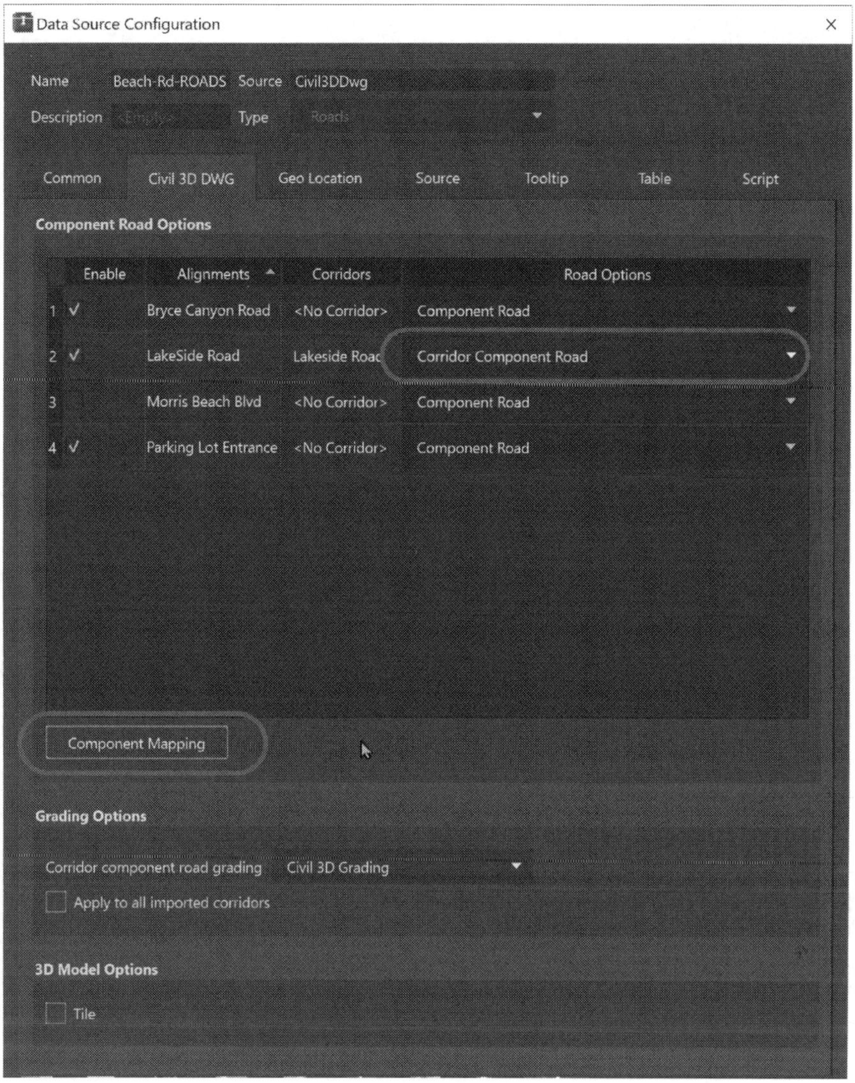

Figure A–50

Before importing the road, you can map how the Civil 3D subassemblies are converted to the InfraWorks road components by clicking the **Component Mapping** button. This will launch the *Component Mapping* dialog box, as shown in Figure A–51.

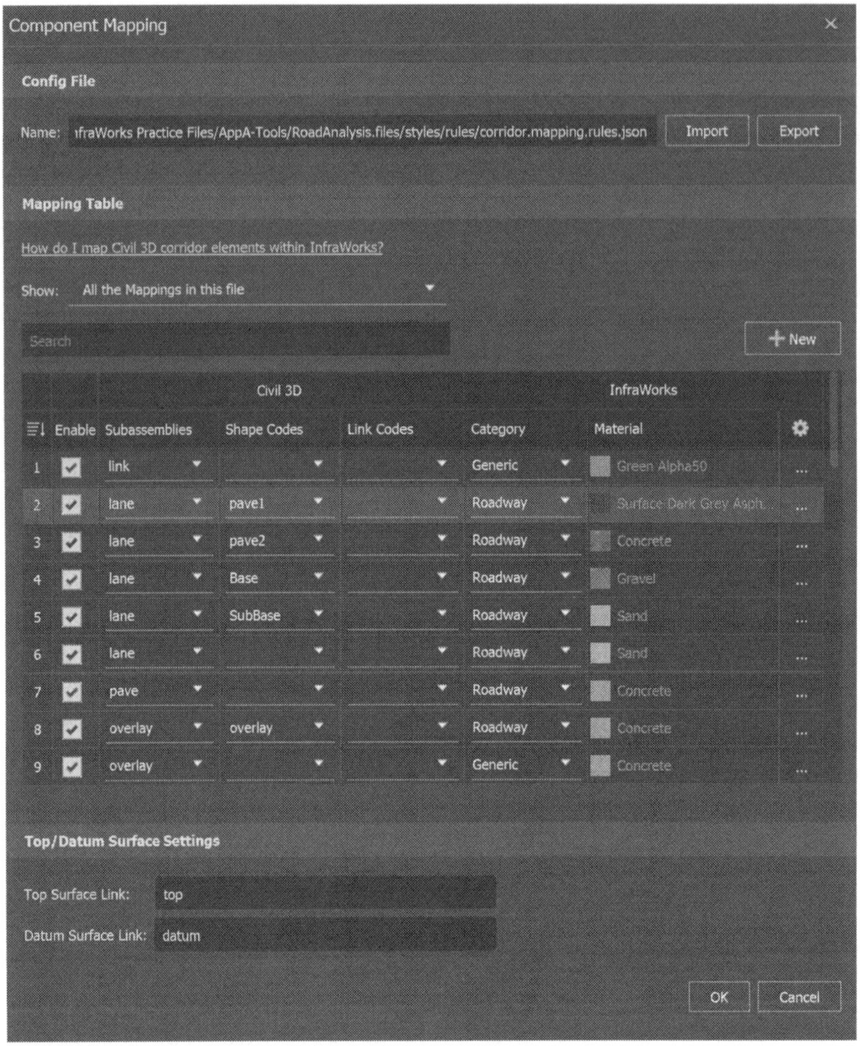

Figure A–51

Choosing the default corridor component road will limit the editing options in InfraWorks as well as cause the road to not interact with other component roads in the file. Consider a corridor component road to be a protected copy/replication of the Civil 3D corridor. It cannot be edited because it is linked to the Civil 3D drawing. Therefore the designers in Civil 3D have control over the corridor.

If, however, the road is configured as a component road, the InfraWorks users can manipulate the road in terms of cross-sections and components.

Note the options that are grayed out for modification, as shown in Figure A–52.

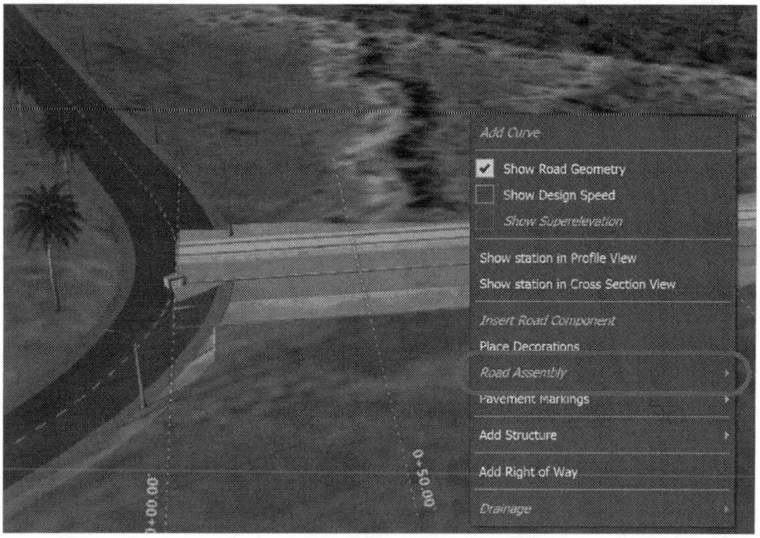

Figure A–52

At any time, the road setting can be adjusted by reconfiguring the imported file and adjusting the road setting. If changed from a corridor component road to a component road, the InfraWorks version of the road will now have all editing options and interact with the other component roads it may have come in contact with, as shown in Figure A–53.

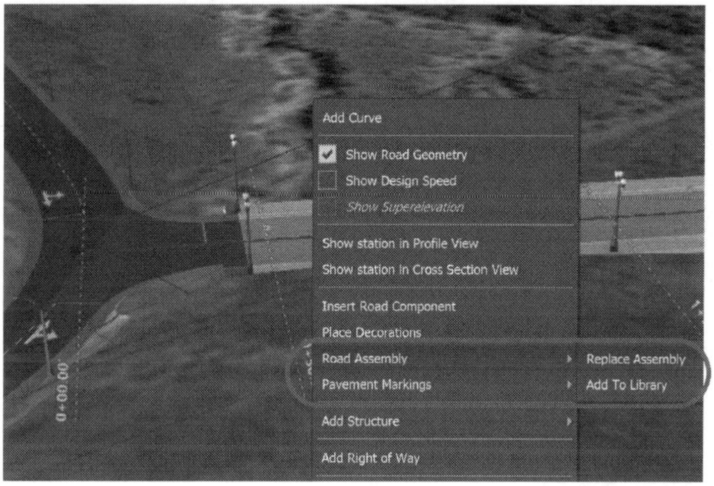

Figure A–53

Note in Figure A–53 that the style has been adjusted to the default assembly. The appropriate assembly can be assigned while configuring or by using **Replace Assembly** in the drawing area.

Hint: Updating Corridors

To update an imported Civil 3D corridor, right-click on the road in the *Data Sources* panel and select **Reimport...**, as shown in Figure A–54, regardless of what type of imported road it is.

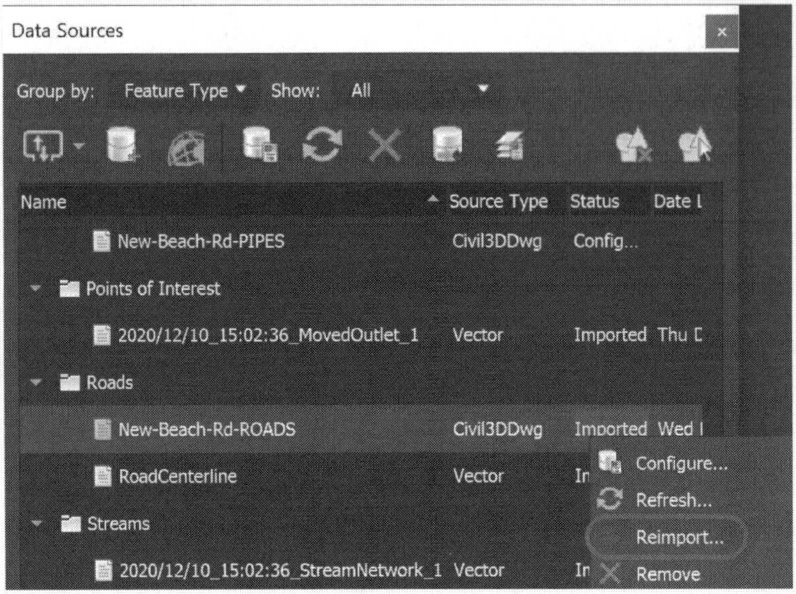

Figure A–54

Drawing Overlays

When the **Autodesk Civil 3D DWG** data source type is selected, only the AEC objects are imported into the InfraWorks model. In order to import other linework (such as parcel lines and utilities other than pipe networks), you can use an **AutoCAD DWG as 2D Overlay** data source type. When working with terrain overlays, you can:

- Move
- Rotate
- Scale
- Align
- Control selectability
- Control transparency, as shown in Figure A–55

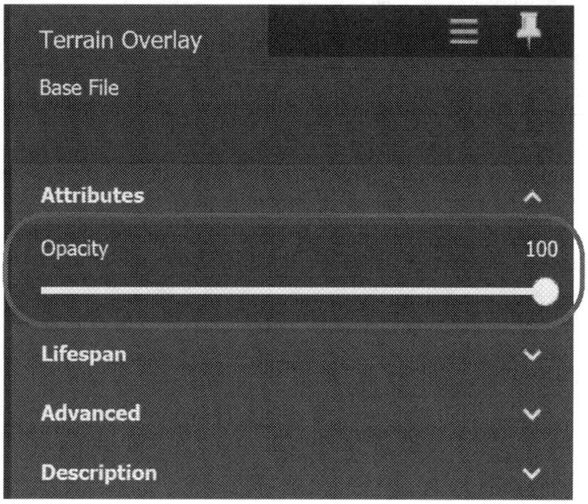

Figure A–55

How To: Import AutoCAD DWG File Linework

1. In the *Manage* tab>*Content* panel, click  (Data Sources) to open the *Data Sources* panel.

   Note: *To use this feature, access to the Internet and Autodesk® 360 account are required.*

2. In the *Data Sources* panel, expand  (Add file data source) and select **AutoCAD DWG as 2D Overlay**.
3. In the *Select Files* dialog box, browse to the AutoCAD .DWG file, select it, and click **Open**.
   - Alternatively, you can drag and drop .DWG files into the InfraWorks model from File Explorer. When you do, a *DWG File Import* dialog box displays that enables you to select what type of data source to use for the file, as shown in Figure A–56. Select the **AutoCAD DWG as 2D Overlay** option and click **OK**.

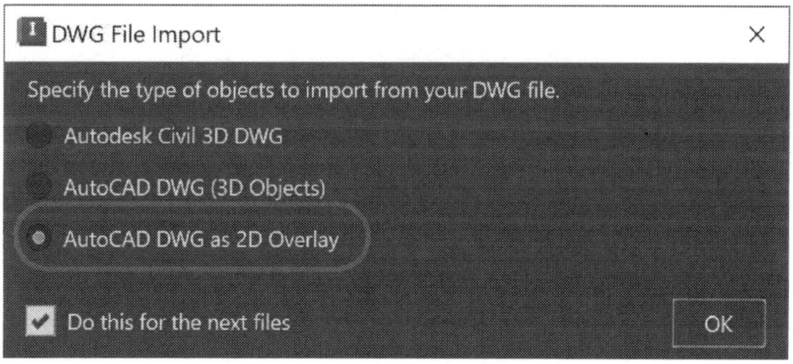

Figure A–56

4. In the *Data Import* dialog box, click **Send** when the following warning displays:
    - *This feature requires an Internet connection and an Autodesk 360 account. By clicking "Send", you will be transmitting data to InfraWorks cloud-based services.*
5. In the *Data Sources* panel, under *Terrain Overlays*, double-click on the imported DWG data source.
6. In the *Data Source Configuration* dialog box, adjust the *Scale* and *Rotation* as necessary. Click **Interactive Placing...** and double-click on a point in the model where the drawing should be located, as shown in Figure A–57.
    - Alternatively, you can set the coordinate system under *Position*, then set the *X* and *Y* coordinate values if you know them. (These values can be found by hovering the cursor over the expected insertion point in the InfraWorks model and taking note of the coordinates in the bottom-left corner of the model window.)

Set the coordinate system and location manually
or
place interactively

Figure A–57

7. In the *Data Source Configuration* dialog box, click **Close & Refresh**.
8. In the model, select the overlay. Then use the gizmos to move, scale, or rotate the overlay as required.

Practice A3
Incorporate a Civil 3D Corridor

Practice Objective

- Import Autodesk Civil 3D AEC objects to display the final design.

In this practice, you will reference data between the Autodesk InfraWorks software and the Autodesk Civil 3D software.

Task 1: Import Autodesk Civil 3D data.

In this task, you will import the Autodesk Civil 3D roads from the detailed design phase of the project.

1. On the *Home* screen, click **Open**. In the *InfraWorks Fundamentals Practice Files\AppA* folder, select **RoadAnalysis.sqlite** and click **Open**.
2. In the Toolbar, expand *Proposal* and select **C_Task1**.
3. Click (Bookmarks) and select **Beach Access**.
4. On the *Manage* tab, *Content* panel, select **Data Sources**.
5. In the *Data Sources* panel, expand (Add file data source) and select **Autodesk Civil 3D DWG**.
6. Browse to the *InfraWorks Fundamentals Practice Files\ Reference\Civil Files* folder, select **New-Beach-Rd.dwg**, and click **Open**.

7. In the *Choose Data Sources* dialog box, uncheck all but **New-Beach-Rd-ROADS**, as shown in Figure A–58. Click **OK**.

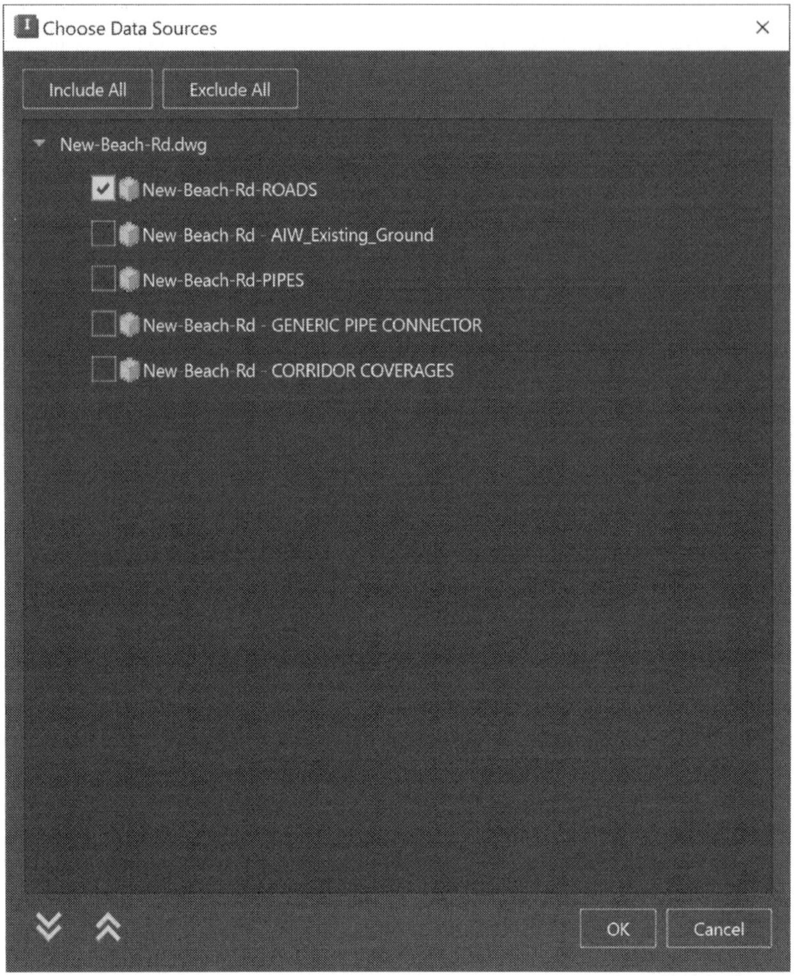

Figure A–58

8. Once the status no longer displays *Processing*, in the *Data Sources* panel, under *Roads*, right-click on the **New-Beach-Rd-ROADS** data source and select **Configure**, as shown in Figure A–59.

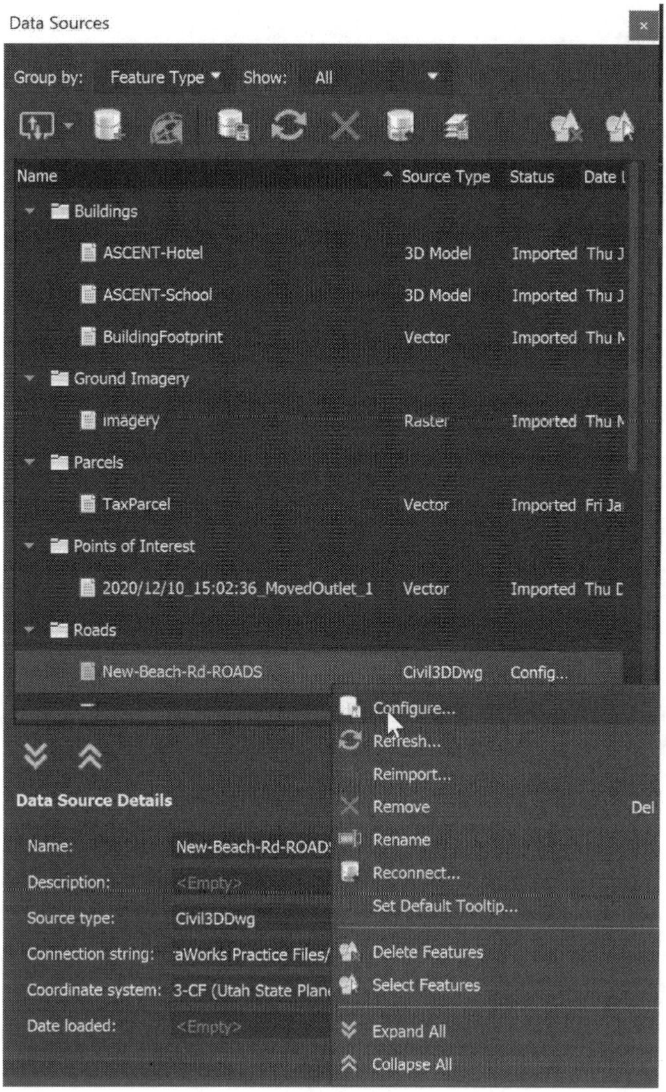

Figure A–59

9. On the *GeoLocation* tab of the *Data Source Configuration* dialog box, verify that the *Coordinate System* is set to **UT83-CF**.

10. On the *Civil 3D DWG* tab of the *Data Source Configuration* dialog box, review the **Component Road** options.

    Note that all but one comes in as *Component Road*. This is because all but one were alignments in *Civil 3D*.

11. Uncheck **Morris Beach Blvd**, as shown in Figure A–60, as it is already in the file as a road.

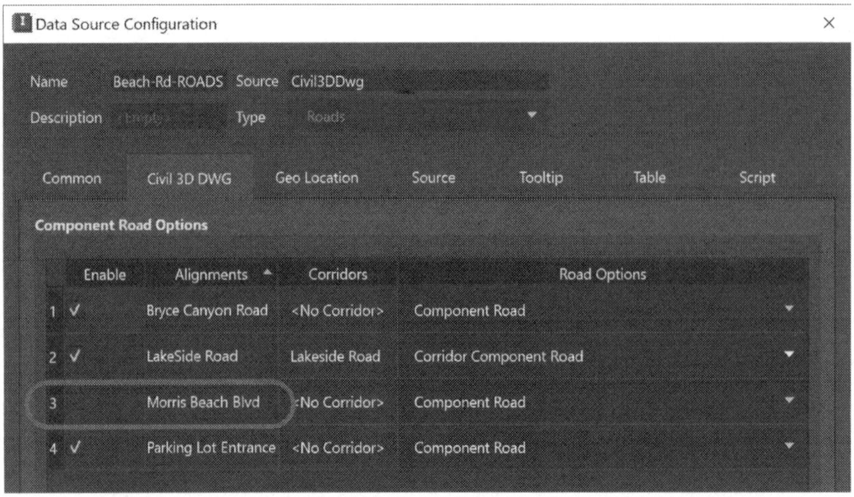

Figure A–60

12. Click **Close** and **Refresh**.

13. Review the road that came in. Note the styling as well as the fact that the road is not creating an intersection with **Morris Beach Blvd**, as shown in Figure A–61. This is because the configuration was set to **Corridor Component Road**.

Figure A–61

14. Click (Bookmarks) and select **New Intersection**. Note how the intersection with **Morris Beach Blvd** is rough and will require some clean-up.

15. Select and right-click on the imported road, as shown in Figure A–62. Review the grayed out editing features.

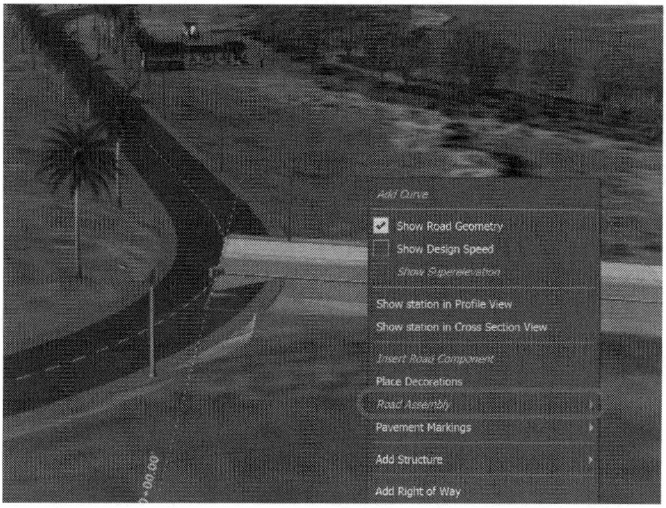

Figure A–62

Task 2: Convert to a component road.

1. Continue working in the same model as the previous task. If you did not complete the previous task, select the **C_Task2** proposal to make it current.
2. In the *Manage* tab>*Content* panel, select **Data Sources** if the panel is not open.
3. In the *Data Sources* panel, under *Roads*, right-click on the **New-Beach-Rd-ROADS** data source and select **Configure**.
4. On the *Civil 3D DWG* tab of the *Data Source Configuration* dialog box, adjust the *Lakeside Road* to be a **Component Road** using the drop-down list under *Road Options*, as shown in Figure A–63.

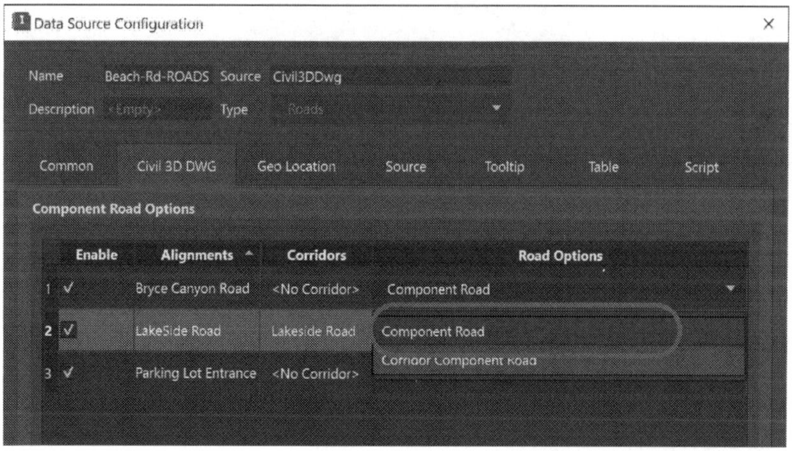

Figure A–63

5. Click **Close & Refresh**.
6. Click  (Bookmarks) and select **New Intersection**.
7. Note the style changes and that the intersection is now corrected at **Morris Beach Blvd**, as shown in Figure A–64.

Figure A–64

8. Select and right-click on **Lakeside Road**.
9. Select **Road Assembly>Replace Assembly.**
10. In the *Select Template* panel, scroll to the bottom and select **ASC-Collector Component/ Custom,** as shown in Figure A–65.

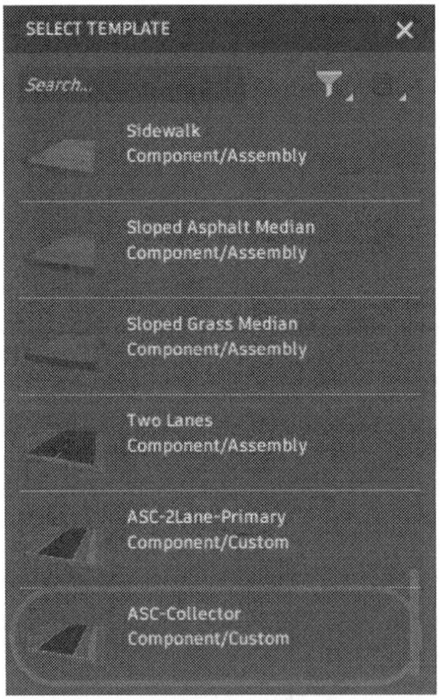

Figure A–65

11. Move the placement box to **0+00** and click to place the box, then drag the highlighted area to the end of the road, as shown in Figure A–66. Double-click to finish the placement.

Figure A–66

12. Review the road with the new assembly and the intersection, as shown in Figure A–67.

Figure A–67

End of practice

A.4 Corridor Optimization

> ***Note:*** *To use this feature, access to the Internet is required.*

The *Corridor Optimization* module provides advanced optimization algorithms for finding an optimal horizontal roadway alignment. This cloud service uses the model terrain and other GIS information in the model to create cost-effective and environmentally friendly solutions. The best available path is calculated by setting the start and end points for the road. The optimal time for performing a corridor optimization is when you are first considering the layout of the roadway.

Advanced Settings

When the *Advanced Settings* are expanded in the *Corridor Optimization* panel, additional constraints can be added to the corridor.

Avoidance zones can be specified to alert the Corridor Optimization that the new road corridor could through environmentally sensitive or other high-cost areas. It may still pass through such areas, but the costs will be higher. These costs can be assigned in the *Coverage* panel for the Avoidance Zone, as shown in Figure A–68.

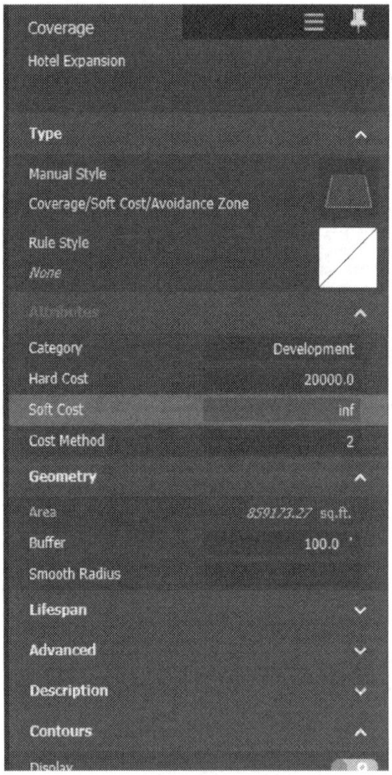

Figure A–68

You can assign Hard Costs to the Avoidance Zone. The Soft Cost is set to **inf** as a default, suggesting that InfraWorks will handle these.

Additionally, they can be activated by opening a suitability map by selecting **Open suitability map**, then selecting the option to **Include the current suitability map**, as shown in Figure A–69.

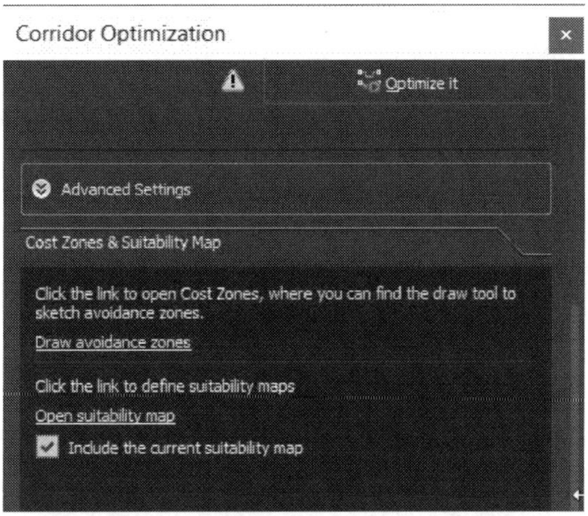

Figure A–69

Hint: Unexpected results

If the Avoidance Zones and Suitability Maps do not achieve the expected results, you can insert a vertex in the path definition through the right-click menu, as shown in Figure A–70.

Figure A–70

Construction Rules

Setting construction rules provides a method of ensuring bridges are placed and tunnels are cut where cut/fill heights exceed a maximum height. Additionally, roadside grading values can be set, as shown in Figure A–71.

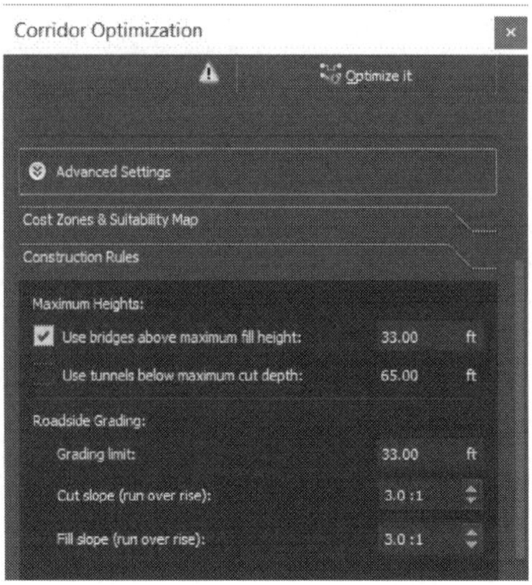

Figure A–71

Alignment Constraints

The *Minimum radius* can be set under *Alignment Constraints*, as shown in Figure A–72.

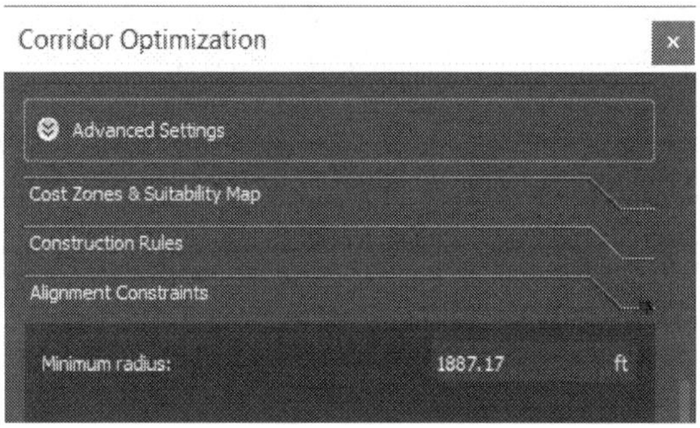

Figure A–72

Profile Constraints

The *Maximum grade* can be set under *Profile Constraints*, as shown in Figure A–73.

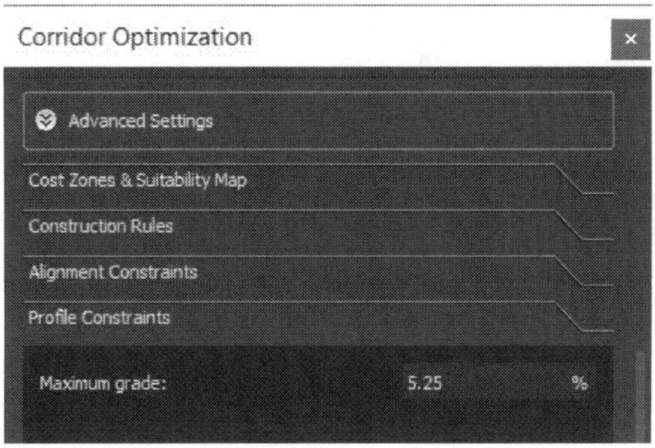

Figure A–73

Construction & Earthwork Cost

Prices for construction and earthwork cost items can be set using the *Construction & Earthwork Costs Settings* dialog box. To access this dialog box, click **Construction & Earthwork Cost**, as shown in Figure A–74.

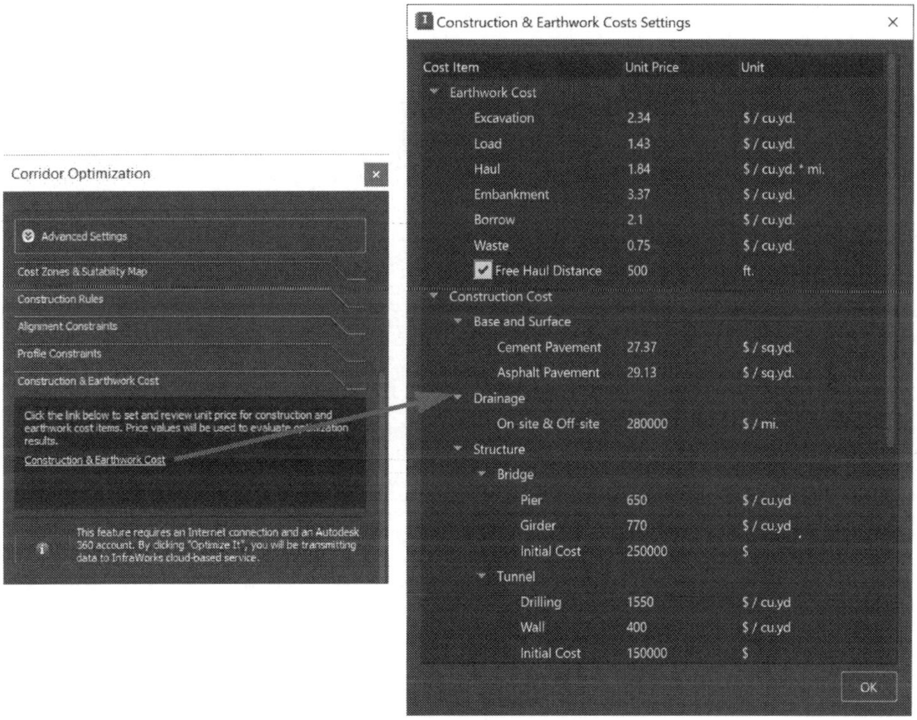

Figure A–74

Job Monitor

The corridor optimization results are communicated through the *Job Monitor* panel, which displays automatically once you run an optimization. The status of all the optimizations that have been run display here, as shown in Figure A–75.

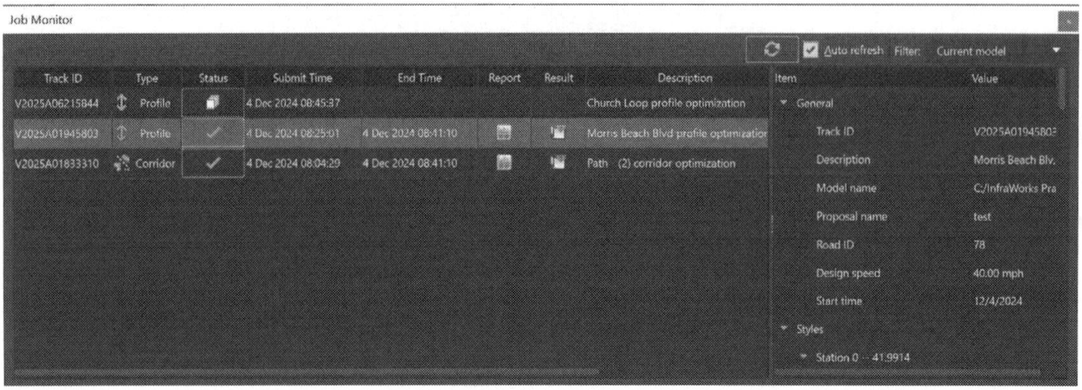

Figure A–75

Status

You will receive an email when from *InfraWorks No reply* when the optimization is compete and the report is ready, a sample of which is shown in Figure A–76.

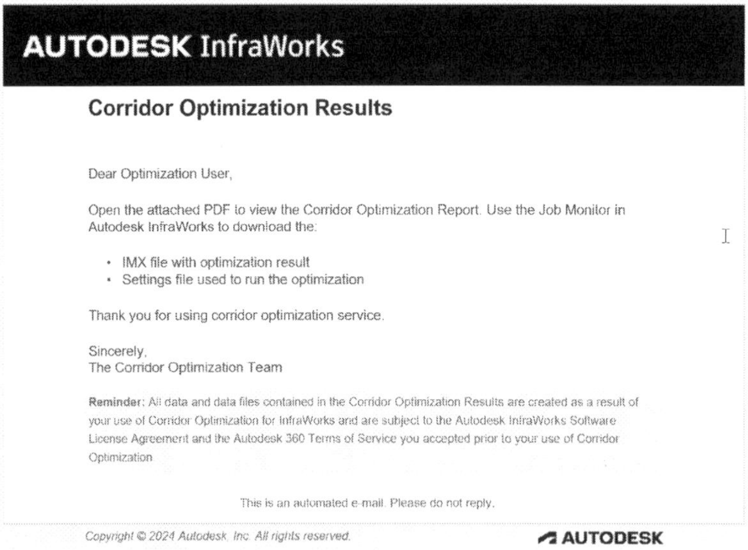

Figure A–76

In the *Job Monitor* panel, click (Refresh) to update the panel.

The *Status* column displays the current status of your optimization. There are three status icons, which are as follows:

Icon	Status	Description
	**Queued**	Indicates that the profile has been sent to the cloud for computing, but has not started yet.
	**In Progress**	Indicates that the profile is currently being optimized in the cloud.
	**Completed**	Indicates that the optimization calculations are complete.

Viewing Results

The results of the optimization can be viewed by:

- Downloading a report.
- Importing the data into a new proposal in the model.

Report

In the *Job Monitor* panel, under the *Report* column, clicking  (Click to download an optimization report) opens a file and displays the results of the calculations. This is the same report that is attached to the notification email. This report displays items including alignment information, profile information, and construction information.

Figure A–77 shows a sample report with the suggested horizontal and profile view for the component road.

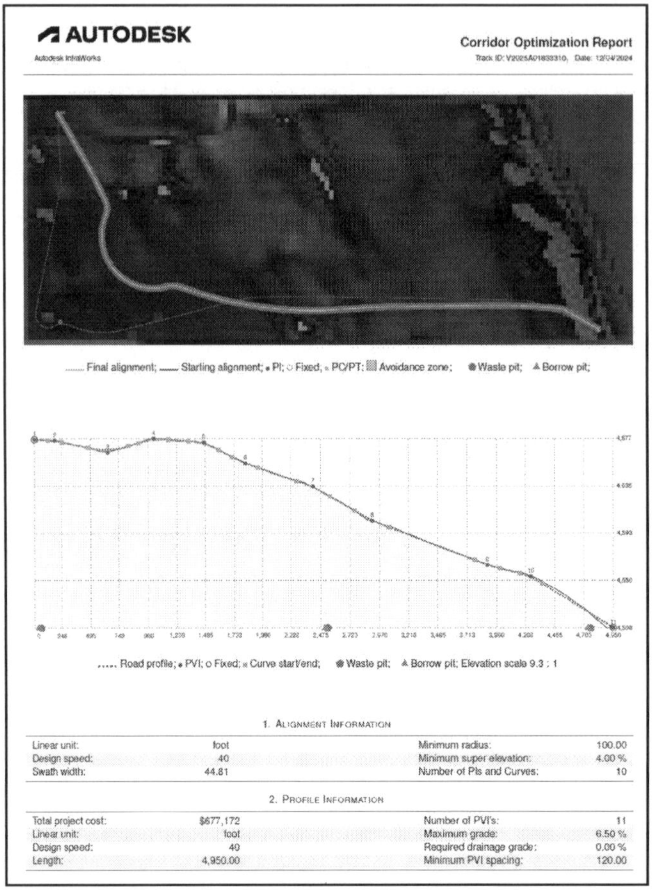

Figure A–77

Create a Proposal from the Results

In addition to downloading the results in a file, you can also view the results by importing the roadway into a new proposal in the model. To do this, in the *Job Monitor* panel, in the *Results* column, click (Create a proposal to view the results in the model).

How To: Run a Corridor Optimization

1. In the *Analyze* tab>*Transportation* drop-down list, click (Corridor Optimization).
2. In the *Corridor Optimization* panel, set the following options (as shown in Figure A–78):
   - Select an appropriate *Design speed* for the project.
   - Select the *Structure styles* for the *Road*, *Bridge*, and *Tunnel*.
   - For the *Path*, click (Define PIs).

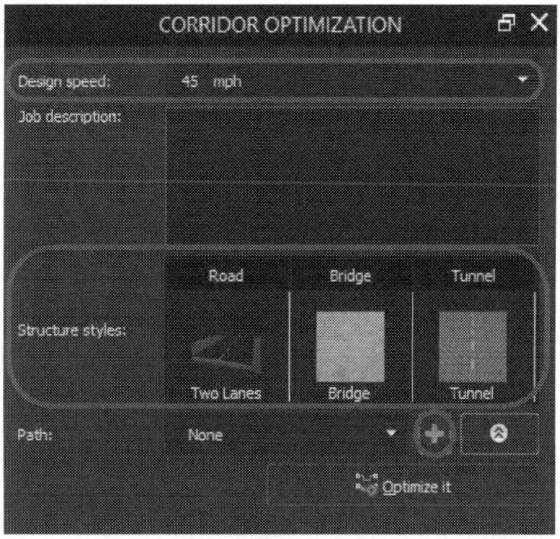

Figure A–78

3. In the model, click to set the start PI and the end PI.
4. In the *Corridor Optimization* panel, expand the *Advanced Settings* area.
5. In the *Cost Zones & Suitability Map* area, click **Draw avoidance zones**.
6. In the *Cost Zones* asset card, click (Draw avoidance zones). In the model, create polylines to define areas to avoid.
7. In the *Cost Zones & Suitability Map* area, click **Open suitability map**.
8. In the *Suitability Maps* asset card, expand the Select a Map drop-down list and select the appropriate map for your needs.
9. In the *Corridor Optimization* panel, select the **Include the current suitability map** option.
10. In the *Construction Rules* area, set the maximum cut/fill heights and the roadside grading parameters, as required.
11. In the *Alignment Constraints* area, set the minimum radius.
12. In the *Profile Constraints* area, set the maximum grade.

13. In the *Construction & Earthwork Cost* area, click **Construction & Earthwork Cost** to open the dialog box and set costing values.
14. In the *Corridor Optimization* panel, ensure that the correct path is selected, then click **Optimize it**.
15. In the *Job Monitor* panel, under the *Report* column, click (Click to download an optimization report) to review the results in a report format.

    Note: *If the Job Monitor panel does not open, in the Analyze tab> Transportation drop-down list, click (Job Monitor).*

16. In the *Job Monitor* panel, under the *Results* column, click (Create a proposal to view the result in the model).
17. Click **Yes** in the *Information* dialog box.
18. Type a name and click **OK** to create the proposal.

Practice A4
Identify the Best Location for a New Roadway

Practice Objective

- Locate the best location for a roadway based on a suitability map.

After seeing the plan, the approving agency requires another option for the roadway that accesses a proposed beach park to the south of the hotel. In this practice, you will use a suitability map in the corridor optimization to find the best location for a new roadway.

> ***Note:*** *To complete this project, access to the Internet is required. Traffic load in the cloud may cause delays in the analysis and results..*

1. Continue working in the same model as the previous practice. If you did not complete the previous practice, select the **D_Task1** proposal to make it current.
2. Click (Bookmarks) and select **New Beach**.
3. In the *Analyze* tab>*Transportation* panel, click (Corridor Optimization).
4. In the *Corridor Optimization* panel, set the following options (as shown in Figure A–79):
    - *Design speed:* **40 mph (from the drop-down list)**
    - *Structure styles, Road:* **Two Lanes (Should already be set as the default)**
    - *Path*: Click (Define PIs)

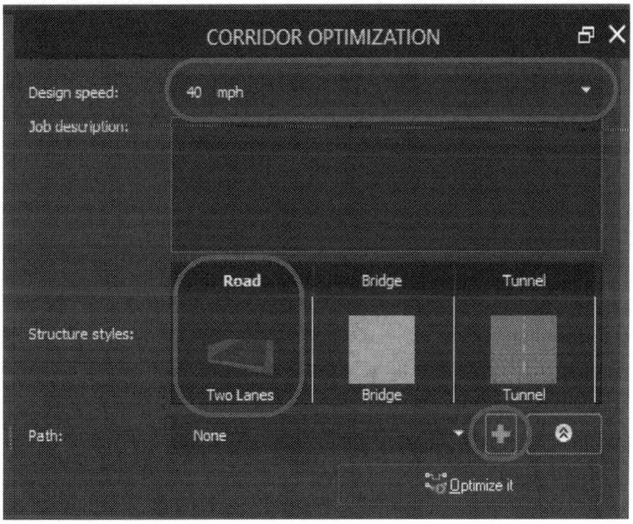

Figure A–79

5. In the model, click to set the *start PI* at **Adams Ave** and the *end PI* south of the **Ascent Hotel** near the lake shore, as shown in Figure A–80. If the yellow alert marker appears warning that the PIs are too close together, move the ending PI further south until the warning disappears.

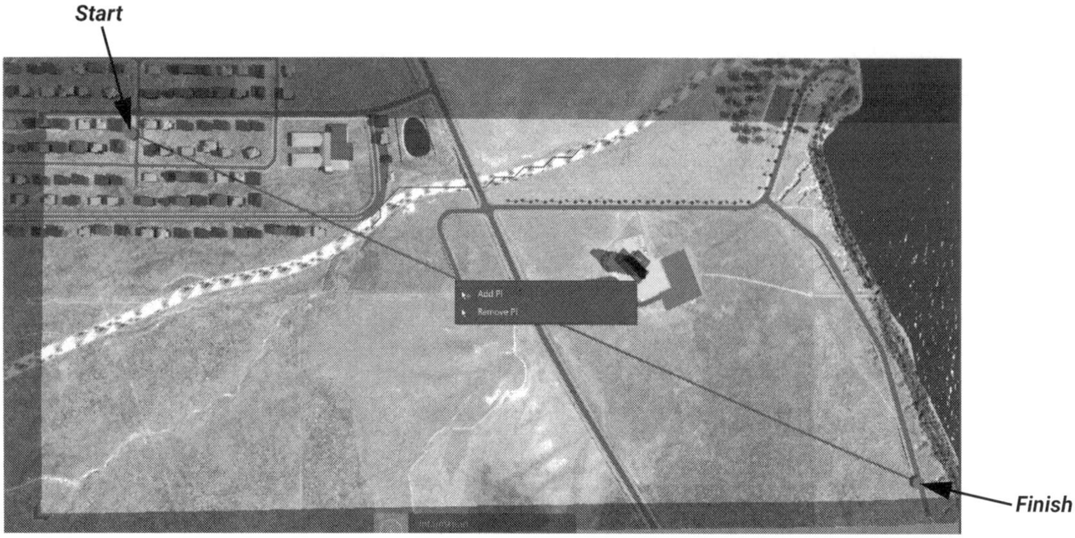

Figure A–80

6. Insert a Point of Intersection (PI) by right-clicking and selecting **Insert**, as shown in Figure A–81.

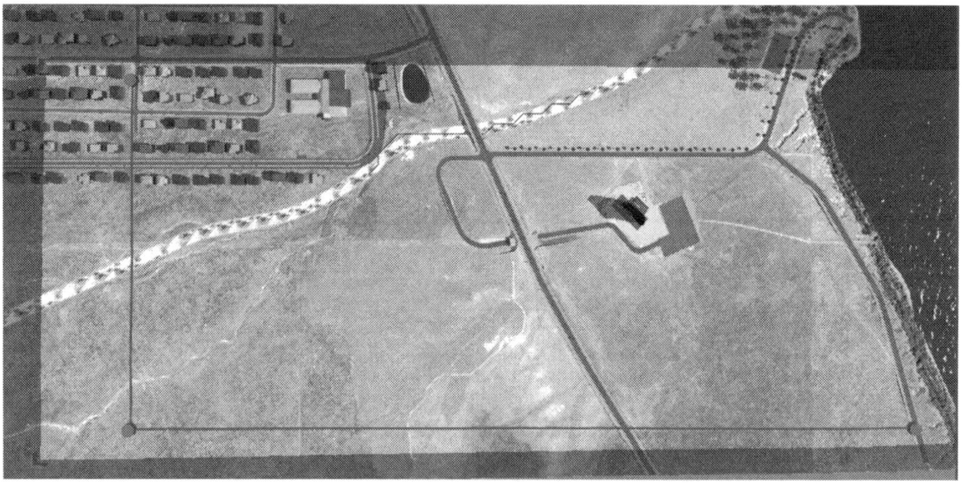

Figure A–81

7. In the *Corridor Optimization* panel, expand the *Advanced Settings* area.
8. In the *Cost Zones & Suitability Map* area, click **Draw avoidance zones**.

9. In the *Avoidance Zones* asset card, click (Draw avoidance zones). In the model, create the area shown in Figure A–82. Ensure that you double-click to finish the boundary.

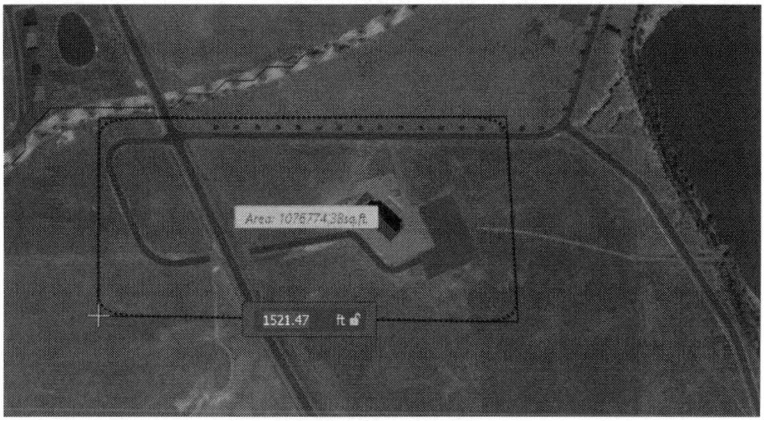

Figure A–82

10. Name the avoidance zone **Hotel Expansion Area**, and assign **120000.0** for *Hard Cost*. The result of the avoidance zone is shown in Figure A–83.

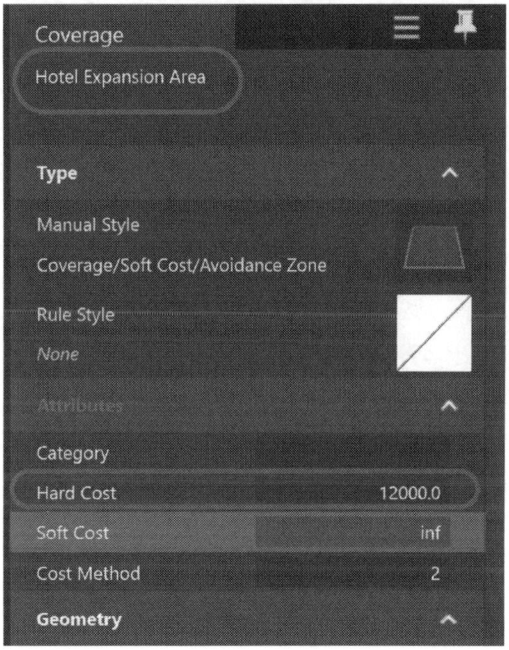

Figure A–83

11. Click on the **X** in the top right corner to dismiss the *Avoidance Zones* asset card.

12. If you want to see the avoidance zone you just created, in the *Manage* tab>*Display* panel select (Surface Layers). Under the *Ground Imagery & Coverages* category, turn on the **Sketched Coverage Areas** layer by clicking (Show/Hide data source contents), as shown in Figure A–84.

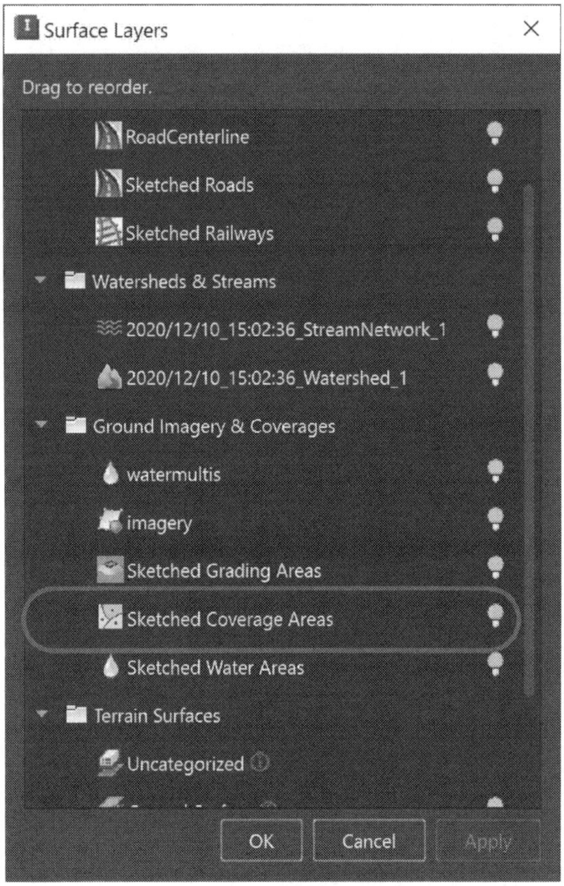

Figure A–84

13. In the *Cost Zones & Suitability Map* area, click **Open suitability map**. In the *Suitability Maps* asset card, expand the *Select a Map* drop-down list and select **Avoid Water & Buildings**.
14. Click **Apply**, then close the *Suitability Maps* asset card.
15. In the *Corridor Optimization* panel, in the *Cost Zones & Suitability Map* area, select the **Include the current suitability map** option.
16. In the *Alignment Constraints* area, set the minimum radius to **100**. You may have to scroll down to find the *Alignment Constraints* section of the *Advanced Settings*.

17. In the *Corridor Optimization* panel, ensure that **Path - (1)** is selected (your path number might be different). Leave all other constraints as they are, as shown in Figure A–85, and click **Optimize it**.

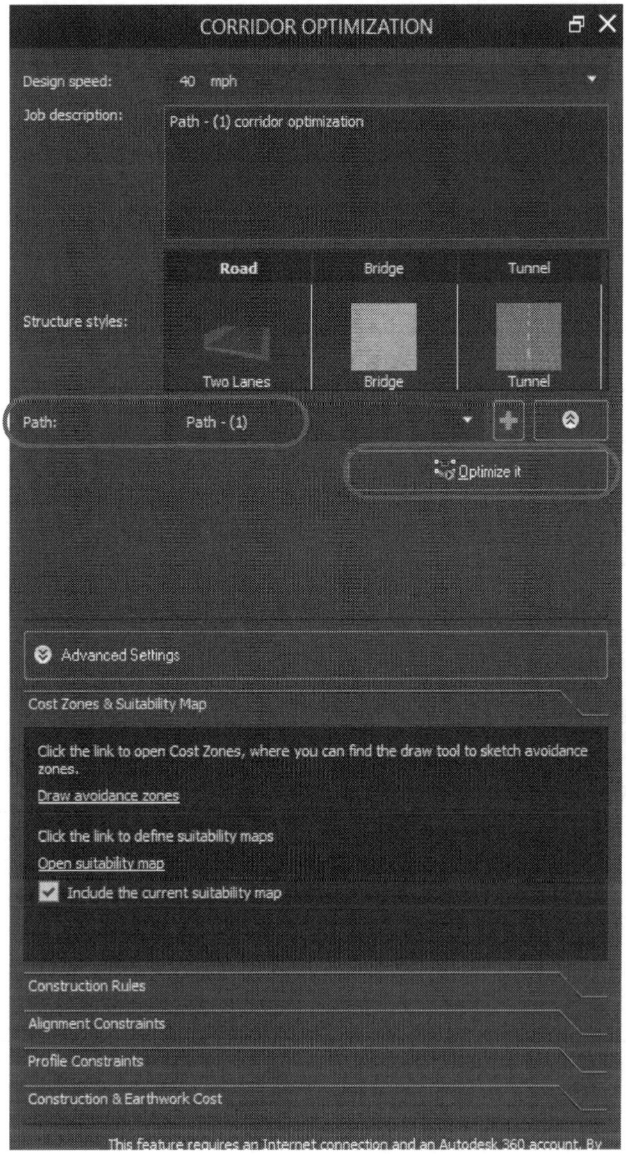

Figure A–85

Note: *This could take as much as 25 minutes, depending on the current load in the cloud. If it takes too long, you can see the* ***New Beach Corridor Report.pdf*** *report in the InfraWorks Practice Files\ References\Reports folder. You can also open the* ***Z_Beach_Corridor_Complete*** *proposal.*

18. Turn off the **Sketched Coverage Areas** layer if you had turned it on earlier.
19. Disable the suitability maps by going to the *Create* tab>*Environment* drop-down list, click (Suitability Maps), then in the *Suitability Maps* panel, toggle off the **Activate Maps** option.
20. If the *Job Monitor* panel does not open, in the *Analyze* tab>*Transportation* drop-down list, click (Job Monitor).
21. In the *Job Monitor* panel, under the *Report* column, click (Click to download an optimization report) to review the results in a report.
22. In the *Job Monitor* panel, under the *Results* column, click (Create a proposal to view the result in the model). Click **Yes** in the *Information* dialog box.
23. Type **New_Beach_Corridor** for the name and click **OK** to create the proposal.
24. Close the *Corridor Optimization* panel, which also hides the proposed path. The result is shown in Figure A–86 (your results may be different).

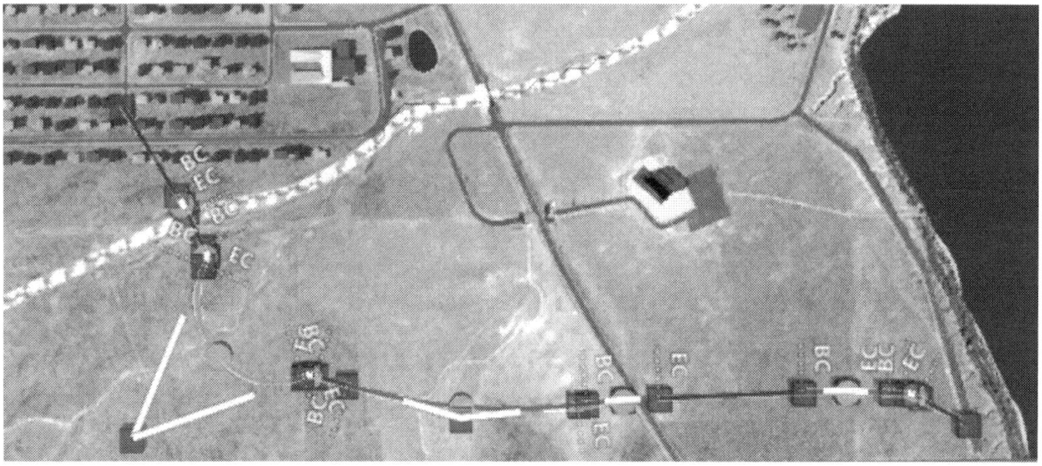

Figure A–86

25. Close the *Job Monitor* panel.

End of practice

A.5 Balance Cut and Fill Along the Roadway

Profile Optimization

Multiple vertical design options can be calculated quickly using profile optimization tools. Running a profile optimization enables you to enter specific cost information for the project area. This information is used to reduce haul charges, thus decreasing the cost of the project. During the analysis process, certain parameters can be set to ensure that project constraints are met.

> ***Note:*** *To use this feature, access to the Internet is required.*

Profile Constraints

A number of profile constraints can be set under the *Advanced Settings* area of the Profile Optimization panel, including:

- Maximum grade
- Minimum PVI spacing
- Required drainage grade
- PVI frequency
- Anchored PVIs

Anchored PVIs are required when the component road must match existing or proposed conditions, such as when the road crosses another road or requires a specific clearance. The *Profile Constraints* area of the *Profile Optimization* panel is shown in Figure A–87.

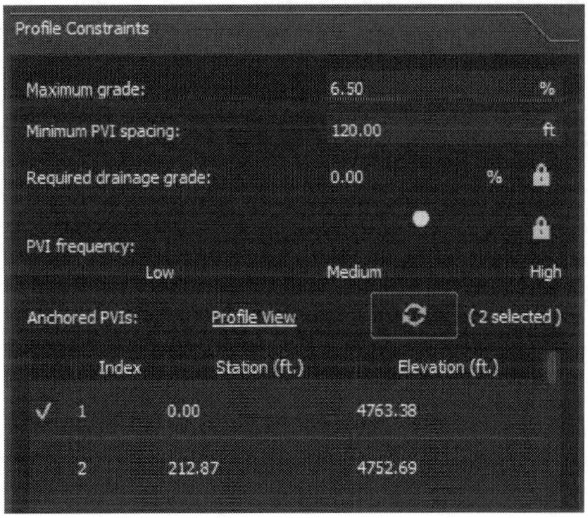

Figure A–87

Quantities Options

Borrow and waste pits can be added to the model at specific stations to reduce mass haul charges. The capacity of each pit and the access distance from the road can both be set in the *Quantities Options* area, as shown in Figure A–88.

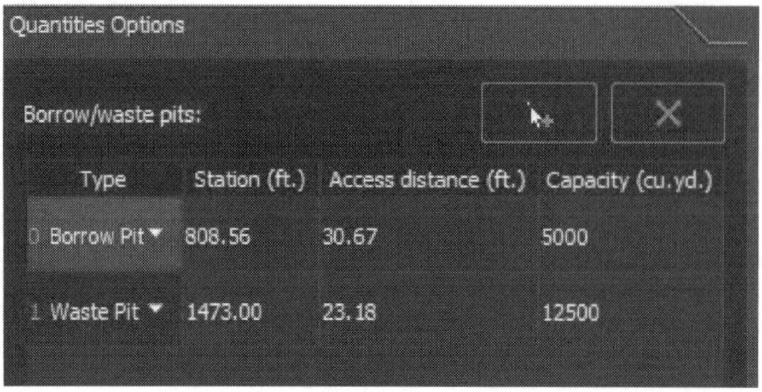

Figure A–88

Construction Rules

Construction rules can be set to determine what to do when a cut or fill becomes excessive. If a fill height is above the specified value, a bridge is used rather than fill material. Alternatively, if a cut depth is beyond the specified value, a tunnel is used to reduce the environmental impact. This is set in the *Construction Rules* area of the *Profile Optimization* panel, as shown in Figure A–89.

Figure A–89

Construction and Earthwork Cost

The cost of the project can be estimated by entering construction and earthwork costs for the area where the project is located. These are defined in the *Construction & Earthwork Costs Settings* dialog box, as shown in Figure A–90.

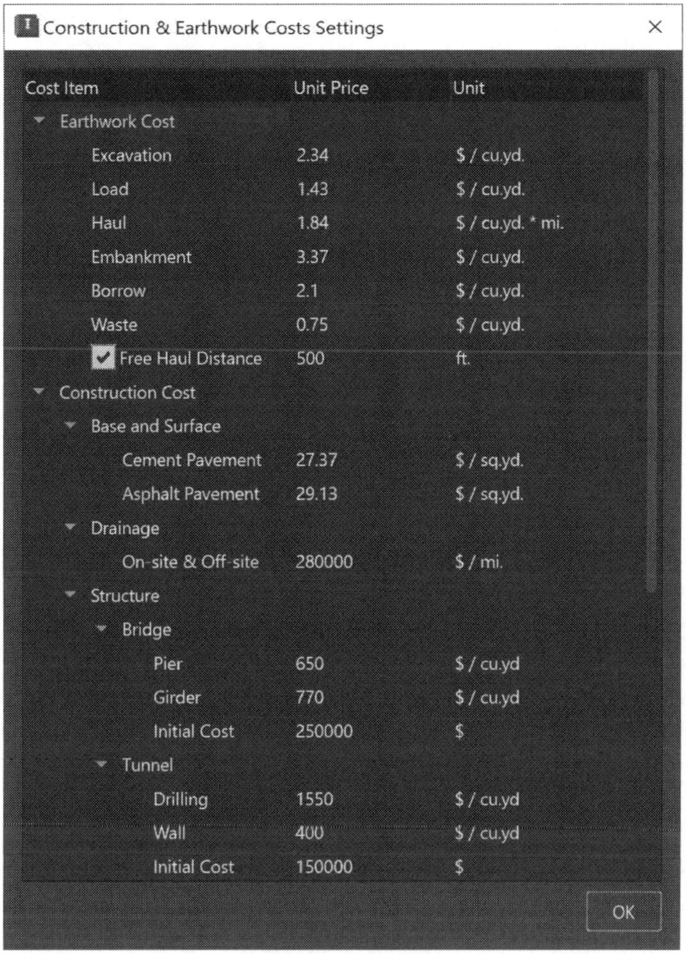

Figure A–90

Optimize It

Once you have entered all of the information, you can send the roadway to the cloud for calculating. Do this by clicking **Optimize it** in the *Profile Optimization* panel, as shown in Figure A–91.

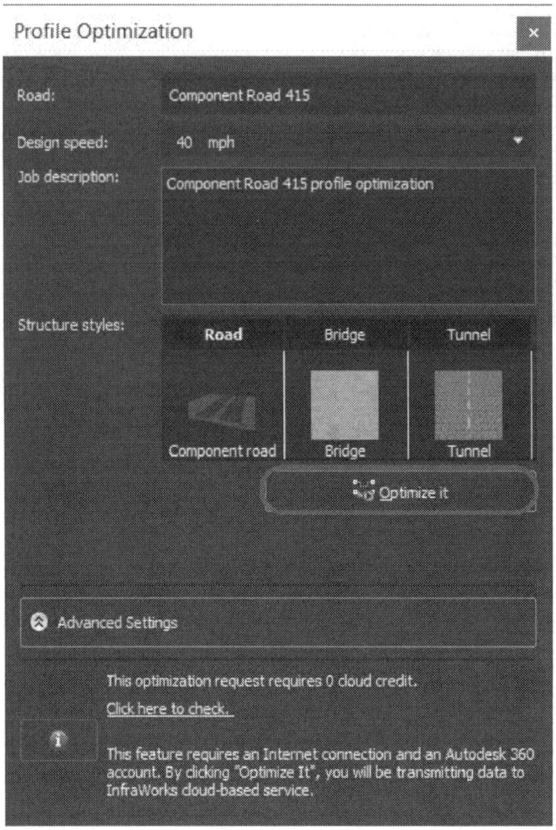

Figure A–91

When you click **Optimize it** within the *Profile Optimization* panel, your design is transmitted to the InfraWorks cloud-based service. The cloud-based service runs the calculations, enabling you to continue working on the design.

Job Monitor

Viewing Results

Similar to a corridor optimization, the results of the profile optimization can be viewed in two different ways:

- Downloading a report.
- Importing the data into a new proposal in the model.

Report

In the *Job Monitor* panel, in the *Report* column, clicking  (Click to download an optimization report) opens Adobe Reader or PDF Reader and displays the results of the calculations. This report displays:

- Total project cost
- Total construction cost
- A haul diagram
- Cut and fill quantities along the roadway
- Additional information

Figure A–92 shows a sample report with the suggested profile view for the component road.

AUTODESK

Autodesk InfraWorks

Profile Optimization Report

Track ID: V2023A03819426, Date: 12/09/2022

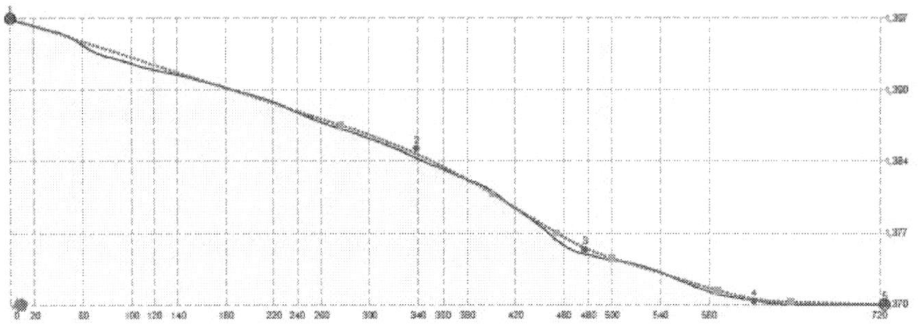

...... Road profile; • PVI; o Fixed; ▪ Curve start/end; ● Waste pit; ▲ Borrow pit; Elevation scale 8.5 : 1

1. PROFILE INFORMATION

Total project cost:	$336,309	Number of PVI's:	5
Linear unit:	meter	Maximum grade:	7.00 %
Design speed:	50	Required drainage grade:	0.00 %
Length:	724.09	Minimum PVI spacing:	31.25

2. CONSTRUCTION INFORMATION

Total construction cost:[1]	$326,887	Use bridges:	Yes
Number of bridges:	0	Use tunnels:	No
Number of tunnels:	0	Sample line distance:	10.00
Number of retainings:	0		

2.1. **Road Assembly Information.** The construction cost for a sample line subsection with a road assembly is l times the road cost per linear unit.

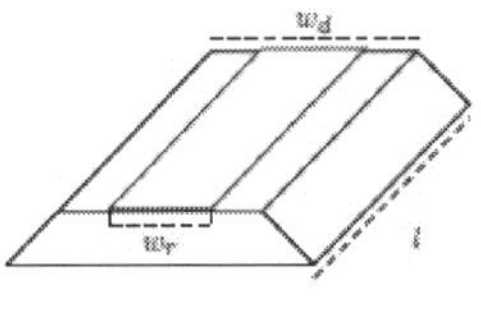

l : Sample line distance
w_r : Road width
w_d : Datum width

Road cost per linear meter:[2]	$447.79	Daylight cut slope:	0.33
Road width:[3]	7.20	Daylight fill slope:	0.33
Datum width:	7.20 – 9.64		

Figure A–92

Create a Proposal from Results

In addition to downloading the results in a file, you can also view the results by importing the corrected profile into a new proposal in the model. To do this, in the *Job Monitor* panel, in the *Results* column, click (Create a proposal to view the results in the model).

Practice A5
Perform a Vertical Optimization

Practice Objective

- Balance the cut and fill quantities for a design roadway.

In this practice, you will run a vertical optimization for the parking lot access road. You will then import the new proposal to view the results, shown in Figure A–93.

> ***Note:*** *To complete this practice, access to the Internet is required.*

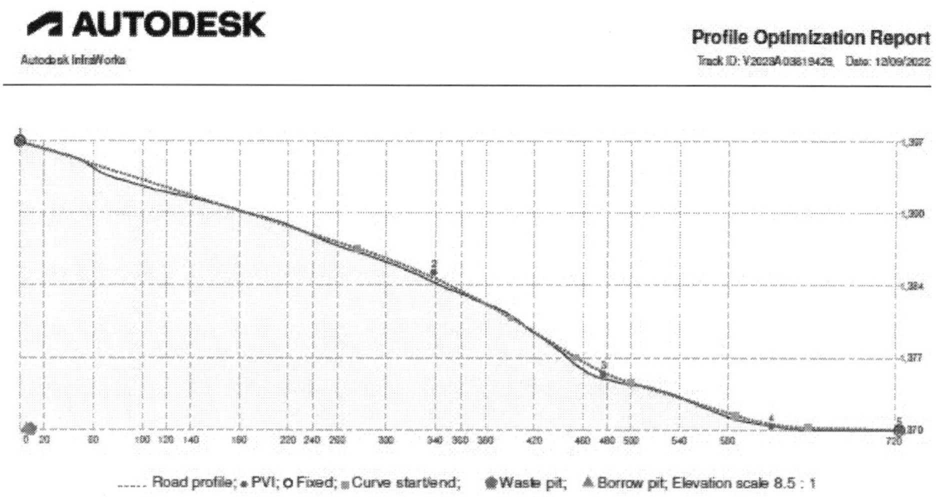

Figure A–93

1. Continue working in the same model as the last practice. In the toolbar, expand the (Proposals) drop-down list and select **D_Task2** to make it current.

2. Click (Bookmarks) and select **New Beach**.

3. In the model, select **Morris Beach Blvd**, as shown in Figure A–94.

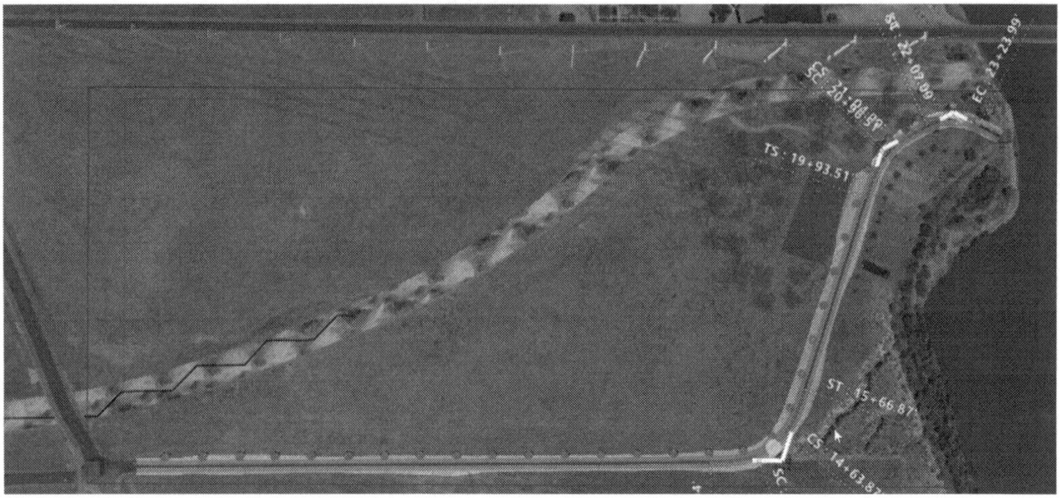

Figure A–94

4. In the *Analyze* tab>*Transportation* drop-down list, click  (Profile Optimization).
5. In the *Profile Optimization* panel, ensure the *Design speed* is set to **40 mph** and the *Structure styles* is set to **Component road**, as shown in Figure A–95.

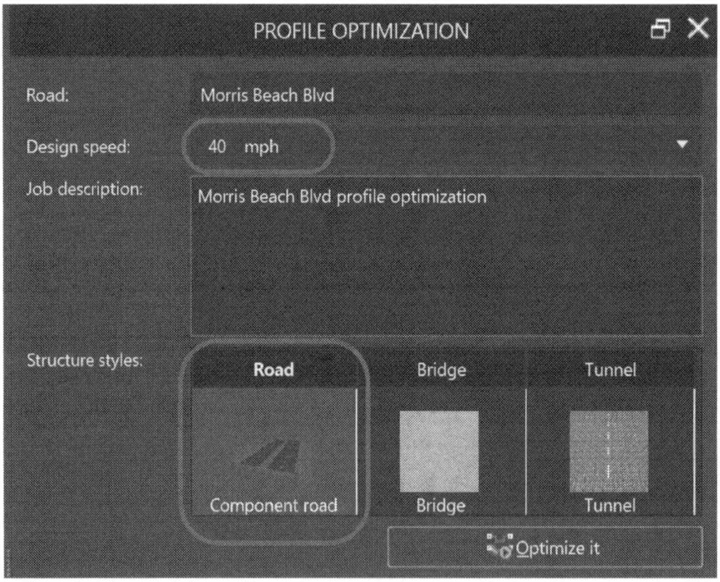

Figure A–95

6. Expand *Advanced Settings*, then expand the *Profile Constraints* area. Set the following, as shown in Figure A–96:
    - *Maximum grade*: **6%**
    - *Minimum PVI spacing*: **130 ft**
    - In the *Anchored PVIs* area, select PVI **4**. This will ensure that the 4th PVI will not be modified. The first and last PVI are automatically selected, as shown in Figure A–96.

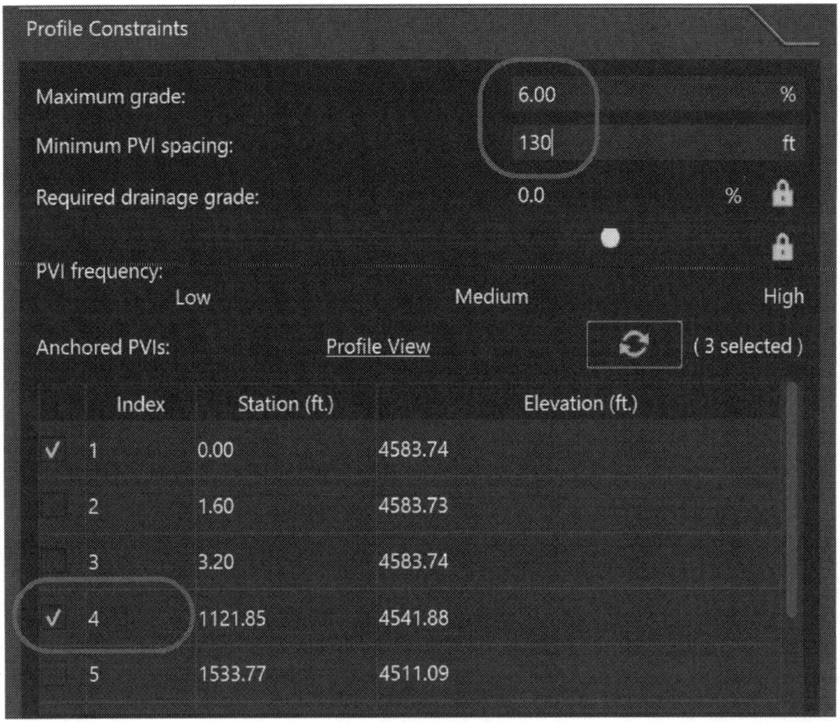

Figure A–96

7. Leave all settings in the other sections as their defaults and scroll back to the top, then click **Optimize it**.

    Note: *The Profile Optimization may take up to 30 minutes to complete. If it takes too long, you can open the* ***Morris Beach Blvd Profile Report.pdf*** *report in the InfraWorks Practice Files\References\Reports folder. You can also open the* ***Z_Morris_Profile_Complete*** *proposal.*

8. If the *Job Monitor* panel does not open, in the *Analyze* tab>*Transportation* drop-down list, click  (Job Monitor).

9. When the Profile Optimization is completed in the cloud, you will receive an email from *InfraWorks Noreply* and the report is ready, a sample of which is shown in Figure A–97.

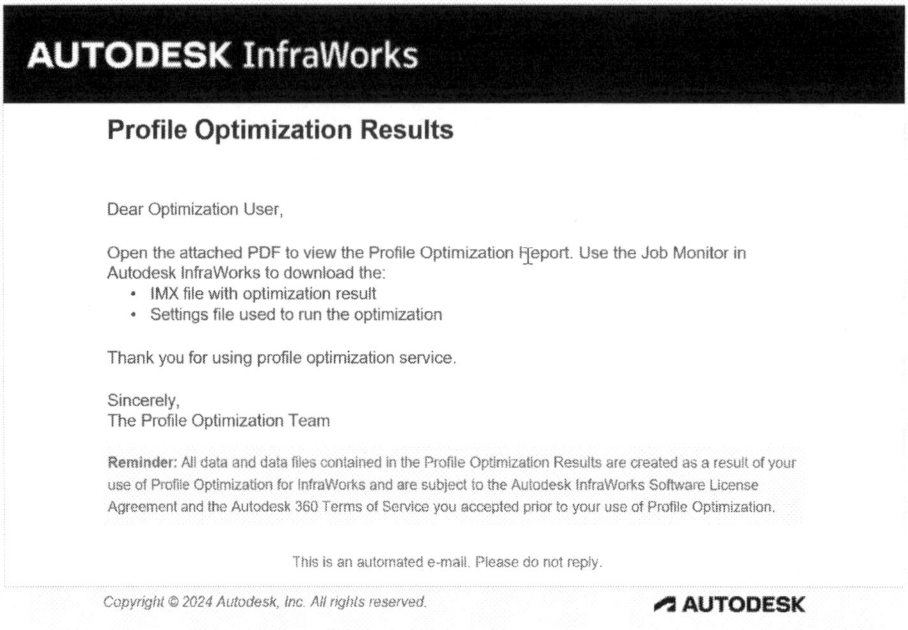

AUTODESK InfraWorks

Profile Optimization Results

Dear Optimization User,

Open the attached PDF to view the Profile Optimization Report. Use the Job Monitor in Autodesk InfraWorks to download the:

- IMX file with optimization result
- Settings file used to run the optimization

Thank you for using profile optimization service.

Sincerely,
The Profile Optimization Team

Reminder: All data and data files contained in the Profile Optimization Results are created as a result of your use of Profile Optimization for InfraWorks and are subject to the Autodesk InfraWorks Software License Agreement and the Autodesk 360 Terms of Service you accepted prior to your use of Profile Optimization.

This is an automated e-mail. Please do not reply.

Copyright © 2024 Autodesk, Inc. All rights reserved. AUTODESK

Figure A–97

10. In the *Job Monitor* panel, click (Refresh) to update the panel.

11. In the *Job Monitor* panel, under the *Report* column, click (Click to download an optimization report) to review the results in a report format.

12. In the *Job Monitor* panel, under the *Results* column, click (Create a proposal to view the result in the model). Click **Yes** in the Information dialog box.
13. Type **Beach_Profile** for the name and click **OK** to create the proposal.
14. Close the *Job Monitor* and *Profile Optimization* panels.

15. Go to the *Profile View* of **Morris Beach Blvd** (right-click on the component road) to examine the new optimized profile, as shown in Figure A–98.

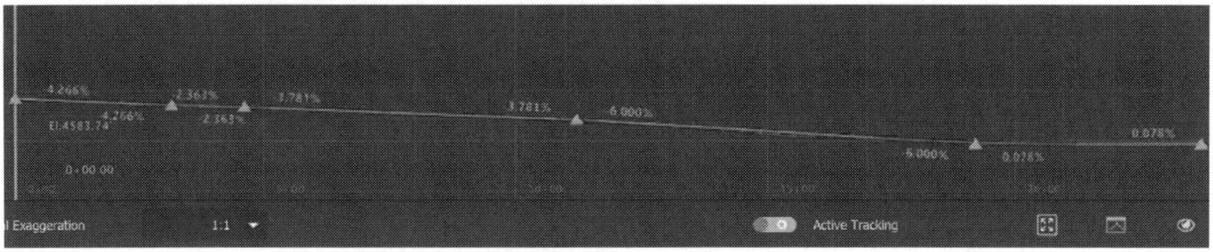

Figure A–98

16. Close the *Profile View* panel.

End of practice

A.6 Sight Distance Analysis

Roadway Sight Distance Analysis

A sight distance analysis is run on component roads to identify blind spots and sight failure zones, where a driver's line of sight is compromised by obstructions. There are six visual options for roadway analysis:

- **Sight Zones:** Displays colors on the analyzed lane to indicate safe and compromised sight zones.
- **Accident Zones:** Darkens portions of the analyzed lane to indicate where sight problems make accidents likely.
- **Sight Envelopes:** Displays colors on a range of required sight distances beyond the road boundary, and shows the effect of obstructions.
- **Sight Regions:** Displays sight regions relative to manually placed sight pins. Darkened areas indicate where the sight line is compromised by obstructions.
- **Sight Lines:** Displays the sight line from the eye point to the target point at the required sight distance. If any obstructions within sight regions negatively affect visibility at the eye point where the sight pin is placed, the first and last blocked sight lines are also shown.
- **Distance Line:** Displays a line from the eye height of manually placed sight pins to the required sight distance.

Intersection Sight Distance Analysis

Running a sight distance analysis on intersections provides visual cues for sight triangles, as shown in Figure A–99. Both visible areas and obstructions display in the model using a set color-coding system.

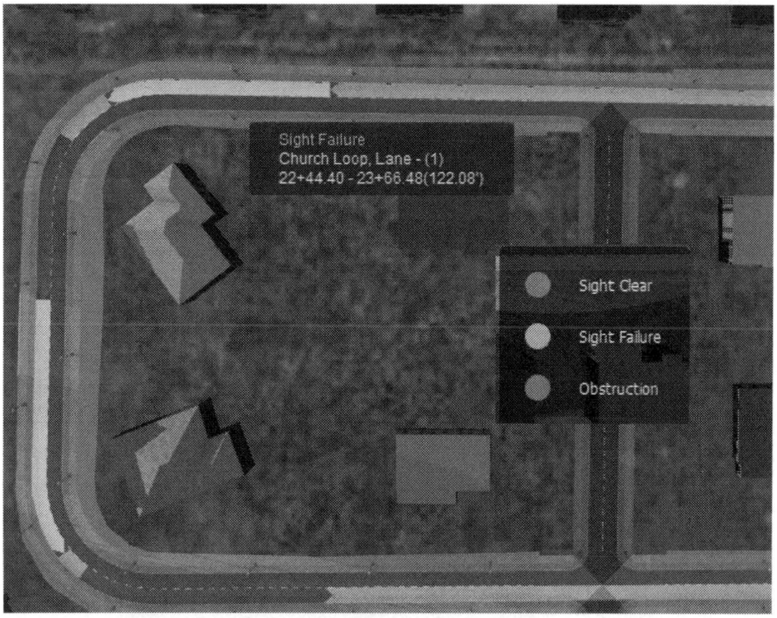

Figure A–99

The table below lists the color codes used for sight distance analysis for both roadways and intersections.

Color	Description
Light blue	Indicates zones with clear visibility.
Yellow	Indicates sight failure zones.
Red	Indicates obstructions.

How To: Conduct a Sight Distance Analysis on a Roadway

1. In the model, select the component road.
2. In the *Analyze* tab>*Transportation* drop-down list, click (Sight Distance).

3. Set the following settings in the *Sight Distance* panel (shown in Figure A–100):
   - *Method:* Select either **Stopping Sight Distance** or **Passing Sight Distance**.
   - *Direction:* The direction of travel (**Forward** or **Backward**).
   - *Lane:* Select which lane to analyze.

   ***Note: Lane (1)** is the lane that is closest to the centerline.*

   - *Obstruction Types:* Select or clear the **Road Decorations** option.
   - Select the obstruction types you want to include in the analysis. The options available in the *Obstruction Types* area vary depending on the road type used, and include trees, barriers, lamps, and other common road elements.

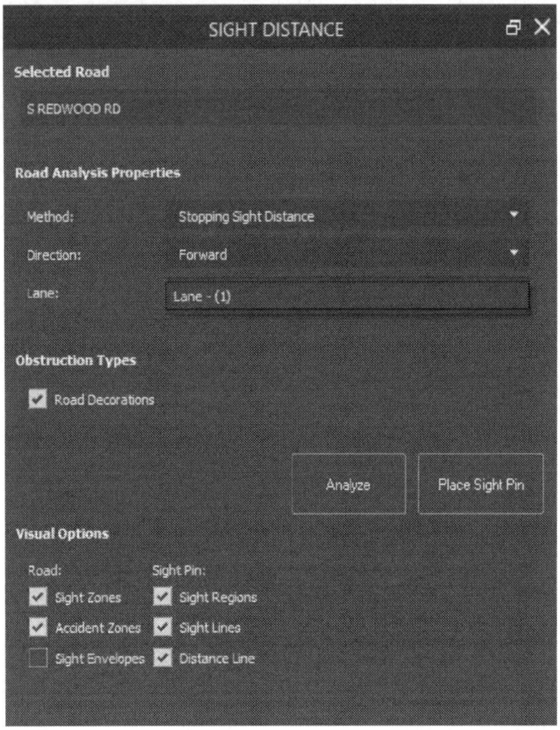

Figure A–100

4. Click **Analyze**.
5. Select or clear the items in the *Visual Options* area that you want to include in the analysis. The items are toggled on/off in the model. You do not need to rerun the analysis if you change the items that display in the model.
6. Click **Place Sight Pin** to place any required sight pins in the model.
7. Close the *Sight Distance* panel to clear the sight analysis.

How To: Conduct a Sight Distance Analysis on an Intersection Object

1. In the model, select the intersection object.
2. In the *Analyze* tab>*Transportation* drop-down list, click (Sight Distance).
3. Set the following settings in the *Sight Distance* panel (shown in Figure A–101):
   - *Approach:* Select the approach road.
   - *Traffic Control:* Select **Stop**, **Yield**, or **No control**.
   - *Maneuver:* Select a maneuver pattern.
   - *Obstruction Types:* Select or clear the **Road Decorations** option.
   - Select which obstruction types to include in the analysis.

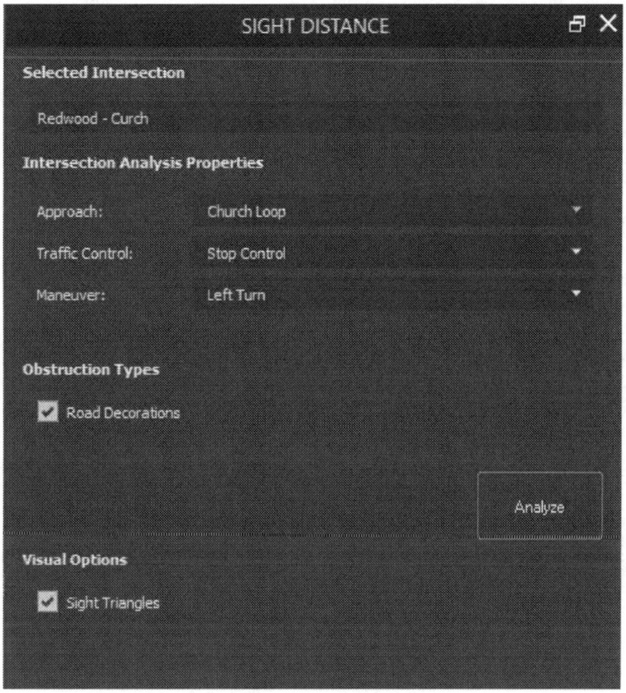

Figure A–101

4. Click **Analyze**.
5. Select or clear the *Visual Options* you want to include in the analysis.
6. Close the *Sight Distance* panel to clear the sight analysis.

Practice A6
Analyze Sight Distance

Practice Objective

- Analyze the roadway and the intersection for sight distance obstructions.

In this practice, you will complete a sight distance analysis for the design roadway and the intersection of the new road with **S Redwood Rd**, as shown in Figure A–102.

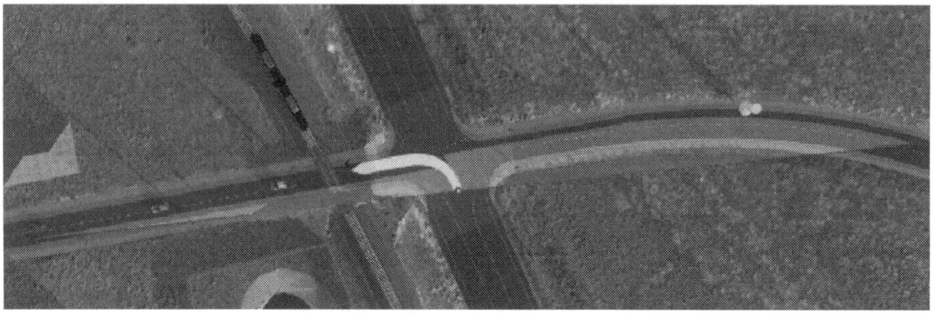

Figure A–102

1. Continue working in the same model as the previous practice. In the toolbar, select the **E_Task1** proposal to make it current.
2. Click (Bookmarks) and select **Project Area**.
3. In the model, select the **Church Loop** component road shown in Figure A–103.

Figure A–103

4. In the *Analyze* tab>*Transportation* drop-down list, click (Sight Distance).

5. In the *Sight Distance* panel, set the following options (as shown in Figure A–104):
    - *Method:* **Stopping Sight Distance**
    - *Direction:* **Forward**
    - *Lane:* **Lane - (1)**
    - *Obstruction Types:* Select **Road Decorations**
6. Click **Analyze**.
7. Select the *Visual Options* shown in Figure A–104.

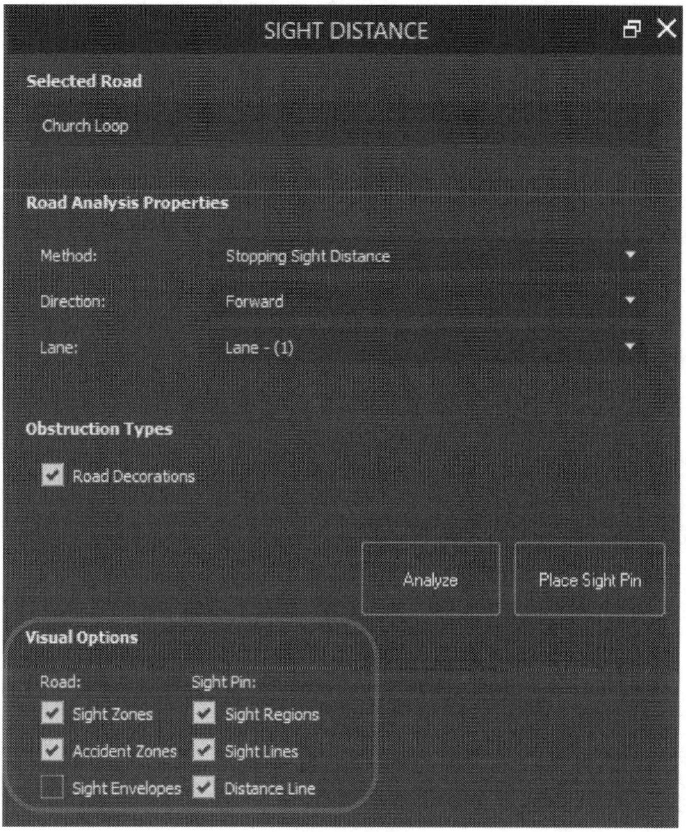

Figure A–104

8. Zoom in to the western part of *Church Loop*. Select and deselect different visual options in the *Sight Distance* panel. Note how the visual tools are added and removed in the model as you do.
9. In the *Sight Distance* panel, click **Place Sight Pin**.
10. Click various points in the model to place sight pins and display the results.

11. Hover over the yellow line and read the tooltip, as shown in Figure A–105.

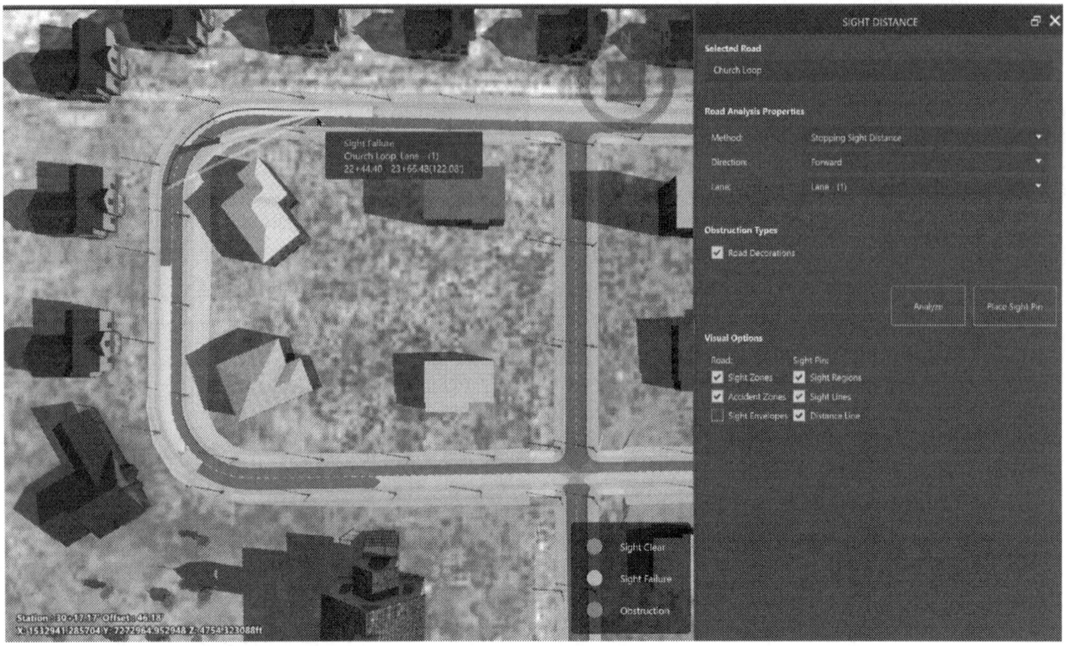

Figure A–105

12. Close the *Sight Distance* panel and press <Esc> to clear the selection.

End of practice

Chapter Review Questions

1. When running a traffic simulation, where do you control the traffic per intersection?
   a. Traffic Simulation asset card
   b. Traffic Analyst panel

2. Where can you find the tools to calculate earthwork and material quantities?
   a.  (Review and modify roadway designs)
   b. Road asset card
   c.  (Perform analysis in preparation for road design)

3. When is the optimal time to perform a corridor optimization?
   a. When you are first considering where to lay out the roadway.
   b. After you have laid out a few alternatives and are ready to compare them.
   c. Right before creating the profile view.
   d. After you have cut plan and profile sheets.

4. Cut and fill quantities can be balanced automatically using which of the following tools?
   a.  (Sight Distance)
   b.  (Job Monitor)
   c.  (Profile Optimization)

5. Which of the following visual options can be selected when running a sight distance analysis on an intersection?
   a. Sight Zones
   b. Accident Zones
   c. Sight Regions
   d. Sight Triangles

Command Summary

Button	Command	Location
	**Corridor Optimization**	• **Toolbar:** *Analyze* tab>*Transportation* panel
	**Earthwork Quantities**	• ***Road* asset card**
	**Job Monitor**	• **Toolbar:** *Analyze* tab>*Transportation* drop-down list
	**Material Quantities**	• ***Road* asset card**
	**Mobility Simulation**	• **Toolbar:** *Analyze* tab>*Transportation* drop-down list
	**Profile Optimization**	• **Toolbar:** *Analyze* tab>*Transportation* drop-down list
	**Sight Distance**	• **Toolbar:** *Analyze* tab>*Transportation* drop-down list
	**Traffic Simulation**	• **Toolbar:** *Analyze* tab>*Transportation* drop-down list

Appendix B

Point Cloud Modeling

Reality Capture software is steadily becoming more a part of the engineering workflow as the technology continues to improve. The Autodesk® InfraWorks® software has the ability to import point cloud data and model objects from it.

Learning Objectives

- Import point cloud data into Autodesk InfraWorks.
- Extract features from point cloud data.

B.1 Point Cloud Preparation

Point clouds are the byproduct of laser scanners, photogrammetry, LiDAR, and other sources. They are used to document realistic conditions of a given environment (existing conditions). Whether you are scanning a building or modeling critical infrastructure, Autodesk InfraWorks has the ability to utilize point clouds in models, as shown in Figure B–1. Before importing most point clouds, they must be processed in the Autodesk ReCap program and saved as either an .RCS (ReCap Scan) or an .RCP (ReCap Project) file.

The native LAS/LAZ point cloud format can be directly imported into InfraWorks without the need of preprocessing in the Autodesk ReCap program.

Figure B–1

Import

Point clouds are one of the few data types that can be imported into an empty Autodesk InfraWorks model. They can be used to create a terrain surface as a base for the new InfraWorks model.

How To: Import a Point Cloud

1. Either start a new model or open the model you want to import the point cloud into.
2. In the *Manage* tab>*Content* panel, click (Data Sources).
3. In the *Data Sources* panel, expand (Add file data source) and select the **Point Cloud** file format, as shown in Figure B–2.

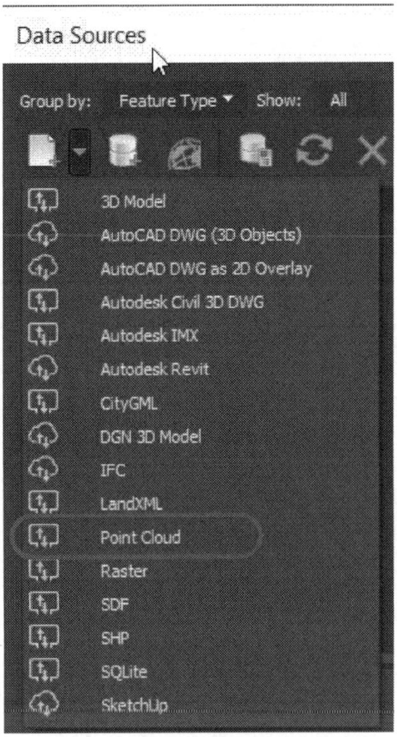

Figure B–2

4. Browse to the directory in which the file is located. Select the required file(s) and click **Open**.

   Note: *Hold <Shift> or <Ctrl> to select multiple files from the directory.*

5. In the *Data Sources* panel, double-click on the point cloud to configure it.

6. In the *Data Source Configuration* dialog box, set the *Position - Coordinate System* (as shown in Figure B–3) or click **Interactive Placing...** to correctly position the point cloud in the model. Point clouds from laser scanners are seldom geo-referenced and need to be positioned manually.

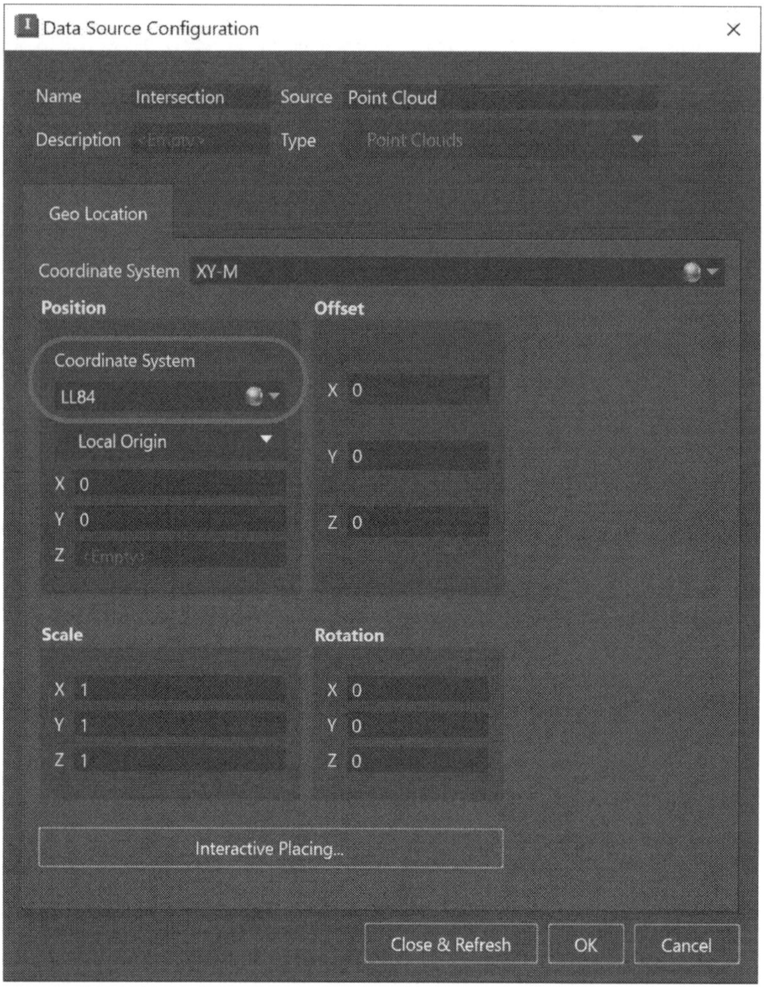

Figure B–3

7. Click **Close & Refresh**.

Point Cloud Appearance

Theme

Theming a point cloud enables you to view its many points using a range of colors. The colors are based on one of the following analysis types:

- **Normal:** Identifies points that are aligned by displaying colors assigned to the X, Y, and Z values associated with the direction of normal for the point. Colors for this type of theme cannot be specified.

  ***Note: Normal** usually refers to the direction in which a surface face is pointing. For points in a point cloud, **normal** is derived from other points that have a planar relationship with a specific point.*

- **Elevation:** Similar to the InfraWorks terrain theme by elevation, it colors points according to their Z value or height. The minimum and maximum values are determined automatically, but can be adjusted as required. The color range can be adjusted or a color palette can be set.
- **Single Color:** All points become the same color and no further options are available.
- **Classification:** This option is only available if a point cloud is classified. Points are colored by their classification ID. The color range can be adjusted or a color palette can be set.
- **Intensity:** Normalizes the intensity values of the points. The color range can be adjusted or a color palette can be set.
- **Elevation + Intensity:** Normalizes the intensity values of the points while also considering the elevation. Colors different from an elevation theme are typically used since saturation is different with the addition of intensity.

Point cloud themes only use the *equal distribution* method for creating ranges.

If you plan to create a surface from the point cloud, it is recommended that you use the **Intensity** option.

How To: Create a Point Cloud Theme

1. In the *Manage* tab>*Point Clouds* panel, click (Point Cloud Themes).
2. In the *Point Cloud Themes* panel, click (Add a New Theme).

3. In the *Theme Properties* dialog box (shown in Figure B–4), define the following settings and click **OK**:
   - *Name:* Type a name for the theme.
   - *Analysis Type:* Select the analysis type.
   - *Palette Type:* Select the palette type.
   - *Number of Rules:* If the palette has not already been set, set the number of rules.
   - *Color Range:* Select the color range. If a palette type is selected, the color range is set and not editable.

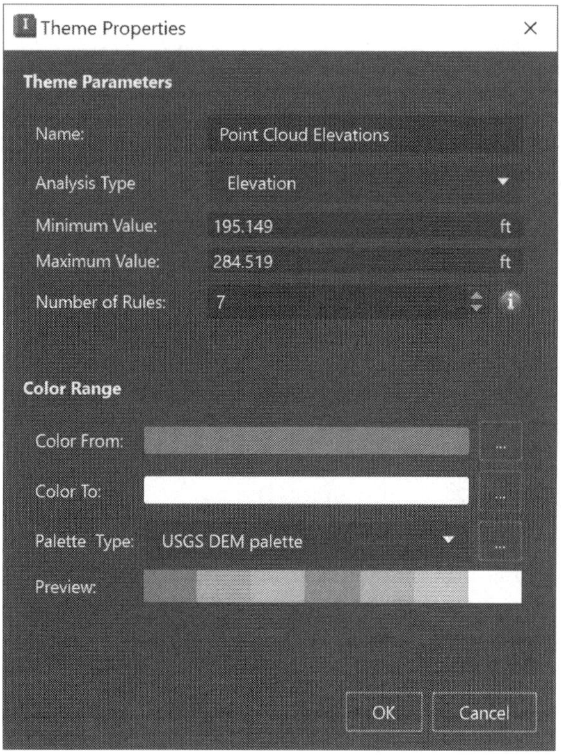

Figure B–4

Size and Density

In addition to point cloud themes, the application options can be used to change the point cloud appearance. Both the point size and density can be controlled in the *Application Options* dialog box, under **Point Cloud**, as shown in Figure B–5.

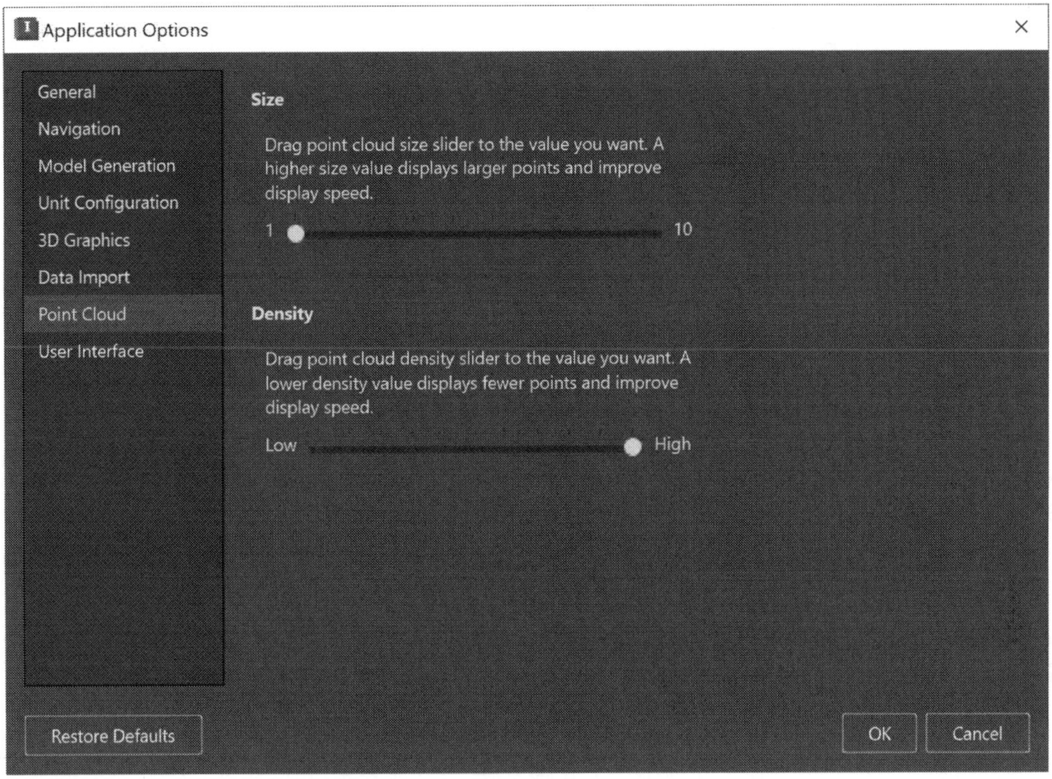

Figure B–5

Practice B1
Point Cloud Preparation

Practice Objectives

- Import a point cloud.
- Create a point cloud theme.

In this practice, you will create a new model from scratch and then add point cloud data to it. Using the point cloud, you will create a terrain and features for the existing conditions model.

Task 1: Import a point cloud.

1. On the *Home* screen, click **New**.
2. Set the following, as shown in Figure B–6:
   - *Name*: **Intersection**
   - *Description*: **Modeling from a point cloud**
   - Select **Work Local**
   - *Work Local:* **InfraWorks Practice Files/AppB-PointClouds**
   - *Coordinate System*: **LL84** (select from the drop-down list)

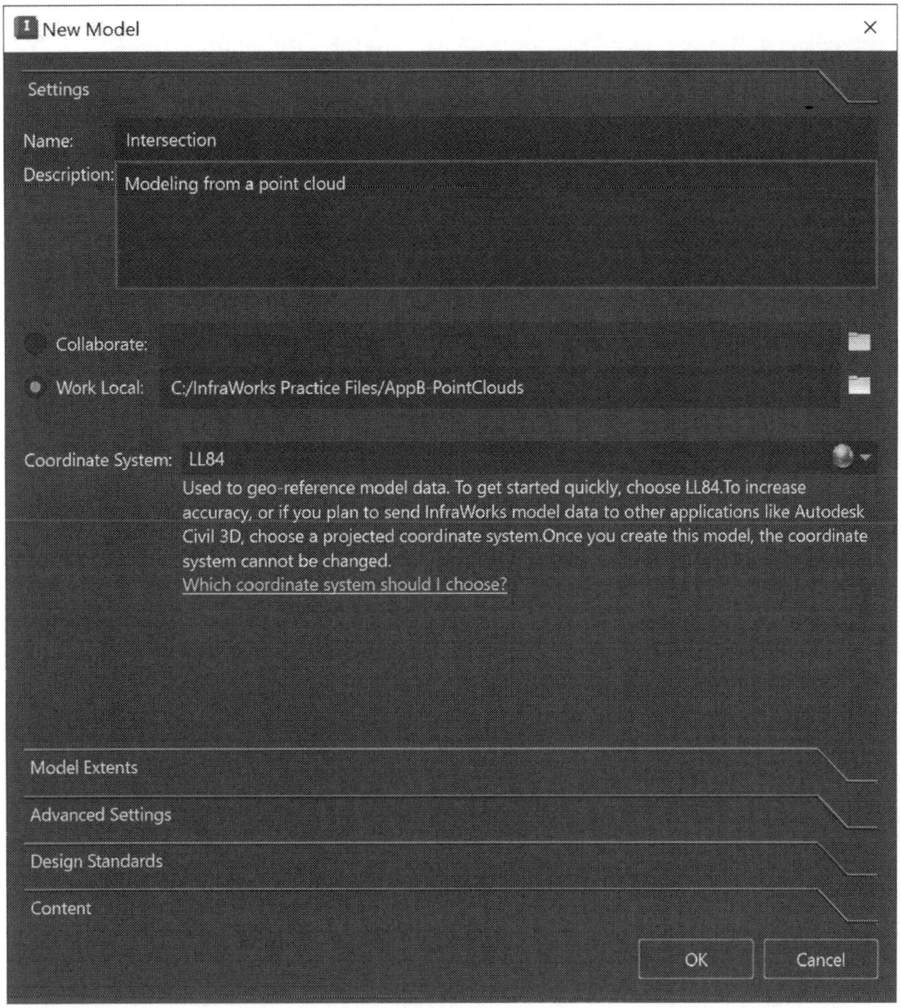

Figure B–6

3. Click **OK** to create the model.
4. If the *Data Sources* panel is not already displayed, in the *Manage* tab>*Content* panel, click  (Data Sources).
5. In the *Data Sources* panel, expand  (Add file data source) and select **Point Cloud**.
6. Browse to the *InfraWorks Practice Files\References\PointCloud* folder, select **Intersection.rcs**, and click **Open**.
7. In the *Data Sources* panel, under *Point Clouds*, double-click on the **Intersection Point Cloud** layer to configure it.

8. In the *Data Source Configuration* dialog box, note that *Type* is set to **Point Clouds** automatically. On the *Geo Location* tab, ensure that the *Coordinate System* under *Position* is set to **LL84**, then type **0** (zero) in the *X* and *Y* fields, as shown in Figure B–7. Click **Close & Refresh**.

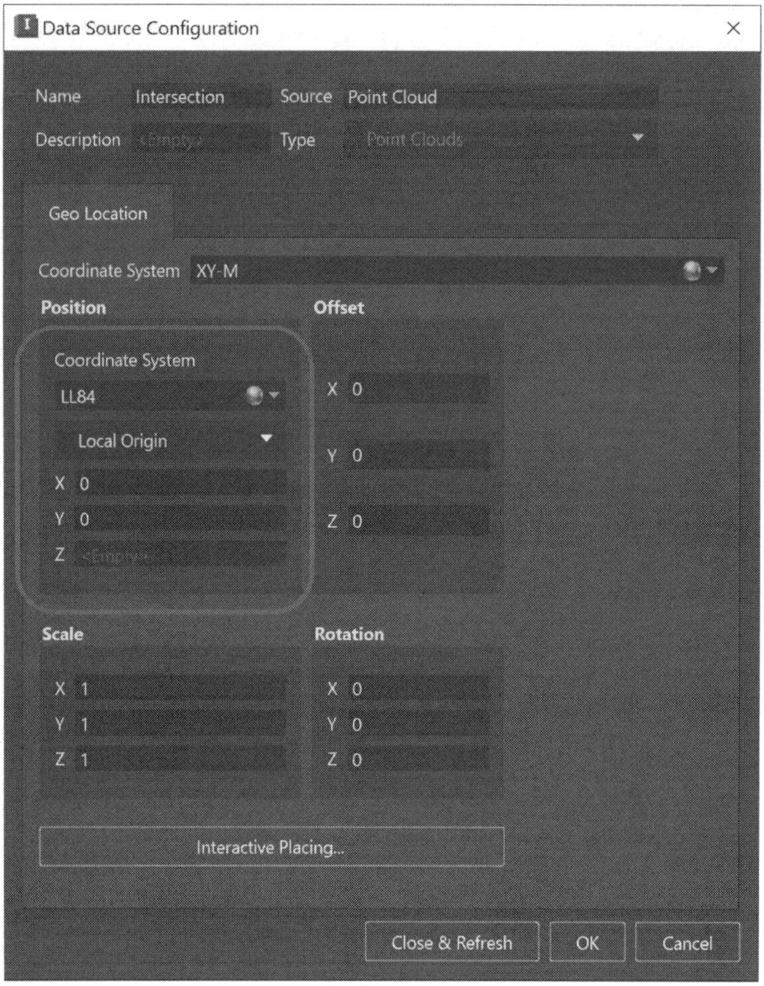

Figure B–7

9. The point cloud is inserted and the model zooms to it, as shown in Figure B–8.

Figure B–8

Task 2: Theme a point cloud.

1. In the *Manage* tab>*Point Clouds* panel, click (Point Cloud Themes).
2. In the *Point Cloud Themes* panel, click (Add a New Theme).

3. In the *Theme Properties* dialog box (shown in Figure B–9), define the following:
   - *Name:* **Intensity**
   - *Analysis Type:* **Intensity**
   - *Palette Type:* **RGB**
   - *Number of Rules:* **10**
   - *Color From:* Click and select a color of your choice.
   - *Color To:* Click and select a complimentary color of your choice.

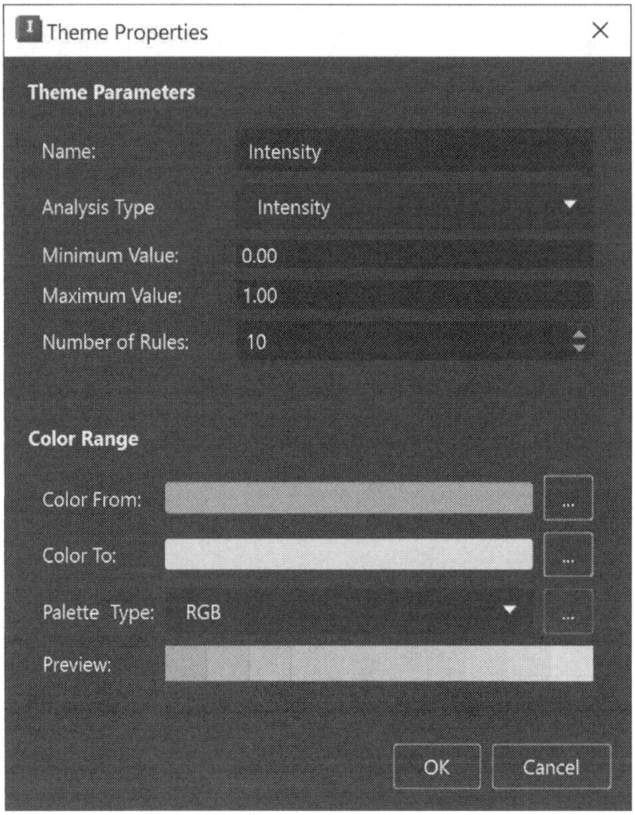

Figure B–9

- *Palette Type:* Select **Cyan Ramped Palette** from the drop-down list, as shown in Figure B–10.
- *Color Range:* Note that you can no longer select a different *Color From* or *Color To* as they are preset by the color palette.

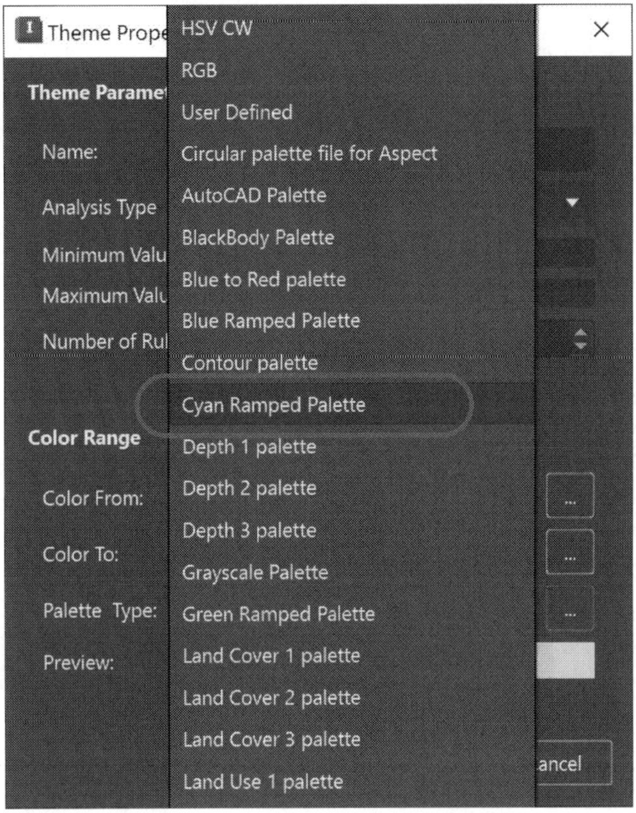

Figure B–10

4. Click **OK.**

End of practice

B.2 Extract a Point Cloud Terrain

The terrain for the model can be created from one or more point clouds. Simply import the point clouds and use the **Point Cloud Terrain** tool to process it. During the processing, you can control how the data is analyzed for each of the three feature types:

- **Ground:** Analyzes point groupings that likely fall on the ground to determine the terrain for the model.
- **Linear Feature:** Analyzes linear point groupings to better understand paint stripping and other linear features.
- **Vertical Feature:** Analyzes vertical point groupings to determine where city furniture (signs, benches, etc.) might reside.

Processing rules determine how much detail within the point cloud to use during the processing. For ground data, you can use the following processing options:

- Less Detail
- Optimum
- More Detail
- Custom

If the **Custom** option is selected, you can set the measurement for the ground detail, the terrain raster resolution, whether or not to fill terrain holes, and the processing window size, as shown in Figure B–11, left panel.

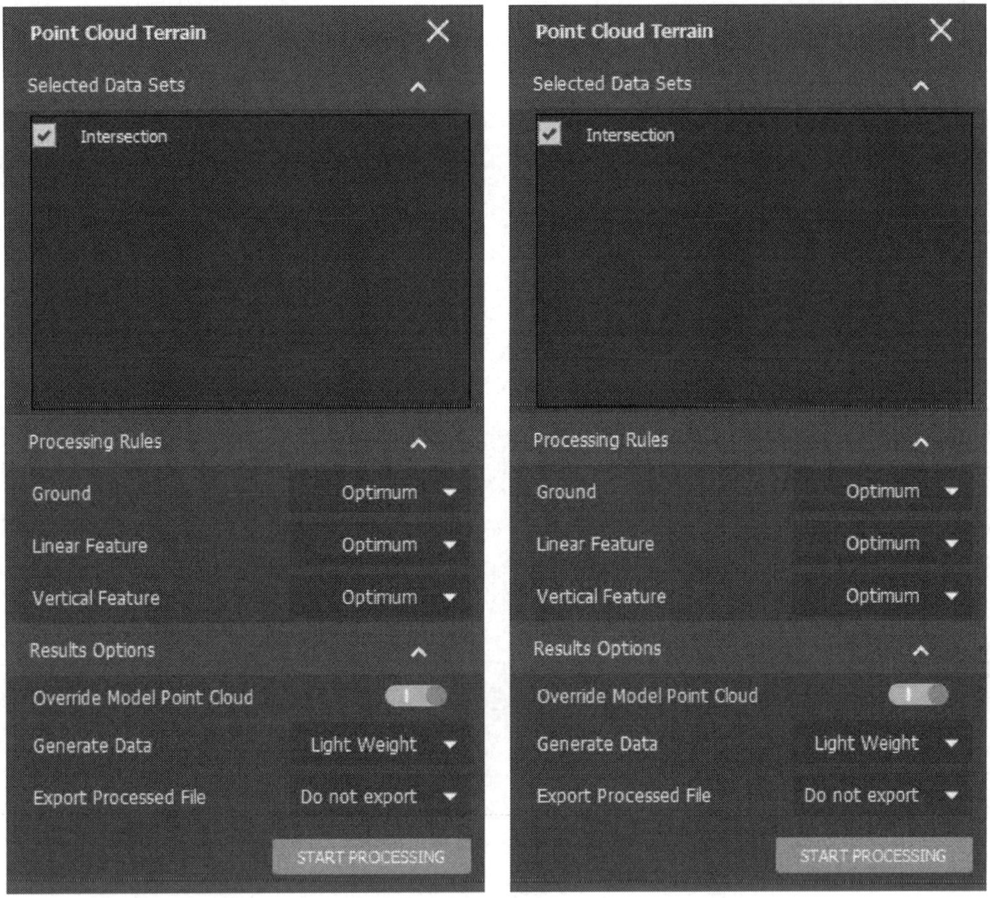

Figure B–11

How To: Create a Point Cloud Terrain

1. In the *Manage* tab>*Point Clouds* panel, click  (Point Cloud Terrain).
2. In the *Point Cloud Terrain* panel, select which processing rules to use for the ground data, as shown in Figure B–11, right panel.
3. Click **START PROCESSING**.

B.3 Extract Point Cloud Features

Once the ground data has been extracted, you can also extract additional features. During the **Point Cloud Terrain** processing, classification IDs are given to points in the point cloud even if they did not exist previously. This can provide more clarity for differentiating features in the model, as shown in Figure B–12.

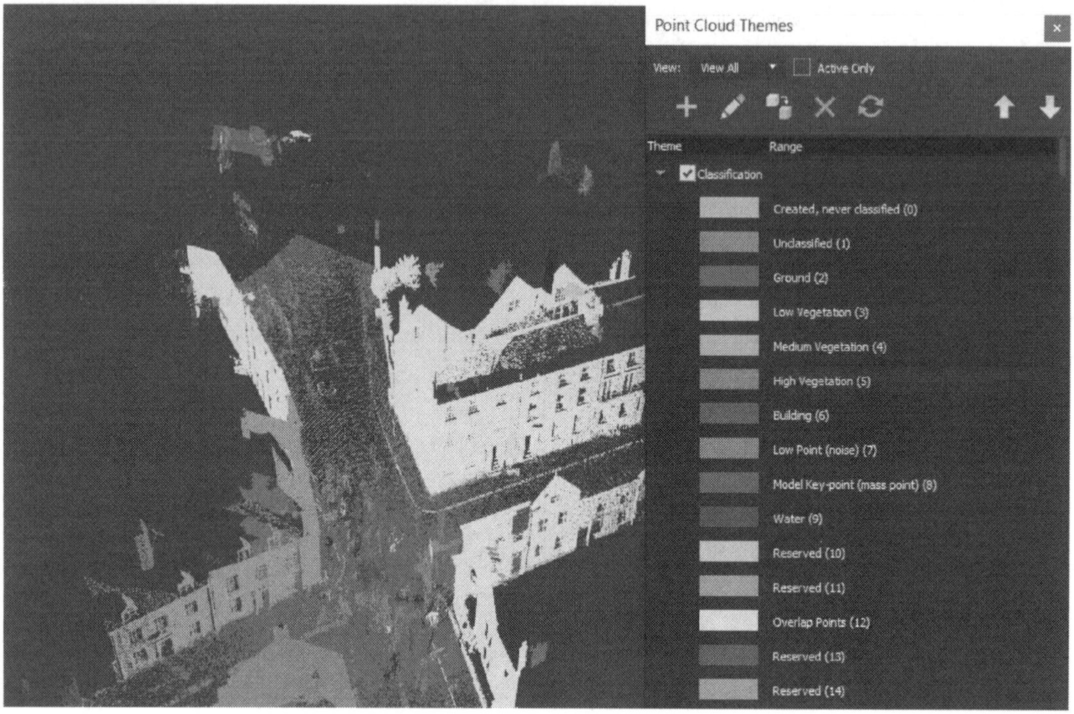

Figure B–12

Point Cloud Modeling

Point cloud modeling analyzes the vertical point groupings to determine where city furniture (signs, street lights, etc.) might reside. Once analyzed, the software automatically zooms to the first feature.

The *Point Cloud Modeling* panel is used to assign categories to found features. If a feature is automatically assigned an incorrect category, you can change the category in the *Point Cloud Modeling* panel, as shown in Figure B–13. Once the category is assigned, the style for the feature can be changed in the feature's asset card, as shown in Figure B–14.

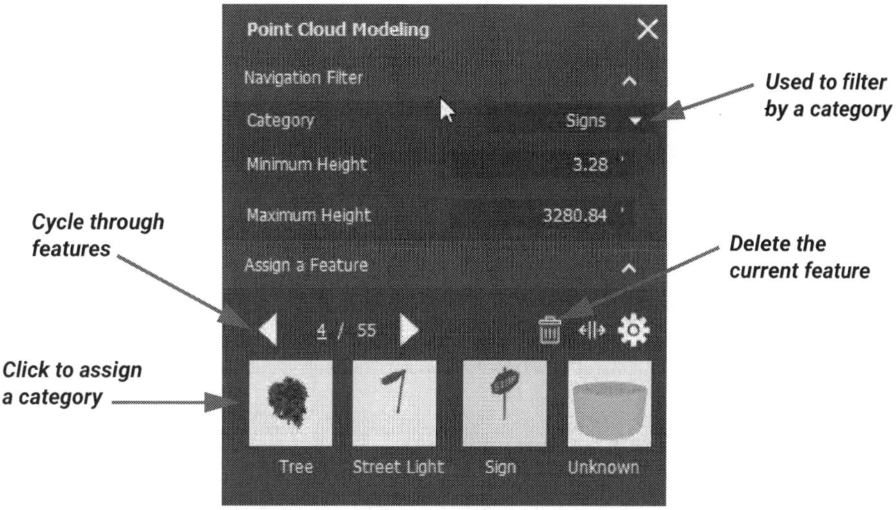

Figure B–13

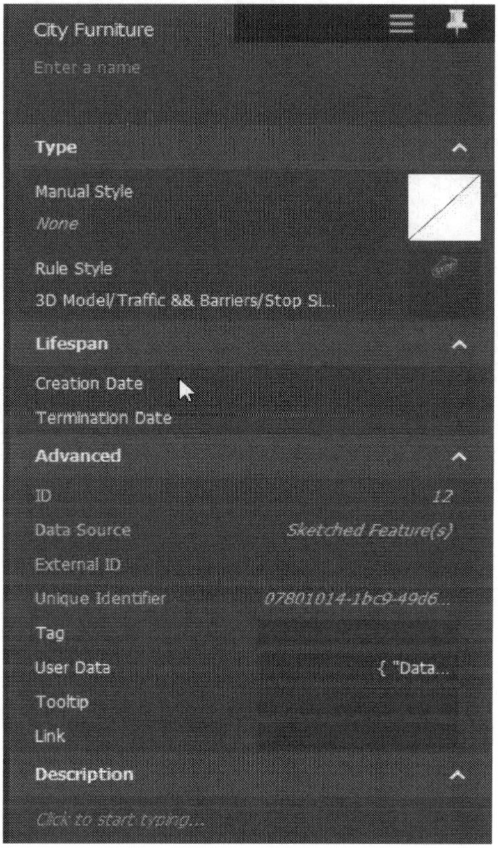

Figure B–14

How To: Extract Point Cloud Features

1. In the *Manage* tab>*Point Clouds* drop-down list, click (Vertical Feature Extraction). The software automatically zooms in on the first feature found and opens that feature's asset card.
2. In the *Point Cloud Modeling* panel, do the following (as shown in Figure B–15):
   - Select which *Category* you want to filter by.
   - Set the *Minimum* and *Maximum Height* values.
   - Under *Assign a Feature*, click on the city furniture to use.

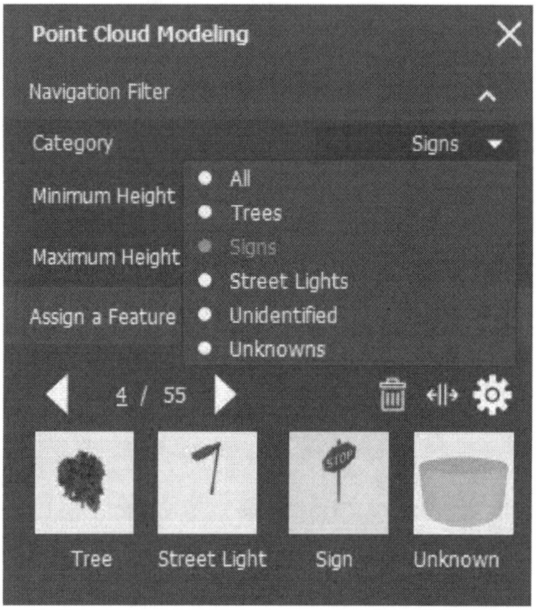

Figure B–15

3. The generic feature box is turned into the selected category. In the feature's asset card, select an appropriate style for the feature.
4. Click (Next) to go to the next found feature.

Hint: Terrain Elevations

Often there will be differences between the modeled elements and the point cloud. This is due to the difference in vertical datum of default terrain in InfraWorks and the point cloud elevation, as shown in Figure B–16.

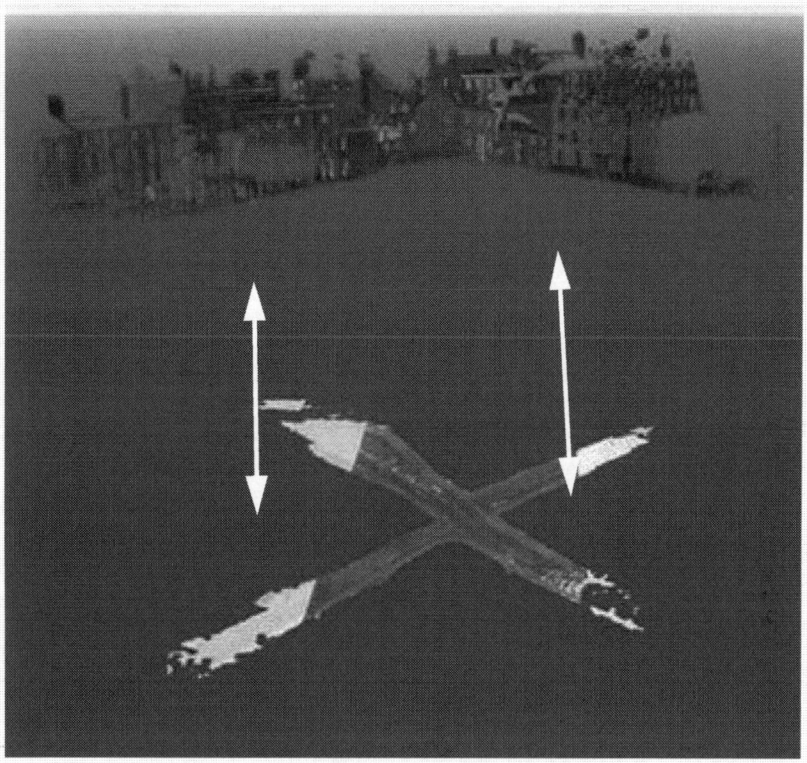

Figure B–16

You can generate a surface using point cloud terrain, which will generate terrain in the same datum as the point cloud to harmonize the ground, the point cloud, and the modeled elements.

Otherwise, you can manually move the point cloud elevation using the configuration window. This is not recommended, however, since every refresh of the point cloud data will need to be adjusted again.

Practice B2
Point Cloud Modeling

Practice Objectives

- Create a point cloud terrain.
- Create features from point cloud data.

In this practice, you will create a terrain from the point cloud and features for the existing conditions model.

Task 1: Create a terrain from the point cloud.

1. On the *Home* screen, click **Open**.
2. In the *InfraWorks Practice Files\AppB-PointClouds* folder, select **Modeling.sqlite** and click **Open**.
3. Click (Bookmarks) and select **Ballard**. Ensure that **A_Task1** is the current proposal.
4. Take some time to navigate around and examine the point cloud.
5. In the *Manage* tab>*Point Clouds* panel, click (Point Cloud Terrain).

6. In the *Point Cloud Terrain* panel, do the following (as shown in Figure B–17):
   - Select the **Intersection** point cloud to use it. (This is only necessary if you have more than one point cloud in your model.)
   - Leave all the *Processing Rules* set to **Optimum**.
   - Under *Results Options*, set *Generate Data* to **All points**.
   - For *Export Processed File*, leave as **Do not export**.
7. Click **START PROCESSING**.

   Note: *If the processing is taking too long, you can abort and use the completed proposal in the next task.*

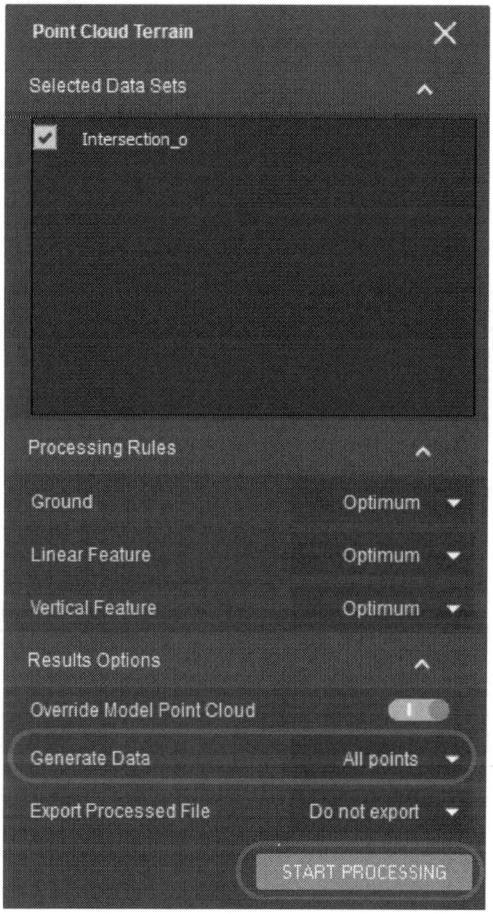

Figure B–17

8. In the *Manage* tab>*Content* panel, click (Data Sources).
9. In the *Data Sources* panel, note that there are now entries under *Terrain* and *Terrain Overlays* (which were not there prior to processing) as shown on the right in Figure B–18.

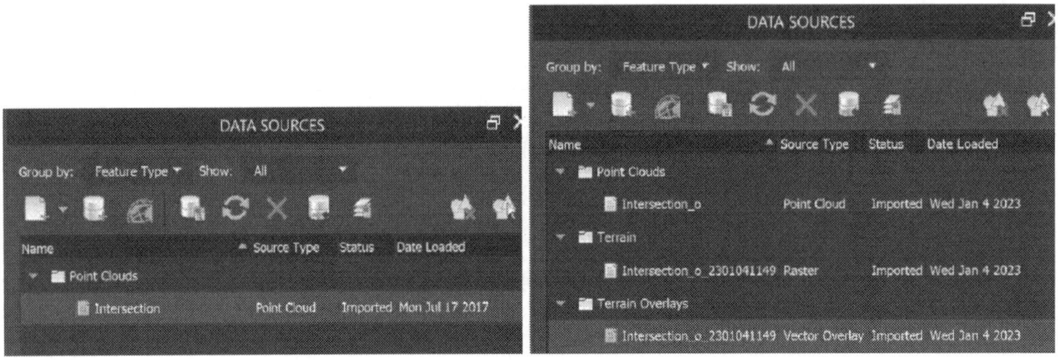

Before processing ***After processing***

Figure B–18

10. Examine the results, as shown in Figure B–19.

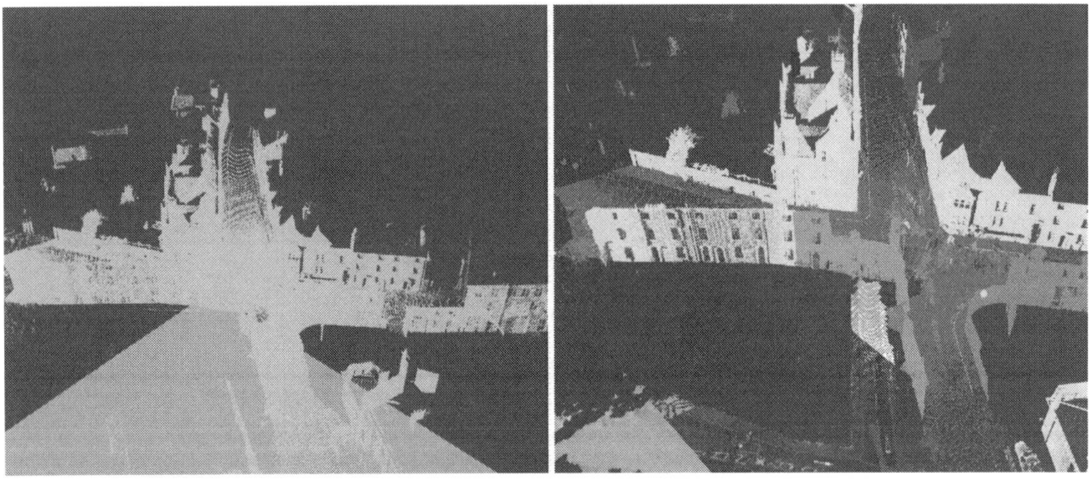

Before processing ***After processing***

Figure B–19

Task 2: Classify the point cloud.

1. Continue working in the same proposal as the last task. If you did not complete the last task, select **A_Task2** as the current proposal.
2. In the *Manage* tab>*Point Clouds* panel, click (Point Cloud Themes).
3. In the *Point Cloud Themes* panel, uncheck the *Intensity* theme if it is still selected from the previous task, and click (Add a New Theme).
4. In the *Theme Properties* dialog box, set the following (as shown in Figure B–20):
   - *Name:* **Classification**
   - *Analysis Type:* **Classification**
   - *Palette Type:* **User Defined**
   - *Number of Rules:* Leave the default settings
   - *Color Range:* Leave the default settings

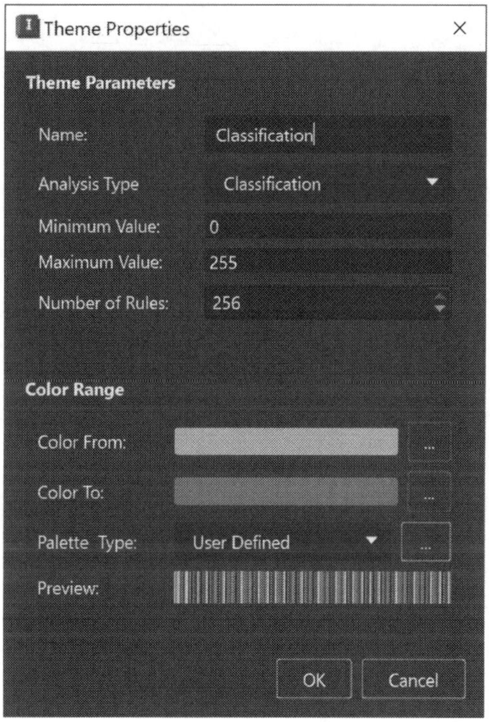

Figure B–20

5. Click **OK**.

6. Examine the results, as shown in Figure B–21.

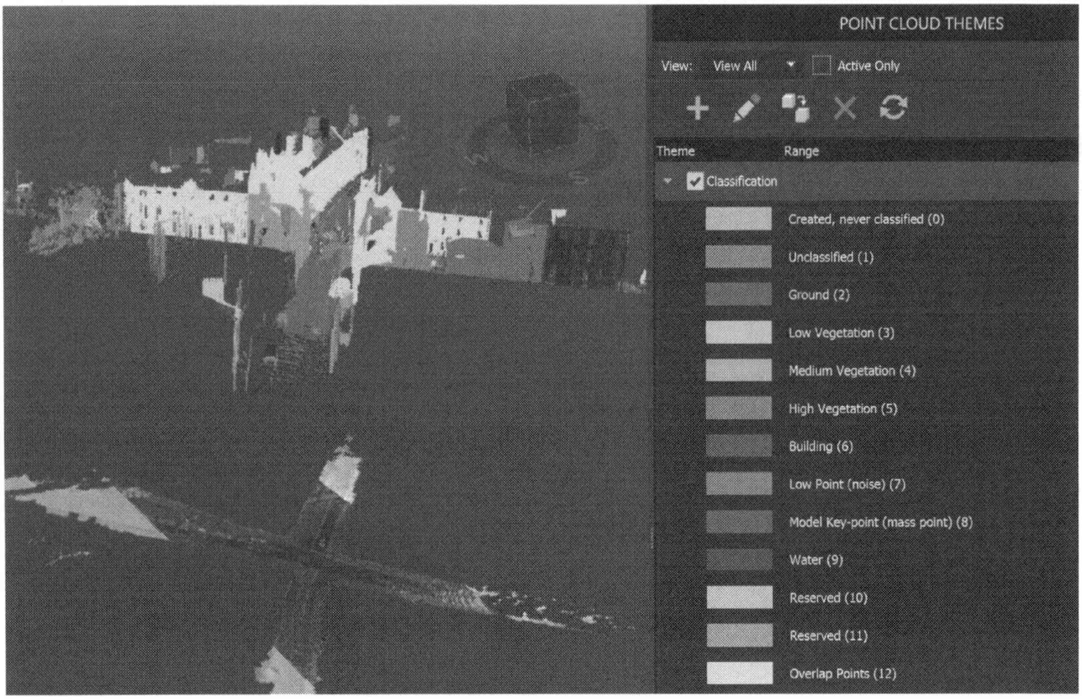

Figure B–21

Task 3: Create features from point cloud data.

1. Continue working in the same proposal as the last task. If you did not complete the last task, select **A_Task3** as the current proposal.
2. Close the *Point Cloud Themes* panel.
3. In the *Manage* tab>*Point Clouds* drop-down list, click (Vertical Feature Extraction).

4. The software automatically zooms in on the first feature found and opens that feature's asset card. Note that there are **111** (plus or minus) features. The number of features found might differ on different systems. In the *Point Cloud Modeling* panel, do the following (as shown in Figure B–22):

   - Set the *Category* to **Signs**. Note the reduction in the number of features to assign when Signs is selected.
   - Leave the *Minimum* and *Maximum Height* values as the default heights.
   - Under *Assign a Feature*, click on **Sign** as the city furniture to use.

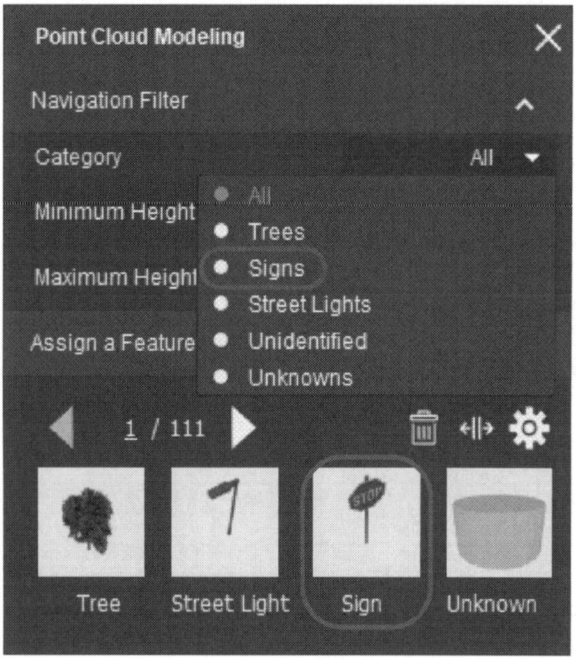

Figure B–22

5. The generic feature box is turned into the selected style.
6. In the *Assign a Feature* area, click  (Next) to go to the next sign feature.
7. For *Maximum Height*, change the value to **10'**. Note that now only 52 objects are found.
8. For *Maximum Height*, change the value to **4'**. Note that now only 12 objects are found.

9. Change the *Minimum Height* to **9'** and the *Maximum Height* to **40'**. Now there are only 4 objects selected and you are zoomed in to one, as shown in Figure B–23.

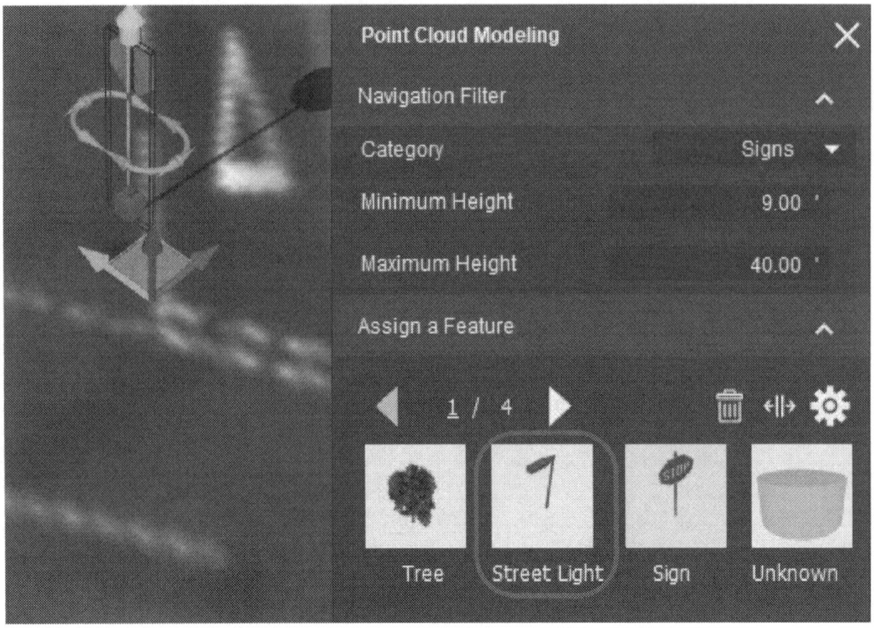

Figure B–23

10. Assign the four objects to **Street Light**.
11. Continue to choose different heights and select different features as time permits.

End of practice

Chapter Review Questions

1. Which point cloud theme is recommended if you plan to create a terrain or features from the point cloud?
    a. Normal
    b. Classification
    c. Elevation
    d. Intensity

2. How do you control the size of the points in a point cloud?
    a. In the *Point Cloud Modeling* panel.
    b. In the *Point Cloud Terrain* panel.
    c. In the *Application Options* dialog box.
    d. In the *Model Properties* dialog box.

3. You can create a terrain from a point cloud.
    a. True
    b. False

4. How do you change a feature style once it has been assigned a category?
    a. In the *Point Cloud Modeling* panel.
    b. In the feature asset card.
    c. In the *Properties* panel.

Command Summary

Button	Command	Location
	**Vertical Feature Extraction**	• **Toolbar:** *Manage* tab>*Point Clouds* drop-down list
	**Point Cloud Terrain**	• **Toolbar:** *Manage* tab>*Point Clouds* panel
	**Point Cloud Themes**	• **Toolbar:** *Manage* tab>*Point Clouds* panel

Index

D

E

F

G

I

L

M

N

Made in United States
Orlando, FL
04 November 2026

90205884R00413